The Amazon

THE BRADT TRAVEL GUIDE

Roger Harris
Peter Hutchison

Bradt Publications, UK
The Globe Pequot Press Inc, USA

First published in 1998 by Bradt Publications,
41 Nortoft Road, Chalfont St Peter, Bucks SL9 0LA, England
Published in the USA by The Globe Pequot Press Inc, 6 Business Park Road,
PO Box 833, Old Saybrook, Connecticut 06475-0833

ISBN 1 898323 71 2

British Library Cataloguing in Publication Data
A catalogue record for this book is available from the British Library

Library of Congress Cataloging-in-Publication Data
Harris, Roger, 1966–
The Amazon : The Bradt Travel Guide / Roger Harris, Peter Hutchison. .
p. cm.
Includes biographical references (p. –) and index.
ISBN 1-898323-71-2
1. Amazon River—Guidebooks. 2. Amazon River—Description and travel. 3. Amazon River Region—Guidebooks. 4. Amazon River Region—Description and travel. 5. National parks and reserves—Amazon River Region—Guidebooks. 6. Natural areas—Amazon River Region—Guidebooks. I. Hutchison, Peter, 1966– . II. Title.
F2546.H28 1998
918.1'10464—DC21 98-37944
CIP

Maps Alan Whitaker
Photographs *Front cover* Poison-dart frog, Family Dendrobatidae (Roger Harris)
Text Roger Harris (RH), Peter Hutchison (PH), Pete Oxford (PO)
Illustrations Oliver Whalley

Typeset from the author's disc by Wakewing
Printed and bound in Spain by Grafo SA, Bilbao

About the Authors

Afflicted with an incurable travel bug acquired during his childhood upbringing in Africa, **Roger Harris** now regularly travels throughout South America – camera in one hand, notebook in the other – on his quest for ever more arcane knowledge. Throughout the book he draws on his degrees in biology and his experience leading dozens of natural history and photography tours to the Amazon and other parts of Latin America.

Peter Hutchison arrived in South America in 1993 after travelling through Central America. He continued his journey south to Bolivia where he worked as a journalist for the *Bolivian Times* for two years before returning to the UK. Despite his attempts to settle in the UK, the attractions of South America continue regularly to pull him back to the region. He now works as a freelance writer and journalist, living in Wimbledon.

THE BRADT STORY

Hilary Bradt

In 1974, my former husband George Bradt and I spent three days sitting on a river barge in Bolivia writing our first guide for like-minded travellers: *Backpacking along Ancient Ways in Peru and Bolivia*. The 'little yellow book', as it became known, is now in its sixth edition and continues to sell to travellers throughout the world.

Since 1980, with the establishment of Bradt Publications, I have continued to publish guides for the discerning traveller, covering more than 100 countries and all six continents; in 1997 we won *The Sunday Times* Small Publisher of the Year Award. *The Amazon* is the 144th Bradt title or new edition to be published.

The company continues to develop new titles and new series, but in the forefront of my mind there remains our original ethos – responsible travel with an emphasis on the culture and natural history of the region. I hope that you will get the most out of your trip, and perhaps have the opportunity to give something in return.

Travel guides are by their nature continuously evolving. If you experience anything which you would like to share with us, or if you have any amendments to make to this guide, please write; all your letters are read and passed on to the author. Most importantly, do remember to travel with an open mind and to respect the customs of your hosts – it will add immeasurably to your enjoyment.

Contents

LIST OF MAPS

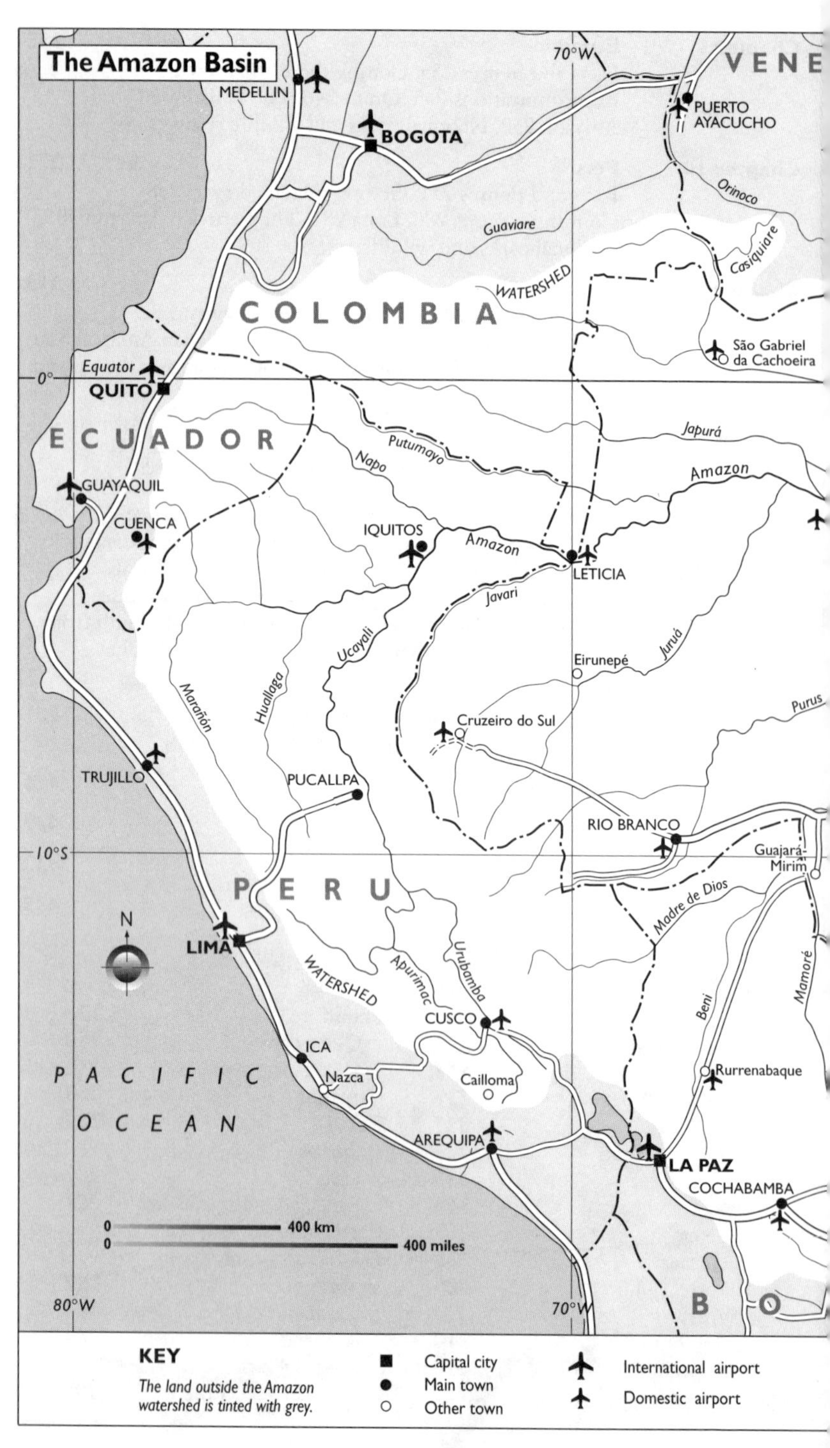

The Amazon Basin
MEDELLIN
BOGOTA
70°W
VENE
PUERTO AYACUCHO
Orinoco
Guaviare
Casiquiare
WATERSHED
COLOMBIA
São Gabriel da Cachoeira
Equator
0°
QUITO
ECUADOR
Japurá
Putumayo
Napo
Amazon
GUAYAQUIL
CUENCA
IQUITOS
Amazon
LETICIA
Javari
Ucayali
Juruá
Eirunepé
Marañón
Huallaga
Purus
Cruzeiro do Sul
TRUJILLO
PUCALLPA
RIO BRANCO
10°S
Guajará-Mirim
PERU
Madre de Dios
N
LIMA
WATERSHED
Apurímac
Urubamba
Mamoré
Beni
CUSCO
ICA
Nazca
Cailloma
Rurrenabaque
PACIFIC
OCEAN
AREQUIPA
LA PAZ
COCHABAMBA
0 400 km
0 400 miles
80°W
70°W
BO
KEY
The land outside the Amazon watershed is tinted with grey.
Capital city
Main town
Other town
International airport
Domestic airport

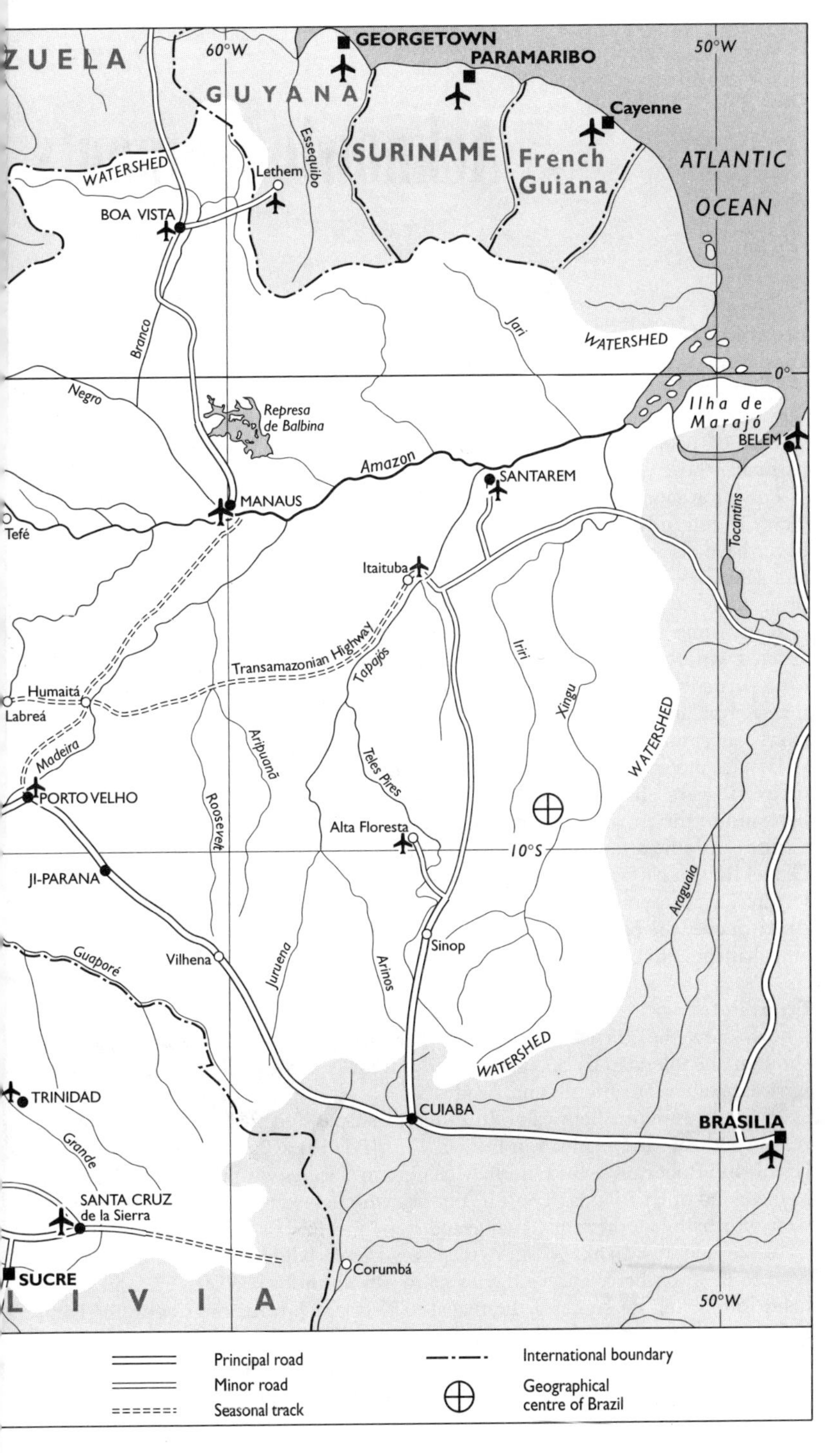
ZUELA
GUYANA
GEORGETOWN
PARAMARIBO
SURINAME
French Guiana
Cayenne
ATLANTIC OCEAN
60°W
50°W
WATERSHED
Lethem
Essequibo
BOA VISTA
Branco
Jari
WATERSHED
0°
Negro
Represa de Balbina
Ilha de Marajó
BELEM
Amazon
SANTAREM
MANAUS
Tefé
Tocantins
Itaituba
Transamazonian Highway
Tapajós
Iriri
Xingu
WATERSHED
Humaitá
Labreá
Madeira
Aripuanã
Teles Pires
PORTO VELHO
Roosevelt
Alta Floresta
10°S
JI-PARANA
Araguaia
Sinop
Guaporé
Vilhena
Juruena
Arinos
WATERSHED
TRINIDAD
CUIABA
BRASILIA
Grande
SANTA CRUZ de la Sierra
Corumbá
SUCRE
LIVIA
50°W
Principal road
Minor road
Seasonal track
International boundary
Geographical centre of Brazil

Acknowledgements

From Roger

I am deeply grateful to all involved in this project. In particular, I thank my family – Mum and Dad in England, my wife Sophie and my sister Jennifer – for their unwavering support.

Lots of people helped make this book possible, and I thank them all, in particular those named below. Any errors remaining are, of course, my own.

For information used in parts of *Chapter Five*, I thank scientists Ryan Hill and Tracy Munn in Ecuador who showed me hidden secrets of the rainforest I might never have discovered otherwise. I also thank Charlie Strader at Explorations Inc and Peter Jenson at Explorama Lodges in Peru, for their contributions to this project.

Ruth Anne Ronk helped in preparatory proofreading of the manuscript and assisted with the drafting of maps. Angelina Kuchar helped proofread early drafts.

In particular I am grateful to Peter Hutchison for his precise comments on the manuscript, and to Tricia Hayne at Bradt Publications, for overseeing the project from conception to completion.

Besides direct experience I have used notes taken from my conversations with native villagers, shamans, local and US naturalist-guides, and travel professionals here and in the Amazon. I especially thank staff and crew at Amazon Tours and Cruises in Iquitos for use of their facilities on many occasions. Naturalist-guide Daniel Rios in particular provided mountains of information during his shipboard lectures. I tip my cap to all those people with whom I have travelled in South America over the past six years, and who provided their experience, good humour and challenges to enrich my life and, I hope, the content of this book.

From Peter

I now know that travel-guide writing is a labour of love and a workload that shouldn't be tolerated by one person without the generous help and support of an intricate network of friends and family.

In South America help came in different shapes and forms from Phil, Alice, Adrian and Alix and Hannah in Bolivia, Vitoria da Riva Carvalho in Alta Floresta, Brazil, and Roberto Carlos Duorte Morinoni in Cacéres, also in Brazil. Thanks go to these and other friends in South America who helped prove that some journeys were worthwhile, others inadvisable and some just impossible or plain stupid.

In England, my thanks go out to the many friends who have helped in too many ways to mention here. Special thanks go to my Mum for her keen eye and steady hand in drawing up some of the maps, to Kris and Jim for their continued and dependable support and to Tessa for her calming influence and love.

Thanks also to Hilary Bradt for her many contributions and comments and to Tricia Hayne for her continued support and patience.

Introduction

The Amazon is a river of superlatives. It carries far more water than any other river in the world, with around 16% of all river water passing through its 320km-wide delta, draining an area almost the size of Australia. The volume of sediment deposited by the river in the Atlantic is so great that it stains the sea for up to 300km from the shore. From its source 5,168m high in the Peruvian Andes – less than 200km from the Pacific Ocean – the mainstream collects the waters from over 1,100 tributaries as it travels the 6,448km (4,007 miles) to the Atlantic. Although the Nile is slightly longer, at 6,670km (4,145 miles), many of the Amazon's tributaries are amongst the world's largest rivers in their own right: the Negro and the Madeira rank as the fifth and sixth largest rivers in the world. Tributaries of the Amazon rise in Peru, Bolivia, Ecuador, Colombia, Venezuela and Brazil, draining 50% of the total area of South America.

For almost half its length the Amazon flows through the world's greatest rainforest, an area larger than the whole of western Europe. The river and the rainforest are inseparable. The Amazon rainforest is as diverse as the Amazon Basin is large, and vast areas remain unexplored and scientifically unresearched.

The Amazon is also home to some of the world's great unresolved myths and tales. From the first European encounters with this 'green hell', the Spanish conquistadors began promoting legends. The first journey downstream by a European, led by Orellana in 1542, recorded tales of warring female tribes that fought like the Amazons of Greek mythology. These female warriors were never found; neither was the tall race of white giants, nor the tribe with their feet facing the wrong way to deceive trackers. The search for the gilded city of El Dorado, meanwhile, continues to this day. With an area so vast and so densely covered in rainforest, who can say with confidence that it doesn't exist?

To travel the Amazon from source to delta is the dream of many: one of the world's great journeys. Others may prefer to strike out into the rainforest, or to explore countries on the outer edges of the Amazon Basin. Those in search of rainforests and wildlife should also consider visiting the pristine jungles of Guyana, French Guiana and Suriname, which, although they lie just beyond the watershed, offer some of the region's least disturbed and most inaccessible rainforest.

Whether you're travelling independently for months or booking a two-week trip to the Amazon it is essential to plan. Visiting the rainforest is an exhilarating experience at any time of year, but if you want to explore the flooded forest you have to get the timing right – April and May are the months to aim for. Independent travel to the region is full of rewards but many of the lodges and riverboat trips get booked up, sometimes months in advance. Spending some time looking through the options in *Preparations and planning* (page 29) should minimise the possibility of disappointments once you arrive in the Amazon.

The deepest reaches of the Amazon are beyond all but the most adventurous traveller but remain a source of fascination for countless people. For those wanting to break out on their own and explore the backwaters of some small tributary, we've given guidelines on *Expedition Planning* (page 67). If you want adventure but don't have the time or the inclination to go alone, rafting opportunities in Peru and Bolivia take you through some of the quietest parts of the river.

The *Natural History* section (page 99) provides an outline of flora and fauna which you might see on the river and in the rainforest, while the chapter on *Indigenous Tribes and Settlers* (page 159) looks at how mankind has adapted to life in the area. The country chapters, in addition to giving an overview of each country and the main gateway city for international arrivals, also provide pointers to the opportunities available in each country and how best to plan them.

Whatever style of trip you plan – whether a one-week riverboat trip or an extensive multi-country tour of the region – your experience will be unique. If you're lucky you may see some of Amazonia's elusive wildlife; more realistically you will come away with just some idea of the sheer scale of the Amazon and the region through which it flows. Whatever your reasons for choosing to visit there is certain to be an occasion when you stand in the rainforest or on your riverboat, mouth agape in disbelief. In Brazil they say *'Opa'* – loosely translated as 'Wow!'

Part One

General Information

History and Background

1

THE AMAZON

From the air, the Amazon appears as a vast, uniform green carpet, embroidered here and there with sinuous, glinting ribbons. Once on the ground, though, you realise it is anything but uniform – this 'carpet' is the rainforest canopy, the crowns of millions of trees; the 'ribbons' are innumerable lakes and rivers reflecting the sunlight from their green, ochre and black waters. Giant columns tower high above, draped with encircling vines. Mysterious squawks, chirps and buzzes break the silence. Warm, damp air envelops you with tropical scents of lilies, orchids, acacias and the musty smell of decaying vegetation… This is the Amazon, place of myth and legend – the Emerald Forest.

Even in our sophisticated jet-set age the Amazon remains a great unknown, inspiring poets, scientists and travellers. Much of it is physically unexplored. Most maps are compiled from satellite photos, and there are great gaps in our knowledge of the region's history; while there still – enticingly – exists the possibility of discovering lost cities and uncontacted tribes.

Biologists are scrambling right now to describe and catalogue its myriad life forms. The Amazon, upstream of Manaus, harbours the world's richest flora and fauna – most of which is yet to be scientifically described. These organisms may yield solutions to seemingly intractable problems of our modern world: food and energy shortages, and currently incurable diseases.

The river

The Amazon is a world of trees and water – life in an abundance unimaginable until seen first-hand and then overwhelming. This is by far the world's biggest river, running through the world's largest tropical rainforest. Even when you are there, its size is difficult to grasp: it is truly awesome!

The Amazon Basin is the earth's biggest freshwater ecosystem and reservoir for a fifth of our planet's fresh water. It drains an area of over seven million km^2, over half the South American continent and three-quarters the size of the continental United States. Its forests – home to the world's highest diversity of birds, insects and plants – comprise the largest remains of primary tropical woodland and half the world's rainforests.

At the river's mouth, water flows into the Atlantic at 160–200,000 cubic metres per second – a flow greater than the world's eight biggest rivers together, or ten times that of the Mississippi. This river could drain Lake Superior – North America's biggest lake – in under two years. As it approaches the ocean the river forms not one but several deltas, as a multitude of tributaries sprawl eastward and fan out to meet the sea. Along the tidal margins of the delta, only tough, salt-tolerant mangrove survives.

The Amazon River is 6,448km (4,007 miles) from source to mouth, second in length only to the Nile at 6,670km. During its journey it receives – directly or

THE SOURCE OF THE AMAZON

The quest to locate the true source of the Amazon, a subject debated by geographers for centuries, now has a new location competing for the title. An international team of scientists, led by the Pole Jacek Palkiewicz, claimed in 1996 that the world's mightiest river originates in an underground glacier near Arequipa. The icy creek, known as Apacheta Crevice, lies at 5,168m on Volcán Chachani. This stream feeds into the Río Apurimac, which becomes the Ucayali and then the Marañon, which in turn flows into the Amazon. In 1971 a National Geographic team placed the source of the river at the Carhuasanta Crevice also close to Arequipa.

The definition of the source of a river is open to debate. Some geographers take it as the furthest point from the river's mouth and others the highest location (of the waters that feed it). An alternative view is that the true source is the river or lake that contributes the most water to the main river. For this reason Lake Lauricocha (4,838m) in Peru is cited in the *Encyclopaedia Britannica* as the source of the Amazon.

indirectly – water from over 15,000 tributaries, 12 of which are over 1,600km in length. The longest, the Madeira-Mamoré-Grande at a length of 3,200km, is the world's longest tributary and 14th longest river. In the flood season some two million kilometres of waterways are navigable.

Iquitos in Peru, a popular starting point for jungle trips, is 2,975km (1,849 miles) from the river's mouth as the parrot flies. For ships, the river's curves and meanders add almost 800km to the distance – a total 3,717km of navigable inland waterway, the longest stretch in the world. By comparison the Rhine, Europe's primary waterway, is just short of 900km.

At Iquitos the river is 7–9km wide during the wet season. Further downstream, in Brazil, the mainstream is 65km wide in places. Unless you're in a plane you rarely get a sense of how broad the river really is, as midstream islands block the view of distant banks.

The depth of the Amazon varies dramatically with seasonal floods, its level rising and falling an average of 12m across the seasons. Despite that, the mainstream is deep enough for ocean-going passenger liners and cargo ships to navigate year-round as far upstream as Iquitos, where the depth varies from 15 to 30m – but with shifting sand bars making navigation a nightmare. The deepest point of the Amazon at 62m is upstream of Santarém, at Obidos.

The rainforest

What is rainforest?

Tropical rainforests are found where temperatures and rainfall are high throughout the year. Such conditions occur only in equatorial regions in a belt 25° north and south of the Equator. All rainforests share similar features – a characteristic layered or stratified vegetation structure and high biodiversity.

Typically, annual rainfall ranges between 200cm (79in) and 1,000cm (394in). The latter extreme is not reached in the Amazon, where the average falls between 250 and 400cm. Temperatures rarely fall below 20°C (68°F), reaching a maximum of 32°C (90°F). This is cooler than many people expect, but the high humidity makes the heat feel worse. Humidity is usually around 80%, though 90–95% is not uncommon.

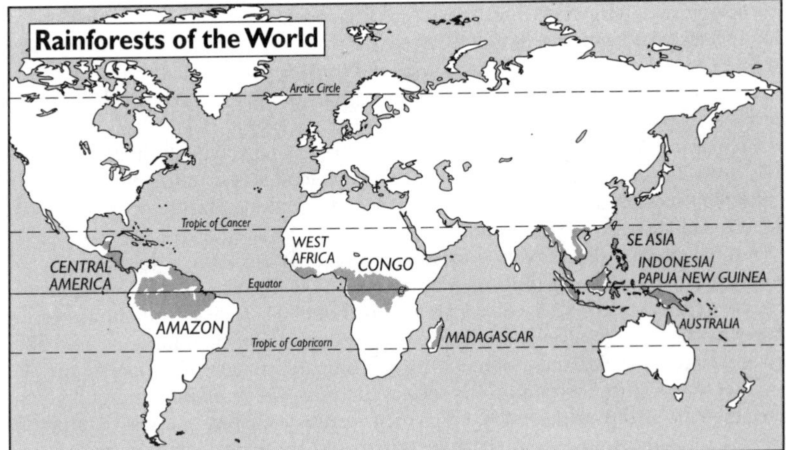

Why is rainforest important?

Since rainforests were first explored scientifically in the 1800s, naturalists have been astounded at the diversity of plants and animals. The overwhelming numbers, variety of colour and form and intricacy of ecological relationships helped inspire the evolutionary theories of Darwin and Wallace (although only Wallace spent significant time in the Amazon). Rainforests occupy less than one tenth of the world's land area but are home to three-quarters of *known* species. As temperate fauna and flora have been researched in considerably more detail than their neotropical cousins, rainforest is clearly the most species-rich habitat on earth.

Plants, fungi, insects and amphibians contain a host of potentially useful chemicals and genes awaiting discovery. Many plant species have genes resistant to disease or drought. Plants with powerful chemicals can provide pharmaceutical products. Agriculturists may find insect species that act as biological pest controls. Particularly in the brave new world of genetic engineering and biotechnology, a wealth of treasures is sure to come from the reservoir of genetic information stored in rainforests.

Besides lifetimes of work for naturalists, rainforest provides hundreds of economically valuable products: lumber, fibre, food, fuel and medicine. Multinational pharmaceutical and chemical companies apply massive efforts to looking for plants with 'miracle' compounds for use in medicine and industry, adding commercial weight to the importance of preserving whole ecosystems.

Many rainforest plants already have industrial uses. Numerous products are made from the rubber tree, *Hevea brasiliensis*. Aviation tyres are composed of 60% natural rubber as artificial rubber alone is too weak to withstand the extreme operating conditions. Other products made from 100% natural rubber include surgical gloves and condoms. Even your boat could be tree-powered: the copaiba tree of Brazil produces a sap that can be used directly as diesel fuel. Trees are harvested for fruits, and palms and brazil nuts, along with many lesser-known species, feed local people and make sustainable contributions to the local economy.

Biodiversity

Perhaps the most oft-cited reason to preserve rainforest is its high species diversity. Indeed, the Amazon rainforest has the world's highest diversity of plant species.

Compared with temperate forests, rainforest has a far greater variety of trees: up to 300 species on a single hectare (2.5 acres) of Amazon forest, or over ten times the number found in the most diverse forests in North America. That's only the trees – the undergrowth also comprises hundreds of species of shrubs, vines, herbaceous plants and ferns.

Actually *on* the rainforest trees is yet another layer of diversity. Epiphytes (plants that grow on other plants) cluster on branches and tree-trunks. They include unknown species of orchids, lilies, bromeliads, philodendrons, ferns, mosses, lichens and algae by the thousand.

Animal species diversity in lowland rainforest is also much higher than in temperate forest. The Amazon supports over 2,000 species of bird – almost a quarter of the world's total – compared with about 700 species throughout North America. Tropical rainforest also harbours more species of mammals (around 300 in Amazonia), reptiles and amphibians than comparable areas of temperate forest.

Insects epitomise the rainforest's species diversity. Of about one million known species, 90% are from the tropics. Scientists estimate that as many as 30 million species remain undiscovered. If true, this would mean that rainforests harbour 94% of all the earth's species, albeit mostly insects!

The Amazon is also unequalled in its diversity of aquatic life. The drainage contains over 2,000 fish species. Despite this being half of all known freshwater species, scientists believe that at least another thousand remain undiscovered. A single Amazon lake might have 200 species, a greater number than found throughout all of Europe.

Climate

The Amazon Basin does not have seasons as such. Apart from a few blips in the overall pattern, rainforest weather is remarkably constant; normally with fine balmy days, and an afternoon thunderstorm once or twice a week. Rain is possible, though unlikely, every day of your trip – so expect the unexpected!

The central Amazon Basin and the eastern slopes of the Andes have a tropical wet climate. The high precipitation in this zone results from low air pressure and wind convergence combined with intense surface heating and the air's high moisture content. Northeast Amazonia, as well as a vast area of southern Brazil and further south, experience both a wet and dry tropical climate, with a distinct dry season that lasts longer with increasing distance from the Equator.

Temperatures

All rainforest climates are characteristically warm (but not excessively hot) with frequent rain. Around Iquitos, 3° south, temperature varies hardly at all. During

AMAZON RAINFOREST – DISAPPEARING FAST

Despite hopes that rainforest destruction was beginning to tail off, figures published in 1998 suggest that the trend is actually on the increase. A Brazilian congressional commission showed that 58,013km² of the Amazon were destroyed through logging, ground fires and thinning of previously virgin forest. Brazil's National Institute for Space Research (INPE) also released long-awaited figures based on satellite images that showed 29,005km² were destroyed in the 1995–96 growing season; with early estimates for 1997 suggesting rates had fallen with 13,037km² cleared.

A COOL WIND

A severe El Niño effect hit South America in 1998; perhaps worse than that in 1982-83, previously the worst to date. Amazon wildlife is affected by such a dramatic change in climate. Some species, especially reptiles, undergo behavioural changes. As surface water temperatures drop, caiman are more likely to bask out in the open to warm themselves in the sun and anaconda emerge from the unusually cool waters, a quite unusual behaviour for this giant snake.

The winds can last for a couple of weeks or so – long enough to cool the surface of lakes and rivers. As the surface cools, the upper layer of cold water descends to the bottom stirring the rich organic ooze of decaying vegetation that traps large amounts of methane. The disturbed mud releases methane and other poisonous gases, creating an oxygen crisis. Desperate fish crowd close to the surface to gasp uncontaminated oxygen, dissolved in a thin layer where water meets air. Even so, vast numbers of fish and freshwater crustaceans suffocate and floodplains become feasting grounds for carrion feeders, especially vultures. This is just one consequence of a sudden temperature drop.

the day it is 'shorts and T-shirt' weather, ranging from 24°C in the morning to 30°C in the afternoon. Occasionally temperatures may exceed 35°C, and at night fall to 21°C but rarely lower.

The one overwhelming factor of the climate is the humidity which can often be an oppressive 80% or higher, inspiring at best lethargy and at worst sleep.

Each year, the intensity of the cyclical weather system off the coast of Peru known as El Niño causes a cold southerly wind (*friagem* in Brazil or *surazo* in Bolivia) to blow from Patagonia. In certain years, daytime temperatures drop as low as 15°C.

Wind

High wind conditions in the Amazon are rare. Forest winds are light and at ground level are more or less non-existent as the forest canopy absorbs most wind energy. This is one reason why pollen and seeds of most Amazon plants are animal-dispersed; wind-dispersed pollen or seeds tend not to travel far.

The strongest winds can occur in the middle of broad rivers and lakes, where there are sometimes severe gusts, especially during rainstorms. Windy conditions on a boat are not dangerous, the greatest concern being motion sickness.

Rainfall

A common assumption is that rainfall in the rainforest must be constant. In fact, it is intermittent though regular, occurring on average three or four times a week, often in the form of short and spectacular downpours. On the coast it can rain at any hour, day or night. Inland, early afternoon is most likely, although rain at night and in the early morning is possible. When it rains, water generally cascades from the heavens; in one hour two or three centimetres (around an inch) may fall. The high levels of precipitation in rainforest are the result of intense individual downpours rather than lighter rain over long periods. If it rains in the Amazon, you get wet; there's rarely the wimpish drizzle found in northern latitudes.

In the upper Amazon, rainfall averages 305cm per year. This seems to have decreased in recent years. In particular 1994 was very dry, possibly because extensive deforestation disrupted local rainfall patterns.

Rainfall is predictably unpredictable. Around Iquitos, with the exception of May, every month recorded as the wettest one year has been recorded as the driest in another. July to November tends to be dry, while the wetter season is from February to April. In Bolivia the wet season runs from December to March. To the north in Venezuela, most rain falls between the months of June and October.

Thunderstorms

Tropical warmth and moisture create perfect conditions for spectacular thunderstorms. Huge cumulonimbus clouds can be seen bubbling above the rainforest and stretching ever further into the sky above, fuelled by rising mists from rivers and vegetation. These formations may rise to 10,000m in a classic 'anvil' shape. These clouds harbour enormous potential energy, released as brilliant lightning displays and ear-splitting thunder.

Sunshine

As the Amazon is equatorial, days hardly vary from twelve hours in length. Of course the amount of sunshine depends on cloud cover, but there are usually nine to eleven hours of sunshine per day. Because the sun is directly overhead, it is more intense than in temperate latitudes. Take precautions to prevent sunburn, especially from reflected sunlight on water.

AMAZON HISTORY

Throughout Amazon history, extravagant wealth and sordid misery are dominant themes. Fortunes were found and lost; kingdoms were defeated; peoples were enslaved and freed. Deadly diseases, fearsome creatures, hostile Indians and rapacious settlers, all within the forest's immensity, set the stage for a fascinating and often turbulent history. Added to this, the overwhelming power of legends attracted conquistadors from halfway across the world in search of the gilded man of El Dorado, while explorers throughout the centuries have searched in vain for the women tribes of the Amazonas and numerous lost cities.

Origins of the Amazonians

Today the Amazon yields few of its past secrets. Unfortunately the heat, together with the damp and acid soils of the rainforest, conspire to decompose organic remains quickly before they can fossilise. Human fossils are virtually absent from the lowland regions, so we have practically no certain clues as to how and when people arrived in the area. Likewise, without animal fossils it is difficult to reconstruct ancient faunas and so we are denied the human picture in its ecological context.

Aboriginal peoples of the Americas are believed to have arrived on the continent around 15–20,000 years ago, between the two most recent ice ages. Migrating east and southwards, the hunter-gatherers made their way across the isthmus of Central America down to South America. This wave of migration gave rise to the Olmec, Maya and Aztec civilisations of Central America which flourished from 1400BC until the arrival of the Spanish conquistadors in the early 1500s. In the eastern coastal regions and highlands of South America the Chimú and Inca, along with many other cultures, left ample architectural and cultural artefacts for us to ponder.

In the last twenty years, chance discoveries and finds of stone tools and ceramics have suggested that large populations were established on the flood plains near the current city of Manaus by 3000BC. Some authorities believe humans have been in the Amazon much longer than formerly thought. David Childress, recounting *The Chronicle of Akakor*, describes advanced civilisations and lost cities in the Amazon dating back over 12,000 years ago!

THE CHRONICLE OF AKAKOR

Tales of fabulous cities hidden in the Amazon permanently enhance the feeling of excitement and adventure that prevails throughout the region. While many lost cities have been found, the Chronicle of Akakor remains perhaps the most fantastic of all the legends.

The Chronicles are written in the tribal book of the Ugha Mongulala, a people 'chosen by the Gods' 15,000 years ago. Arriving in golden airships, white-skinned strangers civilised the tribe and built three great stone cities: Akanis, Akakor and Akahim. The legendary city of Akakor is on the Purus River, in a high mountain valley on the frontier between Brazil and Peru. The city-fortress was one of 26 stone cities stretching from Bolivia through to Venezuela, while another 13 underground cities were linked by an intricate system of tunnels and canals stretching right across South America.

The Chronicles record the existence of a large island to the west of South America, buried under an enormous tidal wave during the first great catastrophe, and predict cyclical devastations each lasting 6,000 years.

The recent discovery of pyramids on satellite images of the Madre de Dios regions correlates precisely with the location of the Lost City of Akakor. The pyramids remain unvisited and several attempts to reach the site have failed, resulting in fatal accidents. Lost cities must always, as everyone knows, be protected by a curse of death on those who enter!

When the city is found, the history of the Ugha Mongulala and the greatest civilisation South America has ever known will finally be revealed and explained in the great tribal book *The Chronicle of Akakor*. Written in Quechua – a skill that eluded even the Incas – the script of the gods will demonstrate irrefutable proof of lost cities throughout the Amazon Basin, as well as of intergalactic travel and visitors from other planets.

The search for El Dorado continues today as several lost cities are still believed to exist, notably Akakor itself and the Lost Mines of Muribeca. Despite the scoffing of establishment archaeologists, in 1986 a lost city in Mato Grosso, Brazil, was actually discovered, visible in satellite photographs. Satellite images have also revealed what appear to be eight huge pyramids in the Madre de Dios region of Peru. But in both these areas expeditions have so far failed to reach their destinations. Faced with such discoveries, established theories and ideas about the arrival and development of humankind in South America are continually being questioned.

A number of scholars believe the Chinese crossed the Pacific over 2,000 years ago and influenced the native cultures. Others think the pattern of migration went in the opposite direction, from South America. Best-known proponent of this theory is Thor Heyerdahl, whose Kon-Tiki expedition across the Pacific in the 1940s proved that a long journey across the ocean was possible with a simple craft made from locally available balsa wood. Still others, notably R Buckminster Fuller, cite evidence of Phoenician voyages to the South American coast around 200BC. We are unlikely ever to discover the whole picture and mysteries will remain.

The indigenous peoples of the Andean regions developed advanced architecture, mathematics, astronomy and agricultural systems unequalled for sophistication and productivity in contemporary South America. Megalithic works – Machu Picchu being the supreme accomplishment – and gold, pottery, textile and stone artefacts show the strength of the Inca and preceding cultures were primarily west of the Amazon.

In the Amazon itself, Inca presence was limited but significant. Well-established around the headwaters of the Putumayo near the Colombia-Ecuador border and along the Napo River, flowing from Ecuador to Peru, Inca outposts promoted trade in gold, pottery, agricultural produce and slaves. In recent decades the eastern slopes of the Andes have become a hot-spot for archaeologists keen to explore links between the high and lowland cultures of South America.

For thousands of years, tribes of the Amazon and the surrounding mountains coexisted as neighbours, albeit as rivals at one time, allies at another. Despite influences from the Inca many remote forest-dwelling tribes remained as hunter-gatherers, as a few do to this day.

In the late 15th century this balance was to be shattered in one swift event: the arrival of outsiders – the Europeans.

The Europeans arrive: paradise lost?

Apparently a shaman, the spiritual healer and leader of each South American indigenous group, prophesied the arrival of a white deity from the east, at the time that Columbus anchored off the shores of Cuba in 1492. If the conquistadors were considered to be gods, it is frightening to contemplate what the activities of evil forces would have entailed. The very first encounters between lowland Indians and Europeans were filled with curiosity from all sides, but the novelty soon wore off and the Europeans quickly demanded control of everything and everyone they encountered. The Indians did not realise the mistaken identity of these fair-skinned deities until it was too late.

The sea voyages of Pinzón, Ojeda and Vespucci had all travelled past the Amazon's mouth by 1500. On April 26 the Portuguese commander Pedro Álvares Cabral made the first landing on the eastern side of South America by a European and is now remembered as the founder of Brazil. But it was not until forty years later that the first Spanish conquistadors entered the Amazon heartland, opening the first chapter of the interior's written history.

Strangers in a strange land indeed, the new arrivals were men the like of whom had never been encountered by the Indians. The magic fire sticks that killed at great distance were a fearsome weapon and the Indians had never seen horses before. Armies thousands strong fell in battles against a couple of hundred mounted Spanish soldiers under the command of Francisco Pizarro. The Spanish conquistadors were the strongest soldiers in the world at the time and, although the odds were stacked against them, the superior firepower of the Spanish made the defeat of the Indians inevitable.

Strength and fortuitous timing assisted greatly in the speedy dispatch of the Incas, who were still recovering from the division of near civil war in their empire. Restless and ready for action, once the battles with the Incas were over, the new Spanish governors turned their energies to in-fighting over new land rights. For war-hungry soldiers the prospect of peace time was uninspiring, and one suitable distraction was for energetic conquistadors to set off to explore new lands.

By 1540, having plundered the Inca empire of its riches and claimed new lands for Spain, the Spanish turned their attentions further inland, while on South America's eastern coast the Portuguese had begun setting up colonies.

The attraction of the lowlands and the first descent

Gonzalo Pizarro, a younger brother and loyal supporter of Francisco throughout the conquest, had been appointed governor of Quito. With the coast to the west a certainty, the eternally curious Pizarro was drawn to the east, spurred on by rumours promising fantastic wealth. Indians spoke of the land of

El Dorado where a gold-dusted king bathed in a sacred lake as his ancestors had done for generations. La Canela was another land filled with spices that were highly prized and valued back in Europe. Pizarro set about planning his trip from Quito.

With time on his hands, the similarly under-entertained conquistador Francisco de Orellana heard of Pizarro's plans in early 1541. Orellana had shown his drive and ambition when he left Spain for the New World at the age of just sixteen and was among the 150 conquistadors who fought under Francisco Pizarro during the conquest of the Incas. Pizarro was happy to have a man of Orellana's stature join the expedition.

Pizarro's expedition force left Quito at the end of February, 1541. The journey, which first had to cross the Andes to the east of Quito before forging a path through impenetrable jungle, was expected to be hard. Some 280 Spaniards, many on horse-back, were accompanied by 4,000 Indians acting as guides and porters. Hundreds of llamas carried supplies, with 2,000 pigs forming a trotting foodstore and just as many dogs to hunt Indians. Strength in numbers seems to be the best explanation for the large expeditionary force, but even so the scale suggests that expectations were high.

The departing procession must have been epic... and Orellana missed it by a few days! Assembling a small band of men and horses, he quickly set out to catch up with Pizarro. Both groups found the journey difficult although presumably Orellana had few problems following the detritus-strewn tracks of such a large expedition. When Orellana was finally reunited with the larger party, Pizarro quickly promoted this man of proven loyalty to second-in-command.

Camping on the Upper Napo, near the modern-day town of Coca (Puerto Francisco de Orellana) in Ecuador, the group explored the area, hacking down jungle, making new paths and building bridges to cross rivers. By the end of 1541 dreams of El Dorado were fading. Most of the highland Indians had died, as had a number of Spaniards. Food was running low and the rains were getting heavier by the day. The search for wealth was replaced by the more basic need to survive.

A turning-point in the expedition came with the decision to build a boat and use the rivers as highways. Despite the fact that every conquistador on the trip had reached the New World by sailing across the Atlantic, inspiration for the decision came from the efficient use of canoes by lowland Indians.

A vessel large enough to carry 60 men and supplies was built. Orellana was given command of the brigantine and, with 57 men and several canoes, set sail in search of food. This was close to Christmas in 1541. Pizarro and some 140 starving men were left on the banks of the river, watching their hopes for survival drift downstream with the current. Orellana never returned.

Orellana moved quickly: 'As the river flowed fast, we proceeded on at the rate of from twenty to twenty-five leagues [110–140km], for now the river was high [from the rains].' By early January 1542 his armada came across a village with food in abundance. As so often with the conquistadors, speed was the deciding factor in arriving before a viable defence could be mounted. When the fleeing Indians returned to their village, through curiosity or otherwise, Orellana's diplomatic skills, a basic grasp of the language and a few traded items encouraged good relations.

Attempts to send a canoe back to Pizarro failed. Whether Orellana had any intention of returning is debatable but he certainly did everything he could to clear his name for the sake of history. He stood down from his command to avoid any possible implications of treachery but was reinstated by the popular vote of his crew. The decision was made to continue with the voyage downstream, since enough was known about South America to assume that the river's mouth was somewhere on the Atlantic.

Back on the banks of the River Napo, Pizarro was in no doubt of Orellana's treachery. He 'displayed toward the whole expedition the greatest cruelty that ever faithless men have shown, aware that it was left unprovided with food and caught in a vast uninhabited region and among great rivers.'

After almost a month as overstaying guests, having stretched the hospitality of their hosts to the limit, Orellana's party set sail once more. Following the current they experienced few problems, apart from the temporary loss of two canoes that strayed too far ahead of the main group and got lost in a maze of streams and islands for a couple of days.

Approaching the confluence of the Napo with the Amazon, Orellana's band once more prepared themselves for conflict. According to the chronicler Friar Gaspar de Carvajal, as they neared one village scores of Indians climbed into canoes 'in the attitude of warriors'. Passing peacefully through the threat of war, diplomacy once more secured amiable relations. While Orellana and his two Friars set about talking to the Indians of Christianity, the crew of professional soldiers began constructing a new and bigger boat in preparation for the sea voyage.

The stay at this cooperative village was made more memorable by the arrival of four white men described as being a span taller than the tallest Christian. Carvajal's records mark the start of the often-told legend of a race of white-skinned, fair-haired giants dressed with gold ornaments living in the Amazon Basin.

The vessel was completed in 35 days, and the two boats, several canoes and crew set sail on April 24. Two months of travel had passed and, although the Indians encountered so far had hardly volunteered food, acquiring it had not proved difficult. But Orellana's flotilla was about to enter the territory of the Machiparo who, according to Indians on the river, had warriors numbering 50,000.

For six weeks the Spaniards were hassled, cajoled, attacked and hijacked. After the warriors of Machiparo, the Indians of the Omagua guaranteed little rest for the tiring travellers. As word of the foreign intruders travelled downstream ahead of the Spaniards, the crew were welcomed by ever more inhospitable Indians and had to resort to increasingly aggressive ways of acquiring food.

Passing the confluence of the Madeira, downstream from what is now Manaus, the crew heard first mention of a tribe of women warriors. 'These women are very white and tall... and they are robust and go about naked, but with their privy parts covered, with their bows and arrows in their hands, doing as much fighting as ten Indian men,' wrote Carvajal.

The account of women in battle may well be true. But such a tribe was not seen after this journey and has not been since. As with the Greek legend of the Amazons, the existence of this fierce female tribe remains firmly placed on a distant boundary somewhere between the limits of geographical knowledge and the imagination. Carvajal's reference to the Amazon archers who cut off their right breasts to facilitate shooting was to become the most memorable tale: a lasting epitaph of this epic journey.

Sensing the ebb and flow of the ocean tide, the Spaniards carried out repair work on the vessels downstream of the Tapajós. On August 26 the two vessels sailed into the Atlantic, completing the first descent of the Amazon by Europeans.

Orellana will always be remembered for the first navigation of the Amazon, but in many ways history has not treated this accidental tourist too well. Orellana's emergence from the Amazon, eight months after his departure from the main group, coincided with Pizarro's return to Quito. Having retraced his route from the banks of the Napo, Pizarro, through pride or anger, paid brief attention to blackening Orellana's name.

A couple of years later Orellana tried to return to the river. With inadequate resources and funds, his second voyage up the Amazon was to cause his death in 1546. Although it was briefly called the Rio Orellana, the river became more commonly known as the River of the Amazons... a name far more fitting for a continent alive with fantastic legends.

Lope de Aguirre claims a new savage frontier

It took almost fifteen years for Orellana's accomplishment to be repeated and with certain parallels. Orellana had joined Pizarro's expedition and by luck reserved himself a place in history. Lope de Aguirre was recruited as just an ordinary member of the crew for the river's second descent but indisputably stole the honour. The expedition of Pedro de Ursúa flirted with disaster from the outset and most problems could be seen to originate from one source – Lope de Aguirre.

Ursúa was the dashing, gallant, Spanish conquistador of history. Ambitious and young, he had already achieved numerous victories in battles throughout the New World. On arriving in Peru his energies obtained him a commission to follow in the footsteps of Orellana, conquer the lands of the Omagua and find, once and for all, that elusive city of gold.

With a motley crew of 300 Spaniards and 2,000 Indians, the trip left Lima in February of 1559 and crossed the Andes to Moyobamba. There they built two boats, flatboats for transporting horses, twenty rafts and several canoes. By October 1560 the river journey had begun but not without warning signs of trouble ahead. Endless delays and frustrations had created a restlessness in camp; four men were sentenced to death for holding the second-in-command at gunpoint even before the river journey had started. Mutiny became increasingly likely and every man watched his back for fear of incriminations and false accusations.

A strong leader would have quashed the insurgents but Ursúa was too wrapped up in his own world, devoting his time to his love Doña Inez de Atienza. For some reason Ursúa had decided to travel with his wife, an act hardly likely to endear him to his crew. And in truth history is not littered with characters who successfully led expeditions with their partners in tow.

Within the crew was the physically crippled and scarred Lope ('The Wolf') de Aguirre. Since arriving in the New World in 1534, Aguirre had successfully managed to avoid gaining wealth and acquiring nobility. His career up to this point was a list of impressive failures, each one contributing to his growing feelings of bitterness and desire for revenge.

With the expedition literally drifting downstream without guidance, Aguirre saw the opportunity for long-sought-after leadership. Heading a band of men who favoured mutiny over loyalty he plotted against Ursúa, murdering him in his hammock with the agreement of the newly promoted Fernando de Guzmán. All friends and sympathisers to Ursúa were similarly disposed of and the group set about searching for the riches of El Dorado.

Guzmán became the new governor and Aguirre took the title of master of the camp. Having plotted against the authority of the King of Spain, the rebels now explored all kind of fantastic ideas. Guzmán was crowned prince and king over the indeterminable territory. The search for gold was just one option, but why stop there? Aguirre suggested the regal forces return upstream to conquer Peru. As far from reality as they were from Spain, this notion slowly gained support. Dissenters, whether identified by rumour or by fact, were killed without hesitation at Aguirre's command. While the new leaders feasted like royalty, delusions of grandeur relegated the search for gold to a lower priority. Despite the lack of food, finances and weaponry, and with just over 200 men remaining, Guzmán and Aguirre explored the possibilities for conquering Peru.

The journey down the Amazon seemed secondary to the omnipresent atmosphere of rebellion. Having played one rebellious group off against another, Aguirre finally tired of Guzmán and murdered his new king. Without competition he took complete command of the group.

Travelling further downstream, Aguirre explored the Negro River seeking a shorter route to Peru. Whether he then continued to the mouth of the Amazon is unknown, but there is a slight possibility that Aguirre was the first European to use the Casiquiare Canal linking the Amazon and Orinoco watersheds.

The chronicles of the journey pay remarkably little attention to the region and its inhabitants, preferring instead to dwell on another first; an intimate demonstration of the phenomenon known as expedition madness. Clearly something had happened to the group. As Smith explains in *Explorers of the Amazon*, 'the expedition was not one of geography but of carnage, of Spaniards killing Spaniards'.

Aguirre's band arrived on the island of Margarita in July 1561. In a rage of anger spiked with paranoia he prepared to march on Peru, looting the city and enlarging the number of recruits to 150. Forces loyal to the Spanish crown finally halted the rebellion as Aguirre and his rebels marched through Venezuela en route to Peru. On the battlefield Aguirre's men were offered royal pardons in return for their surrender. When Aguirre himself was offered the chance to surrender he refused it, preferring to die a leader. He was killed in October 1561 with just one of his loyal soldiers by his side. Just before his death Aguirre penned a letter to King Philip of Spain. Brutally aware of his treachery and somewhat proud of his actions he ventured to offer the king guidance from one great leader to another, urging him 'never to send fleets to that cursed river'.

The upstream struggle

The above two voyages were downriver and Spanish. The more difficult journey upstream was completed in 1637–38 by the Portuguese veteran of the Amazon, Captain Pedro de Teixeira. His upriver journey explains, in part, why half the river, some 3,400km, lies within Brazilian territory.

The Portuguese had not shown a great deal of interest in the portion of South America allotted to them in the Treaty of Tordesillas, which in 1494 divided the sub-continent between the Iberian powers with a straight line. They demonstrated very little concern over the encroachment when, following the tales of wealth and riches in the New World which were common in Europe by the 16th century, French, British, Irish and Dutch navigators were all trying to gain footholds on the quieter eastern side of the continent. But as war spread across Europe, Spain wanted to ensure protection of her overseas territories and, forging Iberian alliance, Spain encouraged Portugal to clear European foreigners from her part of South America. Fort Presépio was built in 1616, in the location where Belém now stands, and by the early 1630s the Portuguese had cleared the Amazon.

Previously unconcerned by the encroachment of other European nations, Portugal was now free to be the sole beneficiary of the riches that flowed from the Amazon Basin.

But in 1637 the arrival of two Franciscan missionaries floating downstream into Fort Presépio unsettled the Portuguese. The missionaries were Spanish and had been working on the Río Napo when illness had forced them to abandon their village. The Amazon would never be free of foreign influence if Spanish missionaries could easily sail a small boat the length of the river, so the Portuguese felt compelled to travel upstream to prevent even greater numbers of Spaniards using the river freely as if it were open sea.

Captain Teixeira left the port of Belém on October 28 1637. Forty-seven canoes, powered by 1,200 Indians and negroes, transported 70 Portuguese soldiers upstream. Even today planning a trip up the Amazon from its mouth is hazardous in the extreme, as several large tributaries can easily be mistaken for the mainstream. Teixeira took with him one of the Spanish Friars who may have been of some help; but, even so, moving the expedition forward must have been a massive task.

On reaching the first Spanish settlement after eight months, Teixeira set up camp. One full year after leaving Fort Presépio, he arrived in the city of Quito.

MAKING THE AMAZON PORTUGUESE

It's a common enough lesson learnt in schools that the Treaty of Tordesillas divided the South American continent between the imperial powers of Portugal and Spain. And so it did... to a degree. The treaty drew a line 370 leagues west of the Cape Verde group of islands – west of the line was Spanish territory, east was Portuguese.

So how did Portugal claim so much land to the west of this imaginary line?

Following the difficulties of Orellana's and Aguirre's descents of the great river, the Spanish were reluctant to mount further expeditions to the Amazon Basin.

The mouth of the river was a natural starting point for exploration to the hinterland. In the 17th and 18th century Portuguese expeditions down the mainstream cleared vast areas of the Indian population while settlements of missionaries and gold prospectors had sprung up throughout the Amazon Basin.

The need to formalise boundaries became apparent as Brazil moved towards independence. On January 13 1751, the Treaty of Madrid between King João of Portugal and King Ferdinand VI of Spain divided the South American continent between Portugal and Spain, marking out the international boundaries roughly as they stand today. Portugal's share was far greater than that allotted in the original Treaty of Tordesillas, and was due largely to the ease of navigation on the Amazon.

The treaty creating this new boundary recognised the difficulty of colonising the region, showing a remarkable openness and indifference to detail: 'without being bothered about a few leagues of deserted lands, in regions where each Crown will have such an over-abundance that they could not be inhabited for many centuries'.

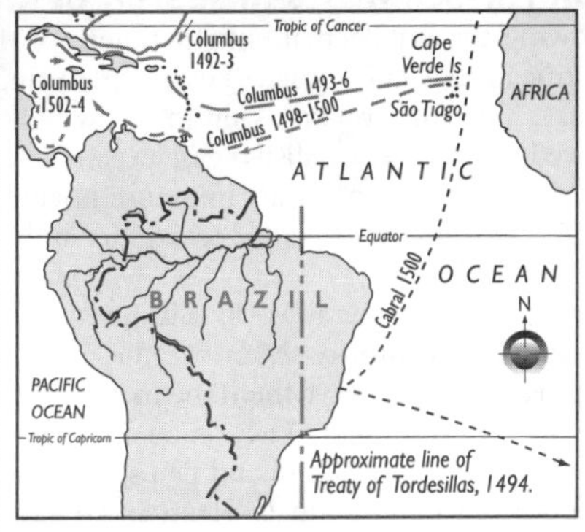

Not surprisingly the Spaniards were as alarmed by the arrival of the Portuguese as the inhabitants of Fort Presépio had been one year earlier. They too wanted to find out how far the Portuguese had wandered west of the Tordesillas line and they sent the Jesuit priest Cristóbal de Acuña to join the Portuguese on their return journey with instructions to record all that he saw.

Acuña's notes create a more detailed record of the region than those from the voyages of Orellana and Aguirre. The Indians encountered receive a generally better press, being credited with using the rainforest to ensure that 'these barbarians never know what hunger is'. He notes their skill in harvesting fruit from the trees and game from the forest. When news got back, Europe was excited by tales of the first encounter with an electric eel, one hundred years before the discovery of electricity in Europe. Old myths were verified and new legends were born. The fierce female Amazons, Acuña was assured by local Indians, did exist but not on the Amazon mainstream... they could be found living to the north in what is now Guyana. Acuña also recorded the existence of tribes of dwarf Indians and yet another tribe with their feet back to front to deceive would-be trackers.

Teixeira's expedition returned to Fort Presépio on 12 December 1639 having been away for more than two years. Stating Spain's claim to the lion's share of the river, Acuña wrote to the Council of the Indies suggesting that Spain waste no time in establishing its right to the river so as to benefit from the river's riches and its value as a route to the Andes. But Teixeira's actions had staked a physical claim to the river, establishing Portuguese settlements as far upstream as possible and guaranteeing Portugal's claim to the River Amazon.

Missionaries followed the early explorers. Jesuits were first, followed by Franciscans and Capuchins. Each order founded settlements and brought Catholicism to the natives. Although many Europeans believed the Indians were savages without spirits, the missionaries were given control over their spiritual development. The Jesuits were the most prominent missionaries, encouraging Indians to descend into villages or *aldeias*, where they could live, work and receive religious instruction. Although the missions were a place of relative safety, missionaries often turned a blind eye to the slaving raids that permitted the collection of legitimate prisoners-of-war from inter-tribal conflicts.

With time these missions became increasingly powerful and vocal in their defence of the Indians. Resentment over their success led to eviction of their leaders from Spanish and Portuguese territory in 1757. With the removal of the Jesuits, slow and steady colonisation of the area was the only European activity in the Amazon.

Explorer-scientists in search of knowledge

Following the intellectual enlightenment of the Renaissance, a new approach to scientific investigation reached its zenith during the Age of Reason in the mid-18th century. The Amazon was seen in a new light: the conquistador's green hell was replaced by the naturalist's green paradise. Such a change reflected a new awareness of the rainforest's immense botanical riches – an attitude to originate with the next group of people to explore and discover the Amazon's wonders: the explorer-scientists.

Regarding the natural world, European views changed profoundly between the 16th and 19th centuries. Men became interested in knowledge for its own sake, while greater wealth gave them the means to pursue their goal to better understand the world around them. These men discovered riches in the Amazon Basin of far greater value than the gold and gems the conquistadors sought in vain. Attracted by reports of strange animals, plants and unknown tribes, they became seekers after knowledge.

LOVE CONQUERS ALL

Travel arrangements in Amazonia don't always go according to plan. Jean Godin des Odonais, a member of Condamine's original expedition, decided that it was time to return to France having lived in Ecuador for several years. Leaving his pregnant wife Isabela in Riobamba in March of 1749, he promised to return when he was certain that passage down the River Amazon was possible and safe. Like his compatriot Condamine he was eternally curious.

After travelling as far as French Guiana he set about returning to collect his wife and family. But the return journey was out of the question. France and Portugal were not friends at the best of times and, without the backing of an official expedition, permission to travel the length of the Amazon was denied. For several years he wrote to friends in high places and government officials seeking permission to enter Brazil to collect his family. He even wrote to the French Foreign Minister advocating war against the Portuguese so France could claim the Amazon.

When a galliot, manned with 30 Portuguese oarsmen, arrived after 16 years of petitioning, Godin feared that his letter inciting war had fallen into foreign hands. Anxious for his own safety he entrusted his friend Tristan d'Oreasaval with funds to travel to Riobamba and return with the beloved Isabela; but d'Oreasaval failed to honour any of his commitments… apart from spending the money.

The vessel made it up the Amazon to Lagunas from where the crew travelled by foot to Quito. News reached Riobamba informing Isabela that transport awaited her in Lagunas. With all her children dead from malaria, yellow fever and dysentery she had nothing to lose.

A party of 41, of which 31 were Indian porters, left Riobamba in late 1769. Isabela's father went ahead to organise river travel and smooth out the journey not knowing that someone in the advance party carried smallpox. When his daughter arrived in Canelos 100km east of Riobamba the pre-arranged canoes were missing and half the villagers dead. The Indian porters then disappeared overnight suspecting the journey was doomed.

Using just one canoe and a raft, the remaining group headed downstream with 200km to travel to Andoas. Hitting a log they lost the raft but recovered their goods and decided to send an advance party ahead to fetch assistance. When help failed to return and with food supplies running low a second raft was built; once again to be smashed to pieces, this time losing all the supplies.

The rest of the group died from illness and no help came. Isabela set off alone through the jungle. After wandering for over a week she was found by Indians, who fed her and transported her downstream, so that she eventually arrived in Andoas two months after leaving Riobamba. In early 1770 she finally boarded the boat in Lagunas that was to take her to her husband.

From there it was plain sailing for Isabela, travelling 3,200km downstream before heading north at the Atlantic and to Cayenne where she was reunited with Godin in mid-1770 – 21 years after they had last seen each other.

Charles-Marie de la Condamine

Among the first and most influential of them was the Frenchman Charles-Marie de la Condamine who explored the mainstream of the Amazon in 1743. Originally sent to South America to resolve an academic argument over the precise shape of the world, Condamine was eternally curious about this stimulating continent and seems to have been incapable of focusing on any one reason for his trip. If there was a way of deviating off a path he took it. Leaving Paris in 1735, the expedition that was originally meant to take just two years returned to Paris a decade later. The man's endless curiosity did much to fill his *Abridged Narrative of Travels Through the Interior of South America*, published in 1745. The book contained the first detailed report of a strange substance made from the sap of a rainforest tree. Along the Japurá River, Condamine observed Omagua Indians using the sap of a tree to make galoshes, rings and even syringes. Although others had seen this wondrous substance used to make bouncing balls and waterproof items, Condamine was the first to take it back to Europe.

Industrialising Europe and the United States soon found invaluable uses for rubber, a substance to which the Industrial Revolution owes much. Condamine also researched and confirmed the existence of a natural canal – the Casiquiare – connecting the Amazon and Orinoco river systems. His reports inspired a generation of scientists to carry on his work.

Alexander von Humboldt

One of the Amazon's greatest explorers was Baron Alexander von Humboldt (1769–1858), a well-to-do Prussian of noble birth. Beginning in 1799, he embarked on a four-year expedition to the Orinoco and the upper reaches of the northwest Amazon Basin. His high-level contacts assured him of every assistance from Spanish officials, giving him greater freedom to travel than Condamine had had some 60 years earlier.

Humboldt's inland expedition began in February of 1800. After seven weeks travelling the wide open expanses of the Venezuelan *llanos,* Humboldt and his companion Aimé Bonpland concentrated their efforts on the great River Orinoco. In particular Humboldt wanted to establish whether there really was a link between the Amazon Basin and the Orinoco.

Travelling up the Orinoco to the Atures rapids – where Puerto Ayacucho is today – Humboldt and his small party recorded suffering the vicious biting insects of the region. Visitors to the area today can still share in the misery of these minute yet ferocious flies known locally as *la plaga*. The suffering eased when the team reached the mission station of San Fernando de Atabapo where the acidic blackwaters of the Río Atabapo fail to support the ecosystems that flourish in the whitewaters of the Orinoco.

Travelling up ever smaller rivers, the canoe was pushed from the watershed of the Orinoco from the River Temi to enter the Amazon Basin on the River Guainía. Downstream Humboldt entered the Casiquiare; he measured the length of this remarkable natural canal and found it to be 322km. The canal, actually 354km in length, proved an arduous journey for Humboldt, with the return of insects reported by one missionary living in the area to be 'the most painful he had felt'.

The verification of the canal, a phenomenon subject to much disbelief in 18th-century Europe, was a considerable success for the Humboldt party but not the only one. His contribution to the field of botany alone ranks as a major scientific achievement, with a collection of over 12,000 plant specimens, most of which were new to science. Humboldt's scientific work was accurate, detailed and exhaustive. No topic was excluded. He wrote on botany, zoology, pharmacology and geology, creating what today is still considered a database of the region. But although Humboldt was a vital contributor to the increased awareness of rainforest, he never actually travelled on or saw the Amazon mainstream.

An explorer's paradise

Following in Humboldt's footsteps, botanists, zoologists and geographers from all over Europe and North America descended upon South America, and the Amazon Basin in particular, to discover its hidden riches. These scientists unveiled a seemingly endless variety of plants and animals. Inspired Western naturalists from humbler backgrounds were to find new species and build their reputation on Amazon discoveries.

Naturalist Charles Darwin, famous for his theory of evolution, sailed past the river's mouth in 1834 on his famous round-the-world voyage in *HMS Beagle*. Alfred Wallace, Darwin's contemporary and co-discoverer of the principle of natural selection, spent four years in the Napo River area of present-day northeastern Peru – near Iquitos.

Wallace's friend, the botanist Richard Spruce, spent much longer in the area. For over fifteen years he collected, drew and noted thousands of Amazon plant species. During his time he fended off unfriendly Indians and recovered from tropical fevers. He is most remembered for obtaining quinine seeds for cultivation outside the Amazon, breaking the South American monopoly on the anti-malarial drug.

Henry Walter Bates, another of Wallace's companions, arrived in Brazil in May 1848. Bates' monumental collection involved the drawing and cataloguing of close to 15,000 insect specimens, more than half of them unknown to science. His lengthy research proved that some species of harmless insects actually mimic other more dangerous species. Now called Batesian mimicry in his honour, this strategy is recognised by biologists today as a fundamental process in the evolution of biodiversity. In 1863 Bates published *The Naturalist on the River Amazons* which is rightly regarded as the best contemporary account of Amazon natural history. The book made him famous and remains highly readable.

Bates' book stirred the imagination of stuffy Victorian England but life in the Amazon itself stayed much the same. However, change was not far off. The discoveries of La Condamine, Humboldt and the explorer-scientists coincided with the surging Industrial Revolution and its insatiable demand for raw materials. The Amazon, its inhabitants and its natural resources were about to become intimately linked to the development of the modern world.

Early rainforest products

For centuries indigenous Indians have passed down their knowledge of herbal remedies, using the vast array of plants available in the rainforest. Of this diverse pharmacopoeia, the first of the Amazon's vegetal treasures to be discovered by the

NATURAL CHEWING GUM

Chicle is the white gooey sap exuded by a couple of species of common rainforest tree. This stuff pervades Western culture as it is the raw ingredient of chewing gum. In the Amazon look for wild *chicle* trees (*Lacmellea* spp. and *Malouetia tamaquarina*). Ask your guide to point one out. Cut the tree bark, roll the sap in your fingers and pop it in your mouth for, hey presto, a somewhat flavourless instant chewing gum – another rainforest first. Chewing gum sold in South America is still called *chicle* today.

outside world was quinine. This bitter alkaloid obtained from the red bark tree (*Cascarilla roja, Cinchona* spp), native to Peru and Ecuador, was an effective treatment against malaria, the scourge of tropical latitudes worldwide.

Malaria was the main disease preventing European incursion into lowland tropical areas throughout the world. With the discovery of quinine these areas became less dangerous. But production was limited to natural harvesting of the tree bark while the South American monopoly maintained high prices and restricted expanded production.

Condamine had tried in 1736 to bring quinine to Europe but failed. The Englishman Richard Spruce finally succeeded in smuggling cinchona seeds from the Amazon in the late 1860s. Plantations were developed in British India and Ceylon (now Sri Lanka) and, with the monopoly broken, quinine dropped in price and became widely available.

Quinine contributed to colonial culture as well as to its medicine chest. The drug was prepared as a tonic and to offset its bitter taste colonials added it to gin, which was readily available and whose strong flavour of juniper berries effectively masked the bitterness of quinine. The gin and tonic cocktail became one of the world's first rainforest products and its popularity spread worldwide.

Numerous other products were, and still are, being discovered and exploited. During the 19th century harvested rainforest products included mahogany, teak and, for perfume, rosewood. Chocolate made from the fruit of the cacao tree (*Theobroma cacao*) became a popular drink among teetotallers, notably Quakers such as Cadbury.

The influx of settlers brought by new industries usually caused disastrous physical changes to the forest, the Amazon ecosystem and its inhabitants. But

THE EXTRAVAGANCES OF MANAUS

Despite the recent growth in Manaus, the city feels as if it is past its prime. Walking around back streets you can still find the crumbling Edwardian buildings constructed in the city's heyday.

At the height of the rubber boom Manaus grew rapidly. With several major Amazon tributaries coming together close by, the city was a natural collection and distribution point for rubber going to Europe and the US. In 1880 production of 10,000 tons passed through the city's port creating revenues of £2,240,000. By 1910 the tonnage had risen to 44,000 and income to £63 million. Such vast amounts of money had to be spent and, with boats regularly making the journey to Europe with cargoes of rubber, what better way could there be to fill the holds on return journeys than with luxury items from Europe.

Cobblestones, marble slabs, tramways and telephone systems were all imported. The new rich of Manaus wanted to display their wealth to the world and expectations were high. Chandeliers, pianos, food, drink and jewellery all crossed the Atlantic and found their way to the heart of the Amazon.

The great symbol of Manaus' extravagance is the opera house which still looks out of place. Started as a modest project with funds of just £3,600, the eventual cost was close to half a million pounds. Everything used had to be the best, imported from Europe. When it was completed, a city with a population of just 30,000 had an opera house that could seat 1,600 people. World-famous artistes including Caruso, Pavlova and Bernhardt were invited to perform in this extravagant building.

despite their value, neither quinine, rosewood nor lumber affected the Amazon as much as Condamine's strange latex.

The 19th-century rubber industry: boom and bust

The story of natural latex parallels quinine's. Like quinine, rubber was known to Indians and used long before Europeans arrived in the New World. Being of great value it was coveted by South American governments and private companies who strictly controlled exports.

The history of rubber in the Amazon is a savage tale. Voracious greed led to appalling abuses of wealth and power. In their lust for profit, powerful rubber barons, with fiefdoms the size of European countries, enslaved and decimated whole tribes .

The worst recorded atrocities were along the Putumayo River in Peru and Colombia, home to the Witoto Indians. The Putumayo was the personal kingdom of Julio César Arana and the indigenous people were his serfs.

Arana was brutal and unforgiving to the local population. Plantation foremen with experience of slavery were hired from the West Indies to capture Indians, beating, torturing and starving them to death if they refused to work at tapping raw latex and preparing it for shipment.

Indians were literally worked to death – indentured to rubber barons living in extravagant luxury. Those who tried to run away, or failed to meet tapping quotas, were brutally punished. Fear and torture were commonly used as examples to anyone who attempted not cooperating.

Indians who managed to survive the brutal physical treatment meted out on the plantations succumbed to equally effective murderers. Millions died from epidemics, against which they had no immunity, of the common cold, influenza, smallpox and venereal diseases introduced by gang foremen.

We have no real idea of the human cost of the rubber industry throughout the Amazon. Alain Gheerbrant calculates that for each ton of rubber exported, seven men, women and children died.

The Peruvian Amazon Rubber Company

Arana – and his company, the Peruvian Amazon Rubber Company – is singled out for particular vilification due to the wanderings of Walter Hardenberg. A young engineer from the US, Hardenberg and a friend were travelling from Ecuador to Bolivia where they hoped to work on the Madira–Mamoré railway line. For adventure, they decided to travel by canoe down the Putumayo to take in the Amazon en route to Bolivia.

The excitement of adventure was quickly replaced by horror as Hardenberg encountered at first hand the indentured labour, whippings, dismembering, murders, crucifixions and rape that were the everyday occurrences of Arana's company.

By 1905 the Peruvian Amazon Rubber Company had adopted a couple of hundred thousand square miles either side of the Putumayo as a result of border disputes between Colombia and Peru. In a territorial no-man's-land, Arana was free to use the population of 40,000 Witoto Indians without interference.

Hardenberg believed few people would tolerate knowing that Arana was treating Indians so badly but, with Manaus' luxuries founded on the wealth of the rubber boom, no-one was prepared to listen to such extravagant tales. Arana was a respected member of society in Manaus. Those who knew of his abuses were only too aware of the consequences of crossing someone who placed so little value on life itself.

With the Peruvian Amazon Rubber Company listed on the London Stock Market, Hardenberg took his story to England. It was published in 1909 and,

THE STORY OF RUBBER

In Europe and America, rubber was initially just a curiosity – slow to catch on. Condamine and other naturalists had noted that the Indians made several items from this strange product but initial interest failed to move beyond mere curiosity.

The Englishman Joseph Priestly found it erased pencil and coined the term rubber. In 1823, Charles Mackintosh rubberised cloth, making the first waterproof mackintoshes. But pure rubber becomes brittle at cold temperatures – a critical flaw in temperate climates – and the market for pencil erasers and raincoats was limited.

In 1839 Charles Goodyear made a discovery that solved the problem of brittleness. Vulcanisation, which introduces sulphur bonds between the rubber polymer chains, creates stronger bonds within the compound allowing the rubber to stay elastic at much lower temperatures than in the untreated product.

More and more uses for the wonder material were developed by new industries in Europe and North America. By 1850, when Spruce visited Manaus, the 'black gold' rush was on and trade was booming. The invention of the first pneumatic tyre in 1888 by John Dunlop was followed four years later with the creation of the first detachable pneumatic tyre by Edouard Michelin.

By the end of the 19th century, industry was mass-producing bicycles and automobiles. Demand for rubber in electrical products greatly increased as new technology took advantage of its insulating properties. The market mushroomed. In the 30 years from 1880 to 1910, rubber exports from the Amazon rose by a thousand tonnes a year to reach a peak of 45,000 tonnes in 1910.

despite attempts to buy him off, Hardenberg determined to stop the atrocities. British authorities, recently shamed by atrocities in the Congo, were looking to limit damage caused by another international scandal.

Parliament sent a Mission of Inquiry to the Putumayo which returned with hard evidence of the atrocities. At the hearing in London Arana turned up in person to defend the family name, with Hardenberg adding eyewitness accounts.

In 1914 the Committee placed all the blame on Arana, conveniently absolving the company's British director of any responsibility. What punishment could be appropriate for such a crime? Even if the question had been asked, Arana had long since returned to South America and by now interest in the Amazon was fading fast... The rubber boom was over.

Beginning of the end

The Amazon rubber industry did not end, shame to say, because of admonitions against the brutality of the rubber barons. It was economic forces that dealt the final blow.

Nature seemed to conspire on the side of the rubber barons as all attempts to grow the trees outside South America failed. The Royal Botanical Gardens in Kew, London, were keen to plant the tree in other parts of the world to reduce dependency on South American suppliers. When officials at Kew came across the notes of the English adventurer Henry Wickham they quickly commissioned him to smuggle plants to London. In 1882 Wickham successfully smuggled 7,000 seeds and saplings of *Hevea brasiliensis* out of South America from Manaus. After a short time at London's Kew Gardens, specimens were despatched to British colonies and by 1889 the plant was being successfully cultivated outside South America. By the turn of the century huge rubber plantations with more efficient tapping techniques and greater economies of scale were providing large quantities of cheap latex in direct competition with the Amazon.

Meanwhile, in South America yields fell due to over-tapping. The cost of tapping larger areas grew and the extravagances of the rubber barons all conspired to put even greater pressure on the South American product.

In 1902 the first rubber from British Malaya reached the market priced at 2s. 8d. (then about US$0.43) a pound. In 1910, when exports from Manaus reached an all-time high, South American rubber was selling for 12s. 9d. (about US$2.55) a pound, almost six times the price of British rubber. Even though rubber from the Amazon was of better quality than the plantation product it could not compete in price. By 1912, although demand was still high, the boom was over. Rubber barons were selling off assets at a loss, financial empires collapsed and local economies followed. Visiting Iquitos in the 1920s F W Up de Graff noted that the population of Iquitos had shrunk to 'a handful of natives' from 20,000 or more at the rubber boom's height during the 1880s. The lords and ladies, riches and luxuries of Manaus and the Amazon Basin drifted downstream back to Europe. Only the jungle remained, mute witness to the terrible human cost.

Indigenous history

Of an estimated seven million when Columbus arrived, fewer than one million Indians currently live in the Amazon Basin. Of their past little is known; the history of the Amazon tends to be the history of the white man's influence and incursion into the area.

Indigenous Indians have consistently been considered last – if at all – when explorers or governments have contemplated expansion, usually with fatal results. Indigenous tribes continue to die from contact with new diseases and are still losing their rights to traditional lands. In Peru and Colombia, major remaining tribes include the Yagua, Witoto, Bora and Tikuna. In Ecuador, the Shuar (Jivaro) people are just coming to grips with the modern world. In Bolivia the Chimane, along with other indigenous groups, have only recently begun to fight for their rights. The Yanomami, who inhabit remote areas along the Venezuela–Brazil border, are one of the largest remaining indigenous groups.

What are the prospects for the Yanomami and others like them? Remnants of tribes not killed off by disease or conquistadors are having their culture and way of life wiped out just as effectively, by the destruction of their forest and rivers or, more insidiously, by the introduction of Western culture and material goods.

It is impossible to turn back the clock. So-called civilisation is reaching into the deepest, darkest corners of the Amazon. The best way of minimising the impact of unwanted outside influence is to extend to indigenous tribes the right to self-determination. With free choice and the protection of traditional land rights, remaining indigenous Indians will have the option to decide how much, if at all, they want to integrate with communities outside their own.

The 20th century

When the rubber monopoly collapsed, many lowland towns became deserted. With Europe and the US preoccupied by two world wars, much of South America was forgotten about by outside influences. Military governments, without needing to seek the popular approval of democracies, ran the countries of South America like personal fiefdoms, with limited regard for the overall welfare of their citizens.

Once Europe had begun rebuilding after World War II, the newly created World Bank, formerly the International Bank for Reconstruction and Development, and the International Monetary Fund looked to help less developed countries with well-intentioned plans to relieve poverty and aid development.

The 1960s saw a wave of projects that pushed into the Amazon in the hope of opening up this new frontier. At a time when ecological awareness was in its infancy, the POLONORESTE project in the state of Rondônia, Brazil, was ploughing a road deep into the Amazon Basin. Retrospectively the colonisation project has widely been declared a failure. In many ways it was a disaster, certainly for the Indians living in the region and for the rainforest that used to grow there.

Almost every country with a share of Amazon territory began colonisation programmes that exerted pressure on the lowlands. The legacy of colonisation projects is a continual steady migration of people into the Amazon Basin. The greatest threats to the rainforest and its flora and fauna are the steady encroachment of settlers, colonisers, ranchers and perhaps tourism.

CONSERVATION IN THE AMAZON

Endangered forests

Most people appreciate the rainforest's aesthetic value. Science too, recognises its worth: rainforests' economic and ecological importance have made them the focus of intense research efforts. Yet, our knowledge is far from complete and sadly may remain so as rainforest is burned, slashed, bulldozed and obliterated. Half the world's original rainforest is already gone and at the present rate of destruction it will disappear completely in 50 years. It is ironic that most deforestation has been during the past 25 years, just as we are beginning to see rainforests for what they are.

GLOBAL IMPORTANCE OF AMAZON RAINFOREST PRESERVATION

Oliver Whalley

Conservation of the Amazon rainforest, like conservation of any primary habitats today, is only a temporary measure unless the man-made causes of climatic change are addressed with the same urgency. The Amazon Basin contains by far the largest area of tropical rainforest left in the world, covering over six million km^2 (2.3 $miles^2$). With more than 1,000 tributaries it must be considered a major arterial system, holding one-fifth of the world's freshwater. The forests generate and regulate this water, and are not, as many people believe, net producers of oxygen. Temperate forests and sea phytoplankton are net producers of oxygen, but tropical forests perform a vital role on the earth in the storage of carbon. Destruction of any forests releases this carbon as carbon dioxide and monoxide into the atmosphere, and so contributes further to global climatic change with all its harmful effects. A secondary effect of deforestation is the loss of the cloud cover, which together with the loss of the forest canopy leads to more of the suns rays reaching the earth's surface, so causing an unnatural heating effect. This extra heat with low moisture content for precipitation may instigate the type of drying out or desertification seen in areas of Africa and other parts of the world.

As you read this, the Amazon rainforest is being cut down or burned at a rate equal to 20 football fields a minute. Many species unknown to science are already extinct. Scientists estimate that deforestation wipes out 17,000 species of plants and animals per year – about 48 a day or two every hour – a mass extinction on a par with the end of the dinosaurs.

Unfortunately, investors obtain best returns when natural resources are converted to cash. It pays more to chop the forest down, invest the profits and collect interest than it does to use the rainforest sustainably – at least under present economic systems. Cost-benefit analyses of development projects consider the forest itself to be worthless, making ranching, mining and hydro-electric schemes seem profitable.

But when the forest is gone we will have lost a potential bonanza of biological wealth. Some 50,000 higher plant species from the Amazon are described scientifically. Only a tenth have been screened for useful drug or pesticide applications and thousands of species remain undiscovered.

Deforestation also affects climate, bringing into question our own long-term survival. Meteorologists tell us that local weather systems depend on forest cover to recycle water and maintain the hydrological cycle. Living rainforests consume vast quantities of carbon dioxide, the main greenhouse gas, helping to offset global warming. Conversely burning rainforest is detrimental to the environment as it returns millions of tons of carbon a year back into the atmosphere, adding to the greenhouse effect with as-yet-unknown consequences for global weather patterns.

False economics of exploitation

As precious minerals and strategic metals become more and more scarce, we mine resources previously considered unprofitable; pushing into increasingly remote areas with drastic consequences for the rainforest and indigenous Indians alike. Mismanaged industrial mega-projects have consistently failed to deliver the expected economic benefits. Henry Ford was unable to make money in the 1930s from his rubber plantation project in Fordlândia on the banks of the Tapajós south of Santarém. In the 1960s billionaire Daniel K Ludwig's paper mill at Jari near the mouth of the Amazon relied on unproven plantation species soon devastated by rainforest pests. More recently the US$1.5 billion bauxite processing plant at São Luís in Brazil, completed in 1984, uses virgin rainforest to create electricity from charcoal. Hydro-electric dams, notably at Carajás in Brazil, have been built with little attention to ecological impacts.

Even conventional cost-benefit studies of these and similar projects show their astonishing expense and lack of profitability. If the actual value of destroyed rainforest is added, the losses become astronomical. Politics and business play a bigger role in these projects than economics or conservation.

Future prospects

Rainforest conservation requires attention to political, cultural and economic agendas. There are countless ways in which intact forest yields positive benefits.

Local people can contribute their knowledge to research and ecotourism, improving their economic and political standing. Several programmes, involving both indigenous peoples and conservation organisations, already help native Indians to run jungle lodges and health programmes, market and distribute crops, and survey their own lands.

New cultivation and logging methods offer practical ways to log and farm rainforest sustainably. Strip logging minimises erosion and maximises natural regeneration of cut areas. Farmers are encouraged to plant perennial shrubs and trees rather than such labour-intensive annual crops as manioc and maize.

Compared with traditional industries of lumber, mining, oil and fisheries, the alternatives provide more jobs, a healthier environment and, over the long term, greater wealth.

Like those of most developing nations, the populations of Amazon countries are growing rapidly. Peru's rate of increase is around 1.8% per year, corresponding to the population doubling in 55 years. Other Amazon countries face similar or greater demographic problems and the demands on governments to provide for such an increase in numbers will place even more pressure on the Amazon lowlands. Just to maintain its present standards of living Peru must double its food supply, available housing, and the number of schools, hospitals and law enforcement facilities – all within 55 years.

Prospects might seem gloomy, but there is hope. Industries are becoming increasingly aware of the need for sound management of natural resources. In 1992 the Brazilian government stopped giving subsidies to lumber and mining corporations, and city dwellers were no longer eligible for grants to farm in the forest. Many believe Rio's 1994 Earth Summit was all politics and no action but at least it happened, which means issues are being addressed. Many governments of the Amazon now appreciate the immense wealth and value of intact rainforest.

The future for the Amazon's sustainable development is promising. Ecotourism is booming. Perhaps 15,000 visit the west Amazon region per year. There may be potential for at least five times that many. Locals are confident of better prospects.

Supplies of oil, precious metals and gems are limited. Even lumber replaces itself only while there is a reasonably intact ecosystem. In theory tourism has the potential to last for ever – as long as rainforest exists, people will be drawn to experience it for themselves.

International reality

To blame the countries of South America alone for the destruction of the rainforest is naive. Every government in the world uses its natural resources to the maximum benefit of the country. And Amazonian countries are no different. Exploiting oil and gas reserves is as useful to Ecuador, Peru and Colombia as it is to the US and Europe. Similarly, now that the US and Europe have destroyed most of their natural forests, do these countries have any right to say that the Amazon should be protected as part of man's patrimony? It is one of the great

HELPING CONSERVE AMAZON RAINFOREST AT HOME

Oliver Whalley

Think 'globally and act locally' could be; 'to act locally is to act globally', this being a key to help conserve what is left of the Amazon rainforest. Every little bit helps, from recycling to just being informed.

- Campaign and support alternatives to fossil fuels and nuclear fuels.
- Steer clear of gold (especially when jungle produced).
- Steer clear of cocaine (millions of hectares of forest are lost for its production to supply the developed world's demand).
- Avoid buying tropical hardwood doors, furniture or plyboard (a lot of packing cases are made of tropical rainforest wood); there is no truly sustainable tropical hardwood harvested yet.
- Contribute to international environmental groups protecting the forest and Indians.

ironies of history that the very nations who first set about clearing the rainforest of the Amazon now clamour for its protection.

The only way these vulnerable areas can be saved from eventual destruction is by new and innovative methods of encouraging countries to leave rainforest standing instead of harvesting it for the quickest return. One promising system which has worked in several Latin American countries allows a portion of the nation's debt written off in return for the protection of part of its rainforest.

On a personal level it is worth asking yourself whether the people you meet in the Amazon Basin can make a living from the standing rainforest. If so, how? If not, what are the options open to them? If you wish, you can also join environmental groups which add to the pressure on politicians to reduce environmental problems at home. Only when countries are serious about their own environmental problems is it possible to believe that interference in the internal affairs of another is motivated by genuine concern. Or, for greater involvement, you can join international organisations which lobby governments and work to find ways of using the Amazon Basin while leaving its riches still standing. Some addresses follow.

In the US

Conservation International 2501 M St, NW, Suite 200, Washington DC, 20037; tel: 202 429 5660/800 429 5660; net: www.conservation.org.

The Ecotourism Society PO Box 755, North Bennington, VT 05259; tel: 802 447 2121; fax: 802 447 2122; email: ecomail@ecotourism.org; net: www.ecotourism.org.

Rainforest Action Network 221 Pine St, Suite 500, San Francisco, CA 94104; tel: 415 398 4404; fax: 415 398 2732; email: rainforest@ran.org; net: www.ran.org.

WorldWide Fund for Nature (WWF) in the US, 1250 24th St NW, Washington, DC 20037. In the UK, Panda House, Weyside Park, Godalming, Surrey, GU7 1XR.

In the UK

Rainforest Concern 27 Lansdowne Crescent, London W11 2NS; tel: 0171 229 2093; fax: 0171 221 4094; email: rainforest@gn.apc.org; web: www.rainforest.org.uk.

Tourism Concern Stapleton House, 277-281 Holloway Road, London, N7 8HN; tel: 0171 753 3330; fax: 0171 753 3331; email: tourconcern@gn.apc.org; net: www.gn.apc.org/tourismconcern

VSO Development Education 317 Putney Bridge Road, London, SW15 2PN. tel: 0181 780 7200; fax: 0181 780 7300; email: enquiry@vso.org.com.uk: net: www.oneworld.org/vso/

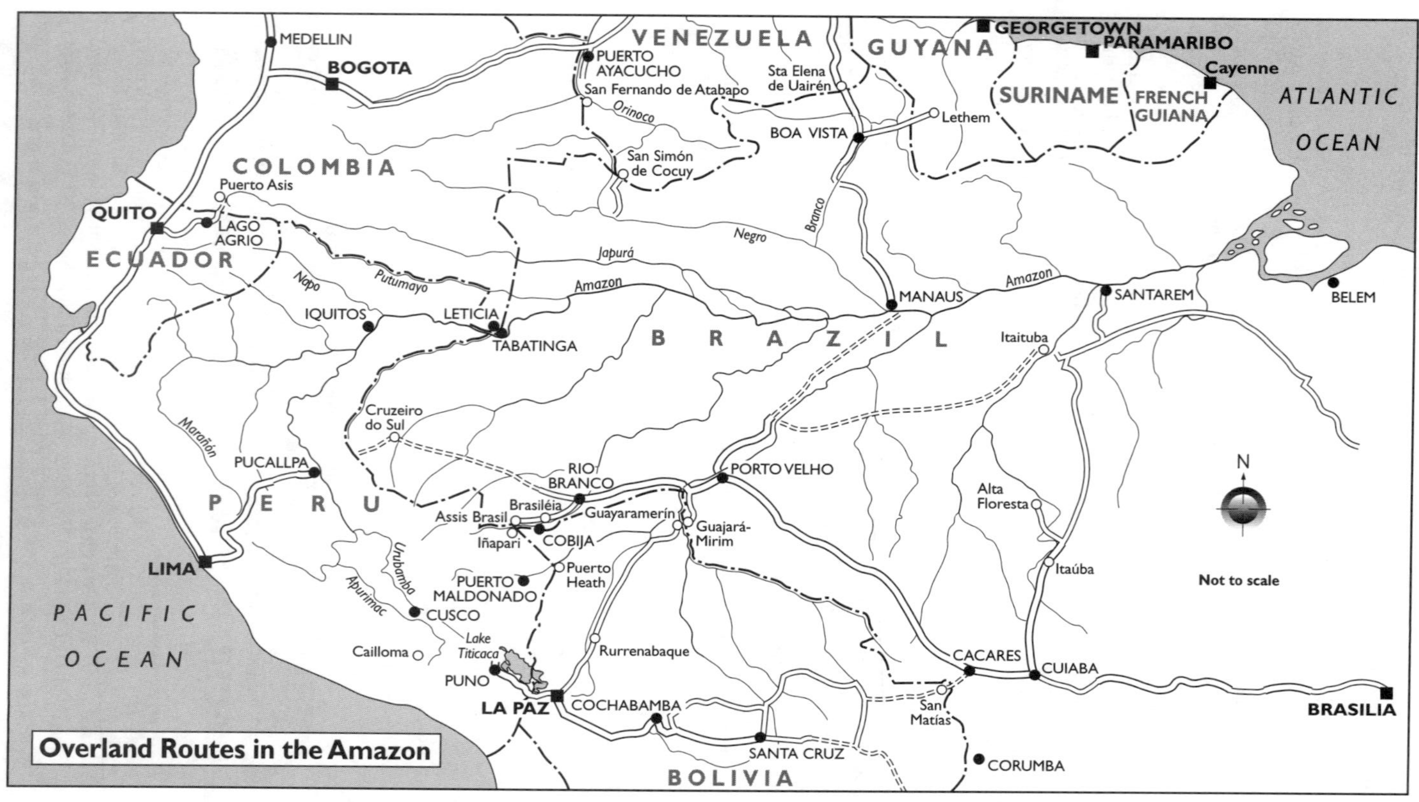

Overland Routes in the Amazon

Practical Information

2

PREPARATIONS AND PLANNING

Red tape

All travellers to South American countries need a **passport** which should be valid for at least six months. **Visa** requirements for specific countries are given below with additional information provided in the individual country chapters.

VISA REQUIREMENTS OF AMAZON COUNTRIES

Country and visa	Nationality USA	UK	Can	Aus	NZ	SA	Fre	Ger	Neth	Jap
Bolivia 90-day	-	-	-	-	-	-	-	-	-	-
Brazil 90-day	+	-	+	+	+	-	-	-	-	+
Colombia 90-day	-	-	-	-	-	-	-	-	-	-
Ecuador 90-day	-	-	-	-	-	-	+	-	-	-
F. Guiana 90-day	-	-	-	+	+	-	-	-	-	-
Guyana	-	-	-	-	-	-	-	-	-	-
Peru 90-day	-	-	-	-	-	-	-	-	-	-
Suriname 60-day	+	-	-	+	+	+	+	+	-	+
Venezuela 90-day	-	-	-	-	-	-	-	-	-	-

Visas required for entrance overland only.

('+' = required, '-' = not required)

If you are travelling overland and require a visa – which you have not yet got – to enter a neighbouring country, you will need to get it from the city nearest to the border. Few frontier towns have the authority to issue visas.

Regardless of nationality, visa requirements can change overnight so check directly with the embassy or consulate of countries you plan to visit. A good tour operator should be able to tell you if you need a visa. Alternatively a visa advisory service can arrange visas at reasonable prices if required. There may be delays so plan well ahead.

Zierer Visa Service tel: (USA) 800 843 9151.
MASTA (Medical Advisory Service for Travellers Abroad); Visa and Passport Information Line for up-to-the-minute advice; tel: (UK) 0897 501 100 at £1/minute.

Entrance to a country is technically subject to you proving that you have a ticket for onward travel and sufficient funds to support yourself for the duration of your stay; in reality proof is rarely requested.

Immunisations are recommended for travel to the Amazon and you should make an informed choice about taking malaria prophylactics. Brazil requires a yellow fever vaccination for travel in parts of Amazonia. Although it is very rare to be asked to show your immunisation certificate the situation would change immediately in the event of an outbreak. In the UK, MASTA also have a travellers' health line; tel: 0891 224 100 at £1/minute.

In South America you have to carry **identification** with you at all times. In most cases a photocopy of your passport is sufficient – with the exception of Venezuela where officials insist on seeing the real thing. Several countries have checkpoints along roads used to travel to the Amazon and you have to show your passport.

Money

Currencies for each country are dealt with in each country chapter. Below are a few general guidelines.

Without exception US dollars are the best currency to have when visiting South America. Travelling with a tour group, most of your costs are prepaid and you should just need currency to pay for drinks, meals and souvenirs. Independent travellers may want the insurance of travellers' cheques – the most widely accepted being American Express.

Dollar bills, in tens, twenties and fifties, should not be damaged or even slightly torn as money-changers and exchange bureaux often refuse damaged notes. Travellers' cheques can be difficult or impossible to change in out-of-the-way places. Credit cards and automatic teller machines (ATMs) are becoming increasingly common, allowing you to get cash out of hole-in-the-wall machines in some of the strangest places. A money belt or pouch is useful for keeping things safe and close to your body.

(The big question has to be how did the likes of Columbus, Orellana and other great travellers move around without plastic? If you can travel through the Amazon without a penny to your name we would love to hear how you get on!)

Insurance

Premiums and coverage levels vary dramatically between different insurance companies so it pays to shop around. In general if something is too precious to lose you probably shouldn't be taking it with you. If you have to spend all your trip in close proximity to your bags, worried that they might be stolen, your trip will hardly be the most relaxing.

Vital, however, is to get cover for emergency treatment and evacuation. Accidents do happen and the cost of emergency evacuation is horrendous. One story tells of an independent traveller who slipped when climbing off the back of a truck in Manu National Park, Peru. Returning home under her own steam with *two* broken legs was difficult enough; having to bear the financial cost as well would have added debt to injury.

When to go

Assuming a flexible schedule, the answer to this really depends on what you hope to get out of your trip.

For a lot of destinations, weather plays a decisive role. Not so with the Amazon. Much of the region shows no great difference in weather from month to month. Equatorial rainforest generally has no well-defined dry or rainy season. Some months are drier than others but you can expect rain any time. The wettest months south of the Equator are between November and April, while north of the Equator the heaviest rains fall between June and October. Humidity is high year-round and temperatures are warm but rarely unbearably hot. During the day, showers are most likely mid-afternoon.

Weather apart, what else can help you to time your visit? Perhaps most important is the dramatic annual change in river level. Every year at the same time the Amazon floods, and the river level rises and falls by as much as 12.5m in places. Floodwaters advance and then recede, creating flooded *várzea* forest with profound effects on the flora, fauna and human inhabitants. As you would expect, the contrast between highest and lowest river levels greatly alters the habitat. (See *Chapter Five* for greater detail on seasonal flooding.)

If your trip is to the flooded forest areas you have three choices of when to go. The 'seasons' are low water, high water and in between. In the central Amazon Basin, the lowest water period is in October and November. The level begins to rise between December and January, reaching high water in April and May. The converse is the case north of the Equator. After several weeks the floodwaters begin to recede. This timing varies slightly from year to year and recently the timing of the floods has become less predictable. Local people say that the rise and fall of the river is becoming more sudden and less smooth than it used to be.

Low water

If aquatic life is your main interest, the low water period (July to February) is best. River channels are narrow and shallow, so fish, caiman and dolphins are more abundant – angling is also better. Land trails are drier at this time and insects tend to be less bothersome.

On the other hand at low water some channels get clogged with vegetation, restricting access to some wildlife areas. At low water your boat may run into submerged sandbanks, but this is more an occasional irritation than anything else.

Animals tend to disperse during low water, reducing the amount of wildlife you may see. On the other hand, isolated water bodies become more attractive to large animals and may be excellent sites to spot game. The time of lowest water, from October to November, is also usually the hottest time of year.

High water

For forest life, high water is best. Tree-dwelling animals have less space and become more crowded so you have a greater chance of seeing monkeys, sloths and birds. Also many inundated riverside trees flower at high water, notably acacias and cecropias. River travel at high water along tree-lined tributaries brings you closer to the rainforest canopy.

During high water, land trails and footpaths may be cut short or totally inaccessible. For a deep forest expedition, camping out at this season is worth avoiding.

Aquatic life is more dispersed at this time, meaning that dolphins, caiman and piranha are locally less abundant. However, all these are encountered on the average trip, whatever the season.

As river levels rise, muddy banks erode and flooded meadows are flushed out. Debris floats downstream, often in spectacular log-jams.

In between

With all these possibilities it is hard to decide when to go. Picking a transitional time, say a month or two before high water, is a good compromise. Weather tends to be less cloudy at this time and it's not too warm. Fish are still moving upstream into newly flooded areas so plenty of aquatic life can usually be seen.

Where to go

The Amazon Basin is a big place. Choosing where to go is difficult but there are some general guidelines that might point you in the right direction. Travelling around the countries in the order of the book, you might want to consider the following:

Venezuela (*Chapter Seven*, page 183)

This is arguably the most developed of Amazon countries. Tourism here is well established in general, so the fledgling industry developing in the rainforests of the Amazon and Orinoco Basins has a good understanding of the needs of the tourist. On the whole the rainforest has not suffered the large-scale logging experienced by many Amazon countries, so much of the rainforest remains undisturbed. Venezuela has a good selection of rainforest opportunities: secluded jungle lodges, floating hotels, bespoke river adventure trips and visits to several indigenous groups that have chosen to accommodate travellers. Throw in a bit of whitewater rafting and the all-round experience is complete. The normally flat relief of lowland rainforest is interrupted in Venezuela by the stunning flat-top mountains called *tepuis*. Unfortunately Venezuela is also one of the more expensive countries in the Amazon as all trips require a permit and have to be guided.

Colombia (*Chapter Eight*, page 211)

This country gets a hard time internationally for being the cocaine production centre of the world. Travelling off the beaten track is generally discouraged for reasons of safety. Consequently the tourism industry in the Colombian Amazon is somewhat underdeveloped. Independent travellers may find visiting the

WHERE TO WATCH BIRDS IN AMAZONIA

Nigel Wheatley, author of 'Where to Watch Birds in South America'

In birdwatching circles South America is known as 'the bird continent' with over 3,000 different species; almost one third of the world's birds, far more than on any other continent. Over 2,000 of them occur no where else. The reason for this incredible diversity lies with the continent's great variety of habitats, which range from the driest desert on earth (the Atacama) and the world's most extensive wetland (the Pantanal) to the luxuriant subtropical and temperate forests on the slopes of the Andes and vast swathes of lowland tropical rainforest. The latter is the most fruitful habitat of all, the richest on earth in fact, and most of it is confined to Amazonia.

The Amazonian forest is not all the same. There are numerous types of subtly different forests, according to local rainfall, relief and soils, and different birds have evolved in these different forest types; so, for example, a set of birds which inhabits one side of a ridge may be completely different from the set of birds present on the other side of the ridge. When one considers the size of the Amazon Basin (some six million km^2), it is easy to imagine how so many different birds evolved in the region.

World bird diversity reaches its peak in west Amazonia, in the eastern regions of Ecuador and Peru, where just 1km^2 supports as many as 300 different species! The world record for the most birds seen in a day, without the use of a light aircraft, is held by Manu Biosphere Reserve in south Peru. A mindboggling 331 different bird species were recorded in the Cocha Cashu area in September 1986. It is possible to get a taste of such terrific birdwatching by visiting the tented Manú Wildlife Centre, accessible by air, or by road and

Colombian Amazon rewarding but should be aware of the risks. Colombia's Amazon gateway town of Leticia is one of the main towns on the River Amazon and in addition to being a main connection point for boats up and down the river, is also a good base for trips to nearby rainforest. Having said that it is probably risky to make Colombia the only country you visit in the Amazon if pressed for time. Colombia is one of the cheaper South American countries, but the distances involved can soon eat up your money especially if you have to take a few flights.

Ecuador (*Chapter Nine*, page 235)
This beautifully compact country has just about got it all. With access to the lowlands possible by road and plane, Ecuador is popular with back-country and group travellers alike. Several Amazon lodges can be accessed easily from the lowland towns of Coca, Tena and Misahualli. Adventure excursions into the rainforest are available and visits to indigenous groups open to travellers can also be arranged. For the truly adventurous, Ecuador is the place to follow in the paddle-wake of Orellana, Teixeira *et al*, but it is currently impossible to cross legally into Peru from the lowlands. Ecuador is one of the cheapest countries for travel in South America. If you are looking for a multi-stop vacation, the unique Galápagos Islands will tempt any nature-lover.

Peru (*Chapter Ten*, page 271)
Peru has a bit of everything. Iquitos in the northern lowlands is a focal point for Amazon visitors, with international flights direct from Miami making week-long visits to the Amazon a realistic possibility. Several jungle lodges, with trails and a

river from Cusco. Over 500 species have been recorded around here in a single year, and nearby is a riverbank macaw lick which is visited regularly by hundreds of parrots, including spectacular macaws.

Manú Wildlife Centre may claim to be the best for birds, at least in terms of variety, but there are plenty of other more comfortable, and consequently more expensive, forest lodges in west Amazonia and elsewhere across the region, where over 500 bird species have also been recorded. During the 1990s three or four new lodges and reserves have opened each year and there are now far too many to list here. More details are in the chapters on individual countries.

It is important to remember that, even though the diversity of bird species is higher in Amazonia than anywhere else on earth, many of the individual species are very thin on the ground, and it is possible to walk for hours in the forests and end up seeing just a few birds. However, If you are fortunate enough to meet a feeding flock of birds then your list at the end of the day should be a lot longer, because these bird waves, as they are also known, may contain over 70 different individuals of 20 or so species. Either way, even veteran birdwatchers see many more birds with the help of experienced guides, and fortunately most lodges employ at least a few local people who are usually first-class bird finders.

Birdwatching novices need not fear being overawed. Such guides are used to showing newcomers the most spectacular species first. So even if you have just the slightest interest in birds it is worth visiting any one of the lodges and reserves mentioned in this book, or some of the many others, because a few days amongst the birdlife of Amazonia may well end up being the most pleasurable experience of your life!

canopy walkway, are within a few hours of Iquitos. Tourist standard riverboats travel the Amazonas (as the Amazon by Iquitos is named), stopping at villages and jungle trails en route, continuing downstream to Leticia on the border with Brazil and Colombia.

If you want to experience the epic length of the navigable Amazon from the confines of a gently swaying hammock, then Pucallpa in the central Amazon region is the starting point. For whitewater adventure kayaking near the headwaters of the Amazon high in the Peruvian Andes, use Cusco as a base. (See page 66.) More sedate rafting through lowland tributaries can also be arranged from the Inca capital as can trips to the internationally famous Manú National Park and Tambopata clay-lick (see pages 310–11). Peru is still one of the cheapest countries in South America, although organised trips to the Amazon Basin can be quite pricey. If venturing as far south as Cusco then don't miss Machu Picchu, the lost city of the Incas.

Bolivia (*Chapter Eleven*, page 313)

This is the cheapest country to travel in, but the most expensive to reach, with the only direct flights coming from Miami. For a long time it was the independent traveller's paradise, but now trail-blazing tour operators are starting to put together trekking and rafting trips through the Bolivian lowlands in the northeast to Madidi and Manuripi Heath National Park, and west to Noel Kempff National Park. A floating hotel serves the central Amazon region near Trinidad. Connecting to the Amazon mainstream along the Grande-Mamoré-Madeira river system it is possible to travel to the mouth of the Amazon, but river traffic is less common than in Peru and Brazil.

Brazil (*Chapter Twelve*, page 345)

This is, for many, the true home of the Amazon. Not surprisingly the opportunities are endless. Budget travel up and down the Amazon and its tributaries is easy, as an extensive network of passenger vessels travels to the border of most Amazon countries. Trips to secluded lodges and Amazon towns by boat or plane are easily arranged either from your home country or from Manaus, which has international air connections with Miami. Brazil is home to more indigenous groups than any other Amazon country, but travellers are not permitted to visit indigenous areas without difficult-to-arrange permission from the government agency FUNAI. Several poor roads stretch across the Brazilian Amazon providing insights into life in growing frontier cities and colonisation communities that are pushing deep into the rainforest. Brazil is currently the most expensive Amazon country to travel in and will continue to be as long as the Brazilian real is pegged to the US dollar.

Guyana, French Guiana and Suriname (*Chapter Thirteen*, page 401)

These countries have, between them, some of the least spoilt rainforest wildlife on the continent. For years closed to travellers and external influence of any kind, the countries, although pricey to travel to and quite expensive once you arrive, offer some of the best chances for seeing wildlife in virtually untouched rainforest. Although even the most basic infrastructure for tourists is limited, new lodges and opportunities are being developed all the time.

GETTING THERE AND AWAY

By air

Countries within the Amazon Basin are served by numerous airlines and prices vary greatly. Limiting your route or the number of days you are available for travel is likely to increase the cost. If you have time, shop around or get in touch with a low-cost specialist travel agent. There are several that now specialise in travel to, within and from South America. If you're able to be flexible and leave at short notice then you may be able to pick up a bargain. There are a number of websites for companies which specialise in cheap flights, including www.cheapflights.co.uk and airtickets.co.uk/offers.htm.

High season, when flights are more expensive, is between May and September, with a mini-peak close to Christmas.

Buying tickets in South America for travel back home is straightforward but discounted prices are rare. If you are uncertain when you expect to return it is possible to buy return tickets valid for up to a year. Open-jaw tickets are available for people who want to arrive in one country but leave from another.

More specific information for each country can be found in the relevant chapter.

From the USA

Most flights connect through Miami with most countries served by the US air carriers American Airlines and United Airlines. Most South America national airlines also have a connecting service. From Miami you can fly straight to the heart of the Amazon, with flights to Iquitos with AeroPerú and to Manaus and Belém with American Airlines.

Prices from the US vary considerably but you may pick up the occasional bargain. Flights to Venezuela, for example, have been available for as little as US$99 one-way in the past. Such halcyon days are unlikely to return but it is worth looking around.

Around the World Travel (tel: 1 800 471 6333) can help with flight details. Airline phone numbers are:

American: 800 433 7300;
Continental: 800 231 0856;
Ecuatoriana: 800 328 2367;
Iberia: 800 231 0856;
Japan Airlines: 800 525 3663;
KLM: 800 374 7747;
Lufthansa: 800 645 3880;
SAETA: 800 827 2382.

From Europe

There are several airlines serving South America from Europe. Aerolineas Argentinas, Avianca, British Airways, KLM, LanChile, Iberia, Varig, AeroPerú, Viasa, American Airlines, United Airlines… the list goes on. Which you use depends on where you are leaving from. Each national airline leaves from, or ends up in, its own country with possible deviations en route. For example, flights with Iberia travel via Madrid, flights with KLM go via Amsterdam. There are direct flights to Brazil, Colombia and Venezuela from Europe. The only way of making the Amazon cities of Iquitos, Manaus or Belém your first port of call in South America is by catching a connecting flight from Miami.

Using a specialist agency helps you get what you want. **Journey Latin America** (16 Devonshire Road, Chiswick, London, W4 2HD; tel: 0181 747 3108; fax: 0181 742 1312; email: sales@journeylatinamerica.co.uk) is an excellent source on flights, tours and travelling in South America. **Trailfinders**, with several offices throughout the UK (tel: 0171 938 3939), can offer a wide range of flights. **Bridge The World** (tel: 0171 911 0900) is also worth contacting. **Wexas** (tel: 0171 581 8761) offers flights worldwide – but you must become a member.

Example fares covering low to high season averages are: Caracas £464 to £619; Quito £531 to £680; Rio £553 to £744; La Paz £679 to £1186; Lima £531 to £680, Cayenne £464 to £767 and Paramaribo £840 plus.

From Australia and New Zealand

Aerolineas Argentinas run a direct service from Sydney to Buenos Aires, and have good connections with several other Amazon countries including Bolivia and Brazil. Alternatively you can use a different airline to complete the last leg.

Airpasses

If you think you will be moving around a particular country, it is worth exploring the option of an airpass. You can currently get airpasses for use in Colombia, Venezuela, Peru, Bolivia and Brazil. Generally there are a minimum number of flights or 'legs' that are purchased as coupons for a set fee. There are usually some conditions in the fine print, a common one being that you cannot repeat any journeys. The Venezuela Airpass, with Avensa/Servivensa, has international destinations on its routes including Miami, Quito, Lima and Mexico City.

At the airport

At the **check-in** desk make absolutely sure your baggage is labelled correctly by the desk clerk. Luggage and passengers go on some pretty spectacular routes around South America and it's worth making sure you know where you and your luggage are next meant to meet. Even then, accidents can happen; so carry any essential toilet and medical items (particularly regular medication, if you take it) in your cabin bag, together with a spare set of basic clothing.

International flights from all South American airports have to pay a **departure tax**. The tax varies between countries and changes without notice. Make sure you find out what the departure tax is before that last minute spending spree. Most countries also have a nominal airport tax ($3–5) for domestic flights. In the past some airports have required payment in US dollars but at present there are fewer restrictions on using local currency.

Overland

Border crossings in the Amazon Basin

The Amazon may be just one river, but that does not mean you can move about Amazonia without restrictions. International border crossings in South America range from barely noticeable frontier huts through to no-go internationally disputed territories where conflicts at times flare up. Sometimes you just have to follow the rules.

If you require a visa to enter a neighbouring country, you will need to get it from the city nearest to the border. Few frontier towns have facilities with the authority to issue visas.

Venezuela has only one generally used crossing to **Brazil**, where buses leave from Sta Elena de Uairen (Venezuela) for Boa Vista and Manaus. A visa is required to enter Venezuela from Brazil. The triple-frontier with Venezuela, Colombia and Brazil is on the Río Negro at San Simón de Cocuy (Venezuela) and, if you do arrive at this point, there is no guarantee you will be able to cross into Brazil. If you do manage it, cargo boats can take you downstream to Manaus.

Crossing the border from Venezuela's state of Amazonas into **Colombia** is considerably more difficult and, even if possible, will require a great deal of smooth talking. There are several crossing points – Puerto Ayacucho, San Fernando de Atobapo, San Carlos de Río Negro – to Colombia, but no road connects the

Colombian side with the rest of the country. Travel on the Colombian side of the border is considered by many to be hazardous.

Colombia's most commonly used frontier in the Amazon Basin is at Leticia, where border crossings to **Peru** and **Brazil** are largely a somewhat overcomplicated formality. Leticia has connections with the rest of Colombia by boat and plane. From Colombia it is possible to travel to **Ecuador** from the village of Puerto Assis, travelling to San Miguel before getting a boat upstream heading for Lago Agrio.

Crossing from **Ecuador** to **Peru** in the Amazon Basin is impossible at present. Frontier disputes flared up again in early 1995, so travellers should consider carefully the risks associated with travel in the area.

In addition to the frontier with Colombia and Brazil on the Amazon mainstream already mentioned, **Peru** has a couple of smaller crossing frontier posts. An adventurous journey into **Brazil** can be organised from Pucallpa; it involves boat travel and a few days' walking in the jungle before you end up in Cruzeiro do Sol. Further south, having completed passport formalities in Puerto Maldonado, you can travel north to Iñapari and cross into Assis Brazil, or Bolpebra in **Bolivia.**

From the Bolivian side, crossing into **Peru** can be completed via Puerto Heath but questions will probably be asked as to why you are in a place that is so completely out of the way. Formalities can be completed in Cobija. Several crossing points into **Brazil** exist, including Cobija and Guayaramerín. Crossing is also possible at San Matías to the north of Santa Cruz which connects to Cáceres in Brazil by bus.

Overland crossings between **Guyana**, **Suriname** and **French Guiana** can all be completed using pedestrian ferries. The southern town of Lethem in **Guyana** is connected to **Brazil** by a road which carries regular buses from Boa Vista. Road connection from Lethem to the rest of the country is along a very poor road that is very often impassable. **French Guiana** has a border crossing with **Brazil** but there is no road on the Guiana side so you need a combination of canoes and walking.

TIME ZONES OF AMAZON COUNTRIES RELATIVE TO GMT

Country	Hours behind GMT
Bolivia	4
Brazil	3 to 5
Colombia	5
Ecuador	5
French Guiana	3
Guyana	4
Peru	5
Suriname	3
Venezuela	4

Of the Amazon countries only Brazil has daylight saving time (equivalent to British Summer Time), but all states of the USA have it.

HOW TO GO

Some travellers have always gone independent and, quite frankly, can't imagine changing. Others prefer the benefits and opportunities that group travel provides. Opportunities for independent and group travel are endless in the Amazon. Some of the pointers below may help you decide which would be best for you.

If you want to take an organised trip with a group there are hundreds of tour operators offering trips to the Amazon. If you're travelling independently, even more possibilities arise. In either case, you can get a trip to suit almost any interest: a river cruise, a canoe or rafting trip, a small plane expedition and even jungle survival courses. There are trips focusing on wildlife photography, birdwatching, native traditional crafts and ethnobotany. You can participate in scientific research on river dolphins or rainforest butterflies. Alternatively you can pursue spiritual development, accompanied by a psychic to get in touch with your 'spirit guide'. Other tours include visits to native shamans providing insight into native beliefs, some of which may actually involve 'trips' on hallucinogens used by the shamans.

Within each country chapter you will find information on tour operators who specialise in that country. First though, you need to have a good idea of the sort of trip you want.

Hard or soft adventure?

How much physical challenge do you want? Do you want to kick back and relax in a hammock, a beer in one hand and a good book in the other? Or maybe you crave the rush of whitewater rafting in the Amazon's headwaters? Could you rise to the ultimate challenge of a jungle survival course? In tour company jargon, do you want hard or soft adventure?

Soft adventure holidays appeal mostly to those seeking a relaxing time with little physical exertion. These are the most popular trips for group travel. Tourist riverboats are a comfortable way to visit remote areas, and several lodges, seemingly in the middle of nowhere, offer exceptional hospitality. Most tours of this type include walks along forest trails and canoe rides. Participants need be only moderately fit, though excursions are more enjoyable if you can at least walk a while without tiring. At a minimum you need at least to be able to clamber in and out of a boat and up steep and sometimes slippery steps, and to carry your own luggage.

Hard adventure appeals to the more active. These vacations involve considerable activity, from backpacking, trekking or hiking through to kayaking and river-rafting. Increasingly popular is a jungle survival course, during which participants live off the land. Most hard adventure trips involve a fair degree of exertion, some being very strenuous. Be sure to double-check with your tour operator on the activity levels and if necessary take up a fitness programme beforehand.

Here, there or everywhere?

Decide if you prefer to stay in one place to get to know it well or if you'd like to visit several places to get a broader perspective. If you travel independently you can visit more places than with a group, and in the order you choose, spending time where and when you want.

Group travel generally has a set itinerary. To find that your riverboat trip from Iquitos down the Amazon misses out the ACEER canopy walkway could be devastating. Ideally, time and money allowing, you would do everything. Whichever type of trip you opt for you must also select areas to visit. How do you decide?

This is where it is important to have as much information as you can lay your hands on about a prospective trip. Leafing through the pages of this book will help. For group travel, a good tour operator will provide enough details for you to make an informed decision.

Ask yourself what you would most like to see and do during your time in the Amazon. To a certain extent, the areas you visit will constrain your activities.

Remote areas have fewer facilities but will offer a greater physical challenge for hard adventurers. Obviously, your own interests will be important. If possible talk to others who have taken the sort of trip you are interested in or, better still, who have travelled with the tour operator you are considering. A good company will provide ample pre-trip advice, such as wildlife information, packing lists, whether you need a visa, inoculation requirements and so on.

Independent or group travel?

Once you've decided on activity levels and where you want to go, the next choice is whether you travel independently or with a group. Each has its pros and cons.

Although a group obviously has greater overall environmental impact than one or two people, the impact per individual may be less. But then, in a group there is less room to apply one's individual ecophilosophy.

RELATIVE ADVANTAGES OF INDEPENDENT OR GROUP TRAVEL

	Independent	Group
Cost	+	-
Flexibility	+	-
Risk	+	-
Exertion	+	-
Variety	+	-
Impact	-	+

('+' = more, '-' = less)

One of the main benefits of group travel is the ability to get to the place of interest with the minimum of fuss and hassle, ideal if you have a time constraint. Most group excursions are between one and three weeks long – though many are optionally longer – which is just about enough time to get out of work mode and relax.

If you decide to travel in a group, try to go with a small one, 15 people maximum, for several practical reasons. Smaller groups are better treated at hotels and restaurants. On wildlife excursions, a large group can crowd you out just as you are about to take that perfect shot – especially important for photographers and birdwatchers. But even small groups can be constraining and in too small a group it's hard to escape from someone you don't get on with.

Group travel

Green or mean?

If you've decided to go for a group trip, your task now is to shop around for a suitable tour operator who runs your sort of trip – easier said than done. We provide tour operator information in each country chapter, with contact details. Get information from as many tour operators as you can, and compare. Cheapest is not necessarily best, as companies differ in their ecosensitivity. A lot of operators promote their trips as 'ecotourism' or 'green' tourism but check to see if this is just hype.

In the US, **The Ecotourism Society** (PO Box 755, North Bennington, VT 05259, USA; tel: 802 447 2121; fax: 802 447 2122; email: ecomail@ecotourism.org; net: www.ecotourism.org) can supply a list of member tour operators; in the UK, contact **Green Globe** (PO Box 396, Linton, Cambridge, CB1 6UL, tel: 01223 890250; fax: 01223 890258; email:

GREENGLOBE@compuserve.com: net: www.wttc.org). If ecosensitivity concerns you, here are the sort of questions you can ask:

- What is the tour operator's environmental philosophy?
- Who will be leading the tour?
- Are excursions changed regularly to minimise ecological damage?
- How does the local economy benefit?
- Is the company dedicated to sustainable development of the tourism industry?
- How ecologically sound is the accommodation?

Tour operators in the US

Country chapters have information about tour operators providing trips to specific countries.

Earthwatch PO Box 9014, Watertown, MA 62272; tel: 617 926 8200/800 776 0188; fax: 617 926 8532; email: info@earthwatch.org. A non-profit organisation offering trips to assist researchers in scientific projects. Also has offices in the UK.

Earth River Expeditions 180 Towpath Rd, Accord, CA 12404; tel: 914 626 2665/800 643 2784; fax: 914 626 4423; email: earthriv@envirolink.org. Well-organised whitewater rafting trips down the Upano (Ecuador) and other Amazon rivers.

Eco Expeditions/Zegrahm 1414 Dexter Av North, #327, Seattle, WA 98109; tel: 206 285 4000/800 628 8747; fax: 206 285 5037; email: zoe@zeco.com; net: www.zeco.com. Top-dollar group tours, including expedition cruises to various Amazon locations.

Field Guides Inc PO Box 160723, Austin, TX 78716; tel: 512 327 4953/800 728 4953; fax: 512 327 9231; email: fgileader@aol.com; net: www.fieldguides.com. Specialist birdwatching tours to South America since 1985 led by professional expert ornithologists.

Focus Tours 103 Moya Rd, Santa Fe, NM 87505; tel: 505 466 4688; fax: 505 466 4689; email: focustours@aol.com. Natural-history and educational tours including birdwatching with local naturalist-guides.

International Expeditions tel: 205 428 1700; fax: 205 428 1714; email: Tgrasse@ietravel.com.

Latin America Reservation Center Inc PO Box 1435, Dundee, FL 33838; tel: 941 439 1486/800 327 3573; fax: 941 439 2118; email: LARC1@worldnet.att.net. Can organise arrangements for lodgings, air and land travel throughout South America.

Maupintour 1515 St. Andrews Dr, Lawrence, KS 66047; tel: 785 843 1211/800 255 4266; fax: 785 843 8351. Group and individual tours throughout South America.

Nature Encounters, Ltd 9065 Nemo St W, Hollywood, CA 90069; tel: 310 247 4540/800 529 9927; fax: 310 247 4543; email: nature21@ix.netcom.com; net: www.phrantic.com/nature. General rainforest tours for groups and individuals.

Nature Expeditions International 6400 E El Dorado Circle, Ste 210, Tucson, AZ 85715; tel: 520 721 6712/800 869 0639; fax: 520 721 6719; email: naturexp@aol.com; net: www.naturexp.com. Ecotourism specialists offering wildlife, cultural and natural history tours, some led by experts from the US.

Ocean Connection 211 E Parkwood, Ste 108 Friendswood, TX 77546; tel: 281 996 7800/800 365 6232; fax: 281 996 1556; email: adventure@oceanconnection.com. Amazon cruises aboard luxury vessels.

Silversea Cruises 110 East Broward Boulevard, Ft Lauderdale, FL 33301; tel: 954 522 4477; fax: 954 522 4499.

Southwind Adventures PO Box 621057, Littleton, CO 80162; tel: 303 972 0701/800 377 9463; fax: 303 972 0708; email: swa@sprintmail.com. Tour operator specialising in South America, with general-interest tours to most countries.

Wilderness Travel 1102 Ninth St, Berkeley, CA 94710; tel: 510 558 2488; fax: 510 558 2489; email: info@wildernesstravel.com; net: www.wildernesstravel.com.

ECOTOURISM?

Oliver Whalley

Tourists on tours in lowland jungle, often having paid a lot of money, expect to see wildlife and, depending on the season, the region, their luck and their guide, they may see many animals or very few. Tropical forests offer many experiences but the pressure on tour operators to provide opportunities to see, photograph or video wild animals is great. In some areas this pressure has led to the retreat of wildlife and a decrease in numbers through disturbance, particularly of their feeding and breeding habits. In Manú National Park in Peru, research done by the Frankfurt Zoological Society and the Munich Wildlife Society found a drop in the number of giant otters, largely as a result of the presence of tour boats. Lactating mothers, stressed by the intrusions, failed to produce sufficient milk for their cubs, resulting in their death.

Tourists or travellers in South America can influence the way the landscape and its ecosystem is used and conserved, especially in the Amazon region. To some indigenous people, they can be role models, coming from developed nations with their 'high' standard of living. This makes the behaviour of tourists all the more important. Yet demand by an increasing number of visitors for the hire of 4WD vehicles and high-powered motor boats has led in some cases to a degradation of the landscape and pollution of rivers. 4WDs have been responsible for severe scarring, often lasting for decades, while wetter regions have been eroded in places not normally accessible to locals. High powered outboard motors, on the other hand, make a surprising amount of noise disruption and pollution, causing problems to river animals such as Amazon dolphins, manatees and otters.

Ecotourism is a much used word in South America; many conservationists have argued that the nature of tourism is bad for any sensitive ecosystem. However, most conservationists can also see that, apart from atmospheric pollution of the hundreds of thousands of ferrying aeroplanes, generally the effects of tourism are beneficial. The overriding positive effect, in the case of the Amazon, is that tourists want to see the high diversity of life that only comes in large areas of virgin rainforest. This means that in order to attract tourists governments and in turn locals must try to conserve the primary or undisturbed habitats.

Tour operators in the UK

Amerindia Steeple Cottage, Easton, Winchester, Hants SO21 1EH; tel: 01962 779317; fax: 01962 779458.

Animal Watch Granville House, London Rd, Sevenoaks, Kent TN13 1DL; tel: 01732 741612; fax: 01732 455441; email: mail@animalwatch.co.uk.

Cox & Kings 10 Greencoat Place, London SW10 1PH; tel: 0171 873 5000; fax: 0171 630 6038; email: Cox.Kings@coxkings.sprint.com. Organise several all-inclusive trips around the Amazon region.

Discovery Initiatives No 3, 68 Princes Square, London W2 4NY; tel: 0171 229 9881; fax: 0171 229 9883; email; enquiry@discoveryinitiatives.com: net: www.discoveryinitiatives.com. Work with conservation organisations to ensure deep jungle trips cause minimal damage. One of the few companies travelling to Guyana.

The EarthWatch Institute 57 Woodstock Rd, Oxford OX2 6HJ; tel; 01865 311600; fax: 01865 311383; email: info@uk.earthwatch.org; net: www.earthwatch.org. Runs environmental research trips to several locations in the region.

Fred Olsen Cruises White House Rd, Ipswich, IP1 5LL; tel: 01473 292222; fax: 01473 292345. Have occasional luxury cruises leaving from Dover in the UK for the Amazon.
Geodyssey 29 Harberton Rd, London N19 3JS; tel: 0171 281 7788; fax: 0171 281 7878.
Interchange 27 Stafford Road, Croydon, Surrey CR4 4NG; tel: 0181 681 3612; fax: 0181 760 0031.
Journey Latin America 12–13 Heathfield Terrace, Chiswick, London W4 4JE; tel: 0181 747 3108; fax: 0181 742 1312; email: sales@journeylatinamerica.co.uk. Organise several trips visiting the Amazon and are the best source for information on flights to South America.
Last Frontiers Swan House, High St, Long Crendon, Bucks HP18 9AF, England; tel: 01844 208405; fax: 01844 201400; email: travelinfo@lastfrontiers.co.uk; net: www.lastfrontiers.co.uk. Bespoke South America specialists who can arrange anything you can imagine.
Overland Latin America 13 Dormer Place, Leamington Spa, Warks CV32 5AA; tel: 01926 332222; fax: 01926 435567; email: worldlspa@aol.com.
Passage to South America 12 Noyna Rd, London SW17 7PH; tel: 0181 767 8989; fax: 0181 767 2026; email: psa@scottdunn.com. Itineraries focusing on the Amazon and others that include several regions of the sub-continent.
Reef & Rainforest Prospect House, Jubilee Rd, Totnes, Devon TQ9 5BP; tel: 01803 866965; fax: 01803 865916; email: reefrain@btinternet.com.
Tribes Travel 7 The Business Centre, Earl Soham, Woodbridge, Suffolk IP13 7SA; tel: 01728 685971; fax: 01728 685973; net: www.tribes.co.uk.
Trips Worldwide 9 Byron Place, Clifton, Bristol BS8 1JT; tel: 0117 987 2626; fax: 0117 987 2627. Also PO Box 17-12-602, Quito, Ecuador.
Wildlife Worldwide 170 Selsdon Rd, South Croydon, Surrey CR2 6PJ; tel: 0181 667 9158; fax: 0181 667 1960; email: sales@wildlife-ww.co.uk; net: www.wildlife-ww.co.uk.
Worldwide Journeys 8 Comeragh Rd, London W14 9HP; tel: 0171 381 8638; fax: 0171 381 0836; email: wwj@wjournex.demon.co.uk. Organise cruises that begin in Brazil and travel the Amazon.

Several other agencies specialise in overland or adventure trips to South America which focus on one country and may involve travel across the Amazon Basin by boat. They include:

Bukima Expeditions 55 Huddlestone Rd, London NW2 5DL; tel: 0181 930 6702; fax: 0181 830 1889; email: Bukima@compuserve.com.
Guerba Expeditions 40 Station Rd, Westbury, Wiltshire BA13 3JN; tel: 01373 826611; fax: 01373 858351.
The Imaginative Traveller 14 Barley Mow Passage, Chiswick, London W4 4PH; tel: 0181 742 8612; fax: 0181 742 3045; email: info@imaginative-traveller.com; net: www.imaginative-traveller.com.
Kumuka Expeditions 40 Earls Court Rd, London W8 6EJ; tel: 0171 937 8855; fax: 0171 937 6664; email: sales@kumuka.co.uk.
Travelbag Adventures 15 Turk St, Alton, Hants GU34 1AG; tel: 01420 541007.

At what price?

The price of a trip is usually the critical factor that decides whether it is booked or not. The lowest-priced trip is not necessarily the automatic choice. For a week-long package tour including airfare to and from Miami, lodge accommodation and all meals provided, you can expect to pay a minimum of US$1,500 (£925). Depending on where you are coming from airfares add upwards from US$300 (£185) to the cost of an Amazon trip. On a pre-paid tour budget U$100–250 per week for airport taxes, handicrafts, souvenirs, tips and bottled drinks.

Independent travel

If flexibility and lots of variety are important, you probably want to travel independently. By shopping around, the independent traveller can travel inexpensively. Bucket shops in the US and throughout Europe usually have good deals that will get you to South America for a reasonable price. From the United States, the Air Courier Association (191 University Blvd, Ste 300, Denver, CO 80206; tel: 303 279 3600; fax: 303 278 1293) brings the cost of flights to South America within reach of even the poorest student traveller.

Independent travellers need to plan and research their trip in more detail than is necessary for group travel, especially if they have a limited amount of time and plan on visiting a particular site or area. Many tour operators will make arrangements for independent travellers, sometimes for no more than it would cost to book yourself. But with email, fax, telephone and international credit cards it is getting ever easier to reserve and pay for flights, hotels and jungle tours before leaving home.

One good compromise is to travel to the country on your own and then join a group on a pre-arranged date for a jungle trip. For those already in an Amazon country, local agencies operate a huge range of tours. Many of the better agencies are used by foreign-based tour operators and can work out cheaper if booked locally.

Independent travellers usually know what they want and are a pretty resourceful bunch. The Amazon is overflowing with opportunities for those with enough time. In general you'll have to do more of the groundwork and a cursory knowledge of Spanish and/or Portuguese is very useful, although not essential. Once you arrive, you are best off using the services of a local guide or someone who at least claims to know the area.

Passenger and cargo boats serve all of the major Amazon tributaries and most of the small ones. Swinging in a hammock while gazing into gallery forest is a strangely hypnotic experience.

Travelling on smaller rivers and using a canoe to explore the waterways gives a great feeling of independence and has the thrill of stumbling over the occasional new surprise. If you would like a degree of explanation or increased chances of seeing something in particular take a guide, or convince a local that he can do the job.

Moving off the water, walking in the rainforest is an exhilarating and stimulating experience. Even if you pay attention to where you're walking – which would mean you don't get to look at the rainforest – there is a very real likelihood of getting lost. This prospect, or even the thought of it, gives some people a real buzz. Fine, but for most sane people it's just plain scary.

One technique to avoid getting lost is to mark any trail blazed by using a machete to chip away at tree bark or breaking and snapping palms, ferns and branches en route. For the experienced this certainly works, but it's not uncommon for guides to get lost using this method. If you're on your first trip into the jungle and fancy trying this technique there'll be a few panicky moments before you're really confident. The purist ecotourist may baulk at this drastic method, so you're best off with a native guide who knows where he's going.

The financial realities are that independent travel in the Amazon is rarely cheaper than an organised tour. You can certainly travel through the region on a tight budget, but if you include any activities it is unlikely there will be much difference in cost by the time you get home. Going off foot-loose and fancy-free is all very exciting but it does tend to be the most expensive way, and perhaps riskier too.

Travelling with children

Children put a constraint on the type and length of vacation. The Amazon is great fun for youngsters of, say, ten and over, but any younger and they tend to be somewhat overwhelmed. An Amazon holiday with children would probably turn out best if the family stays at a good jungle lodge. The tourist riverboats are ideal for families.

US readers can get specialist travel equipment for children from **Tough Traveler**, 1012 State St, Schenectady, NY 12307, USA; tel: 800 468 6844/518 377 8526; fax: 518 377 5434, email: service@toughtraveler; net: www.traveler.com. In the UK readers can contact **Nomad Travellers Store** at 3-4 Wellington Terrace, Turnpike Lane, London N8 0PX; tel: 0181 889 7014; fax: 0181 889 9529; email: nomad.travstore@virgin.net.

For the truly adventurous

There are some fairly unique individuals who, like Orellana and other legendary travellers, just fancy the idea of exploring the Amazon or one of its tributaries with a canoe and a companion for months at a time. It's possible and people do, more often than not, come back alive… well, that's what John Harrison, author of *Up the Creek*, claims.

Expeditions into the Amazon represent serious adventure. If you want pointers on how to organise such a fantastically hare-brained idea read the next chapter, *Expedition Planning*. Tanis Jordan and her husband Martin started travelling along Amazon tributaries back in the 1960s and their adventures can be read in more detail in *Out of Chingford*.

Additional information

For practical travel hints the **South American Explorers Club** (126 Indian Creek Rd, Ithaca, New York, NY 14850l, USA: tel: 607 277 0488; fax: 607 277 6122; email: explorer@sameexplo.org; net: www.samexplo.org) is a mine of information, with current unbiased advice from all over South America on tour operators, hotels, security and travel problems. UK residents can join through Bradt Publications; tel: 01494 873478.

Staff can help with trip planning and assist members seeking travel companions or experts in a particular field. They can put you in touch with local rainforest conservation organisations who can up-date you on recent environmental issues. To get all this you need to be a member which costs US$40. Annual subscription buys the quarterly club magazine and use of the Quito and Lima clubhouses which are both packed with books, trip reports and other travellers. Club addresses are in the Ecuador and Peru chapters, pages 246 and 284.

Latin American Travel Consultants (LATC) PO Box 17-17-908, Quito, Ecuador; fax: 00 593 2 562 566; email: LATC@pi.pro.ec; net: www.amerispan.com/latc/. They publish the quarterly *Latin American Travel Advisor* (LATA) newsletter and provide up-to-date country information pamphlets, also maps and books on all aspects of travel in the Amazon and rest of South America.

Maps

Maps in this book are approximate to give an idea of a layout and geography. For adventure activities, high resolution, accurate maps of the Amazon are necessary, but hard to come by. The best practical sources are universities and government military institutions. Unless you've grown up in the Amazon, finding your way around the back-country with anything less than a 10m accurate GPS is virtually impossible, and then pretty pointless if you don't have a map. Hence for backpacking or hiking in the lowland Amazon, most travel will be along rivers and with a guide.

International Travel Map Productions (ITMB Publishing, PO Box 2290, Vancouver BC V6B 3W5, Canada. tel: 604 687 3320; fax: 604 687 5925) publish an excellent map of the Amazon Basin which has been used to produce some of the maps in this book.

General-interest maps of the Amazon Basin can be obtained (or ordered) from travel bookshops or mail order companies. In the UK **Stanfords** is the best travel bookshop and handles international mail order. Tel: 0171 836 1321; fax: 0171 836 0189.

Guides

Seasoned travellers often baulk at the idea of using a guide. This phobia must be overcome for a trip to the jungle. A guide is essential for gaining some deeper understanding of the jungle. The naturalist-guide leads visitors along trails, takes them on canoe rides and helps them to spot wildlife. While it is possible to move around developed areas and between various Amazon towns independently, for any type of extended trip to remote areas a local or native guide is essential. The quality of guides can make or break the rainforest experience, so choose carefully.

Native local guides

Virtually everyone who visits remote areas of rainforest will be accompanied at some time or other by a local guide. The average local guide knows the area well, can identify most animals and some plants and can talk with the indigenous Indians in the area.

The experience and quality of local guides varies considerably. The best are highly knowledgeable and are able to talk at length on the ecology of rainforest species, scientific topics and native cultures. The worst guides – and they do exist! – drink on duty, promote their own business, speak little English, and have poor knowledge of wildlife and a nonchalant attitude to clients' well-being.

Independent travellers can ask others for recommendations. Group travellers should check suitability with tour operators.

University-trained guides and tour leaders

Owing to the lack of local guides with broad scientific knowledge, some travel companies offer group tours escorted by a qualified naturalist-guide. Some lodges and reserves may employ American or European researchers working on-site. They usually have expert knowledge in specific fields, such as ecology, ornithology or entomology.

As with local guides, the experience and background of biologist-guides or tour leaders is highly variable. The best are university-trained, have experience of travelling in the area and knowledge of tropical biology, and speak Spanish or Portuguese.

WHAT TO TAKE

By and large, what you take to the Amazon depends on what you'll be doing there, and where you'll be staying before and after. If you're travelling independently a daily set of clean clothes isn't that crucial. If you're on one of the luxury liners that cruises up the Amazon mainstream then forgetting the tuxedo could be a real *faux pas*.

Some of the out-of-the-way lodges have luggage limitations, so knowing what is essential and useful is fairly important.

Packing

Before you even get out the bags, have an effective and efficient method of packing and aim to minimise what you pack. A traveller's rule of thumb is to pack what you think is essential and then halve it.

CHECKLIST

Clothes

Broad-brimmed hat; rain jacket; T-shirts or tank tops; shorts; long pants or trousers/skirt; long-sleeved shirt/blouse; sweater; socks; underwear; swimwear; set of 'smart' clothing

Shoes

Deck/beach shoes or sandals or trainers; walking shoes or rubber boots

Toiletries

Whatever you normally carry with you when travelling; plus a bar of biodegradable soap. Don't forget: shampoo, contraceptives, tampons, sanitary towels. If you use glasses or contact lenses, take spares.

Medical equipment *(see also Chapter Four)*

Malaria prophylaxis; anti-diarrhoea remedy; itch-ease; sunblock (SPF 15–30); moisturising cream; lipsalve; general painkillers; antibiotic ointment; a small first-aid kit; antihistamine cream or tablets; pre-sealed sterile towelettes; required prescription medicines

Travel documents

Passport (with visa if required); tickets; travellers' cheques, credit card, cash; money/document pouch; photocopies of all important travel documents, kept in a different place

Miscellaneous

Sunglasses; insect repellent (see page 91); torch/flashlight (for night excursions and badly lit lodges); strong one-litre water bottle; small backpack (for jungle excursions); large waterproof zip-lock bags (5 or 6); small towel (quick-drying); penknife; ear-plugs; cheap wristwatch; travel alarm clock; binoculars (vital to enjoy birdlife and wild animals); dictionary/phrasebook (see page 53); travel games (chess, checkers, Scrabble, backgammon, cards); ball of string (multiple uses...)

Photographic equipment *(see also pages 49–51)*

SLR camera with 50mm lens; 75–210mm zoom lens; 25 or 35mm wide angle lens; daylight (UV) filter; polarising filter; flash unit; spare batteries; film (as much as you think you will need for the trip); point-and-shoot camera (for back-up and spontaneous shots); camera bag; packet of silica crystals (to absorb moisture); ziplock bags (to keep used film in); lead bag (to protect fast film from airport X-rays); tripod or monopod and/or beanbag (to rest the camera on); cable shutter release

After this drastic measure, other methods reduce the load further still. Eliminate useless packaging, such as film boxes, by putting films in a water-tight container. Repackage items so you carry only as much as you need for the trip. For lotions and liquids, put the necessary amount in a small used container, such as a food jar, film canister, or pill bottle.

Clothing

Clothing should be lightweight and dry quickly. A pair of synthetic or cotton (some people are prone to heat rash wearing synthetics in a humid climate)

athletics trousers is ideal. Light enough to stop you getting hot and sweaty and long enough to keep the insects off, they reduce the chances of scratches and infections when out on the jungle trail. They're easy to wash and dry very quickly.

Two or three lightweight cotton-mix shirts/blouses with long sleeves are ideal for your top half. Pull-over shirts minimise the risk of getting snagged in the jungle. Also take a few T-shirts or tops to wear when you're not on the move and a lightweight jumper to keep the occasionally chilly nights bearable.

A pair of shorts are good for the quieter, flyless moments and some people actually prefer to trek in them.

In the rainforest you don't need expensive hiking or trekking boots. Running or tennis shoes or trainers with a lightweight sock are ideal. When you're not trekking or hiding every inch of your body from the insects, thongs or rubber sandals give your feet a breather and are good for tramping around boats, towns and villages.

Take a swimsuit or shorts if you like swimming, plus something to cover your shoulders in case of sunburn.

A lightweight, compact raincoat or poncho is good for the inevitable downpour and a broad-brimmed hat offers protection from the sun.

If you'll be passing through one of the capital cities you ought to take a smartish set of clothes for posher restaurants and hotels. A pair of casual trousers and a shirt – or separates and/or a dress, depending on your gender – along with a pair of clean shoes will get you into most restaurants. Check with your tour operator about the

DON'T HAM IT IN THE HAMMOCK

Most lodges and tourist riverboats have spots where you can sling a hammock to relax and pass the time. Usually the hammock is already rigged up for you. On budget trips and when travelling by boat you will probably sleep several nights in a hammock. Having your hammock fall while you are asleep in it is one of the funniest things… about two days after it happened. There is a technique to putting it up and, if you're not sure how, ask crew members or lodge staff for a bit of advice. Basically you need a couple of pieces of string/rope to connect the end-loops of the hammock to a post or something. Ideally it should be hung level at hip height, without too much sag. On passenger boats hammocks may be stacked two or three high so you can't always achieve the ideal.

Once you have your hammock up, you need to master the art of getting in and out, and staying in it comfortably. Like eating with chopsticks, it is one of those things a lot easier to do than to explain! Similarly, everyone has their own technique and you will develop your own. Here is Roger's tried and tested method:

Getting in: Pull the hammock together and press down in the middle, hike a leg over the hammock's lowest point, and stand astride. Stand on one leg, place the other in the hammock, sit down and spread the material to give enough room for your body. Once your weight is taken by the hammock bring the other leg in. Not very dignified, but this procedure is easier than it sounds. To save yourself backache, lie diagonally across the hammock which should just about have you sleeping level.

Getting out: Sit up, put a leg down, bring the other leg across so you are sitting sideways on the hammock, and get up without putting any weight on the hammock.

Try it!

dress code in riverboats and lodges. In the Andean cities the altitude can make it quite chilly at night so you'll need to take a jacket or fleece if you're staying there.

For expedition clothing see also page 72.

Medical equipment

Medical essentials include anti-malarials (see pages 81–2) and of course insect repellent. The active ingredient in repellent is DEET which is highly toxic – a concentration of 30–50% should be adequate for use on the skin, but clothes may be impregnated with 100%. A natural option is citronella oil which achieves mixed results. More suggestions are in *Chapter Four*, page 81.

Hammocks and camping equipment

If you intend travelling on local riverboats a hammock is indispensable, so take yours if you have one. Otherwise, strong cotton hammocks are available for sale in most South American towns at incredibly low prices (usually under US$20). The lightweight hammocks available from survival shops tend to be uncomfortable and crucial pieces of string break fairly easily.

An outline of things to take if you plan on sleeping out is included in *Chapter Three*, page 67.

Luggage

A personal choice this one. If the bag is really just a way of getting your stuff from A to B, taking a case is useful especially if you might want to bring back fragile things. If you're on an adventure trip a duffel bag is best as it will stand up to a battering.

If you are hiking, doing significant amounts of walking, or will be carrying your own luggage for most of the time, take a rucksack.

More and more bags of all types are lockable. In reality your luggage is most vulnerable at the international airport either in your own country or in South America. If it can be locked this will deter the casual thief.

A small rucksack/daypack is ideal for keeping hold of important things like passports, tickets and so on, when logistics require you to be separated from your main luggage. In any case take a daypack for walks.

IN AMAZONIA

Hunting and shooting... with binoculars and camera

To maximise your enjoyment of Amazon wildlife we provide some tips on the only way for visitors to hunt and shoot wildlife... with binoculars and a camera.

Viewing Amazon wildlife

Most large animals and birds you expect to see in the Amazon are rare, elusive and wary. To maximise the chances of spotting animals on your hunt, remember the following:

- Be quiet! Most wild animals hear, see or smell us long before we are aware of their presence. Talk in low tones and step carefully.
- Be attentive! Many Amazon creatures are masters of disguise. Dense vegetation and low light in the forest make it hard to see well-camouflaged animals such as sloths and tree-snakes. Keep your eyes (and ears) wide open.
- Stay together! In the forest, many eyes are better than two, so in a group you are more likely to see interesting wildlife. People spread out across a distance scare away animals more than a compact group. Keep up with your guide who is more likely to spot animals.

YOU NEED BINOCULARS

You may prefer to travel light but, whatever you do, *don't* forget your binoculars. There are times when, as you spend a quiet few moments resting away from other people, a solitary bird may accidentally wander within a few metres of you. These moments are unforgettable. But most birds, indeed most wildlife, that you see will be a considerable distance away – and hard to study with the naked eye.

Modern, compact binoculars are very light. Buying yourself a small, pre-Amazon adventure present (eg: 12x24) will bring the world of the rainforest considerably closer to you... literally.

- Look and listen closely! You may not see any big mammals or reptiles but the rainforest is a treasure chest of nature's smaller jewels. Observe closely a fallen rotting log, under leaf litter or among the leaves of a shrub and you are bound to find something.
- Avoid perfumes! Animals are often spooked by an unusual scent so wearing your favourite after-shave or cologne is only going to put more distance between you and what you have come to see.
- Early to rise! Makes you healthy, wealthy and wise... and you get to see more. Not only is it more peaceful, but birds and monkeys are more active around dawn, which is at sixish in the Amazon. Also, early morning light adds contrast and atmosphere to photographs.
- Wear 'quiet' clothes! Clothing subdued in colour, such as khaki, greens or browns, is less visible to animals. Primates and birds see colour, so bright blue, orange or yellow may frighten them off. (Avoid camouflage gear which will make locals wonder whether or not you are a soldier!)

Photography

Shooting the wildlife... with a camera. If you follow the above advice then with a bit of luck there will come the thrilling moment when you encounter a wild rainforest animal. You may well be happy with memories alone. But some people want to record the event and the most popular way is with a camera. However, to be pleased with results you should keep your expectations in proportion to your experience.

Nature photos matching magazine publishers' standards are taken after years of experience and are not likely on your first foray into the jungle. Professionals use expensive equipment, spending hundreds of arduous hours in blinds and tree-houses. Talent and imagination can make up for some of this, but most average photographers must practise and experiment for years. Whatever film or camera is used and whatever one's experience, it is almost impossible to capture the forest's grandeur on film. Bear this in mind and you'll be happier with your own initial efforts.

In the jungle most wildlife is too far off or well-concealed for good pictures. Without a telephoto lens, a sloth, bird or monkey will appear as a blur or blob on most photos taken in the field. The least you need is a good camera (SLR) and zoom lens (minimum 70–210 mm). Unless you have a suitable lens and tripod (to steady the camera for the slow exposures needed with a long lens) and lots of time, the best way to use your film is to go for scenic views or close-ups of flowers and leaves. On the occasions when you do see some interesting wildlife, it is often better to enjoy the animals with binoculars rather than waste film.

As mentioned, good equipment, patience and lots of luck are needed for the best wildlife pictures. However, it is still possible to take pictures of animals with a point-and-shoot automatic camera if you can get really close. Mostly, these are invertebrates, some of which are exquisite and highly photogenic. Beetles, leaf insects and butterflies make good topics.

For close-ups you need a macro lens or extension tubes to magnify the subject, a flash to compensate for reduced light and a tripod when using slow shutter speeds.

Some amphibians also make beautiful subjects. Brightly coloured and relatively fearless, poison-dart frogs (eg: *Dendrobatidae*) can be approached quite closely. Unfortunately, their minute size makes it hard to get well-lit and composed photographs. Poison-dart frogs – or any amphibian to be on the safe side – should not be touched. They are easily damaged by handling and there exists a danger of poisoning from the highly toxic compounds secreted by their skin.

In addition to uncooperative wildlife, lighting conditions often conspire to frustrate the Amazon photographer. Darkness on the forest floor or glare from the river cause incorrectly exposed shots. To overcome exposure problems, automatic shutter speed settings can be altered on most modern SLRs and combined with filters, flash and the right film speed. For the best natural light, dawn and dusk give ideal conditions. Close to the horizon, the low sun bathes the subject in a soft, golden glow and enhances contrast as it casts deep shadows.

On a casual level, whether to use print or slide film is down to personal preference. If there is any prospect of the photographs being reproduced, slide film is a must. Buying film in major cities in South America is, generally, perfectly safe. Whatever risk there is will be determined by the size, style and the location of the place you are buying it. Prices tend to be more expensive than in the US or Europe so the best bet is to take what you think you need. Some people would recommend as much as two rolls a day but keeping up that rate for three weeks or longer could be difficult.

Be selective with the film speed you use for specific shots. River and open village scenes with lots of light are best shot with ISO200 or ISO100. Slower film works fine, giving better definition and reproduction, but demands more light than fast film.

Under the canopy, a faster film is needed for low-light situations, so you might choose ISO400. For any slower film, a flash is definitely needed for photography in the jungle as the forest floor is too dark for ordinary film. Try experimenting with superfast black-and-white film such as ISO1000 for interesting grainy effects.

With slow film or a telephoto or zoom lens more light is needed. Hence scenic shots will require longer exposures. To prevent blur with exposures longer than 1/60th second (1/125th with telephoto or 1/250th for action shots), you must use a tripod or other support, plus a cable release. Tripods are generally bulky and heavy. A good alternative is a monopod, placed directly in the ground or leant against a tree. A beanbag is an even cheaper option and one you can make at home. It is placed on a wall or branch of a tree with the camera set on top.

An ultraviolet (UV) or daylight filter is useful to protect the lens, while a polarising filter greatly improves scenic shots. It reduces glare from the river, preventing over-exposure, and adds definition to clouds. The polarising filter gives a picture with contrast closer to what the eye perceives. Without the filter, many landscape shots turn out with the sky over-exposed or the river and forest under-exposed.

Annoying malfunctions can be avoided by caring for your camera equipment. Before departure, clean and check everything works correctly. If your camera is old, you might consider having it professionally overhauled or serviced before departure. Few things are as frustrating, and almost unresolvable, as your camera breaking down in the middle of the Amazon.

In the forest humidity can be a problem. Fungal growths on lenses may occur in very damp conditions. Put a sachet of silicon crystals beside the camera to absorb excessive moisture. With this precaution you're unlikely to experience any real difficulties.

Photography etiquette

It can be quite disconcerting, whoever or wherever you are, to have a camera stuffed in your face. When photographing local people, ask permission. To break the ice, let them look through the viewfinder first, and even take a picture of you. Children love the immediate results of Polaroid.

Generally people do not mind being photographed and rarely ask to be paid. Courtesy dictates that you ask, and respect demands that you honour the person's wishes. Tour operators prefer you not to offer money simply for a photograph. The best trade option is to offer to send the person a copy of the photograph, and of course remember to do so. Professional photographers, on the other hand, have a different moral dilemma to consider.

A walk in the dark: identifying wildlife at night

As you will hear from the cacophony of sound in the jungle at night, many Amazon animals are nocturnal. Most tours include a night walk or an excursion

ANIMAL	EYESHINE	LOCATION
Mammals		
Brocket deer	brilliant yellow-white	swampy areas, riversides
Capybara	yellow to red (dim)	near water with aquatic plants
Jaguar	green-yellow	trails in wet forest areas
Kinkajou & olingo	bright orange	forest canopy
Margay	yellow	dense forest
Night monkey	reddish-orange	river edges, open areas
Ocelot	pale yellow	trails in forest and scrub
Opossums	yellow-orange, yellow	various habitats
Paca	bright yellow-orange	swamps, near rivers, occasionally forest
Peccary	reddish (dim)	wide range of habitats
Porcupine	faint dull red	secondary dense growth
Puma	pale yellow	widespread, many habitats
Rat	bright yellow	forest, inhabited areas
Tapir	yellow (dim)	water-edge forests
Birds		
Owl	yellow	widespread
Potoo	glowing orange	humid forest borders
Others		
Caiman	red	water margins, floating meadows
Spider	pale green (small)	water margins, floating vegetation

by boat. A powerful torch is useful and you really need your own; a headlight is ideal since it concentrates the beam at eye level and leaves your hands free. Animals are spotted mainly from eyeshine caused when a portion of their retina reflects back the light.

Night walks are the best opportunity to see cats. After dark they are most active and like to prowl along footpaths. They have a bright eyeshine which makes them easy to spot. To help you identify cats and other common nocturnal animals in the field, we give a summary opposite of animals most likely to be seen at night with descriptions of their eyeshine and preferred habitat.

Fishing in the Amazon: a different angle

Many visitors come to the Amazon expecting to fish and they are rarely disappointed. Virtually all organised tours include an excursion to fish for the infamous piranha with fishing tackle provided.

The tackle could not be simpler: a bamboo rod, line and hook. No weights, reel or floats. Even with this primitive set-up piranha fishing is often successful. Let your guide remove the hook. Local fishermen are often missing a piece of toe or finger because a piranha fancied a nibble.

Also caught with the bamboo rod are small catfish, called *squeakers* because they make a high-pitched sound out of water. More dangerous than they look, squeakers have a sharp, poisonous dorsal spine.

Angling enthusiasts who want to do some serious sport fishing should take their own rod and tackle. The guide will provide chopped meat for bait and basic fishing equipment. With better equipment you can catch a greater variety of species, such as the larger catfish or better still the delicious *tilapia* (Cichlidae). The latter are highly valued as food and a large *oscar* is a real prize. Most treasured is the *tambaqui* which requires much practice and patience. Natives have the skill to mimic the splash of the falling nuts that are this species' sole food.

Most fish in the Amazon use smell or electric signals to detect food. Artificial lures for visually-oriented fish are usually unsuccessful, unless designed for certain species, such as peacock bass.

Most organised fishing tours in Brazil are organised from Manaus (book through **Rod & Reel Adventures**, 3507 Tully Rd, Ste B6, Modesto, CA 95356; tel: 800 356 6982/209 524 7775; fax: 209 524 1220). Here the peacock bass (*Cichla ocellaris*) is large and abundant. This species is the most popular for sports fishing being aggressive and putting up a fierce fight. It needs specialised equipment such as heavy line, oversize topwater lures and stiff rods. Large fish, they average 2.7kg but specimens weighing 4.5–9.0kg are caught regularly. World record sizes (up to 12.3kg) are reported from the area. Away from the madding crowd, Alta Floresta in the southeast of the Brazilian Amazon has a specialist fishing lodge with excellent fishing in the nearby rivers.

THE VALUE OF SPORT FISHING

If carried out sustainably, sport fishing could eventually help to save animals in the Amazon.

Fishermen will pay a lot of money to catch peacock bass, and this hard cash speaks louder than cries to preserve the ecosystem for its own sake, laudable sentiment though that is. This species illustrates the value of intact habitat.

THE PEOPLE

Languages and customs

Languages

You can travel anywhere in South America, or the world for that matter, without knowing the language. Getting from A to B is easy enough if that is all you want to do. But if you're curious enough about a country to go there, why not have a shot at its language?

Spanish is the lingua franca throughout South America except in Brazil (Portuguese), Guyana (English), Suriname (Dutch) and French Guiana (French). The type of Spanish spoken in South America is slightly different from European Spanish, but the differences are manageable.

In Brazil Portuguese is the official language but, as with Spanish, there are considerable differences from the mother-tongue in Portugal. Brazilians can usually understand Spanish if you speak it but understanding their reply to you is pretty difficult. Some people find making the leap between Spanish and Portuguese easy, others find it impossible.

With the expansion of tourism and industry in recent years, most guides in the Amazon's popular tourist areas speak some English.

The most widely spoken native language in the western Amazon is Quechua, for which bilingual dictionaries are available. Given the difficulty of pronouncing Quechua, with its many guttural rasps, the short-term visitor is easily deterred from further linguistic experiments.

In Amazonia, whichever country you are in, the language is generally used differently from in the more populated parts. The introduction of slang, slight changes in accent, innovative developments in the concept of grammar and a host of other influences conspire to make it sound like a completely new language.

Just a few words and a natural ability to make a complete fool of yourself will get you far closer to people's hearts than linguistic perfection. And making a fool of yourself can lead to some fairly amusing situations, like going to the cinema for a haircut, going to a barbecue for a bus, or confusing your heart and a sausage.

Language dictionaries

Berlitz publish compact travellers' dictionaries specifically for Latin-American Spanish and Portuguese, with useful phrases and a phonetic pronunciation guide. Some of the basics are in *Appendix 2*, page 427.

Local customs and mannerisms

The *Latino* (a Spanish-speaking person from the Americas; feminine is *Latina*) is typically less reserved and more voluble than the American or North European. A quick hug or *abrazo* is a normal gesture among men who know each other. A handshake is considered formal but suitable for most occasions, including greeting and parting. When men and women greet, they hug with a quick kiss on the cheek, or just hold hands and touch cheeks. For strangers, this is reduced to a shoulder grasp, leaning forward, first to the left, then the right.

Beckoning is opposite to the northern European gesture: Latinos typically beckon with one hand palm down, waving the fingers.

Begging and trading goods

It's not uncommon for tourists in South America to be confronted with begging. Asking for sweets, food and presents in general may appear to be a natural response of villagers to a few seemingly wealthy gringos arriving in town. But as soon as you've been to somewhere truly out of the way, you'll realise it isn't.

Gift-giving by tourists, in whatever form, creates a dependency culture. Once established, the procedure is expected. It becomes a source of disappointment for locals – and a hassle for tourists – if gifts are not given. If you want to contribute to this impression of tourism, that is your choice. Simply saying 'no' usually stops the begging.

If the reason for giving gifts is to create temporary friendships, then with time on your hands and a creative mind you can devise plenty of ways of sharing experiences across cultures that don't relegate one half to the status of beggars.

If you do get to spend time with new 'friends', photographs of family and postcards of home are always interesting. A Polaroid camera's instant snapshot is a truly personal gift. If you want to help with cash, you can donate to local schools or hospitals or, back home, to conservation or health organisations who work locally.

Contacts with local people

South Americans are a passionately laid-back people. The routine of life has created a culture that focuses on the importance of *mañana* with an impressive indifference to haste that frequently frustrates Westerners. Let's face it, rushing around while doing something rarely gets it done any quicker in reality. For the traveller on the receiving end this indifference can come across as a lack of concern. Lateness is almost institutionalised in South America and your visit will be far more enjoyable if you relax into that way of life. Buses and taxis don't go faster with stress, so if you have a plane to catch, leave slightly earlier.

Whether meeting people deep in the Amazon Basin or in a city, the conventional greeting is *buenas dias* – often shortened to just *buenas* – in all but Brazil where *bom dia* or *boa tarde* are used. In a social setting you will normally be introduced to everyone. For introductions and new acquaintances, men and women both greet with a handshake. The next step up, showing particular appreciation and strong friendship, is a rather intricate combination of handshake and pat on the back which stops just short of an all-out hug. Female friends greet with a kiss to each kiss often accompanied in more formal settings by a small handshake. These gestures also cover separations.

Tipping

Tipping varies greatly across the region. Airport porters, hotel staff and restaurants all rely to a certain extent on the wage top-ups that come from tipping. Taxi drivers do not generally expect a tip although a few will probably do their best to encourage you. Agreeing on a price before you travel will reduce the chances of your bags being held to ransom.

Gifts

If you are lucky enough to be invited into someone's home you will almost certainly be confronted with a banquet that is the best the house can provide. It is easy to feel slightly guilty about contributing nothing to the feast but nothing will be expected. If you spend time with new-found friends, any hospitality you receive will be freely given. There are plenty of ways of returning the generosity without resorting to money. Sending a gift from home, or taking a photograph and sending it through the post, are two options. If you promise to send a picture make sure you do.

Buying souvenirs

Shopping in South America is a lot of fun! The most popular souvenirs among Amazon visitors are native-made handicrafts. Wood carvings are widely available in

THE ANIMAL TRADE

Oliver Whalley

In the Amazon region many animals are exploited, often illegally. Live animals and animal parts are exported in large numbers but also supply local, mainly urban, demands and the tourist trade. The market for live animals is not always as pets or for zoos but often for scientific research; cruelly this includes various species of monkeys. Recently pharmaceutical companies have started collecting large numbers of animals, such as poison-arrow frogs, severely threatening their survival in certain areas.

As a traveller in the Amazon region you may see such animal abuse and exploitation; please report the sale of species, particularly protected endangered species, to conservation groups locally and at home and also to the local authorities.

Do not buy any of the following:

- Animal skins of any sort, part or whole
- Any animal parts, including parrot feathers, skulls (especially jaguar and caiman skulls, teeth and claws), toucan beaks, turtle shells, heads or fins
- Any insects, often sold mounted in glass cases. Particularly under threat from over-collection are species of very large or brightly coloured beetle such as the harlequin beetle or the hercules beetle, the large iridescent blue morpho and the large black and yellow/green papillon butterflies, and tarantula and other large spiders.

city shops and even remote forest villages. The commonest woods are mahogany, genipa or balsa.

Other local handicrafts include palm fibre baskets, mats and hats, woven goods, pottery and simple adornments made out of collected wild seeds, shells and insect parts. Animal teeth, feathers, claws and skin are sometimes used. On ecological, and in some cases legal, grounds, items incorporating animal parts should not be bought.

Except in town shops, bartering is commonplace but optional when purchasing souvenirs. If you like something and are happy to pay the asking price no one is likely to complain.

Other good buys are 'naive' paintings on postcards (Colombia) and woven goods (Peru and Ecuador). Gold and some gemstones, especially emeralds, sapphire and topaz, are good value (Colombia, Brazil). Basketry is very good in Venezuela. Textiles in Bolivia are probably the best on the continent although they are not widely available in the lowlands.

SLEEPING AND EATING

Accommodation

Finding a place to rest your head for the night in the Amazon, indeed throughout South America, is rarely a problem. As you'd expect from a continent of contrasts, the range covers the extremes. Major cities and large towns all have comfortable accommodation, with five-star standards occasionally found in the most out-of-the-way places. But comfort costs, and in some countries the best hotels will set you back over US$100 a night. Most towns have a number of mid-range hotels costing US$20–45. Although some of the luxury comforts may be lacking, it's unlikely that you'll notice if you're out and about exploring during the day.

The bottom end of the market is a delightful game of chance. While some are efficiently run small hotels that hold cherished reputations for friendliness and cleanliness, others cut costs in every way possible, cramming beds into the smallest of spaces. Genuine flea-pits are rare but the only way to avoid them is to have a look at the rooms first.

Away from towns, the priorities of the traveller take a back seat and hotels or *residencias* target locals passing through. Function takes priority over form. Small towns may have a variety of options, most of which will be acceptable to all but the pickiest of travellers. The very smallest settlements are likely to welcome you with little more than a wooden shack and something dubiously called a 'mattress', or even straw-stuffed flour sacks, with the river providing a rather handy all-in-one washroom-cum-bathroom.

Accommodation in the jungle varies greatly. The very best lodges offer excellent accommodation and food but most leave you wanting for some of the comforts of life. The best solution is to immerse yourself in the rainforest and avoid thinking about the largely irrelevant temporary discomforts.

The cheapest and arguably the best jungle experiences will have you sleeping in hammocks under thatched huts or, if the season is right and the insects not too numerous, the stars. Although hammocks are comfortable for most people once you get the hang of them, some people might not like the idea of a fortnight suspended between two trees, so check the style of accommodation offered before booking any trips.

Youth hostels, or affiliated organisations, can be found in Brazil, Colombia and Peru, with an associate organisation in Ecuador. For the latest information contact a local branch of the IYHA in the UK on (01727) 855215, or in the US on (202) 783 6161.

Accommodation in this guide is divided between the top, middle and bottom end of the market relative to each country· twenty dollars spent on a hotel in Bolivia will get you far more than it would in Brazil. Avoiding comparisons on price across countries, we have opted to focus on the relative comforts available in each area.

In all but the very best hotels you should always ask to have a look at the rooms and the bathroom first. The vast majority of places are comfortable but there are a few that are so grubby that you'd be lucky to find any sleep, rest or comfort.

On a more personal level, plumbing can be beautifully erratic in the Amazon region and heated water is rare. Given the temperatures and humidity this is unlikely to cause a real problem. Where hot water is available, it is usually barely more than a trickle. The 'Frankenstein-switch' that will be somewhere close to the shower offers heated water should you feel like it. The system may look very low-tech and more than a little disconcerting to the non-electricians amongst us, but actual shocks are uncommon! Toilets throughout the region are not designed to flush paper, so use the basket next to the toilet.

Some accommodation – most in Venezuela – has air conditioning, but a fan is more commonly available to help you cool down. The best way of staying cool is to get up early, rest through the hottest part of the day, then get active again towards the end of the afternoon. It's what the locals do.

Food and drink: a taste of the Amazon

Food in Amazonia is varied and tasty, healthy but rarely 'haute cuisine'. Many foods in the Amazon are familiar – bread and eggs are widely eaten, as well as most well-known vegetables, which are grown locally or imported from other parts of the country.

MARVELLOUS MANIOC

Versatile, ubiquitous and easy to grow, manioc is the ultimate multi-purpose vegetable. With over 140 varieties under cultivation, manioc, or yucca as it tends to be called outside the Amazon (or cassava in Africa), is the principal ingredient in 14 foods and 13 beverages. Throughout Amazonia it is prepared into a ground course flour and sprinkled on virtually all food as *farinha*. This is guaranteed to test your dental fillings, but the taste benefit is negligible.

That manioc ever found its way to the Amazon table is surprising. Eaten as harvested, some types are highly toxic. Preparation requires two days of soaking before the root is pounded to a paste and dried.

Many indigenous groups believe the plant seeks the souls of children for nourishment, and needs to be carefully tended to keep the spirit of the plant under control. You may well doubt this, but if you dig up a manioc root following the death of a young child you will see red in the veins of the plant. What greater proof could you need?

Tomatoes, lettuce, cabbage, potatoes and onions are all available. Restaurants and lodges which cater to international tourists serve wheat bread, invariably white; whole-wheat is non-existent in the Amazon. Meat served at tourist facilities is usually beef or pork. Vegetarians can ask tour operators to arrange non-meat dishes but make sure you point out that chicken is meat – many people in South America do not think so.

Breakfast tends to be something simple like eggs, bread and tea or coffee. A typical main meal served at jungle lodges and on tourist riverboats might include salad or soup to start, and a kind of beef and vegetable stir-fry, with corn tamales wrapped in banana leaves.

Certain foods are not found in the region. Virtually all the cattle in Amazonia are raised for beef, which, combined with the lack of refrigeration, means dairy produce is rarely available. Outside dairy-producing regions in the Andes foothills, cheese and fresh milk are scarce. Evaporated or powdered milk is normally used instead.

With wheat not being readily available, river people bake a flat loaf made from manioc flour. Try it if you get the chance although it can be rather bland and rubbery. Local meats exclusive to rainforest areas include wild iguana, turtle, tapir and peccary. Due to hunting laws, with the exception of iguana these species are out-of-bounds for a law-abiding chef unless a tribal Indian. For poultry, locals occasionally keep currasows in captivity.

Not surprisingly the main source of animal protein in the region is fish, which is usually just filleted and fried. At restaurants and lodges it is sometimes cooked in batter which, along with manioc 'french fries', makes an acceptable 'fish and chips'. *Pirarucú* and *tambaqui* are the tastiest fish, and a *dorado* catfish or large silver dollar fish make a good meal. Piranha is high on the adventurous gourmet's list of 'must try' Amazon foods. Somewhat bony and oily, it can be made into a rich, brothy soup.

Local foods are generally inexpensive and nutritious. One of the best local dishes is fresh heart of palm salad. This excellent dish is often served for lunch or dinner at hotels and lodges. The raw ingredient is an ivory-coloured cylinder about a metre long, harvested from the heart or growing point of a *chonta* (*Euterpe* spp) or palm tree. In the case of *E. precatoria* this results in the death of the tree after 20–30 years. However, *E. oleracea* produces multiple stems and can be harvested sustainably.

Usually served on its own, the palm heart is shaved into thin ribbons. These are slightly crunchy, with a mild, delicate flavour. This dish is usually very safe as the vegetable is peeled and does not need to be washed.

You might want to try some of the jungle insects as food, including honey ants and the Amazon delicacy of palm grubs – a traditional native Indian food and a regional speciality. The grubs are beetle larvae harvested from the heartwood of rotting palms. The creamy-white delicacies are collected by locals, prepared and eaten.

In the larger cities such as Iquitos and Manaus the urge for Western-style food can be satisfied. In most cases, it is convenient to dine at hotel restaurants. Here, the food is generally palatable but sometimes boring, so you might want to look elsewhere if time and budget allow.

Apart from fruit, few choices for dessert are found in the Amazon culinary repertoire. Ice-cream and slushy iced drinks are popular, and from street vendors you can buy pastries or sugared popcorn. You can also get sweet bread, cakes and cookies topped with powdered sugar, from most food stores and markets.

Eating out

Breakfast in restaurants or cafés tends to be a simple affair, as in the lodges; normally just bread and jam with coffee. A pre-set three-course lunch consisting of soup, a meat dish, and something for dessert is filling and enough to keep you going for the day. Available throughout South American countries, *almuerzos* can be found for as little as US$1 if you hunt around. Supper tends to be a lighter snack, and although pre-set meals can be found, it is less common and you will tend to have to find an eatery and choose from the menu. (Each country chapter has more specific details on eating out.)

Buying food

If you are camping, buying food is rarely a problem, although fresh vegetables can be difficult to find. Even the smallest towns will have a store of some sort selling a few tinned goods, pasta and rice. As the towns get bigger so does the choice.

The standard rules apply with all food you buy: peel it, boil it, cook it or forget it!

Drinks

Water is plentiful in most areas but remember to drink only purified, bottled water and never untreated tap or river water. Bottled water is not always available so you will have to plan ahead, take water from a river or ask locals where they get their water. If you are not sure about the quality of the water, purify it.

Given the heat, it is important to drink more water than usual. At the better lodges and hotels drinking-water is available 24 hours a day. Fizzy drinks and beer are widely available. Alcohol dehydrates, so it is worth holding back a little if you have an active schedule.

Fruits of great variety, in some cases harvested from the forest, are used in beverages, for either a potent alcoholic brew or a refreshing soft drink. Numerous plant products are fermented, such as the ubiquitous manioc, and made into a drink of variable strength called *chicha* or *masato.*

Local beverages

The variety of beverages locally available in the Amazon is among the greatest anywhere in the world. Literally hundreds are made from unheard-of tropical fruits such as *naranjilla*, *guayaba*, *uvilla*, *obos*, *taxo*, and *morete* from the fruit of the moriche palm (*Mauritia* spp).

Guaraná is a widely consumed soft drink originating from tropical South America and made from juice of the *guaraná* or *cupana* (*Paullinia cupana*). Raspberry coloured, it is high in caffeine and locals swear it has magical and aphrodisiac properties. Whatever its powers, *guaraná* is a pleasant alternative to the ubiquitous Coke and Fanta.

Guanábana, also known as soursop or custard apple (*Annona* spp), makes a tasty beverage or can be eaten fresh or in ice-cream. It's about the size of a grapefruit, with a hard skin, and covered in blunt spines. The firm flesh is yellowish with a few large black seeds.

The oval dull-yellow **cupuasú** fruit, about the size of an avocado, is a member of the cacao or chocolate tree family (*Theobroma grandiflorum*). A dozen large black seeds cluster inside. Its whitish creamy flesh is made into fruit juice. The drink has a distinct taste of citrus and locals drink it before a hunt or a day's fishing for its energising properties.

Also known as passion fruit, ***grenadilla*** is a popular fruit that mixes well with alcoholic drinks and is often used in ice-cream.

Called the ***tomate de arbol***, the tree tomato fruit grows on a plant and looks like a giant tomato. Not too dissimilar from the common garden tomato, the fruit is pale green with a lip-smacking flavour. It yields a tart, delicious juice, which tastes better with some honey or sugar.

Other Amazon drinks

Incakola is Peru's answer to Coca-Cola and in Peru is almost as popular.

Exclusively made by natives, ***masato*** is not, as yet, produced commercially. In fact, as the drink is normally only produced for special occasions, visitors can consider themselves most fortunate to be offered it. The gruel-like alcoholic brew is made from chewed manioc. Masato manufacture is the exclusive province of women who sit around, chewing and spitting wads of masticated manioc into a container. Saliva is the special ingredient supplying yeast to ferment the manioc's sugars. Water is also added and the mix is left to ferment for three to four days.

Drinking the soupy brew may take some courage. F W Up de Graaf, in a turn-of-the-century expedition to the River Napo, describes a friend who 'took exception to the *masata* [sic] prepared by an old hag who had but a few teeth left and did the work with her gums'.

Soaking the roots of various plants in rum (minus the spit) creates **root tonics**. The result is a pleasant tasting brew with punch. The tonic's potency depends on the number of different plants used in the infusion.

For a country of Spanish descendants, the wine available in most parts of the Amazon leaves a lot to be desired. On average, it is simply awful – vinegary and cloudy. Wine is available at tourist lodges and on riverboats but can be pricey (about US$10–15 a bottle) and can rarely be recommended. Beer, on the other hand, is the drink of the *latino* and is usually cheap, good and refreshing.

Coffee is widely grown in the Colombian and Brazilian highlands and rates among the world's best. Colombia and Brazil rank as the world's biggest coffee producers but both countries export most that they produce. Although good coffee can be bought in most towns in the Amazon many lodges and hotels do not serve fresh coffee. Tea is usually available.

TRANSPORT

If you're taking a group trip, most operators include transport within the cost of the trip, so logistics and cost of transport need not be a cause for concern. For independent travellers, moving around the region is rarely difficult... as long as comfort, cost and time are not an issue. But in reality there are usually limitations on at least one of these factors.

Buses

An extensive road network serves the Amazon region from the more populated areas of each country. Some of the countries – Brazil and Ecuador – even have a half decent network of roads within Amazonia itself. But while the network may look good on maps, the roads are often no more than well-travelled dirt tracks. In some cases, local weather conditions mean the tracks may have hardened to provide near smooth, almost dust-free roads down which buses and trucks thunder with little concern for passenger comfort. More common, though, is the creation of tyre-chewed mud-pools in the rainy season that dry and bake to create ornately rutted tracks in the dry season. Travelling along these roads is rarely comfortable and the buses on these routes are usually the more battered of a company's fleet. Bus companies may have impressive air-conditioned, Marco Polo, buses in their fleet, as demonstrated in their adverts... they just don't send them into Amazonia. Check with the bus company when you buy your tickets if some degree of comfort is important.

Air conditioning is available on buses travelling from major cities in some countries, but as soon as you move into the less-populated areas the buses tend to become little more than travelling boxes with seats.

Systems of bus travel in the region and in connecting cities vary greatly. Most towns and cities – except Lima – have a central *terminal* or *rodoviária* for long-distance buses. The terminal houses the ticket offices of all the bus companies, so you will probably need to visit both to get times and prices, and for the departure and arrival of buses.

In Brazil and Venezuela bags are usually stored in luggage compartments under the bus; in all other countries luggage is usually put in a rack on the roof. Although neither system is automatically safer, you do get a luggage receipt in Brazil and Venezuela which at least gives you peace of mind. Staying outside with your luggage until it is stored in the luggage compartment or loaded onto the roof is the best way to stop someone walking off with it. Bags are unlikely to go missing and padlocking bags will stop opportunistic pilfering.

All long-distance buses stop for food every few hours. The food available is usually authentic regional fare ranging from the acceptable to the inedible. This option is worth trying at least once. Alternatively you can take your own food to eat on the bus.

Bus schedules and reliability are one of the endearing characteristics of travel in South America. Schedules are generally just a rough estimate of when the bus might leave, but you can bet that the time you turn up late is the one occasion on which the bus leaves on time. Exceptions are Brazil and, to a lesser extent, Venezuela, where you can set your watch by the time the buses leave.

Bus travel tends to be fairly reliable. Sometimes roads are washed out in the wet season but when this happens buses tend to stop running the route. While you can rely on reaching your destination, don't place any great importance on the estimated time of arrival. Only in Brazil and Venezuela can the duration of a journey be considered any more than a guesstimate.

The merits of city buses depend on the city and are discussed in each chapter in more detail.

Taxis

Taxis are common throughout the Amazon region and can be found even in the smallest towns. Prices and quality vary greatly, from gas-guzzling air-conditioned US-made hand-me-downs through to battered early Japanese production models on their last legs. Safety isn't normally a real problem, but it has been known for the steering wheel to come off in a taxi driver's hand! 'I'll just fix that *Señor,* it won't be five minutes.' A consistent piece of advice is to agree on a price before you start your journey.

In a few smaller towns, motorbikes can be hired to provide pillion rides across town but there are obvious restrictions and dangers for travelling with heavy luggage. Iquitos in Peru offers a quirky solution with converted motorbikes called *motocarros* working as motorised rickshaws ferrying people and goods around the city.

River travel

With the growth in road building and the increased use of air transport the amount of river traffic has declined in recent years. Tourist-standard riverboats operated specifically for foreign travellers are comfortably fitted out, providing good food and cabin arrangements as they follow a set itinerary.

Moving about on the river independently depends on the volume of traffic on a particular stretch of the river. This in turn depends on the number of people using a route and whether alternative modes of transport are available. If road transport is available for a particular route, river traffic is often minimal.

The busiest section of the river – between Iquitos and Manaus – is served by regular cargo boats that take several days for the journey. If you're in a hurry, express taxi boats will whisk you from Iquitos to Leticia on the border with Brazil in just a few hours. All major tributaries of the Amazon mainstream have regular passenger services, while quieter rivers tend to have less traffic.

Travelling by riverboat is a joy for some, a painful memory for others. Riverboats make money in at least two ways: carrying cargo and carrying people. More people means more money. Most passengers sleep in a hammock and on medium- to larger-sized boats you will find yourself packed and stacked like sardines. If you didn't have any travelling companions when you started the journey you will have by the end. On smaller boats and tributaries you sleep on the cargo deck and tend to have more space.

Cabins, which cost slightly more than hammock space, are available on all but the smallest boats. The only clear benefit is a sense of privacy if you have the cabin to yourself, as the beds are often uncomfortable and the cabins cramped.

Food on riverboats lacks imagination, variety and taste, but what it lacks in stimulus for the primary senses it makes up for in challenges to the stomach, with serious stomach upsets a possibility. Drinking water is provided but there is no guarantee that it is any more hygienic than the food. Some foreign passengers prefer to take their own food and water. Most riverside towns and villages sell a variety of tinned goods and fresh fruit and bread that can be purchased as you travel.

Although it's a relatively relaxing way to travel and an ideal way to get a sense of the size of the Amazon, riverboat travel gives little feel for the jungle and is best used as a lazy means of getting from one place to another. When water levels are low, delays are commonplace as boats get stuck on shifting sandbanks. Ten days or more on a riverboat can start to stretch your sanity.

Hitching

It's popular to discourage hitching, but for some it is the best way to travel and in parts of the Amazon region it may be the only way. The basic rules of hitching hold true here and throughout South America: don't hitch alone, and don't hitch from large cities where you clearly look out of place and perhaps rather vulnerable.

Petrol stations or checkpoints where cars and lorries are stopping are a good spot to look for a ride. If you find yourself at a checkpoint, the soldiers or police on duty are often quite helpful in trying to get you a lift.

In Andean countries people 'hitch' rides on the back of trucks. Cargo carrying *camionetas* are often packed with people paying a small fee for the ride. It's a dusty, bouncy and often slow mode of travel, but as there is usually a link between speed of travel and appreciation of detail that isn't always a problem.

Hitching on the river is an Amazon variation on the theme which could get you to – and leave you in – the most inaccessible places. Asking around at ports should reveal whether there are boats travelling along certain rivers that look interesting. Get an idea of how long a journey is before you travel so you can buy enough food for the trip.

Internal flights

With so much of Amazonia inaccessible to all but river traffic, the use of the occasional internal flight can quickly get you to the heart of the region. Charter

THE AMAZON: THE WAY IT WAS

Hilary Bradt

When I told this elderly woman I met at a San Francisco party in 1969 that I was going down the Amazon her face lit up. 'Oh, I've always wanted to go to Africa,' she said. For the last year I'd been wanting to make the trip – ever since I'd read a book about Indians with bones through their noses slipping silently through the jungle to hide stores of gold. I could hardly wait!

By the time I got to Pucallpa I'd been travelling alone for two months and realised that the gap between fact and travelogue was immense. But I owe it to *The Rivers Ran East* that I'd hung on to the ambition to boat it down as much of the river as possible. This meant, in those days, Pucallpa to Belém. My diary of the trip describes long days on the river and longer nights being bitten by mosquitoes (I proudly report the total count one morning: 116). There were no Indians with bones through their noses and no wildlife except what the crew caught and loaded on board for dinner.

I well remember the excitement and enjoyment of the first boat, from Pucallpa to Iquitos. We three gringos shared a cabin, with slatted bunk beds covered with dirty straw mattresses, but the boat was spacious enough to walk around on, and the food, rice and plantains, wasn't bad. It took five days to reach Iquitos, stopping at several Shipibo Indian villages. We reached the first one at dusk, and I recall the villagers running down the riverbank from their huts with goods for sale, followed by an enthusiastic cloud of mosquitoes. The Shipibos were selling their beautiful and distinctive pottery and live animals, including a charming (and sad) albino squirrel monkey. All that trip I was struggling with myself not to buy an animal companion. My diary records that I resisted a coati and a baby kinkajou, as well as parrots and macaws.

We stopped each night and anchored by a different village. Dawn would come like early morning on a farm: first the cocks would start crowing, then the pigs would want their breakfast and the ducks would get enthusiastic about their prospects of a swim. These animals were all part of the passengers' baggage. At one place about fifty turtles were brought on board and stored on their backs in the shower. Once I was woken to watch a display by the freshwater dolphins which were playing around the boat. Wonderful! The flight prices are rarely prohibitive and when you take into account the spectacular views from the air then the extra cost could be justified as an essential part of any trip. The largest settlements in all Amazon Basin countries get regular flights, often several times a week. Smaller towns throughout the region also have flights operated by the national military airline who, space allowing, are usually happy to take passengers.

Where there are no regular flights you may have to get an air taxi which can be expensive. Prices are charged by the hour so it is most economic to make sure all the seats in the plane are filled. Depending on your destination, the air taxi may land on a highway or even on the river itself.

THE AMAZON FROM SOURCE TO MOUTH

It's a major ambition of many travellers to travel the full length of the Amazon from headwaters to delta. This may be to emulate the great explorers such as Orellana and Teixeira; or more recent celebrities like Joe Kane, author of *Running the Amazon*

captain told me that if a pregnant girl sees one of these river dolphins she will give birth to one (likewise if she sees a sloth; both offspring sound preferable to a human baby).

We waited ten days in Iquitos, lured by promises of a free ride on a luxury boat. When it didn't materialise we took *El Socio*, an overworked little craft hardly larger than a pedalo and towing two barges. It was loaded with oil-drums but just had room for us and five other passengers to sling our hammocks. The one loo was occupied by a hen, and drinking water was scooped from the river. The cook was enormous and bad tempered, and produced different versions of sludge at mealtimes. We had to provide our own crockery and utensils. We enjoyed *El Socio*; she was a companionable little vessel and being forced to spend your days and nights in a hammock (there was no room to walk around) wasn't so bad. The journey to Leticia, in Colombia, took three days.

Someone took us to an Indian village where they practise the hair-pulling ceremony at the onset of puberty. As far as I could gather, everyone gets roaring drunk and the women of the village pull the poor girl's hair out until she is completely bald. One rather sad-looking child had her head covered by a headscarf having recently been through the ceremony. In some villages she would have been deflowered at the same time. I was even more intrigued by a little girl clutching her favourite soft toy to her chest. It was a giant frog – or ex-giant frog – stuffed with kapok.

From Leticia we crossed the river to Benjamin Constant, in Brazil. Our last boat was the classic 'bird-cage' vessel, the sort that still plies the lower waters of the Amazon. The villages – small towns even – along the river became more interesting, with decaying signs of the rubber boom in some of their fine churches and other buildings. Things were always happening in the villages: women weaving palm thatch, pots being fashioned from the riverside mud mixed with powdered charcoal, a cow being butchered, a hen riding around on the back of a pig, and a parrot fluent in Portuguese swearing, laughing and coughing.

We reached Manaus on July 16. On July 20 at 4.30pm, all the church bells in town rang out. The Americans had landed on the moon. I told an old man about it. Oh no, he said, you can only go to the moon after you die. It's not for the living.

(Pan, 1997), who kayaked down the Amazon from its source to the mouth; or the late Jacques Cousteau. Or it may just be one of those things you want to do. Beyond the kudos of completing this epic trip, the journey confronts you with paradoxes and environmental problems which are both common to humanity and at the same time specific to the unique conditions prevalent in the Amazon.

If you want to follow the mainstream by local riverboat for the longest distance, the starting point is Pucallpa in Peru, which is easy to reach by bus from Lima. The journey is often given the title of 'Most Boring Trip in South America' and for some such a title is apt and justified. It is true that a trip down the mainstream will not provide the intimacy and excitement of a two-man canoe down some unexplored tributary, but there can be no better way of getting a real impression of the vastness of the river. Travelling by boat along a river without being able to see

RUNNING THE AMAZON

Paul Cripps of Amazonas Explorer, Cusco

The first kayak descent of the Apurimac – the Amazon's longest tributary – is credited to a French couple, Michel Perrin and Teresa Gutierrez, who in 1953 attempted probably the hardest section of the river from below Puente Cunyac. Teresa was drowned after their wooden and canvas kayak turned over not far from their starting point.

More successful was a party led by J Calvin Giddings, whose book *Demon River Apurimac* is a gripping account of their epic attempts on two different sections of the river in the mid-1970s. Paddling long, fibre-glass kayaks they struggled through incredible hardships to conquer most of the upper canyons of the Apurimac.

Later in 1981 the Polish Expedition 'Canoandes 79' ran from even further up than the Giddings expedition. Finally, in the early 1980s, a Polish–South African–American team finally made a complete descent from source to sea. Two books have been written about this journey: *Running the Amazon* by Joe Kane, an interesting tale from the non-rafter's viewpoint, is probably most notable for his account of the internal conflicts that plagued the expedition, while a similar book by expedition leader François Odendaal sharply contradicts Joe Kane's account and really makes you wonder about the true story.

With the advent of the virtually indestructible plastic kayak, various expeditions have run many of the different sections of the river. Most of the first descents concentrated on the hardest section of the Rio Apurimac, the notorious Accobamba Abyss, where the sheer canyon walls rise thousands of metres above you, rockfalls are common in the afternoon and the rapids are all but unrunnable.

In 1997, an extraordinary South African appeared with tales of swimming the length of the Apurimac (including walking in from the Pacific) on a hydro-speed – a kind of surfboard. Fishing for food and carrying everything on his back (including a mobile satellite phone), he matter-of-factly told of getting stuck in whirlpools for up to half an hour, of having his helmet sucked off his head whilst travelling through a 40ft-long rock siphon and of having to cut off his fins to escape being sucked into an undercut. He was last heard of heading for the Atlantic with some 3,000 miles still to go. Having survived the worst of the rapids the Amazon could throw at him, his greatest threat in the lower stretches of the river will be the huge cargo ships – and boredom.

the banks is awe-inspiring: it is, after all, a river not an ocean. But there are moments when time can drag, so make sure you have plenty of books, entertainment and the energy to maintain an intensive Spanish- and Portuguese-language course for several weeks.

With planning and foresight it is possible to plan small excursions on your route downstream. Stopping off at any of the larger towns and cities along the river, and many of the smaller ones, you will be able to arrange a trip down some of the smaller tributaries and to less disturbed areas.

One of the best reasons for travelling this route is to get an idea of the working river. People travel vast distances to visit relatives, in search of work and for hospital treatment. Cargo is transported up and downstream along a seemingly chaotic distribution network, but all the time the river flows on.

Boats leave Pucallpa from La Hoyada docks for the 3–4 day journey to Iquitos. The journey itself is fairly straightforward and best achieved in a number of short legs, changing boats at Iquitos, Tabatinga/Leticia, Tefé (optional), Manaus and Santarém before arriving in Belém. The journey downstream will probably take around three weeks, or longer if you allow for sightseeing. Smaller boats tend to stop at smaller villages en route but also take a little longer. The cost will vary according to the type of boat and the time spent in cities but the bottom line is US$400–500 for transport, and another US$250 for food and spending money.

As a bare minimum you'll need a hammock, a sheet or sleeping bag for sleeping at night and a small library of books. Spending in excess of three weeks in a hammock is not an exciting prospect for some and the journey by riverboat is certainly not comfortable. On some legs of the journey it will be possible to get cabin accommodation if you need a break from the hammock, but don't rely on it. Taking your own supplies of food – essential if you're a vegetarian – will add to the bland and unadventurous menu. Buying clean water or using purification tablets is also advisable. Don't stock up for the whole journey as you can easily buy extra supplies downriver in the larger towns.

A more expensive, comfortable and convenient option is to book passage on one of the luxury passenger vessels that sail from Belém to Iquitos. For well-off ecotourists the best vessel for a full-length trip is the *M/V Explorer*. The 90-passenger purpose-built vessel uses inflatable Zodiac dinghies to take passengers into remote tributaries and lakes inaccessible to the mother ship. The ship's amenities include comfortable accommodation, a large dining room, well-stocked bar, lecture theatre and library. The bridge is open to passengers and offers excellent views as well as the chance to examine charts of the river and navigational equipment. Although travelling upriver is recommended, the current-assisted downriver trip is cheaper and takes a couple of days less. For the 18-day upriver cruise with Lifelong Learning (see page 353) the cheapest cabins are US$5,125 (Belém–Iquitos), while downriver for 16 days the same cabin is US$4,695 (excluding US$149 port charges). If these are beyond your budget, you could opt for the half-trip, from Iquitos to Manaus, of US3,640, or upstream for US$3,895. A similar trip is offered by OdessAmerica (page 354).

A halfway house option is a combination of small-plane, canoe and riverboat travel. To avoid the nightmarish logistics of doing this independently, your best bet is to take a package such as that offered by Nature Expeditions International (page 354). This trip begins in Belém, followed by a flight to Santarém, then to Manaus. A tourist riverboat takes you from Manaus to visit Ariau Jungle Tower. From Manaus you fly to Leticia for an overnight stop, plus city and jungle tour, before travelling to Iquitos for visits to Explorama Lodge and Explornapo Camp. For 17 days, this trip is good value at US$2,990 excluding international airfare.

Running the headwaters of the Amazon

Only seriously fit and experienced adventurers with adequate back-up should consider starting their trip at the Amazon's source in the Peruvian Andes (see box on page 64). This involves a major expedition, such as the one described in *Running the Amazon* (see *Further Reading*, page 432). However, the less intrepid (or masochistic...) can visit the Amazon's headwaters for some whitewater kayaking, and then pick the river up again at Pucallpa and continue downstream from there. Companies to contact for kayaking in the headwaters are:

Amazonas Explorer PO Box 722, Cusco, Peru; tel/fax: 00 51 84 236826. email: amazonasexplorer@compuserve.com; website: http: www.amazonas-explorer. com. UK contact: tel/fax: 01437 891743. An Anglo-Peruvian-Swiss operation specialising in environmentally and safety-conscious expeditions in inflatable kayaks to the source of the Amazon, and rafting the Apurimac; always off on 'exploratory expeditions' to new and exciting locations. Also operate the Tambopata and Cotahuasi rivers in Peru and, in Bolivia, the Río Tuichi. Cater largely to overseas bookings.

Apumayo Expediciones Emilio Cavencio 160, Of. 201, Lima; tel: 00 51 4423886. The new boys on the block who seem fairly well organised, though they recently closed down their Cusco office to concentrate on overseas bookings. But probably, if they open again, the best of a pretty dodgy bunch.

Eric Adventures Plateros 324, Cusco; tel: 00 51 84 232244. If you thought Instinct were cheap, try these guys. Complete cowboys with one fatality under their belt (a guide); an accident waiting to happen.

Explorandes San Fernando 320 Miraflores Lima 18; tel: 00 51 4458683. The grandfathers of rafting in Peru, somewhat reflected in the age of their equipment and guides. A very good trekking agency that sells largely overseas and fancies itself as a rafting operator. Upmarket (clients and prices) 6-day trips down the Apurimac, largely so long because their guides go so infrequently to the river that they have to spend hours inspecting and portaging a number of rapids. Used to be the best. Now should gracefully retire!

Instinct Procuradores 50. Cusco; tel: 00 51 84 233451 just off the Plaza de Armas. At the cheap end of the market, owner Benjamin Muniz was largely responsible for bringing rafting the Apurimac to the backpacker market with his big group, low-budget trips.

Mayuc Expediciones Plaza de Armas, Cusco; tel: 00 51 84 232666. One of the longest-running companies, was responsible for two fatalities last year.

3 Mounting your own Expedition

Tanis Jordan

Tanis Jordan, with her husband Martin, has been making independent, self-financed expeditions since the late sixties. She has travelled extensively and made expeditions of several months' duration in Brazil, Venezuela, Peru, French Guiana, Guyana, Suriname, Morocco, Algeria, Cameroon and the Caribbean. To date she has had two travel books and four children's books published. A Fellow of the Royal Geographic Society, she has lectured there on several occasions.

In recent years Amazonia has opened up to travel. There is no shortage of companies that will take you there. You can rough it or smooth it, watch wildlife, visit Amerindian villages, go up mountains or down rivers; you name it, they arrange it. But perhaps that isn't what you want.

Picture this. Imagine waking at dawn, when it is just getting light. You are warm and cosy in your sleeping bag as you peer out at the day. Strange fantastical tree shapes appear and disappear as the morning mist swirls slowly over the river and hangs in the trees. Just the occasional whistle of a tapir to its mate or the splash of fish jumping in the river disturbs the stillness. Then you hear the flap of wings and raucous cries as red and blue macaws fly across the river in twos and threes to their food trees. In the distance an eerie roar begins, coming closer and closer until it is deafeningly loud – then high in the treetops a troop of red howler monkeys appears, marking their territory.

You leave your hammock. The ground is damp and cool. You bang your shoes to remove scorpions, ants or cockroaches, fill the kettle from the river, then take your machete to chop driftwood and build a fire. After breakfast of coffee and oatmeal you wash the dishes in the river, while shoals of tiny coloured fish nibble at your hands. Checking that no unwanted guests have dropped into the boat overnight, you break camp, load up, start the engine and chug off into the hot sunshine to the next set of rapids, with absolutely no idea who or what the day will bring.

This is what it's like to go it alone, to mount your own expedition to Amazonia. It will take endless planning and organisation, be tedious, frustrating and potentially dangerous; and when you do get there, jungle life is hard work. But the rewards are many. When at last you put your boat on the water and push off from the bank for the very first time, there is no other feeling quite like it, and one way or another it will change your life forever.

PLANNING AN EXPEDITION

The most important requirements for a successful trip are to have a purpose and a plan. Your expedition must have a definite goal otherwise you will just drift around and never get properly motivated. Ask yourself why you want to mount your own expedition. If it's so that you are free to go where you want when you want, to stay away as long as you wish and to be in total control of your own destiny, then to achieve that much freedom you will need to finance it yourself. If you are sponsored, commissioned or under contract to carry out some sort of research you won't have complete choice in where you go and what you do.

Most working expeditions make use of local guides, porters and boatmen. For a first-time independent jungle trip, travelling, camping and daily chores will take up most of your time and all your energy; you would need experience to be able to carry out project work as well. If you plan to write a book when you return home or make a film while you're there, then you will have to compromise your freedom. We've found that even the obligation of taking an occasional photograph gets in the way of just enjoying the moment. You may also spend days worrying that nothing exciting will happen to fill your book or film; and nights plagued with fearful dreams of what might.

Choosing your destination

For us it is usually an area of jungle or a river tributary as remote as possible and far away from towns and people. The more information you can gather about your destination the better equipped you will be to handle any unforeseen circumstances that arise – and arise they will. The most common form of transport for jungle expeditions is by boat, with forays of days or weeks spent exploring in the jungle. Buy the best maps available and plan your route, then start doing the detective work. Contact embassies, ministries, tourist boards, but keep your enquiries brief and concise. Write letters, send faxes or search the web for any information about the river and the area. In most out-of-the-way places there is very little information available, but whatever you can get hold of will help you prepare. If you want to make an expedition walking from A to B then find out if there are rivers to cross and, if so, whether there are any settlements where someone can ferry you across. Once you reach B, is there any way of getting back without retracing your journey? If it's a river trip can you find a boat there? If you want to use an outboard engine will fuel be available? For expeditions in really remote areas we have learned to take everything with us – on a five-month trip inside Manú National Park, Peru, we took ten five-gallon cans of gasoline in the back of a truck on a two-day journey across the Andes mountains, and one of us had to stay awake at all times to make sure nobody stole it.

Gaining permission

Whether or not you need a visa to enter the country itself, you would be well advised to make thorough enquiries about requirements to enter the area you wish to visit. Some officials are sensitive if there is logging or mining activity. If you wish to travel in a national park, a protected area or the home of indigenous tribal people then gaining permission to enter can sometimes take six months or even longer. Be patient, polite and persistent and remember that some of the most interesting places cannot be visited on a whim by casual travellers. On the Trombetas river in Brazil we met a group of Spanish anthropology students who had decided to visit an Amerindian village high up in the Tumucumaque mountains. At great expense they hired a boat to bring them up the river to the highest navigable point and then a light aircraft to take them to their destination. Despite tearful begging and pleading, their plane was not allowed to land because they had not requested permission in advance. This aborted journey cost them thousands of pounds and could have ended happily if they had done some more research.

Some countries have limits on how many 'expeditions' are allowed in per year. I once telephoned an embassy in Britain to ask what permission was needed to make an expedition in its country to be told that 'absolutely no expeditions would be allowed in until further notice'! We quickly became two tourists on holiday.

When to go

Whether to go in the dry or rainy season is an important consideration. In the dry season the rivers will be low, sometimes so low that the riverbed is exposed, making river travel arduous. Hauling boats up rapids or unpacking the boat and carrying everything around the rapids overland (portaging) takes a lot of time and a phenomenal amount of energy. But in the dry season you will see lots more wildlife and camping is pleasanter because it's not raining all the time and more jungle bank and beaches are exposed. It's very tempting to camp on those beautiful sand beaches but there is a very real danger of flash floods that arrive with no warning, often caused by rain far away in the mountains. Your pretty jungle stream may rise three metres in an hour and become a raging torrent or, worse, a wall of water may pour downstream engulfing all before it. In Peru we pitched our shelter on the edge of the jungle at least thirty metres from the river and tied the boat to an enormous fallen tree fifteen metres long. We were woken in the night by water swirling at our feet and both boat and tree had floated away. NEVER camp on beaches.

In the rainy season it rains heavily nearly every day and there will be plenty of water in the rivers; too much of it, in fact. Rivers will be fast flowing and the jungle may flood. Clothes that get wet take ages to dry, while mould grows on camera equipment and film.

But the rainy season does have its compensations, particularly if you are visiting a waterfall. All the river trips to Angel Falls in Venezuela, the highest waterfall in the world, are made in the rainy season. We travelled to it in the dry season when, to quote the late 'jungle Rudy' Truffino, 'in the rainy season it's the most impressive sight in the world, but in the dry season my dog can do better'.

Choosing your boat

Dugout canoes are the most common means of travel on Amazonian rivers. They are strong, and respond well under power, but they are heavy and sit quite low in the water. Sometimes the sides are built up with planks, which makes them far more stable but even heavier. If you plan to paddle upriver or portage around rapids then you will need to be fairly strong. Dugout canoes are usually available in riverside towns and (sometimes) villages. Because they are not commodities with fixed market values, the price you pay depends on who sold it, where you bought it, the country you were in and so on. The only useful tip is that you will probably get a better deal buying a secondhand canoe from a local person than a new one from an established river trader. If you are returning to your starting place an alternative may be to try and hire a canoe for your trip, the cost of which will vary greatly depending on availability and duration.

Fibreglass, plastic and aluminium canoes are light, fast and responsive under power. But they are not so readily available and are much more fragile than dugout canoes. Take this into consideration if your choice of river is a rocky one. If this type of boat is your choice then you will probably have to take one with you. The alternative to all this is to hire a boat and boatman to take you, but it will be expensive and your expedition will not be the same kind of experience.

Inflatable boats are excellent, particularly for the novice. They rarely capsize even when punctured or full of water; they bounce off rocks, carry enormous weights and are repairable and comfortable to sit on day after day, month after month. But on fast water they slide, they spin, they are slow and almost impossible to paddle. However, for a first trip my choice would be an inflatable powered by an outboard engine light enough for one person to carry. We fold our inflatable as small as possible and carry it as ordinary luggage. It's easier to buy the engine out there.

CANOEING

John Harrison

The advantages of paddling quietly along the Amazon rivers are many. The wildlife doesn't hear you coming and you can hear the rustles and calls that betray an animal's presence. You don't have to sit in a haze of petrol fumes, or be a slave to available fuel supplies. Being self-propelled gives a sense of satisfaction, and puts you on a shared level with the locals. There's no great haste, so why rush along pursued by the banshee wail of a two-stroke?

Admittedly it's quite hard work at first – but within a week you become fit enough to paddle six hours a day at a steady, economical rhythm. By the end of the trip you'll have a torso to die for, supported on a couple of spindly, atrophied legs.

My early canoeing in the Amazon was done in dug-outs or in canoes I made myself from locally obtained planks. Both craft are heavy and only suitable for rivers without rapids. Two people can barely lift them and some rapids require portages of several hundred metres.

In Brazilian Amazonia it's almost impossible to buy aluminium or fibreglass canoes. It's best to take alternatives from home that can be carried on aircraft as personal baggage. Never send canoes or anything else as unaccompanied freight to South America. You can waste half your holiday trying to get it out of customs.

Granta Canoes (Ramsey, Huntingdon, Cambridgeshire, UK; tel: 01487 813777) produce excellent plywood canoe kits for 5m, and 6m 'Canadian'

If you opt for a canoe get some practice first, as a South American river is not the place to learn basic boating skills. Whatever your choice of craft, wear buoyancy aids and tie everything in, including the engine. Tie heavy bags securely. If you don't and the boat capsizes, the bags will hang down like anchors and make it very difficult to flip it back over. We learned this particular lesson when we capsized a fibreglass canoe on the Marowijne river in Suriname, couldn't right it, lost everything including the canoe and both nearly drowned.

When you want to leave the boat and spend time in the jungle, take the boat out of the water if possible and hide it in the jungle. Tie the painter – the rope on the front of the boat – fairly high up a tree so that if the river rises and floods the bank the boat will float up. If it's not possible to take it out of the river then cover it with some greenery. If you plan to leave it in the river for some time, make sure you leave plenty of slack in the rope. If you don't and the river drops while you are away, you may come back and find your boat hanging in the air halfway up a tree. Don't forget to take a repair kit for your boat if appropriate.

If you plan something ambitious like crossing from one river to another, bear in mind that there is usually a hill or even a mountain range between river valleys or vast distances of jungle. Everything must be carried including the boat. If you are travelling upstream near the source, the going will become steeper, rockier and less navigable and you may even run out of river before you reach the source. This happened to us on the Mapuera River in Brazil when our river journey turned into a hiking trip.

What to take

It may be possible to buy most of the things you will need in established frontier towns, but if an item is essential to your expedition, or you, then take it with you. Where new roads have been built through the jungle new settlements will have canoes. Capable of carrying two people and 300kg, they can be supplied with a squared-off stern to take a small outboard motor if you must (at least then you have a craft that can be paddled easily when the fuel runs out). The only drawback is that assembly is completed using fibreglass which, because it can't be taken on airlines, has to be obtained in Amazonia. In Manaus, in 1987, I found only one factory that would sell me some of their stock – it wasn't sold in any stores. Availability may well have increased now. The Granta is easily repairable with fibreglass if damaged on the river.

Folding canoes and kayaks

There are several folding kayaks on the market, but they don't have enough carrying capacity for a long trip. The only folding canoe that I know is the excellent Norwegian 'Ally'. It will also carry two people plus 300kg of gear. Not cheap – £800 (US$1,300) or so, but ideal for taking on planes and bringing home with you afterwards (the Granta can't be dismantled). Bergans Sports, Ovre Eikerve 92, Drammen, Norway 3001 (tel: 010 4732 826010). The Ally is repaired with stick-on patches. In the US folding canoes are sold by **Pouch Faltboote** (1931 SW 14th St, Ste 3, Portland, OR 97201; tel: 503 274 2313).

Paddles

Take a paddle from home. The local ones are hewn from a piece of hardwood and are very heavy.

sprung up, but don't rely on buying vital equipment there. In French Guiana we found a shack selling only Chanel perfume and ten-year-old French Cognac; nice, but not terribly useful. In Brazil, in what was marked on the map as a fair-sized town, we planned to buy wood to make a floor for our boat. It was impossible to find anything suitable. In desperation we searched close to the jungle's edge and found a packing case washed up that was perfect.

Rucksacks and kit bags

Your choice of rucksack for an expedition is purely personal. There is a vast array of rucksacks available today but still not one that I know of that is completely waterproof. Wrap everything in plastic first; self-seal bags are ideal for this. Take plenty of strong plastic bags. Don't have too many dangly straps or bits sticking out, as they will catch on bushes and trees and really impede your progress through the jungle, as will rucksacks that protrude above your head.

For boat travel take plenty of kit bags. Waterproof bags are available at camping shops but we make our own from the cloth that boat sails are made of. They are light, strong, waterproof and you can customise them to suit. If you need to travel on trucks or buses to reach your embarkation point it's a good idea to have bright-coloured bags that are easy to keep in view. Our bright yellow kitbags travelled quite a few kilometres downriver on their own when we tipped that canoe on the Marowijne River. Eventually we found them washed up on rocks and our sleeping bags were still dry! Things wrapped in sealed plastic bags will usually float, which is another advantage. If you are planning a river/land expedition it might be worth looking at combination bags that convert to rucksacks. Anything too fiddly or complicated might not stand up to a lot of hard use, but a really strong, simple design could serve both purposes quite well.

Clothes

I have made many expeditions where the absence of biting insects meant that I spent all day in a bikini and the evenings in shorts and T-shirt. But in Manú National Park, Peru, we had to cover up from head to foot to avoid the night-time mosquitoes and day-time blackflies that never ceased their biting activities except for the two blessed 40-minute change-over periods at dawn and sunset. Upriver, near Tayakome, there were 24-hour mosquitoes and we had to walk up and down the beach eating our food.

If you have never been in the tropics you may not realise quite how hot it can feel. When you get off the air-conditioned plane it is like a hot, wet blanket enveloping you. There is absolutely no need to spend a lot of money on specialist clothing except for trousers. Trousers designed for travellers today are exceptionally good, light and strong, with lots of zip pockets, and they dry incredibly quickly. I prefer a polyester/cotton mix because it's strong and dries very quickly. I never wear heavy cotton in the jungle, as it holds the water, is slow to dry and tends to rot quicker than man-made fibres.

Take long-sleeved shirts that button right up as protection against sun and insects, a warm sweater or sweatshirt for cooler nights and a hat with a brim or a peak – with a chin strap or you'll lose it – to protect you from the sun. We only ever wear simple no-frills tennis shoes (one pair lasts about two months) and have never worn jungle boots. At night (and possibly day) if there are biting insects you will need to cover up. Wool socks are comfortable but man-made dry quicker. Make sure they are long enough to tuck your trousers into them. Put repellent on your socks and cuffs. A tropical rainstorm will drench you in seconds so a fully-waterproof poncho is more useful than a jacket.

Take two sets of clothing: one to wear during the day that will get wet and dirty, and a clean set to put on when you make camp. Keep the spare set dry at all times and never be tempted to put them on instead if your day set is wet and clammy. Dry clothes at the end of the day will keep you sane, and your body is less likely to go mouldy and develop fungal infections if you stay dry. The underwear you wear at home will be fine in the jungle. The way to keep clear of rashes, sores or fungi is to keep clean and dry and let the air get to your body as often as you can.

Sleeping equipment

Hammocks Whether in the jungle or in a village hut, the most comfortable way to sleep is in a locally bought hammock of woven cotton. Before buying, check that the ropes and cords that gather the ends are strong, as these are usually the first to break. Try to keep your hammock dry as dampness weakens them drastically. Hang your hammock high and tight as they drop at least a metre when you get in, and lie diagonally across it. Don't hang your hammock under dead wood – you don't want branches crashing down on you in a storm. Likewise, amusing as it may sound, there have been several fatalities caused by people slinging hammocks between coconut palms. Check nothing worrisome is living in the trees above you; we slept without nets in Brazil and spent a night with large cockroaches dropping into our hammocks at regular intervals. In another camp we picked out dozens of pairs of eyes in the trees above and surrounding us. Investigation revealed them to be the eyes of huge black furry spiders.

Mosquito nets With the ever-present danger of malaria, mosquito nets are very important. Hammock nets are available in most South American countries but I would recommend taking a tried and tested one. There are several companies that now make purpose-built hammock nets which are available from good camping shops. Nets I've bought in Amazonia were either so flimsy that they split or so thick it was unbearably hot and like sleeping in a fog. Some had mesh so wide that while they kept out the mosquitoes, biting blackflies flitted joyfully through. The net must be large, loose and seal you in completely. Anywhere that the net is in contact with your skin will be bitten. The slightest hole and mosquitoes will be queuing up to feast. Nets impregnated with repellent, usually permethrin, will prevent this but will need to be re-treated after about three months. The repellent loses its strength after a couple of washes so avoid washing nets unless essential. If you must wash them don't do it in the river as the repellent can be harmful to fish and amphibians. Take plenty of rope for hanging the hammock and thin nylon cord for hanging the mosquito net high enough above the hammock to give you plenty of headroom. It is possible to get hold of hammocks that have a built-in mosquito net and waterproof covers. Personally I have never managed to get on with them but I know at least two jungle veterans who wouldn't use anything else. Depending on the length of your trip you can either take a large sheet of plastic to cover your hammock or make a proper shelter to take with you.

Take two large pieces of lightweight waterproof cloth (3m by 6m each), edged all round with Velcro so that they fit together to form a square or an L shape. Punch eyelets around the edges large enough to take rope. To hang the shelter, tie a rope at a high point between the two trees that support your hammock and drape the shelter over it. Tie the edges of the shelter securely to trees or bushes or it will take off in a tropical storm.

Tents One disadvantage with a hammock as opposed to a tent is that when biting insects get the munchies you may have to retire under your net. There are things you can do in a tent that are difficult in a hammock: you can read, write or eat by candlelight and seek protection from insect pests. In addition, if you are ill or the weather is bad it's more comfortable to spend time in one. You have privacy. The vast variety of tents available means that you can select one most suited to your needs. When we first travelled to South America the only tents available were windowless, net-less canvas heavyweights and we made our own. Now we use a one-touch Khyam Highlander, though for a long boat trip I would choose a three-man version of the same dome-type tent. Always secure the tent especially if you are leaving it for any time, as a tropical storm could whisk it up and blow it away, even in deep jungle. Bear in mind that tropical rain can be devastating to a single-skin tent and tropical heat can bake you in a double. Mosquito-net panels for ventilation are essential and a removable fly sheet advisable. Even in the Amazon, nights can be surprisingly cool up-country, so a sleeping bag is better than a blanket and a synthetic filling dries more quickly than down.

Night comes quickly in the tropics: sunset around six and total darkness not too long afterwards. If you leave it too late to look for a place to camp you will find yourself working in the dark. It can take a couple of hours to make camp, light a fire and cook a meal.

Food

In more populated places along the rivers you will find trading posts and travelling shops on boats, but they may not have what you want and goods will probably be relatively expensive. One we met in Brazil sold only beer and biscuits. In villages where people grow their own food there may not be enough produce available to sell to visitors. If you plan to be away from civilisation then you must take all you need with you. It is completely impracticable for even experienced travellers to live off the jungle. Unless you are an authority on the subject or advised by a local you

FISHING

John Harrison

With over 1,750 species – all the rivers of Europe hold only 150 – Amazonia has fish ranging from tiny blue aquaria specimens to monsters weighing 300kg or more.

While I wouldn't advise anyone to hunt to supplement their food supplies, I personally think fishing is acceptable, and a valuable source of protein. It's also great fun and a world away from the dull, damp activity pursued by bored individuals along the streams of England.

Methods

Fish can be caught by almost any method. The locals might fish very skilfully with a handline, but I think it's worth taking a rod and reel from home. A two-piece boat rod and a fixed-spool reel holding 15kg breaking-strain line is enough.

Depending upon what you're trying to catch, bait is a piece of meat, dead fish, or, in season, certain fruits and berries. It's wise to have a length of metal wire above the hook to prevent your catch biting through the nylon line. With the bait resting on the river bed you will generally catch one of the 500 species of catfish, piranha or *traira* – a mottled tube with big teeth and pink eyes that you'll recognise when you see it. Predators are caught with little live fish (caught first with a tiny hook and *farinha* bait), or metal lures that are drawn through the water to imitate small wounded fish. Buy lures that have detachable treble hooks, and take a lot of replacement hooks to replace the ones the piranhas have mauled. The advantage of spinning is that you don't need to carry a putrid piece of dead fish in the canoe to use as bait. The drawback is that a lure will only catch four or five species, but one, the *tucunare* or peacock bass, is one of the great sport fish and among the tastiest.

Almost everything you will catch is edible. Most fish get their revenge with a wealth of forked bones that seem designed to lodge in the throat, or be used to pin snakes to the ground. Eating a plate of fish stew in the flickering, feeble light of a camp fire is a challenge.

The best fishing spots are the eddies and patches of turbulence below a rapid or at the confluence of two rivers. The best time to fish is at night from a canoe. This is a magnificently spooky activity on a moonless night and it's best to keep a knife and torch handy. Not because caiman or anaconda might pluck you out of your seat (that's an improbable scenario that your imagination can't let go of), but because after a 15-minute tussle that has left your arms aching and towed the canoe a hundred metres, you will want to examine the fish as it rolls exhausted to the surface. Only then can you decide whether you really want that toothy great thing snapping and flapping around your bare feet in the dark.

will probably poison yourself. And as for 'eating what the monkeys eat' – if you are prepared to climb five metres or more up a tree every time you feel hungry you will have a very busy time.

Food becomes very important on long jungle trips and the variety of dried food available means you can eat very well indeed. Lots of small packs are better than large ones as, once opened, their contents absorb moisture from the air. Take oatmeal for breakfast: it's light, nutritious, filling and usually available wherever there are places that sell food. Rice, beans, pasta, coffee, salt, spices, soups, flour, dried milk and sugar will give you a varied basic diet. Take some luxuries as well for an occasional treat and anything else that you just can't live without. If you can't carry fresh fruit or vegetables then take vitamin supplements. It's easy to dehydrate in the hot sun or if you lose fluids because of sickness, so sachets or tablets of rehydration mixture will be useful. We've never become ill or weak from eating this way for months at a time. Store your supplies off the ground in camp, as rodents are quite capable of demolishing plastic containers and devour the strangest things: on one occasion our whole supply of candles and a bar of carbolic soap.

Hunting

In a word – don't. If you can't get by in the jungle without killing wild animals, you shouldn't be there. Amazonian wildlife is under enough pressure without the added burden of being hunted. It's better to observe the wildlife than eat it. It's extremely dangerous and probably illegal to hunt while travelling through indigenous people's land. They do not take kindly to all the goldminers, loggers and prospectors who invade their territory and decimate their food supply by hunting and you will be regarded as no different from them. It's perfectly possible on a boat to carry all the food you will need for up to five months; we've done it on many occasions.

Water

'If you drink the water of the Tapanahoni river you will be sure to return to Suriname one day,' said the Bushnegro Granman as we bade him farewell. He was right and we did. We also picked up the 'Suriname shuffle' medically known as *giardiasis*, proving that water can be dangerous stuff. A reassuring fact is that we've only ever become ill when living in populated areas, never in quiet jungles far away from towns or villages. Always fill your water container upstream of any settlements. The most effective way to sterilise water is to boil it thoroughly. This is not always possible and water-sterilising tablets are the next best option. Double the dose when you think the water may be very polluted. Chlorine-based tablets have less after-taste than iodine but take longer to become effective. Ones based on silver are tasteless but take two hours to work. Always leave the tablets for at least the required time and preferably longer.

Other equipment

In our experience gadgety tools don't stand up in the field; if you are going to need a tin opener then take a tin opener. Take a knife; it doesn't have to do everything, so the less complicated the better. Tweezers are useful for removing thorns and splinters. A compass is no good at all if you don't know how to use it; practise with it before you go. Lightweight torches designed for divers float beam up. A candle lantern when in-camp saves batteries. Have a sharpening stone for the long bladed machete you will buy out there, as metal files clog up and wear smooth quickly. Take a bit of rubber tyre; you can shave bits off to start campfires. Carry sun-block that you know is effective for you. If your nose is vulnerable take a total zinc-based sun-block; the flesh-coloured ones won't make you look quite so ridiculous.

Travelling companions

A common problem is the animosity that develops between members of even the least arduous expeditions. You are stuck with the same people for weeks, possibly months, and it's hard to believe the hostility that can build up unless you've experienced it first hand. Your friends' endearing ways can become unbearable habits that you cannot stand. We were on a large expedition in Brazil when one normally charming man attempted to strangle and drown his best friend simply because he had borrowed his toothpaste without asking. Competition can build up as to who can paddle faster, or go on longest without a break, turning an enjoyable

IT'S NOT ALWAYS A BREEZE IN THE AMAZON

Amazing it is, but the South American rainforest is not always the paradise that people make it out to be. Trouble and strife can result in the most extreme reactions and disagreements between friends as this excerpt from Redmond O'Hanlon's adventures of travelling between the Orinoco and the Amazon in Venezuela, titled *In Trouble Again*, points out:

> 'Why the hell should I put up with all this? That's what I want to know! You tell me! I can't stand it. Why should I? Why should I be stung by ants and wasps and hornets and bees all day? I've been thinking about it. It's nothing but rain and mosquitoes and the same bloody awful trees and endless rivers and disgusting food and being wet all the time. There's no comradeship. There's no wine and no women and no song and nowhere sensible to shit.'
>
> 'I'm sorry,' I said, 'you'll think differently in the morning.'
>
> 'No I bloody won't,' said Simon, his eyes white in the murk, 'oh no I bloody well won't! I've been thinking about it for four weeks. It's not that I'm frightened. It's not really your fault. It's just that I can't bear to go back in there' (he waved the bottle in the direction of the landing-stage and the uncut jungle) 'and why the hell should I?'
>
> 'Do you think you are so unstable already,' said Juan, in his most precise way, his beard outlined in the light of the kerosene lamp, pressed forward in interrogation, 'because of the sudden withdrawal of drugs and alcohol on this journey?'
>
> 'You stupid dago,' said Simon, exasperated, 'how the hell would I know?'
>
> 'Don't do it,' I said. 'You'll feel bad about it later. About deserting me.'
>
> 'Redmond,' said Simon, relaxing, 'I'll handle all that with the first pint of cognac.'
>
> 'Don't be silly. You'll never forgive yourself.'
>
> 'Oh yes I damn well will. I have already. Redmond – I've cried four times in my adult life. Once when my father died; once when my wife left me; once when Pinky my cat was run over in front of me; and every night when we were lost up that stinking pitsville of a swamp.'
>
> 'What about the Yanomami? What about your pictures?'
>
> 'I don't want to see the Yanomami. *I can't stand all the poverty*. These people are bad enough. *They don't own anything*. And anyway, my cameras are totally, but totally full of mould and gunge and parasites, and the odd fish too, I shouldn't wonder. It's the pits.'

Do you still want to go?

trip into a contest of endurance. Some of our worst rows were over who was doing it wrong on rapids, and I know of two men who got on so badly they were reduced to writing derogatory observations and complaints about each other in their diaries and leaving them about to be read. It helps a lot if you genuinely like the people you intend to travel with, so that at least when things get a little touchy there's a chance you will sort the problems out.

Hazards

A river expedition through uninhabited jungle can be an exhilarating experience. It can also be a nightmare. But it's said that 'adventure' begins when your plans go wrong – plans often do go wrong. It would not be fair to imply that everything on a river journey is absolutely safe. The river and the jungle demand respect and care should always be taken with both.

Man

When we started making expeditions in South America nearly 30 years ago the main human dangers were from the odd criminal, miners or gold prospectors (the mercury used in gold extraction affects the central nervous system and sends them mad). But there are new dangers now, in particular, the fact that crops of drug plants are often grown and processed in remote and inaccessible jungle areas, just the sort of places adventurous travellers like to visit. Also, if there is any kind of civil unrest in a country there are likely to be armed and potentially dangerous people in the most remote regions. It is popular but unwise to make yourself look like a soldier or guerrilla by wearing camouflage clothing or army fatigues.

In the jungle

The small things (see also pages 89-92)

I once lost five of my toenails thanks to **chiggers**, female sand fleas that lurk in damp, shady, sandy places.

Scorpions, while they are not aggressive unless provoked, have a habit of crawling into unlikely places like shoes, bags or through open tent fronts. This is easily rectified by shaking out boots and bags, and keeping tents at least partially closed. Take care if you turn over logs or rocks where scorpions may live.

Ants usually pose few problems, unless you bring a nest of tiny biting, stinging fire ants down on you while cutting a trail. The *tocandira*, a giant ant an inch long, is aggressive and known as 'ant 24' in Venezuela because its sting can produce pain and fever lasting up to 24 hours. It is quite easy to see and avoid. To come across army ants on the march is an amazing sight – they eat all small creatures in their way. Leaf-cutter ants are common, numerous and harmless.

If you are lucky you might come across the dinner-plate-sized bird-eating **spider**, and you will certainly see lots of smaller versions, none of which poses any serious danger except for black widow spiders. These small – about 24mm or one inch – satiny black spiders have hour glass shaped red markings on their abdomens. They have a habit of occupying dark, quiet places like sheds and outbuildings. I know someone who was bitten by a black widow that had spun a web across the seat of an outside toilet. Though the bite is painful it is rarely fatal.

Take care with **tropical wasps and hornets**. They sometimes construct their nests low down, hidden on the backs of leaves where the unwary might walk into them. Some of these insects can inject extremely potent venom. I was stung by a black hornet, two inches long; the pain was tremendous but didn't last long, although it threw my body's defences into overdrive. If you should accidentally disturb a wasp's nest this advice given to us by a Guyanese 'porknocker' (gold prospector) may help. 'Drop everything, cover one eye with one hand, shut your mouth, run like hell to the nearest water and dive in!'

The bigger things

Large **mammals** are generally not dangerous in Amazonia. The largest South American cat is the shy and seldom aggressive **jaguar**. The **ocelot** is arguably the most beautiful of Amazonia's cats, much smaller than the mighty jaguar and renowned for its gentle and timid nature in the presence of humans. There is no reliable record of an ocelot ever harming a human. If you are very lucky you might glimpse a jaguar or ocelot.

In the water

In the river there may well be **stingrays** that lie flat and still in shaded mud and sand shallows. Their sting is excruciatingly painful and can take months to heal. Shuffle your feet when you walk in the river and look carefully before you jump out of the boat.

Electric eels are related to catfish and can grow up to two metres long. A large specimen can render a human being unconscious by the power of its shock. They are usually found in deep, slow moving waters.

Pity the poor **piranha** fish which has been given such a bad image by Hollywood. Yes, it can and does bite, but usually only when someone is trying to remove a fish hook from its mouth. The idea that piranhas are waiting to devour anyone who so much as puts a toe in the water is hugely exaggerated. However, in the dry season when the rivers dry up, leaving large pools cut off from the main body of water, piranha fish trapped there will be extremely hungry and you should exercise caution. In places where local people warn you about piranha fish, take their advice.

I do not recommend swimming naked in the rivers, not from any sense of modesty but because of the ***candiru***, a tiny parasitic fish that wedges itself in the gills of larger fish. The *candiru* is reputed to swim up any human orifice, usually the anus or the urethra, and open its needle-like barbs.

Amazon snakes

Many snakes in the jungle are beautifully coloured and patterned, and if you are lucky enough to see one it will enhance your memories of the trip. We have come across many snakes during our travels and, though neither of us has ever been bitten, we were always conscious that a snakebite would be a very serious problem far from medical help. Because there is such conflicting advice about what to do in the unlikely event of snakebite I have consulted internationally recognised herpetologist Mark O'Shea, who says:

> 'Snakes are often found near water, especially at dawn and dusk. They lack ears and rely on ground vibration. Despite popular local myths, most snakes don't chase people and would far rather save their venom for prey than bite you. If you want to look under logs, roll them toward you rather than away so a hidden snake can't strike at your legs. Wear boots and gloves while collecting firewood. If by some misfortune you do sustain a bite the most difficult advice to follow, but perhaps the most important, is not to panic. Many bites can be from non-venomous snakes and even venomous snakes often inject no venom or sub-lethal doses.'

As Mark O'Shea says, the DON'Ts are far more important than the DOs and his advice is:

- DON'T cut the bite with a knife or a razor, or apply a tourniquet, or give electric shock. Don't use ice or extreme heat or potassium permanganate, or alcohol.
- DON'T suck or use any sucking apparatus. It's instinctive to suck a bite but this isn't proven to do any good. Once the venom is in, it's in, and you can no more suck it out than you could suck out a tetanus serum that a doctor injects in your backside.
- DON'T give aspirin.
- DON'T mess with snakes.
- DON'T kill snakes unnecessarily; most snakes are harmless.

Venomous Amazonian snakes to be cautious about

Specifically, the pretty, banded **coral snakes** are related to cobras but they don't hood. Their venom contains neurotoxins which cause respiratory failure. They are usually red, black and yellow in bands while some are blue and black. Forget all the poetry used in North America – 'Red to yellow kill a fellow, red to black venom lack' – it doesn't apply to South American coral snakes. Fewer than one in a hundred venomous snakebites in Amazonian Brazil are caused by coral snakes. Coral snakes have great difficulty in biting through clothing but they have been known to come into sleeping bags on the ground. Bites are often on the fingertips or between the fingers and because the bite doesn't hurt, you may not even realise you have been bitten. Later symptoms are when the eyelids begin to droop and the tongue and the face muscles become paralysed. You can apply a pressure bandage as you would for an ankle sprain, so that you can still get a finger comfortably underneath. It's important not to cut off blood circulation. Don't use a tourniquet.

Pit vipers are a sub-family of vipers. They have heat-sensitive pits on their heads which are extremely accurate prey-locating receptors. Their venom attacks the blood and tissues, bites can bleed and there will be massive swelling, severe pain and discoloration. Keep the limb elevated but NEVER apply a pressure bandage because as the limb swells this will fast become a tourniquet.

In all cases of snakebite get the person to hospital as soon as possible. Don't waste time. If possible kill the snake and take it with you in a secure box for identification, but don't rush around in a panic trying to catch it. Record what it looks like, colours, patterns, length, time and location, but don't risk another bite. To measure swelling, put a tape measure around the victim's limb, mark the edges with a pen, remove the tape measure and continue to monitor the swelling this way. Reassure victims that they will be alright.

If all this seems rather alarming, remember that people manage to spend entire lifetimes living in Amazonia without being bitten by a snake. Here are some snakebite statistics and the snake groups usually responsible:

- Fer de lance and relatives – 90% – all habitats
- Rattlesnake – 9% – prefer savannah but have been found near jungle edge
- Coral snakes – 0.9% – primarily forest
- Bushmaster – 0.1% – deep forest

Most non-venomous snakes will bite to defend themselves, and large species like boas and anacondas can inflict painful, bloody bites but they are harmless wounds. Wash with an antiseptic.

IS IT WORTH IT?

There will be days when it rains. Even in the jungle, it sometimes gets cold. In places the riverbank is slippery and you get covered in mud, the jungle is murky and threatening, wet and clinging, all the trees seem to be thorny and there's nowhere to camp. You fantasise about the food you will eat when you get back to a town – how could there have been days at home when you didn't know what to eat, with everything in a supermarket to choose from? You miss newspapers, TV, the radio and your family and friends. You can't face another rapid, another uncomfortable night, another mosquito bite. Physically and mentally exhausted you wonder what you are doing there, and begin to feel miserable and just a bit frightened.

But if thoughts of snakes and spiders, rapids and roaches haven't put you off, then picture this. You pull your boat up the beach. In the cool jungle away from the hot sun you have your pick of trees from which to hang your hammock. You gather wood, light a fire and cook a meal. Later, sitting on the beach with a drink, you can see the stars as never before. Caimans slip into the river with hardly a splash, a cacophony of frog voices fills the night and in the jungle a deer barks. That night you are woken by a snuffling sound and a cough, then a sound just like somebody snoring, but you drift back to sleep. In the morning, all around your camp are huge paw prints, even between the hammocks hanging only a metre apart. A curious jaguar has visited in the night. It could come true, it happened to us and it could happen to you.

Health and Safety 4

Written in collaboration with Dr Jane Wilson-Howarth

Health and safety concerns put off many people who would like to travel to the Amazon. True, within rainforests lurk a wide variety of nasty parasites and viruses absent from more sanitised parts of the world. Most tropical diseases are rare, preventable and treatable. Health does matter, but for Amazon visitors it need only concern those who have other medical problems, are frail or have just watched lurid movies about deadly tropical viruses. The scariest diseases are unlikely to trouble the short-term visitor if you follow a few standard hygiene practices. Far more likely are the usual travellers' woes. This section looks at potential risks and necessary precautions for travel in Amazonia.

HEALTH

Before you go

Malaria

Malaria is characterised as a serious, acute and chronic relapsing infection; symptoms include fever, chills, anaemia, and sometimes fatal complications. It exists throughout the Amazon, but there is a risk travelling anywhere in the region. Because malarial mosquitoes cannot breed at cold temperatures, the risk is less the higher you go, and they and malaria are absent from areas above about 2,500m (8,250ft).

The disease is transmitted via the saliva of the female *anopheles* mosquito when the insect takes a blood meal. The microbe enters the bloodstream and infects the red blood cells. A blood sample usually diagnoses malaria infection.

Strains of malaria

Four strains of malaria commonly infect humans of which only two, *Plasmodium vivax* and *P. falciparum*, are found in South America. *Falciparum* malaria is the commonest and most dangerous. The symptoms appear from one week to four months after exposure and consist of high fever, shivering, chills, profuse sweating and nausea. In severe cases, hallucinations, headache, numbness in the extremities, and/or diarrhoea and vomiting may also be experienced.

Given prompt treatment, adequate rest and good nursing care, most people (99%) recover from malaria. Following recovery *falciparum* malaria does not recur.

The *vivax* strain of malaria is less common than *falciparum*. Symptoms are similar to *falciparum* malaria, though usually less severe. If the patient is initially healthy the case may be no worse than a bad flu. Onset of the disease can occur any time from one week of being bitten. However, this type of malaria is resistant to therapy and can recur over a period of several years.

Prophylaxis and treatment

A number of effective drugs are available to treat malaria. Indeed quinine, the active principle in the Amazonian *cinchona* (Peruvian bark) tree, was widely used from 1700, before the disease was understood. Among the more important are chloroquine, paraquine, pyrimethamine and amodiaquin. These are active against malaria parasites in red blood cells. Many *falciparum* strains and some *vivax* strains are now resistant to anti-malarial drugs. The disease is spreading even faster where mosquitoes have evolved resistance to insecticides.

The preventative most widely prescribed in the US is **mefloquine** (sold under the brand name **Lariam**). This is a recently developed drug. It is taken once a week, for two weeks before and after the trip as well as during. Drawbacks of mefloquine are side-effects, including sleep disorders, frightening dreams and mood changes; also some people find it too expensive.

Depending on the strain of malaria, there are a number of alternatives to mefloquine. Commonest are **paludrine** and **chloroquine**. The number of people experiencing the side-effects of nausea and appetite loss are less when compared with those using mefloquine. These drugs also cost less than mefloquine. Paludrine is taken daily, and chloroquine weekly and, like mefloquine, they need to be taken for a month after leaving the malarial region. As mentioned above, there is chloroquine resistance in some South American malaria strains.

Fansidar is used in the treatment of malaria. It is not safe to use as a prophylactic but, if you are travelling independently a long way from medical centres, you should consider carrying three tablets per person for emergency treatment, and check with your doctor on the correct usage.

Drug stores in some Latin American countries sell anti-malarial drugs over the counter, but don't count on the drug being in stock.

Malaria can be fatal if not treated promptly. Familiarise yourself with the symptoms and, if any occur within four months after travel, suspect malaria and seek medical attention immediately.

Preventing mosquito bites

A traveller on a short visit would be very unlucky to catch malaria. It is not common in most parts of the Amazon. In addition to taking an appropriate course of prophylactics, the best prevention is to avoid bites from pestiferous carrier mosquitoes between dusk and dawn. At dusk, put on long clothes and apply insect repellent under the socks and to exposed areas of skin. Sleep under insecticide-impregnated mosquito nets. Clothes impregnated with mosquito repellent act as a buffer zone, while boats mid-river are too far for mosquitoes to fly and provide welcome relief. If necessary, burn mosquito coils at night.

Immunisations

Many people think they need a dozen jabs to venture safely into the rainforest. So they are surprised to learn that, for a week-long organised tour, immunisations are not really necessary. Some visitors get four or five shots before they go; many have none.

Yellow fever, **hepatitis A** and **tetanus** immunisations are recommended, especially for travellers staying longer than one month or who intend roughing it. **Rabies** vaccination (see page 90) may also be warranted and many doctors will recommend **typhoid** immunisation although this is only 60% effective. The **cholera** vaccination is ineffective and unnecessary.

Yellow fever

Transmitted via mosquitoes like malaria, yellow fever is much rarer. This acute infectious tropical disease is caused by a virus. Widely regarded as originating in Africa, earliest reports of yellow fever were in fact from Central and South America during the 16th century. In the 1930s, studies of yellow fever's transmission cycle showed it to be endemic over much of the Amazon and Orinoco river basins.

There are two types, according to the mode of transmission: urban or classical yellow fever, transmitted from person to person; and jungle yellow fever, transmitted from a mammalian host (usually a monkey) by mosquitoes to humans.

After an incubation period of several days the virus multiplies within the body. The initial attack includes headache, fever, nausea and vomiting. After two to three days the patient may begin to recover. If not, the disease enters a serious stage, marked by high fever, slow pulse rate and vomiting of blood. Death may follow within ten days after the first symptoms. Because the disease attacks liver cells, jaundice (bile pigment is deposited, turning skin and eyes yellow) is common, hence the disease's name.

Treatment relies on keeping the fever as low as possible and preventing dehydration. Convalescence can take a long time but recovery is complete and the patient acquires a life-long immunity. Mortality varies greatly according to the strain of virus and individual genetic resistance.

Yellow fever is completely preventable by immunisation which is effective for ten years.

Many countries require travellers who have visited an endemic zone to be immunised and to carry an international immunisation certificate at all times.

NOTE Travellers on tourist riverboat day-trips from Peru into Leticia (Colombia) and Tabatinga (Brazil) do not need these certificates.

Hepatitis

This illness is basically inflammation (*-itis*) of the liver (*hepat-*). It is in fact a complex of acute viral and chronic diseases of differing rarity, severity and modes of transmission.

Hepatitis A and B are acute diseases caused by two different viruses, called (you guessed) A and B. These are the two commonest types of hepatitis.

Travellers are at greatest risk from hepatitis A. Though the least dangerous type of 'hep' it can really knock you out, and recovery takes several weeks or months. It is most often contracted from contaminated food or water; immunisation against hepatitis A is recommended especially for those travelling rough. The virus inhabits the digestive tract, is passed on via faeces and is subsequently swallowed by the next victim. Hepatitis A appears within 20–40 days after exposure. Initial symptoms include upper stomach pains and mild fever, usually accompanied by chills and fatigue. Headache, muscle aches and appetite loss follow, and then later the classic symptoms of yellowish eye-whites and skin.

During this time the immune system produces antibodies against the virus. Treatment relies on rest and good care, as there is no cure. During recovery, the lost liver tissue regenerates and liver function returns. Once someone has caught hepatitis A they become immune to this type.

Immunisation with gammaglobulin works by providing antibodies against hepatitis A; it does not stimulate your body's immune system so provides some protection for a maximum of about six weeks. It is much cheaper than active immunisation (with Havrix), so is worth considering for those travelling infrequently, short-term. Havrix provides good protection against hepatitis A for ten years.

Hepatitis B has a longer incubation period than type A, taking around 90 days to show symptoms. It is transmitted via blood transfusion, contaminated hypodermic syringes, through dentistry, acupuncture, tattooing or sexually. This virus populates blood serum, semen, and saliva. Effective vaccines are available. Hepatitis B vaccination requires three shots over six months.

Tetanus

This is a disease caused by bacteria commonly found in soil and animal dung. Infection arises via a wound contaminated with dirt. Puncture wounds with little bleeding to flush out bacteria can result in tetanus. Symptoms consist of involuntary spasmodic contractions of various muscles, especially those of the neck and jaw giving rise to the more common name of lockjaw.

Tetanus vaccination is effective and recommended for visitors on extended Amazon stays.

Teeth

Get a dental check-up before travelling as going to the dentist on holiday is a waste of time. You might want to take an emergency Dental Repair Kit, available from camping stores and good chemists. Anything you can do to avoid dental treatment in South America is a wise precaution.

Health clinics

UK

MASTA (Medical Advisory Services for Travellers Abroad), London School of Hygiene and Tropical Medicine, Keppel Street, London WC1E 7HT; tel: 0891 224100. This is a premium line number, charged at 50p per minute. For a fee, they will provide an individually tailored health brief, with up-to-date information on how to stay healthy, inoculations and what to bring. MASTA also sells basic travel supplies including mosquito nets and medical equipment packs.

British Airways Clinics There are now 32 BA clinics around Britain, and three in South Africa. To find your nearest one, telephone 01276 685040 (UK). Apart from providing inoculations and malaria prophylaxis, they sell a variety of health-related goods.

Berkeley Travel Clinic, 32 Berkeley Street, London W1X 5FA (near Green Park tube station); tel: 0171 629 6233.

Fleet Street Travel Clinic, 29 Fleet St, London EC4Y 1AA; tel: 0171 353 5678.

Nomad Travellers' Store and Medical Centre, 3–4 Wellington Terrace, Turnpike Lane, London N8 0PX; tel: 0181 889 7014.

Trailfinders Immunisation Clinic, 194 Kensington High Street, London W8 7RG; tel: 0171 938 3999.

Tropical Medicine Bureau This Irish-run organisation has a useful website specific to tropical destinations: www.tmb.ie

USA

Centers for Disease Control This Atlanta-based organisation is the central source of travel health information in North America, with a touch-tone phone line and fax service. Travelers' Hot Line: (404) 332 4559. Each summer they publish the invaluable *Health Information for International Travel* which is available from the Center for Prevention Services, Division of Quarantine, Atlanta, GA 30333.

Connaught Laboratories PO Box 187, Swiftwater, PA 18370; tel: 800 822 2463. They will send a free list of specialist tropical medicine physicians in your state.

IAMAT (International Association for Medical Assistance to Travelers) 736 Center Street, Lewiston, NY 14092, USA; tel: 716 754 4883. Also at Gotthardstrasse 17, 6300 Zug, Switzerland. A non-profit organisation which provides health information and lists of English-speaking doctors abroad.

Australia

TMVC has 20 clinics in Australia, New Zealand and Thailand. For the nearest clinic phone 1300 65 88 44, or try their website: www.tmvc.com.au.

Sydney, Dr Mandy Hu, Dymocks Building, 7th floor, 428 George St, Sydney, NSW 2000 (tel: 2 221 7133; fax: 2 221 8401).
Brisbane, Dr Deborah Mills, Qantas Domestic Building, 6th floor, 247 Adelaide St, Brisbane, QLD 4000 (tel: 7 3221 9066; fax: 7 3221 7076).
Melbourne, Dr Sonny Lau, 393 Little Bourke St, 2nd floor, Melbourne, VIC 3000 (tel: 3 9602 5788; fax: 3 9670 8394).

Travel insurance

Anyone travelling to the Amazon would be advised to get adequate travel insurance. Full coverage is best but if you need to save money the premium can be apportioned. Emergency transport home and medical expenses are obviously more important than baggage or trip cancellation coverage. Count on a minimum of US$1 million worth of cover for medical emergency and evacuation.

Whether or not an emergency evacuation is possible depends on where you are and also whether you are well enough to be evacuated. But in the end, the chances of an accident or mishap on an average Amazon trip are minimal – no more and no less than in a concrete jungle.

Water sterilisation

Drinking clean water reduces the possibility of contracting several troublesome diseases. One reasonably safe option is to buy and drink bottled water; it is available in all but the smallest towns and villages and is reasonably priced. You should make sure the seal is not broken. Even this regime isn't foolproof as studies in some countries have shown that mineral water may be contaminated.

If you are worried about the water take along your own purification tablets which are available from camping stores and good pharmacists. Chlorine-based purification tablets do not kill amoebic cysts so you may want to take iodine. Tincture of iodine is widely available throughout South America. Add two drops to one litre of water and leave to stand for one hour. Alternatively you can buy iodine crystals or tablets from camping shops back home. Read the label as instructions can vary.

If you are camping, carrying sufficient water is unrealistic so you will need to boil the water or use iodine to kill off the bugs.

There are several water purification pumps available on the market now. It is probably worth testing a few before you find yourself in the middle of the Amazon with a pump that requires so much effort that you sweat more water than you have cleaned. Make sure the pump incorporates iodine in the system somewhere, as at present no pumps on the market are capable of removing giardia.

First-aid kit

A good kit should include: Band-aids (plasters) of various shapes and sizes; bandages; absorbent pads; a good drying antiseptic such as iodine, or potassium permanganate crystals to dissolve in water; antibiotic cream; soluble aspirin/paracetamol (as painkillers, for gargling and to reduce fever); and burn lotion.

Several companies market first-aid kits of various shapes and sizes. Depending on your needs, purchase a basic first-aid kit packed small for travellers, or a larger 'expedition' size kit.

Remember that clinical thermometers (containing mercury) can't officially be carried on aircraft. One traveller mentions having had hers confiscated twice. Use a digital thermometer instead.

Minor ailments

Eating and drinking safely

The golden Amazon rule for good digestive health is to take scrupulous care over what you eat and drink. Basic precautions are:

- PEEL IT, BOIL IT, COOK IT OR FORGET IT!
- Eat only fruits and vegetables you have peeled yourself
- If you eat meat ensure it is hot, cooked through and fresh from the kitchen
- Order a la carte rather than eat from a buffet
- Do not drink unpurified water (never straight from taps or rivers)
- Do not use ice unless you know it was made from purified water

Avoid lettuce and beware of salads unless you know all vegetables were cleaned and soaked in iodine or potassium permanganate. Salad food at lodges and on tourist boats is treated to eliminate germs and parasites.

Traveller's diarrhoea

The trots, runs or Montezuma's Revenge, call it what you will, this is one of the commonest ailments to strike the Amazon visitor. The condition usually indicates contaminated food, rather than 'your stomach flora adjusting to the new environment', as at least one travel brochure nicely puts it. The cause is often food prepared by someone with dirty hands or in unsanitary conditions.

On a week-long Amazon trip, diarrhoea may afflict one in a group of ten people. If you are in the region for longer you will probably experience 'a period of acclimatisation'. Even being careful one can be unlucky and come down with a tummy bug. In addition to diarrhoea, symptoms may include stomach cramps, nausea and fever.

Depending on the severity, dealing with diarrhoea is straightforward. As fluid loss is an inevitable consequence, it is important to replenish fluids, ideally with a rehydration salts mixture. These can be purchased ready-made in sachets, or made from a mixture of sugar (40g) and salt (3.5g), mixed in a litre of water. Milk, fatty foods and alcohol should be avoided and, if possible, rest certainly helps the healing process. Glucose tablets provide an instant source of energy – ideal if you are feeling run down due to diarrhoea.

When rest is not possible or when you have to travel, blockers such as Lomotil, Kaopectate or Imodium can be taken. They physically plug you up by paralysing the bowel but in overdose they paralyse the breathing muscles too. These drugs should be taken as a last resort, as they usually prolong the illness by keeping diarrhoea-causing bugs inside you.

Most cases of diarrhoea clear up in a day or two. Should the illness continue for more than a few days, see a doctor, as chronic symptoms indicate worse but treatable trouble. If it is impossible to see a doctor a three-day course of antibiotics such as norfloxacin or ciprofloxacin may clear up the problem but self-diagnosis should be a last resort.

Independent travellers should carry a roll of toilet paper, as many public toilets (and some budget hotels and lodges) in Amazonia lack this rather essential item.

Altitude sickness

If arriving for your trip to the Amazon through one of the Andean cities there is a possibility you will experience altitude sickness for the first few days. In general this only affects people arriving at altitudes above 3,000m directly from sea level. Visitors to La Paz (4,000m) in Bolivia should be aware of the risks; people travelling to Quito (2,850m) or Bogotá (2,650m) should also be aware of altitude sickness although the risk is reduced. Acetazolamide (Diamox) can be taken to speed up acclimatisation, but people with blood or breathing related illnesses should see a doctor before flying directly to La Paz.

Symptoms include breathlessness, insomnia, headache, appetite loss and possibly nausea. When arriving at altitude make an effort to rest. The onset of altitude sickness can occur after a few hours even though you may be feeling fine initially.

Sunburn

Perhaps the commonest affliction of Amazon visitors is sunburn, especially with the reflective sunlight from rivers. Take sensible precautions. Use sunblock. SPF15–20 (SPF = Sun Protection Factor, eg: SPF15 offers 15 times your own skin's protection) is best. Fair-skinned people need a higher SPF than those with darker complexions. Severe sunburn may cause skin blisters which could lead to infection and it increases the chance of skin cancer. Wear sunblock whenever you go out in the sun. This is good advice even at home, but especially important in equatorial regions such as the Amazon where the sun is stronger.

In the short term, mild sunburn is at worst an inconvenience; but heatstroke can be a lot more serious. This is when the body temperature rises too high and, although it is often misleadingly called sunstroke, it need not be associated with too much sun. Initial symptoms are headache, faintness, dizziness and nausea. If heatstroke is suspected, move into a cool place and drink plenty of non-alcoholic fluids.

Dehydration

High humidity and warm temperatures tax your body's natural cooling system and most people perspire more than usual, especially in the first week in the tropics. To compensate drink more water. Never rehydrate with alcohol. Drink before you feel thirsty (the first sign of dehydration).

You should consider taking a bit more salt than you normally would to help keep electrolyte levels in balance; just a little extra on your food should be enough. If you are feeling low on energy due to dehydration, glucose-containing sports drinks help, although fruit juice or non-caffeinated soda are just as good.

Minor cuts and bruises

Owing to the constant heat and humidity, bacteria and fungi flourish, so it is vital to treat even small cuts or insect bites immediately to prevent potentially dangerous infection. Wash any cuts with clean water, rinse and allow them to air-dry. Don't use antiseptic creams, as they are less effective in the tropics, and replace the dressing daily. A standard first-aid kit should be enough to cope with most minor emergencies.

Fungal infections

The constant heat and humidity have far-reaching effects. Just as bacteria and fungi respond by colonising the rainforest, given half a chance they'd take over your body too. Bathing often and giving the body a chance to breathe are the best ways of avoiding infection. Symptoms include itchiness and flaking skin around the armpits, crotch and between the toes. Treatment requires a fungicidal cream and powder.

Motion sickness

The water is calm enough on lowland Amazon rivers to prevent motion sickness being a problem, but expedition cruise vessels coming from the open ocean may hit a bad squall. Occasionally, when the water is rough, a ride in the *collectivo* motor boats can be a bit bouncy if they travel fast. Take motion sickness pills or use a hyoscine patch if you suffer from motion sickness; these need to be taken well before you feel the symptoms. Some motion sickness pills (eg: Dramamine) may cause drowsiness; others (eg: Stugeron) don't. Ginger is also claimed to be effective.

In a small plane where the ride can be very bumpy, there may be no flight crew aside from the pilot, so remember to take your own pills.

Bus rides will certainly be bumpy so, if you are a sufferer, be prepared.

More serious problems

Medical emergencies

Most Amazon tours are run by responsible tour operators with years of experience and well-trained guides so it is highly improbable a serious emergency will arise over a week or two's visit. However, this is a remote area and you are further from help than in most places back home.

Tourist lodges and riverboats usually have no staff nurse or doctor, but they do have two-way radio in case of emergency. In direst and potentially life-threatening situations not too far from a town or city, it may be possible for a helicopter or float-plane to evacuate a patient to a city within a couple of hours. Make sure you have insurance.

If you are travelling independently in the Amazon, unless you are close to one of the larger towns or cities you will probably be relying on your first-aid knowledge and initiative. If you have adventurous travel plans do your best to be prepared for any eventuality.

Sexually transmitted diseases and AIDS

The status of AIDS in the Amazon is poorly known. Its rate seems to remain low among rural populations but is rising around cities. Brazil's high rate of AIDS – well over one million – is mostly in coastal cities such as Rio de Janeiro and São Paulo. Only a handful of AIDS cases have been reported in the Amazon.

Using a condom protects against AIDS and other sexually transmitted diseases. Condoms, when available, can be bought from pharmacies but quality may be questionable. It is best to bring condoms from home so that you know they will fit; women may like to travel with a few femidoms.

If you are planning on having any injections or vaccinations in the Amazon consider taking a sterile needle pack to avoid the possibility of infection through shared needles.

Filth-to-mouth diseases

Giardiasis is a parasitic intestinal disorder commonly acquired from contaminated food or water. Associated with severe and intermittently persistent diarrhoea and eggy burps, this parasite can be quite insidious and may lie dormant for a considerable period before infection is apparent. If you believe you may have contracted *giardia* you need to see a doctor.

Prevention is by avoiding unhygienically prepared food or heavily contaminated water.

If a case of severe diarrhoea persists for more than a few days, coupled with stomach cramps and fever, **dysentery** could be the culprit. This waterborne disease has two forms – amoebic and bacterial – which show similar symptoms: severe inflammation of the mucus membrane of the large intestine, resulting in bloody evacuations. The bacterial form of dysentery responds well to a week-long course of ciprofloxacin antibiotics but the amoebic form requires treatment with Flagyl (metronidozole). Self-diagnosis and treatment of dysentery (or any serious disease) are not advisable and, if suspected, a doctor should be consulted.

Cholera has plagued dense human habitations throughout the world for millennia but, although it has a very bad reputation, it tends to kill the ill, starving or debilitated. In 1993–94 Peru suffered the most severe outbreak the country had seen. It is most often acquired through contaminated food or water. Any type of cholera-like watery diarrhoea requires lots of fluid replacement and a medical consultation if the illness seems bad. Most of the cure is through constantly drinking clean water with rehydration salts. Constipatives, to prevent diarrhoea, are dangerous. Another source of cholera is seafood contaminated by untreated sewage dumped into rivers or oceans. This was the cause of Lima's mass outbreak. Raw fish, used in the popular local dish *ceviche*, was directly responsible for thousands of cases. Hence, travellers to Peru are advised to avoid raw fish unless 100% certain it is uncontaminated.

Typhoid – also called enteric fever – is an acute, infectious fever, with symptoms of severe intestinal disturbances, pink spots on the chest and abdomen and physical exhaustion. Infection is usually through contaminated food. A vaccination is readily available but is only 60% effective. Typhoid is treated with antibiotics (chloramphenicol or ampicillin), rest and a balanced diet.

The nasty side of nature

Chagas' disease, also called *trypanosomiasis*, received some notoriety as the apparent cause of Darwin's lassitude upon his return to England after the Beagle voyage. It is very possible Darwin contracted the disease in South America, where it is endemic in many rural areas. It is extremely rare in travellers. The disease is transmitted by an insect belonging to the same order as assassin bugs. The parasite is passed on when the bug takes a blood meal, typically on the face around the cheek. Rather than being transmitted by the bite itself, the parasite is ejected in the bug's faeces and deposited close to the wound. Scratching by the unwitting victim rubs the faeces into the wound, admitting the parasite into the bloodstream where it remains, often for many years, before symptoms become apparent.

The symptoms are acute and chronic. Initially, during the acute stage, infection causes a flu-like fever, although there may be no symptoms at all. At this time the disease is treatable.

Avoid scratching bites, especially those not from mosquitoes, and wash them with alcohol or antiseptic. In the absence of any cure for this disease, prevention is the only medicine. Avoid sleeping on the floor of poor adobe huts.

Leishmaniasis is caused by sandflies (*Lutzomyia* sp) which transmit this parasite. Symptoms are chronic if untreated. Not usually a fatal disease, it can cause severe disfigurement by sores that refuse to heal, particularly around the face. Prevention is based on avoiding the sandflies, easiest achieved by liberal applications of insect repellent in areas where they are present. Additional protection is conferred by long trousers and a long-sleeved shirt. Although very unlikely to be caught on an average-length Amazon visit, *leishmaniasis* is a real risk for those staying in certain areas for more than a few weeks. Sleep under an insecticide-impregnated bed-net in high-risk areas.

Dengue fever is an increasingly common mosquito-borne disease that can be very debilitating, and potentially fatal. Flu-like symptoms include headache, fever, and pain in muscles and joints; hence it is also called 'break-bone fever'. There is no cure and no vaccine for dengue so avoid being bitten by the day-active *aedes* mosquito vector. Aspirin and related medications such as ibuprofen should not be taken if you think you have dengue.

On account of the diseases they transmit, **ticks** (*Acarina*), although tiny, are among the most dangerous arachnids, understated by Bates as creatures of 'great annoyance'. The **cattle tick** (*Margaropus annulatus*) and ticks of the genus *Ixodes* occur throughout the Americas and infect livestock and humans with a number of dangerous pathogens such as tick fever. Ticks are not common in forest, and it is unlikely you'll be bitten on a typical jungle trail. In grassy open areas where cattle are present it's a different matter, and you should check your clothing and any exposed skin regularly for pests. Upon discovering a tick, remove it very gently to avoid infection. This is age-old advice from Bates himself, who observed 'serious sores are caused if care is not taken in removing them as the proboscis is liable to break off and remain in the wound'. To do this, slowly pull the tick out, making sure the tweezers are tight up against the skin, and it will hopefully come off in one piece. If you forget tweezers, insect repellent (applied to the tick) or a lighted cigarette also work well.

Rabies is an acute, ordinarily fatal, viral disease of the central nervous system (CNS). The disease is also called *lyssa* or *hydrophobia*. It is usually transmitted via domestic dogs, although wild carnivorous animals and bats frequently carry the disease. The active virus inhabits the salivary glands and is thus transmitted with a bite.

The virus propagates along nerve tissue near the wound and soon establishes itself in the CNS. After an incubation period of anything from ten days to several months (usually four to six weeks), the virus reaches the brain and full-blown symptoms develop.

Best of the available vaccines is the HDCV (Human Diploid Cell Vaccine), grown on human cells. Two injections are enough to immunise the patient, although four injections is a standard course. Initial HDCV treatment is followed with a series of vaccinations.

If you are bitten by any animal, treatment is simply to wash the wound immediately for five minutes and apply disinfectant. This removes infective saliva before too much virus has entered the blood, reducing the chances of contracting the disease. If rabies is properly treated prior to the onset of symptoms recovery should be complete. Without treatment, rabies is nearly always fatal once symptoms start.

Snakes The Amazon has *only* 23 poisonous species and most of these rarely inflict a lethal bite. Many people have an instinctive revulsion to snakes but you will be lucky if you see one, and equally unlucky if you are bitten by one. But even people with ophidophobia have no reason not to visit the Amazon.

Snakes are abundant, but excellent camouflage and reclusive behaviour make them all but impossible to see under normal conditions. Most species are wary and quietly slither off as soon as they sense ground vibrations from human footsteps.

But on the principle 'anything that can go wrong...', educate yourself as best you can regarding snakebite and focus attention on keeping the patient calm and rested. Identify the snake if possible and get medical professional help as soon as you can. Few cases of snakebite are life-threatening provided treatment is prompt. (For detailed advice, see pages 78–9.)

Keeping creepy-crawlies at bay (see also pages 77–8)

'For your enhanced enjoyment...', as they say, insect repellent is necessary on jungle walks or night excursions by boat. Failing that it may keep you just this side of sane. Use products containing 30–50% DEET, though clothes may be impregnated with 100%; you can reduce the amount of repellent you need to apply by wearing long clothes. An alternative is repellent containing citronella oil. At some lodges liberal amounts of repellent may be needed when insects are abundant, especially in the rainy season.

If spending several days at a lodge, take mosquito coils which can be bought from camping shops and are available in the larger lowland Amazon towns and cities. They are long-lasting, compact, economical and environmentally safe. (Pressurised aerosol repellents are banned from jet planes and not always ozone-friendly.) One coil lasts through the night.

Sandflies are especially bothersome pests. The bite hurts out of all proportion to the creature's size. This insect is often abundant around pasture or inhabited areas. It carries a parasitic disease, *leishmaniasis*, so wear long clothes and apply repellent to any bare skin whenever walking on land, especially where there are grassy areas grazed by animals or in forest.

The same regime should minimise attack by another 'no-see-um' pest of open pasture: **chiggers**. Without you feeling a thing, these mites burrow under the skin to appear as a tiny mole-like spot about the size of a pin-head. You can remove the creature with a pair of tweezers but make sure none of it is left behind. Applying ammonium hydroxide (Itch-ease®) reduces the itching. If the spot is not scratched – easier said than done – it disappears without a trace. If not treated carefully, the bite may become seriously infected. **Botflies** also like to burrow into the skin and set up residence. Several remedies are claimed to work, including smearing a petroleum jelly over the entrance hole to suffocate the creature out, or placing a piece of fresh meat over the wound in the assumption that a piece of juicy steak is more appealing than the inside of your arm! After treks it is worth doing a quick check over your body to remove uninvited freeloaders.

Any insect bite may become infected in the tropical warmth and humidity. If a wound reddens and weeps, clean thoroughly with a drying antiseptic and apply antibiotic powder or ointment immediately.

Although most **spiders** are harmless, some Amazon species have a big enough bite to inject venom. A bite is most likely on a jungle walk or in bed (shake out the bedding and mattress). Usually harmless or just a nasty inconvenience, a few spider species have venom which kills cells around the bite site and so prevents wounds from healing quickly. If a spider bite is not healing get professional medical attention. Dreaded 'tarantula' types of spider are very common in Amazonia but none is a threat. Their bite is usually too weak to penetrate our skin and their venom is not especially potent.

Scorpions are renowned for their deadly stings, but once again fears are out of proportion to the risk. Most scorpions can sting but inflict no harmful wound. Yes, a few are dangerous, but these species are rare and generally restricted to dry areas. To avoid being stung, simply don't put your hands and feet in dark nooks or areas where the arachnids may be hiding. If you're lucky you might see more than the odd cockroach.

Occasionally you may be stung or bitten by an **ant**. On jungle walks, watch out especially for the huge bullet ants, an inch or more long. Insect repellent does not deter these gargantuan monsters, which wield an excruciating sting. Luckily, the effect of a sting is not permanent. The pain takes a while to subside and the area goes red and throbs for a day or so but no lasting damage arises. The same goes for bites from tree-dwelling ants, such as *azteca*, which inhabit Cecropia trees. If stung you can always adopt the stoic attitude of one lady who, after the initial shock, declared she was '...happy to have been initiated into the rainforest'. Better still, watch your step and avoid being stung in the first place.

If you suffer from severe allergic reactions consult your doctor for appropriate medication before visiting the Amazon.

When you get home

If for any reason, on return to your home country, you suspect you may have picked something up, go to your doctor. It is surprising how often visitors to the Amazon take home new friends they did not even know they had met.

SAFETY

Theft

It is easy to see where South America's violent reputation comes from. The infamous government death squads, the activities of various drugs cartels – not limited, as some would have you believe, to Colombia – and the murder of street children have all made the international press. But keeping the threat in perspective can be an eye-opener. Peru's per capita murder rate is just one third of New York City's!

Travel in South America, and the Amazon in particular, is essentially safe. The reality is that most people do not experience problems first hand and have to satisfy their listener's curiosity by passing on travellers' tales which grow hyperbolically with the telling. Some are amusing.

One such tale is of a traveller who, wary of being robbed, had placed his money strategically around his body; in his pocket (the mugger's money), in his money belt, in a leg pouch, in a secret pocket sewn into the back of his trousers, even under the instep of his shoe. While he was sitting on a bench, two men sitting on either side of him stood up, asked him to strip naked and left him in just his underwear. If a thief wants your money he will take it somehow. If you are threatened with a weapon or outnumbered, the best advice is to cooperate.

Tourists are a source of rich pickings throughout the world. Violent assaults against the person are rare. If you do have any problems the worst you are likely to experience are petty crimes such as bag snatching, pick-pocketing and theft. It is most likely that any theft will occur near the airport, in the city, close to money-changing facilities or in any setting where the novelty of the situation may cause you to relax your natural levels of awareness. Here are a few tips to consider:

- Use a hotel safe for valuables when there is one. Although you may feel safer when close to your valuables they are more likely to be stolen from you when on your person.
- Take a small padlock or combination lock to secure the doors of cheaper hotels. You should also find a way of locking luggage to stop opportunistic thieves having a quick rummage through your bags.
- Leave all expensive jewellery and watches at home. If you need a watch there are plenty of cheap ones available in South America.
- Take a money belt, pouch or whatever you feel most comfortable with. It isn't the best idea to have all your money in one place whether that is your money belt or your pocket. Keeping a small amount of money close at hand for casual spending avoids digging away for your money belt in the middle of the street.
- Take copies of all important travel documents, including passport, air tickets, travellers' cheques and credit cards. Keep them in a separate place from the originals. Note down ticket and travellers' cheque numbers along with serial numbers of any electronic or camera equipment.
- If you have a daypack to carry around your camera and other items, wear it on your front when in towns and cities. Hanging off the back it is an easy target

for bag-slashers who are quite capable of cutting your bag, emptying it and disappearing without you noticing.
- Stay with crowds at night. Although wandering around at night is enjoyable, you do tend to be slightly more vulnerable. Unless you know an area well you are more likely to become disorientated at night. Taking taxis at night instead of buses is preferred by some travellers.
- When using long-distance buses, check that your luggage is loaded before getting on the bus. Some companies provide luggage receipts which offer some peace of mind.

If you have a problem you should report the theft to the police or a local authority who will provide you with the official bits of paper. Although small consolation for the bag that has disappeared, the report is essential for any insurance claim.

A couple of things to watch out for...

The art of distraction has been perfected by criminals working in gangs. Be wary of any sudden spurt of activity that may distract you. Items dropped in your path, mud 'accidentally' thrown on to your clothes, babies being handed over... the list is growing and becoming more creative. While you are distracted, a member of the team sets about relieving you of any valuables.

Thieves in major South American cities have been known to impersonate police officers, accusing victims of drug possession and demanding an on-the-spot fine. Presumably similar types of crimes occur throughout South America, but as yet no similar incidents have been reported outside of major cities. Ask police for identification. If you are asked to go to the police station try, whenever possible, to go with a friend.

Drugs

Refuse any offer of drugs – it could be a set-up; sentences are long, jail conditions appalling and chances of help from your own country zero.

Drug use – or abuse – is not as widespread in South America as may be thought. Most cocaine produced is for use in the US and Europe. Drug use is illegal in all South American countries, and if you are found guilty of possessing drugs your embassy will do its bare minimum to support your case. To avoid problems, avoid drugs.

On occasion, in laid-back tourist hang-outs, travellers have been drugged and awoken to find all their personal belongings have disappeared, or worse. Don't accept medicine or drinks from anyone who is even remotely suspicious.

Drug production in South America is widespread. The coca leaf – a harmless plant, with medicinal and cultural uses – is the raw material for cocaine. Production of the leaf is not limited to Colombia. There is widespread cultivation in Peru and Bolivia – where growth of the plant is legal in certain locations – and there is no reason why it couldn't be grown in all other Amazon countries. Any 'traveller' wandering around likely production areas tends to be viewed with suspicion and may well be accused of being an undercover antinarcotics agent. Whatever your claims for being in the area, they may be ignored. Fortunately most coca-leaf production areas are well away from any tourist trails.

The Shining Path and terrorism

Pucallpa in Peru was potentially dangerous during the 1980s when the Shining Path were active, but the organisation's demise has removed the problems. Terrorism and hostage-taking activities in Colombia tend to be well away from the Amazon region.

In the wild

Close encounters of the wild kind

People often worry about a possible encounter with a wild animal, such as a snake, jaguar or caiman. Such an encounter is, in reality, highly unlikely. Most creatures are terrified of humans – we are, after all, their major predator. As a rule, wild animals attack humans only if they are cornered or they think their young are threatened.

If you do encounter a jaguar or other cat it is most likely to be on a trail at night. It is more than tempting to tell you just to sit still and enjoy the privilege. Should you feel threatened, shout, wave your arms around and make as much noise as possible. Do not run away, as the cat may sense fear and give chase, but such attacks are extremely rare.

Among the Amazon's crocodilians, only the black caiman grows big enough to pose a fatal danger to people. This reptile, up to 5.5m long, has largely disappeared from the Amazon, except in remote places far from people. As with snakes, caiman are unlikely to attack unless their nest is threatened. It is wise to keep your distance from the water's edge in areas where large caiman are known to be present. Sandy banks during the nesting season (low water) should be approached carefully as nests are well-camouflaged and the female may be out of sight but lurking somewhere nearby.

Safe jungle walking

Forest trails and paths are usually safe and are well-known by guides, but not all guides remember to give a safety talk. Because of certain dangers, mostly mere inconveniences, there are some simple precautions for safe jungle walking. The basic rules are:

- Do not 'grab' at vegetation to steady yourself; many plants have thorns or spines or harbour hordes of aggressive stinging ants.
- Take care where you step on the trail; it is easy to slip on mud, trip on tree roots or end up standing in a column of army ants if you don't look where you are going. Staying on the trail helps you keep an eye out for potential hazards and minimises your impact on surrounding forest.
- Take plenty of water with you, and on longer walks, a small snack; it is easy to get dehydrated as the humidity, heat and exertion increase perspiration.
- Wear appropriate shoes for the walk; you do not need hiking boots. Some lodges and tour operators supply guests with rubber boots, which are ideal as they keep your feet dry. Old trainers or tennis shoes will get wet and dirty. The soles need grip for muddy paths.
- Wear appropriate clothes and apply insect repellent to exposed body parts before a jungle walk and take some repellent with you. Be assured that mosquitoes will attack whatever bits of you are unprotected.
- Always take a waterproof with you. A sunny day can turn to a tropical deluge in minutes. It is warm rain but out in the open with a slight breeze it can feel chilly, especially on a launch. A poncho is good as it also covers your daypack, camera, etc.
- On jungle walks at night take a torch to avoid roots and puddles. Not only does the light help you see where you are going but it illuminates weird and wonderful nocturnal creatures not usually seen by day. A climber's torch worn on your head is ideal for camping, but walking in the jungle at night it attracts insects to the light beam and you may find a couple of hundred insects buzzing around your face quite disconcerting.

Safe swimming

'I swam in the Amazon!' is a great party line. Indeed, to swim in the famous river is the goal of many visitors. Danger from piranha is much exaggerated, so should not deter the prospective Amazon bather. After all, a swim in the world's biggest river (or one of its tributaries) is the thrill of a lifetime.

There is no danger from piranhas unless you are bleeding or have an open wound. Sting-rays, electric eels and the notorious candiru – which allegedly lodges itself in body orifices – can also be a risk to swimmers. However, these species are rare and do not pose a significant threat.

The two greatest risks of swimming are strong currents and water-borne microbial parasites. Ideally, the current should be a slow crawl, anything near walking pace means the current is too fast for swimming. All rivers should be treated with respect and the Amazon is no exception.

To avoid parasites, do not swim near villages and towns, particularly downstream. Most parasites are orally ingested so if the site is not ideal, try to avoid swallowing river water.

Boat safety

A lot of your time in the Amazon is spent aboard canoes, small boats or ships. You are usually provided with a life-jacket, most often used as a cushion on long canoe rides. A few basic precautions if you're not used to boat travel are:

- When getting into a canoe, make sure only one person boards at a time, that they step into the middle of the canoe and are seated before the next person gets in.
- Once under way, never stand up. You don't want to 'rock the boat', after all! Always have your life-jacket to hand and wear it on open water or in rough weather.
- Upon disembarkation, only one person should get out at a time – and carefully, especially if you are disembarking on to a muddy riverbank or unsteady floating pier.
- When manoeuvring through overhanging vegetation along narrow streams, watch out for projecting branches which, besides poking you in the eye, are home to biting insects, notably ants which end up falling into the boat.

CAUTION Cecropia, a popular host plants for ants, is a riverside plant, so must be avoided on canoe rides to avert a serious ant invasion. In the worst-case scenario, you would have to 'abandon ship' temporarily.

Further reading

Wilson-Howarth, J *Bugs Bites & Bowels: healthy travel,* Cadogan Guides (1995)
Wilson-Howarth, Dr J and Ellis, Dr M *Your Child's Health Abroad: A Manual for Travelling Parents*, Bradt Publications (1998)

Part Two

Wildlife and People

TRIPS
worldwide
YOUR TRAVEL EXPERTS IN
GUYANA & SURINAME
HAVE YOUR TAILOR-MADE
HOLIDAYS ORGANISED BY
SOMEONE WHO HAS BEEN THERE
WE ORGANISE RAINFOREST, WILDLIFE,
BIRDWATCHING, ADVENTURE AND
CULTURAL TOURS OF
GUATEMALA • BELIZE • COSTA RICA
CUBA • DOMINICA • HONDURAS
MEXICO • TRINIDAD & TOBAGO
PHONE: 0117 987 2626
FAX: 0117 987 2627
E-mail: enquiries@trips.demon.co.uk
WWW.trips.demon.co.uk

Natural History 5

'...the greatest evolutionary theatre in the world.'

Michael Goulding, *Amazon: the Flooded Forest*, Partridge Films, 1989

ORIGINS OF THE AMAZON RIVER BASIN

To get a full picture of how the Amazon ecosystem came into being let's look at its history. How were past conditions different? How did all the diversity come about? How long did it take?

Scientists believe that parts of the Amazon are ancient, hardly changed in 100 million years; as the rainforest's living fossils testify. We see evolution's fantastic tapestry, woven from billions of threads: plants, animals, decomposers and all their relationships. The origin of this complexity is in the forest's beginning.

When dinosaurs roamed the earth, over 220 million years ago, a huge river flowed west across what is now South America, into the Pacific. At that time, southern continents were joined, like pieces of a jigsaw, in a super-continent called Gondwanaland.

According to the theory of plate tectonics, continents and ocean floors form gigantic rocky rafts, or plates, that are moved by convection forces in the planet's interior. Sudden earthquakes and dramatic volcanic eruptions mark their boundaries as the plates bump and collide, sliding over, under or around each other. But the plates move extremely slowly. During our lifetime, a continent moves only three metres or so. Yet speed this up, and the landmasses wander and pirouette across the globe.

By about 150 million years ago, South America had become a huge island isolated from neighbouring landmasses. The continent's isolation had profound effects on its fauna. Primitive mammals, notably marsupials and edentates, proceeded to evolve in niches elsewhere occupied by more successful placental mammals. All the marsupials of the Americas are now extinct except opossums, while the last surviving edentates are sloths, armadillos and anteaters.

About 15 million years ago, tectonic movement caused huge eruptions and earthquakes all along the continent's west coast as the Pacific and South American Plates collided. Pushing against each other, the Pacific Plate was forced downwards while the South American Plate crumpled upwards. The Andes began to rise (and continue to do so) and during the Pliocene epoch – between 5.3 and 1.6 million years ago – blocked the westward-flowing river and so created a huge inland lake, the biggest ever. Marine animals were now trapped in a freshwater environment. Some adapted and remain to this day. Hence, the rivers are home to freshwater sting-rays and dolphins, and other animals normally found only in marine environments.

Around 5 million years ago, South America joined North America, forming the Panama Isthmus. Ocean currents changed and climate patterns altered. Placental mammals invaded southwards leading to the extinction of many of the previously isolated primitive mammals. Some 1.6 million years ago, tectonic movement tilted the entire South American Plate, and the river flowed east, in its present direction, into the Atlantic.

Over time the highlands on the basin's edges eroded. As sand and mud collected, the underlying rock sank under the weight and yet more silt piled on the deposits built up over millions of years when the area was an inland lake. Immensely deep alluvial deposits fill the vast network of ancient valleys that comprise the present-day river system – in the Amazon, you're on a pile of mud 4km deep.

The last great geological events to sculpt the lowland landscapes were the ice ages, the most recent of which ended 10,000 years ago. The sea-level was 30m or more lower than today, causing the river to run much faster. Huge torrents cut deep channels in the mud, leaving hills and rises as the sea level dropped. Carved by primordial floods, the high banks your boat sails past are above today's highest flood levels. Beyond the reach of seasonal flooding, the forests on firm ground, or *terra firme* forests, are quite different from the *várzea* forest found in flooded areas.

Geography of the Amazon: flat, flooded and forested

With a shallow gradient along its course, gravity means that the Amazon barely flows. From Iquitos to the mouth, the river drops by a mere 70m, a gradient of 1 in 50,000... basically flat! The entire area's hydrology ultimately depends on snowfall in the Andes.

Sunlight warms lofty peaks. From on high, huge quantities of thawed snow rush downhill on a long journey to the sea causing the lowland river levels to rise dramatically. According to Michael Goulding, author of *Amazon: The Flooded Forest*, about 2% of the Amazon watershed is under water during seasonal floods. A small portion, but it adds habitat variety and hence species diversity.

Water is the forest's life-blood. Rivers annually deposit nutrient-laden silt to fertilise vast lowland areas. The enriched soils can support some agriculture and enhance the growth of natural vegetation. With every season's flood, the flow of the river changes. Where the flow is diverted, the river leaves behind ox-bow lakes and newly formed land. New channels create 'edge' habitat essential for certain wildlife. Strong currents during annual floods or heavy rains scour weed-clogged streams and lakes. The river itself is a natural corridor along which animals migrate, be they fish, birds, or even small mammals, on floating rafts of dislodged vegetation.

Floods speed up erosion and deposition. Without large rocky areas, a lowland river's course is unstable. On the river's outside curve the current runs faster, eroding the bank and eating up to 30m of forest a year. Where the riverbank has collapsed trees lie askew in the river, a tangle of trunks and vines, ready to be swept away by the current. On the inside bend, the current slows, dropping silt, floating vegetation and anything else carried by the water. The inner banks grow, become exposed when waters recede, and new land is created. As the process of erosion and deposition continues, year on year, the meanders of the river make their way downstream, picking sediment up from the outside of one bend and depositing it on the inside of another, further downstream.

The process overall is a complex 'shifting mosaic' of innumerable islands, ox-bow lakes, rivers, streams and sand bars – a wide variety of habitats for plants and animals. The constant change of occasional disturbance through seasonal flooding creates conditions that promote speciation.

Some 2,960km from north to south, the Amazon Basin's outer margins comprise montane forest to the west and dry grasslands to the north and south. The vast, flat interior is mostly covered in dense tropical rainforest across which giant rivers gently wind thousands of miles.

Undiscovered until 1953, the source of the Amazon is high in the Peruvian Andes around 160km from the Pacific. (See box on page 4.) Waters gather and merge until they meet the westernmost major tributary, the Ucayali. About 100km west of Iquitos in Peru, this joins the mainstream, now called the Solimões by Brazilians – and Amazonas by Peruvians. It is then another 3,720km from Iquitos to the mouth at Belém; the world's longest stretch of navigable river.

Soils of the Amazon River Basin

Amazon soils remain largely unsurveyed. But we can make some generalisations. Along lower floodplains so-called inceptisols dominate. These fertile alluvial soils are young, comprising primarily inorganic silt and freshly decayed humus. Regular input of fresh deposits from seasonal flooding supports intensive agriculture without the frequent manuring needed to cultivate soils of unflooded areas.

Older oxisols and utisols dominate the non-flooded Amazon making up three quarters of the soils found in the region. With good drainage, the mineral content of these soils has been washed out or leached, and they are subsequently of limited agricultural value. In extreme cases, when forest cover is removed and compacted, these soils are subject to laterisation, in which the sun bakes the surface into a brick-like substance. Good for making bumpy roads, but not that great for agriculture.

In rainforest, breakdown of vegetative matter is continual and the nutrient cycle is efficient, so there is never much time for soil to accumulate. Heavy rainfall leaches untrapped nutrients and concentrates certain elements, notably iron and aluminium. Although the lush vegetation of the rainforest creates the impression of mineral-rich soils, the success of the ecosystem relies on the efficient recycling of minerals close to the soil's surface.

Consequently the soils of the Amazon risk laterisation and toxification if not carefully managed. Recommended agricultural techniques are small-scale shifting cultivation and agroforestry (crops and trees grown together). Some experts believe oxisols are best utilised for sustainable timber sources and forest products.

Physical measurements of the Amazon river today

Over millions of years, geological and meteorological events laid the foundations for the Amazon's physical characteristics. Here we describe the present-day conditions as background to discuss an abundance and variety of life unequalled on earth.

Flow rate

The current speed depends on the combination of local terrain, flood conditions and recent rainfall. Gravity barely affects flow rate because the terrain is so flat and the current averages just 2–3kph along the river's mainstream. Similar speeds are measured for most lowland rivers. After heavy rains or during floods, flow rates rise to as high as 8-10kph.

Depth

River depth varies greatly due to annual floods. Sand bars shift unpredictably making navigation a nightmare. Even so, the mainstream is deep enough (undredged) for ocean-going luxury liners and cargo ships to sail year-round to Iquitos, where depth varies from 15m to 30m. The river's deepest point, 91m, is near Manaus, where the Rio Negro meets the mainstream. The average depth from Iquitos to the mouth is 36m, according to Captain Todd's measurements made during the 1900 expedition in the gunboat *USS Wilmington*.

Seasonal floods

Due to cycles of snowfall and thaw in the Andes, river levels rise and fall on a seasonal basis throughout the lowlands. Around December, the river begins to rise until it peaks in April or May. At Iquitos, the highest water level is around 6–10m above the lowest and almost double this at Manaus. Peak levels downstream occur some weeks after as the bulge of floodwater takes time to make its way downriver. In June or July, the river subsides until October when it reaches its lowest levels. Then it starts to rise again. Recently the timing of annual floods has been more erratic than was historically the case.

Flooded-forest flora and fauna adapt to yearly inundation. Trees stop photosynthesis. Acacia leaves droop, as though they are wilting. The high-water period is when many trees redirect energy stores to producing blooms and fruits. Rising waters reduce available habitat for arboreal animals. Local population density of animals increases along with the chance of a tree being visited by pollinating and fruit-dispersing animals.

Forest on land permanently above flood levels is called *terra firme* forest. It receives water only through rainfall and flowering seasons for its trees are less predictable.

Silt load

The amount of silt – called the silt load – carried by the Amazon varies enormously. Rivers are categorised by their colour, determined by the type and amount of silt. In the early 1980s, scientist Jacques Cousteau calculated that around 400 million tonnes of silt are discharged from the river's mouth every year. A giant fan-shaped mountain of mud extends 800km from the delta, descending 4,500m (14,764ft) to the floor of the ocean.

Geochemistry of Amazon rivers

The geochemical composition of a river depends on its origin and the types of habitat in its watershed. The types of suspended silt and detritus vary according to its course through the rainforest so the water colour tells you something about the river's chemistry. The Amazon's rivers and lakes are classified into three distinctly different types.

Whitewater

In this case, 'whitewater' has nothing to do with politics or rafting down rapids. Most whitewater rivers (eg: Ucayali and Huallaga) rise in the Andes then flow east through the upper river basin. Heavy silt loads are fed by large quantities of loose rock eroded from the mountains. The Amazon mainstream is classed as whitewater. Despite the name, these rivers are a pale murky yellow-brown, similar to *café au lait*. The water is close to neutral (pH7.0) and contains a high concentration of microbes and inorganic particles. The typical silt load of a whitewater river is 10–20mg/litre. When whitewater rivers flood each year, they renew soil fertility, replenish dried-out rivers and swamps and bring new life to the forest. The characteristic flora of forests flooded by these rivers is termed *várzea*.

Blackwater

Evidently named for its colour, the Rio Negro is the biggest tributary of the Amazon mainstream and the biggest blackwater river. This type of river occurs over vast sandy areas common across northern Amazonia. Sandy soils lack the micro-organisms to break humus down into chemicals. (Humus is mostly decayed plant remains with few inorganic particles.) Heavy rain washes humic matter into

CLOUDFOREST

Oliver Whalley

The vast lowland rainforest of the Amazon Basin is swathed to the west by a band of higher, montane forests on the Andes. These montane cloudforests are often bathed in swirling mists and are an integral part of the regions ecosystem.

Up to an altitude of about 900m the rainforest is similar in appearance and generally considered lowland rainforest; in the western Amazon this rises to an altitude of about 1,700m. From this altitude the forest begins to change. From 900m to 2,000m, lower montane forest dominates before being replaced by upper montane forest between 2,000m and 3,200m. Subalpine or elfin forest reaches from 3,200m to 3,800m before the forests dwindle at the upper limit creating the tree or timber line. It is through the dense cloudforests that the headwaters of the Amazon seep and at times roar in cascading streams and towering waterfalls from the watersheds high in the Andes.

At altitude the forest canopy height drops considerably. In the low montane forest the height of trees is around 25m, whilst trees in hot lowlands reach 60m or more. In the tropics the temperature gradient is between 0.4–0.7°F (0.7–1.3°C) for each 100m rise. This change in temperature and air composition, combined with heavy rainfall, less evaporation, and higher winds, reduces metabolism and growth. The rate of decomposition and the release of nutrients is also slowed down.

There are other changes too; the number of species of insect drops enormously and there is often a reduction in the numbers of bird, amphibian and reptile species. Fruit eaters, scavengers and predators also decline rapidly with altitude. The number of species of omnivores stays approximately the same but there are large increases in the number of species of hummingbird and certain forms of plant life, especially epiphytes like mosses, ferns, lichens, bromeliads and orchids. In cloudforest epiphytes make up about 40% of the total plant biomass. Cloudforest trees are often completely covered in epiphytes, with as many as 50 different orchid species on a single tree.

High montane forest, although unsuitable for many mammals like monkeys, is home to endangered mammals like the spectacled bear and the very rare mountain tapir. The cloudforest with its dense ecology is an essential part of the mountain ecosystem, the loss of which can create devastating changes. Approximately 95% of annual rainfall is detained temporarily in a complete cloudforest watershed. This water-detaining ability makes it essential for the regulation of water, especially during the drier seasons. Acting like a sponge, it sustains both itself and that below, allowing water to trickle through, and preventing flash flooding, severe erosion and landslides. With its thick complex of roots and humus it literally holds soils to the steep slopes thus preventing them slipping away under the assaults of pelting rain, high winds and the tremors or quakes of the growing Andes. These rare magical forests are not only fragile but irreplaceable. Already Ecuador has less than 1% of its original Pacific watershed forest and Brazil less than 10% of its southeast Atlantic coastal forest.

rivers, staining water blackish or a very dark brown – like dark tea. The colour derives from dissolved plant compounds of tannins, caffeines and phenols. The acidity of blackwater rivers (pH4–5) limits microbial activity and growth of aquatic flora and fauna, notably mosquito larvae. Their silt load (20–30mg/litre) is about twice that of whitewater rivers. The name *igapo* is given to flooded forest along blackwater rivers and lakes.

Clearwater

This third type of river has very low levels of humic matter, a tenth that of blackwater rivers. Most clearwater rivers rise in the Brazilian highlands (Xingu, Tapajós, Tocantins). Despite their often murky appearance, clearwater rivers have the least silt and humus because all the movable material in these mountains was eroded long ago. They vary from acidic to alkaline (pH4.5–7.8). Vegetation along clearwater rivers is of highly variable composition.

Meetings of the waters

The difference between river colours, most obvious when they meet, creates an impressive natural phenomenon. At the 'meeting of the waters', the two rivers maintain their independence, preferring to flow side-by-side yet sharing the same channel. To begin with the only mixing is along the meeting edge as the different current speeds create eddies and swirls to merge the waters of different densities. The most spectacular 'meeting of the waters' is close to Manaus where the Rio Negro, the largest blackwater river, flows into the mainstream. More modest meetings of waters occur locally throughout the Amazon Basin and are fairly common.

Geology of the Amazon

Deep sediments cover most surface rock in the lowland floodplains. Significant rises begin only in the Andean foothills, around 300km west of Iquitos. From the east the broad basin stretches north to Venezuela and Colombia and south to the Andean foothills of Bolivia. Past the confluences of the Negro and Madeira with the mainstream, the floodplain narrows like an hour-glass on its side until it is only 100km across. Constricting the plain are two massive ancient rock formations, the Guyana (or Orinoco) Shield to the north and the Brazilian Shield to the south. The floodplain widens again toward the mouth.

Surrounded by riches

As the rapacious Spaniards discovered, El Dorado is a myth. But throughout the Andes of South America and in the highlands of Brazil and Guiana is wealth beyond even the greediest conquistador's imagining. In addition to gold and silver are such strategic metals as tungsten, molybdenum and uranium. Gemstones mined in the area include emeralds (for which Colombia is world famous), sapphires, topaz, tourmaline and the lesser-known tanzanite, citrine, rubellite, andalusite and heliodor. Semi-precious stones include amethyst, aquamarine, opal, lapis lazuli, agate, malachite and crystalline quartz.

The glamour of jewels need not outshine humbler minerals and ores that are of greater value to national economies. Peru is a major world producer of copper. Brazil has the world's biggest iron ore deposits, and important reserves of aluminium, tin and gypsum. Huge projects are under way, or planned, to mine and process ores for export. Ecuador's Oriente is oil-rich but exploitable metal reserves are lacking. Colombia's mineral wealth is concentrated in the highlands and few attempts at oil exploration have been conducted in its portion of Amazonia.

AMAZON FLORA: THE SECRET LIFE OF AMAZON PLANTS

Virtually all life depends on green plants. With their leaves plants harvest the energy in sunlight to power photosynthetic reactions. Inside leaf cells, molecular alchemical factories transform light, air, water and earth into living matter. Animals in turn depend on plants for energy from food and life-giving oxygen.

Warmth, strong light and lots of water speed up photosynthesis in rainforests making them extremely productive. One square metre produces up to 3.5kg of living material (dry weight) per year – the most of any ecosystem except coral reef. This figure – technically 3,500g/m^2/year – is the ecosystem's productivity. Biomass is the total weight of living matter in a given area. In rainforest mean biomass is 45kg/m^2, the highest of any habitat. Tropical forests contribute 29% to the world's primary production, holding over half the world's biomass, despite covering less than 5% of its area.

Trees

Trees are the foundation of the rainforest as we experience it. Trunks, stems, branches, leaves, fruits and roots are all micro-habitats for animals and smaller plants. On a broader scale, the rainforest absorbs and releases so much water, it determines the amount of rainfall – one reason to suspect deforestation as a cause of changes in weather patterns.

Rainforest trees need specific environmental conditions: year-round high temperatures and heavy rainfall. Floristic compositions of forests are based on terrain and the geochemistry of rivers. Of the three main biomes, *terra firme* has the

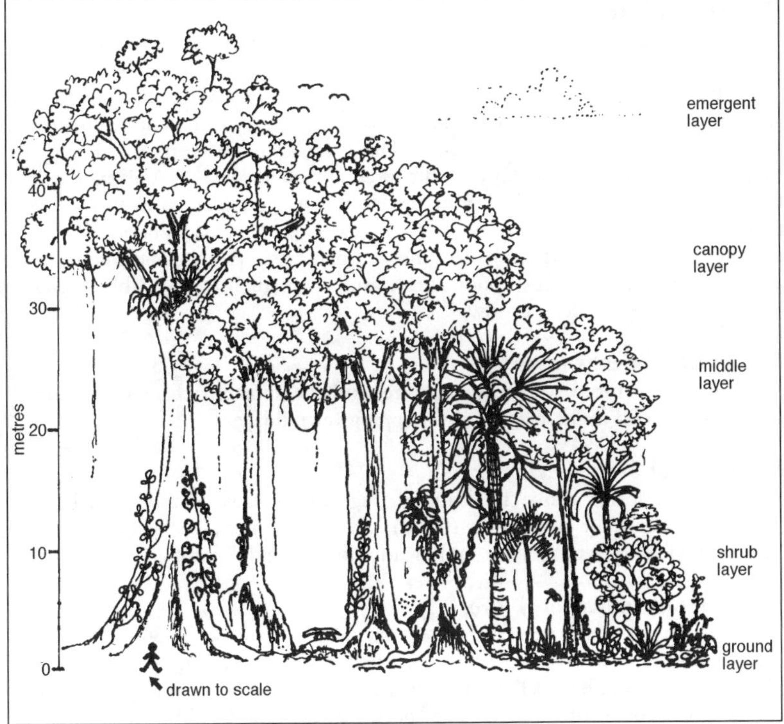

most species, although a layman would have trouble telling the difference from *várzea* or *igapo*. Scientists believe the biodiversity of *terra firme* is highest in northwestern Amazonia – the most species-rich region in the world.

Structure and function, diversity and design

When you walk through rainforest you feel overwhelmed by the abundance of plant life. At least 50,000 woody plants are recorded from the Amazon, around a fifth of all those known. Indeed, around Cuyabeno, Ecuador, *terra firme* rainforest harbours the world's greatest variety of trees, with over 100 species per 0.4ha – at least ten times the variety found in an equal area of temperate forest.

Most rainforest trees are broad-leafed evergreens that shed leaves continually, a few at a time. Groups not found in temperate forests, like palms and acacias, add to the variety. Yet the strikingly similar appearance of many rainforest trees hides their true diversity. Remember when you walk along forest trails away from rivers, you pass through *várzea* or *igapo* (floodplain forest) to *terra firme* (upland forest), but because of the trees' similarity the change seems imperceptible. Typical trees have straight trunks and smooth grey-to-brown bark splotched with moss and lichen. Leaf structure is also remarkably invariable – dark and narrow, with pointed 'drip-tips' and a waxy surface to help heavy rain run off easily, inhibiting colonisation by fungi and epiphytes.

Here and there, huge broad crowns of trees called 'emergents' rise above the canopy. Few have very thick trunks. Instead, to support themselves in thin soil too shallow for a tap root, forest giants have stabilising flared bases and buttress roots. Impressive root systems branch out for great distances. Extensive roots also increase the area available for absorption of nutrients from the leaf litter on the rainforest floor.

Plenty amid starvation

Look under the mat of rainforest litter and you find bare clay. Termites, fungi, algae, insects and worms rapidly decompose the thin layer of rotting leaves. Dead vegetation decomposes 60 times faster than in temperate coniferous forests. Minerals and nutrients are so quickly incorporated into plants that most organic matter is locked up in living organisms. This is how infertile tropical soils support plenty of growth. So effectively does the forest absorb nutrients that plants use 98% of the phosphate dissolved in rain before the water reaches the forest floor. Innovative ways of maximising nutrient use have evolved. Certain kinds of symbiotic fungi (mycorrhizae) surround and penetrate epiphyte and tree roots to greatly increase the root absorption area. Nitrogen-fixing bacteria enable acacias to thrive in nitrogen-deficient soils.

Life in the forest's layers

Trees form the forest's vertical structure, and the apparent chaos of growth is actually organised in three or five overlapping vertical layers.

Emergent (or overstorey) layer

Forest giants tower above the canopy. Fig (*Ficus*), teak (*Tectona*), mahogany (*Swietiana*), kapok or silk-cotton (*Ceiba*) and many others reach 40m or more. Epiphytes cloak lower branches, and greatly add to floral diversity.

Middle (or closed-canopy) layer

These uniform-looking trees form the main canopy, growing 12–30m tall. This is the site of highest biodiversity, where over 90% of the forest's photosynthesis takes place. Canopy trees have tall, narrow crowns, to efficiently occupy space between each other. Crowns of the same tree species at the same height never overlap or

CLASSIFICATION

Biologists have created a strict set of rules to identify organisms precisely. This is called classification or taxonomy and an understanding of its principles will help clarify the descriptions in this book.

The first division, called a kingdom, is very broadly defined, for instance, animal, plant or fungi. Each subsequent division then becomes more precisely defined, until the organism is identified: this is called the species. Here are two simplified examples from the Amazon region.

Southern two-toed sloth

Kingdom:	Animalia
Phylum:	Chordata
Class:	Mammalia
Order:	Edentata
Family:	Bradypodidae
Subfamily:	Megalonychidae
Genus:	*Choloepus*
Species:	*didactylus*

Anaconda, or water boa

Kingdom:	Animalia
Phylum:	Chordata
Class:	Reptilia
Order:	Squamata
Famioly:	Boidae
Subfamily:	N/a
Genus:	*Eunectes*
Species:	*murinus*

Given in Latin, the universal language of biologists, only the genus (plural: genera) and species are quoted. This constitutes the 'scientific name' and is written in italics. The genus name always begins in upper case, while the species name is written entirely in lower case. If the genus is known, but not the species, it will be written thus: *Choloepus* sp, or if the description includes several members of the same genus (congeners), it will be written: *Choloepus* spp.

Some species are divided into subspecies or races. Often these groups have been separated for long periods, perhaps by geographical barriers, and evolution has changed, say, their colour. In this instance, the subspecies name is written after the species name.

cover each other, an arrangement called 'crown shyness'.

Most amazing of all 'trees' is the strangler fig (*Ficus americana*). Seeds dropped by frugivorous birds germinate on a branch. From the seedling, shoots grow out and around the main trunk of a host tree. Ever-tightening, these tendrils encircle the trunk, cutting into the bark, and block vital cellular water channels. Doomed, the victim is eventually enshrouded under tightly woven roots and stems. After several years the host tree dies and decays leaving behind the shell of the living fig tree. This allows the fig to grow to canopy level much quicker than if it had to wait for the light and warmth created by a forest gap. According to Forsyth and Miyata, in *Tropical Nature*, the strangler fig is not all bad. Once grown, its maze of tangled roots and trunk crevices offer shelter for a wide variety of lizards and insects, especially the wasps *Polistes* and *Stelopolybia*. Indeed, the maligned strangler (subgenus *Urostigma*) is closely related to the common and popular houseplant, weeping fig (*F. benjamina*).

Tall palm and acacia crowns contribute to this level. Around 900 palm species are described from the lowland rainforest. The common stilt palm or *cashapona* (*Socratea exorrhiza*) has stilt roots to help support it in the thin soil. The moriche palm (*Mauritia flexuosa*), called the 'Tree of Life' by Alexander von Humboldt, has among the largest leaves of any plant that can be put to a wide variety of uses. The plant's fruits are edible, consumed fresh or as a juice, and the petiole is used to make mats and candles. Other palms important for income or subsistence include thatch palm (*Lepidocaryum tessmannii*), fibre palm or *chambira* (*Astrocaryum chambira*) and heart palm or *chonta* (*Euterpe* spp).

Understorey (or shrub layer)

At this level widely spaced treelets and shrubs reach upward from one to six metres. In forest undamaged by axe or saw, understorey plant growth is sparse. Small palms include the commercially valuable ivory palm (*Phytelephas macrocarpa*) and others with edible fruits (such as several *Astrocaryum* spp). Tree-ferns (*Cyathea* sp) and cycads (*Cycas circinalis*) also comprise this layer.

Ground level

In mature forest, dense closed canopy cuts off most light – up to 98% of it – so only shade-tolerant herbs, ferns, tree seedlings and fungi grow at ground level. Many herbs have long, narrow, often variegated leaves. Look for the beautifully variegated *Calathea* and *Caladium*, members of the arum family and popular as houseplants. Some terrestrial arums provide edible corms, notably arrowroot (*Maranta* spp), used in cooking as a natural thickener. The corm of the huge, pale green elephant's ear (*Xanthosoma* spp) is made into a taro-like flour.

Piper is a genus of low-growing shrubs with pointed, oval, shiny leaves with four parallel veins and swollen nodes (where the leaf meets the stem). It's among the most diverse plant genera, with over 1,000 species described, many from the Amazon. Mushrooms or *hongo* come in all shapes and sizes from classically-shaped *Agaricus* to jelly-like forms, of which tree-ear (*Auricularia* spp) is common. Selaginella and club-moss (*Lycopodium cernuum*) are abundant ground-dwelling mosses.

Forest edges and gaps

Where light is abundant, layered growth breaks down; creating 'edge habitat' – home to numerous specialised plants and animals.

Related to beans (family *Fabaceae*), acacias and mimosas are trees 4.5–30m tall, dominant along rivers and lake edges. Acacias often have elaborate red-orange flowers and many have large, attractive seed pods, like giant beans. The scarlet-flowered coral tree (*Erythrina* spp) has hard, red-and-black, poisonous seeds used in native handicrafts, such as necklaces, bracelets and earrings. A most unusual long, thin fruit is produced by the ice-cream bean tree (*Inga* spp), which grows to 15m or more. Break open the pod to find a delicious white flesh. It's light, almost fluffy, and edible fresh; or can be used as a flavouring in, you guessed it, ice-cream.

While you can sip away at an orange juice and champagne Mimosa cocktail, a botanist will tell you there are hundreds of different kinds of mimosa endemic to the Amazon. Indeed, related mimosas grow diverse in form. Some species are small and shrubby, while others grow to sizeable trees up to 10m high. The globular yellow or creamy-white flower sprays produced by mimosas – the inspiration for the cocktail – are one way to tell a mimosa from the closely related acacias. Another distinction is that mimosas usually have delicate, feathery leaves. Their pods are generally small and fragile. Retama (*Cassia* spp) is an unmistakable yellow-flowered legume with large oval leaflets, and very common along slow-moving whitewater rivers. Because legumes tend to have low levels of phytotoxins, many of these trees and shrubs are defended with large sharp thorns, home to their second line of defence: hordes of stinging ants. Another line of defence is exhibited by the rather sensitive shrubby plant *Mimosa pudica* which has leaves that close when touched.

THE TREES THAT DEFIED TIME

A recent study has revealed that the trees of the Amazon are much older than anyone previously believed, with some growing for at least 1,400 years. Using carbon-dating techniques, a team from the University of California in Santa Barbara found that most of the trees felled in an area near Manaus were 500 to 600 years old, with a couple exceeding 1,000 years.

Scientists believe the discovery could have implications for forest management. Armed with this knowledge, loggers could leave the older slower-growing species behind to maintain the canopy, harvesting only the faster-growing ones.

Reaching heights of 20m, the cecropia or *cetico* (several species in Cecropiaceae) is one of the commonest trees of river edges. Easy to recognise, it has large five-lobed leaves, a greyish stem and a noticeable absence of epiphytes. It too gives food and shelter to aggressive stinging ants inside its stems.

Edge habitat is spectacular for sheer exuberance of growth and much closer to our idea of 'jungle'. On the flood plains, well-lit glades are home to the *Heliconia,* an impressive jungle plant with huge leaves similar to those of banana trees. The flowers are coloured bright red and yellow and are similar in shape to crabs' claws, giving rise to the more popular name of crab-claws. The flowers attract birds and bats, making the plant an essential part of the edge habitat ecosystem.

Multiple roles for animal players

Animals inhabit ecological niches corresponding to the layered forest structure.

Life in emergent tree crowns consists mainly of birds and insects. Swifts and swallows race through the air in pursuit of insects straying too high above the canopy. Small primates are active at night, as raptors prey on them by day.

Site of highest biodiversity, the canopy harbours birds, mammals and reptiles. Tiny poison-dart frogs inhabit tree-holes and bromeliad tanks. Plants provide food and shelter for animals who in turn help the plants to reproduce. Rodents, bats, hummingbirds and insects pollinate flowers. A unique characteristic of trees in the tropics is the production of tough blossoms directly from the trunk. By not placing flowers on the end of branches high up in the canopy, *cauliflory* makes it easier for pollinating mammals and birds to reach the fruit, which helps seed dispersal.

In the canopy's shade, small arboreal carnivores such as the ocelot and margay prowl thick branches preying on sloths, monkeys and rodents. This habitat is ideal for tree-dwelling snakes hunting camouflaged tree-frogs.

Ground-dwelling forest mammals have compact bodies to help them move through tangled undergrowth. Mice, shrews, tapir, deer and peccary are hunted by jaguar and puma on the forest floor. Anteaters flourish on the abundance of ants and termites while, in the soil and leaf litter, fungi and a host of invertebrates quickly decompose organic matter to provide vital nutrients to fast-growing vegetation.

Below the canopy, lianas, bark, branches, leaves of certain shrubs and tiny twigs are colonised by opportunistic shade-tolerant miniature ferns, along with mosses, lichens, algae and other simple plants. Within this mini-habitat live detritus-feeding micro-animals: isopods, springtails, silverfish, millipedes and earth-dwelling oribatid mites. They break down a lot of dead plant matter and in turn are hunted by micro-predators: centipedes, hunting spiders, pseudoscorpions and predatory mites. Non-arthropod fauna are there too: tiny worms, nematodes and minute molluscs.

Epiphytes: living the high life

Among the treetops there is enough light to allow smaller plants to grow – ideal habitat for epiphytes (wrongly called 'air plants'). Incessantly reaching for light above gloomy lower layers, epiphytes perch on tree limbs but are not parasitic. Rooted in soil accumulated on branches or crevices, they take all their nutrients from rainwater, leaf litter, and dead microbes and insects. Epiphytes depend on their host tree to raise themselves to canopy height but do not directly harm it. Yet, they sometimes festoon boughs so heavily that their weight is up to one third of the tree's.

Although the 'high life' has its advantages, things are not that easy. Epiphytes must withstand the rigours of life in the treetops – the dangers of desiccation from winds and hot sun, and fierce competition for space among the branches.

Among the higher plants (ie: those having a vascular system with specialised water transport cells), the biggest epiphytes are bromeliads and arum lilies. In total some 28,000 higher plants are epiphytes including orchids, philodendrons, peperomias, forest cacti and ferns.

Smaller, more primitive inhabitants (lower, non-vascular plants) cram the remaining space. Velvet-green moss carpets every surface, and crusty lichens and primitive algae encrust branches and tree-trunks. Some of these, called epiphylls, live only on the leaves of bigger plants. Many lower plants can tolerate complete drying out.

Bromeliads: aerial aquariums

High in the branches of trees you notice the most conspicuous epiphytes: bromeliads. Often growing large enough to obscure the host tree's branches, bromeliads produce spear-like blossoms and some can be cultivated. Bromeliads are easy to spot with leaves clearly arranged in a rosette. The bright green, waxy, strap-like leaves are often lined with thorns along the edges. Also called 'vase' plants, the Bromeliaceae family includes the pineapple. To mimic how rain falls in nature, gardeners pour water into the central vase-like water reservoir.

In the biggest specimens the vase holds as much as eight litres. This aerial mini-aquarium supports water ferns, algae and microscopic plants. They in turn are grazed by larvae of aquatic insects, food for small arboreal frogs who depend on bromeliads for a place to hide, mate and raise tadpoles. Sometimes you will find a poison-dart frog within a bromeliad.

Being epiphytes, bromeliads do not actually damage the host tree but the weight of the plant can indirectly cause damage. After heavy rain, water accumulates in the vases of huge bromeliads and the extra strain causes branches to break and even trees to fall.

Orchids: evolution's sculptures

Orchids or *orquídeas* are best known for their blooms. Their exquisite forms, colours and wonderful fragrance seemed mysterious to early botanists. Today we know their beauty results from intricate relationships with pollinating insects. The insect is often a small euglossine bee, but some orchids have intricate pollination relationships with wasps, beetles, butterflies, flies or even birds.

To prevent access by the wrong insect, flowers often have traps and passages. The insect must often negotiate a veritable obstacle course before it fertilises the flower. Each flower uses a unique method to attract the insect and to ensure pollen is placed on its body. Some orchids provide nectar or extra pollen to persuade their pollinators to make the effort, but the most interesting species, at least from an evolutionary view, offer no reward but rather trick the insect into pollination.

To be pollinated, orchids deceive the male insect. An orchid mimics the female bee in size, shape and colour pattern; even its perfume smells like her pheromone.

So convincing is the deception, the male bee buzzes from flower to flower in futile attempts to mate. Over time orchids have evolved to mimic perfectly the female insect. In this way, tight bonds have evolved between orchids and insects.

With hot sun and drying winds, orchids are in constant danger of drying out so have unique structures called *pseudobulbs* to help them conserve water. In addition to these swollen leaf bases, their thick, waxy leaves minimise evaporative water loss. White, light-resistant roots affix the plant to branches and absorb nutrients from dripping rain. On a cellular and molecular level, orchids are rather like cacti. Like those of their prickly cousins, the leaf pores of orchids close during the day to reduce evaporation.

Visitors to the lowland rainforests often expect trees to be adorned with thousands of brightly coloured orchids. In reality, they are not easily visible from the ground. Most rainforest orchids grow on branches in the middle and upper canopy, high up and hidden by dense vegetation. Only a few flower at any one time, so we see mostly leaves. The truth is that orchids are not very diverse in lowland rainforests. Only 125 kinds have been found around Iquitos. Orchids are most diverse in moist upland forest commonly called *cloudforest* which has ideal conditions for them.

From a conservation perspective, orchids are among the most threatened plants. Epiphyte species tend to be rare and orchids are no exception. Their beauty has meant that collectors have pushed populations to extinction. The problem has reduced slightly as the trade in wild botanicals is controlled but persistent habitat destruction continues to threaten orchids.

Commercially valuable ornamentals from Amazonia include *Cattleya*, *Laelia*, *Odontoglossum*, *Miltonia*, *Cymbidium*, *Oncidium*, *Epidendrum* and *Maxillaria*. An important non-ornamental is vanilla (*Vanilla planifolia*), cultivated for its aromatic pods.

Ferns: graceful simplicity

Some ferns grow as epiphytes, others are soil-bound at ground level and some are flexible enough to not mind either spot. Familiar as house plants and cultivated by interior designers who love their graceful feather-like leaves, ferns do not have flowers.

Because their reproductive cells need free water during the crucial fertilisation phase, they are less restricted in moist tropical rainforests than in dryer habitats.

Familiar to indoor gardeners is the terrestrial maidenhair fern (*Adiantum capillus-veneris*). Notable for its thin deltoid leaves and wiry black stems, it is used by natives for a variety of purposes including mosquito repellent. Bird's nest fern (*Aspelenium nidus*) has the form of a bromeliad but without the vase to hold water.

Tree-ferns (*Cyathea* spp) are puny compared with real trees. Their dignity arises instead from an immensely long lineage as 'living fossils', relics from the age of the dinosaurs. A botanical curiosity, they are more fern than tree, their crown of typically fern-like leaves supported by a tall, black stem about 3m high, thick as a man's wrist and covered in coarse black hairs. Over a thousand species are known from tropical areas around the world.

Other epiphytes

Other vascular epiphytic plants include philodendrons and monsteras, several of which are cultivated. You can recognise these plants by their heart-shaped, leathery leaves, climbing stems and long, stringy roots dangling down to the forest floor. Monsteras, also known as Swiss cheese plants because of the holes in their deeply divided leaves, have a dark and a light side. When growing on the forest floor, they prefer the darkest places, such as between the flat buttresses of tall rainforest giants which are ideal for providing support as the plant grows upwards.

Arum lilies are not climbers but they grow to huge sizes. Their shiny, dark-green, arrowhead-shaped leaves can grow to a length of 2m. The flowers are white or yellow, and unmistakable with a single petal or 'spathe' curved around the fleshy, finger-like head of pollen-bearing flowers. Arums (family Araceae) are a highly diverse and numerous group and many are raised as houseplants. As you might expect with epiphytic plants, many arum lilies are found in trees. However, because many tolerate low light, another place to look for these plants is on the forest floor where they are quite common, often being found along jungle trails.

Lianas and vines: living walkways

As we have seen, epiphytes live entirely *on* other plants. In contrast, ground-rooted vines and lianas get their nutrients from the thin forest soil. Rather than get to a high spot by chance distribution of seeds in the manner of epiphytes, lianas and vines germinate close by taller plants, choosing to grow up them.

These plants add much to the forest's botanical diversity and interest. They serve to physically connect trees, providing living walkways and highways for ants, caterpillars and arboreal mammals. You will often see a trail of leaf-cutter ants disappearing up a liana high into the canopy. On the other hand, their dense growth at forest edges impedes larger animals on the ground, including humans!

Lianas

Like ropes entangling the masts of some fantastic sailing ship, knotted stems straggle up thick trees and vanish high into the canopy. These are the stems of lianas, woody plants that grow up into the canopy but choose to cheat in the race for light. To avoid expending energy on growing a huge trunk of their own, lianas hitch a ride upwards on new trees growing in forest gaps or work their way up the trunks of existing trees. Large trees thus provide habitat for lianas and give them access to brighter levels. Lianas grow in all types of forest, living for over a hundred years in some cases, and develop intricate networks across the rainforest canopy. Woody lianas can reach a length of over 900m, trailing over acres of trees.

A liana can literally be the downfall of a tree as the weight of the plant, with its matrix of interconnections with other trees, spreads the stresses and strains of swaying action across several trees. When one tree falls, connections between lianas may also pull down others. In deep *terra firme* forest, some lianas grow to be as big as trees and are strong enough to support a person's weight; Tarzan swings on lianas, not vines.

Yet even Lord Greystoke probably couldn't count all the types of liana, with over 15,000 in the Amazon, many of which are distinguished only by flowers or leaves hidden from sight in the canopy. Some, including the water vines (*Doliocarpus* spp, *Pinzona coriacea*), contain water within their hollow stem. But drink with caution – a similar liquid is used in curare, a paste used for poison on the darts of blowpipes. The spirit vine, vine of the soul or *ayahuasca* (*Banisteriopsis* spp), is widely used in religious ceremonies because of its powerful hallucinogenic properties.

Growth forms vary from slender stems to massive trunks in the shape of a simple cylinder or with helical twists, or two or three plaited together. Monkey ladder (*Bauhinia guianensis*), which grows in *várzea* forests, has a flattened wavy stem. A few lianas have protective thorns or spines, while others have hooks and suction cups on the end of long thin exploratory shoots to get a firm hold on nearby trunks and branches. Inevitably, some trees have evolved a defence. The smooth bark and frequent shedding of bark by such trees as the holy stick (*Bursera*) and *Terminalia* are believed to inhibit liana growth as well as epiphyte colonisation.

Vines

Some 90% of vines are tropical. In the Amazon these fast-growing plants are generally restricted to high light areas around forest edges. They have thin, spindly, often thorny stems and most are short-lived. They drape trees and shrubs with a mass of green, enveloping river banks and forest glades. Missionaries believed the passiflora blooms of the passion flower symbolised Christ's Passion, confirming the Lord's blessing on their New World endeavours. Several passiflora or *granadilla* (*P. edulis*) have edible fruits used to make soft drinks.

Cissus, with three-lobed leaves and sprawling tendrils, is a true vine (grape family, Vitaceae), but relatively poor in species. Morning glories (Convolvulaceae) grow fast, with papery, heart-shaped leaves. Delicate trumpet-shaped flowers open early in the day, attracting bees for a frenzy of nectar-feeding and pollination. It's all over in just one glorious morning. Of the many commercially important vines, one is the *camote* or sweet potato (*Ipomoea batatas*). Related to cleavers (family Rubiaceae), the *uña de gato* or cat's claw (*Uncaria* spp) shows promising medicinal properties. It, along with several other vines, is becoming rare around towns and cities due to over-collecting. Another important family of vines is the Cucurbitaceae or cucumbers. Amazon cucs don't give rise to anything like the familiar vegetables we see in our supermarkets, and wild cucumbers are small, bitter, and in some cases poisonous.

Floating meadows and water plants

Water plants form an integral part of the unique floating meadows of the Amazon, providing food for fish, arthropods and the world's only herbivorous aquatic mammal, the manatee. Underwater roots shelter small fish, amphibians, crustaceans and molluscs. Above-water vegetation supports arthropods and other invertebrates, in turn sustenance for vertebrate predators.

Water plants quickly colonise ox-bow lakes and slow-flowing rivers. This process is even faster if manatee are absent. Flood-tolerant *carricillo* (*Olyra latifolia*) cane first takes over, accompanied by forage grasses (*Paspalum* sp, *Eleusine indica*). If floods do not dislodge floating vegetation, it remains and eventually claims the waterway for the forest.

Only a handful of aquatic plant species are abundant, notably water hyacinth (*Eichhornia crasippes, E azurea*) and water lettuce (*Pistia stratiotes*). The mosquito fern (*Azolla*) has pairs of simple leaves, only 1mm wide, the smallest leaves of any plant. In the mainstream's lower reaches, water chestnut (*Montrichardia arborescens*) is common along sluggish *igapo* rivers. This arum, with typically arrowhead-shaped leaves, grows on a tall, stout stalk with a huge, edible, pineapple-like spadix.

Giant water lily

The Amazon or Victoria water lily (*Victoria amazonica*, previously named *V. regia*) is the mother of all water lilies. In permanent *várzea* swamp, the pads grow up to two metres across. Blackwater lilies, although impressive, are smaller, usually no more than half the size.

The pad's underside and the stalk bristle with large spines to deter manatees and herbivorous fish. Its network of supporting ribs is said to have inspired the design of the Crystal Palace for London's Great Exhibition in 1851.

This water lily's sordid sex life involves bribery and kidnapping, perhaps justified as 'crimes of passion' as they ensure cross-fertilisation. White melon-sized flowers open in the evening, exuding a strong perfume. Nectar bribes scarab beetles to enter and feed within the flower. During the feast, pollen adheres to their bodies, sticky from the sweet nectar. With the beetles inside, the flower closes, kidnapping the beetle overnight.

Once pollinated, the flower turns purple and loses its scent. Next morning the flower opens again and the freed scarabs fly to white first-day flowers and continue the process of cross-pollination. Both organisms benefit. The beetle has a meal and secure home for the night and the lily gets pollinated.

Ecology of forest gaps and river edges

To understand rainforest biodiversity it is important to understand the significance of forest gaps and their role as one of the dominant evolution-promoting ecological phenomena. What is a forest gap? How are gaps made? How do competing plants fill gap space? What are the important evolutionary forces at work in gaps?

It seems esoteric, but gap ecology is useful to forestry managers. It provides models of how to reclaim damaged habitat using suitable plants, and offers guidance on how to optimise harvests of lumber or other forest products. During your visit to rainforest, look at gaps and forest edges in various states of disturbance and notice how they differ from mature forest. Nature repairs this natural and man-made damage with techniques evolved over aeons.

How gaps are made

When a large tree falls, it tears a hole in the surrounding forest. Dozens of other trees often fall along with it – dragged down by entwined lianas. Even without human interference, trees inevitably fall from old age, lightning, rotten branches and the domino effect of a downed tree.

When a gap is made, light increases dramatically. Shady areas are suddenly illuminated, along with plants used to the dark forest floor. Cool, damp conditions are replaced by a warmer, drier micro-climate. Vegetation decay from existing leaf

SEED DISPERSAL

Forsyth and Miyata in *Tropical Nature: Life and Death in the Rainforests of Central and South America* unravel the complexities of seed dispersal ecology, pointing out that seed dispersal serves a number of functions; it allows the seedling to avoid competition with the parent and its other seeds; it moves the seed away from predators and disease that may be lurking near the adult plant; and, of course, dispersal can get the seed to a gap – optimum conditions for successful germination and growth.

As they do for pollination, many forest plants, especially with big seeds, rely on animals for seed dispersal. This is where fruits come in. Red fruits, which are often small-seeded, tend to attract birds, while mammals go for larger-seeded green or yellow fruits. By tempting highly mobile monkeys and birds to eat the seeds, the plants ensure maximum dispersal distance for their progeny. Better still, habitat preferences of many animals ensures seeds are more likely to be dropped in an environment similar to that which favoured the parent's growth.

A tree may depend on more than a few species for dispersal of its seeds. In western Ecuador, 23 bird species were counted eating fruits of a single *Castilla* tree. Animals disperse seeds for about half of all rainforest trees.

litter speeds up and releases nutrients. Seeds germinate and trees regenerate. Almost immediately, the forest begins to reclaim the open space. Taking place in an area previously occupied by other plant communities, this process is called 'secondary succession'.

How gaps are filled

With the increase in warmth and sunlight, dormant saplings spring to life. Without the light and warmth of forest gaps, seed energy raises baby trees only a short way. The energy required for them to attain canopy height depends on micro-climate change caused by forest openings.

Gaps create niches occupied by different plants. Early on, the gap is dominated by one or two types of short-lived trees. Vines, herbs, grasses and pioneer shrubs also colonise, their seeds rapidly introduced into the area by bats and birds.

After ten years or so this community is replaced by another distinctive tree flora of five to ten species. Their seeds, often brought in by rodents and squirrels, lie dormant in the litter until a gap appears. These trees are short and are unable to close the gap in the canopy. After two or three decades, they are outgrown by slower-growing but taller ones. Alive for 100 years or more, these eventually die. By this time more large trees have established themselves, with attendant lianas and epiphytes, to finally repair the gap created so long ago. Succession is complete and the gap becomes mature, high-diversity forest.

Old-growth rainforest was previously thought of as a balanced, steady-state ecosystem. A more accurate picture is provided by the shifting mosaic model, wherein the forest consists of various gaps of different size, stage of regeneration and species composition.

The road to recovery

If not disturbed too extensively, woodland recovers fully, although complete restoration takes time. Only specially adapted organisms can take advantage of changed conditions caused by gaps in the forest. Gap reclamation involves a 'competitive lottery' for space. The properties of a tree's seeds and an element of luck determine how and where it will end up. Small, widely distributed seeds (eg: wind or bird dispersed) are specialised to arrive quickly in large gaps, while large seeds (mammal dispersed) tend to be moved shorter distances and end up in smaller gaps, which are more common than big gaps. Variation of seed dispersal ability prevents overall dominance by just a few species. The 'lottery' winners are those to arrive first. But although they may be first off the line, it is the plants with the stamina to climb up to the canopy that are the eventual victors.

At any one time, new gaps cover about 2% of the tropical rainforest. Between 60 and 140 years pass before a falling tree opens up new space at a given spot, making rainforest a mosaic patchwork in various stages of regrowth. A patch's age determines its successional stage and species composition. Light-loving plants do well in the new gaps whereas gap-intolerant plants bide their time and do best in older gaps. Forests in various stages of succession constitute a quarter of lowland rainforest.

Reclaiming the beaches

Besides tree falls, water action intermittently disturbs the forest ecosystem. The various forces of water – rain, rivers, floods and erosion – all alter forest structure. Water creates unique habitats, adding to biodiversity. Waterbodies are reclaimed by the forest (see *Floating meadows*, page 113), beginning with primary succession, where colonisation begins on new land. A similar scenario occurs on the beaches. On bare beaches, fast-growing tessaria trees (*Tessaria integrifolia*) quickly create an

THE BIODIVERSITY CRISIS

Protecting the precious biodiversity of the planet is often cited as the reason for creating national parks, defending ecologically sensitive areas under threat. While it is easy to have sympathies for cute-looking animals and beautiful birds, why should we care about the destruction of trees, insects and other animals that in the vast majority of cases we will never see? It is almost certain that the biodiversity of the rainforest holds cures for current illnesses of the world and doubtless ones that have not yet evolved.

E O Wilson of Harvard University explains the reality of the biodiversity crisis with academic authority:

> 'Among the hundreds of experts on biodiversity I know, everyone, without exception, agrees that the world is in the early stages of a massive extinction of ecosystems and species. If not ameliorated in the next several decades, it will equal the last great natural spasm recorded by palaeontologists, which ended the Age of Reptiles 65 million years ago. Furthermore, the loss will not be replaced by evolution in any time that has meaning for existing humanity. In all five of the previous great extinction spasms, spread over the past 450 million years, it took evolution about 10 million years to make up the loss in full.
>
> With each species lost or doomed to early extinction (now in the tens of thousands yearly), humanity is recklessly discarding priceless scientific information and other benefits that we are only beginning to appreciate. Of at least equal concern is the destabilisation of the biosphere. It is possible that when enough of the natural ecosystems are erased, the process might continue autonomously, triggering changes that will be catastrophic for *Homo sapiens*. We should be worried about these consequences.'

A sobering thought indeed.

even-aged stand about 6m high. A stout cane (*Cana*) then invades the tessaria within three to five years. The cane dominates for 15–20 years after which large, slow-growing trees take over, as for rainforest gaps.

People and diversity together

Many plants need forest gaps to survive but, in turn, a community of mammals, birds and insects specialises and depends totally on gap habitats. Native peoples have known this since pre-history, basing shifting agricultural methods on natural gap formation and succession. The light and warmth created by forest clearing favours the cultivation of legumes, rice, banana, plantain and manioc. Later, farmers plant fruit trees, shade-loving herbs and plants found only in natural gaps. These in turn attract such game animals as peccary and tapir. At a sustainable level, the gaps created by slash-and-burn shifting agriculture increase biodiversity, as much as, if not more than, the forest's natural gaps.

Mysteries of biodiversity

That tropical rainforests are dynamic ecosystems in a constant state of change over space and time is beyond dispute. But it is the geography of an area combined with the interaction of vegetation and animals that encourages a biodiversity far greater than is found in temperate forests. The absence of true seasons in the tropics encourages a process of continuous evolutionary development that in more temperate regions is interrupted by the changing seasons.

Any disturbance tending to isolate populations is likely to promote speciation and hence biodiversity. Millions of years ago, the continent's isolation set up initial conditions for South America's unique fauna to evolve. Plant isolation encouraged by seed dispersal encourages faster evolution of new species than the interbreeding of plants all located in the same area.

Intermittent disturbances in the rainforest canopy therefore increase the potential for diversity. In the Amazon, large and small-scale disturbances produce evolutionary hotspots. Forest gaps are 'islands' of unusual habitat that, although sparse in a mature forest, offer opportunities for genetic isolation. Given this set-up, forest openings and edges are ideal places to test new evolutionary combinations.

Biodiversity also arises through ecological specialisation. Most tropical organisms occupy narrow niches. For example, only one part of a tree may be a suitable micro-environment for a particular epiphyte species. Many animals can complete their entire life-cycle in the rainforest canopy, because a year-round supply of fruit allows monkeys, birds, bats and others, to keep to a wholly frugivorous diet. Where winters end the annual fruit supply, as they do in temperate zones, the year-round strictly frugivore niches are simply unavailable; which reduces the overall diversity of these areas.

The extensive river networks of the Amazon Basin are another essential contribution to greater biodiversity, creating an important physical isolating mechanism. They can stop migration and movement, prevent interbreeding and promote isolation. The ranges of several mammals and birds stop at wide rivers, creating isolated populations that can then evolve into new species. Small land animals on islands in the middle of rivers may be cut off from the main group. Those stranded on floating mats of vegetation can be transported far from their territory and so establish new colonies.

Life has invented wonderful ways to enhance its chances of survival. The techniques of water lilies and orchids demonstrate elaborate mechanisms that ensure cross-pollination. Such systems allow individual genes to combine with each other in novel ways. Animals use sex for the same purpose. Forsyth and Miyata suggest that the chief virtue of sex is the production of genetic diversity. New gene combinations provide raw material upon which natural selection acts. Cross-pollination promotes genetic diversity: essential for adaptation to changing conditions.

On the other hand, offspring of self-pollinated plants are clones, genetically identical to their parents and each other. A population of clones is more prone to extinction because it lacks the genetic variability necessary to adapt quickly. A varied population improves the chances of at least some individuals possessing traits that will help them to survive in a changed environment passing on successful genes to future generations. This principle is the core of evolutionary theory and explains, in part at least, the great biodiversity found in the Amazon.

ANIMALS OF THE EMERALD FOREST

Most of us have heard of the astounding biodiversity found in the world's tropical rainforests. Globally this habitat harbours at least 50% of all known animal species, a figure that would probably exceed 90% in the unlikely event that all the fauna were ever described.

Rainforest mammals

Walking through the rainforest it is so quiet that you wonder where the 200 kinds of mammals (excluding bats) you read about are. You see almost none, for several reasons. Most rainforest mammals are inconspicuous and hard to spot being small, well-camouflaged, shy and nocturnal. Populations are patchily distributed and you have to be in the right place at the right time. Even sizeable creatures can be overlooked because of dense vegetation. Around inhabited areas most mammals have been over-hunted. But animals there are, and with luck, patience and a good naturalist-guide you will probably spot at least five or ten of those described here.

Canopy mammals

Canopy mammals interact broadly with their surrounding flora. Many pollinate flowers. Trees attract pollinators with large, strongly-perfumed, cauliflorous blooms coloured white for bats or rodents. Luscious fruit tempts monkeys who inadvertently disperse the seeds.

Sloths

Given the title of the world's slowest land animals, sloths barely manage 2m a minute, although when pushed they can race along branches at a staggering 4.5m a minute. Nature's couch-potatoes, they save energy and decline to move at all for much of the time. They are the world's laziest creatures, spending up to 80% of their lives asleep or dozing, suspended from the branches of trees. Like that of reptiles their body temperature varies with the environment. Minimal movement and a slow metabolism enables sloths to survive on a low-energy diet of leaves; clearly a highly successful strategy as they constitute two-thirds of all canopy mammal biomass.

Sloths must eat large quantities of leaves to meet their nutritional needs, but their peg-like teeth are poorly suited to the job – undigested leaves make up to a third of their body weight. They feed on relatively few trees because their digestive system can neutralise only a few toxic chemicals at a time. This may be why the non-poisonous cecropia is a favourite tree despite vicious stinging ants.

Easy prey for predators, sloths are well-camouflaged. Their grooved fur encourages algae growth creating a greenish hue. Opposite to that of other mammals, their fur grows up the back to help heavy rain run off the upside-down sloth. Small animals make a living in the sloth's fur, including moths, spiders and several mites.

Sloths high in the canopy often suffer aerial assaults from eagles on the wing, while rainforest cats look out for sloths on the forest floor as they move to new feeding trees or while making their weekly trip to ground level to defecate. For arboreal niche specialists, sloths are good swimmers and fearlessly paddle across rivers and ponds. Their first line of defence is to avoid being seen; their colour and ability to remain motionless for hours protect them from predators but also make them hard to find on field trips. Still, sloths are the commonest large canopy mammal, so you should see at least one or two.

Hoffman's two-toed sloth

Of four types of Amazon sloth, visitors are most likely to see the **brown-throated three-**

toed sloth (*Bradypus variegatus*). It is absent in eastern Amazonia, replaced by the very similar **pale-throated three-toed sloth** (*B. tridactylus*). Hoffman's two-toed sloth (*Choloepus hoffmanni*) has the smallest range, west of Iquitos to the Andes and the Napo. The **southern two-toed sloth** (*C. didactylus*) is the least known.

Sloths belong to the Xenartha order of primitive mammals which include anteaters and armadillos. Typified by primitive or absent teeth, these animals survived the Pliocene invasion of placental mammals some five million years ago.

Tamanduas

These edentates are small arboreal anteaters, specialist predators on ant and wasp nests. Related to the giant anteater, they share adaptations: powerful claws, long snouts and jaw-bones fused into a tube for the long, sticky tongue. Thick fur and small eyes and ears provide protection against aggressive stinging insects. Tamanduas are primarily arboreal and have a coiling, prehensile tail, adapted for grasping. Only the **collared or southern tamandua** (*Tamandua tetradactyla*) is found in the Amazon, with a range that stretches as far south as the Argentine highlands.

Southern tamandua

Pygmy anteater

The smallest anteater is the **silky or pygmy anteater** (*Cyclopes didactylus*). No more than 20cm long and weighing 283g, it scores high on the cuteness quotient, with lustrous, silky, grey-gold fur. Despite a wide distribution in Amazonia, pygmy anteaters are rarely seen; they live solitary, mainly nocturnal lives out of sight in the canopy.

Primates

The expectation of seeing monkeys or *monos* swinging from the branches of every tree is quickly lowered on a walk in the rainforest. Monkeys are common but their activities rarely bring them within sight or sound of humans, unless at remote lodges or where they have become tame. In areas where they have been heavily hunted, they are extremely wary and disappear into the forest before you realise they were there. Elsewhere in the wild, monkeys may be as curious of you as you are of them. If your guide knows the correct call he may, with a bit of luck, attract a troop closer to your binoculars. However, you have to watch out because, following a territorial threat display, the creatures could defecate or pee on you – considered an honour by some! Three Amazon primates are officially endangered (CITES I) and the rest are threatened (CITES II).

The dominant primate family is the neotropical Cebidae. Characteristic of the cebid monkeys is a prehensile tail acting as a fifth limb. Marmosets and tamarins comprise the other important group. Some 30–35 lowland forest monkeys are known, with new ones still being discovered. The **Maués marmoset** (*Callithrix mauesi*) was discovered in 1993 in Brazil, the third new discovery in two years. By 1996 seven new species had been discovered in just five years.

The primate most often seen is the common **squirrel monkey** (*Saimiri sciureus*). Squirrel-sized and slender, it has a handsome coat coloured gold-green, and yellow-orange forelimbs. Though classified as a cebid, it lacks a prehensile tail. During the

Squirrel monkey

day, they roam in troops, on the look-out for fruiting trees. Often kept as pets, squirrel monkeys roam free at the zoo in Leticia where their antics provide amusing entertainment.

All six species of **saki monkey** are relatively rare. The **monk saki monkey** (*Pithecia monachus*) has a hairy crest around its naked face with the appearance of a monk's cowl. It may be spotted in the wild because the long, fluffy, non-prehensile tail dangles down when it sits on a branch. The **equatorial saki monkey** (*P. aequatorialis*) has the narrowest range, along the western upper Napo River.

The large black **spider monkeys** (*Ateles* spp) have long, thin limbs and coarse fur. A punk hair-do doesn't hide their curiously human expression. To add grip, there is a patch of skin on the tail's underside. The black spider monkey (*A. paniscus*) is common where not hunted. Captured specimens are often kept as pets by locals.

The **woolly monkey** is superficially similar to the spider monkey, with a prehensile tail and skinny body but with thick, dense, dark-brown fur. The **common woolly monkey** (*Lagothrix lagothricha*) feeds in groups at middle to higher canopy levels. Tastiest of monkeys, this is the most intensively hunted primate and is rare or extinct in much of its former range west of the Río Negro.

Black spider monkey

Howler monkeys (*Alouatta* spp) often appear in nature films about the rainforest, and with good reason. Their impressive calls resound for great distances through the dense forest. Indeed, howler monkeys are arguably the world's noisiest creatures, audible for a distance up to 16km. The calls signal status and territory, allowing the howlers to communicate through dense vegetation where visual gestures would be useless. Howlers are sometimes heard during thunderstorms, adding their cacophony to the crescendo of thunder and hiss of pelting rain. The **red howler** (*A. seniculus*) is found only in northern and western Amazonia. East of the Purus River in Brazil is the **red-handed howler** (*A. belzbul*). Further south, the **black howler** (*A. caraya*) replaces it. Intensively hunted for meat, they are rarely sighted.

Attractive-looking, smallish, and grey-brown with a pale face and a prehensile tail, the **capuchin monkey** is the organ-grinder's monkey. Its hair resembles the cowl or *capuche* worn by monks. **Brown capuchins** (*Cebus apella*) are found throughout the Amazon Basin, except in Venezuela where they are replaced by the **wedge-capped 'weeping' capuchin** (*C. olivaceus*) also found in the Guyanas and northern Brazil. **White-fronted capuchin** (*C. albifrons*) range through central Brazil to the Andes. Capuchins are intelligent, noisy monkeys, foraging destructively in the mid to lower canopy for small animals as well as fruits and nuts.

Both the **black uakari** (*Cacajao melanocephalus*) and **red or white uakari** (*C. calvus*) are on their way to extinction in the wild. Quite large, with stumpy tails, uakaris are habitat specialists restricted to flooded forest, making them easy prey when hunting from boats. They are probably the primate species at greatest risk in South America (CITES I). Embarrassingly for the English, the red uakari's pink naked face and corpulent body inspired its nickname *mono Ingles*. It lives along the Javari River, north up to the Solimões.

The **night or owl monkey** (*Aotus* spp) – the world's only truly nocturnal monkey – has nine recognised species at present. Grey-brown in colour with three black stripes down the face, the *douroucouli* is often kept as a pet. Night monkeys have enormous eyes to enhance night vision, and lack prehensile tails. They feed mostly on fruit, insects and nectar.

Marmosets and tamarins

The 14 Amazon marmoset and tamarin species, despite often being referred to as monkeys, are placed in a different family from true monkeys. They are small to tiny, with non-prehensile tails. Unlike monkeys, they have claws instead of fingernails.

The **pygmy marmoset** (*Cebuella pygmaea*) is tiny with a maximum body-length of only 15cm and weighing no more than 141g. Its tawny-yellow to reddish colour and mane around its face give rise to the local name *leoncito,* meaning little lion. Often kept as a pet, its nature is most un-leonine. It is quite common and found between the Japura and Purus rivers. Too small to hunt, it prefers lowland flooded-forest areas and is potentially at risk as a result of deforestation.

The **saddle-back tamarin** (*Saguinus fuscicollis*) is the primate most likely to be seen in the wild after the squirrel monkey. So-called because of its large 'saddle' of dark red-brown fur on its shoulders, it has a black head and forelegs and a white muzzle.

Pygmy marmoset

Porcupines

Four types of these familiar rodents inhabit the rainforest canopy. All are in the same genus (*Coendou*). Typical characteristics include thick, sharp spines, long-clawed feet, tiny ears and a prehensile tail. Typical is the widespread **Brazilian porcupine** (*C. prehensilis*). Porcupines are not often spotted in the wild as they are quiet, slow-moving and nocturnal, preferring to spend the day curled up in a tree hole or an empty termite nest.

Squirrels

The six squirrel species are similar in appearance and difficult to tell apart. They resemble northern temperate squirrels, red to brown in colour with bushy tails, and feed primarily on nuts and seeds. Squirrels perform useful ecosystem functions. The southern Amazon **red squirrel** (*Sciurus spadiceus*) buries and gnaws large, hard nuts, continuing the reproductive cycle of nut-bearing trees, especially palms.

Racoon family

Here we briefly discuss lowland rainforest racoons along with the semi-terrestrial coati. (See also the crab-eating racoon, page 153.)

Although it suffers an identity crisis as a racoon, the **kinkajou** (*Potos flavus*) is the clear winner of the cutest rainforest animal contest. Thick golden fur, wide brown eyes and a docile manner endear it to all. Its diet is equally benign, consisting of fruit and a few insects. Uniquely in the family, the strictly arboreal kinkajou has a prehensile tail, helping it to find food among high canopy branches. About the size of large house cats, kinkajous are found in a wide range of forested habitats, even close to human settlements.

Kinkajou

With a similar niche and sometimes mistaken for a kinkajou, the **olingo** (*Bassaricyon gabbi*) is actually about three-quarters its size, brown, with a faintly banded non-prehensile tail. It is uncommon and restricted to western Amazonia; scientists believe the population may comprise several species.

More terrestrial than the olingo, the **coati** (*Nasua nasua*) accordingly demonstrates several more racoon-like characteristics, having a ringed, tapered tail and long low body. It takes a wide variety of food, from insects and small vertebrates to fruits, nuts and flowers, and is equally at home probing for food with its long snout under leaf litter or among canopy branches. Easily tamed, coatis are often kept as pets.

Coati

Bats

The bat or *murciélago* gets a hard time from many quarters, but these little winged mammals perform important ecological as well as mythical services. Bats are renowned as specialist predators of nocturnal flying insects and, with such an abundance of prey, tropical bats reach a high degree of diversity.

Depending on the exact boundaries and details of classification, 150–200 species are recorded from Amazonia: the most diverse bat fauna in the world and 40% of the region's total mammals. The majority are insectivorous. Notable are the **Vespertilionid** bats, found across the Americas, and the **spear-nosed bats** (*Phyllostominae*) who have complex ears and 'nose-leaves' to emit sound. Yet in this hotbed of evolution all these kinds of bats do not coexist on one food source.

Best-known alternative niche occupants are **vampire bats** (*Desmodus* spp), inspiration for dozens of Hollywood horror movies. Of course, a preferred diet of fresh mammal blood does nothing to endear them to us, but reality is more complicated than legend. Vampires rarely attack humans – their usual victims are cattle or wild mammals. They do not suck blood. So gently do a vampire's sharp incisor – not canine – teeth cut a small flap of skin, it does not startle the prey. The bat then laps blood as it seeps from the wound, while anti-coagulant saliva prevents clotting.

The largest Amazon bat, the **greater bull-dog** or **fishing bat** (*Noctilio leporinus*), plucks fish from the water in the manner of an osprey. Besides piscivores, sanguivores and insectivores, there are frog-eating bats, bird-eating bats and even bat-eating bats.

Many are fruit- and nectar-feeders. Neotropical fruit bats belong to the order Microchiroptera. They evolved from insectivorous bats, rather than a separate ancestor as is believed to be the case with Old World megachiropterans. Frugivores disperse seeds and nectarivores pollinate many trees. Bat-pollinated flowers are often cauliflorous, large, white and heavily perfumed. Many bats leave their hiding-place just before or after dusk to forage overnight, spending the day roosting in well-hidden spots, including tree-holes, leaf-tents or caves.

Forest floor mammals

Porcupine, coati, tamanduas and related species cross easily from tree to forest floor. These medium-sized animals are equally at home among lofty branches or in shady undergrowth. Larger animals tend to stay on the ground, but not always. If scared, tapir charge headlong into water, whereas a jaguar or puma bolts into a tree.

The **giant anteater** (*Myrmecophaga tridactyla*) is the largest edentate and among the largest rainforest animals, up to 2.8m long and weighing 39kg. Strictly terrestrial, it searches the forest floor where ants and termites are most plentiful. Insects are no match for the anteater whose claws rip open nests in seconds, while tough hairy skin protects it against stings and bites. With a long snout and sticky tongue it probes for its abundant food. If you walk off a forest track a short way you often see holes where an anteater has dug through an ant's nest. Its digging tools also come in handy to defend itself and it can easily kill a dog. Rare in rainforest and locally extinct in many places, the giant anteater is threatened (CITES II). Anteaters are easiest to see in grassland savannah habitats.

In the same order as sloths and anteaters, **armadillos** are well-known to US southerners, familiar with the nine-banded armadillo (*Dasypus novemcinctus*) whose range from South America, stretching ever further north, makes it the most widespread armadillo. The largest is the **giant armadillo** (*Priodontes maximus*) at over 1.5m long from head to tail and up to 30kg in weight. Due to over-hunting the giant armadillo is extinct over much of its former range (CITES I). Armadillos are rarely seen, on account of their quiet, nocturnal and solitary habits. If you do see one it will more than likely be curled up in a tight ball to protect the vulnerably soft parts of its body. Broadly omnivorous, they feed on ants and other insects, various small animals, carrion, fungi and fruit.

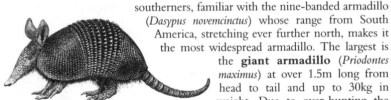

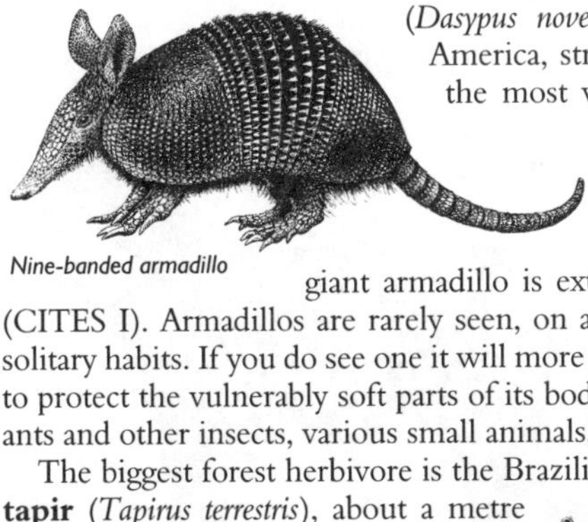

Nine-banded armadillo

The biggest forest herbivore is the Brazilian **tapir** (*Tapirus terrestris*), about a metre high at the shoulder and weighing up to 250kg. Tapir are related to horses but have an elongated, highly mobile snout, useful when searching out fruits, berries, tubers, fungi and herbs. Heavily hunted, tapir are rarely seen.

Brazilian tapir

Peccaries or *sajino* (*Tayassu* spp), also called boars, are smaller than tapir, weigh around 30kg and are related to pigs. Commonest is the widespread **collared peccary** (*T. tajacu*) which is omnivorous

Red brocket deer

and consumes any edible plant, small animals or carrion. Roaming in groups of ten or more, pungent cheesy smells reveal their presence long before sight or sound. Aggressive animals, they can inflict serious wounds with their 8cm-long tusks. Intensively hunted for meat, peccaries are listed as threatened (CITES II).

Red brocket deer (*Mazama americana*) venture into forest clearings or even to the edge of gardens and plantations. Although common and widespread, deer are shy and retiring (CITES III).

Carnivores

Carnivores are well represented, with the main terrestrial ones being cats or weasels. The dog family, with two rare and obscure species, is relatively insignificant.

The cat family (Felidae)

At the top of the food chain, wild cats are uncommon everywhere. Their conservation prospects are worsened by over-hunting. All South American felids are officially endangered (CITES I). Four are spotted cats; golden-yellow with black spots or stripes. Two others are uniform in colour.

For many, seeing a cat would be the ultimate goal of a trip to the Amazon, but cats are extremely unlikely to be seen in the wild on an average-length visit. They are rare, wary of humans and in the main nocturnal, but observe carefully and you can pick up evidence of activity. Look for tracks by muddy rivers or claw marks on a tree. Cats may be seen on trails at night or around water margins in remote areas. Local zoos sometimes display captured jaguars and smaller cats.

The **jaguar** (*Panthera onca*) is South America's biggest and best-known feline and its only 'big cat.' Extinct over much of its former range, it is thinly distributed but widespread across the neotropics. Jaguar, up to 1.8m in length and weighing up to 136kg, are the only predators big enough to tackle full-grown tapir, pouncing to break the spinal cord behind the neck. The name **jaguar** comes from the Indian word *yaguar* meaning 'he who kills with one leap'. Natives tell tales of titanic struggles between jaguars and anacondas, stories seemingly from the pages of an Edgar Rice Burroughs novel. The second largest rainforest cat, the **puma** (*F. concolour*), also known as the cougar or mountain lion, is the most widespread New World feline, with scattered populations throughout the New World.

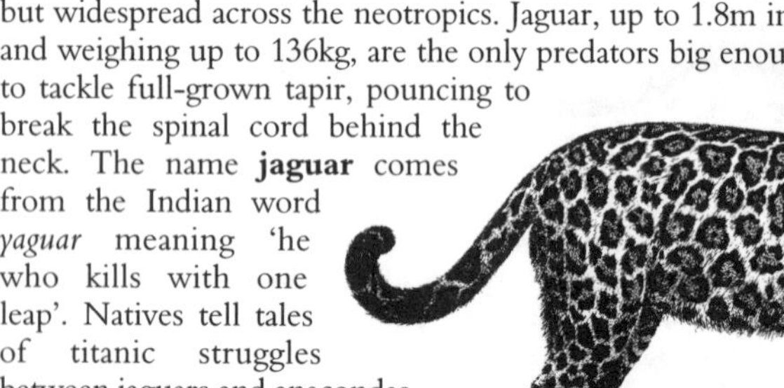

Jaguar

The **ocelot** (*Felis pardalis*) looks like a miniature jaguar and grows to just over one metre but with a less muscular build weighs comparably less at around 11kg. It ranges through the neotropics up into the southern US. The **margay** (*F weidii*) looks similar to the ocelot but is smaller and somewhat rarer. Both the ocelot and margay are nocturnal, making sightings somewhat rare. The **jaguarundi** (*F. yagouaroundi*), about the same size as a margay but without spots, is a far more likely sighting being

Jaguarundi

Ocelot

diurnal in nature. Interestingly, populations display a wide range of colour morphs: grey, red, tawny yellow, brown or even black. These cats prey on rodents, small reptiles, birds and the occasional snake.

The elusive **oncilla** (*F. tigrina*) is about the size and build of a house cat with markings similar to an ocelot: dark spots arranged in lines on a tawny coat. Its range is poorly known beyond coastal regions of Venezuela, the Guyanas and southern Brazil.

Dogs (Canidae)

The two wild rainforest canids are the **bush dog** (*Speothos venaticus*) and the **short-eared dog** (*Atelocynus microtis*). Both are small and racoon-like, but very little is known of their natural history with virtually all information coming from captive animals or dead specimens.

Weasels

These carnivores (*Mustelidae*) perform a vital role in the rainforest food chain, with each occupying a different ecological niche. The **grison** or **huron** (*Galictis vittata*), looking more like a skunk or a honey-badger than a weasel, eats small animals and sometimes fruit. The **tayra** (*Eira barbara*) resembles the grison but is larger and darker, with longer legs and tail. A more generalist feeder on small vertebrates, insects and fruit, it occasionally climbs trees.

Tayra

Large rodents

On trails or canoe rides, a creature resembling an over-size guinea-pig on a diet is occasionally seen by a sharp-eyed observer. The animal is most likely a large rodent, of which the capybara is the best-known. Characteristically, species in this group are strictly terrestrial and uniformly coloured, with a low stance, long legs and either a small or no tail.

Capybara

The **capybara** (*Hydrochaeris hydrochaeris*), the world's largest rodent, weighs up to 113kg and can grow to be 1.4m long. Tan to yellow-brown, it feeds on grass and leaves and has a squarish muzzle. Easily tamed by natives as pets, the capybara could soon be bred commercially in ranches as food as a sustainable rainforest industry, to the benefit of the eco-system.

Agoutis (*Dasyprocta* spp), **paca** (*Agouti paca*) and **acouchys** (*Myoprocta* spp) are coloured orange-red to grey to black. Of these only the widespread paca has any markings: rows of white spots. No agoutis overlap in distribution with the **black agouti** (*D. fulignosa*) limited to western Amazonia, with the **red-rumped agouti** (*D. agouti*) prevalent only in Brazil and the Guyanas. Feeding on a variety of seeds and forage foods, agoutis use their sharp incisors to open the tough coconut-sized outer shell of the Brazil nut.

Opossums

Normally associated with Australia, the New World marsupial opossums are the living survivors of the time before South America became an island continent; when South America, Africa and Australia were conjoined. While Australian marsupials have flourished, their distant South American relatives have lost out to placental mammals. There are at present 41 species of opossum. Amazon opossums, like most species, are nocturnal, sleeping by day and foraging at night.

Rainforest birds

In lowland Amazonia, there are at least 1,800–2,000 types of birds (excluding the 250 or so aquatic species; see page 134). Compare this with 500 species in all of Europe, an area half as big again as the Amazon Basin. The number increases seasonally with migrants from Patagonia or North America. Alarming declines in US songbirds, notably the **summer tanager** (*Piranga rubra*) and the **yellow-billed cuckoo** (*Coccyzus americanus*), are attributed partly to destruction of Latin American rainforests in which they overwinter.

Even non-ornithologists want to see toucans, macaws and parrots. However, these and most other birds are hidden until they fly out across a river or forest gap. There are a few birds that are easier to spot perching in the open, especially at water margins. These include hawks, kingfishers, orioles, flycatchers and anis. Small birds can be very hard to tell apart, even in the hand. Differences in song or behaviour are sometimes the only clues to identity.

Parrots and macaws

Endowed with a remarkable ability to mimic human speech, parrots are the quintessential tropical bird. Indeed Amazon parrots are common and diverse, with several dozen species. They use their powerful curved bill to break open hard nuts and seeds, notably those of the mucuja (*Acromia lasiospatha*) and tucumá palms (*Astrocaryum tucuma*). These are a favourite food of the **hyacinth macaw** (*Ara hyacinthus*) as described by the Victorian naturalist Bates in 1876. Found only in the lower Amazon Basin, this is still, as Bates puts it the 'finest and rarest species of the parrot family'. Words do not do justice to the shimmering purple-blue bird around 100cm in length, with a distinctive white eye-ring. It is very rare and at present considered endangered.

Better-known **macaws**, widely distributed and still quite common, are the largest parrots. With long tail-feathers, and nearly always in pairs, the fairly common **scarlet** or *guacamayo rojo* (*Ara macao*), **blue-and-yellow** (*A. ararauna*) and **red-and-green** (*A. chloroptera*) macaw are easily identified by their colouring.

Other parrots are smaller than macaws, have short tail-feathers and prefer to fly in flocks. Common parrots include the **festive parrot** (*Amazona festiva*) and **mealy parrot** (*A. farinosa*). Along rivers in the evening you frequently see flocks of **canary-winged parakeets** (*Brotogeris versicolurus*) flying to their evening roost. **White-eyed parakeets** (*Aratinga leucophthalmus*) and **tui parakeets** (*B. sanctithomae*) feed on coral-tree blossoms and can often be found close to moriche palms. Most parrots are difficult, if not impossible, to distinguish in the field. They are usually flying overhead so you only see silhouettes and little colour; and most are greenish and similar in appearance. Differences are mostly in head-feather colours.

One of the best places to see parrots and macaws is at the famous clay-lick on the Tambopata River, Peru, where hundreds of parrots, mostly macaws, gather on clay walls along the riverbank. (See page 311.) The birds are present mostly from late July to late September. This cycle is believed to be based on seasonal availability of food plants and the birds' need to supplement minerals or perhaps detoxify the 'pre-season' unripe fruit which contains toxins. Less well-known are the parrot lick on the banks of the upper Napo in Ecuador (page 254) and a smaller one found close to Rurrenabaque in Bolivia.

Parrots and macaws, with clipped wings to prevent them flying away, are often kept as pets in hotels, lodges, or jungle villages.

Toucans

Their huge colourful bills have made toucans familiar rainforest icons often used to promote conservation or sales of rainforest products. Toucans have the biggest bills, relative to body size, of any bird, in some cases as long as the body itself. The bill is partially hollow, reinforced by an internal honeycomb structure, making it very light for its size.

Fruits are the toucans' main food and their long bill is ideal to reach figs and berries at the ends of thin branches. Distantly related to woodpeckers, toucans roost and nest in ready-made tree-holes. In addition to a diet of fruit, they will prey on small animals and even eggs and nestlings of other birds.

One of the biggest is the **white-throated toucan** (*Ramphastos tucanus*), black with a white chest, yellow rump and blue ring of bare skin around the eye. As long as the body, the bill is black with a yellow ridge on top. The white-throated toucan's frog-like croak is one of the few ways to avoid confusion with the nearly identical **yellow-ridged toucan** (*R. culminatus*) which has a polysyllabic yelp. A local guide should be able to point out the difference. Smaller toucans include the **chestnut-eared araçari** (*Pteroglossus torquatus*) and the beautiful **golden-collared toucanet** (*Selenidera reinwardtii*).

Hummingbirds

Considered by some pre-Colombian cultures as messengers to the 'gods' or spirits, hummingbirds are rarely seen for long. They are small and flit among vegetation, almost too fast for the eye to follow, and you will probably hear one before you see it. The humming is caused by their incredibly fast wing-beat, the fastest of any bird: up to 80 beats per second. Hummingbirds are beautiful and also useful. Indeed they're ecologically essential to many trees, shrubs and epiphytes of which they are primary pollinators. Hummingbirds are attracted to red, orange and yellow flowers such as crab's-claw (*Heliconia* spp) and *Aphelandra*.

Many hummingbirds are less than 8cm long and have a precarious existence. To remain alive, they need a meal every two hours. Only pure nectar has enough energy to maintain their fast metabolism. At night, they remain torpid until the morning. Their legs are virtually useless for walking, so they fly even the shortest distance. Woven from down, tiny plant fibres, lichen, moss and even spider's silk, their nests are tiny, as small as 2.5cm across, and sometimes hung from the underside of a banana or heliconia leaf. Snug inside, the eggs are the size of peas.

Hummingbird diversity is highest in cloud and montane forest of the eastern Andes where, in Ecuador alone, over 100 hummingbird species are recorded.

Contrary to what most people expect, lowland rainforest is relatively poor in hummingbirds. Still you may get lucky and hear one flit by or, if you're lucky, have one hover in front of you for a few precious seconds. Their charming names often refer to exquisite plumage; **glittering-throated emerald** (*Amazilia fimbriata*), **golden-tailed sapphire** (*Chrysuronia oenone*) and **black-eared fairy** (*Heliothryx aurita*) can be found around Iquitos.

Harpy eagle

Raptors

The **harpy eagle** (*Harpia harpyja*) is the world's most powerful bird of prey. Adults stand a metre in height, with a wingspan of over 1.8m, and have huge yellow talons. They are major predators of monkeys and sloths. Perhaps luckily for our furry friends this majestic eagle is rare, but is sometimes seen soaring above undisturbed old-growth canopy in search of prey.

Amazon raptors include other eagles, hawks, kites, falcons, vultures and owls. Commonest are the **yellow-headed caracara** (*Milvago chimachima*) which is a type of falcon, the **black-collared hawk** (*Busarellus nigricollis*) and the **roadside hawk** (*Buteo magnirostris*). In undisturbed swampy areas, the **slender-billed kite** (*Helicolestes hamatus*) perches high in a tree when not searching for freshwater snails.

The **turkey vulture** (*Coragyps atratus*) is abundant around settlements especially, not surprisingly, at rubbish tips. The biggest lowland scavenger, with a wingspan up to 2m, is the **king vulture** or *condor de la selva* (*Sarcoramphus papa*), the royal title confirmed by an appropriately grotesque crown of orange, yellow and purple wattles. Away from towns the most common vulture is the **greater yellow-headed vulture** (*Cathartes melambrotus*).

Hoatzin

The unmistakeable **hoatzin** or *shansho* (*Opisthocomus hoazin*) is a large, portly bird about the size of a turkey. Its head bears a prominent scruffy 'mohican' crest. Large blue eye-rings of bare skin add to its comic appearance.

They are poor flyers, as the pectoral muscles of the hoatzin are too small for sustained flight, limiting the seemingly clumsy bird to short, gliding flights. The reduced musculature makes room for the bird's oversized crop which stores its diet of 60% leaves. Gut bacteria ferment the material for up to four times longer than most birds. Fermentation by-products are believed responsible for the hoatzin's unpleasant smell and its rather unkind nickname, the 'stinkbird'.

Raptors and arboreal predators can make an easy meal of the weakly-flapping hoatzin, which therefore is quite wary, and often flies off as soon as it is disturbed. But when the prospect of mating comes along, hormones throw caution to the wind and shyness is reduced. Flocks of up to a dozen birds squawk clumsily among trees, especially along borders of permanent *varzea* swamp, cooperating in nesting with the mating pair assisted by a number of 'helpers'.

The nest is built over water and, when threatened by a predator, the chick flings itself into the water below. It swims back to the nest tree where it uses its bill, feet and special wing-claws to climb back up. This latter unique and apparently primitive characteristic is believed to have evolved independently and is not evidence for the widespread belief that the hoatzin is related to the fossil bird *archaeopteryx* – one of the first birds that evolved 120 million years ago – or is itself a 'living fossil.' Indeed egg protein analysis suggests it may be recently evolved from cuckoos. However, the bird is still weird enough to be classified in a family of its own, Opisthocomidae.

Hoatzin

In some places where there's ideal habitat, hoatzin are very common. During non-breeding periods they form flocks of 25 or 30 at times, seeming to totally ignore benevolent human presence.

Orioles

In the Icteridae family, which includes orioles and blackbirds, **oropendolas** are common riverside birds, coloured brownish with gold (*oro* in Spanish) on the tail feathers, with a loud burbling call. Their woven nests hang 2m or more, like large pendulous fruits, from the branches of trees. Most likely you will see the widespread **russet-backed oropendola** (*Psarocolius angustifrons*), common along *várzea* borders, or in *terra firme* forest the **olive oropendola** (*Gymnostinops yuracares*).

Caciques, with dark plumage and gold tail bars, resemble the oropendola but are smaller. Their rumbustuous behaviour and loud calls make them hard not to notice. Caciques nest communally in riverside shrubs and trees, often around villages and jungle lodges, producing woven nests of compact globular form. Other birds in this family include true **orioles** (*Icterus* spp) and **yellow-hooded blackbird** (*Agelaius* sp). Cowbirds such as the **shiny cowbird** (*Molothrus bonariensis*) are common in ranches, cultivated and pasture areas. In the manner of cuckoos, these are brood parasites, and lay eggs of a size, shape and colour which mimic the unfortunate host's product.

Night birds

Several owls (Strigidae) are endemic to the Amazon. The tropical **screech owl** (*Otus choliba*) has a high-pitched whistle often heard just after nightfall or before dawn. **Nighthawks** (Caprimulgidae) are often seen at dusk, flitting through the air catching insects on the wing. In poor light they are often mistaken for bats.

Similar to nighthawks but in a family of their own (Nyctibiidae), **potoos** (*Nyctibius* spp) hide during the day by mimicking a dead branch. Their grey splotched plumage and stiff, upright stance enhance the deception. **Nightjars** are similar to nighthawks and have loud calls. These birds roost on riversides at night, and are easily picked out by their eye-shine reflected in torchlight. The **pauraque** (*Nyctidromus albicollis*) is the most widespread. The **sand-coloured nighthawk** (*Chordeiles rupestris*) is often seen at dusk around villages, towns and even airports.

The **oilbird** (*Steatornis caripensis*) looks a lot like a nighthawk, to which it is related. However, the oilbird can use echo-location to navigate and it nests solely in caves. Moreover it is the world's only nocturnal frugivorous bird: as the one species of oilbird, it is placed in its own unique family.

Other forest birds

Numerous other forest birds inhabit the jungle. Of these, the following are the more commonly encountered.

The neotropical family of **antbirds** (Formicariidae) reaches its greatest diversity in Amazonia; a daunting array of 150 or more small birds of dull plumage that forage for prey flushed out by army-ant raids. Many resemble other birds, leading to the appropriately named antshrikes, antwrens and antpittas. In June 1998 a US team of ornithologists added to the diversity, finding a new species of antpitta in the cloudforests of Ecuador. A typical species, the **ash-breasted antbird** (*Myrmoborus lugubris*), has greyish underparts and black throat and cheeks. In open areas along the Amazon's mainstream you may see it forage under Heliconia plants. Among the commonest antwrens in the upper Amazon is the **white-flanked antwren** (*Myrmotherula axillaris*), which is black with white wing bars and makes a living gleaning the middle and lower canopy.

Barbets (Capitonidae) are most diverse in Africa and tropical Asia, but a few are neotropical residents. They are robust birds about the size of a starling, brightly coloured, usually with bars or spots on the chest and wings. Typical is the **black-spotted barbet** (*Capito niger*), replaced in *várzea* forest by the **scarlet-crowned barbet** (*C aurovirens*).

The only Amazonian crow or corvid is the **violaceous jay** (*Cyanocorax violaceus*).

The diverse **cotinga** family (Cotingidae) of tree-dwelling birds has a broad range of habitats. Most are fruit eaters, but are highly variable in appearance and behaviour showing marked sexual dimorphism. Diverse in humid montane forests of Peru, Colombia and Ecuador, lowland species are numerous. Two attractive examples are the **purple-throated fruitcrow** (*Querula purpurata*), the female of which lacks the male's magenta throat fan, and the **plum-throated cotinga** (*Cotinga maynana*), the male of which is shiny turquoise while his mate is dull brown-and-grey. Both these species occur around fruiting trees. Another common cotinga is the **screaming piha** (*Lipaugus vociferans*). This bird's call is a quintessential sound of the Amazon – a very loud, three-syllable 'weet-wee-ooo,' with the last note trailing away. The **black-tailed tityra** (*Tityra cayana*) is commonest of its genus in lowland forest, especially around villages or tourist lodges, often with orioles. The strangest cotinga is the **umbrella bird** (*Cephalopterus ornatus*) named on account of its large parasol-like crest. This, along with a pair of dangling throat wattles, are used for courtship. The male's dating paraphernalia are considerably larger than the female's – another example of sexual dimorphism. As described by Bates, the wattles help amplify its 'singularly deep, loud, and long-sustained flute note'. Quite common, the umbrella bird often lurks around its nest in riverside trees.

Cracids typically look like a cross between a turkey and a chicken. **Chacalacas** and **guans** are several species of similar-looking cracids that resemble a streamlined chicken and likewise readily become semi-domesticated, although in the wild they spend most of their time in trees. **Curassows** are pheasant-sized, dark-coloured, semi-arboreal forest birds, widely hunted for meat. The **wattled curassow** or *pauji* (*Crax globulosa*), has large, spherical yellow wattles. Curassows are intolerant of disturbed habitat, and their conservation status is causing concern.

Finches and **sparrows** are typical members of the order of perching birds (Passeriformes) and include one of the world's most widespread birds, the **house sparrow** (*Passer domesticus*). They are largely disregarded as boring and unimportant 'little brown birds'. Members of the family Fringillidae have thick, robust bills specialised to crack open hard seeds, especially grains. They are commonest in drier savannah-type habitat where grasses are more abundant. In the

Amazon, there are a dozen or so common species plus a handful with spotty or patchy distributions.

Most likely to be seen in the field is the **red-capped cardinal** (*Paroaria gularis*). Its entire head and throat are scarlet, while the rest of the body is glossy blue-black above with white underparts. It's common along shrubby lakes and stream banks, in marshy areas with partially submerged branches on which to perch.

Cuckoos (Cuculidae) comprise 15–20 species, mostly cryptic and rarely seen, except for the uncuckoo-like **smooth-billed** (*Crotophaga ani*) and **greater** (*C. major*) **anis**. The greater ani is very common along vegetation-lined waterways. Anis are the size and build of a magpie but pure black. Unlike most cuckoos, anis are non-parasitic. Quite the opposite, they are social and gregarious, feed together and breed communally.

Perhaps the most species-rich Amazon family, there are at least 200 **flycatchers** (Tyrranidae) of diverse colour, occurring in every New World habitat from tropical lowlands up to the snowline. Many share the same technique to catch aerial insects: perching until one flies by, then sallying forth to catch it before returning to enjoy the meal. Others glean foliage or take fruit.

Flycatchers are commonly seen along rivers or the edges of large, open lakes. Many are attractive yellow-breasted birds with a prominent black eye-stripe. The **greater** (*Pitangus sulphuratus*) and **lesser** (*P. lictor*) **kiskadees** and **tropical kingbird** (*Tyrannus melancholicus*) are common along waterways. Birdwatchers will want to spot the distinctive **vermilion flycatcher** (*Pyrocephalus rubinus*).

Foliage-gleaners (Furnariidae) of the New World inhabit deep forest. Of about 70 species, 25 or so occur in lowland forest, many restricted in range. These small birds are also called ovenbirds, a collective name which includes foliage-gleaners, horneros and spinetails.

Despite the uniform appearance of these birds, they show a remarkable diversity of nest architecture from the dome-shaped mud nests of the horneros – hence the name ovenbirds – to the big tangled stick nests of spinetails and thornbirds. The nest of the **pale-legged hornero** (*Furnarius leucopus*) is smooth and oven-like with a side entrance that spirals inward. The structure is often seen at the cleft of a branch in a cercropia tree and may be mistaken at first for a small termite nest.

Diverse in the Old World, only four or five species of **gnatcatchers** and **gnatwrens** (Sylviidae) occur in the Amazon lowlands. All are insectivorous, as implied by the common name. Gnatcatchers are small, sprightly birds living in the middle- to upper-level canopy in lighter woodland. Gnatwrens, found in lower canopy, are wary and shy making identification somewhat more difficult.

Honeycreepers are related to tanagers and woodwarblers but placed in an artificial family (Coerebidae) which also includes **dacnis**. Some authors ally them to wood warblers. The most widespread species is **bananaquit** (*Coereba flaveola*). They feed on flowers, being mostly nectivorous, but will take fruit and some invertebrates. Many honeycreepers pierce the flower's petals near the base with their bill to suck out nectar. This cheats the plant since it does not get the reward of pollination in return for its nectar. Purely arboreal, honeycreepers have a deeply cleft tongue that is fringed or brush-tipped to help lap up nectar. Plumage varies from blue, purple, yellow and green, with considerable sexual dimorphism. The male **green honeycreeper** (*Chlorophanes spiza*) and **short-billed honeycreeper** (*Cyanerpes nitidus*) are both a dazzling purple with black wing coverts and throat.

The New World family of **jacamars** (Galbulidae) comprises several common kingfisher-like birds with small, compact bodies, lance-like bills and glossy green plumage. Jacamars catch insects on the wing like flycatchers. You might see the

white-eared jacamar (*Galbalcyrhynchus leucotis*), perched among vegetation along a river or stream.

Manakins are a diverse group of small, highly mobile canopy birds (Pipridae) rarely seen from the ground. Manakins feed on fruits, berries and the occasional insect. Their breeding behaviour includes 'lek' formation where the male clears an area of rainforest floor to display his courtship dance. They are often black above with colourful head and throat, but females of most species are dull green. The **white-bearded manakin** (*Manacus manacus*) is found throughout lowland western Amazonia.

Motmots are small and chunky, their unusual tails ending in two racquet-shaped tufts. A scarlet breast and dark green wings characterise the **broad-billed** (*Electron platyrhynchum*), **rufous** (*Baryphthengus ruficapillus*) and **blue-crowned** (*Momotus momota*) **motmots**.

Among the most familiar birds, **pigeons** and **doves** (Columbidae) rarely get much attention. But in the wild, they're fruit-eating specialists playing critical roles in the ecology of many rainforest trees. About a dozen columbid species occur in lowland rainforest. Pigeons and doves typically fly fast and direct, manoeuvring with fan-shaped tails. They are robust in appearance except for their weak bills and small heads. Generally dull-coloured, grey or brown, pigeons and doves feed among trees or forage on the ground for fruits and the occasional insect.

Many rainforest species are shy and rarely perch in the open. The **plumbeous pigeon** (*Columba plumbea*) is occasionally seen, but it's more common in humid forest and on forest borders with advanced secondary growth. It is virtually identical to the **ruddy pigeon** (*C. subvinacea*) and impossible to distinguish in the field.

Terrestrial columbids include **ground-doves** and **quail-doves**, the latter being more terrestrial. The **ruddy ground-dove** (*Columbina talpacoti*) is associated with open areas and scrubland and is spreading in Amazonia, apparently because of deforestation.

Puffbirds (Bucconidae) have a tuft or *puff* of bristles around the bill. This presumably helps to catch aerial insects. They are small-to-medium, robust birds with thick, slightly-hooked bills. Most are plain and drab in colour or have camouflaged or *cryptic* plumage. The **swallow-winged puffbird** (*Chelidoptera tenebrosa*) is sometimes seen in open *várzea* woodland. The **black-fronted nunbird** (*Monasa nigrifrons*) is unmistakable, as the only all-black bird with a scarlet bill.

Swallows and **martins** (Hirundinidae) are characterised by a streamlined shape, small head and beak, but large gaping mouth. In flight they can be recognised by deeply forked tails and swept-back, pointed wings. They resemble swifts in some respects but are less well adapted to aerial life. Swallows like to perch on branches, telephone wires and roofs. Most are gregarious and gather in groups or large flocks. Amazon species nest in cavities or holes and, unlike northerly species, tend to avoid using man-made structures.

Two notable species are **white-banded** (*Atticora fasciata*) and **white-winged** (*Tachycineta albiventer*) **swallows**. These are seasonally common, appearing in large numbers at certain times of year. At other times, they will be completely absent. The **brown-chested martin** (*Phaeoprogne tapera*) is quite common in areas with some vegetation, usually around water.

Swifts (Capodidae) are supreme aerial insectivores, spending almost their entire life on the wing. Agile and rapid fliers, they are perfectly adapted to life in the air. Unable to perch, swifts cling to vertical surfaces or hop around on small weak legs. Indeed, males of some species never return to earth, even mating on the wing. Only for breeding do females return to ground. Swifts rarely rest – it is believed that some species even sleep on the wing. Swifts differ from swallows in two main respects easily picked out in the field: swifts have a blunt, squarish tail and have more curved, scythe-shaped wings.

Apodids are often overlooked because of difficulty in field identification. Look for **white-collared swift** (*Streptoprocne zonaris*), a large species, 20cm long, with a notched tail. It's black except for a white collar around the neck. The **fork-tailed palm swift** (*Reinarda squamata*) has dingy brownish plumage but is gracefully built with a long tail, usually held closed in a point. This swift associates closely with **Mauritia** palms within which it roosts and nests. It is seen alone or in small groups, common over clearings and towns in forested areas.

Back down to earth, there are a dozen or so unusual ground-birds called **tinamous** (Tinamidae). Tinamous have rounded bodies, small heads and short tails. Being poor flyers they rely on dull brown-black plumage to avoid predators. Shy, furtive and hard to see, their loud calls are heard many times before they appear. Most widespread are the **great** (*Tinamus major*), **little** (*Crypturellus soui*) and **undulated** (*C. undulatus*) **tinamous**. In a sex-reversal role, tinamou males incubate eggs and raise the young while females lay in several nests.

Tanagers are a diverse family (Thraupinae) of small birds akin to finches. Most of the 125 lowland species feed on fruit, making them important agents for seed dispersal. Perhaps the most beautiful is the **paradise tanager** (*Tangara chilensis*), with turquoise underparts, a scarlet rump and apple-green cheeks and crown. Among palm trees near clearings and villages look for **palm tanagers** (*Thraupis palmarum*), often found with **blue-grey tanagers** or *azulejo* (*Tepiscopus*), the commonest type. The **magpie tanager** (*Cissopis leveriana*) looks just like its European namesake. Other family members include the more strictly frugivorous euphonias, a genus of some 15 species of tanager-like birds.

The New World family of a dozen or so species of **tapaculos** (Rhinocryptidae) is mostly confined to the southern half of South America. Tapaculos are terrestrial insectivores, in habit similar to antbirds but wren-like in appearance with a cocked tail. Only one species is known from the upper Amazon, the **rusty-belted tapaculos** (*Liosceles thoracius*). One of the largest, at 19cm long, it's dark rufous brown above, with flanks and abdomen heavily barred brown-and-white.

Familiar back-garden birds of almost cosmopolitan distribution, only a handful of **thrushes** (Turdidae) occur in the Amazon lowland rainforests. These birds are renowned for their fine songs. A typical thrush diet consists of fruits, seeds and insects, occasionally taken on the ground. Open cup nests in trees or bushes are typical. Shy inconspicuous birds, most thrushes remain out of sight, except for the **black-billed thrush** (*Turdus ignobilis*).

Trogons are easily identified, with multicoloured plumage and straight tails, barred black-and-white on the inside. The most famous of these beautiful birds (Trogonidae) are the quetzals. Lowland Amazonia is home to the **pavonine quetzal** (*Pharomachrus pavoninus*) and the **collared** (*Trogon collaris*), **black-tailed** (*T. melanurus*) and **blue-crowned** (*T. curucui*) **trogons**. These birds are fruit- and insect-eaters, and take both foods on the wing, having weak feet. They nest in disused insect nests or woodpecker holes.

The **trumpeter bird**, lo and behold, has an extremely loud call, enabling this highly sociable bird to communicate through thick undergrowth. The **grey-winged trumpeter** (*Psophia crepitans*) prefers dense woodland where it forages on the ground for a variety of fruits and invertebrates. They are occasionally kept as pets, making useful alarm animals.

A handful of species of **vireos** and **greenlets** (Vireonidae) are found in Amazon rainforest. All are rarely seen. Primarily arboreal insectivores, some are also seasonally frugivorous. One vireo species which might be seen in humid lowland forest is the **red-eyed vireo** (*Vireo olivaceus*) of small chunky build. It has rather plain plumage distinguished by a grey crown and white eye-stripe. All vireos are characterised by sluggish behaviour and dull plumage.

As the name implies, **woodcreepers** forage up and down trees. They use their specialised bills to prise out insects hidden in crevices. Hence the shape of the bill varies somewhat, ranging from short and wedge-shaped to long and sickle-shaped. Strong legs with angled toes similar to a woodpecker's help the woodcreeper grip tree-trunks. Like woodpeckers these birds have a stiffened tail with projecting spines that aid climbing. These poorly known arboreal insectivores and bark foragers are rarely seen, being cryptically coloured.

About 20 species are known from Amazonia. Common in disturbed areas is the **straight-billed woodcreeper** (*Xiphorynchus picus*), which is 20cm long with a straight, whitish bill. The song is described as a series of descending whistles. This species may be in pairs or in mixed flocks, and is seen climbing smaller branches in lower and mid-elevations of the canopy.

As might be expected from the world's biggest tropical forest, **woodpeckers** (Picidae) are highly diverse. They have long, sticky tongues to snare insects stuck in crevices. Some occasionally turn to fruit or specialise on tree-borne ant or termite colonies. With heavy, chisel-like bills, these birds are specialist excavators of old wood and their brains are thickly cushioned to prevent damage from the continuous pounding. Invariably, loud drumming first reveals their presence, but they prefer thick forest cover and are hard to glimpse, let alone identify. The **chestnut** (*Celeus elegans*) and the **lineated** (*Dryocopus lineatus*) **woodpeckers** may be spotted by a keen-eyed twitcher. Included in the family are the **piculets**, a group of hard-to-identify, cryptically coloured birds.

Small to tiny birds, **wrens** (Troglodytidae) are remarkable for their beautiful calls, trills, whistles and warbles: members of both sexes often sing duets. Of small build, these chunky birds have small bills and cocked tails. Eight species are known from the upper Amazon but most are not often seen, though they may be heard.

Most likely to be spotted is the **black-capped donacobius** or mocking-thrush (*Donacobius atricapillus*) which is one of the biggest species in the family. It is 22cm long, and is a slim jay-like bird with a strong bill and long tail. Noisy, with a wide variety of cries and whistles, it has a distinctive yellow eye-stripe, chocolate-to-black on the side of the head and pale-yellow-to-buff underparts. It is common in marshy areas, around pools with vegetation, often seen low down or on the ground.

Aquatic birds

A world of rivers, streams, lakes and swamps, the Amazon is haven for some 250 or so species of aquatic and shore birds. Many are easy to identify, including herons or *garzas*, the most diverse group.

Most common are the **great** (*Casmerodius albus*) and **snowy** (*Egretta thula*) **egrets** and the **little blue heron** (*Florida caerulea*). Morning boat rides along quiet rivers and streams disturb the elegant **white-necked heron** (*Ardea cocoi*). It flies fruitlessly ahead of the boat, then tires and flops on to a branch. The compact, well-camouflaged **striated heron** (*Butorides striatus*) opts to stay perfectly still. Also striped is the rufescent **tiger heron** or *pumagarza* (*Tigrisoma lineatum*), sometimes flushed out by a passing boat.

At night look for **black-crowned night heron** (*Nycticorax nycticorax*). Also crepuscular is the **boat-billed heron** (*Cochlearius cochlearius*, family Cochleariidae) which indeed has a huge prow-shaped bill, ideal, foraging through water for shrimp, fish, insects and other small prey. The beautiful **zig-zag heron** (*Zebrilus *undulatus*) is among the smallest Amazon herons and a special rarity birders often seek to tick off their list.

Of storks, the only common species is the **jabiru** (*Jabiru mycteria*), a tall, primitive-looking white bird with a huge black bill, with black skin covering the head and swollen neck. It prefers drier areas and is often seen flying in flocks above ranchland.

The **sunbittern** or *tanrilla* (*Eurypyga helias*), the only member of the Eurypygidae family, is a graceful waterbird sometimes spotted along the margins of shady streams and quiet lakes. Another solitary member of its New World family (Heliothornidae) is the **sungrebe** (*Heliornis fulica*), whose short legs and lobed toes suggest its ancestor was an evolutionary step towards web-footed ducks and geese.

Along muddy banks, **sandpipers**, **snipes** and **plovers** and other shorebirds forage for titbits left behind as the flood waters recede. **Ibises** and the diverse rail family (Rallidae) including **crakes**, **rails**, and **gallinules** are also present.

Around lakes several birds hunt for fish including the **osprey** (*Pandion haliaetus*), the **anhinga** or snake-bird (*Anhinga anhinga*) and the **olivaceous cormorant** (*Phalacrocorax olivaceus*).

Classic riverside birds, **kingfishers** are among the commonest birds of waterways and lake margins. They are stout, with short necks and long, pointed bills. Kingfishers perch on a branch waiting for a fish to swim by before plunging into the water after it.

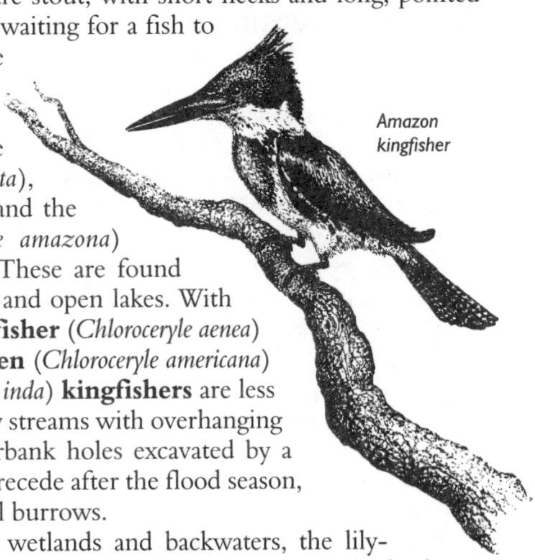

Amazon kingfisher

The entire Amazon has only six species. Most common are the **ringed kingfisher** (*Ceryle torquata*), which grows to a length of 38cm, and the **Amazon kingfisher** (*Chloroceryle amazona*) which is slightly smaller at 28cm. These are found along the edges of wide deep rivers and open lakes. With luck, you will spot the **pygmy kingfisher** (*Chloroceryle aenea*) that is just 14cm in length. The **green** (*Chloroceryle americana*) and **green-and-rufous** (*Chloroceryle inda*) **kingfishers** are less often seen as they prefer small, shady streams with overhanging vegetation. Kingfishers nest in riverbank holes excavated by a burrowing catfish. When the waters recede after the flood season, the holes are exposed and make ideal burrows.

A common bird of undisturbed wetlands and backwaters, the lily-trotter or **wattled jacana** (*Jacana jacana*) is a chestnut-brown crow-size bird. With long, skinny legs, it looks like a moorhen on stilts. Common and easily observed, the jacana is well-adapted to open, swampy habitat where its long, thin toes spread the weight, stopping it sinking through floating vegetation.

Because of its unusual physical and behavioural traits, taxonomists place the jacana in its own family, Jacanidae. It has a polyandrous mating system; females mate with many males and maternal duties become the male jacana's responsibility. Males incubate eggs and tend the young. Unlike most eggs, the jacana's float so they are easier to recover; the male's job, should an accident occur. When danger looms, the male runs away, skinny legs propelling him rapidly with the chicks tucked under his wings.

The **horned screamer** (*Anhima cornuta*) is another oddity in its own family (Anhimidae). It is a large goose-sized bird, greenish-black with a white belly, neck and shoulders, and with a prominent quill or horn projecting from the forehead. Its very loud call sounds a bit like 'Yoo-hoo!' Having trouble getting airborne, this

ANACONDAS DON'T EAT PEOPLE ... AS A RULE!

It is said that anacondas do not eat people but travellers to various towns in the Amazon may find themselves gazing at a photo while topping up on film supplies. As is common in photography shops throughout South America, copies of the best shots processed are displayed in the shop. The 12m anaconda straddled across the back of a lorry surrounded by people, who adequately provide scale, is a poorly constructed photograph, but there is no disputing the large bulge halfway down the serpent's body. On opening up the snake, the body of a 76kg Indian, missing for three days having left his village on a fishing trip, was found.

But then the Amazon is filled with myths...

mostly vegetarian bird makes a memorable sight as it flaps clumsily through trees and shrubs among vegetation-lined swamps, lagoons and lake margins. When alarmed they quickly try to move to higher branches before flying away on thermals like vultures.

Rainforest reptiles

Reptiles are successful due to their relative independence of open water. Their scaly skins and eggs are waterproof, enabling them to colonise areas without relying on the presence of free water. Many get all the water they need from their food. Reptiles also have a slow metabolism, reducing water and food requirements. Their distribution and activity are limited because they are 'cold-blooded'. But reptile blood is not cold and the animals behave in such a way as to regulate their body temperature. When they need to warm up they bask in the sun, and to cool down they seek shade; useful clues on when and where to look for them. Land reptiles are snakes, lizards and tortoises, all represented in the Amazon. Aquatic reptiles are covered later in the chapter.

Snakes

The most famous South American snake is the **anaconda** (*Eunectes murinus*), which was fantastically represented recently in a film of the same name. This huge non-venomous constrictor reaches up to 10m in length and, according to Guinness, is the world's heaviest snake weighing over 225kg. Bates measured a 5.7m specimen that he regarded as 'not very large', but reveals a typically Victorian attitude to the snake, remarking that 'the reptile has a most hideous appearance'. Although not poisonous, their bite can inflict a serious wound. They kill prey by crushing it within powerful coils, so tight that it can't breathe and dies of suffocation. The process is swift and the victim is quickly despatched whole.

Among the most beautiful and common constrictors is the **rainbow boa** or *boa arco iris* (*Epicrates cenchria*). Between 1.5m and 2m long, and dark brown with black-purple circles along its back its iridescent skin shimmers and reflects all colours of the spectrum. The **emerald boa** (*Corallus caninus*) is blue-green or red-orange with green flecks that appear with maturity. This species is nocturnal, hunting small mammals, birds and lizards near water and in wetlands. On its upper jaw are several heat-sensing pits enabling it to hunt warm-blooded prey at night. The pits, called labial thermoreceptors, are possessed by several types of snakes. The emerald boa is *ovoviviparous*; like several boas it does not lay its eggs, but carries them internally until they hatch so the female gives birth to live young.

The **boa constrictor** (*Boa constrictor*) is a big snake, though rarely over 4m. It is diurnal and hunts mostly large rodents. The subtle shades of dark greens and browns blend together creating a diamond pattern across the upper parts of the snake's body. The ovoviviparous females have been known to give birth to as many as 80 young but 20 is average.

The **garden boa** (*C enhydris*) is totally arboreal and has a prehensile tail able to curl tightly around branches. Individuals come in a wide variety of colours from orange to grey. Females are ovoviviparous. It is noted for irritability and a serious bite.

Venomous snakes are in fact mostly harmless to humans and in rainforests do not generally pose a threat. In Amazonia, 23 snakes are considered dangerous including pit vipers, colubrids and coral snakes. **Pit vipers** (Viperidae) have a notorious reputation. These snakes have pits in their snouts helping them detect body heat emitted by prey. The **fer-de-lance** or *jergon* (*Bothrops atrox*) grows up to a length of 2m and is responsible for most attacks, very few of which are fatal. These snakes, light brown with darker diamond patterning, are most active around twilight and just after dark. Fer-de-lance are very common especially around riverbanks, cultivated areas and near human dwellings. More dangerous than the fer-de-lance is the much rarer **bushmaster** (*Lachesis muta*), the world's largest pit viper and Amazonia's biggest poisonous snake growing to over 3m. Other vipers include the **speckled tree snake** (*Bothriopsis taeniata*), a striking species with bold black and gold markings. This snake is nocturnal. Another nocturnal species is the **two-striped forest pit viper** (*Bothriopsis bilineatus*) marked by two bright ventral lines. This snake is ovoviviparous, producing six to eight young per litter, and is highly venomous.

Colubridae are the most diverse snake family, with about 50 genera in South America which are mostly harmless. Canopy-dwellers include the extremely slender vine snakes (*Oxybelis*, *Leptodeira*). The slow-moving but beautifully patterned **sibon** is just fast enough to outrun its main food staple of snails. **Green tree-snakes** (*Thalerophis*) are less slim but swift-moving. When threatened, non-venomous ***Lystrophis*** displays alarmingly and strikes vigorously with loud hisses; but if molested ceases action and plays dead. **Spindle snakes** (*Atractus*) are well-adapted to burrow in the forest floor.

Colubrid ground-dwellers include the **brown** and **indigo snakes** (*Drymarchon* spp) and **false coral snakes** (*Erythrolamprus*). **King snakes** (*Lampropeltis* spp) mimic the poisonous coral snake but are impossible to tell apart unless examined in the hand, as the only clear difference is the fangs in the back of their mouth.

True **coral snakes**, numbering over 50 species, are in the same family (Elapidae) as the most venomous snakes: cobras, kraits and mambas. Growing to a maximum length of 1.2m these South American elapids have powerful venom but very rarely inflict a bite deep enough to cause life-threatening symptoms. **Coral snakes** are ringed with bold red, white and black bands, as clear warning of their threat. They may be active day or night and are most likely to be found under logs and rocks.

Iguanas and other lizards

The prehistoric-looking **green iguana** (*Iguana iguana*) often basks on a tree branch overhanging a river and dives in at any hint of danger. Their long toes and nails grasp branches to help them stay aloft. Individuals grow large, over 1.8m long, of which more than half is the tail. The green iguana is also known as the *chicken of the forest*. Tests show that meat yields from forest-raised animals exceed those from cattle raised on an equivalent parcel of land. No doubt idealistic, the hope is for iguana to replace beef and so eliminate one cause of deforestation.

PRECIOUS POISONS

Poison-dart frogs are perfect examples of why we must preserve biodiversity. Only now do scientists recognise that frog-skin toxins yield biochemicals potentially useful in medicine and industry. Amphibians' damp skins produce agents to inhibit fungal colonies and are under close scrutiny as sources of new fungicides. Furthermore, frogs and toads yield neurotoxins produced as a defence against predators. The Ecuadorian *D. tricolor* exudes an analgesic 200 times as powerful as morphine yet non-addictive. Chemicals found in amphibian skin secretions are often unknown to science and undoubtedly many are yet to be discovered.

Several factors exacerbate frogs' vulnerability to extinction. Their reproductive success depends on water availability. Permeable amphibian skins readily absorb environmental pollutants and have little protection against the sun's ultraviolet radiation. Small frogs tend to have very limited ranges. Hence habitat loss, low rainfall, rising pollution and loss of the ozone layer could all damage frog populations. Reports of worldwide declines in amphibian populations worry ecologists who think they represent an early warning of ecosystem malfunction.

Most lizards are small and furtive. Geckos (Gekkonidae), generally nocturnal, are often seen prowling around lights on walls and ceilings of hotels and lodges. Quite cute-looking and with friendly faces, they cling to the wall munching their way through any insect that comes too close. They range in size from 5cm to 15cm.

A large lizard inhabiting most types of forest, especially during the dry season, is the **black-and-gold tegu** (*Tupinambis* sp). This large, robust lizard has shiny grey-green scales and forages noisily among leaf litter for a variety of invertebrate prey, fruits, caiman eggs or anything else it can eat.

Smaller lizards include **ameivas** (*Teiidae*), beautifully mottled in a wide range of colours. The diminutive **anoles** (*Anolis* spp) are slender, fast moving insect-eaters. Uniform pale green, they are able to change colour slightly, so are sometimes incorrectly called chameleons. Males contend for territory or females with jerky push-ups while thrusting out their orange-red dewlap.

Tortoises

These familiar inhabitants of drier climes are poorly represented. The yellow-footed tortoise (*Geochelone denticulata*) is found in rainforest throughout northern Amazonia. Breeding males fight in ponderous competitions for females who lay 15–20 eggs. The tortoise's carapace, up to 45cm long, is sometimes seen discarded by a dwelling, the animal being a popular delicacy.

Rainforest amphibians

People are rarely ambivalent towards amphibians. To many they are sluggish and slimy, on top of which many Amazon amphibians have the liability of being poisonous. Others admire them because most are active, beautiful and, on the whole, harmless.

Amphibians were the first vertebrates to live on land and still need water to reproduce. To overcome this limitation they evolved ingenious strategies and fill a myriad of ecological niches. Today amphibians are the most diverse and abundant terrestrial vertebrates and are at peak biodiversity in the lowland tropical rainforests.

Poison-dart or poison-arrow frogs

So-called poison-dart frogs, of the families Dendrobatidae and Phyllobatidae, are exquisitely coloured to warn predators of their highly poisonous skin. *Dendrobates tinctorius* of French Guiana is shiny black, mottled with yellow stripes, *D. azureus* of Suriname is iridescent turquoise, splotched with irregular black spots, and the Peruvian *D. fantasticus* is orange-gold decorated with black filigree. Compared with families of frogs in temperate climates, poison-dart frogs are highly diverse. However, fewer than you'd think are poisonous. Of 135 known types only 55 are toxic. Many are tiny, from just 1.5cm to 7.5cm long, ranking among the smallest terrestrial vertebrates.

Dendrobatids and their relatives are hardly ever seen, being arboreal and so small. Many live out their complete life-cycle in the canopy, making pools of water in bromeliads or tree-holes their base for life and reproduction. Looking in fallen or cultivated bromeliads may reveal a frog living inside. A few live closer to the ground or breed among leaf litter.

These frogs care for their young rather than abandon them to chance it in a pool of water as do most amphibians. From two to 20 eggs are laid. In some species of dentrobatids the fertilised eggs are attached to the male's back where they hatch before he releases them in a suitable bromeliad plant or tree-hole. Females of some species lay a sterile egg in the water to sustain the tadpoles while they adjust to their new home. Other species make sure that each tadpole is placed in a separate plant increasing the chances against their all being taken by one predator.

While Shakespeare's witches used frog skin in a prophecy-inducing brew, native Indians use frog skin to make curare, a black poisonous substance smeared on tips of arrows or blow-gun darts. In some cases the Indian just rubs the dart tip on the frog's skin. Indeed, these are among the most poisonous of vertebrate animals. For example, *D tinctorius* of eastern Amazonia yields a poison of which 0.0001g is sufficient to kill a man. Just handling the golden-yellow Colombian *Phyllobates terribilis* could be lethal.

Tree-frogs

Chemical 'warfare' is not the only way to escape predators. Tree frogs use other strategies. Many blend in superbly with vegetation, or mimic natural objects. Hylids have feet with sucker pads for acrobatic climbing. *Hyla riveroi* found in the western Amazon and the widespread *H. granosa* are, like all hylid frogs, almost entirely insectivorous.

To avoid unnecessary competition, different frogs have become very fussy about their preferred habitat. A niche might be ephemeral pools on the forest floor or among reeds of waterside vegetation. Some frogs lay hard, crystalline eggs, like a cluster of miniature pearls, on the side of a tree. Eggs are laid at low water just before the river begins to rise. This strategy keeps the eggs safe from aquatic predators until tadpoles develop inside. When the flood waters rise up to the eggs, the shells dissolve and release the tadpoles.

The 24 neotropical **glass frogs** (*Hyalinobatrachium* spp, previously *Centrolenella*) eschew most of their colour. Typical is the *H. fleischmanni*, found in most of the northern neotropics. The colours of the plant it rests on go right through the transparent skin and muscles, revealing the heart, digestive system and bones of the frog.

Other frogs

Large frogs do not usually have toxic skin secretions so rely on camouflage to hide from predators. Many are also nocturnal so, if frogs are your thing, you will have to go out at night to find them on floating vegetation or on a river bank. You might discover the **Amazonian horned frog** (*Ceratophrys cornuta*), a giant 20cm long. Going down in scale, some horned frogs are not much more than 2.5cm long.

You may not find one on your trip but you do not have to go far to hear them. Frog and toad voices are a distinctive part of the rainforest chorus. Come dusk, croaks, whistles, trills, burps and grunts prove the abundance of frogs of all sizes as they prepare for amorous encounters of the night. Expandable throat pouches greatly amplify their calls. The male call attracts the female who chooses the best-sounding croak. Different call types ensure species remain separate, so a skilled listener can tell frogs apart by call alone.

Mostly insectivorous, adult frogs and toads are voracious and will eat almost any moving thing they can swallow – even each other. Some mimic other frogs' calls so when a curious female arrives she is promptly eaten!

A strong contender for the title of Weirdest Amphibian is the **Surinam toad** (*Pipa pipa*), shaped like a pancake with legs. Coloured black-brown it blends in perfectly with dark mud. Its 'fingers' have filaments at the end, greatly adding to tactile sensitivity. This adaptation allows it to find food in soft mud or the murkiest water. Its breeding method is equally bizarre. The female's skin grows over the eggs so each rests in a little water-filled pocket of its own. The young emerge as mini-adults, without gills or a tail, as they pass the entire tadpole stage within the female.

Other large toads include **narrow-mouth toads** (Microhylidae) and **true toads** (Bufonidae). Two so-called narrow-mouth toad species of **leaf-frogs** (*Phyllomedusa* spp), inhabit the forest floor, where a wide triangular head and cryptic camouflage blend in perfectly with dried leaves.

Once native to French Guiana, the **giant cane toad** (*Bufo marinus*), growing to around 12cm is now cosmopolitan throughout the tropics. It preys on birds, reptiles and even small mammals. Being so large it would normally be considered a worthwhile meal itself so has developed skin toxins for protection.

Caecilians

Their name sounds as if they come from a certain Mediterranean island, but caecilians are only found in tropical South America. Up to five species may coexist together in rainforest. They are mysterious worm-like amphibians, with a worm-like lifestyle burrowing through leaf litter in damp, shady forests. But they do not eat earth and instead search for standard amphibian fare: insects, spiders and the like. Caecilians vary in length from 10cm to 150cm and are coloured blackish to pinkish tan. Unlike other amphibians, their fertilisation and embryonic development take place within the female. These are the only viviparous amphibians. Even more bizarre, embryos eat the oviduct wall for nourishment.

Rainforest insects and other invertebrates

Let's face it, most people dislike creepy-crawlies. Many find insects and spiders repulsive, scary, or simply uninteresting.

A visit to the rainforest could change that. The beauty of invertebrates – creatures without a backbone – comes in many guises. We can easily appreciate the exquisite colour and form of butterflies and moths. But there is a more subtle beauty in the inter-relationships between insects and other rainforest organisms. The interdependence of rainforest inhabitants lies in their ecological roles as symbionts, predators, prey, herbivores, parasites, mutualists, commensalists or any number of these together. Insects are normally in the relationship somewhere.

Arthropod diversity is at least ten times that of all other groups combined. Recent estimates, based on studies of rainforest canopies, suggest 30 million insect species. Just the insects comprise 34 orders compared with 16 orders of mammals. There are 20 families of flies (order Diptera), compared with seven families in the order Primates. We almost know more about rocks on the moon than about forest insects...

Whatever we feel about insects, without them life on land would quickly collapse down to a few simple plants and microbes and the rainforest would not function or even exist.

Incessantly active, countless tiny hexapods sustain our world unthanked. Forest insects recycle nutrients, maintain soil structure and fertility, pollinate plants, disperse seeds, control populations of other organisms and are a major food source for birds, mammals, reptiles, amphibians, other insects... even carnivorous plants. Tight, mutually beneficial interactions are common among rainforest organisms, but especially between plants and insects. Indeed, some plant-insect relationships are almost unbelievably elaborate.

Beetles

The famous English biologist J B S Haldane remarked 'God must have been inordinately fond of beetles', and with good reason as beetles are the most diverse group of terrestrial animals. Indeed, far too many beetle species exist for a systematic treatment here. The exercise would require a book, several books, and this has not, as yet, been attempted. Of the 1.75 million species so far described, some 60% are insects and a third of these are beetles, amounting to about 350,000 known beetles. Of these perhaps half are from the tropics. On a single leguminous tropical tree entomologist Terry Erwin found 1,500 beetle species, 163 of which specialised on that tree alone. Such discoveries are the basis of seemingly extravagant claims that rainforest holds 95% of the world's species.

Despite the wide range of shapes and sizes among beetle species, they all have a single pair of membranous wings covered by a pair of hard chitinous plates called elytra. This gives the order its name *Coleoptera,* meaning sheath-wing. The tough elytra are moulded by evolution into a wide variety of forms to exploit an equally varied range of niches.

Among others, an especially favoured life-style which provides both food and shelter is that of wood-boring. The **palm beetle** (*Rhynchophorus palmarum*) lays its eggs in fallen euterpe and bactris palms. The grown beetle larvae are harvested by Indians for a handy, nutritious snack.

Among the most exquisite specimens is the **golden tortoise beetle** (Chrysomelidae). This looks like a living Egyptian scarab, carved in gold, under a curious transparent tortoise-shaped carapace. Chrysomelids, or **leaf beetles**, are among the most diverse beetle families. Many feed on live plant material and some are pests, though others have been employed to control weeds and others to pollinate flowers.

In the same superfamily as chrysomelids are the **long-horned beetles** (Cerambicidae). Among the longest insects, these giants of the beetle world include *Titanus giganteus* which is up to 20cm long and comes from northern Brazil and French Guiana.

Although the golden tortoise beetle may look like a jewel scarab, real scarabs are usually quite plain, though some are pretty. This family, the Scarabidae, consume dung and are important recyclers in the nutrient cycle. Large scarabs tend to be black or dark brown, smaller ones vary from green to orange or blue. They all share the dungball-rolling ability and powerful limbs to push this precious cargo around. This is buried in a suitable spot where the female scarab lays her eggs, from one or two to a couple of dozen, depending on the species. But not all scarabs have scatalogical tendencies; one species (*Cyclocephala* spp) pollinates the giant water lily.

Fire-flies, also called lightning bugs, are neither flies nor bugs but beetles (Lampyridae) responsible for spectacular displays along river edges and lowland areas at certain times of year. The light is generated by a non-heat-producing enzyme reaction. Each species has its own identification code of short and long flashes, used to attract mates. Iridescent **click beetles** (Elateridae) are also bioluminescent.

Another important beetle family is **coccinellids** or ladybirds. Coccinellid adults and larvae are important predators of aphids, voracious pests. **Weevils** are notable pests of stored grains but wild species abound. Indeed, the weevils (Curculionidae), numbering some 60,000 described species, have more species than any other beetle family, about a fifth of the entire order of Coleoptera. Weevil lifestyles vary widely. In nature, they use their snout to bore into plant leaves, stems, seeds and roots for feeding or oviposition. These beetles look like miniature tanks, armed with a large nozzle-like proboscis, antenna and a set of jaws attached to its end, and a rounded carapace lined with small longitudinal pits.

Among the most beautiful insects are the woodboring beetles (Buprestidae) including the above-mentioned palm beetle. Serious pests of wooden buildings, in nature their feeding habits help speed up decomposition of dead wood. Popular with collectors, buprestids are also called **jewel beetles** because of their dazzling iridescence. Natives use metallic green elytra from a buprestid, *Euchroma gigantea*, for necklaces and other adornments.

The **rhinoceros beetles** (*Megasoma actaeon, M. anubis*) are large, robust beetles up to 8cm long. The males' impressive antlers occasionally end up in handicrafts. The so-called **ground beetles** (Carabidae) are a cosmopolitan group of small to medium-sized, shiny black, fast-moving predators of other insects and small invertebrates. Despite the name, many carabids are found in trees.

The **rove beetles** (Staphylinidae) can be recognised by their foreshortened elytra which leave the posterior abdomen exposed. This seems no hindrance to success as they are very diverse, ranging in size from tiny (under 5mm) to over 2.5cm. Some are black and dull, others may be iridescent green or blue. Aggressive predators of other insects, rove beetles are creatures of dark, damp crevices and corners, living among leaf litter, under rocks and logs and along muddy waterways. **Darkling beetles** (Tenebrionidae) are found worldwide and eat dead or dry vegetation, ideal for the rainforest but not so good in your house.

Wasps

Wasps can be nasty stinging pests spoiling a summer's day, but they are just one of a group of insects, including ants and bees, or Hymenoptera, the second most diverse insect order (circa 100,000 described species).

It's hard to generalise about such a diverse group. Wasps vary greatly in size from the tiny to the worryingly large. Some species build large intricate nests, others build simple ones and many build none at all.

A few wasp species are solitary, such as **potter wasps**. Most are communal, living in hives of from five or ten individuals to many tens of thousands. Although hive wasps operate a caste system incorporating a queen, workers and so on, each species has its own unique life history. Some live by scavenging, others live by robbing ants or other insects of larvae. Minute non-communal parasitic wasps, able to fit in this printed 'o', lay their eggs in a caterpillar which then produces dozens more tiny wasps instead of a moth or a butterfly. Before they emerge from the caterpillar, the tiny maggots are in turn parasitised by another kind of wasp – a hyperparasite.

Another highly specialised group of tiny wasps (Cynipidae) – gall wasps – lay their eggs in tree branches and, by some unknown chemical means, force the tree to produce a spongy amorphous tissue called a gall. Safely within this chamber the wasp maggot will develop into an adult to continue the cycle. That is if it escapes predators or parasites, at least one of which may well be another wasp.

Some wasps have coevolved, creating fascinating relationships. **Fig trees** (*Ficus* sp), fairly common in the rainforest, display a remarkable symbiotic relationship with fig wasps that are about the size of a match-head.

Inside the hard and gourd-like fig are minute, composite flowers which are female, male or sterile. Despite having male and female flowers side-by-side pollination cannot occur because the female flowers mature earlier than the males. A few of the flowers are sterile and are used by the previous generation of female fig wasps to lay eggs in. The male wasps hatch first and inseminate the still unborn female wasps. As the females hatch at precisely the same time that the male flowers reach maturity, they exit the flower laden with pollen in search of another fig. Searching for a sterile flower in which to lay her eggs, the female deposits her precious pollen cargo on female flowers. After laying her eggs the female fig-wasp dies, at least if she isn't finished off first by one of the parasitic male fig wasps roaming around inside the fig looking for partners to mate with.

Each fig tree relies on just one species of wasp to do the pollinating. According to tropical biologists Forsyth and Miyata, around 900 kinds of neotropical fig tree are known, so there must be at least 900 fig wasps to go with each tree species.

Ants

A dominant aspect of ant biology is that no species directly consumes conventional plant matter such as leaves and stems. Ants are secondary consumers and rely on other organisms to convert plant matter into edible fare. There are at least three different ways to do this. Some live in a plant utilising specialist cells to provide food. Others consume the waste products of herbivorous insects, and others eat a primary consumer, usually herbivorous insects or another organism able to break down the plant into edible matter. In many cases, social organisation of the ants facilitates their exploitation of a food source.

With these strategies and endless variations, and well-adapted to darkness and high humidity, ants so successfully exploit forest production they are the most abundant rainforest insect. Indeed, they comprise up to a tenth of total animal biomass. Ants are very species-rich in tropical rainforest. In the lowland rainforest of Peru, scientists counted 30 to 40 species per hectare. In Tambopata Reserve, a single leguminous tree yielded 43 ant species. The entire Amazon fauna could number as many as 2–3,000 species. Ants are the dominant insects, and indeed, are second to none.

A fascinating symbiosis involves the common riverside **cecropia tree** (see *Forest edges and gaps*, page 109) and **ants**, typically *Azteca* or *Pseudomyrmex* spp, which are particularly aggressive and defend the tree accordingly. The cecropia's hollow stem serves as army barracks, mess and headquarters. The interior is furnished with automatic, inexhaustible food dispensers in the form of special glands which exude nectar. Modified leaf structures provide protein-rich rations in little ant-sized packets. The tough dry stem makes an ideal nesting place and the ants depend entirely on cecropia, the only place they survive.

In return, stinging ants fearlessly defend the host tree from hungry caterpillars, beetles, leaf-cutter ants and mammals. Workers snip away at every sprouting epiphyte or entwining vine tendril. Tap the trunk and hordes of small, reddish-brown ants gather around your finger and immediately start stinging. Only the sloth and a few

JAWS

Matthew Parris, author of 'Inca Cola'

Many have walked down the Mapiri Trail from Sorata to Mapiri in the foothills of the Bolivian Andes, but nobody who has ever recorded the trip has made the journey up. We decided to try this. We left Mapiri with the fat restaurateur who runs the chicken shack on the corner running after us shouting 'You're going to die! You're going to die!'

It was incredibly hot. You toil up the road towards San Juan until you reach a hairpin bend. Just before this the path departs, to the right. At first you are walking up and down hilly, cultivated land, crossing streams.

Then you begin to climb. Our backpacks were loaded with a week's provisions and it was the end of a long, wearisome afternoon. We decided to camp in a clearing burned for agriculture: open and flat, with excellent views up towards the Andes and down over the rainforest. I pitched my tent, threw off my sweaty clothes, slung my underpants – red, pretty cool – over a singed bush outside, unrolled my sleeping bag, climbed in and passed out.

In the small hours I awoke, disturbed by what sounded like something grinding its teeth under my ear: a very faint gr-gr noise, just by my right ear, which would stop whenever I moved my head. I poked around but could find nothing. Could it be from under the groundsheet? I drifted back to sleep.

The dawn was clear and fresh. I leaped naked from my tent. One does find – does one not? – that under these extreme conditions one can get two days out of a pair of underpants, not to say four. But where were they?

Hanging from the bush was a sort of rag, full of holes and as woebegone as a discarded washing-up cloth. Moving across the ground beneath was a line of leaf-cutter ants, each waving a small red flag. They had also eaten a corner of Keith's towel and half of Tim's cap.

'Ah,' said Louis, who keeps the Residencial Sorata, when we limped in seven days later, 'the tent-eating ants. You passed through their kingdom, at the bottom of the trail. You were lucky. Others have lost the groundsheets to their tents.'

I checked mine. There was one small, neat hole, just beneath where my right ear would have been positioned. Obviously this leafcutter ant had made a start, then opted for my underpants in preference. These had been, after all, Calvin Klein. Cutting edge.

insect-eating birds find the tree approachable. Some woodpeckers and antbirds feast on arboreal ants, so you often see several perched on a single tree at one time.

Ant dairy farmers

Rather than protect plants in benign symbiosis, many kinds of ants contribute to their demise. For example, species of the cosmopolitan genus *Formica*, which includes **honey ants** (subfamilies Camponotinae and Dolichoderinae), the **Argentine ant** (*Iridomyrmex humilis*) and the **fire ant** (*Solenopsis saevissima*), tend plant-sucking hemipterans, mostly aphids and scale insects. These pests literally drain a tree's resources. When ants are about, they get especially abundant, clumped around a young shoot like a bunch of grapes. Like miniature dairy farmers, the ants *milk* their charges as they collect honeydew sugars excreted by plant-suckers. As a farmer defends his livestock from wild beasts, so ants defend their charges from ladybird larvae and adults, hoverfly larvae, parasitoid wasps and flies. Some ants even go as far to build protective covers as 'barns' for their valuable livestock. That the ants effectively help destroy the plant is beyond doubt. Plants with aphids protected by ants suffer much more from the ravages of herbivorous insects than plants without aphid-tending ants.

Agricultural ants: farming for fungi

They can defoliate a whole shrub in a few days, but **leaf-cutter ants** (*Atta cephalotes*) are strictly speaking not herbivorous. Worker ants harvest leaves, cut them piece by piece into neat shapes, then carry these back to cavernous underground nests. They always leave some leaves for the tree.

But why do the ants work so hard? They cannot actually eat the leaf pieces because they lack the enzymes to break down plant toxins and the cellulose in leaf cell walls. Instead, they use leaf pieces as a compost for mycelia fungus (*Leucoprinus* spp). The fungal mycelia feed every ant in the colony and are incessantly tended by workers. Leaf-cutter ant nests go deep beneath the soil, to where conditions are ideal for fungal growth. Nests stretch over distances of 50m, and last up to 20 years or more, housing as many as eight million ants. The fungus grows only in the ant nest and the ants depend entirely on the fungus. Their activities have a major impact on the forest by defoliating whole trees and creating forest gaps, sometimes extending for several metres around their nests.

Ant armies on the march

Other conspicuous rainforest ants include army ants (*Eciton*, *Labidus* and other genera). The nest-raiding activities of *Eciton rapax*, *E legionis* and the two commonest species *E hamata* and *E drepanophora*, are described by the naturalist H W Bates. He tells of 'eager freebooters' who plunder other ant nests for eggs and larvae. Bates also discusses a dwarf species (*E praedator*), who move in 'dense phalanxes', rather than in the long columns of other ecitons. Huge colonies of up to a million individuals form bivouacs in tree-holes and hollow trunks. Tens of thousands of worker ants hook limbs together to form the living walls of a nest. Within, the queen and her progeny are dutifully tended.

At daybreak, the horde decamps and workers and soldiers sally forth in dawn raids, fanning out from the tree trunks and consuming all edible prey in their path. One entomologist describes army ant raids as 'an attack of 50,000 miniature wolves'. The flurry of activity caused by insects trying to escape the raiders draws insectivorous birds, like the antbirds, and parasitoid flies to the scene.

Common on the forest floor is the huge **bullet ant**, dark brown to glossy black in colour, measuring up to 25mm in length. Its excruciating bite is presumably the origin of its name (though it's given a colourful list of largely unprintable names by people who get bitten!), but there are actually dozens of different species of these ants – true Amazon giants. The really big black ones, such as *P clavata* (in the genus *Paraponera*), are found in the lowland rainforest of Ecuador. Bates describes a related species, *Dinoponera grandis,* as having a sting 'not so severe as in many of the smaller kinds'. Paraponera are solitary by day, presumably scouting out their territory for prey opportunities, and at night, they gather in small bands of a dozen or less and sortie out to collect the booty. Ants such as **carpenter ants** (*Camponotus*) and the lesser-known genera, *Solenopsis*, *Monacis* and *Paratrechina*, are semi-nomadic, setting up camp for a while before moving on.

Ants are ubiquitous in the rainforest and in many ways crucial to its ecology. The sooty antbird (*Myrmeciza fortis*) and many other specialists of this niche follow army ants to glean insects trying to escape the horde. Old ant nests provide nest sites for birds and arboreal animals.

Insect architects

Some insect constructions, particularly nests of social insects, rival human buildings in complexity. Ants, bees, wasps and termites are renowned for architectural skills. All social insects have a caste system delegating work in the nest to queens, workers, soldiers or drones. Each individual is efficiently communicated its task from chemical signals which emanate from the queen.

Wasps build combs similar to those of bees but of chewed wood-pulp paper. A **common wasp** (*Chartergus* spp) builds finger-shaped nests 2m long. Others, notably the **potter wasp** (*Polybia* spp), use clay to build compact globular nests. *P. emaciata* from Colombia moulds a spherical clay nest about 10cm in diameter which, being covered in a cement of clay and sand, is virtually impenetrable, except via a small entrance or flight hole. Another species of the upper Amazon, *P. singularis*, has rectangular clay nests 30 x 15cm or larger, distinctive on account of the long slit-like flight hole. English naturalist H W Bates described several species of potter wasps. *Trypoloxon aurifrons* and *T. albitarse* are big black wasps that build little pot-like structures much like those of **mason wasps**.

THE ETERNAL ARMS RACE – BUTTERFLIES, MOTHS AND THEIR ENEMIES

Stories of fairies and angels could have been born of the most beautiful insects: butterflies and moths (Lepidoptera). Behind the myth and beauty lies a biology marvellous and near-miraculous but at the same time somewhat sinister. Lepidoptera metamorphose from larva to pupa to adult, so the first phase of life is spent as a caterpillar. Its sole purpose is to accumulate enough food and energy to complete pupation, making it little more than an 'eating machine'.

Caterpillars generally feed only on one or two plant species. They specialise because most rainforest plants produce toxic, sticky or indigestible substances which deter herbivorous insects. So as not to starve, the caterpillar has counter-measures – an array of toxin-neutralising enzymes. But these are expensive on energy so the caterpillar can make only limited quantities. It just can't make enough enzymes to neutralise the defences of more than a few different plants. As one plant evolves greater defences, the caterpillar must produce more and more enzymes to deal with it. Inevitably, the caterpillar evolves to become increasingly specialised to feed from one or two plants, creating a natural arms race between the plant and caterpillar. Such runaway coevolution is believed to be an important speciation-promoting mechanism. In terms of diversity, Lepidoptera rank about equal with Hymenoptera, with about 100,000 described species.

As the caterpillar munches away out in the open, it cannot help leaving evidence of its activities. These eventually catch the watchful eye of a bird or predator. Now begins the second arms race, as the caterpillar tries to avoid becoming a meal itself. Two basic strategies are used.

Lying is one strategy, more properly called **mimicry:** relying on the victim deceiving a curious predator. Mimicking species copy a particular natural object. Many look like twigs. Other species mimic parts of bigger animals. One species of moth caterpillar resembles the whole head of a snake complete with wiggling tongue-like appendage. To get a meal their predators must become

From Santarém in Brazil, Bates collected *Pelopaeus fistularis*, a 'large black and yellow wasp with a remarkably long and narrow waist'. He goes on to describe how this solitary species builds its 50mm long pouch-shaped nest, containing a single large grub. These wasps paralyse other insects, then leave them in the nest as fresh baby-food for the larvae. Other kinds of wasps, including the **sand wasp** (*Bembex* spp), anaesthetise prey for their young, placing it in a tunnel dug in soft dry ground wherein its offspring – usually only one per nest – is ensconced. Bates mentions *B ciliata*, a small pale green wasp, and a solitary species that excavates its nest 'with wonderful rapidity' throwing sand from 'out beneath their bodies…in continuous streams'.

Stingless bees (Meliponinae) build combs in nooks and crannies of trees such as the strangler fig. Others use silk from their own larvae to weave nests from folded leaves.

And precious dwellings should be protected. Certain tree-dwelling ants have a caste of 'doorkeeper' ants. These stalwarts block the entrance hole with square-shaped heads employed for no other task. Some ants live on the outside of trees. Often seen on canoe rides, triangular mud nests are shaped around the underside of branches so rain does not enter and they point down to help the water flow off.

better and better at spotting deception. To avoid detection the caterpillar must become more and more like the object it mimics – an epitome of the art of camouflage in the eternal battle between hunter and hunted.

Some caterpillar species opt for a second strategy by using poison and bright warning colours to defend themselves, often acquiring their toxins from the host plant. Rather than starve, predators evolve ways to deal with poisons so, in turn, the caterpillar becomes ever more poisonous. Moving into the realms of chemical warfare, this arms race carries on as each species stakes its survival on the next generation improving on the last. Although clearly a haven of fascinating chemical developments, little research is devoted to the properties of the insect pharmacopoeias.

Out in the open, butterflies or *mariposas* and moths are again targets. Now we have aerial warfare. Mimicry, using spots creating the image of a bird's eye, is a common defence. *Caligo* spp have owl's eyes emblazoned on their wings' underside and the hairy thorax mimics the owl's beak. A particular form of mimicry is when a non-poisonous butterfly has almost the exact appearance of another related but genuinely toxic species. First discovered among Amazonian insects by Bates, Batesian mimicry is particularly widespread among butterflies and moths.

Moths have also entered the 'arms race' with their main enemy. Bats emit sound clicks to detect their environment at night and of course to hunt slow-flying aerial insects. Some poisonous butterflies actually emit a warning click to announce their unpalatability. How do non-poisonous moths protect themselves? When tiny hairs on the moth detect air vibrated by the bat's click, the moth instantly drops from the sky, beyond the bat's flight path. You can probably guess the scenario as the bat's sonar gets better and better. It's one explanation for why bats have such huge ears.

Who knows the end result of this life-and-death struggle? One thing is certain. As long as plants and caterpillars, butterflies, moths and their predators exist, nature's 'arms race' will continue.

Termites (Isoptera) are not ants but they *are* master builders. In dry areas, their 3m mud mounds are equipped with a queen's chamber, living quarters, nurseries, gardens, defensive walls, waste disposal and air-conditioning. In flooded forest, termites build their ball-shaped nest up a tree trunk; lower down it could be washed away by floods. These nests employ delicate free-form architecture to maximise available space, minimise weight and maintain structural strength. Related to cockroaches, termites lack tannin in their chitinous shell so they are easily damaged by light. To avoid sunburn, they remain in the nest. To move afield, they construct long mud tunnels, sometimes tens of metres up a tree-trunk.

Butterflies and moths

Among rainforest butterflies and moths, several evolutionary strategies are more or less in play continually (see box below). We do not know precisely the number of species recorded from the lowland Amazon, let alone the true number. Accurate measures may never be possible. Lepidoptera is perhaps the best-known invertebrate group, with about 112,000 species worldwide, of which some 4,000 butterflies have been described from Peru alone.

Among the biggest Amazonian 'leps' are moths, notably the splendid **saturniid moth** (*Tysania agripina*), with a wingspan up to 30cm in the largest species. Occurring throughout much of the Americas and Europe, **hawkmoths** are very large and resemble a hummingbird in form and size, so closely in fact that Bates 'several times… shot by mistake a hawkmoth instead of a bird'. The biggest hawkmoths are sometimes called **hummingbird moths** as they 'hum' due to rapid wingbeats while hovering. This behaviour allows them to feed on flowers while out on nocturnal forays. Indeed this is the nocturnal equivalent of the hummingbird's ecological niche, and to attract the moth flowers are usually white and pungent.

Another interesting group of Lepidoptera are the Pierid butterflies, a family in which most species appear to have only four legs compared with the normal six of virtually every insect. In fact the forelegs are held close to the body and only the two pairs of rear legs are used to stand.

Rainforest savants are familiar with **morpho butterflies**, distinguished by their large size and wings of iridescent blue, which may be 15–20cm across. But despite being obvious in flight the resting morpho is cryptic, showing only the underside of its wings, and almost indistinguishable on the trunk of a tree. These magnificent creatures seem barely able to fly under their own impressive size and weight; their looping flight path appears both laborious and strained. Typical upper Amazon species include *M. achilles*, *M. negro* and *M. didius*. These butterflies are highly diverse with over 80 species of morpho within the subfamily *Morphinae*. Another subfamily (Brassolinae) includes *Caligo* spp which has superb eye spots – perfect replicas of owl eyes – while the rest of the wings and body complete the deception, mimicking the bird's 'ears' and beak.

In the Nymphalidae family, along with morphos, is the beautiful Heliconiinae subfamily, or **longwings**, which have a convoluted evolutionary interaction with their passiflora vine host plant. Cyanide compounds produced by passifloras put off most insect herbivores but not the heliconiids. Female longwings lay eggs on the leaves of the vines, which try to prevent this by producing, direct from the leaf, tiny protuberances that look like eggs. Fooled into thinking that these are real eggs, the female wrongly decides the plant is already taken. She moves on and the plant has saved itself from an army of hungry caterpillars.

But of course, there is strong selection for females who are not easily deceived and, when they can tell the difference, plonk, down go the eggs. Selection favours the plant that produces a more realistic fake egg, and the butterfly evolves to get better at detecting the fake and we have another evolutionary arms race. Some passion vines produce nectar to attract ants and wasps that attack butterfly eggs and caterpillars.

Many heliconiids are highly poisonous, 'a flying cyanide capsule', in the words of Diane Murawski (1996), an expert on South American butterflies. Exactly how they acquire the poison is unknown, but it is believed to depend on toxins produced by the host plant, ingested by the caterpillar or butterfly, and sequestered for later use.

Now it gets really interesting. Different species of poisonous heliconiids have evolved to mimic each other, sharing similar wing patterns. In the Amazon of southern Colombia and western Brazil, two different species, *Heliconius erato* and *H. melpomene*, each have a race (or subspecies) that share virtually identical wing patterns. Hence the two races *H. e. reductimacula* and *H. m. vicinus* look the same. Müllerian mimicry was first discovered in the late 19th century by the German naturalist Fritz Müller.

One or two tastes of either of these two poisonous species and predators associate the 'search image' used to recognise food with poison; subsequently all butterflies which share the pattern will benefit from being off the menu. Thus, natural selection favours like-looking individuals whether or not they're different species.

Trays of mounted insects are sold by hawkers who hang around tour operator offices and airports. Some insects – notably morphos – and large beetles like Cerambycidae and Lucanidae species, especially the 'Goliath' (*goliathus*) beetles are at risk or threatened from over-collection, so don't buy them.

Other insects

There is an academic appeal to **cockroaches** which in any other sphere are seen as pretty revolting creatures. Cockroaches have a most distinguished lineage having existed on the planet for some 300 million years. Cosmopolitan pests, they are persistent and hardy, able to survive considerable maltreatment, as anyone who has tried to kill one knows. Aside from various species found around huts, homes and hotels, guests would probably not want to encounter the world's largest cockroach, *Megaloblatta longipennis*, recorded from Colombia at 9.68cm long and 4.50cm across. Curiously, this fact is never cited in tour operator brochures.

John Krichner in *A Neotropical Companion* stretches out an olive branch to the beleaguered insects saying: 'They do not bite or sting, nor do they carry vile diseases. So relax and enjoy them. You might as well. In the Neotropics, at least, they are always close by.'

It is said some people have been driven mad by the ever-present electronic rasping of **cicadas**, with the appearance of huge flies. Our intrepid reporter Bates thought they had a 'harsh jarring tone… a long and loud note resembling the steam whistle of a locomotive'. Like the rest of their order (Hemiptera), cicadas possess a sharp, hypodermic proboscis to suck plant fluids. They are diverse, varying in size from about 10 to 50mm, and sound out different songs according to species to mark territory and attract mates. Assassin bugs (one of which causes Chagas' Disease) use the implement to suck animal fluids, usually from other insects.

Most hemipterans are less than 10mm long but you can see them if you examine closely a green stem or leaf. Here you will also find **aphids**, such as **greenfly** and **plant-lice**, **leaf-hoppers**, which jump as you go to touch them, **scale insects**, which look like tiny shields and **mealy bugs**, which are fluffy or spiky, covered with a whitish woolly substance. Most sedentary plant-suckers produce some type of defensive chemical as a defence against predators and parasites.

Suddenly, a twig moves without a breeze, and you look closely to notice it is a 15cm long **stick insect**, to which are related **leaf-insects** (*Phasmida*), another twist in evolution's game of hide and seek. **Mantids** are voracious predators of other insects and mimic leaves, sticks or even flowers to ambush prospective prey as well as hide from their own predators.

Flies (Diptera) appear mostly around your food or rubbish pits, but less-obvious parasitoid flies attack pest insects like leaf-cutter ants. **Blowflies** hasten the decomposition of dead animals and **fruit-flies** help break down rotting flowers, fruit and fungi. **Mosquitoes** are probably the most troublesome members of this order.

Grasshoppers, **katydids** and **crickets** (Orthoptera) are abundant and highly diverse. Many are nocturnal and have long, whisker-like antennae. Most are cryptically camouflaged. These plant eaters do not swarm locust-like but whole fields can be stripped overnight to satisfy their voracious appetites. Go on a walk after dark to look for **katydids**, of which an incredible number emerge as night descends.

Here we have touched on the best-known insect groups: social insects, butterflies, beetles. But these are the tip of the iceberg, with dozens of other insect orders. Mostly these are inhabitants of places biologists have difficulty reaching; for example, the high canopy, or middle of swamps, or dark, dank places. The true diversity of these cryptobugs is anyone's guess. One could start looking at tiny soil insects such as **springtails** or **thrips**, or look for bigger ones: **earwigs** or **mayflies**, or **scorpionflies**. These are just a few orders of insects that have yet really to come under scrutiny of tropical entomologists, whose task to catalogue and name but a fraction will surely occupy many, many years.

Spiders: a real web sight

The Amazon has an endless fascination for the select few arachnophiles who admire spiders. Admittedly we do not all share a love for them but we ought to respect these eight-legged arthropods. Spiders are major predators of pest insects and are an important food source for many birds.

On jungle walks or canoe rides, everyone notices huge, funnel-shaped webs, up to a metre across. The finely meshed traps are woven by communal spiders, thankfully much smaller than the web size implies! Huge stretches of nature's finest cloth, tattered here and there, hang down and around trees at forest edges. The webs are shaped to catch prey dropped from the canopy. Collectively, dozens of tiny spiders dash out, inject the victim, then suck out its juices.

Communal spiders would not get the prize for the most beautiful webs. This is awarded to the **orb-weaving spiders**, like those you see in your house and garden. But the rainforest, in characteristic profligacy, harbours orb-weavers much bigger and more striking. Elegant *Nephila* species, some coloured black and yellow, with elongated bodies and long black legs, spin perfect giant webs stretching across forest gaps and trails. (Try not to walk into one, it is one of the more disconcerting sensations a rainforest can provide!) These catch large insects and the biggest, up to 2.5m across, can snare small birds and bats.

Big, robust and hairy, **tarantulas** fit our preconception of a rainforest spider. They do not spin a web but actively hunt for prey in swamp vegetation or other damp habitats. Mostly harmless, tarantulas are more fearsome in appearance than in actual bite. Take care though; they should not be handled because their hairs irritate skin. Amazon species include the world's biggest spider, *Theraphosa leblondii*, weighing 120g and with a legspan of 28cm. Recent work has shown tarantulas, notably the **Peruvian pinktoe** (*Avicularia urticans*), are major predators of tree-frogs. A number of tarantulas, the so-called **bird-eating spiders**, also prey on tiny

Left Red and green macaws, *Ara chloroptera*, on salt lick, Madre de Dios River, Peru (PO)

Above White-throated or Cuvier's toucan, *Ramphastos tucanus* (PO)

Below Tiny hawk, *Accipiter superciliosus*, Yasuni National Park, Ecuador (PO)

Above left Hoatzin, *Opisthocomus hoazin*, Manú National Park, Peru (PO)

Left Mealy (*Amazona farinosa*), yellow-crowned (*A ochrocephla*) and blue-headed (*Pionus menstruus*) parrots and dusky-headed parakeets (*Aratinga weddellii*) on salt lick, River Napo, Ecuador (PO)

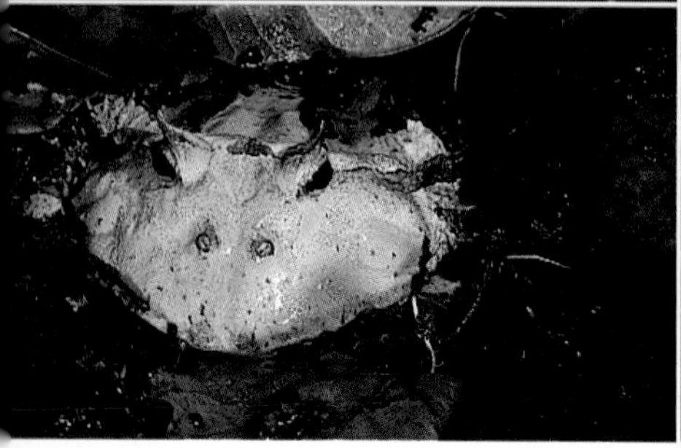

Top left Leaf frog, *Agalygnis craspedopus* (PO)

Above Amazon horned frog, *Ceratophrys cornuta* (PO)

Below Glass frog, *Centrolenelid* sp (PO)

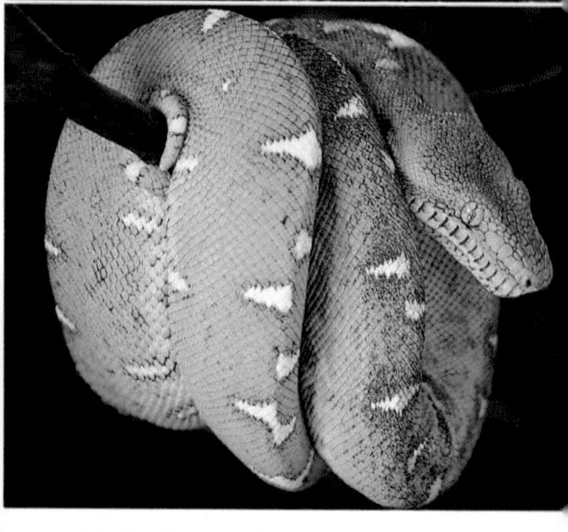

Top right Double-striped forest pit viper, *Bothriopsis bilineatus*, eating mouse (PO)

Above Emerald tree boa, *Corallus coniuis* (PO)

Below left Black caiman, *Melanosuchus niger* (PO)

Below Iguanid lizard, *Enyaloides laticeps* (PO)

Above left Katydid, *Tetigonidae*, resembling a dead leaf (PO)

Above Butterfly, *Dryas iulia* (PO)

Left Owl butterfly, *Caligo eurilochus* (PO)

Above Broad-winged katydid, *Tetigonidae*. Note resemblance to species top left. (PO)

Below Spider (PO)

Above Giant otters, *Pteronura brasiliensis* (PO)

Above right Pygmy marmoset monkey, *Cebuella pygmaea* (PO)

Below Brown-throated three-toed sloth, *Bradypus variegatus* (PO)

Right Ocelot kitten, *Felis pardalis* (PO)

Below Baby tapir, *Tapirus terrestris* (RH)

birds, stalking nests or by ambush. Scholars at first dismissed early reports (Bates *et al)* of spiders big enough to eat birds as clearly the stuff of legend. These species (*Mygale avicularia*) are, in Bates' words 'large and hairy' with 'coarse grey reddish hairs'. His Victorian distaste shows through in his description of the spider's kill, in which one of the birds killed 'lay underneath the body of the spider… and was smeared with the filthy liquor or saliva exuded by the monster'. Whatever Bates' feelings, these are impressive creatures.

Some small spiders are dangerous. A number of species have cytolytic venom that dissolves cells. This causes cells to break down and die, hindering the healing process. Untreated, the wound spreads and ulcerates. A few spiders are life-threatening, but only two or three species out of tens of thousands. One of these species happens to be the world's most venomous spider: the **Brazilian wandering spider** (*Phoneutria fera*), which lives in the thatch or walls of jungle huts.

A group of spiders not commonly known to bite people are the **hunting** or **wolf spiders**. These occur throughout the world, and produce neatly spun funnel-shaped webs between clumps of grass or, in the Amazon, against tree trunks or among leaf litter. These are the spiders' lairs. Here they wait patiently for feckless insects to wander by. Then, faster than you can say 'Wolf!', the spider leaps out, grabs the prey, injects it with venom and drags it back into the funnel, all in one swift, smooth move.

Other arachnids

Despite its large size, about 10–15cm long, and terrifying appearance, the **whip scorpion** (Amblypygidae) is all bluff. The beast is apparently harmless and lacks a sting. Fearsome in looks and reputation is the **scorpion**, an arachnid of which dozens of species are known from South America. They are generally animals of drier climates. (See page 85.)

Millipedes and centipedes

These arthropods (Myriapoda) look like armoured caterpillars. **Millipedes** are usually round in cross-section, shaped like a cylinder. In contrast, a common rainforest species, greyish and up to 13cm long, is flattened, with horizontal projections from each segment. Millipedes have two pairs of legs per segment of which there may be as many as 60. They feed on dead vegetation. If threatened they eject an unpleasant-smelling fluid and roll up but they are harmless.

Centipedes are flattened in cross-section and have only one pair of legs per segment. They prey on small insects and other invertebrates. Most are harmless but some species have a vicious sting.

WATERWORLD

The Amazon is so big that early explorers thought it was actually a giant lake. Now we know it's the world's biggest river with the most diverse freshwater fauna on the planet. There are at least 2,000 fish species with perhaps a thousand more to be described. By comparison, about 150 fish species are known from all of Europe's rivers.

Aquatic mammals

Freshwater dolphins

Although Amazon dolphins do not take as much interest in people as their open-water relatives, they occasionally tolerate humans and often allow people close. To this day, these fun-loving creatures thrive in the Amazon, largely left alone by man who generally has taboos against hunting or eating dolphin. However, fishermen occasionally do kill them by accident or deliberately when dolphins become entangled in nets.

Worldwide, there are five freshwater cetaceans of which the Amazon has two, in most lowland rainforest rivers and lakes. They are smaller than their marine relatives, but are still formidable predators. River dolphins prefer clearwater rivers, but they also roam blackwater rivers, being least common in murky whitewater rivers. Size, colour and behaviour distinguish the two.

Natives call the **pink dolphin** (*Inia geoffrensis*) *bôto*. About 2.4m long and weighing around 160kg, it has a low dorsal ridge in place of a fin. The pink dolphin swims slowly while flat triangular pectoral fins guide it along the river bottom where it does most of its feeding, using sonar to search for fish, crabs and turtles. According to experts, the dolphin stuns prey with sound bursts from the 'melon' organ in its bulging forehead. Pink dolphins are active day and night, and you will often see a bachelor male, or sometimes a family pod of three or four, swim by. When they leap, their body does not clear the water, giving the impression that they are less agile than their saltwater relatives.

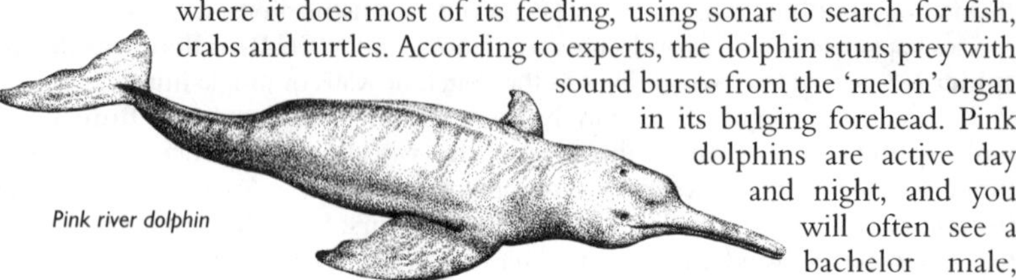

Pink river dolphin

Locally called *tucuxi*, the **grey dolphin** (*Sotalia fluviatilis*) is about 1.5m long and weighs 53kg. Tucuxis are pinkish when young and turn dark grey to black with adulthood, which can create a little confusion if you're trying to work out which Amazon dolphin you have seen. Greys are shaped more like a marine dolphin, with a curved dorsal fin and small pectoral fins. When they jump, their bodies clear the water, reminiscent of marine park performances. Grey dolphin feed mainly on fast-swimming fish close to the surface, reducing competition for feeding between the two species. Found throughout the Amazon and in the lower reaches of the Orinoco, grey dolphins also venture along the Atlantic coast of South America.

Manatee

Once forgotten by all except lonely sailors who mistook them for mermaids, recent attention to its imminent extinction has put the unphotogenic manatee in the limelight. As most Florida residents know, these huge, gentle herbivores are in a highly precarious situation.

RIVERINE ROMEOS

As with their ocean-faring cousins, the Amazon dolphins are widely revered and respected by the indigenous peoples of the Amazon. Believed to have mystic powers and abilities the freshwater dolphins are not hunted in the river leaving population numbers healthy and unmolested.

One myth would suggest that the dolphin's offspring are even greater in number. A widespread belief is that the dolphins are able to transform themselves into handsome men capable of leaving the waters of the Amazon temporarily. Free to roam beyond the banks of the river they seduce young girls making sure they return to the waters of the river rather than face the responsibility of parenthood. Freshwater dolphins are often blamed for unwanted pregnancies.

There are two species (*Sirenia*) in tropical America. The **West Indian manatee** (*Trichechus manatus*) is found in coastal waters from southern Florida to the mouth of the Amazon, while strictly freshwater **Amazon manatee** (*Trichechus inunguis*) is found only in the river basin.

Weighing up to 500kg and 2.7m long, the manatee is the largest Amazon mammal, and wins no beauty contests. Its squarish, whiskered muzzle bears nostrils at the top to allow breathing while the barrel-shaped body and head remain mostly submerged. A powerful paddle-like tail moves it ponderously through the water. Manatees are purely vegetarian and consume over 45kg a day of water weeds. In the absence of manatee grazing, water weeds quickly clog rivers and streams.

Unlike the dolphin, no taboos protect the manatee. Docile, slow-moving and conspicuously swimming just under the surface, it is easy hunting. To make it even easier, floating dung leaves a convenient trail. When hunted the peacefully munching beast is harpooned from a boat. Panicked and hurt, it swims off with the harpoonist hanging on. The huge bulk of the manatee has strength to tow its burden for an hour or more. As the manatee tires, the hunter closes in and stuffs the nostrils with wooden plugs. Suffocation is slow but certain. Packed in old petrol cans, manatee meat keeps for years, preserved in its own oil. Most is sold at market. A high price is a strong incentive to hunt, an opportunity a poor *riverño* cannot afford to pass up.

The long-term outlook for wild manatees is not positive and both species are endangered (CITES I). Despite this, their hunting remains virtually uncontrolled.

Otters

The **southern river otter** (*Lutra longicaudis*) is dark brown above, with creamy-coloured underparts. It feeds on fish and crustaceans in clear rivers and fast streams, and can be found throughout the Amazon and Orinoco Basin. The **Brazilian** or **giant otter** (*Pteronura brasiliensis*) is the world's largest otter, up to 34kg and 1.9m long. Highly social and gregarious, their loud playful antics do little to disguise their whereabouts from hunters. Formerly common and widespread, both species are endangered (CITES I) as a result of hunting for their pelts and their supposed competition for fishing stocks.

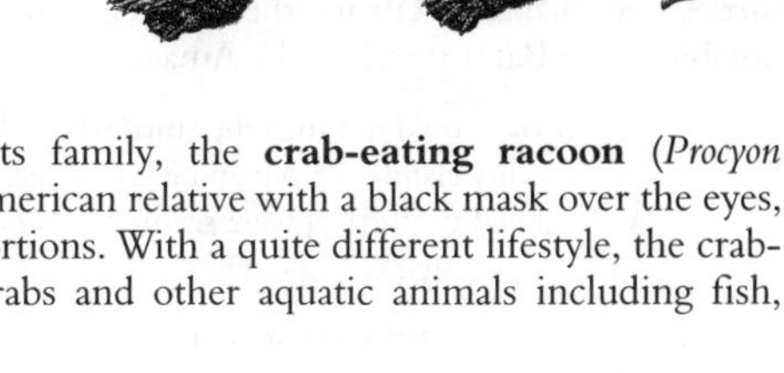

Giant otter

Crab-eating racoon

The only aquatic member of its family, the **crab-eating racoon** (*Procyon cancrivorus*) resembles its North American relative with a black mask over the eyes, ringed tail and similar body proportions. With a quite different lifestyle, the crab-eater is specialised to prey on crabs and other aquatic animals including fish, molluscs and amphibians.

Water opossum

One of 40 or so opossum species, the **water opossum** (*Chironectes minimus*) is the only one to have an aquatic lifestyle, feeding on fish, crabs and insects. Curiously it has exceptionally fast gestation: 12–13 days, the shortest of any mammal, of course facilitated by marsupial biology which produces young born at an earlier stage than placental mammals.

Aquatic reptiles

Tropical freshwater is ideal for aquatic reptiles. The two main groups are crocodilians and turtles. Their Amazon representatives are unique and mostly endemic species, evolved from ancestors isolated when South America became an island continent.

Caiman

Among the most impressive Amazon reptiles are **caiman**, the South American crocodilians. The four species differ in size, enabling them to use different ecological resources and so coexist in the same habitat. All caiman eat fish, but turtles, frogs, other reptiles and anything else that gets in the way are also considered suitable prey.

The largest is the **black caiman** (*Melanosuchus niger*), an awesome creature at its full-grown length of 6.1m, but populations are under severe pressure due to hunting. Bates was impressed with the 'cunning, cowardice and ferocity of this reptile…' but admiration was not among his feelings as he considered 'the enormous gape of their mouths…' believing 'the uncouth shape of their bodies makes a picture of unsurpassable ugliness'. This seems somewhat unenlightened in our conservation-minded age, but it shows how much our attitudes differ from those of the first naturalists to explore the Amazon.

On night boat rides you will probably see the red eyeshine of the **common** or **spectacled caiman** (*Caiman crocodilus*). They grow up to 2.5m, but the majority are considerably smaller. If you manage to see one close up, you will see that the bony ridges above the eyes convey a bespectacled appearance. These caiman are found throughout the Amazon and Orinoco Basins. They lay communally on the same beach. Caiman lay 30 to 60 eggs at a time – food to attract many predators. Egg mortality is high (50–80%) and even after hatching, juveniles have a slim chance of making it to adulthood. Wading birds and especially tegu lizards take their toll, with perhaps just one or two individuals in a clutch surviving to adulthood. Two species of **dwarf caiman** (*Paleosuchus* spp) are widespread in Amazonia, but relatively rare.

River turtles

An abundance of ideal habitats and food makes the Amazon perfect for *tortugas*. The 13 Amazon species of river turtle are all side-necked turtles, so-called because they retract their head sideways into the shell. This primitive group's fossils date back to the Cretaceous period over 140 million years ago, a time when river turtles were abundant throughout the Amazon Basin. Traditionally, Indian tribes kept turtles and farmed them for their oil, eggs and meat. Their abundance was still notable when Bates travelled the Amazon:

> 'Cardozo… could not turn the [turtles] on their backs fast enough so that a great many clambered out and got free again. However, three boatloads, or about eighty [turtles] were secured… When the canoes had been twice filled, we desisted…'

As Bates discovered, turtle meat is 'a most appetising dish', a fact that has led to its downfall. Turtles still occur in many parts of the Amazon, but are rare in most places. Even where common, they tend to be shy and you'll catch but a glimpse of a trio lined up on a rock or branch before they see you and quietly slip into the water.

Your best bet to see turtles in the wild is in remote, protected areas, with lots of lakes and rivers. Where left alone, they may even come to tolerate human presence, allowing you close enough to take a good photograph. At La Selva Lodge in Ecuador turtles regularly bask on branches protruding from the nearby lake.

Largest representative is the **giant river turtle** (*Podocnemis expansa*), over 0.9m long and weighing 75kg. This species has potential to be farmed for meat, eggs and shell, with projected meat yields far exceeding those of conventional cattle ranching. Sadly, these marvellous prehistoric creatures continue to be over-exploited in the wild. Each of the four *Podocnemis* turtles are listed as threatened (CITES II).

The **snake-neck turtle** or *matamata* (*Chelys fimbriata*) has a neck longer than its backbone. The snout is long and tube-like to act as a snorkel. Its carapace has pointed peaks on the top, camouflage to hide it among floating leaves in wait of prey. It feeds on fish by opening its wide mouth suddenly to draw in small fish like a vacuum cleaner. Related species include *charapita de aguajal* (*Phrynops nasuta*), a small, nocturnal piscivorous turtle, and the **mud turtle** or *charapa de fango* (*Platemys platycephala*).

Fabulous fishes

Over 2,000 endemic Amazon fish species have been catalogued – making the Amazon Basin the most diverse freshwater fauna in the world – and scientists estimate as many as two thousand more remain to be described.

From relatively few ancestors Amazon fishes evolved and diversified into a multitude of niches in a process called *adaptive radiation.* Around 80% are characins, neotropical freshwater fish. To these belong such diverse groups as catfish, lungfish, gaudy aquarium fishes and the less alluring but more famous piranha.

Characins

Piranha

If we were to believe B-movies, we would think there is only one type of Amazon fish, the deadly and vicious piranha. There are in fact some 25 species of piranha lurking in lowland rivers: a few are specialist carnivores, one type feeds exclusively on fish fins and some are even vegetarian.

The most famous piranha is the **red-bellied** or *pana roja* (*Serrasalmus nattereri*), which ranks as the world's most dangerous freshwater fish. Its best-known attribute is extremely sharp teeth, serrated and triangular, just like a shark's, but no more than 6mm long. They grow to 20–23cm and are diamond-shaped with a silvery back and an orange-red underside. Very easy to catch with a piece of raw meat, and with seemingly hundreds of tiny bones, piranha are neither enjoyable nor particularly tasty food. **White piranha** or *pana blanca* (*S. rhombeus*), lack the red belly.

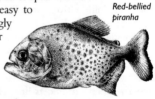

Red-bellied piranha

In blackwater lakes some piranha attain impressive size. Luckily these are not flesh-eaters, but instead patiently wait for fallen fruits. Indeed, most species feed only on floating fruits, berries or insects.

Piranha detect the splash of potential food as it falls into a stream or lake and smell it in the water. They attack prey only if it is bleeding and moving erratically. The famous flesh-stripping abilities depend on fish numbers, carcass size and season. Low water-levels are likely to reduce food availability and increase competition. Nevertheless, piranha partly deserve their reputation as aggressive, ferocious fish; proven by the number of fishermen in the Amazon missing toes and fingers. Piranha attacks have injured people, but records show not one fatality.

Electric eel

On the other hand, a number of documented cases report fatalities caused by the infamous **electric eel** (*Electrophorus electricus*). This stunning fish discharges a shock of up to 1,000 volts to knock out or kill prey; also an effective defence against predators. The current is usually between 0.5 and 0.75 amperes, non-lethal for humans, but powerful enough to cause temporary paralysis. As most encounters are in water, the immobilised victim is drowned rather than electrocuted. Rarely encountered, the fish is a bottom-dweller in sluggish channels and streams, although surfacing every now and then to breathe air, or rather absorb it through specialised buccal filaments.

Able to move backwards is the **knife fish** (*Carapus* sp), a relative of the electric eel and an electro-navigator but lacking a significant current.

Parasitic catfishes: leech-fishes, water vampires and living arrows

The notorious candiru family (Trichomycteridae) are small, scaleless fish. A few species are free-living but others have various obnoxious lifestyles. Some attach themselves to other fish, using spines on their gill openings, and rasp away at scales and flesh like fishy leeches. Half a dozen or more wriggling, slimy appendages infest an afflicted fish. Another candiru lives in gill filaments of larger fish, vampirically feeding off the blood supply.

Most notorious of this group is *Vandellia cirrhosa*. This extremely thin fish normally dwells within another fish's waste tract but is believed to wriggle up urogenital and, some say, other orifices of human swimmers. Apparently attracted by the warmth of the urine, it zooms inside the body opening, whereupon its sharp spines project into the tender flesh. Stuck like a living arrow, the fish is only removable by surgery. In areas where vandellia are present natives wear protective garments and menstruating women do not swim as they believe blood attracts the fish. Attacks are virtually unheard of but just to be safe, don't pee in the water.

Other catfishes: giant fish, gold fish and talking fish

Catfish make up the majority of neotropical characins. Several are important food species. Those mentioned here are but a few of the hundred or more catfish species that differ greatly in size, colour and ecology. Most catfish are bottom-feeders, and use their long whiskers (barbels) to search the river mud for worms, crustaceans and snails.

The largest catfish, and one of Amazonia's biggest fish with a scientific name to match, is *Brachyplatystoma filamentosum*. Individuals grow up to 3m long. Good to eat and a popular catch their huge jaws can easily wound the careless fisherman. But size is no indication of danger where catfish are concerned. Small free-living species called **squeakers** have poisonous, stinging dorsal spines.

Not all Amazon fish are horrible nasty creatures. The **dorado** is a common catfish, reaching a metre in length, coloured pale gold along its flanks with a silvery back. More practically, it is a staple food fish for people along the river, and often served at tourist lodges and river boats. Species in the Doradidae family have fat bodies and four to six barbels. The **talking catfish** (*Acanthodorus spinosissimus*) makes grunting sounds in and out of water. Aquarium species include the **arch-backed catfish** (*Corydroras* sp) and the **hassar** (*Callichthyes*).

In fish markets you may see the **carachama** (*Chaetostomus* sp), dark brown and up to 30cm long. Its heavy scales bear ornate horns and each pectoral fin has curved, toothed bony projections. The fish probably uses them as anti-predator defence; locals use them in handicrafts. Other heavily armoured catfish include *Plecostomus,* a popular aquarium species.

Living gems of murky *igapo* waters, **jewel tetras** (*Hyphassobrycon* spp) are among the most sought-after aquarium fish. Under lights these tiny specimens glow brilliant primary colours, giving rise to names like **cardinal tetra**, **neon tetra** and **glo-lite tetra**.

Shaped like a miniature barracuda, the **dog fish** (*Rhaphidon vulpinus*), 30–45cm long, is coloured silvery-yellow and possesses two long canine-like teeth. It uses these weapons to stab prey, typically other fish, up to half its size. Unrelated to small sharks of the same name found only in oceans, dog fish are often seen in a fisherman's catch or on sale at city fish markets.

Flying hatchet fish (*Carnegiella*) use their pectoral fins as wings to propel them through the air. This seems to be a defence against predatory fish but they will often fly high and far enough to land in a speeding canoe. Others behave equally strangely. The more sedate **headstanders** (*Abramites*) spend the majority of their lives with their tail up in the air, whereas **pencil fish** (*Poecilobrycon*) live mostly head-up.

Bony-tongued fish

Bony-tongued fish (Osteoglossidae), with fossils dating back to the Cretaceous era, are South America's most primitive piscines, now represented by relatively few species. Their diagnostic feature is a hard, stiff, bony tongue, stiff scales and a dorsal and anal fin continuing almost to the tail.

Arapaima: armour-plated lung-fish

Few of us know the Amazon boasts one of the world's largest freshwater fish, called **paiche** in Peru or **pirarucú** in Brazil (*Arapaima gigas*). Shaped like a huge pike they are predators of other fish. Specimens up to 4.6m long and weighing 250kg were known but this fish's huge size and tasty flesh have led to its demise. Most caught today are usually less than 2.5m weighing *only* 90kg.

Their greenish-bronze scales turn white when removed. As big as your palm and hard as plastic, they evolved as armour plating against caiman or dolphin attack, and are ideal for decoration or jewellery. They also make a good nail file. Natives use arapaima's rough bony tongue as coarse-grade sandpaper.

A type of lung-fish, arapaima can breathe air if necessary. When water warms up, oxygen levels drop, which encourages the fish to gulp air which is absorbed through a modified air bladder. Other lungfish use this ability to crawl across land when waters recede. Arapaima aestivate, relinquishing its fish lifestyle for a while, choosing to hibernate through warm, dry periods; they burrow deep in the mud, curl into a ball and stay cocooned until the river returns.

Arowhana: mouth-breeding water monkeys

Many rainforest fish consume insect prey and hunt among the tendrils and roots of floating vegetation or rely on insects floating on the water's surface. The **water monkey**, locally called the *arowhana* or *arahuana* (*Osteoglossum bicirrhosum*), depends not on a chance meal to fall from overhanging vegetation: it jumps. Up to a metre long, it leaps a full body length out of the water to gulp unsuspecting meals perched on a leaf or branch. Given the opportunity it will catch small reptiles, birds or even baby sloths.

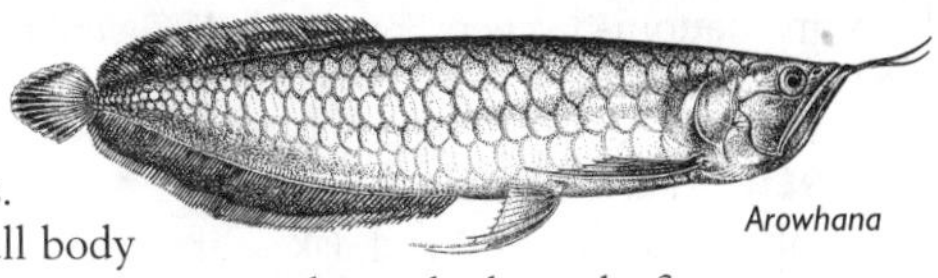

Arowhana

Unlike most fish, the arowhana is a mouth brooder. After the eggs hatch, the male scoops the tiny larvae into his mouth to protect them. When the yolk-sac is consumed the male releases fry for sporadic feeding and guides them back to safety by waving barbels on his lower jaw, a successful strategy to protect the young against natural predators. Human fishermen, who capture fry for sale to foreign aquaria, catch and behead breeding males for their conveniently packaged fry. Predictably, arowhana are a threatened species.

Cichlids

Cichlidae is an important family of tropical freshwater fish with some 150 cichlids described from the Amazon. Many species are commercially important either as food or sport fish, or for the aquarium trade.

Flooded forests are important habitat for fruit-eating fish. ***Tambaqui*** (*Colossoma macropomum*) is said to be the best-flavoured of fishes and has been over-fished around Manaus. Found in blackwater rivers, it grows to a length of 1.0m weighing up to 30kg, and is golden-yellow with black dorsal bars and a prominent eye-spot on the tail. Experiments show the eye-spot decreases predator attacks.

Other cichlids with eye-spots are ***acarahuasú*** (*Astronotus ocellatus*) and ***tucunaré*** or ***oscar*** (*Cichla monoculus, C. temensis*). Bates encountered the *tucunaré* along the Tapajós River, during his exploration of the Amazon. He says little of it except to note it is 'a most delicious fish… esteemed by natives'. Of economic importance is the **peacock bass** (*C. ocellaris*), the biggest neotropical cichlid.

Discus fish (*Symphysodon* spp) have a round, compressed body. Their attractive markings make them popular with aquarium hobbyists. Two species are found in tributaries of the mainstream that provide parental care for their young by producing a mucus exuding through the skin on which the young feed.

Other Amazon fishes

The **leaf fish** (*Monocirrhus polyacanthus*) mimics a dead leaf floating on water. Drifting around, pointing downward, it preys on other fish as they swim by oblivious to the danger. A transparent tail and pectoral fins allow it to move without being detected.

Common in quiet streams with overhanging vegetation, the **four-eyed fish** (*Anableps*) is uniquely equipped to spot danger in or out of the water. Each eye is divided in two so one half is above water with the other half below.

Four-eyed fish eye

The tiny **killifish** (*Cyprinodontei*) spend most of their lives as tough, drought-resistant eggs in shallow, ephemeral ponds. Some killifish have adapted to hatch, grow, mate, lay eggs and die in places where water persists for a mere two or three weeks. (And you think your life is hectic?)

Sting-rays or **dasytid rays**, notably of the strictly freshwater genus *Potamotrygon*, are the only freshwater cartilaginous fishes (although sharks roam upriver from the ocean). The 'sting' is a venomous barbed fin at the base of the tail. Rays are bottom-dwellers, resting half-covered in sand on the beds of shallow rivers.

Aquatic arthropods

Tropical rivers, streams and lakes are among the least biologically explored habitats. Ecologists lament how few land arthropods are studied relative to their diversity, but forget there is a community of largely unknown species among the weeds and floating meadows. Who knows how many species are to be found? Lift up a mat of floating vegetation and you see water snails, diving beetles, water boatmen, aquatic stages of flying insects, paleomonid shrimp and other crustaceans.

Indigenous Tribes and Settlers

6

The Amazon is commonly referred to as one of the last frontiers of humanity, but the notion of an empty area, devoid of people is a myth. True, the Amazon Basin is not packed with people, but neither is it empty. More than 30 million people live within its 7.3 million km^2 watershed. Indigenous tribes, rubber tappers, gold prospectors, cattle ranchers and forestry workers all make the headlines from time to time. But in the cities, life continues pretty much the same as in any city of the world.

Every person living in the Amazon Basin arrived there through migration, the majority of them in their own lifetimes. A consistent factor of these migrations is the adaptation of each group, within the limits of technologies and vision, to the environment. Some seem to manage a little better than others.

ORIGINS

The original inhabitants of South America arrived from Asia via North and Central America, crossing the continental divide during the last ice age, around 22,000 years ago. As migration pushed further south, tribal groups adapted their lifestyles to the wide variety of environments encountered. The first arrivals to the Amazon Basin reached the open plains and southern regions 12,000 years ago, having followed the line of the Andes southwards before heading east through modern-day Bolivia. Ceramics found in the Upper Xingu River and the Madeira River suggest that communities could have begun to move down these major tributaries as early as 8,000 years ago.

Archaeology is difficult in the Amazon Basin. Organic remains rot quickly in the warm, wet climate and fieldwork, often in remote areas, is difficult to support and sustain over long periods of time. Piecing together fragments found so far, by 5,000BC communities were well-established along the Amazon mainstream when the core languages of the region began to fragment and diversify. The warlike and aggressive Tupi pushed north from their Paraguayan homelands to contest the central plains of Brazil. Preferring a quiet life, the Gê-speaking Indians dispersed from the central plains and moved in a westerly direction towards the heart of the Amazon, allowing the Tupi to occupy territory as far north as the Amazon mainstream. By the time the Gê moved into the Amazon, Carib and Arawak tribes had long since settled in the region from their Caribbean homelands having followed the coastline of South America to the river's mouth. Warfare and migration subsequently distributed groups throughout the Basin.

But in this huge and complex area little is absolutely certain. An alternative route for migration to the Basin, and one that is more conventionally accepted, is the Andean route. According to this theory, Arawak tribes are believed to have taken the overland route, migrating from their Central American homelands through what are now Colombia and Venezuela. Other groups migrated from Ecuador down the River Napo and other tributaries into the Amazon Basin.

It is easy to see how migration was the dominant vehicle for change. Using the rivers as highways, even today village communities and families can collect their belongings and rapidly move from one location to another in a very short period of time. With different Indian tribes advancing and retreating, fragmentation and dispersal of groups occurred quickly and easily.

Although migratory patterns are uncertain, the existence of trade and warfare between the Indians of the Amazon and those of the mountains is beyond dispute. The eastern slopes of the Andes in Ecuador, Peru and Bolivia are littered with defensive forts and trading posts marking strategic points. The oral history of the Incas mentions raiding parties by jungle Indians. The eastern quarter of the Inca empire was called *Antisuyo* and its inhabitants were known as *Antis*; from where the Andes mountain range gets its name. The rainforest lowlands, even for the Incas, were considered an impenetrable mass, and it was to the jungle that the last Inca fled when seeking protection from the invading Spanish.

When the Portuguese arrived the indigenous population of the Brazilian Amazon was between 1.5 and 7 million. Today across all Amazon countries the figure is below one million. Of the 2,000 different indigenous tribes that existed at the time, fewer than 400 remain.

Languages

The dominant languages of the Amazon Basin are Spanish and, in Brazil, Portuguese. Brought in by conquering European powers these languages are, beyond doubt, the most widespread.

In the Andean highlands the Incas made Quechua the *lingua franca* of their empire. As a result many communities and some Indian tribes on the eastern slopes of the Andes and nearby lowland areas use Quechua as the dominant language.

But more generally the number of languages across ethnic groups in the Amazon reflects the diversity of the region. The majority of dialects spoken by Brazilian Indians derive from one of four languages: Gê, Tupi, Carib and Arawak. Gê- and Tupi-speaking Indians arrived from the south of Brazil and fought for domination of the coastal regions. The Tupi, being the more aggressive and warlike, were more expansionist in outlook, pushing Gê-speaking tribes further inland.

Linguistic variety was further enhanced by Carib-speaking tribes, linguistically related to the original inhabitants of the Caribbean, and the arrival of Arawak tribes from Central and North America. While most indigenous languages are based on a mixture of these four languages, there are a number of languages throughout the Amazon that bear no relation to these four core groups.

BELIEFS AND CUSTOMS

To generalise about Indian beliefs and customs is difficult. Many Indians are animists, believing that all living things – animals, plants and humans – possess a spirit. A complex hierarchy of spirits governing the natural world makes the hunting of certain animals completely taboo. Songs, chants and dances are used to keep evil forces at bay, offering protection on hunting trips and safe passage when travelling.

Upsetting the balance can arouse vengeful spirits, which make themselves known in several ways. Dreams are one medium of communication with the spirit world, offering insightful perspectives on the illness of a child or the prospects for a hunting expedition. Illness is also attributed to malevolent spirits, and caused by unnecessarily upsetting the spirit world or by a curse from a neighbouring village or community. Either way, healing comes from special songs, dances and herbal concoctions administered in ceremonies conducted by the shaman spiritual healers.

Shamans have the ability to see the invisible magic darts that cause pain, curses and illness, a skill enhanced by the use of hallucinogens. Experience and strength determine the power of a shaman to fight off illnesses and defend his village against the darts of vengeful shamans from neighbouring villages. He spends his life building up an armoury of magic darts, each one equipped with special powers to deal with specific situations.

The effect of order and responsibility in the spirit world is reflected in daily life. Social interaction is highly ordered, relying heavily on ritual. Domestic life too is ordered, with responsibilities clearly divided between the sexes. Men hunt, fish and build new homes; women tend the garden, prepare food, look after the children and manage the house. (So there are quite a few cross-cultural similarities.)

In such a carefully ordered world, stepping over the line that constitutes responsible and acceptable behaviour demands revenge, usually resulting in raiding parties and death. As a result many Indian tribes have been described as aggressive and warlike. At a cursory level there often appears to be an excess of violence, but it is rarely violence for its own sake. A system of honour prevails and, when placed in context, there are usually complex and justified reasons for the warlike behaviour.

Life and death

Indians have a wide range of myths and legends to explain their place in the universe. The creation myths of different tribes usually reflect some part of the natural environment, if not from the area currently occupied then from a region lived in by earlier generations. The existence of an afterlife is common, but judgement on whether it is paradise varies greatly.

Birth is a difficult affair. When women have given birth they commonly have to observe strict taboos restricting them from eating especially nourishing foods. Added to that, birth often takes place without special precautions and care. While the woman bears the infant and returns to her daily chores often immediately, the men carry the responsibility of making sure the 'empty soul' is not occupied by evil spirits: an exhausting and difficult job which requires their complete attention for several days.

Infanticide used to be widespread, especially with female babies. Although a young girl is free to enjoy sexual freedom, society will not support any illegitimate child. Infanticide was also practised if several same-sex babies were born concurrently, or if twins were born and if a baby was handicapped.

Death too requires a flexible outlook to achieve understanding of some apparently bizarre practices. The Yanomami of Brazil and Venezuela cremate their dead, consuming the ashes several months later and thus enabling the dead to continue their lives through the living. The Achuar of Ecuador bury their dead but dispel the spirit of the dead from their world and their memories. The French anthropologist Philippe Descola explains that this 'reflects the notion that the living cannot be truly living if the dead are not truly dead'. For other groups the Indian spirit travels to a village in the sky where the spirits of all the dead live. The journey confronts the spirit with dangers so he is buried with his bow and arrow.

But once the celestial village has been reached, the spirit requires no further nourishment or assistance. The rivers and forests, without fish or game, are there for nothing more than the memory of the soul as it dances to the rhythm of eternity.

INDIGENOUS TRIBES TODAY

The Yanomami are probably the best-known Amazon Indian tribe. Numbering around 22,000, they live in an area bridging the borders of Brazil and Venezuela. Inhabiting highland areas of *terra firme* forest, Yanomami live communally in *shabonos* which are generally made up of several extended families.

Social structure is based on the independence, rights and obligations of the individual. A careful balance between these three core values creates a self-sustaining society that speaks out against wrong, yet understands the importance of sharing. Such an egalitarian society requires no central authority and resorts to the use of chiefs only at times of conflict. When disagreements rise to unacceptable levels, defending self-respect is essential and may escalate, leading to permanent division of the community.

The social structure of the Yanomami recurs in various guises throughout the Amazon. Their society, as one well-researched tribe, offers a point of comparison across the highly varied lifestyles of indigenous tribes.

Amazon indigenous lifestyles can broadly be divided into two groups: those occupying *terra firme* rainforest, like the Yanomami, and those that live on the river, using *várzea* (flooded) forest.

Tribes living on in *terra firme* forest primarily rely on slash-and-burn agricultural systems to supply an important part of their food requirements from plant cultivation. Clearing small plots, about half a hectare in size, with axes and machetes, they burn the vegetation, while large trees are kept and used as firewood. With the thin soil fertilised by the ash of the rainforest the garden is planted with a variety of crops, including manioc, plantains and sweet potatoes. The Yanomami plant a range of crops that mature at different speeds. Maize is ready to harvest in four months. Sweet potatoes, manioc, bananas and plantains are all ready for harvesting within a year, with palms taking as long as three years to become productive.

Plots generally have one staple crop covering 80% of the garden. Manioc is by far the most popular throughout the Amazon with other tribes, such as the Yanomami and the Shipibo of Peru, preferring plantains, and a few (including the Araweté of Brazil and the Amawaka of Peru/Brazil) choosing maize.

As with all crops, the gardens need constant attention to keep weeds at bay and to prevent the forest and its malevolent spirits reclaiming the cleared land. After a few years, the soil's productivity falls and the community moves on. Although subject to leaching and erosion from heavy rain when being farmed, the plot is quickly reclaimed by the forest when left untended. The forest regains the appearance of primary rainforest within 50 years but takes another century or so to reach its original structure.

Although the plot is left to be reclaimed by the forest, the community returns to it to harvest crops with a longer growing-life. Typically a single community works a young plot, a mature plot and an old plot.

Agricultural production is supplemented by hunting and fishing, with foraging providing seasonal fruits.

Agriculture is also practised in *várzea* areas. Rice, beans, peppers and cocoa are planted to maximise benefits from the annual floods. The varieties of manioc planted mature in six months rather than twelve, taking advantage of the shorter growing season caused by annual flooding.

Várzea communities have the benefit of seasonal floods to constantly review the waning fertility of agricultural land. The ready availability of protein from fish, caiman, turtles, and birds, along with hunting of mammals visiting the water's edge, removes the need to periodically shift to new areas.

INDIGENOUS POPULATIONS TODAY

It is impossible to obtain universally agreed figures on how many indigenous groups live in the Amazon and the size of their populations. Organisations and governments have different definitions of what constitutes an ethnic group, based on linguistic or cultural differences. Some authors divide ethnic groups into smaller groups. National census figures are unreliable, and in some countries do not even require statement of ethnic group. When population figures are compiled they are usually best guestimates.

A widely agreed figure puts the Indian population at just under 700 thousand. Current populations vary dramatically in size ranging from less than a hundred to over 40,000.

The largest ethnic groups in the Amazon

Ethnic group	*Population*	*Location*
Chiquitano	40,000	Bolivia
Kampa	31,919	Peru, Brazil
Mojeño	30,000	Bolivia
Achuar/Shuar	30,000	Peru/Ecuador
Tukano	27,000	Colombia, Brazil
Tikuna	25,637	Brazil, Colombia, Peru
Arguarana	25,000	Peru
Shipibo	20,000	Peru
Yanomami	19,727	Brazil, Venezuela
Makuxi/Makushi	15,132	Brazil, Guyana
Wapishana	13,467	Brazil, Guyana

Although disease, encroachment of tribal lands and violence against Indian groups has been highlighted in recent years, comparison of figures between 1970 and 1990 show that Indian populations have, as a general trend, increased over the last twenty years. Explaining the increase is difficult. Significant improvements in health services are rare and inconsistent across the region and environmental conditions tend to have deteriorated. One suggestion is that groups have now acquired resistance to imported disease.

The number of populations that are disappearing is relatively small – some 6% of the total. Some of these groups, such as the Pakaguara of Bolivia, will soon disappear.

(This information has been taken from an EC-funded report looking at the state of indigenous populations living in rainforest areas. Data on population statistics for Amazonian Indian tribes varies widely.)

Várzea communities living close to the Amazon mainstream were the first groups encountered by Portuguese and Spanish explorers and were quickly decimated by diseases. Before the Europeans arrived these groups farmed fish and turtles in pens. As might be expected, social organisation reflected seasonality. Social conflict was at its highest during annual floods when food stocks were at their lowest and warring parties would often raid neighbouring communities for food. But in times of plenty, *várzea* communities were capable of supporting large populations that developed complex technologies and social hierarchies.

In reality, no Indian society in the Amazon today relies entirely on agriculture or hunting and fishing alone. Pressure on wildlife has actually increased the importance of agriculture in recent years to the extent that no Amazon tribe relies on hunting or fishing for more than half of its dietary needs.

Social groups

Social structure among Amazon tribes varies greatly with some sharing common features. The Yanomami live in communal structures called *yanos* or *shabonos* that are home to the whole village of between 25 and several hundred people. Several families live within each dwelling and social interaction is an essential part of life. The huge 'o' shaped houses, thatched with palm leaves, have a wide open space in the middle. The space is reserved for dancing and ceremonies, with festivals often lasting for days. Festivals are essential to maintaining a sense of community.

Other tribes choose smaller structures. The Achuar of Ecuador use individual family dwellings and the head of the house takes two or three wives with other men occasionally living in the house.

Social groups vary from settled villages with large numbers of people and elaborate dwellings, to nomads living in bands of 30 to 40 and moving every few days without the need for permanent houses.

Dwellings built with forest products provide shelter from heavy rains, hot sun and seasonal floods. Tall, straight tree-trunks are ideal for sides of buildings and stilts raise houses above the flood level.

As many as 20 different tree species are used to construct a traditional house, without using a single nail. Leaves of the thatch palm or *irapay* (*Lepidocaryum tessmannii*) provide palm fronds for roofing. Split down the middle rib they are doubled over and then laid pointing downwards on parallel roof beams.

Simple housing suits the subsistence life led by most forest dwellers. People usually move to a different place long before their organic house becomes affected by termites and fungi. More often a settlement is vacated due to floods or declines in the yields of crops and game. When it is time to move, the old house is left behind and another constructed in a new site from nearby materials. A palm-thatch stilt house may last up to ten years before returning to the forest whence it came.

Living off the land

Indigenous groups live in apparent harmony with the surrounding habitat. Hunting and foraging upset the ecological balance of the rainforest, but the smaller population size has a reduced impact on the rainforest from which it is easier to recover.

Hunting

The work of men, hunting is carried out primarily with a bow and arrow. The bows are made from the strong, flexible wood of palms, with bowstrings fashioned from braided palm fibres. Arrows are made from cane, found in the wild or grown in the garden, fletched with primary feathers of birds. Bows and arrows are generally used to shoot terrestrial game, such as rodents, deer, tapir and peccary, and arboreal game including monkeys and birds. They have even been adapted for the water species including fish, turtles and caiman.

Blow pipes are used throughout the Amazon and are particularly common in the western Amazon although guns are slowly, but increasingly, being used. Over nine different species of plant are used in the construction of blow pipes, with the darts made from slivers of the wood of the *inayuga* palm (*Maximiliana venatorum*).

CURARE

In the right hands the blow pipe (*Strychnos toxifera*), from the wourali root, is a highly efficient method of killing birds and mammals. But the darts that shoot out of the barrel of the blow pipe seem barely capable of breaking the skin, let alone causing death. The potency of the blow pipe as a weapon lies in the curare-tipped darts. Curare is a muscle relaxant that induces paralysis. Not only does the curare kill the prey, it also relaxes the muscles, thus reducing the chance of muscle spasms keeping the prey out of reach in the rainforest canopy – and wasteful hunting is sure to activate vengeful spirits.

Although numbers are unknown, there are probably over a couple of hundred toxins used in hunting made primarily from plants and even frog-skin secretions. In the Colombian Amazon at least 75 plant species are used in the preparation of curare. A mixture of different lianas, including *Strychnos toxifera*, utilising the bark and wood of the plants, are treated to create a resinous substance. Remarkably the highly effective poison is most potent when it is slightly bitter, a quality assessed by taste.

Western doctors have used curare derivatives in a number of ways in Western medicine, where it is used as a muscle relaxant for surgical operations and to relieve paralysis, multiple sclerosis, lockjaw, epilepsy and Parkinson's disease.

Using down from kapok (*Ceiba* sp) seeds creates an airtight seal. Bags for carrying the curare-tipped darts are made from fibre palm (*Astrocaryum chambira*) and chonta (*Euterpe* spp).

Hunting itself is carried out in a number of ways. Men may go on short solitary hunting expeditions. Dawn or dusk, when birds and animals are most active, are the favoured times for the hunt. Silent stalking or mimicking bird or monkey calls are advanced techniques used by skilful hunters.

Hunting expeditions lasting several hours or even days require planning and support. As most Indian groups live communally, hunting doubles up as an opportunity to spend time with a partner. The pair follow the sounds, tracks and droppings of animals. With experience comes the ability to differentiate between animal spoors, and further examination reveals how recently the animal was in the area, also whether it was feeding or just passing through. Guans and curassow, along with macaws, parrots, toucans and doves, are common prey taken by hunters travelling in pairs. Monkeys are also taken.

The introduction of hunting dogs has added a new dimension, enabling a hunting couple to tackle larger prey that previously required hunting in large groups. In some groups the breeding and care of hunting dogs is the women's responsibility, with the performance of a woman's pack directly reflecting her status. The women, with the overall responsibility for food production, would generally quarter the larger animals before carrying them back home in backpacks instantly made from forest plants.

Prior to the arrival of missionaries, most cultures were polygamous. An invitation to go hunting showed favour to the chosen wife and created an opportunity for intimacy away from the communal home.

Hunting expeditions for herding animals such as peccary are usually carried out in groups. They are aggressive animals when cornered and travel in groups of ten or more, so the opportunity to bag so much valuable meat would be wasted on the solitary hunter. With a hunting group it is possible to trap the herd, killing several animals.

Fishing

The most widespread means of catching fish is with nets, although poisons are also used. The roots of the *barbasco* (*Lonchocarpus*) plant are pounded into a thick, white liquid. The mulch is then released into a river that has been blocked off downstream. Stupefied, but not dead, the fish are then picked out of the water as they float towards the barrage. The mild toxin in *barbasco* does not permanently affect the fish so causes no permanent damage to fish that are not caught and, importantly, is not toxic to mammals.

The use of ichthyotoxic plants is widespread throughout the Amazon but especially in the smaller rivers on the Andean foothills. Fishing expeditions are most common at times of low water. Virtually all Indian groups that have fish in their diet use poisons. A few have developed the use of harpoons and bow and arrow, especially in slow-running, blackwater rivers where visibility is better.

Gathering

The impression that the jungle is a tropical Garden of Eden with fruits hanging from the boughs of every tree should, by now, have been truly dispelled. Wandering through the forest is unlikely to produce impressive yields of fruit. But gathering is a crucial activity for Indian societies. In addition to seasonal plant foods, wild honey and eggs, edible insects such as palm grubs are harvested, as well as shellfish. Plants for medicine and poisons for hunting are also collected. And it is the natural environment that provides Indians with weapons, the structure and roof of their houses, rafts and boats, as well as the materials for making baskets, dyes, strings and ropes, handles for tools, clay for pots and an infinite variety of other products.

Clothing

Religious zealots in Amazonia saw the absence of clothes as savagery rather than innocence. For many Indian groups, with limited or reduced contact with the outside world, clothing is replaced by adornments made from bird feathers, palm and grass fibres.

Certain types of cloth are also used for ceremonies or dances. The Bora of Peru wear skirts made of bark cloth which comes from a fig tree called *chuchuara* (*Ficus yoponensis*). Yagua on the other hand, wear 'grass skirts' and other accoutrements made from chambira palm leaves, shredded into long fibres.

Some *várzea* communities encountered by the early Spanish and Portuguese, in particular those of the Omagua upriver from the mainstream's confluence with the Rio Negro, were reported to grow cotton and were recognised for their weaving skills.

Dyes are used for painting cloth and baskets, as well as body decorations used at festivals. Juice pressed from the fruit of the Genipa tree makes a deep blue-black colour, while orange-red colours come most often from urucum seeds (Bixa sp) which provide annatto used as food colouring.

Feathers from brightly coloured tropical birds, including macaws and toucans, are used to create dramatic and impressive head-dresses bound together using plant fibres and beeswax.

Flutes fashioned from bamboo or from the hollow leg-bones of animals provide music for ceremonies. The maraca is made from a small gourd filled with seeds or pebbles, and wooden drums are widespread.

Material wealth

Recent anthropological studies have developed an opinion of Indian tribes as lacking in material wealth, preferring to see them as rich in ingenuity. Hence, from rainforest materials a basket can hastily be assembled if the hunting trip turns out to be successful. With the bare minimum of material goods, Indian groups exist comfortably at subsistence level without having to 'work' for more than 40 hours a week.

Further reading

Describing the indigenous tribes in general terms loses much of the subtlety and completeness of Indian life in the Amazon. For a deeper understanding of Indian

HEAD-HUNTERS

Head-hunters are as much part of Amazon lore as giant snakes and vicious piranhas. The practice has long been banned in Peru and Ecuador, where it was formerly practised by the Achuar/Shuar tribal groups. These inhabitants of the upper Marañon watershed were the most feared head-hunters although other tribes performed the rite.

Head-hunting was widely written about but little understood. When discovered, the ritual was taken out of context by sensationalist film makers who portrayed frenzied savages immobilising victims with deadly blow darts, and viciously slicing off heads to shrink at weird cannibal rites. All of this is pure fiction.

In fact, the reason for head-hunting revolves around the spirit world. Indians believe the soul resides within the head which is beautiful and revered. The body is merely a vessel for the head. To own an enemy's head is therefore to possess his soul and use its power… if you know how.

In 1960, Jack Walker went to the headwaters of the Santiago and Pastaza rivers in Ecuador to live for some two years in an Achuar village, where he underwent the rituals to become a fully-fledged Achuar warrior. His accounts give one perspective on their rituals, taboos and sacred procedures.

First, blow darts are for hunting game and not to be used on humans, as the enemy must be nobly killed with hand weapons. The shrinking process is straightforward, requiring the removal of all fat and muscle from the head by boiling. What remains of the head is filled with burning sand which begins to contract and harden as water is removed from the tissues. The victor must conduct interminable magical rites to control the victim's soul, resident in the head. The eyes and mouth are sewn shut to imprison the soul in the head, as it would otherwise haunt the possessor's dreams. Long periods of celibacy and isolation are also necessary.

Three years of incantations, rituals and potion-making must pass before the head is fully empowered as a magic fetish.

Complexity and risk in head-hunting rituals deterred tribes from actively seeking victims, and taboos affect whose head can actually be chosen to make into a trophy. A head can only be taken as an act of revenge and, although the subject must be a member of a local tribe, the individual cannot be personally known.

A person whose relative dies by weapon or witchcraft is justified in seeking vengeance and only the murderer's head can be taken and shrunk. Thus, head-hunting was a ritual which served as a social control, apparently rare even before it was actively suppressed.

THE INDIAN PHARMACY

The potential of the rainforest as a medical pharmacy seems infinite. Whether you choose to believe in or try any of the medical concoctions available depends on your outlook and condition at the time. The existence of ichthyotoxic plants for fishing and the removal of toxins from manioc are just two examples that show the sophisticated use of knowledge accumulated over generations.

Indigenous remedies tackle a wide range of maladies including bug bites, back pain, diarrhoea, intestinal parasites – and many more. Given that quinine, until recently the primary defence against malaria, comes from the Amazon, it is reasonable to assume that other medicinal break-throughs are waiting to be made, research and funding permitting. Ethnobotanists are certain of the need to explore the rainforests and the minds of the shamans to garner what information remains.

One of the more widely known products of the rainforest is hallucinatory drugs. In some tribes only shaman or elders consume the sacred drug. In most, only men are permitted to partake. Used for ritual purposes the hallucinogen induces vivid hallucinations which assist in experiencing the spirit world. The shaman communicates with spirits to prophesy or divine, protecting the tribe against sickness, making hunters alert and discovering the identity of enemies.

There are several different plant genera recognised as having hallucinogenic properties. The best known is *ayahuasca* or the vine of the soul (*Banisteriopsis caapi*), common in the western Amazon. Pieces of stem are cut up, ground and boiled as the main ingredient of the powerful brew used by the shaman to reach a state of altered consciousness.

Ayahuasca frees the soul from corporeal confinement, to wander and return at will. Ingestion of the brew causes nausea and vomiting. With intoxication

culture, the best option is to pick up one of the many excellent books that study in detail the culture of individual Indian groups. There are several which give considerable insight and make perfect reading for an Amazon trip. (See *Appendix 3*.)

WAVES OF SETTLERS

The first Portuguese forays to Brazil took Europeans to the southern Atlantic coast close to Illhéus and present-day Salvador. Ocean currents and trade winds made approaching the mouth of the Amazon directly from Europe difficult, so the earliest colonisation southward began from 1530. As pressure on the southern lands grew, colonies pushed northwards closer to the mouth of the Amazon.

Early encounters with Indians relied on bartering metal tools and beads in return for the precious *pau do brasil* or brazilwood, used to produce valuable reddish dyes for sale in Europe. As healthy Indian communities were decimated by contact with European diseases, the need for more 'workers' to clear land and work on farms became apparent. With time the system of bartering labour for goods became one of slavery.

With the arrival and settling of the Spanish on the western coast of South America from the 1540s, exploration had focused on the search for El Dorado. The explorers didn't know whether El Dorado even existed, but the fantastic quantities of gold taken from the Incas was insufficient to quench the lust of the conquistadors.

Early forays into the Amazon did little to dispel the rumours of El Dorado. Orellano's first descent of the river by Europeans encountered tribes who told tales comes power of prophecy, divination, sorcery and healing. Frequently, the shaman will see overpowering visions, including attacks from huge snakes and jaguars, which humble him as a mere man.

From *ayahuasca*, chemists have isolated several active compounds called *indoles*, resembling LSD in their molecular structure – scientific confirmation of the powerful hallucinogenic properties of this plant. Due to the large number of tribes that use hallucinogenic drugs, the vine is known by many other names including *natema* among the Ecuadorean Jivaro and *yajé* by the Desana of Colombia.

In the western Amazon and upper Orinoco, another vine, *Virola elongata*, along with several other virola species, is widely used to make a snuff. Bark-scrapings are collected, boiled, simmered and refined into a fine powder. It is administered by blowing a charge down a pipe into the nostril – and the symptoms look bad. It induces heavy production of tears and mucus. In Amazonian Peru and Colombia it is used by the Bora and Witoto for similar purposes to *ayahuasca*. A related plant processed into *yoppo* snuff is used by the Yanomami and Amerindians of the Caribbean.

The Amazon lowlands provide another plant called *ipadu* (*Erythroxylum coca var ipadu*) which is the base material for cocaine. While cocaine is seen as a problem internationally, in South America coca has a wide range of medicinal and cultural properties. The leaf of the plant is chewed or taken as a brew which releases the alkaloids in it. Nutritionally, chewing coca provides a range of vitamins and minerals, and is also believed to reduce fatigue and counteract altitude sickness. Chewing coca or drinking the brew is not the same as taking cocaine. The proportion of active alkaloids in the coca leaf are minimal.

of great cities laden with gold. Whether the yarns recounted were based on fact or simply a way to ensure the quick movement downstream is not important; they simply served as more fuel to the fire.

Orellano's descent took place in 1542, several years after the Portuguese of the eastern coast had fully embraced slavery of the indigenous peoples for agricultural production. With large indigenous populations along the mainstream, rumours of increasingly unwelcome visitors from foreign lands undoubtedly would have spread up and down the river, its tributaries and inland to smaller settlements.

While rumours of El Dorado and matriarchal Amazon tribes lived on only in the deepest recesses of the European mind, the heavily populated banks of the rivers were to produce a new wealth to fund Portuguese expansion through Brazil. The labour of the Indians and the fruits of their land were essential to the success of European colonisation, as sure as if the blood of the Indians had been gold itself.

Sickness and disease

Early chroniclers recorded the large numbers of Indians and villages found throughout the region, theorising that if it weren't for the bellicose nature of many of these cultures, the land would be incapable of supporting so many mouths.

From the moment the Europeans arrived, indigenous populations were affected by European illnesses. When the Europeans stepped ashore they brought with

FROM NOBLE SAVAGES TO SLAVES

The first encounters of the Europeans with the Indians of the New World fostered the image of the noble savage: a people who ran naked in the world, living without greed and without reference to poverty. Indian tribes seemed happy to help the Portuguese harvest the precious *pau do Brasil*, in return for simple iron tools. But this utopian image, the creation of 18th-century philosophers, became fashionable after it was too late for the Indians.

At the time of their arrival, the Portuguese entered an area recently conquered by an aggressive tribe called the Tupi. Fighting was a way of avenging past wrong-doings and of kidnapping enemy tribes. The wars achieved a degree of territorial balance and fighting kept population levels down to numbers the land could easily support.

The outcomes of tribal wars were an abhorrence to the European mind. The spoils of war involved the ritual killing of prisoners by their captors. Once killed, the victims would be eaten, as would any creature of the rainforest. The eating of a prisoner was an intolerable insult against the defeated tribe and demanded revenge, continuing the cycle of war. Although cyclical aggression and cannibalism were not uncommon throughout the Amazon, the Portuguese based their opinions on the particularly aggressive Tupi.

As demand for wood rose, so the Indians were less inclined to travel further into the forest to collect it. The need for workers became even more apparent when Portuguese settlers began growing sugar cane. The planting and harvesting of sugar plantations required labour and, conveniently, the Portuguese believed they could eliminate the savage practice of cannibalism by using prisoners-of-war to work on plantations. Metal tools were no longer traded for work or wood, but for prisoners who became slaves.

As labour demands rose, the Portuguese incited inter-village rivalry, thus ensuring a steady supply of prisoners-of-war. Before long, whole villages were forced to accept 'protection' against imminent attack in return for working for Europeans.

For the Indians, however, the reality was different, as the French Capuchin missionary Yves d'Évreux noted in a conversation with an Indian. This extract is taken from John Hemming's *Red Gold: The Conquest of the Brazilian Indians*: 'When you are dead you no longer feel a thing. Whether they eat you or not is all the same to a dead man. But I should be angry to die in bed, and not in the manner of great men, surrounded by dances and drinking and swearing vengeances on those who would eat me before I died.'

And so begins the tragic history of enslavement of the Amazon Indian, despite the fact that few Indian communities practised the ritual eating of human flesh like the coastal Tupi.

them smallpox, influenza and a range of Eurasian and African diseases to which the Indians had no natural immunity. While the Jesuit priests proclaimed the maladies were punishment for lack of faith, the Indians were in no doubt that the Europeans had brought these evils with them.

This pattern of illness accompanying encounter still continues today. In an increasingly populated region, uncontacted Indians somehow manage to avoid contact with fatal diseases. When contact is made, the consequences are dramatic. Recent incursions by gold prospectors into Yanomami territory introduced smallpox and measles, accounted for a dramatic rise in malaria cases, and caused thousands of deaths.

Protection of indigenous tribes

Today the legal status of lowland Indians and the protection of their lands varies greatly across the region. Countries such as Colombia and Ecuador offer a degree of protection to Amazon Indians under the umbrella of active indigenous organisations.

In Peru, which has the highest proportion of the Amazon Basin within its national territory, the need to delimit and demarcate indigenous lands is recognised but is carried out by government officials. There is no consultation with indigenous tribes.

Bolivian indigenous rights have been subject to an attitude of *laissez faire* until recent Marches for Dignity put them on the political agenda.

In Brazil, recognition of territorial rights provides a degree of federal protection. However, obtaining recognition requires a lengthy and tiresome procedure which, without government support, is difficult to obtain. Of the 87 million hectares claimed as indigenous territories, just 17 million have been recognised.

Historically Brazil has recognised the need to address indigenous issues for some time, with the formation of the Indians' Protection Department back in 1910. This was replaced by the National Indian Foundation, FUNAI, the government agency responsible for Brazil's Indians. Although the recent work carried out by the employees of FUNAI is widely seen as good and well-intentioned, the attachment to government prevents the organisation acting in a truly independent way. The lack of funding has resulted in inefficiency and corruption, doing little to engender the belief that FUNAI is the real guardian of indigenous peoples.

A new law in 1996 changed the legal position of the Indian lands. Any person or organisation who could prove they had a legal claim to indigenous lands could claim their part of the reserve. Objections from international and indigenous groups failed to produce a change in the position of the government.

The Amazon frontier

The early settlers of the Amazon, in addition to the colonisers who set up Portuguese forts to defend the waterway, were the missionaries. Formed in 1534, the Society of Jesus introduced young, ambitious and intelligent men dedicated to spreading the Christian word. Soon after their arrival in South America in 1549, control over the Indians was delegated to Jesuit-run Indian villages or *aldeias*. By the time the Society was expelled from Brazil in 1757, the Jesuits had more than 60 *aldeias* housing thousands of Indians along the banks of the Amazon.

Charged with their welfare, Jesuit missionaries encouraged Indians to move to the missions where they would live and work within mission society. Indian labour supported and sustained mission communities. The accumulated wealth of missions with hundreds of head of cattle contrasted dramatically with the problems experienced by colonists who failed to develop agricultural systems on the poor soils of the Amazon.

But although the Jesuits were the best European friends the Indians had, it wasn't beyond them to turn a blind eye. Slaves to work for newly arriving settlers were kidnapped by *bandeirantes* in raids along the Amazon mainstream. With the support of government officials, raids would take only bonded captives – the prisoners-of-war from inter-tribal conflicts.

INDIANS OF AMAZONIA TODAY – RAPE OF THE LOST WORLD

'The white man built roads, houses, farms and opened the way to disease, poverty and death.' So said Waldir Tobias, a Makuxi Indian of Raposa-Serra do Sol, Brazil.

The Makuxi are a hunting and farming people who live in a hilly region known as the Guyana Shield, near Mount Roraima on the border between Brazil and Guyana. There are an estimated 22,000 Makuxi, of whom nearly 15,000 live in Brazil and the rest in Guyana. In Brazil, they are concentrated in the Raposa-Serra do Sol Indigenous Area in the border state of Roraima, north of the Amazon rainforests. Theirs is a spectacularly beautiful land of mountains, tropical forest and savannah, where they raise cattle.

Makuxi believe that they, and the neighbouring Ingariko people, are descended from the brothers Macunaima and Anique, the children of the sun. Macunaima and Anique discovered a tree known as *Waxaca*, the Tree of Life, which is the origin of all the plants and wild fruits on which the Indians' lives depend. The brothers left behind them some good legacies, including the gift of fire, but they also created disease and the hardships of nature. The Makuxi believe that *stkaton*, the life principle, governs everything and comes from the sun.

Raposa-Serra do Sol has two distinct seasons; winter, with heavy rainfall from May to September, and a long dry summer between November and March. In summer, the Indians plan hunting and fishing expeditions and visit friends and relatives in neighbouring villages – such visits are not possible in the rainy season. Fishing is a favourite Makuxi activity, both as a pastime and as an essential source of food, but it is often made difficult by the drying-up of rivers and streams.

Makuxi villages are linked together by a complex network of paths and tracks. They range in size from settlements of two houses to large communities with clusters of houses built around central courtyards. These communities are based on ties of marriage and family. Makuxi extended families hunt together, but the planting of crops for personal use is done by individual households. Houses are built and repaired during the dry season, when the Indians have easier access to wood and clay for the walls and can gather palm leaves for the roofs.

When Makuxi marry, they live in the wife's family's village and submit to the authority of their fathers-in-law. A young husband has to provide his father-in-law with game and carry out domestic services like house maintenance. When the couple have children, they can move to their own plot of land. The father-in-law is the most important figure in the Makuxi kinship groups. When he dies the group often dissolves, and married men return to their original villages, taking their wives and children with them.

Since their 'discovery' by European invaders, and their colonisation by the Portuguese in the 18th century, the Makuxi have experienced land theft, murder, torture and slavery. Today, they are still fighting for recognition of their most basic human rights. Although the indigenous area is officially demarcated, neither the federal nor the state authorities of Brazil make any attempt to stop the advance of ranchers and gold prospectors.

Jesuits were present to act as witness, supposedly to ensure only bonded captives were rescued. Either through intimidation from the *bandeirantes* or the demonstrated execution of uncooperative captives, Indians were obliged to say they were captives. This kept them alive as slaves for the immediate future at least.

By the late 1750s, the Portuguese economy was beginning to falter. The Jesuits, wealthy and powerful from the labour and conversion of countless Indians, were suitable scapegoats to take the blame for shortcomings of settlers. The removal of the Jesuits, it was argued, would make Indians available as labour for all colonisers.

With the Jesuits dispatched from all Portuguese territories in 1757, the last remaining restrictions on further exploration of the Amazon and at least a notion of fair treatment of the indigenous Indians were removed.

The first settlers

With the removal of religious pontificating, the colonisation of the Portuguese territory could continue quickly without obstruction.

By the 1750s land-hungry plantations using Indian labour had begun to encroach on the Amazon Basin. Rice plantations in the lower Amazon made Portugal self-sufficient in this staple crop. As cocoa became a fashionable drink in Europe, the harvesting of *cacoa* first wild from the forest and then on plantations made this an important crop, before epidemics finished off the contribution local Indians could make to its cultivation. As the Indians died, slaving raids went further and deeper along the Amazon mainstream.

Sugar and cattle were produced on ranches, with the enforced assistance of Indian peoples and the introduction of slaves from Africa. The success of plantations encouraged colonists to look for suitable sites, and they spread rapidly through the rivers of the Amazon. By the 1770s attempts were made to establish villages on the grassy savannahs near the headwaters of the Rio Branco. North of Boa Vista, the state capital of Roraima, the now familiar system of colonisation was introduced. Indian groups were enticed to live in villages in return for tools and comfort. The attractive offer was accepted by members of the Carib-speaking Paravilhana and Purukotó who joined the village, only to desert the settlements within a couple of years.

In the mid-1840s the wave of enlightened thinking that gripped Europe nearly saw the introduction of legislation to protect the Indians and their right to tribal lands. But by now the march of colonising settlers was too strong.

At this time the seeds of current problems were sown. The late arrival of the 19th-century idea of the 'noble savage' living in a primitive Utopia had little effect on the rainforest reality. Brutal frontiersmen hell-bent on personal gain and satisfaction were outside the control of any law. As is the case today, any legislation designed to protect the rights of individuals requires adequate resources to enforce it.

Adequate legal protection was nearly introduced, but economies elsewhere in the world were growing at a fantastic rate and Europe and the US needed one Amazon product that would ensure their economies continued to grow.

Rubber goes boom

By the 1850s, as the boom in rubber hit Amazonia, the high ideals of protection for the Indians of Brazil were promptly forgotten in a quest for wealth. Europeans migrated to the region rapidly, to benefit from the rich pickings of the rubber industry. However, Indian communities were not forthcoming in working for the rubber barons. Rubber tappers or *seringueiros* migrated from the coastal areas to take advantage of the booming work opportunities.

With the crash of the rubber boom, the majority of rubber workers and their entourage left the Amazon as quickly as they had arrived. Hemming concludes 'the rubber boom was not as catastrophic to the native population as might have been expected… Ecologically, rubber tapping caused almost no damage'. However, when the rubber barons deserted the Amazon in droves, many of the *seringueiros* remained stuck in conditions of debt bondage where they continued to toil with minimal reward.

Interest in rubber waned as profits fell and investment moved to the south of Brazil. Despite the brief increase in production to supply the allied armies in World War II, by the 1960s the last remaining estate bosses had relinquished ownership of their activities in the Amazon. With the ties of debt bondage cut, rubber tapping families effectively owned their own stand of trees. With new freedoms came new opportunities. In addition to the regular visits to the rubber stands, nuts, fish, hides and a range of products could all be harvested from the rainforest. A new type of Amazon settler, with a new set of territorial land rights, had been created.

Recognising the land rights of rubber tappers

In the 1970s governments began to promote the modernisation and integration of Amazonia into national economies. In Brazil, generous financial incentives focused interest on ranching and settlement in southern Amazonia.

Advancing cattle ranchers encountered rubber tappers defending what were now their traditional lands. A long history of ignoring traditional land rights offered little hope for the rubber tappers. Resistance in the form of *empates* or stand-offs, organised by newly-formed unions, raised temperatures in the conflict zones. In 1988 the murder of Francisco Alves 'Chico' Mendes, as leader of the Xapuri Rural Workers' Union, brought the plight of the rubber tappers to the attention of the world.

The death of Chico Mendes occurred at a time when international protests against the rapacious destruction of the Amazon rainforest were at an all-time high. The global publicity resulting from his murder quickly produced the recognition and value of protected extractive reserves as proposed by rubber tappers' unions.

By 1990 four extractive reserves covering two million hectares and providing an income to around 23,000 Brazilians had been recognised. These areas are: the Juruá valley in northern Acre; the Chico Mendes reserve in southern Acre, Rio Ouro Preto in Rondônia; and Rio Cajarí in Amapá, north of the Amazon's mouth.

Large-scale colonisation projects

In recent decades government programmes have worked hard to integrate the Amazon regions into their national economies. From a national perspective this is almost the natural thing to do. Three-quarters of Bolivia and Peru lie within the Amazon Basin. Nearly 60% of Brazil is within the Amazon, while for Ecuador the figure is just under 50%. As such a large part of a nation's resource, it is hardly surprising that governments have encouraged economic growth in the Amazon lowlands.

The result has been massive migration. Manaus and Belém on the Amazon mainstream in Brazil both have more than one million inhabitants, while Porto Velho in the southern Amazon has nearly half a million. Iquitos in Peru, even without a road connection, has 600,000 inhabitants, and to the south Pucallpa has grown dramatically following improvements to the road from Lima in the last decade. Santa Cruz in Bolivia is mushrooming, currently with around 600,000 inhabitants; it is expected to be Bolivia's largest city early in the 21st century. The momentum for growth has taken the region's population up to 30 million and shows no sign of stopping.

Other new arrivals to the Amazon Basin include farmers, settlers and gold prospectors. The vast majority of these migrants are first-generation. When travelling around the Amazon Basin, particularly away from the rivers, it is quite difficult to find someone of working age who was born in the area. As families grow the pressure on land is certain to increase.

The colonisation process is greatly assisted by road-building programmes. The road-building in itself causes relatively little damage. Parts of the Transamazonica Highway between Itaituba and Humaita have been reclaimed by the rainforest through lack of use. But in most locations road-building is quickly followed by a period of colonisation. Once a critical mass of settlers moves down loosely defined highways, roads are quickly improved, increasing the likelihood of migration.

In southern Brazil the road between Cuiabá and Porto Velho has been asphalted since the mid-1980s. Heading out to the west the road steadily deteriorates but buses, lorries and a few shaky cars transport people and supplies to new settlements springing up along the road. Previously rainforest, vast tracts of land alongside the road are now completely cleared.

The history of colonisation globally has gone hand in hand with the destruction of forested lands. In the USA colonisation destroyed 95% of natural forests before any were protected.

Farming and settling – clearing the forests

Currently some 20% of the Amazon population are farmers or *campesinos*. The majority are poor farmers working small plots of land. Although land is promised through government programmes *campesinos* often have no legal right to the land they farm. Where possible, they will seek seasonal work on larger farms. A large number of small farmers move spontaneously, settling haphazardly along new highways.

Medium- and large-scale plots are also widespread and commonly used as ranches. With the use of fertilisers and more advanced technologies these can be productive year-round operations. Agriculture and livestock production is extensive but yields are low. As with many colonisation projects, applying temperate-climate agricultural technologies to the rainforest rarely works.

In the 1970s, the Brazilian government used subsidies to encourage the creation of large-scale ranches in excess of 20,000ha. Although no longer actively encouraged, the subsidies still cost the Brazilian treasury over US$2.5 billion annually. And meat output from the ranches is just 9% of what was projected.

Although such projects are clearly recognised as failures, the legacy to the region extends far beyond the clearance of rainforest. When rural projects fail, migration to urban areas increases, increasing pressure on the stretched services of cities like Manaus. Alternatively, when bad economic policies depress agricultural production, then highly profitable illegal activities can result such as the production of coca – the raw ingredient of cocaine – which is common in parts of the Peruvian and Bolivian Amazon.

Urban settlers

Within the wide expanses of virgin rainforest, the bulk of the Amazon population is urban, between 50 and 60%. Most of the large population centres – Manaus, Belém, Iquitos and Porto Velho – are relatively old, established during the colonial era or more recently in the years of the rubber boom.

THE EXPERIENCE OF AN AMAZON SETTLER

Some agricultural settlers in the Amazon have managed, very successfully, to flourish in their new lands. More common, however, is this review by the international Amazon Cooperation Treaty of abandoned plots within the large-scale colonisation of POLONORESTE (Northwest Region Integrated Development Programme) settlements in Rondônia, in Brazil's southern Amazon.

'Attracted by government publicity seeking to encourage settlement of rural communities in the Amazon, settlers are told the land is fertile. If they move to Rondônia the colonisation programme will provide 30 or more hectares of land, with technical assistance and credit to hand.

Settlers often arrive in the Amazon accompanied by a wife and several small children with neither money nor family goods. Untrained and normally illiterate they settle on the land.

The land assigned to them by the colonisation agency has been carved from jungle, located beside a path barely wide enough for a cart. There is no water at the site, so it must be brought long distances until a well is dug. The settler-turned-farmer naturally builds his first hut close to the road.

Clearing the jungle is tiring and exhaustive work. In addition to this, to support a period with no income, the family will have to look for income from wherever it is available. If the season is right, felled trees can be burnt and the first crops of rice, corn and beans are planted. In between seasonal work and the demands of farming, if the opportunity arises a small house can be built from wooden planks, with palm thatch for a roof.

In the background, all the hopes for prosperity are slowly fading. The promised health clinic and school have closed or, worse still, never opened. The family is probably suffering from a variety of intestinal parasites. It is also possible, indeed highly likely, that the settler and some of his family have contracted malaria, greatly reducing their ability to work. And the farmer can consider himself extremely lucky if no member of his family suffered a serious accident felling trees.

If the first crop was good, it is possible, if the marketing centre is operational and the freight costs are not too high, that produce over and above subsistence requirements can be sold to prepare for the second crop. More than likely, however, is the reality that through planting at the wrong time of year, poor crop maintenance and lack of help, the crop is poor.

The optimistic words of agricultural technicians seem ill-founded as the high returns offered by permanent crops such as coffee and cacao are barely worth it, given the time requirements. The rosy picture of agroforestry in harmony with nature is blocked by the presence of too many obstacles.'

These, along with others, like Pucallpa in Peru, Riberalta in Bolivia and most lowland towns in Ecuador, have grown rapidly following colonisation and road-building programmes. Mining has also fuelled urban growth, with mining settlements, especially with gold prospectors, setting up new towns almost overnight.

The population of the principal cities is a mosaic of races of different origins who have migrated there for a number of reasons. Local migration occurs as a result of failed colonisation projects, while others move from areas of poverty believing the rapid growth of lowland cities is proof of better opportunities. A walk round any of the Amazon cities quickly proves that without a bit of luck in finding work, the reality is very different.

Some cities have experienced a fifty-fold increase in population since 1940, becoming important commercial and communication centres in their own right. Rapid growth has led to a proliferation of slums inside and around urban areas with the predictable consequences of insecurity and poverty. The population increase places staggering demands on water, sewage, rubbish and electricity services. In the wrong conditions, infectious and contagious diseases fester, creating epidemics of cholera, hepatitis and dengue fever.

Miners – still seeking El Dorado

Relatively unexplored and generally undeveloped, the mining potential of the Amazon is extensive. The potential for easy pickings such as gold and precious gems has seen the number of *garimpeiros* or gold prospectors explode. Estimates put the numbers searching throughout the Brazilian Amazon at between one and two million, operating 25,000 pieces of equipment over an area of 160,000 million hectares. An estimated 30,000 people prospect for gold in the southern Amazonian department of Madre de Dios in Peru. When prospects elsewhere are close to zero, it's easy to understand the attraction of striking gold despite the hardships.

Travelling around the Amazon you find that most medium-sized towns have shops buying and selling gold. A friendly conversation on a bus, truck or boat heading towards one of these towns may reveal that despite the poverty-stricken appearance of the man sitting next to you, he actually has a small fold of paper holding gold dust, or a small ingot worth several thousand dollars in his pocket. He is unable to pay the bus fare in cash, so the bus driver makes a detour, stopping at a shop so the gold can be sold and the fare paid.

In addition to the numbers prospecting for gold, the provision of supporting services in construction, maintenance services, logistical support, transportation and prostitution, employs vast numbers. Around 30% of the population of the Amazon Basin is believed to be directly or indirectly employed in the gold sector. In the Brazilian Amazon gold mining is the most important economic and social activity.

Territory invasion

With such a large number of prospectors it is hardly surprising that invasion of indigenous territories by gold prospectors is widespread. The invasion of Yanomami land by 40,000 *garimpeiros* in the 1980s made world headlines. This sudden incursion led to outbreaks of malaria, other diseases, and violence. Despite the creation of the Yanomami Park restricting the entry of uninvited visitors, incursions still occur, with periodic expulsion of *garimpeiros* occurring when international pressure groups are most vocal. But the reality is that keeping the prospectors out permanently is almost impossible.

In 1993 as many as 70 Yanomami were murdered by *garimpeiros* in what became known as the Haximu Massacre. In recent years more than 1,500 Yanomami – 2% of the population – have died from malaria, TB, influenza and other diseases. Pollution resulting from the mining has also reduced food supplies to the hunter-gatherer community. As recently as 1997, new camps of miners had entered the park, many of them crossing the international border with Venezuela.

Environment devastation

The wholesale destruction of ecosystems is an additional cause for concern. The techniques used to extract gold by small-scale operations can have disastrous consequences. The extraction of two grams of gold requires the removal of one cubic metre of sediment. Dredges excavate the riverbed and the banks, completely destroying the flow of water and watersheds. As they go, oil pollution from machinery filters into the river systems. An estimated 7,000 dredges work the River

DANGER … TOURISTS!

All too often a visit to Indian villages results in awkwardness. Asking if you can take photographs leads to feelings of embarrassment by those on both sides of the camera. It is a difficult situation: one that demands stepping outside the singular goal of getting good shots from your holiday.

Tourism need not be a destructive force for tribal peoples but unfortunately it usually is: if it violates their rights it should be opposed. Tourism must be subject to the decisions made by the tribal peoples themselves. Here are a few guidelines issued by Survival International:

- **Do be respectful.** Tourist companies should insist their staff and clients behave respectfully towards tribal peoples. (In practice, many tourists who visit tribal areas simply have their false stereotypes reinforced.)
- **Don't demean, degrade, insult or patronise.** All tourism and advertising which treats tribal peoples in an insulting, degrading or patronising manner (for example references to 'stone-age cultures', 'untouched by time', etc) should be opposed. They are demeaning and wrong.
- **Do ask permission.** The lands lived in or used by tribes should not be entered without the free and informed consent of the tribal peoples themselves. Obtaining this consent can be lengthy; it requires money, respect, tact and honesty. Bribery should never be used.
- **Do pay properly.** Tribespeople should be properly recompensed for their services and the use of their territory. Payment should be agreed in advance with their legitimate representatives. Where profits arise from using tribal areas, this should be properly explained to the tribes who may want a share. Anyone who is not able to accept tribal peoples' own terms for payment should not be there.
- **Do recognise land rights.** Tribal peoples' ownership of the lands they use and occupy is recognised in international law. This should be acknowledged irrespective of whether the national government applies the law or not (governments are amongst the principal violators of tribal rights). When in tribal lands, tourists should behave as they would on private property.
- **Don't bring in disease.** Care must be taken in areas where tribal peoples' immunity to outside diseases may be poor. Some contagious diseases which affect tourists only mildly – colds and influenza, for example – can kill tribespeople.

Survival International, 11–15 Emerald St, London WC1N 3QL, UK; tel: 0171 242 1441; fax: 0171 242 1771; email: survival@gn.apc.org

Madeira in southern Amazonas, Brazil, dumping around five million litres of oil into just one tributary of the river every year.

The processing of gold, carried out close to mine sites, also carries a heavy environmental toll. Mercury is used to separate fine gold particles from river sediment. When the gold-mercury amalgam is burned to recover the precious material, mercury vapour is released into the atmosphere. In this form the mercury is either inhaled causing direct personal harm, or released into the atmosphere from where it eventually returns to the ground in precipitation. Then it pollutes the rivers, infects the fish and works its way up the food chain. ultimately to the local people.

A new type of prospector

While many rivers in the Amazon have some *garimpeiros* dredging and sifting through sediments, the majority of gold remains out of reach of the small operator. This explains why prospectors push ever further into new lands. In many regions, however, the hey-day of the small-scale *garimpeiros* has passed. On the River Tapajós in the state of Pará, state records show production for the small prospector falling rapidly, with new production coming from large companies. The state government is marketing the mineral wealth of the state in the hope that the concessions given to large multinational companies like Rio Tinto Zinc, Placer Dome and Anglo American will eventually provide much-needed royalties for the state's economy.

When large mining companies move to the Amazon, a new period and type of migration will begin, placing even greater pressure on the region's resources.

Mega-mines

Once such mega-mine, the Grand Carajás project, is already in existence. In the eastern Brazilian Amazon, southwest of the town of Marabá on the Tocantins River, the world's largest mining complex has been built to extract the estimated 18 billion tonnes of iron ore reserves. The project's level of success depends on whom you ask. Around 15,000 direct jobs have been created since the project's inception in the 1970s. It has required the development of a rail network, hydro-electric dams and agro-livestock enterprises in an area equal in size to France and Britain combined.

For the rainforest the project has been a disaster, as land has been cleared to make way for the mega-mine and associated services. Entrance to Carajás itself is heavily controlled but the effect on the region is clear. The nearby town of Marabá has boomed from just 10,000 people in the 1970s to over 200,000 and is still growing. Power to support the region's growth comes from the massive Tucuruí hydro-electric dam which creates 8,000MW annually, a project that in itself supports a town of 65,000. The creation of the 12km-long dam flooded 2,360km^2 of rainforest.

In addition to the widespread environmental destruction created by such a large project – a cause for concern in itself – some 22,000 people were moved from their homes without discussion or concessions.

Oil and gas prospectors

Oil and its extraction are increasingly important to the region. Most operations are in the western Amazon and cause particular concern amongst environmentalists. Oil companies in Ecuador are regularly criticised for the environmental damage caused to the rainforest and indigenous land through mining operations. Exploration is also stepping up in Colombia and Peru, with Bolivia only just beginning to explore opportunities in the lowlands.

The Camsea gas field in the southern lowlands of Peru exemplifies the problems of lowland development perfectly. It is judged to be one of the world's largest gas fields, and the Peruvian government is keen for Shell to begin production that could see investment of US$8 billion enter the national and local economies. Unfortunately the gas field is close to Manú National Park and infringes on the traditional lands of the Nahua and Kugapakori Indians. Some of these groups are still uncontacted, while early encounters with others have produced whooping cough and influenza epidemics which killed off 50% of the population.

On the plus side, however, in early July 1998 the Royal Dutch/Shell/Mobil consortium announced its decision to pull out of its Camsea gas field project in the Peruvian jungle after an investment of US$250,000. The relief may be only temporary, but it may indicate that the cost of extracting hydrocarbons in this type of environment is prohibitively high.

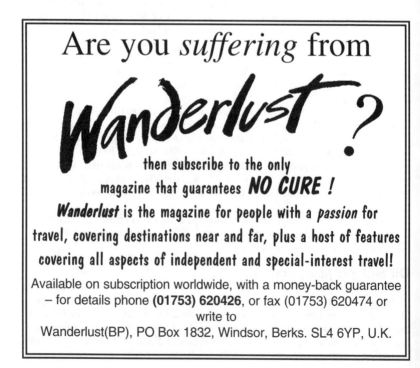

Part Three

Countries of the Amazon

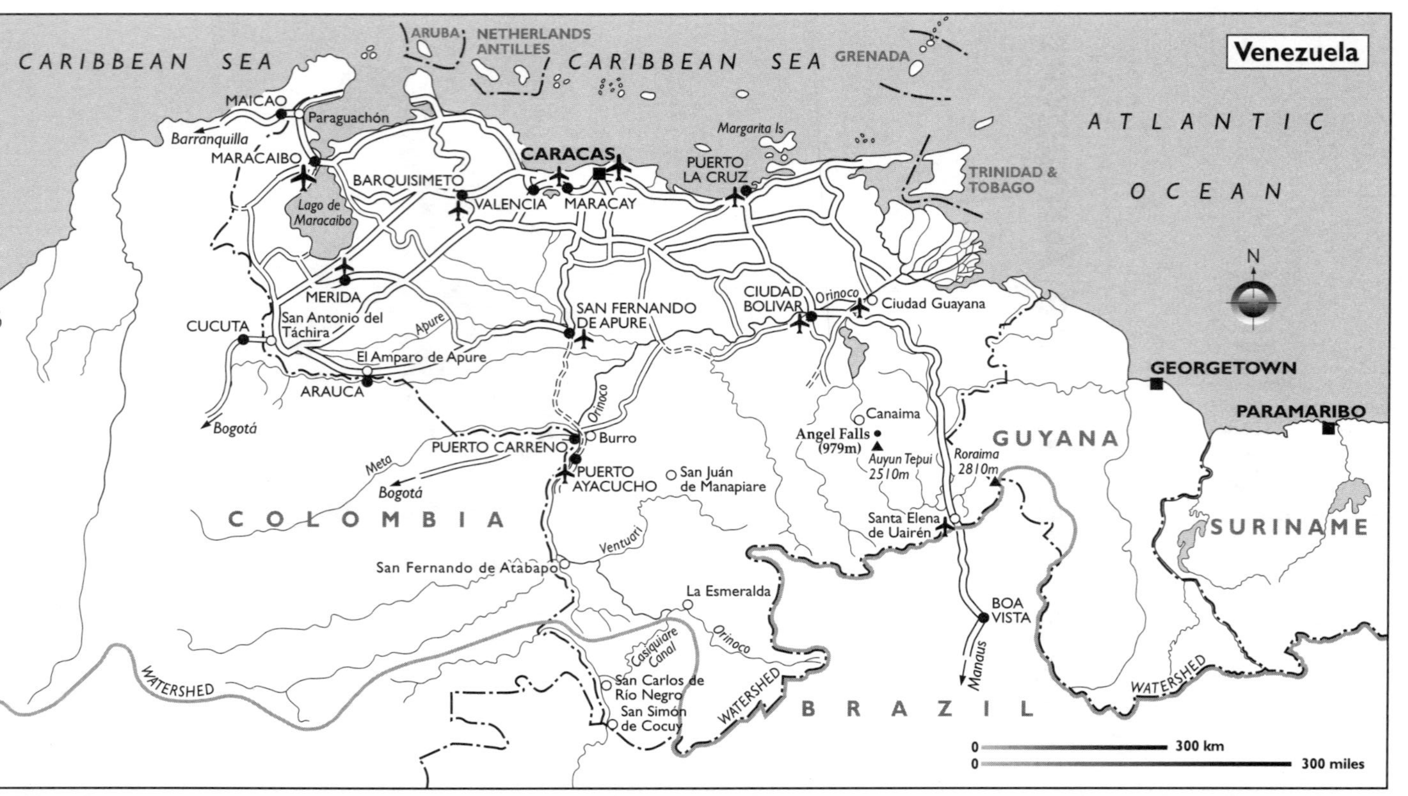
Venezuela
CARIBBEAN SEA
ARUBA
NETHERLANDS ANTILLES
CARIBBEAN SEA
GRENADA
ATLANTIC
OCEAN
TRINIDAD & TOBAGO
Margarita Is
N
MAICAO
Paraguachón
Barranquilla
MARACAIBO
Lago de Maracaibo
BARQUISIMETO
CARACAS
VALENCIA
MARACAY
PUERTO LA CRUZ
MERIDA
CUCUTA
San Antonio del Táchira
Apure
El Amparo de Apure
ARAUCA
Bogotá
SAN FERNANDO DE APURE
CIUDAD BOLIVAR
Orinoco
Ciudad Guayana
GEORGETOWN
PARAMARIBO
Orinoco
Burro
PUERTO CARREÑO
Meta
Bogotá
PUERTO AYACUCHO
San Juán de Manapiare
Canaima
Angel Falls (979m)
Auyun Tepui 2510m
Roraima 2810m
GUYANA
COLOMBIA
Santa Elena de Uairén
SURINAME
Ventuari
San Fernando de Atabapo
La Esmeralda
BOA VISTA
Casiquiare Canal
Orinoco
Manaus
WATERSHED
San Carlos de Río Negro
San Simón de Cocuy
WATERSHED
BRAZIL
WATERSHED
0 300 km
0 300 miles

7 Venezuela

Venezuela promises lofty Andean peaks and crisp, clean Caribbean beaches in abundance for the vertically and horizontally inclined. For those seeking a rumble in the jungle, Venezuela is just as much a place of extremes and unique opportunities. The truly adventurous can spend two weeks paddling in the canoe strokes of the great Prussian explorer Baron Alexander von Humboldt, while more genteel options include treks of just a few days that give a flavour of the jungle.

Venezuela was introduced to written history in 1498 when Christopher Columbus landed on the Península de Paría close to Trinidad. The name, Venezuela, literally translated as Little Venice, was inspired by sightings of Indian communities living in huts on stilts in Lake Maracaibo.

FACTS AND FIGURES

Geography

The geographical diversity of Venezuela is staggering. The north has idyllic Caribbean coastline with a large number of developed and undeveloped beach resorts. Along the coast the humid tropical warmth of the east contrasts with the dry deserts found in the west.

Lake Maracaibo towards the border with Colombia, with an area of 21,470km^2 (8,286 miles^2), is the largest lake in South America. The highest peaks of the Cordillera de Marina reach an altitude of 5,007m.

BASIC FACTS

Official name República de Venezuela
Area 912,050km^2 (352,144 miles^2)
Population 21,177,000 (1994)
Capital Caracas
Largest city (population) Caracas (2,784,084)
Main Amazon city Puerto Ayacucho
Official language Spanish
Date of independence 5 July 1830
Major industries Oil and derivatives, manufacturing and mining
GDP per capita US$2,994
Currency bolívar (US$1=Bs533; £1=Bs850)
Major attractions Isla Margarita; the Gran Sabana; Angel Falls; the Orinoco/Amazon Basin
National holidays Carnival (Monday and Tuesday before Lent), Easter, Apr 19, May, Jun 24, Jul 5, Jul 24, Oct 12, Dec 25

The flat expansive *llanos*, found to the south of the Cordillera and north of the River Orinoco, make up a vast low-lying savannah scattered with ranches. The life of the *ranchero* is dictated by extremes: widespread flooding in May contrasts with the dry season between December and April that leaves riverbeds dry and livestock parched.

To the south of the Orinoco lie the Guyana Highlands, the remains of a sedimentary layer which was first laid down around 1.7 billion years ago and has experienced extensive erosion. Vertically-sided *tepuis* (flat-topped mountains) rise abruptly to an altitude of 3,000m, their summits hosts to hundreds of endemic plants including numerous insectivorous species.

Angel Falls cascades for almost one vertical kilometre off the side of Auyán *tepui*, and Mount Roraima, on the disputed border with Guyana to the east, was the inspiration for Arthur Conan Doyle's *The Lost World*.

The Guyana Highlands drop away to the southwest giving way to flat tropical lowland and the state of Amazonas, comprising almost a fifth of Venezuela's national territory, where occasional *tepuis* break the green carpet of tropical forest. The highest, with an altitude of 3,014m (9,888ft), is Pico da Neblina on the border with Brazil, just a degree north of the Equator.

Rivers

In Venezuela the Amazon River plays second fiddle to the Orinoco. Virtually all of the country, and a considerable part of neighbouring Colombia, is a watershed draining into the Orinoco and out to the Atlantic via the Orinoco Delta.

The Orinoco flows along a giant fishhook-shaped channel for over 2,100km. From its headwaters in the Sierra Parama on the Brazilian border, the river is forced to travel in a westerly direction round the immovable Guyana Highlands, before turning back on itself to head northeast through the heart of the country.

Such a prominent main artery has proved vital to the economic development of the Venezuelan heartland. The Orinoco is navigable by ocean-going ships for 240km upstream and by river steamers for up to 1,100km. A series of rapids prevents navigation beyond Puerto Ayacucho, the state capital of Amazonas.

Prior to the road link with the north of Venezuela, Puerto Ayacucho was just a transit point where cargo was unloaded and taken by land to the port of Samariapo, 63km upstream beyond the rapids. From Samariapo hundreds of boats ferry cargo to river communities upstream.

The Amazon Basin proper constitutes a very small part of Venezuelan territory – just over a quarter of the territory of the state of Amazonas. The small part that is an Amazon tributary comes courtesy of the natural Casiquiare Canal which diverts one third of the Orinoco's headwaters south to join the Río Negro.

Climate

Temperatures in Venezuela are fairly constant, allowing for geographical differences. The dry season runs roughly from December to April, with the wet season taking up the remainder of the year.

A more important consideration is the local topography, in particular the altitude. For example, the hills around Mérida have comfortable day temperatures of around 20°C, while the night can bring a slight chill. Coastal regions are comfortably warm with temperature increasing as you travel further west. Maracaibo can be uncomfortably hot, at over 30°C.

To the south the Guyana Highlands and the state of Amazonas experience rain that is sudden and often dramatic. Temperatures on the Gran Sabana are around the mid-20s°C. Amazonas is around the high 20s, but this can be oppressive when humidity rises.

Flora and fauna

The easiest place to see large animals is in the *llanos*. The flat, open and normally dry savannahs concentrate animals around water channels. Capybara, armadillos, tapirs, caiman and jaguar are all found in the region. Piranha are abundant and sightings of freshwater dolphins are common.

Venezuela is home to over 1,300 bird species (some 44% of South America's avifauna). Many of the cloud and lowland tropical forests in the hills of the north are within the protected boundaries of national parks.

In Amazonas birdwatchers can see the lek of the Cock-of-the-Rock, as well as the Amazonian umbrella bird, Amazonian kingfisher, macaws, toucans and parrots. Over 670 bird species have been recorded in Amazonas, more than half of all Venezuela's known species.

Over 30,000 species of insect have been recorded so far including 1,200 species of butterfly. Perhaps the most impressive and memorable is the incandescent blue morpho butterfly with a wingspan approaching 15cm. According to locals, tarantulas used to be very common throughout the area but numbers are reduced somewhat by the Piaroa Indians, who see the spiders as both a food delicacy and a protective spirit.

Aquatic animals are also in abundance with over 3,000 species of fish. Freshwater turtles include the curiously horned *matamata,* and freshwater dolphins, caiman and snakes can all be seen in the region. Over 190 mammal species have been recorded including nine species of primate, along with tapirs, peccaries and jaguars.

Land use

Venezuela's dependence on the oil sector has done a great deal to discourage development of a viable agricultural sector. Although a variety of products are produced throughout the country about 60% of food is imported.

Tropical forest regions produce orchids, wild rubber and timber while on the *llanos* to the north the beef and dairy industry is being developed. The hilly and mountainous regions to the north produce a wide range of agricultural products including basic staple crops, cocoa, coffee and bananas.

The people

Population

Over 90% of Venezuela's population lives in urban areas. Population is growing by 2.6% annually and just under half the population is under 20. The average Venezuelan woman has 3.6 children. Population density varies greatly, peaking at 1,090 per km^2 in Caracas and falling to below five per km^2 in the states of Amazonas, Bolívar, Apure and Delta Amacuro.

Over two-thirds of the population are of mixed Indian-European descent known as *mestizos*; one-fifth are Europeans; 9% are blacks; and indigenous Indians make up 2%.

Of the indigenous Indians, 29 groups total around 200,000, with 21 distinct indigenous languages. The main groups of the south include the Yanomami, Piaroa and Pemón, located in the southern states of Amazonas and Bolívar.

Languages

Spanish is the official language of Venezuela. Many of the officially recognised indigenous languages are being wiped out as increasing acculturation introduces Spanish into groups that are numerically strong but linguistically vulnerable.

Education

With the tightening of the economy, education funding has been cut back in recent years. State-funded institutions of the 1970s and 1980s had hoped to put Venezuelan universities among the best in the world; however, cash restrictions have put an end to that dream.

Education is free and compulsory between the ages of five and 13, with secondary education lasting an additional four years. There are 11 state universities in the country and 13 private higher educational institutions.

Culture

Whether monuments of a recently passed glory or inspiration for future prosperity and dreams, the towering modern architecture of Caracas is certainly impressive. The clean-cut lines and extensive use of mirrored glass create an air of prosperity and modernity, but the push for modernisation did much to destroy most of the city's colonial heritage.

Art also reflects a drive for modernisation. The success of the kinetic artist Jesús Soto in recent decades has done much to promote Venezuela on the international scene. Several modern sculptures are found in public places throughout Caracas, particularly in Sabana Grande.

When South America caught the soccer bug, Venezuela was elsewhere. The country's close association with the US has made baseball the national sport.

The drive for modernisation in the economic heartland of the north has protected southern lowland areas from the colonisation programmes common throughout much of the Amazon Basin. The cultural heritage and welfare of indigenous groups takes a back seat in the national consciousness; a situation that has allowed some Indian groups to preserve their way of life, maintaining a strong sense of cultural identity with less interference than many groups in neighbouring countries.

A brief history

Pre-conquest

Pre-Hispanic populations were primarily located in three areas. The coastal regions were occupied by fishing cultures practising shifting agriculture, while the *llanos* were home to groups of hunter-gatherers. As with much of South America, in Venezuela the Andes was the cradle for more developed cultures. The Timote-Cuica used terracing and agriculture to increase agricultural productivity on the sloping terrain.

Smaller groups living in the lowland areas to the south included the Yanomami, Piaroa and several other groups, along with the Pemón Indians of the Guayana Highlands. Most of these groups have only recently experienced large-scale influences on lifestyles maintained for thousands of years.

Post conquest

Columbus' arrival in 1498 marked the European discovery of Venezuela. The country's apparent lack of wealth and the absence of large indigenous populations to work on plantations reduced the level of exploitation at the hands of the Spanish. Venezuela suffered considerably less than many other countries of the New World.

The first permanent Spanish settlement was Nueva Cádiz on the island of Cubagua, close to Isla Margarita where local Indians were forced to dive for pearls from the rich beds found in the coastal waters.

Colonisation continued at a gentle pace, with Europeans creating a number of coastal settlements.

Independence

The general state of calm prevailing in Venezuela was to be upset by the hunger for independence which swept the continent in the late 18th century. Taking orders from Spain was an increasing source of frustration. Feelings of resentment brought to the fore one of South America's truly great men, Símon Bolívar. This legendary figure, born in 1783, travelled to France and the USA at the turn of the century, experiencing at first hand the euphoric feelings that came with liberation and independence.

Peaceful attempts to bring about independence failed. Bolívar's army achieved independence for Colombia in 1819, securing Venezuela's liberation within two years.

In 1830 *El Libertador*, as Bolívar became known, was sent to exile in France. Before boarding his ship he became ill with tuberculosis and, although he died a quiet and lonely man, the timing of his illness meant that at least he could die in his homeland.

The 20th century

Venezuela's boom came in the 1920s when the discovery of oil below Lake Maracaibo thrust the country on to the world economic stage. From the mid-1920s until World War II, Venezuela was the world's biggest exporter of oil. Governing over the period of the oil boom, General Juan Vicente Gómez seized power in 1908. When he died in 1935, having diverted some of the profits from oil, he was one of the richest men in the country; setting a precedent for governments that lasted for much of the 20th century.

Little wealth from the oil boom filtered down to improve the general standard of living. Demanding accountability from its leaders, Venezuela experienced an eight-month period of democracy in 1947 before the military regime of General Marco Pérez Jiménez took control, entering into a period of oil-funded public investment. Jiménez commissioned the first skyscraper erected in Caracas, setting the tone for the architecturally impressive urban development that dominates the city today. Economic incompetence, corruption and repression forced the regime to stand down in 1958.

The return to democracy under a new political system favoured cooperation rather than adversarial power-broking. The formation of the OPEC oil cartel in 1960 saw Venezuela dramatically increase its revenues from oil. The Arab-Israeli War of 1973 caused the price of oil to rise from US$1.76 in 1970 to US$10.31 in 1974. In that year Venezuelan income rose by 40% and government revenues by 170%.

With new levels of wealth, government spending went through the roof. The oil industry was nationalised, Venezuelans were encouraged to share in the high life and imports of foreign goods rose dramatically. What the government could not afford to pay for immediately would be paid back from future revenue, dramatically increasing government borrowing.

As revenues from oil fell, the taste of the high life for many Venezuelans was difficult to forget. Government debt continued to rocket to over US$30 billion; inflation rose; and by the end of the 1980s a sense of foreboding had gripped the country.

Austerity measures aimed at restructuring the economy were introduced by President Carlos Andrés Pérez but riots in the streets in 1989 demonstrated public objection to the reforms. Sections of the military also demonstrated their dissatisfaction with the state of the country. Venezuela teetered on the edge of a new military regime as two attempted coups in 1992 saw war planes flying between the skyscrapers of Caracas.

In 1993 Pérez was impeached for using defence funds to play the currency market, making himself US$11 million in the process. His replacement, Raul Caldera, elected president in December 1993, found himself overseeing the near complete collapse of the banking sector. In 1994, 13 major banks went to the wall, with several others following in 1995. Caldera declared a 'state of economic emergency' until stability was restored.

Despite measures to remove structural economic weaknesses and the devaluation of the currency, the economy continues to limp along. Inflation is currently hovering in the mid-30s and a further currency devaluation is believed to be imminent. Privatisation has been promoted as the country's salvation, with the government looking to the petroleum industry to lead Venezuela out of the economic wilderness as it has before.

Venezuela goes to the polls in December 1998, when long-time statesman President Rafael Caldera, now 82, will have to stand down. The 1993 election demonstrated a shift in support away from the traditionalist parties of Venezuelan politics. The 1998 election is expected to exhibit even greater decentralisation as more groups of diverse interests push to generate a more participative democracy.

Practicalities

Money

The bolívar continues to limp along in a state of flux. Currency controls in place in 1995 have been removed, squeezing out the black market. Although exchange rates have stabilised recently, the weakness of the bolívar remains a problem. The implications for the traveller can be dramatic. If you are in Venezuela for several weeks, change your money slowly as the falling exchange rate will almost certainly work in your favour. Although there are no currency restrictions at present, check for the latest information before travelling.

Cash dollars, travellers' cheques and credit cards are the most convenient way to carry your money. Changing travellers' cheques is straightforward in *casas de cambios* throughout Caracas. Using a bank, usually the only option outside the major cities, will leave you standing in long queues. Credit cards are widely accepted in the better hotels and shops and can be used for cash advances. ATM machines are widespread, although don't rely on your plastic 100%. Branches of Banco de Venezuela usually have cash dispensing machines, even in out-of-the-way Puerto Ayacucho.

The cost of living in Venezuela makes the country very affordable. Budget travellers can get by on US$30 a day, rising to a minimum of US$50 per day when taking excursions. From that bottom figure the sky's the limit. There is no shortage of hotels and travel operators willing to relieve you of substantial sums in return for very high standards and genuinely unique experiences.

Accommodation

Hotel pricing in Venezuela definitely favours group travel. A *simple* (single room) for one person is usually available only in the cheapest hotels and is rarely cheaper than a *doble* (two single beds) or *matrimonio* (one large bed).

Highlights

Sticking with the rainforest, the standard options are fairly limited but tailor-made travel opportunities are restricted only by your imagination. The rainy season in Puerto Ayacucho is from June to October.

All jungle trips go through Puerto Ayacucho, from where you can spend a couple of weeks relaxing in one of the top quality jungle lodges and venturing out to the rainforest for the occasional foray. Several tour operators arrange boat trips lasting three or four days to the region south of Puerto Ayacucho, taking in visits to Indian villages, treks through the rainforest and trips to Cerro Autana.

The truly adventurous can explore the Humboldt Route for ten days or so, taking in the Casiquiare Canal and Venezuela's part of the Amazon Basin proper. Judging by the bite-covered bodies of returning travellers, the insects are as vicious as Humboldt recorded back in 1800.

If you have a day or two in Puerto Ayacucho, consider a half-day whitewater rafting trip down the Atures rapids on the Orinoco.

Venezuela is also home to what must be *the* most luxurious rainforest travel experiences. For the truly extravagant, helicopter and light-aircraft tours will take you to any part of the lowlands, giving aerial tours of Cerro Autana and flying close to Pico da Neblina.

In Amazonas, technically you need a permit for travel south of La Esmeralda. Depending on your ability to look harmless and talk sweetly you may be able to travel to San Fernando de Atabapo and beyond without one.

Outside Amazonas, if you want to see animals you can spend a few days in one of the *hacienda* ranches on the *llanos* that are set up to cater for tourists. For trips to Angel Falls, travel to the nearest town of Canaima can be easily arranged from Caracas or Ciudad Bolívar.

On the coast, the beach town of Choroní in Henri Pittier National Park is a quiet alternative to the more commercial resorts of Puerto La Cruz and Isla Margarita to the east, where you can sunbathe, windsurf, scuba dive and dance throughout the night if you want.

Tour operators

Several agencies operate in Puerto Ayacucho for those wanting to turn up and book on the spot. Details are in the Puerto Ayacucho section on page 200. If you'd prefer to book internationally here is a selection of agencies handling travel to and in Venezuela:

In Venezuela

Alpi Tours tel: 00 58 2 285 6067; fax: 00 58 2 285 6067; email: tours@alpiturismo.com; net: www.alpiturismo.com. Can organise a wide variety of trips in the Amazon including boat trips along the Casiquiare Canal.

Charles Brewer Carias tel: 00 58 2 978 0129l fax: 00 58 2 977 1298; email: 70501.3522@compuserve.com. The *crème de la crème* for travel opportunities in Venezuela with an impressive list of previous clients.

Eco Voyager tel: 00 58 2 762 1571/1397; fax: 00 58 2 762 4967; Also in the US on 1 800 326 7088; email: ecotour@ecovoyager.com; internet: www.ecovoyager.com. Have trips to several jungle lodges in Amazonas.

Expediciones Guaharibo Av Francisco de Miranda, Torre Dozsa, piso 4, El Rosal, Caracas; tel: 00 58 2 952 6996/952 7895; fax: 00 58 2 953 0092; email: guaharib@telcel.net.ve. One of Venezuela's exclusive operators that treasures its reputation for giving VIP treatment 100% of the time.

Orinoco Tours tel: 00 58 2 761 8431; fax: 00 58 2 761 6801; email: info@orinocotours.com; net: www.orinocotours.com. This company, with offices in Caracas, organises rainforest tours based from the Orinoquia Lodge on the banks of the Orinoco, south of Puerto Ayacucho.

Tobogan Tours Av 23 de Enero #24, Puerto Ayacucho; tel: 00 58 48 214865/214553; fax: 00 58 48 214553. One of the few agencies in Puerto Ayacucho geared up to take international bookings. They can arrange trips throughout the state and to surrounding jungle lodges.

In the US

Field Guides Inc PO Box 160723, Austin, TX 78716; tel: 512 327 4953/800 728 4953; fax: 512 327 9231; email: fgileader@aol.com; internet: www.fieldguides.com. Organise specialist birding trips to lodges deep in Amazonas.

Interconnections Travel 975 Osos St, San Luis Obispo, CA 93401; tel: 800 345 7422; fax: 805 543 3626; email: tours@crconnect.com

In the UK

Geodyssey 29 Harberton Rd, London N19 3JS; tel: 0171 281 7788; fax: 0171 281 7878.

Interchange 27 Stafford Road, Croydon, Surrey CR4 4NG; tel: 0181 681 3612; fax: 0181 760 0031.

Kaminski Air Safaris are one of the premier travel opportunities. Boris Kaminski is an experienced bush pilot and with your own pilot you can travel to the most remote corners of the country. Organised through Last Frontiers (see below).

Last Frontiers Swan House, Long Crendon, Bucks, HP18 9AF; tel: 01844 208405; fax: 01844 201400; email; travelinfo@lastfrontiers.co.uk; net: www.lastfrontiers.co.uk. A specialist tour operator, focusing on tailor-made itineraries throughout Venezuela for independent travellers.

GETTING THERE AND AWAY

By air

Venezuela is without doubt the easiest, though not the cheapest, South American country to travel to, from both the US and most of Europe.

From the US

Flights are channelled through Miami which is just four hours from Caracas. Prices change and strong competition on this route means good bargains can be found. It is unlikely that the US$99 one-way prices of the early 1990s will return but it is worth asking in more than one travel agent to check. One-way tickets are currently around US$450, with returns starting at US$700.

From Europe

Competition here is also hotting up. British Airways offers a direct service from London. Other airlines include Varig, Iberia, Air France, Alitalia, United Airlines. For the best and latest flight deals contact one of the specialist South American tour operators such as Journey Latin America (see page 42). Prices from London start at around £450 return.

Airpasses

Avensa has an Airpass that includes international destinations. A minimum of four coupons needs to be bought but, as one of these can include Miami, travelling to Venezuela can be very cheap. Miami, Caracas, Puerto Ayacucho and back using the airpass costs just US$250. Other international options include New York, Bogotá, Quito, Lima and Mexico City. The price for international sectors varies. Details from travel agents.

Overland

Entering the state of Amazonas directly from Colombia is technically possible only through Puerto Carreño, arriving in the small town of Burro. On the border further south, immigration offices can be found at crossings between Guaviare in Colombia and San Fernando de Atabapo; also between the Colombian town of San Felipe and its Venezuelan neighbour San Carlos de Rio Negro. At both points there are no road links to the rest of Colombia which makes getting there a tough proposition – but your mere presence will create a fair amount of interest and curiosity. Obtaining the necessary stamps and permission could depend on the mood of the officials. Other crossing points from Colombia are between Maicao and Paraguachón, north of Maracaibo; at San Antonio del Táchira in the mountains; and a little further south where the Venezuelan town of El Amparo de Apure and the Colombian town of Arauca sit either side of the Brazo Guárico.

Entering southwestern Venezuela from Brazil is possible, but again is subject to the suspicions of officials. The crossing point is San Simón de Cocuy, connected to Puerto Ayacucho by a weekly flight. Entering Venezuela on this route requires a visa which can be obtained in Manaus. Officials may also want to see a permit for travelling in the restricted region. The more widely used overland frontier with Brazil is in the far southeast of Venezuela near Santa Elena de Uairén. A good road links the town with Boa Vista in Brazil and beyond. For those entering Venezuela, roads lead north to Ciudad Bolívar, from where you can get a bus to Puerto Ayacucho.

There are no border crossings between Venezuela and Guyana.

Customs and immigration

There are currently no visa requirements for US or European nationals entering Venezuela by air. However, if you wish to enter Venezuela overland you do need a visa, which you should obtain from a Venezuelan consulate either in the neighbouring country or in your home country.

Security

When travelling in Venezuela you should always carry your passport with you. Spot checks are common throughout South America and in Venezuela authorities insist on seeing the real thing. It is not uncommon for police to arrange impromptu spot checks in the street or in bus stations, especially in areas close to any of Venezuela's borders.

Getting around

Travel in Venezuela is very easy. Roads are good and internal flights serve most towns. Puerto Ayacucho has road connections with major cities in Venezuela but for the sake of speed you might want to consider taking a plane at least one way.

By bus

Hundreds of intercity buses criss-cross the country. The air-conditioned buses leave on time, arrive on time, and usually show a video. The air-conditioning is a definite bonus and a break from the stickiness of travel in humid climes, but take extra clothing in case you feel cold.

If you are at all curious about the difference, travelling by the only slightly cheaper buses that use good, old-fashioned windows for ventilation will help you decide.

Venezuelan bus travel has an element of security not shared with some of its South American neighbours… a luggage ticket. Bus stations are busy, frantic places where luggage can easily go missing. If you put your bags in the 'hold', you will get a receipt that is checked when you collect them.

Travelling to Puerto Ayacucho is easy. Long-distance buses make the journey from central Caracas (US$13), Ciudad Bolívar (US$10), Valencia (US$13) and Maracay (US$12). Should you find yourself in the *llanos* you can catch a bus from San Fernando de Apure (US$7).

Hitching

The adventurous and curious could hitch from Caracas down to Puerto Ayacucho, but finding a good starting point would be difficult. It's probably better to start from a smaller city. Hitching is a great way to meet people you wouldn't otherwise come across. The usual commonsense rules apply: there is safety in numbers, and women travellers do run an extra risk, especially if travelling alone.

By air

Internal flights in Venezuela are convenient and reasonably affordable. Regular scheduled flights travel to all the major cities and towns. Several companies provide internal flights from Caracas to Puerto Ayacucho. Avensa run a daily service from Caracas costing around US$70 one way. Tickets can be bought from the domestic terminal, next to the international airport near Caracas, or from travel agents in town.

Once you're in small towns there are usually air taxis that can take you to smaller towns. In Puerto Ayacucho, flights can be arranged with Aguaysa (tel: 00 58 48 21026/21443) near the Plaza de los Indios. They also have some charter flights to small settlements in the region. Air taxi services can be found at the airport.

If you're planning on visiting several parts of the country, Avensa's Airpass is a good deal. Buying a minimum of four coupons costs US$160.

COMMUNICATIONS

For a country displaying all the visual signals of a modern economy, Venezuela's prosperity is severely restricted by its poor communication networks.

Mail

Postal services are run by Ipostel and are infamously slow and expensive. Three weeks is the minimum time for a postcard to reach the US or Europe. Parcel post is expensive. Not surprisingly, private courier companies offering alternative services have sprouted up.

Telephones and fax

The CANTV-operated telephone system is good... when it works. Telephones use magnetic *tarjetas* ranging in value up to Bs5,000. Cards are sold by vendors close to phone boxes, in hotels and at news-stands. International calls can be made direct from call boxes. The main problem is finding a telephone that works. Not surprisingly mobile telephones are becoming extremely popular.

Both the terrestrial and mobile systems are overstretched and numbers seem to alter monthly as digits are added, codes are changed and tempers fray. If you are having problems contacting a company in Venezuela check with international operators for changes to the network. If you are in the country, hotel staff may be able to help.

Fax machines are widespread in the better hotels and in the regional offices of CANTV. As with the postal system, private companies have set up fax services which increases availability.

The international country code for Venezuela is 58.

Internet

A system that has proved a lifeline for many other isolated countries has failed, as yet, to make a real impression in Venezuela – probably as a result of unreliable telephone lines. Having said that, several of the international tour operators have email facilities.

In Puerto Ayacucho, the Amazonas Informatic Center (Av Aguerrevere) is planning to set up an Internet service in early 1999.

Television and radio

Venezuelan television is dominated by *telenovellas,* movies and baseball. There are five channels coming out of Caracas but not all of them can be received countrywide. Satellite has added to the appetite for more soap operas, movies and baseball. News on television is notable by its absence.

As on radio in so many countries, a few popular tunes are played endlessly. It's a good way to pick up on the latest trends, so why not buy a CD of your favourite group to listen to while reminiscing over your Venezuelan vacation photos!

Newspapers

Several newspapers are available throughout the country, with *El Universal* and *El Nacional* being the main ones from Caracas. *The Daily Journal* is an English-language daily available in Caracas, with good coverage on Venezuelan and international issues.

CARACAS

Caracas is a vibrant, modern city nestling in a valley 900m above sea level. The altitude makes for fairly comfortable temperatures hovering in the low 20s Celsius despite being only 11° north of the Equator. The view of the coast just 35km away is blocked by the deep-green hills of El Avila National Park which loom over the city, rising to 2,765m. To the south, lower and slightly less steep hills are laden with shanty towns which cling precariously to the unstable slopes.

The city sprawls through the valley in a long ribbon stretching from west to east. The impressive modern skyscrapers, highways and urban design of the city centre have, in many ways, succeeded in masking the chaos of life with shiny facades. But despite the attempts of urban planners to design out all signs of poverty, shanty towns have built up in the empty spaces of the city centre around the main bus terminal.

The main areas of interest to the passing tourist are **Central Caracas** and **Sabana Grande**, a few kilometres to the east.

Central Caracas is home to the remaining colonial heritage of the city. The focus of attention is Plaza Bolívar – an essential feature in every Venezuelan town or city – where there are several museums, some interesting architecture and significant places of history. Accommodation in the city centre tends to be on the scruffy side and the streets can be eerily empty at night and weekends.

In contrast Sabana Grande is a lively district packed with restaurants, several good hotels and plenty of things to do at night. The central boulevard has several *alfresco* restaurants ideal for people-watching and letting the world pass you by.

Caracas has a reputation as a dangerous city and, from what its residents say, this is justified. Walking around on your own, particularly at night in quiet areas, should be avoided. Take precautions to avoid attracting attention, and if you are not sure of your bearings just take a taxi.

At the airport

Símon Bolívar International Airport is 35km outside Caracas near the Caribbean coastal town of Maiquetía. A bus service leaving from outside the terminal building and serving the city centre costs US$2. When returning to the airport the bus leaves from a rather eerie lay-by under Avenida Bolívar close to the Museo de los Niños. Very few people in the street know the service exists and even fewer can

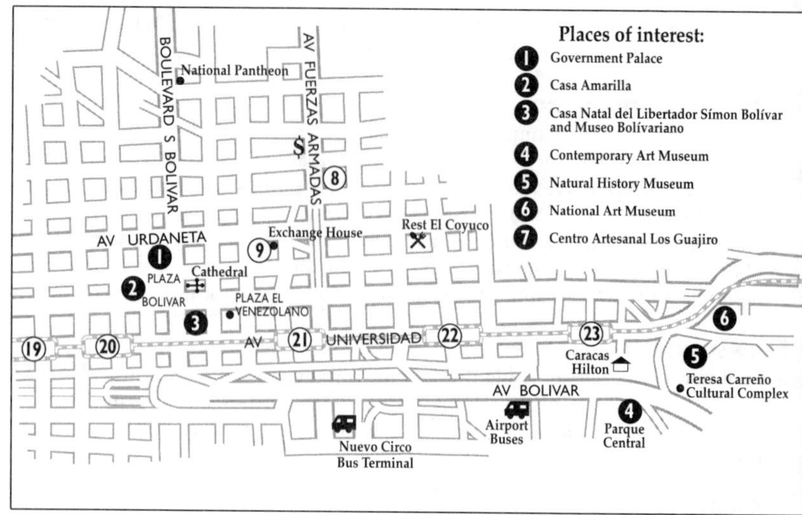

give instructions on how to find it. The evening service stops 'when there are no more passengers' so, if your plane travels late at night, leave early.

The alternative is to get a taxi to or from the city. This costs around US$18 and has the added benefit of getting you direct to your hotel.

The airport departure tax changes often. It is currently US$30, the highest of any of the Amazon countries. There are cash dispensing machines that take credit cards upstairs in the terminal building.

City transport

Taxis and buses can take you all over the city and both are fairly cheap, but the streets are usually close to gridlock. Clean, quiet and efficient, the Metro passes within walking distance of most places of interest in Caracas and is worth using even if just for the few stops between Sabana Grande and Central Caracas.

Metro La Hoyada is closest to the central district of town, Metro Sabana Grande closest to most hotels in Sabana Grande. Metro Bellas Artes is the stop closest to the airport bus service.

Where to stay

The most convenient place to stay is Sabana Grande. The atmosphere is pleasant and any trips to Central Caracas are just a few stops away on the Metro.

First class

Caracas Hilton tel: 02 573 5702; fax: 02 503 5003. Midway between Sabana Grande and Central Caracas. A mere US$200 a night… but they can arrange specials if you are planning to stay for a few days!

Middle range

Hotel Kursaal Avenida Casanova esq Calle El Colegio; tel: 02 762 2822; fax: 02 762 5715. Just off the main Boulevard de Sabana Grande, this is a clean and tidy 3-star hotel three blocks south of Metro Sabana Grande. US$36 for a double.

Hotel Luna Calle El Colegio; tel: 02 762 5851; fax: 02 762 5850. A 3-star hotel just round the corner from the Kursaal but with a friendlier atmosphere. US$28 for a double.

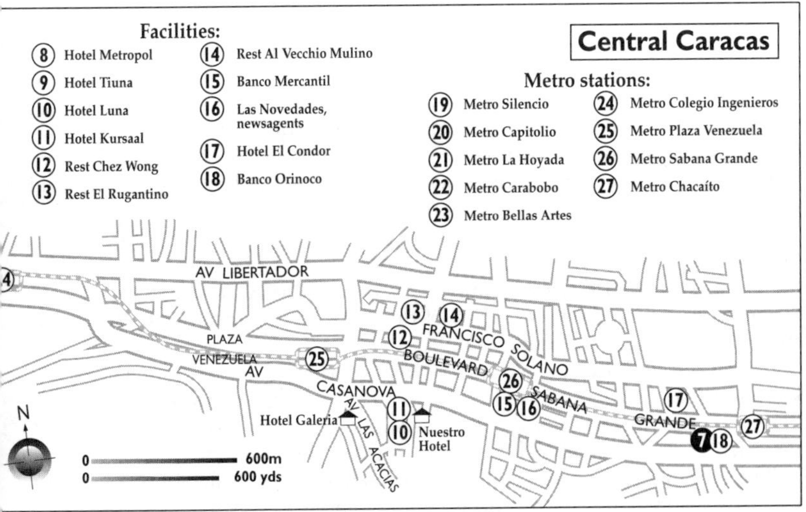

Hotel Gabriel Av Sur Las Acacias. The best hotel on a street packed with possibilities. US$26 for a double.

Hotel El Condor 3ra Av Las Delicias; tel: 02 762 9911-15; fax: 02 762 8621. Towards Metro Chacaíto. A very comfortable option, US$30 for a double.

Budget

Budget travellers will find plenty of cheap hotels down Av Sur Las Acacias. **Nuestro Hotel** on Calle El Colegio opposite Hotel Luna is one of the friendliest budget places in the area. The really cheap hotels are found one block south of the Nuevo Circo Bus Terminal. It's not the most relaxing part of town and you don't feel that comfortable moving about at night. If you want to be in Central Caracas, the old part of town, a good hotel is hard to find. These two are reasonable.

Hotel Tiuna Av Urdaneta esq La Pelota (near McDonalds). Basic, but cheap, friendly and helpful. US$12 for a double.

Hotel Metropol Av Fuerzes Armadas between Plaza Lopez and Socorro. An alternative if the Tiuna is full. US$16 for a double.

Where to eat

Breakfast is one meal that Caraqueños have got down to an art form. *Pastelerías* serve pastries and cakes with a small cup of potent coffee. The early morning rush can be amusing. Um and er for too long and you'll be lost in a flurry of activity.

Arepas are small fried cornmeal rolls filled with vegetables or meat and great for snacking throughout the day. Lunch or *almuerzo* is usually a set menu served with soup, a main course and dessert. Eating out in the evening tends to have fewer set menu options.

Around Sabana Grande there is no shortage of eating options. Alfresco restaurants fill the main boulevard between Metro Plaza Venezuelana and Metro Sabana Grande. One street north, the Avenida Francisco Solano, is packed with more atmospheric restaurants costing from US$15. **Restaurant Al Vecchio Mulino** is an Italian restaurant decorated with a windmill that stands out. Others along the same street include **El Rugantino** and **Chez Wong** on the other side of the street. There are too many to list. Take a walk and make your choice.

Finding food in the centre can be a bit of a chore in the daytime. There are several *pastelerías*, pizza places and *tasca* bars along Avenida Urdaneta. Juice bars serve tasty *batidos* refreshments to keep tired feet on the go for the afternoon bout of sightseeing. The choice of fruits is bewildering.

A must for an evening meal in Central Caracas is **El Coyuco** which is usually filled with *caraqueños*... always a good sign. Their speciality is grilled meat brought to the table on your own personal charcoal grill. Wash it down with an ice-cold *Polarcita* beer and you're halfway Venezuelan!

What to see

Many tourists go to Caracas because they have to rather than for any wish to explore the city, but there are plenty of things to see that encapsulate Venezuela, ancient and modern, perfectly.

Essentially within a few blocks lies what remains of the colonial heritage of Caracas. **Plaza Bolívar** is a shaded plaza with a statue of Venezuela's national hero Símon Bolívar on horseback. The hustle and bustle of the city seems quite forgotten in this peaceful and quiet small square. Bordering the plaza are several buildings of interest including the **Casa Amarilla**, currently the foreign ministry, which was the house of the nation's president before Miraflores Palace was constructed. You can also see **Caracas Cathedral**, and the **Museo Sacro** displaying a collection of 17th-century artworks.

Two blocks west is the uninspiring Plaza El Venezolano. Facing the plaza on Calle San Jacinto is **Casa Natal del Libertador Símon Bolívar**, where the legendary figure was born on 24 July 1783. The restored house is home to several paintings and items paying tribute to the man and his life. Next door the **Museo Bolívariano** also houses memorabilia in homage to the great liberator.

Several blocks north of Plaza Bolívar is the **National Pantheon** in which rest the ashes of, you guessed it, Bolívar. As precious as the man's memory is to the nation, the building is in a pretty sorry state and is surely due for refurbishment once the government's finances are in better shape.

A visit to **Parque Central** takes you from the ancient to the modern. A city within a city, seven skyscrapers are filled with homes, offices, shops and museums, with people quietly moving around the buildings like rabbits in hundreds of concrete warrens. The complex was part of Venezuela's vision for a brave new world. Several museums are in Parque Central including the **Museo de los Niños** (Children's Museum) and the **Museo de Arte Contemporáneo** (Contemporary Art Museum), which includes significant collections from international artists including Picasso.

Slightly north of Parque Central and close to the Caracas Hilton is the **Complejo Cultural Teresa Carreño**, a modern performing arts centre. Its neighbours include the **Museo de Ciencias Naturales** (Natural History Museum), and the **Galeria de Arte Nacional** (National Art Museum).

Shopping

Central Artesanal los Guajiro is a small craft market selling hammocks, clothes and other items in Sabana Grande, close to Metro Chacaíto. For the best shopping, you're better off going to El Hatillo.

Excursions from Caracas

El Hatillo

El Hatillo is a suburb of Caracas some 13km south of the city. Regular city buses leave from Av Humboldt close to Metro Chacaíto in Sabana Grande. Quaint streets and colonial buildings painted in vibrant pastels give a cosmopolitan feel to the village-like atmosphere. El Hatillo is very calming: a welcome break from the chaos of Caracas.

The main reason for visiting El Hatillo is for shopping. There is no shortage of places selling all things Venezuelan, ancient and modern, traditional and contemporary. Everything is within two blocks of the main plaza.

For excellent handicrafts and service seek out Hannsi at Calle Bolívar #12. The shop sells crafts from throughout Venezuela including those from the Indian tribes of Amazonas. There are Yanomami carrying-baskets with their characteristically strong geometric designs; the straw-fringed masks of the Piaroa paying tribute to the tarantula; as well as blowpipes, carvings, hammocks and even dug-out canoes.

Larger items can be shipped home, and Hannsi take credit cards. It's the kind of place where vacation budgets get thrown out the window.

Leaving town

Buses to Puerto Ayacucho – and most other places in Venezuela – leave from the Nuevo Circo Terminal on Av Lecuna. The nearest metro stop is La Hoyada. Internal flights depart from the domestic airport next door to the international airport.

Buses for eastern destinations leave from Terminal de Oriente, 8km out of town. A local bus takes passengers from Metro Petare to the terminal.

PUERTO AYACUCHO: GATEWAY TO THE VENEZUELAN AMAZON

Officially founded on December 9, 1924, the creation of Puerto Ayacucho as the administrative and distribution centre for the region naturally led to growth. A Salesian missionary living in the region since 1932 remembers when Puerto Ayacucho was just a tiny hamlet with a population of 200. Now the capital of the state of Amazonas, the dusty town of 60,000 people is not the kind of place you fall in love with for its natural beauty. Although geographically near the Orinoco, the heart of the town is a long way from the river. The town has little of the noise and atmosphere of most lowland settlements, despite being close to the rainforest which starts some 80km to the south.

Puerto Ayacucho owes its existence to the Orinoco. Boats can travel unhindered up to the town from the Orinoco Delta, which is 900km downstream. But beyond Puerto Ayacucho the Atures and Maipures rapids churn up the smooth waters and make the river unnavigable for 60km. All cargo being transported by river has to be unloaded, moved overland some 60km upstream to Samariapo above the rapids, and then reloaded on to vessels to continue the journey through the river's headwaters that stretch for a further 1,160km. So when roads stretched as far south as Puerto Ayacucho, the port was no longer used, removing the town's *raison d'être*. As often happens with towns in the Amazon, the arrival of the road ripped the sense of purpose out of the place. Puerto Ayacucho is now a river port without any real reference to the river. Although it now relies on road and air connections, the town still functions as the main distribution centre for the state of Amazonas.

The central part of the town is very compact – nowhere is more than ten minutes' walk away – making it very easy to get around. The town centres on Plaza Bolívar from where the statue of Simón Bolívar keeps watch over the comings and goings of visitors to the government buildings, the faithful and sinners to the Salesian Mission and students to the library and school.

The average temperature is 27°C and, despite being more than 900km away from the Atlantic, the town is just 110m above sea level. The city gets rainfall of almost 2,200mm annually with the rainy season running from June to October.

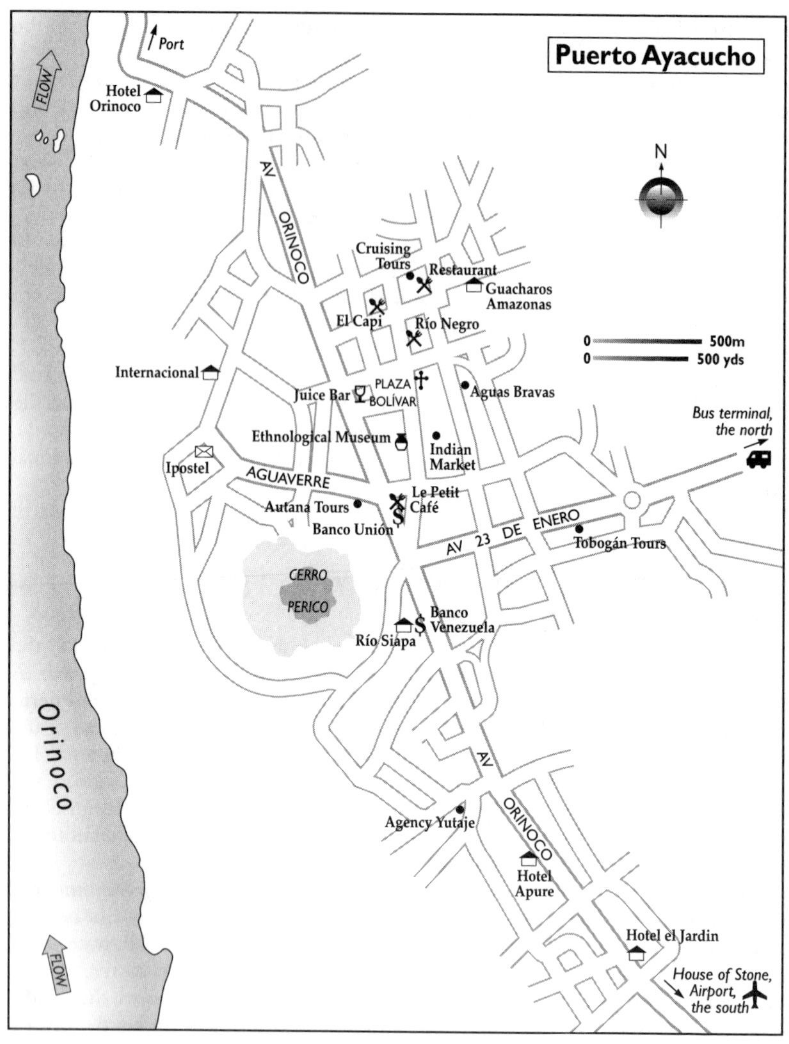

The area in the immediate vicinity of Puerto Ayacucho is plains savannah covered with grasses and green moriche palm trees. The rocky terrain around the town limits soil production and a number of crystal clear rivers flow through the region.

Getting there

Puerto Ayacucho airport is 5km south of the town. Taxis make the journey for around Bs3,000 (US$6). The small bus terminal is a few kilometres east of town. Local buses marked *Centro* regularly run the route for Bs70 from the main road outside the terminal. Taxis charge Bs700 for the trip.

Where to stay

There is a surprising number of hotels in Puerto Ayacucho providing for all but luxury budgets.

Middle range

Guacharos Amazonas Resort at the end of Calle Evelio Roa and Av Amazonas; tel: 048 210328; fax: 048 210155. Recently refurbished, the hotel has a swimming pool, restaurant and bar. A little overpriced starting at US$33 for a *doble* with A/C and TV.

Hotel Orinoco at the bottom of Av Orinoco near the port; tel: 048 210285. Comfortable and quiet. A fair hotel that has seen better days. *Dobles* start at US$16 with A/C and TV.

Hotel Apure Avenida Orinoco on the way out to the airport; tel: 048 210516. A well-kept hotel that caters for organised tours. Quite a way from the centre of town. *Dobles* with A/C and TV are US$25. Probably the best comfortable hotel in town, although there is no restaurant.

Hotel Restaurant 'El Jardin' Av Orinoco close to Hotel Apure; tel: 048 213373. A new hotel which has a restaurant and a patio garden. *Dobles* with A/C and TV are US$25.

Budget

Residencia Rio Siapa Calle Carabobo (no sign); tel: (00 58 48) 210138. Comfortable and friendly. Very popular with visiting Venezuelans. *Dobles* with A/C and TV are US$10.

Residencial Internacional Av Aguerrevere 18. The budget travellers' favourite. The rooms aren't much, but it is a good place to meet up with other travellers. *Simples* are US$8, *dobles* US$10 and *triples* US$12.

Out of town

An alternative option is to stay at one of the many jungle-style lodges in the area using them as a base for trips to the jungle. Most can be booked internationally or from Caracas. **Tobogan Tours** (Av 23 de Enero #24, Puerto Ayacucho; tel: 048 214865; fax: 048 214553) can advise on availability if you are in the area.

Just out of Puerto Ayacucho is the popular resort of **Campamento Tucán** also called **Campamento Genesis** (tel/fax: 048 210409). Set amongst trees with spotless rooms, a pool and a thatched dining room based on the traditional *churuata* round-houses of the Piaroa Indians, this is a relaxing retreat: an ideal way to start and finish trips to the rainforest. Prices from US$80pp. Book in Caracas through Alpi Tour (tel/fax: 02 2856067).

Further south is **Campamento Las Garzitas**, tel: 048 214958, overlooking the rapids of the Orinoco. At US$40 it's slightly cheaper than other lodges and can help arrange bespoke trips throughout the region. If you call in advance they will arrange transfers from the airport. They share an office in Puerto Ayacucho with Siapa Amazonas Expeditions on Plaza de los Indios.

Nearby is the new **Orinoquia Cacao Lodge** on the banks of the Orinoco, with headquarters in Caracas (tel: 02 977 1234; fax: 02 977 0110; email: info@orinocotours.com; net: www.orinocotours.com). Six very comfortable *churuata* bungalows in a riverfront setting. Double and triple rooms all have private bathrooms. The Lodge also owns *Islas Garcitas,* a beautiful 12-acre island in the middle of the Orinoco. Prices start at US$42 pp for bed, breakfast and supper. US$85 pp provides airport transfers, three meals and two excursions a day. Other packages are available on request.

Camturama Resort, tel: 048 210266, is the largest resort with air-conditioned chalet-style rooms, a large restaurant, bar area and disco. On the banks of the Orinoco, day fishing and birding trips can be arranged, along with jungle excursions. Prices from US$85pp including meals. Enquiries and bookings can be made in Caracas (tel: 02 9418813; fax: 02 9435160).

Where to eat

El Capi on Calle Evelio Roa is a small restaurant on a covered terrace. There's something special about relaxing on a terrace while the full power of a tropical rainstorm does its best to wash the town downriver. **Tasca Restaurant Rio Negro** on Av Rio Negro, close to the plaza, is an intimate little place. The early evening is quiet and relaxed; later at night live entertainment keeps going till the early hours.

Restaurant El Angoleño is a restaurant and bar close to Guacharos Amazonas Resort. Walking towards Guacharos down Calle Evelio Roa it is the last road on your left. There is no sign to guide you so you may have to ask. The food is good and covers a wide range of fish and meat dishes and the service is very friendly.

For snacks, **Le Petit Café** on Av Orinoco sells very tasty *arepas* with a wide selection of fillings. There are several bakeries/juice bars in town, the best of which is on the corner of Av Bolívar and Av Orinoco.

Money

Banco Union and Banco Venezuela, both on Av Orinoco, change cash and travellers' cheques. If you want to avoid queuing use their ATM machines that take Visa and MasterCard. Most of the tour agencies accept travellers' cheques.

What to see

Mercado Indigena is on Plaza de los Indios one block south of Plaza Bolívar, selling a wide range of items from the area. You can pick up Piaroa, Guahibo and Yanomami crafts. The distinctive red-and-brown basketry of the Yanomami is finely crafted. There are several different sizes of *guatura* or *wii* for sale. An ingenious flexible tube, woven out of palm fibres, that springs shut to hold fruit and vegetables or can be used to squeeze toxic juices out of soaked and mashed manioc.

Opposite the market is the **Museo Etnológico del Amazonas**, open Tuesday to Saturday all day, and in the morning on Sundays. It's a small museum but packed with information about the Indian tribes of the region. There are several rooms with models and artefacts reflecting the main indigenous cultures of the region including the Piaroa, Guajibo, Yanomami, Arawak and Ye'kwana Indians. On Plaza Bolívar itself is the Salesian Mission and the library, with displays and videos about the region.

Not too far from the centre of town is **Cerro Perico**, a small hill with a viewing post at the summit which gives an excellent view of the surrounding area and the Orinoco. To get there follow Av Aguerrevere west looking to the left until you see the hill. The road meanders round the hill becoming a path towards the top. The view is impressive and best visited at sunrise or sunset.

On the road out to the airport is the rather eccentric **Casa de La Piedra** (House of the Stone). It is not in itself remarkable, but the building, constructed in the 1960s, sits atop a massive boulder balancing precariously 10m above the ground. The house is currently being renovated and, if funds don't run out first, the plan is to use the building as a hotel or hostel.

Tour operators

In Puerto Ayacucho the tour agencies seem to open and close daily. Most of them can help with almost any enquiry or request. It is worth comparing a couple of agencies for price and level of service. Here are a few of the recommended agencies in Puerto Ayacucho in addition to **Tobogan Tours** mentioned on page 199 and those at the beginning of the chapter (page 189).

Turismo 'Yutaje' Monte Bello 31; tel: 048 210644. This agency has been around for quite a while and is trying to stimulate interest in the importance of sustainable ecotourism in the Venezuelan rainforest.
Cruising Tours Tel/fax: 048 210443. Close to Guacharos Amazonas Resort, this new agency is getting good reports.
Autana Tours has a good reputation, has been popular for a while and seems to move offices almost weekly. Ask in Puerto Ayacucho where their latest offices are.

Indigenous groups of Amazonas State

In 1992, government figures estimated the indigenous population of Amazonas at 43,366, comprising 17 different ethnic groups. The largest populations are of Ye'kuana (4,000), Yaruro (4,859), Curripaco (2,623), Piaroa (8,030) and, the most numerous, Yanomami (10,000 plus). Each ethnic group has a different language and a different set of beliefs, usually based on a complex inter-relationship between spirits of the forest.

The Yanomami inhabit an area of forests and mountain valleys that cross the Venezuelan-Brazilian border, straddling the headwaters of the Orinoco in Venezuela and several tributaries feeding into the lower section of the Río Negro in Brazil. Yanomami live in communal houses called *shabonos* which may be home to as many as 400 people. Oval in shape, they have steep walls to protect an inner area open to the sky.

The Yanomami are semi-nomadic, living off manioc, bananas and other crops tended in gardens close to the *shabono*. They hunt with bows and arrows tipped with *curare* – a natural poison made from forest plants that attacks the nervous system. The Yanomami decorate their faces with wooden plugs and their bodies with red paint made from vegetable dyes of *onoto* seed and *curare*. They also use a hallucinogenic snuff called *yoppo*.

NO WAY TO DECIDE...

Beata Pawlikowska, a radio personality with the Polish radio broadcaster Vheadline/VENews.

It's easy – you get on a plane and fly to Caracas. Then you go by bus as far south as it can take you. Finally, you go to a local travel agency and say that you want to go and see the Yanomami Indians. You pay a substantial sum of money, get on a boat and after a few days you arrive at a Yanomami village.

You see slim dark-skinned people, barely dressed, men with scars on their heads, women with wooden sticks put in their cheeks and chins. You see the shacky *shabono* houses, thatched with palm leaves. You see the bows and arrows, naked children grimy with soil, and you think: 'Oh my goodness! They are so poor, dirty, lazy and primitive!'

But stop and consider this:

Some civilisations focus on changing the environment around them so that it serves all their needs. Other civilisations make the effort to adapt themselves to the existing conditions.

There is no way to decide which is better: people who burn and cut the forest to build a city with shops, streets, concrete houses and an airport; or people who make the jungle their home.

Once you are born in either of these civilisations, you will never be able to comprehend the nature of the other.

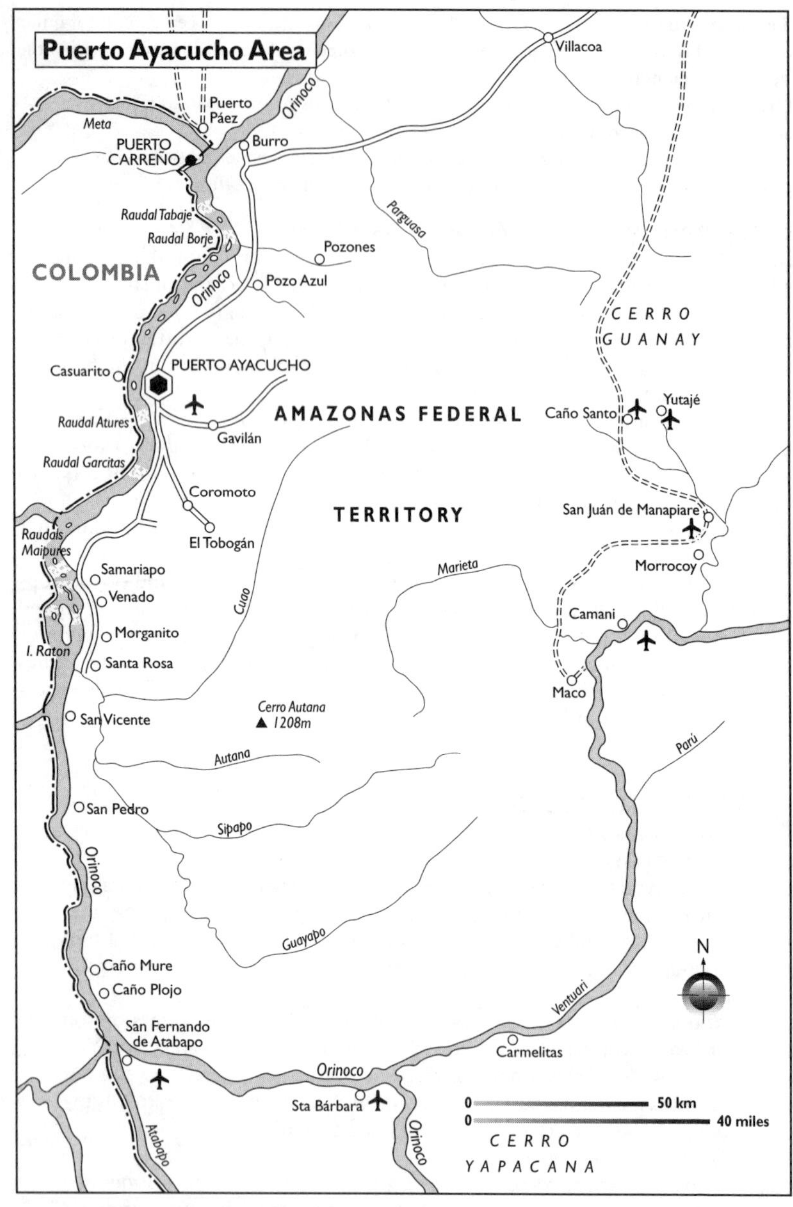

The Piaroa, like the Yanomami, are semi-nomadic, clearing land for settled agriculture before moving on after four years or so. The land is cleared by burning and then cultivated as a garden or *kanuku* to produce around 50 different types of vegetable, mainly bitter manioc, corn and sweet potato. For fishing they use poisons and for hunting rely on blowpipes and darts coated with curare – a product for which the Piaroa were once famous within the Amazon. Their spiritual leaders or shamans also have a good reputation amongst indigenous groups and use hallucinogenic substances in rituals and healing. Circular communal houses or *churuatas* built from hardwoods and thatched with palm fronds reflect the status of the chief and can be large enough to house 100 people.

Excursions near Puerto Ayacucho

El Tobogán de la Selva, 30km south of Puerto Ayacucho, is a huge rock escarpment with a river running down its face. Erosion has created a natural water-slide almost 100m in length – it's great fun if you can handle a few bumps and bruises. Towards the top of the slide are a couple of natural jacuzzis that look just like shallow puddles but are actually several feet deep, and at the summit is a natural diving pool. There are shelters with barbecue racks and picnic tables, but the place does get crowded at weekends and holidays. Camping is allowed but there is no food for sale close to the area.

El Tobogán is not served by any public transport. To get there hitch a ride south to the turn-off at Kilometre 30 and then walk or hitch the remaining 6km. There is an hourly jeep that travels south down to Samariapo from Av Orinoco (near Banco Venezuela) which stops at the turn-off. Alternatively trips can be arranged through agencies or with a taxi. Hitching is easiest at weekends and by far the best way of making new Venezuelan friends.

On the way to El Tobogán is the **Piedra de la Tortuga** which is a couple of rocks which, from the right perspective, appear to be a giant tortoise. It's about 8km out of town. From the wrong perspective, however, they appear to be a couple of rocks…

About 17km south of town you can also see **Cerro Pintado**, home to prehistoric petroglyphs. It is best to visit the site with a guide as some of the images can be difficult to see.

Another swimming hole called **Pozo Azul** is 30km north of town. The water appears bluish and if you go mid-week you may have the place to yourself. There is regular traffic on this route so catching a ride is fairly easy.

Expediciones Aguas Bravas (Av Río Negro; tel: 048 21541) offer half-day trips down the Atures rapids. Traditionally rafting is paddle-powered but Aguas Bravas use outboards to make the trip considerably less strenuous. In the dry season (December to April), stops are made at Sardinata Island to see the petroglyphs. Trips are tailored to each group's preferred level of excitement and all equipment and training is provided.

Jungle tours

The amount of competition between agencies in Puerto Ayacucho is great news for travellers visiting the area. There are several set itinerary options to pick and choose from, but for something a little more adventurous or just the idea of following a particular tributary on a map the agencies in Puerto Ayacucho will do anything they can to help. A few moments pondering over the map of Venezuela published by ITMB Publishing (see page 45), produces endless exciting possibilities. The downside of competition is that the environment normally loses out so don't forget your ecotourist hat.

Travel in the region is restricted and only allowed with a permit. Travel down to San Fernando de Atobapo by boat and further south to Maroa and San Carlos de Río Negro by light aircraft is permitted. Any travel west of this route and further south without a permit is outside the protection of the law.

A couple of days

The simplest option includes a short two-day, one-night trek in the jungle. Most of these stay fairly close to Puerto Ayacucho and don't actually get into lowland rainforest but reports are generally good. Trips include visits to Piaroa communities to experience the culture at first hand, including the use of blowpipes and the medicinal use of plants and natural materials. These 'anthropological tours' start at around US$40 per person per day. As with most of the jungle tours, the night is spent in a hammock which may be on a river beach or in a hut. Mosquito nets are generally provided but check first.

Four days

A more rewarding option is to visit Cerro Autana, called Wahari Kuawai by the Piaroa, 80km south of Puerto Ayacucho. This trip takes you to see the sheer cliffs of one of Venezuela's *tepuis*, rising dramatically to over 1,250m above the rainforest lowlands. In a landscape that is often uniformly flat this striking feature knocks the senses. A three- or four-day trip takes you up the Orinoco, Sipapo and Autana rivers in a *bongo*. Originally the name for the traditional dugout canoe used by people above the rapids, this now equates to almost anything that travels on the water. Accommodation is in hammocks with local Piaroa communities. The trips include visits to nearby waterfalls and walks in the jungle looking for tarantulas; increasingly difficult as they are not only revered by the Piaroa as protectors of the rainforest but also eaten as delicacies.

Trip prices start at US$40 per person per day.

The geology of Cerro Autana is complex and recent aerial expeditions have discovered a horizontal cave passing through the *tepui* from one side to the other, impossible to see from the ground. Air taxis and helicopters can be hired from Puerto Ayacucho for a flying tour.

One extended alternative is travel by boat to San Juan de Manapiare. It is five or six days upstream, depending on how many smaller tributaries you explore along the way, but the main route follows the course of the Orinoco before heading north up the Ventuari. Flights from San Juan de Manapiare to Puerto Ayacucho are around US$60 one way. Prices for the expedition are about US$80pp per day.

Over a week

A more adventurous option is to follow the *Ruta Humboldt*; retracing the journey of Baron von Humboldt in the early 19th century when he made the crossing between the Amazon Basin and the great Orinoco river system by way of the Brazo Casiquiare. This natural canal waterway diverts up to one third of the River Orinoco's volume down the 354km-long canal from Tamatama, flowing on to join the River Negro, one of the Amazon's major tributaries. The waterway is thought to be unique and goes against more generally accepted rules of hydrology.

It's a fantastic journey and *enjoyed* by the most hardy of fools. The region is pristine rainforest and the insects do their best to keep people away – a couple of hundred bites wouldn't be uncommon. Fortunately if you are travelling by motorised boat the insects can't keep up.

Heading upstream from Puerto Ayacucho, the canoe travels to San Fernando de Atobapo and beyond, following the River Temi to Yavita. A road link crosses to Maroa on the River Guainía which flows down to meet the Casiquiare when both rivers merge to become the Río Negro. Heading up the Casiquiare against the current, the route rejoins the Orinoco before heading back down to Puerto Ayacucho.

You need to take food for the journey, supplementing it with fish caught while travelling and supplies brought on the expedition. En route you can stay with Piaroa, Yanomami and several other indigenous communities.

In total the journey takes at least eight days or maybe longer. There are several smaller tributaries that make for interesting exploration and, innumerable blood

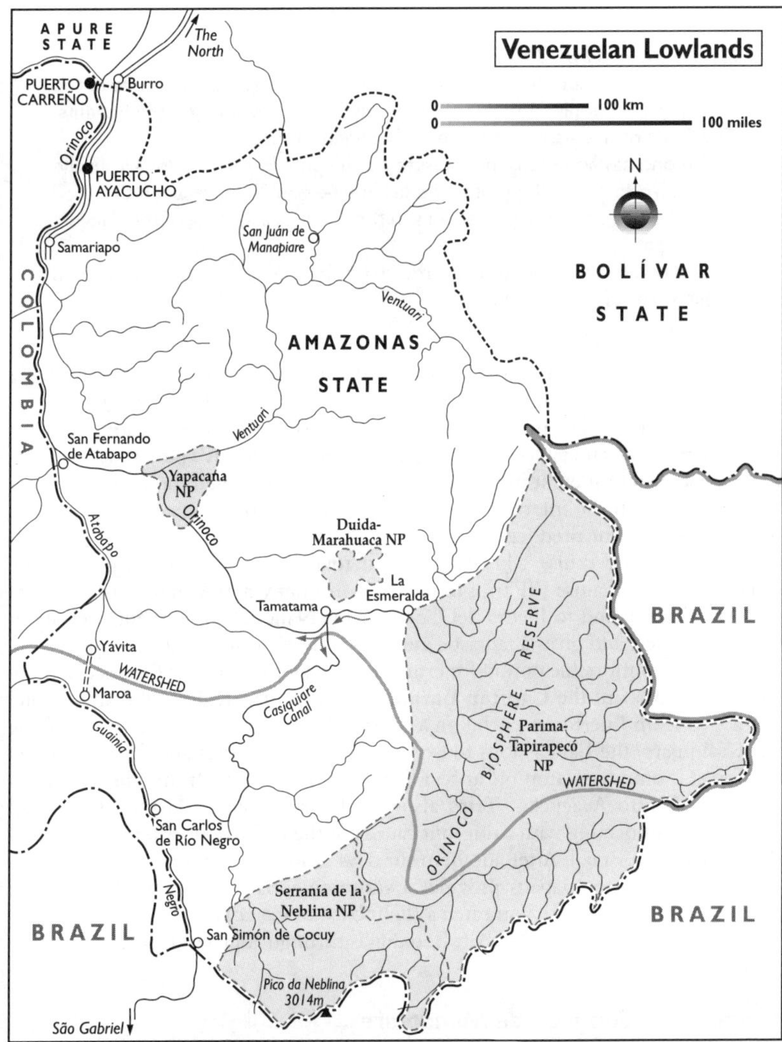

sacrifices to the local biting insect population. Animal life goes beyond insects, with dolphins, giant otters, jaguar and tapir all found in the area. There are also hundreds of butterflies, birds and other rainforest wildlife to see on the smaller tributaries. Prices start from around US$100 per day.

Ruta Humboldt and cruising in style

The Ruta Humboldt is adventure travel . The trip is best organised through one of the operators in Puerto Ayacucho. **Expediciones Guaharibo**, based in Caracas, travel the route in style. (See page 189.) The journey begins in Puerto Ayacucho and takes in Autana *tepui* and several small Indian villages and communities en route to the mission outpost of La Esmeralda, before turning round and heading down the Casiquiare. Stopping to explore tributaries and lakes, and with time for

AUTANA – THE TREE OF LIFE

The local Indian legend tells of a giant tree that offered all the fruits of the world to the people of the earth. Nobody had to work to get the benefits. The fruits of the giant tree were within hand's reach.

But one day ambitious men possessed the people and decided to cut the tree down to get all the fruits. The fallen tree couldn't give any more food to the people and its trunk remains in the earth as a symbol of the dangers of ambition.

Today all that remains of the tree is the *tepui* Autana, indeed reminiscent of a giant stump.

fishing and swimming, the trip follows the Casiquiare downstream before flying you back to Puerto Ayacucho from the town of San Carlos de Río Negro.

With Guaharibo the emphasis is on comfort. VIP service means eating meals at a table with chairs and tablecloths along with waiter service. It's rather incongruous to see a table laid for eight in the heart of the rainforest. When the water levels are right, meals from the international menu are taken as the waters of the Orinoco gently massage your tired feet.

The Casiquiare cruise takes ten days in total costing US$1,670 per person. Guaharibo also organise VIP trips to the triple frontier where Venezuela, Colombia and Brazil meet, and to Piedra del Cocuy. This National Monument rises 400m above rainforest and gives a fantastic view of the rainforest lowlands.

A second comfortable option for cruising the waterways of the Orinoco and the Amazon is to board the **Capitán Barata**. This Brazilian-registered floating hotel is reached from Puerto Ayacucho on a charter flight to Tamatama. Cruising along the Casiquiare, the Barata stops to explore smaller tributaries and for treks in the rainforest. Some trips stop off at San Carlos de Río Negro from where you can return to Puerto Ayacucho. Trips also travel further south, visiting Piedra del Cocuy and connecting with a dug-out canoe for the eight-hour trip to São Gabriel de Cachoeira in Brazil. After another four days of local excursions in the Brazilian rainforest, flying to Manaus provides a stunning aerial view of the heart of the Amazon rainforest before you catch a flight back to Caracas.

Trips run from July to October. Booking is through Alpi Tours in Caracas. (See page 189.)

Lodges near San Juan de Manapiare

Jungle lodges close to San Juan de Manapiare are targeting the comfortable end of the market. The lodges are all in the middle of the rainforest; ideal places for combining true relaxation with the occasional burst of, albeit mild, energy.

Campamento Camani is on the banks of the Ventuari south of San Juan de Manapiare and claims to be 'the cure against civilisation'. Surrounded by rainforest, the lodge is perfectly located for treks into the jungle. Excursions include boat trips to the Caño de Piedra and Tecuna waterfalls, along with shorter walks to indigenous communities and sites of special natural interest. Fishing can also be arranged. The luxury *churuatas* have hot water and electricity and the international menu is spectacular. There is also a swimming pool. The lodge costs US$140 per person per night, plus charter flight to the airstrip. The journey from Caracas takes two hours and requires a minimum of six people for the charter flight. From Puerto Ayacucho it is 50 minutes. Details from Tobogan Tours in Puerto Ayacucho (see page 199) or in Caracas (page 189).

Nearby is **Junglaven**, which is slightly less comfortable but gets rave reviews nevertheless. The area is perfect for birdwatching and the owner has compiled a bird list that now includes over 420 species. The camp also offers excellent sports fishing for peacock bass, payara, catfish and pacú between November and May. There are ten *churuata* cabins each with private bathroom and shower. Birding and general trips are US$120pp per night, fishing trips are US$250pp. Flights can be organised from Caracas or from Puerto Ayacucho. Details in Caracas on: tel/fax: 02 9918478; fax: 02 9915083; cellular: 016 6291814. Field Guides in the US (see page 190) has trips to Yunglaven for 12 days from US$2,750 (land only).

North of San Juan de Manapiare is **Yutajé Camp**. Set up in 1967 for private visitors, the camp is now open to visitors. The accommodation is simple but the rainforest remains unspoilt and is home to large numbers of birds along with giant otters and river dolphins. Trips can be made to the nearby Yutajé Falls which cascade off the southern rim of the Guyana Shield. Four-day packages to the camp, based on five passengers and including the flight from Caracas, cost US$480. In Caracas contact EcoVoyager (see page 189) who have flights departing every Sunday. For flights in Caracas contact Roques Air in Caracas; tel: 02 952 4315; fax: 02 952 5923.

Independent travel

Non-boat trips

For those wanting the freedom of independent travel without restrictions the options are rather limited, and there is always the chance of being turned back by one of the many checkpoints. On the other hand, there is something nice about going somewhere without a guide… book.

The most straightforward destination is San Juan de Manapiare. Its population of 1,200 lives in temperatures in the high 20s. The region produces the majority of Amazonas' agricultural produce. San Juan de Manapiare is surrounded to the east, north and west by the most westerly outcrops of the Guyana Shield. Although at just 140m above sea level, it is some 1,400km to the Orinoco delta. The combination of rainforest lowlands with the steeply sided mountains of the southwest Guyana Shield rising to over 2,400m has made this an ideal place for guided treks. Salto Yutajé is one of the many waterfalls in the area worth exploring. Flights for San Juan de Manapiare leave several times a week from Puerto Ayacucho and cost US$60 one way.

For the really adventurous, Cruising Tours in Puerto Ayacucho (see page 201) can organise treks on foot or horseback between Puerto Ayacucho and San Juan de Manapiare, or north to the town of Guaniamo. Both trips involve trekking over parts of the Guyana Shield. Prices vary depending on the number in the group.

South towards Brazil

Several communities live along the road that connects Puerto Ayacucho with Samariapo upstream of the Maipures and Atures rapids. None offers hotels or services but they could be good places to stop if you are camping through the region.

At Samariapo there is little more than a few huts, selling soft drinks and meals. Any other produce you can see is probably in transit. There is no accommodation. The biting insects are vicious, making it uncomfortable to stand still, which is another excellent reason for moving on.

Boats regularly travel to the small community on the unfortunately named Island of Rats (Isla Ratón). There is a mission and small school on the island but not much else. The island is close to the River Sipapo which goes towards Cerro Autana and it may be possible to catch a ride with a small supply boat.

Upstream you come to San Fernando de Atobapo, a small town with a couple of hotels. The last surviving communities of Piapoco and Piunave Indians live nearby. Just in front of the town is a clearly defined meeting of the waters where the blackwaters of the Atabapo River meet the brown-coloured waters of the Guaviare flowing in from Colombia. Transport from Puerto Ayacucho with Camani Transportes near the electricity generator cost Bs7,000.

Maroa, founded in 1760 by Chief Maruwa, is an island settlement that acts as a transit point between San Fernando de Atabapo and San Carlos de Río Negro. It is possible to get to Maroa by boat, pushing up to Yavita, then making the land crossing over the watershed between the Orinoco and the Amazon to the town.

San Carlos de Río Negro is a small town downriver from Maroa with a square, church, a small hotel and not much else. Founded in 1759 by Colonel Solanos this is the oldest town in the region, and is the closest to the outlet of the Casiquiare Canal. The area is home to the Baré Indians.

The triple frontier with Colombia and Brazil is further south in Cucuí.

San Fernando de Atabapo, Maroa and San Carlos de Río Negro are all served by regular flights with Aguaysa from Puerto Ayacucho. There is a landing strip just north of the frontier in the town of Santa Lucía.

NATIONAL PARKS AND WILDLIFE RESERVES

Nationally Venezuela has a vast range of habitats, protected by 42 National Parks. In addition to parks there are 41 natural monuments, including Cerro Autana and Piedra del Cocuy, nine forest reserves, including the Sipapo reserve south of Puerto Ayacucho, and five wildlife reserves.

Within Amazonas there are four national parks, all of which require permits to visit.

Yapacana National Park

Created in 1978, this park covers 320,000ha close to the merging of the Orinoco and the Río Ventuari. The park includes extensive savannah and the region is believed to have among the higest levels of biodiversity in Venezuela.

Duida-Marahuaca National Park

This 210,000ha park touches La Esmeralda to the south, and stretches north to include the peaks of Duida (2,232m) and Marahuaca (2,890m), western outcrops of the Guyana Shield. The park has a series of tube-shaped mountains similar to *tepuis,* and there is a wide diversity of flora and fauna in the region.

Mount Neblina National Park

On the southernmost tip of Amazonas State, this park of 1,360,000ha encompasses craggy landscapes, deep rich valleys and views of Pico da Neblina.

Parima-Tapirapecó National Park

*(also called the **Alto Orinoco-Casiquiare Biosphere Reserve**)*

Formed in 1991, this national park protects 3,420,000ha of jungle and savannah encompassing the headwaters of the Río Orinoco. In addition to protecting a wide range of flora and fauna, about which very little is known, the boundaries form part of the territory of the Yanomami Indian communities. There are strict controls regarding entry to the park.

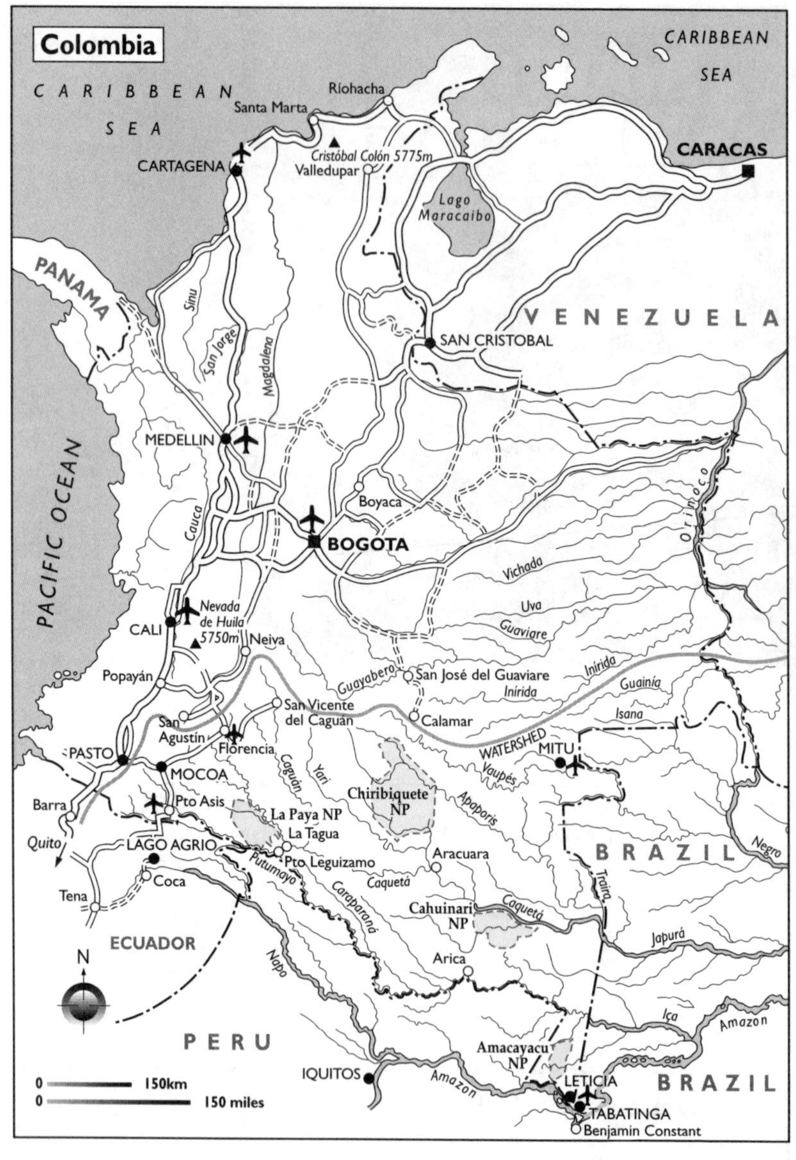
Colombia
CARIBBEAN SEA
CARIBBEAN SEA
Ríohacha
Santa Marta
CARTAGENA
Cristóbal Colón 5775m
Valledupar
CARACAS
Lago Maracaibo
PANAMA
Sinu
San Jorge
Magdalena
VENEZUELA
SAN CRISTOBAL
MEDELLIN
PACIFIC OCEAN
Cauca
Boyaca
BOGOTA
Vichada
Uva
Guaviare
Orinoco
Nevada de Huila 5750m
CALI
Neiva
Popayán
Guayabero
San José del Guaviare
Inírida
Inírida
Guainía
Isana
San Vicente del Caguán
Calamar
San Agustín
Florencia
WATERSHED
MITU
Vaupés
PASTO
MOCOA
Caguán
Yari
Chiribiquete NP
Apaporis
Barra
Pto Asis
La Paya NP
La Tagua
Quito
LAGO AGRIO
Pto Leguizamo
Aracuara
BRAZIL
Negro
Putumayo
Caquetá
Traíra
Coca
Tena
Caraparaná
Cahuinari NP
Caquetá
Japurá
ECUADOR
N
Napo
Arica
Iça
Amazon
PERU
Amacayacu NP
0 150km
0 150 miles
IQUITOS
Amazon
LETICIA
BRAZIL
TABATINGA
Benjamin Constant

8 Colombia

Although named after the 'discoverer' of the Americas, Colombia was never visited by Christopher Columbus. Presumably he had no idea what he was missing, for even today Colombia compels the attention and fascination of the curious traveller. It is indeed the land of emeralds and legends of El Dorado. From its snow-capped volcanoes and sunny beaches to the vast tropical woodlands, Colombia – more than most countries – merits the tour brochure's description, 'a land of contrasts'.

FACTS AND FIGURES

Geography

Colombia is South America's fourth biggest country, just over twice the size of France. Neighbouring countries include Peru and Ecuador to the south, Venezuela to the north and east, and Brazil in the southeast. Colombia's shortest frontier is with Panama, where South and Central America meet. The Isthmus of Panama splits Colombia's 2,890km (1,800 mile) coastline between the Pacific to the south and to the north the Gulf of Darien in the southern Caribbean.

Inland from the coast, the terrain graduates, by fine degrees, up through every major biome, from tropical rainforest to temperate woodland to alpine.

Colombia's interior is divided by several mountain ranges or *cordilleras*. From the south, the northern Andes spread out into three diverging ranges that separate western Colombia from the eastern lowlands. From the border with Ecuador, the Cordillera Occidental continues north toward Panama. Cordillera Central heads

BASIC FACTS

Official name República del Colombia
Area 1,141,748km^2 (440,831 miles^2)
Population 34,520,000 (1994)
Capital Bogotá
Largest city (population) Bogotá (4.5 million)
Main Amazon city Leticia
Official language Spanish
Date of independence 1819 (Spain)
Major industries coffee, oil and natural gas, cotton, sugar, mining
GDP per capita US$1,316
Currency peso (US$1=1,100 pesos; UK£1=1,750 pesos)
Major attractions Cartagena Old Town, emerald mines
National holidays January 1, March 19, May 1, July 20, August 7 & 15, December 8 & 25

north-northeast, toward the Caribbean. Longest of the ranges, Cordillera Oriental veers northeast toward Venezuela.

To the north of Cordillera Oriental a separate geological formation, Cordillera de Mérida, rises on the Colombia-Venezuela border. A low series of hills and valleys to the southeast of Cordillera Oriental form a large plateau. The southern part of this formation, the department of Amazonas, is the northernmost extent of the Amazon watershed in Colombia, accounting for about 6% of the watershed's total area. The northern part of this plateau, the *llanos* (or Orinoquia), gives rise to numerous tributaries of the Orinoco River that flows through Venezuela.

Rivers

Colombia's natural waterways reflect its complex topography and comprise no less than five major watersheds.

In northwest Colombia, the Magdalena begins between the Cordilleras Central and Oriental, flowing northwest into the Caribbean. The Río Cauca flows along the central valley between the Cordilleras Central and Occidental and into the lower reaches of Río Magdalena. West of Cordillera Occidental the Artaro heads north, parallel to the coast, into the Gulf of Darien by the Panama border.

Colombia's other major rivers originate in the Cordillera Oriental. High in the southern half of this range are sources for several major tributaries of the upper Amazon, which flow eastwards in the river basin. In southeast Colombia, the Putumayo forms the southern border with Peru. This is the Colombian Amazon's most used river as it is the region's second longest and navigable for most of its 1,800km length.

Rivers rising in the northern half of Cordillera Central are claimed by the Orinoco flowing through neighbouring Venezuela.

Climate

Colombia's climate is as variable as its habitats, from alpine to dry savannah to tropical rainforest.

In the Amazon lowlands, annual temperatures average 23°C while rainfall is around 2,500mm and tends to be heaviest in late December to January. Beginning in July or August and lasting anywhere from two to eight weeks, the *veranillo* is a short period of lower precipitation during which temperatures can get very warm. The upper Magdalena Valley, Atlantic lowlands and *llanos* region share a tropical savannah climate of alternating wet and dry seasons. The dry season is from November to April. Weather in the mountains depends on elevation. Temperatures drop about 0.6°C for every 100m of ascent.

Flora and fauna

Ever since the early 1800s when Alexander von Humboldt first described Colombia's wildlife, naturalists have been impressed by its variety and abundance of life forms. Varied climate, soil and topography support an extraordinary diversity of plant and animal communities. Mangrove swamps dominate tidal zones, La Guajira is desert scrub, while the Atlantic Lowlands and eastern *llanos* support savannah grasslands and gallery forest. Montane ecosystems are found among Andean slopes and valleys, while the Choco region and Amazonas are primarily tropical rainforest.

For the visitor to the Colombian Amazon, there is the usual panoply of tropical South American animals. Colombia's birdlife comprises some 1,500 species (about one sixth of the world's total) over a third of which are found in lowland Amazonia. Dozens of North American songbirds and flycatchers overwinter in Colombia but most species are endemic. About two hundred mammal species are known, and the same number of reptiles. Aquatic life is rich, in contrast to the overfished and polluted Magdalena and Cauca.

Mountain habitats support a different variety of animals, although some of the larger mammals range from low to high elevations. Montane vegetation of *páramo* regions is a highly diverse alpine flora, including a large number of endemic species.

Conservation efforts in Colombia are highlighted by the Amacayacú National Park and extensive investment in biopharmacology and ecotourism. However, pollution and deforestation are taking their toll, notably outside protected areas. In particular, illicit cocaine labs, well-hidden in remote forest, utilise toluene, benzene and a variety of other unpleasant solvents and reagents. Used chemicals are just dumped into a river.

Legal extractive operations have also seriously disrupted local ecosystems, mostly along the flanks of the Andes. Colombia's diversity of plants and animals is largely unknown. As recently as 1995, a 75m-high tree (*Pseudomonotes tropenbosii*) was found deep in the Colombian rainforest by two graduate students. Though not new to science, the species was known only from Africa previously. Scientists concluded the tree must have evolved before South America and Africa separated – it is a living fossil.

Land use

About a third of Colombia's land area is considered permanent pastureland, while 5% is suitable for crops and about half the country is forested. Most arable land is in scattered patches among the high valleys of the Magdalena and Cauca rivers. A significant proportion of Colombia's land remains uncultivated due to poor soils or unsuitable weather or terrain. The Amazon lowland soils are lateritic and clayey, except in fluvial plains, where regular deposits of silt maintain soil fertility. However, Amazonia's sparse population limits agricultural activity.

The people

Population and ethnic groups

South America's third most populous country, Colombia has the second highest population density, around 30 people per km^2. Most people (65%) live in upland cities, notably Bogotá, which has some 15–20% of the country's population. This is a reversal from the case just 20 years ago when the majority of the population was rural.

Originally, some 75 tribes inhabited Colombia. But today, pure-blood Indians are a mere one-fiftieth of the population – the smallest share for any Andean country. Some 80% of the population is mestizo, 12% white of Spanish descent, 5% black and a small percentage Asian.

Languages

Castilian Spanish is the official language but over 180 indigenous dialects and languages are spoken. Major linguistic groups include Arawak, Chibcha, Tupi-Guaraní and Yurumanguí. There are around 50 tribes in the Amazon region, the largest groups of which are Tikuna and Witoto living near to Leticia. In isolated hinterlands to the north are less well-known and populous tribes including Makuna, Yukuna, Barasana and Desana, while Ingara and Cofan live in the Ecuador border region.

Education

Schooling is a high priority for Colombians, both officially and among the people. Virtually all children attend kindergarten, primary school and secondary school. At 87%, the adult literacy rate is among the highest in South America. Public universities include the National University of Colombia (founded in 1867), the Central University and the Women's National University. Most universities are in Bogotá.

Culture

Understanding the principle that to conquer a people you must control their culture, the colonials assaulted pre-Columbian secular and religious arts, strongly suppressing weaving, basketry, ceramics and musical crafts. In 1583, Chibcha – the mostly widely spoken language – was banned. The early 20th century saw a revival in traditional arts.

Bogotá is the country's cultural capital, with Cali, Medellín, Manizales, Cartagena and Tunja all making important contributions as art centres. The arts are well-funded and the Banco de República is renowned for its contributions to museums, art galleries and the performing arts. The country's rich literary heritage is reflected in the achievements of such authors as Gabriel García Márquez, awarded the 1982 Nobel Prize for Literature. Considered among the best South American writing, his award-winning novel, *One Hundred Years of Solitude,* tells the story of family life in a small jungle settlement.

A brief history

Prehistory

We know from archaeological evidence that the uplands were inhabited at least 2,000 years ago, probably much earlier. These inhabitants were predecessors of the Chibcha and other tribes who settled the area.

Indigenous peoples developed an advanced culture, in the apparent absence of any outside influence. Because they used wood for building, little evidence of their achievements remains in the humid tropical climate. Unlike nearby Central America and Andean countries to the south, Colombia was considered to be devoid of large stone structures. This changed in 1976 with the stunning discovery on Colombia's Caribbean coast of a 600ha 'lost city', built around AD900 by the Tairona, an advanced offshoot of the Chibcha tribal group.

Conquest

During 1500–01, Rodrigo de Bastidas sailed along the northern coast of Colombia and the Gulf of Darien and in 1525 Bastidas founded Santa Marta on the north coast, the first European settlement in South America.

Cartagena, a major outpost of the Spanish empire, was founded by Pedro de Heredia in 1533, and by the mid-1500s, all major coastal cities along with connecting roads had been established. Bogotá, the first major upland city, was founded in 1538 by Gonzalo Jiménez de Quesada.

By the time the Spanish arrived, several tribes inhabited what is today Andean Colombia but they had neither the resources nor the manpower to resist the Spanish invasion. The conquistadors imposed the *audencia* with its accompanying *encomienda* system. Initially, due to disease and the Spaniards' bad treatment of the Indians, Colombia's population declined precipitously. During the early 18th century this trend reversed. Mining, agriculture and textile industries were established and slaves were imported to meet the labour demand.

Independence

In 1794, Antonio Nariño led the call for independence, publishing, in Spanish, a translation of Thomas Paine's 'Declaration of the Rights of Man'. Spain was hard-pressed to maintain control. When Napoleon Bonaparte invaded Spain in 1808, replacing King Ferdinand VII with his own son, Joseph, the colonialists refused to recognise the new monarch and Colombian towns began to declare independence. By 1810, several parts of Colombia had seceded from the Spanish empire. Colombia achieved full independence from Spain in 1819, after the Battle of Boyacá in August that year in which the Venezuelan Simón Bolívar was hero of the day.

Post-independence

Despite Nariño's ideals, the aftermath of independence saw upheaval and struggle. By 1840 civil war broke out, followed by counter-revolutions, dictatorships and mass repression. The 1886 constitution declared Colombia a republic, and set up the country's political system as it is today. Two major political parties, Liberals and Conservatives, became established at the time, but did nothing to ameliorate the situation. By 1899, another war erupted, the so-called 'Thousand Days War' that dragged on until 1903 and during which an average of 100 people a day died.

The 20th century

After the turn of the century, Colombia's political scene remained stable until 1948, when disagreements again erupted into open hostility, ceasing only when the Liberals and Conservatives united during 1957–74 to defeat the dictator Gustavo Rojas Pinilla. In 1974 Colombia resumed its traditional two-party system.

Despite continued Liberal-Conservative rule during the second half of the 20th century, Colombia's ruling powers have been dominated, indeed intimidated, by military juntas and their main funding source, the *narcotraficante* cocaine barons. Adding to the sense of violence are the Marxist insurgence groups, notably the Colombian Revolutionary Armed Forces and the National Liberation Army.

In late 1992 a state of emergency was declared, then renewed in February 1993 and again in May, a total of 180 days in under a year. The army claimed to have killed or captured over 1,200 rebels. In August 1995 a National Conciliation Committee was established to examine proposals for peace between various factions. Since then, President Ernesto Samper has maintained a firm rule, and the country has prospered for the most part. However, his tenure continues to be marred by allegations of government corruption and enrichment through the drug trade.

Renewed fighting broke out in 1998 between rebel forces and government troops, in which hundreds died. Skirmishes were concentrated in central Colombia, in jungle east of the city of Villavicencio in the foothills of the Andes.

Colombia's well-reported 'drug problem' flourishes on poverty. Land and wealth are concentrated among a small minority. Welfare services are inadequate, living standards low and awareness of Western wealth increasing. All these exacerbate dissatisfaction among the poorer people. If world prices slump or trade embargoes are imposed, farmers cannot profitably sell legal produce such as coffee so have little choice but to turn to growing coca (the raw material for cocaine) and cannabis to make a living.

The 1886 constitution declared Colombia a republic and vested power in executive, legislative and judicial branches of government. The president is head of state and elected for a single four-year term. All citizens over 18 are eligible to vote. Guaranteed civil rights include the right to strike, to assemble, to petition and to

COCAINE, COLOMBIA AND THE WORLD

Despite it being an admirably democratic and free society, Colombia's constantly changing government destabilises the country and has helped cocaine attain high importance in the country's politics and economy – a touchy subject but essential if one is to have any understanding of Colombia's recent tumultuous political history.

Cocaine has been a mainstay of Colombia's illicit drug exports. This provides great wealth for giant underground corporations who are wealthier and better equipped than the government. Police, judges, lawyers, politicians and businessmen are bribed or threatened – many lawmen have lost their lives – and the cartels retain their power. With so much money at stake, someone always pops up to replace captured or killed drug lords. When the head of the Medellín cartel, Pablo Escobar, was killed by police in 1993, the rival Cali cartel quickly stepped in to take Escobar's business.

One approach to this persistent problem would be to eliminate the huge profits (some experts advocate legalisation as the only way to achieve this) and incentive for organised crime to produce and sell drugs. However, locals are quick to point out that the responsibility for the present situation lies as much with those countries where cocaine is consumed as with those where it is produced. Families growing coca are generally growing the crop that gives them the best return for their work. As long as coca can be grown in the labyrinthine hills and valleys of the rugged Andes, as long as people will pay lots of money for tiny amounts and as long as there are crooks to exploit the system, the drug trade will continue.

exercise freedom of speech. Colombia's portions of Amazonia comprise five departments (of the country's total 32): Amazonas, Putumayo, Caquetá, Vaupés and Guaviare.

Economy

Colombia has one of the healthier economies in South America. It possesses every major natural resource in abundance: valuable metals and gems, coal, rivers for hydro-electric power, freshwater and marine fisheries, oil reserves, forest for plant products, and coastline for maritime trade and recreation.

Private enterprise is more important than the public sector. Agriculture and manufacturing contribute each about a fifth of the GDP. Coffee is the mainstay of Colombia's legal agricultural exports, with about 15% of arable land devoted to its cultivation. Fresh flowers are increasingly grown in highland valley greenhouses. Exports of illicit cannabis and coca products are estimated at twice the value of coffee. Gemstones are important to the economy, especially emeralds, of which half the world's total comes from Colombia.

Practicalities

Money

Colombian currency is the peso, with US$1=1,100 (compared with 850 pesos to US$1 in October 1995) and likely to increase. US dollars are widely accepted but you tend to get a better price paying with pesos.

Changing pesos back into dollars or other currencies can be difficult outside Colombia so get only as many pesos as you think you will need for your trip. Most banks will not exchange cash dollars for pesos, but they will cash travellers' cheques or give advances on Visa or MasterCard. Credit cards tend to get a better exchange rate. As a rule of thumb, use a credit card or travellers' cheques for hotels, tours and large expenses, and carry small US$ bills for souvenirs and emergencies.

Colombia has two exchange rates for the peso: the official rate and the 'free market' rate. The official, lower rate is what you get for cash (when accepted) or travellers' cheques at banks. You get the better free market rate for cash from *casas de cambio*, which is 100% legal, although travellers' cheques are not always accepted.

Highlights

Colombia has as much to offer as any South American country, with idyllic tropical beaches on its Pacific and Caribbean coasts, tall mountain ranges, rainforest and native tribes. It is, some say, the source of the legend of El Dorado, as the Spanish observed the Muisca Indians conducting a ceremony where a gold-covered 'king' bathed in the waters of Lake Guatavita in northern Colombia.

Because of the underdeveloped infrastructure in the Colombian Amazon, travel in the country can be a challenge. First-time visitors to the area, particularly non-Spanish speakers, are better off taking a package tour, with all arrangements made.

Exploring the Colombian Amazon is the realm of independent travellers who can handle the absence of tourist facilities. There are two points from which to start. The first, and most popular, is Leticia, reached by air from Bogotá, or by ship from Iquitos or Manaus. Starting from the Andean foothills, Florencia or Mocoa offer an alternative route and can be readily reached by bus from Bogotá. Much of the area along the Florencia–Mocoa road is heavily settled and potentially risky due to coca-growing activity so it's best to head east immediately.

WARNING While some of the world's best coffee is grown in Colombia the country is just as famous for its illegal product, cocaine (see box opposite). The coca plant does not grow well in lowland rainforest but the dense cover is ideal to hide clandestine processing facilities. The military are active in these areas and should be avoided by inexperienced travellers. Remote areas should not be entered without an experienced local guide, preferably a member of the Colombian military.

Tour operators

Several companies in Bogotá and Leticia can organise trips.

Tierra Mar Aire (TMA) in Bogotá have offices at the Hotel Tequendama and on Carrera 7, #35-20; tel: 00 57 91 288 2088; fax: 00 57 91 288 2461; email: tma0020@colomsat.net.co.
Viajes Chapinero Av 7, #124-15; tel: 00 57 91 612 7716; fax: 00 57 91 215 9099; email: iduque@colomsat.net.co

In Leticia **Anaconda Tours**, **Amaturs** and **Amazon Explorers**, all close to the Hotel Anaconda, can help to arrange trips to nearby areas.

GETTING THERE AND AWAY

By air

Non-stop flights to Bogotá depart from Miami (Avianca: US$499–656 return, low/high season) and several other US cities, including New York. From the UK there is a daily service with British Airways, and several airlines from Europe have direct services including Avianca, Air France, Iberia, Alitalia and Lufthansa. Prices from London start at £540 in the low season. The **Avianca Airpass** makes internal flights considerably cheaper.

From Ecuador, Avianca has daily flights from Quito to Bogotá (US$68).

Overland

Road connections from Venezuela are in the north, to Paraguachón from Maicao (north of Maracaibo). In the mountains you can cross to San Antonio del Táchira and further south the Venezuelan town of El Amparo de Apure links with Arauca. Puerto Carreño on the Río Meta is accessible from El Burro, north of Puerto Ayacucho.

Leticia in the heart of the Amazon is on the border with Brazil and Peru. It is also possible to cross from Lago Agio in the lowland regions of Ecuador to Puerto Asís.

The Pan-American Highway links the southern Colombian highlands with Ecuador at Ipiales.

Customs and immigration

Colombian entry procedures are fairly relaxed, especially since visa requirements were lifted for all except Chinese nationals. For last-minute enquiries contact a Colombian consulate. In Colombia, the DAS (Departamento Administrativo de Seguridad) is in charge of immigration affairs. Day-visitors to Leticia on tourist boats from Peru and Brazil do not need to complete border formalities.

Airport departure tax in Colombia must be paid for in hard currency. It is US$17 if you stay under 60 days, US$30 for longer.

Getting around

Colombia's transportation system ranges from relatively efficient, in large cities, to primitive or non-existent in remote rural areas. In many cases the only feasible way to reach remote areas is by air.

By bus

Roads between major cities are surfaced and in good-to-fair condition, but minor roads connecting remote jungle towns are unsurfaced and vary from bad to terrible. The major towns in the western highland regions are served by relatively comfortable buses, connecting major towns. Around one sixth of the roads are paved, and the condition of the remainder depends on a fine interplay between the depredations of the elements and the occasional efforts of road repair crews.

Hitching

Sadly, hitching in Colombia cannot be recommended. Although in reality you are unlikely to experience problems away from trouble spots, the risk of getting involved in Colombia's internal affairs is too great.

By air

The country is well-connected domestically. The national airline is Avianca, South America's oldest, founded in 1919. Several other domestic airlines are in operation including SAM, Aires and the military airline Satena. There is one flight a day (Avianca) from Bogotá to Leticia (US$100). Several local carriers offer scheduled or charter flights between Bogotá and Leticia. It is possible, though not easy, to get on a cargo or military flight. Domestic air travel is considerably more expensive than in Peru or Ecuador, and most independent travellers choose to move around the country via the extensive bus system.

In Bogotá the Avianca office is at Carrera 7, #16-36; tel: 091 2669700. SAM's offices are at Carrera 10, #27-91; tel: 091 2669600. Satena have flights to the remoter parts of Colombia which can be booked at their office at Ave 19, #13A-

18; tel: 091 2835557. Airline offices close at weekends. Your best strategy is to have all your flights and travel arrangements organised before even leaving for Colombia.

By river

Lowland rivers remain important conduits for people and goods. For transport the rivers are most important in the eastern lowlands. The Putumayo, Caquetá and Vaupés rivers conveniently connect up with the Amazon's mainstream giving access to Brazil and eventually the Atlantic.

COMMUNICATIONS

Mail

Mail is reliable and efficient enough in Colombia, especially if you've had to deal with the post offices in Peru or Brazil. Adpostal runs the service and rates are reasonable. Within the Americas a postcard costs US$0.50 and a letter just US$1, taking about a week. Packages cost about US$12 per kilo. To all these prices, add about 15–20% for destinations outside the Americas. Surface mail is the cheapest way to send large packages but it takes five times longer.

Telephone, fax and email services

Telephone and fax services are widely available at most hotels, while email is just catching on among tour operators and travel agents. To phone outside Colombia it is cheapest to use the public phones of the state telephone service Telecom. These are found throughout the large cities, but don't expect every phone to work…most don't. Finding the nearest Telecom offices will make things considerably easier. Telephone cards for public phones are also available from the Telecom office.

The international country code for Colombia is 57.

Internet services in Colombia are limited, although tour operators or hotels may give you access.

Television and radio

Easier to control than print media, and arguably more influential, Colombia's broadcasts reflect a stricter degree of control than is exerted over newspapers and periodicals. Regarding government, television and radio strive for a balance between patriotic support and guarded criticism. Programmes are professionally produced, although the domestic productions are a stale fare of soap operas and chat shows.

Newspapers

All Colombia's major newspapers and magazines are in Spanish, but English-language publications from the UK or US are available in larger cities, and at some hotels and airports.

Colombia's press freedom has historically depended on the government in power. However, freedom of expression is generally respected, a privilege that extends to the press. At present it is free to criticise the government – and does. Widely circulated Bogotá newspapers are *El Tiempo* and *El Espectador,* both considered supporters of the Liberal Party.

BOGOTÁ

After losing four-fifths of his men in the gruelling journey along the Magdalena River, in 1537 Gonzalo Jiménez de Queseda reached the mountain valley that was

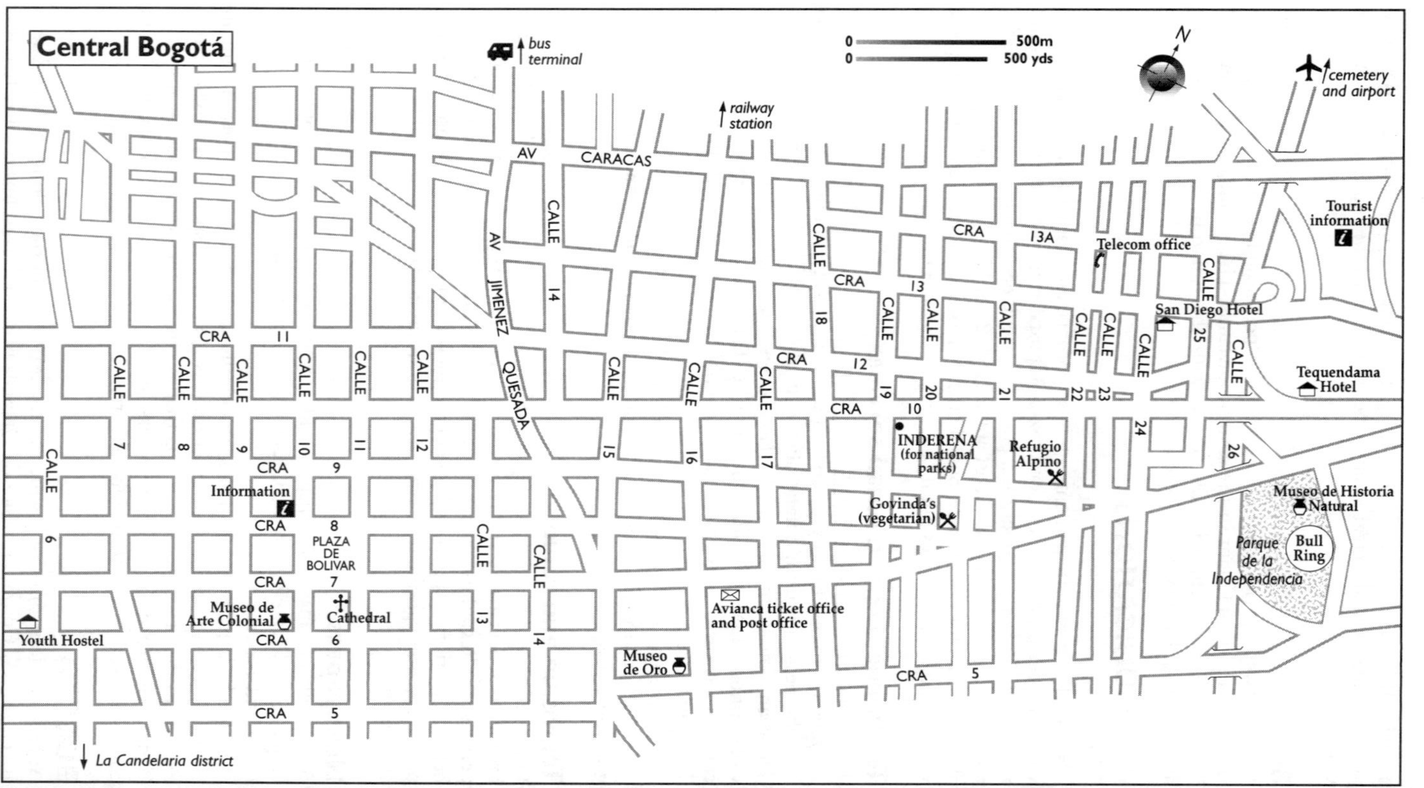
Central Bogotá
bus terminal
0 500m
0 500 yds
N
cemetery and airport
railway station
AV CARACAS
AV JIMENEZ QUESADA
Tourist information
Telecom office
San Diego Hotel
Tequendama Hotel
INDERENA (for national parks)
Refugio Alpino
Govinda's (vegetarian)
Museo de Historia Natural
Bull Ring
Parque de la Independencia
Information
PLAZA DE BOLIVAR
Museo de Arte Colonial
Cathedral
Youth Hostel
Avianca ticket office and post office
Museo de Oro
La Candelaria district
CALLE 6
CALLE 7
CALLE 8
CALLE 9
CALLE 10
CALLE 11
CALLE 12
CALLE 13
CALLE 14
CALLE 15
CALLE 16
CALLE 17
CALLE 18
CALLE 19
CALLE 20
CALLE 21
CALLE 22
CALLE 23
CALLE 24
CALLE 25
CALLE 26
CRA 13A
CRA 13
CRA 12
CRA 11
CRA 10
CRA 9
CRA 8
CRA 7
CRA 6
CRA 5

to become the site of Bogotá. Today it has a multiple personality, with a huge contrast between the new Bogotá and the older parts of the city.

In a bowl among the Andes mountains, Bogotá (elevation 2,652m) is one of South America's great cities. Packed with an overcrowded six million people, it is also becoming one of South America's worst cities. Drugs, violence and pollution are all major problems facing this sprawling conurbation.

As Bogotá is at such a high altitude, its climate is mild and cool, but the equatorial location (4.36° north, 74.05° west) keeps temperatures within narrow limits around 14°C. Bogotá is relatively dry compared with other parts of Colombia and has total annual rainfall around 1,100mm.

At the airport

El Dorado International Airport is located 12km from town, about 20 minutes' ride. To get into town is not easy. There is no good bus system so budget to take a taxi (US$5, US$7 after dark). It is accepted practice to ask a policeman to note your taxi's registration number. He will then give you a piece of paper stating the fare. A reliable taxi driver should have no problem with this. Do not take unregistered taxis or use porters not in uniform.

To get *to* the airport is a bit easier. Your hotel can book a taxi or you can take a bus. Marked 'Aeropuerto', these depart regularly from Avenida 19 between Carreras 3 and 10.

City transport

Public transport in Bogotá is good enough to get around on your own and very inexpensive. However, it is imperative to take the utmost care before jumping in a taxi or *colectivo* (a communal taxi with set routes like a bus), especially on your own.

Make sure taxis are registered and if possible agree on the charge before you start on the journey. The police are helpful in ensuring you are not over-charged.

Frequent and reliable buses are the cheapest way of getting around. Pick up buses at the red and yellow signs (marked 'Paradero') or else flag them down as you would a taxi.

Security

Bogotá challenges the traveller to stay aware of surroundings and people. There are several no-go areas in the city. Beware in particular of the area near the railway station, especially between Carreras 15 to 17 and Calles 15 to 18. Never take out money or passports on the street. Keep valuables and money at the hotel. If you are approached by someone in uniform asking to see documents politely refuse and say you will be happy to go to the police station and show any papers there. If the request is from a uniformed official and is for a legitimate reason (eg: at a road-block), common-sense dictates compliance.

As a rule of thumb, the western part of Bogotá is more industrial and rougher than the eastern half and, in the main sightseeing area, the Montserrate district is unsafe any time except weekends. Daylight muggings are reported from this area. Other dangerous areas are in the southwest, older part of the city (west of Carrera 13 and south of Calle 12). The new part of the city is relatively safe.

Where to stay

Hotels in Bogotá range from expansive and expensive (US$100+ per night) to dirty and dirt-cheap (US$10 and under). To remain in the safety zone, stay in the northern part of the city. Book in advance if at all possible, so that you have somewhere to go and someone is expecting you.

First class

Bogotá Royal Ave 100, #8-01; tel: 00 57 91 2183261. The poshest hotel and said to be among the best hotels in South America.
Charleston Hotel Carrera 13, #85-46; tel: 00 57 91 2180590. More centrally located than the Bogotá Royal.
Tequendama Carrera 10, #26-21; tel: 00 57 91 2837740. This has a very good restaurant.
Orqidea Royal Carrera 7, #32-16; tel: 00 57 91 2870788. Run by Trusthouse Forte. It has a heated swimming pool, gym and French restaurant.
Cosmos 100 Calle 100, #21-A41; tel: 00 57 91 2574000. This has the best views of the big hotels and among the friendliest staff.

Middle range

Las Terrazas Calle 54, #32-16; tel: 00 57 91 2555777. Has a nice view.
San Diego Hotel corner of Carrera 13 and Calle 24; tel: 00 57 91 2842100. More centrally located, near Parque Independencia and close to the Natural History Museum.

Budget

There are many budget hotels to choose from and new ones open practically every day.

Internacional Hotel Carrera 5, #14-15; tel: 00 57 91 3418731. Offers a lot for the price.
Virgen del Camino Calle 18A, #14-33; tel: 00 57 91 2824450. In a quiet safe area, with pleasant helpful staff.

International Youth Hostel Association members can stay at the **youth hostel** (Carrera 6 #10-32, seventh floor; tel: 00 57 91 2821787) for about US$4.

Where to eat

Restaurants serving local dishes are most numerous but several cater to foreigners. International food is served at the excellent **Refugio Alpino** (Calle 23, #7-49), and **La Fragata** at the World Trade Center (Calle 100) has good seafood, but neither restaurant is cheap.

Chinese restaurants have good inexpensive food – try **Bambú**, on the corner of Carrera 7 and Calle 62. Some fast-food restaurants offer a take-away service, but when in Colombia, why not do what the Colombians do… and eat *al fresco*. Try **Tony Romas** (Calle 93, #13-85) or wander along Carrera 15 where there are several options including **Café Oma**.

Govinda's (Carrera 8, #20-56) is an international chain serving tasty, healthy vegetarian food at an unbeatable price. **El Trópico** (Carrera 8, #17-72) offers wholesome food and **Acuarius** is a small chain with several restaurants that specialise in vegetarian food. Try the one near Plaza Bolívar (Carrera 8, #11-19).

Most restaurants are closed Sunday evenings.

What to see

As the cultural centre of Colombia, Bogotá has much to offer the visitor. Historic buildings, art galleries and museums offer examples of Colombia's past achievements and unique artistic heritage.

Museums

Bogotá's museums rate among the best in South America so are a 'must' if you can fit them in. Most museums are either free or charge a small admission fee, usually under US$1. Museums are closed on Mondays. Here is a selection of some of the best:

Museo del Oro (Gold Museum) at Parque de Santander, Calle 16 and Carrera 6-A, houses the world's largest and finest collection of worked gold, with over 30,000 pieces. Open Tue–Fri 9.00–17.00; Sat 09.00–13.00; Sun and holidays 9.00–12.00.
Museo de Arte Colonial (Museum of Colonial Art) at Carrera 6, #9-77. An impressive collection of Creole religious sculpture and painting housed in a building that beautifully exemplifies colonial architecture. Open Tue–Sat 10.00–13.00; Sun 10.00–17.00.
Museo de Historia Natural (Natural History Museum) at Parque de La Independencia, Planeterio Distrital. For wildlife enthusiasts, this is a 'must'. Although some of the stuffed animals need a little patchwork, they give a good idea of the country's biodiversity. Open Tue–Fri: 9.00–18.00; Sat and Sun: 10.00–18.00.
Corporación de Araracuara at Calle 20, #5-44. Although not a museum this organisation holds the best sources of information on the Colombian Amazon. The library comprises several thousand books, journals and articles on natural history, tribes and history.

Cathedrals and churches
Architecturally, Bogotá's religious buildings offer the visitor an impressive range of styles. Most notable is **La Catedral**, completed in 1807 and with strong classical influences. In the sacristy, you can see a banner carried into Bogotá by de Quesada on his campaign against the indigenous people. La Catedral is located in the district of the same name on Calle 10 between Carreras 6 and 7. Behind it on the same block is the serene **Chapel of El Sagrario** dating from the late 1600s.

Other things to see in Bogotá
For views of the city, make your way to the top of **Montserrate** on the east side. This area is only safe at weekends and especially dangerous after dark. A funicular railway saves the walk but before mid-afternoon a long wait is usually necessary, especially at weekends.

Shopping
The best places to shop for folk art and handicrafts is at the state-run **Artesanias de Colombia** in the San Diego church (Carrera 10, #26-50). Next to the Church of the Waters (Iglesia d'Aguas) is **Almacén Las Aguas** with a wide range of well-priced handicrafts. Less expensive still are the street markets, such as the one on Carrera 15, and on Carrera 7 opposite the Tequendama. If you are off into the jungle you can pick up most of your supplies in Bogotá. The best place to get a hammock is at **Pasaje Rivas** (Carrera 10, #10-54).

Leaving town
Long-distance buses depart from the terminal at Av Boyacá west of the city centre. This area around the bus station is not safe so time your arrival and departure for daylight hours. Numerous buses run up and down Av Boyacá, but you would probably prefer to get a taxi (quite safe from your hotel or the airport).

You can take a bus to the Colombian Amazon as far as Florencia, a 12-hour journey (cost US$25, one way). A recommended bus company is Coomotor, with offices both in Florencia and at the terminal in Bogotá. Despite the discomforts the bus is certainly a cost-effective way of seeing the country and meeting Colombians.

THE COLOMBIAN AMAZON
Although Colombia's Amazonian territory, west of the Cordillera Oriental, is small compared with that of Brazil or Peru, it covers a third of the country. Amazonas is Colombia's largest province, some 110,000km^2, over four-fifths the size of England. About 95% of this vast region is uninhabited and visited only by

prospectors, missionaries and occasionally a curious traveller. The total population is about half a million, most of whom live along the Andean foothills in the provinces of Caquetá and Putumayo far to the west.

Half of Amazonas state's 60,000 people live in Leticia. Due to the heavy traffic on the mainstream and the Putumayo, the town is the commercial – but definitely not the physical – centre of southeastern Colombia. The peculiarly wedge-shaped boundary, established in 1922, covers just 130km or so of the Amazon River (Solimões). Nevertheless, Colombia is proud of its small foothold on the world's biggest river, and indeed seems to value its rainforest; Colombia has stringent controls and more enlightened conservation policies than most Amazon countries.

On the Putumayo and other Amazon tributaries, water levels rise as much as 7m during flood season. River levels fall from August to January, then rise rapidly from April to June and peak mid to late July. A minor rise is usually experienced during October or November.

Leticia: Gateway to the Amazon

Originally in Peru, Leticia was founded as San Antonio in 1867. The town has a parallel history with Iquitos and Manaus: jump-started into industrialisation by the rubber boom of the late 19th century. Now with around 30,000 inhabitants, Leticia is Colombia's largest settlement east of the Andes and the second largest, after Iquitos, in lowland Amazonia west of Brazil. Below the fourth parallel, it is also Colombia's southernmost town.

The nearest international airport is Iquitos in Peru, just over 400km from Leticia as the parrot flies: by river, the distance is about 560km. The town marks the turn-around for regularly scheduled tourist riverboats. Its airport and status as Colombia's centre for Amazon tours have led to rapid growth.

Tabatinga, just inside Brazil, is Leticia's poor relative. Because of the lack of border formalities, it is difficult to tell when you have gone from one town to the other; or from one country to another. This area is a free-trade zone with the nickname Tres Fronteras ('Three Frontiers') because the boundaries of Colombia, Peru and Brazil meet here.

Getting there

Leticia, stuck out on its own in one of Colombia's most distant corners, poses problems of access from within Colombia which probably create the main reason to visit.

For those who want to travel by air, Leticia is served by an airport, but then you miss the experience of river travel.

By boat

To reach Leticia by boat from within Colombia you have to travel from Puerto Asís, close to the border with Ecuador, and take a boat down the Putumayo (see Puerto Asís, page 231).

Internationally by riverboat, it takes seven days to reach Leticia from Manaus (Brazil), or three days downstream from Iquitos (Peru). If approaching Leticia from Manaus, you will arrive at Tabatinga after transfer through the town of Benjamin Constant, 34km south of Leticia. If travelling on a local riverboat, you complete Brazilian exit formalities at Benjamin Constant (sometimes at Tabatinga), then register with Colombian immigration in Leticia (see next section). If travelling from Peru you complete exit formalities at Santa Rosa.

By expedition or cruise ships, the voyage from Manaus to Leticia takes four days, or two from Iquitos, and the crew usually take care of the paperwork.

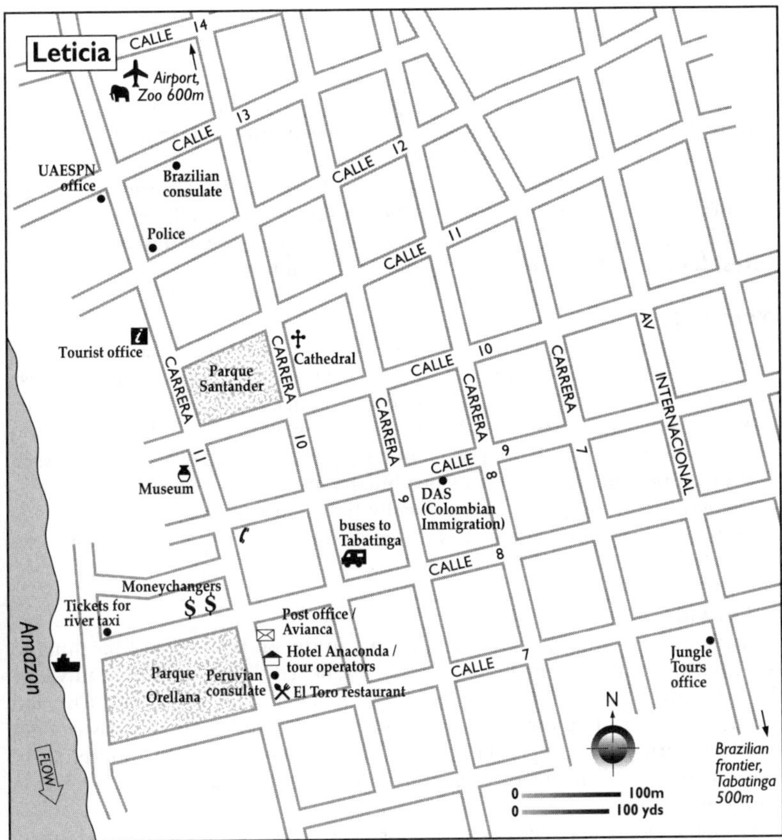

By road

Although accessible by road, Leticia is not served by any buses. Road travel beyond is restricted to a few outlying towns. Because of poor road maintenance, transport by vehicle is unreliable and possibly hazardous, especially during the flood season. Leticia is a long way from anywhere and to reach it overland is a major expedition.

Getting around

Local taxis are good for one or two trips but for a city tour you are better off letting the tour operators make arrangements. Tour operators use VW minibuses to take up to seven passengers on day tours departing from Hotel Anaconda.

For independent travellers, the local taxi system must suffice to get around town. You can rent a motorcycle or car but this is pointless unless you are going to stay a while. In any case you can walk to most places provided it's not in the heat of the day.

Where to stay

Like everything else in Leticia, accommodation is expensive by Amazon standards. But then the quality of rooms and food is a bit above average. Bargains are few but, if you're on a shoestring, you could hunt out a cheap *residencia* for under US$10. There are about a dozen hotels to choose from.

For most travellers and tour operators the usual choice is the **Hotel Anaconda** on Carrera 11. It has above-average facilities, including a swimming pool, restaurant and bar. Sadly, the reception staff and waiters win no awards for friendliness. Per person it costs US$53 (twin) or US$90 (single) per night for air-conditioned rooms, but no hot water. It is conveniently located, with a tour agency, bank and post office nearby and a small shopping mall next to the lobby.

For the budget traveller, there are several options. Recommended is the comfortable and friendly **Residencias Fernando** on Carrera 9, between Calle 8 and 9. Per person it is US$23 (twin) to US$33 (single) per night. Also worth a try is **Residencias Internacional** on the road to Tabatinga.

Where to eat

The Hotel Anaconda has a restaurant where the food is reasonable. Elsewhere in the town are several bars and restaurants that serve inexpensive meals or snacks. Fresh fruit and vegetables can be bought very cheaply in markets or stores around town.

A couple of restaurants along Av da Amizade (main road to Tabatinga market) serve reasonable food at a fair price, but check what locals pay before you order. Often the prices increase the moment a hungry gringo walks through the door!

Beyond Leticia, you'll have no difficulty finding a couple of bars and cafés in most jungle towns you visit. Unless travelling independently, you'll probably not want more than a soft drink or beer.

In Leticia

Varying in mood from bustling jungle town in the pleasant cool of morning to lazy backwater during long hours of a heat-drenched siesta, Leticia's beauty is in the eye of the beholder. It's clean by comparison with most Amazon towns, and cobbled together of breeze-blocks and concrete, or wood, nails and plastic – not smart, but friendly enough. This is a working town, somewhat indifferent to tourists, perhaps sensing that they are temporary like all previous Amazon economic booms.

Strolling along cracked pavements or half-surfaced streets are tradesmen, fishermen and the occasional sailor. Filling the grid of streets, oriented north-south along Carrera 11 and the airport road, nondescript flat-topped blocks of variously coloured and windowed concrete house the shopkeepers, restaurateurs, tour agents and hoteliers of most interest to the traveller.

Apart from the standard city tour, which takes in the museum, zoo, fish market and border crossing, there is not much to entertain outsiders, unless you are into cockfights.

Along the divide of the upper part of Calle 8 are a number of small wooden booths which could be mistaken for espresso carts. They actually house moneychangers who exchange cash dollars for pesos, or Peruvian or Brazilian money. The booth occupants are honest enough and there's not much difference

COLOMBIAN COFFEE

On the corner of Calle 8 and Carrera 11 (turn right from the Hotel Anaconda) is a small supermarket where you can buy excellent Colombian coffee. The best brand is Sello Rojo ('Red Seal'), at about 5,200 pesos per kilo. Other brands are cheaper but not as good. Whole bean is scarcer than ground coffee which is available only in one consistency – very fine – suitable only for espresso or filter machines.

between them. They may refuse to change travellers' cheques or amounts under US$10. If you need to change travellers' cheques, banking hours (and times for the post office and museums) are from 08.00 to 12.00 with a long siesta until 14.00, after which places stay open until 18.00.

Lively activity surrounds the Hotel Anaconda, which overlooks the large Parque Orellana plaza with a bust of the park's namesake Francisco Orellana, the first and most famous full-length Amazon voyager. A small portion of the park is paved with a concrete map of Amazonian Colombia, where you can stand on Leticia.

Go left out of the Anaconda and you pass the unfortunately named Amaturs tour company and the Peruvian consulate. Nearby is the Wild West saloon complete with traditional swing doors called *El Toro* ('the bull'). Sip the excellent local lager beer, Antarctica, which should be served as cold as its name suggests, while you sit outside and watch life go by.

What to see

Along the airport road, about 1.5km from the Anaconda, is the **Jardín Botánico Zoológico** (Botanical and Zoological Garden), right next to the airport. Fortunately, there are few flights and the inconvenience seems not to bother the animals.

Jet noise apart, the zoo is worth a brief visit if you have time to spend in town. As well as squirrel monkeys, a friendly giant anteater and three-toed sloths roam – or more precisely in the case of the sloth, sleep – freely. More dangerous animals are caged, notably a jaguar and pair of ocelots. Other mammals you can see here include peccary, tapir, kinkajou, coati and sometimes a capybara or agouti.

Reptiles include the spectacled caiman, matamata turtle and a couple of medium-sized anaconda. Most impressive are several huge black caiman up to 5.5m long. For a ghoulish treat, time your visit around mid-morning to coincide with the beasts' feeding time.

On display in a couple of pools toward the rear of the grounds are a small piracucu and several armoured catfish. There are some birds, such as harpy eagle, macaws, curassow and a yellow-ridged toucan.

The 'gardens' include a small selection of local plants; nothing more than in nearby parks and gardens, mostly acacia trees and lilies. Still, there are often a few nice blooms to be found.

The **Museo del Hombre Amazonico** (Museum of Amazon Man), funded by the Banco de Colombia, is on Carrera 11. The museum consists of one room which houses a small but well-displayed collection of post-Columbian Indian artefacts. Overall they give a good sense of how indigenous people use rainforest materials to survive day-to-day.

For those more interested in local culture than animal rights, Leticia's **cockfight ring** on Avenida Internacional holds matches every Sunday evening. Huge amounts are bet and emotions run high. These performances are not for the faint-hearted or squeamish, as blood is usually drawn and contests frequently end in the death of the losing cock.

Shopping

On the right of the Anaconda Hotel lobby is a small arcade with souvenir and jewellery shops, where you can buy a T-shirt claiming 'I survived the Amazon', a giant carved balsa parrot or precious stones.

Nearby on the same block as the hotel are a couple of curio stores. These are Aladdin's caves for the souvenir hunter, packed from floor to ceiling with masks, carvings, palm fibre baskets and hammocks, seed necklaces and less desirable items like caiman skulls and mounted piranha.

Whether or not you have souvenirs on your shopping list, visit the Amazonas curio shop around the corner (turn right) from the Anaconda on Calle 8. As you enter, there is a glass case, with regularly changing occupants which at one time housed a rainbow boa. On a later visit, the incumbent was a small electric eel to which two electrodes could be applied to light a small lamp. Beyond shelves and cabinets of fairly ordinary souvenirs, behind a curtain towards the back of the store is a small 'museum' with dozens of bizarre exhibits, in varying states of preservation. One wall is adorned with a variety of huge wasps' nests and on shelves opposite are fossils, birds' nests and animal parts, including skulls, claws, shells and skins. A glass cabinet holds dozens of pieces of native pottery, some of it allegedly 'pre-Columbian'.

Several shops along Calle 9 adjacent to the museum sell strong cotton hammocks, which are more comfortable than the native ones and unbelievably cheap from US$15.

If you are travelling up to the highlands, and need some warm clothes, goods from the Andes area are worth considering: sweaters, gloves and hats will keep out mountain chill. In the central commercial area several shops sell a wide range of leather goods of excellent quality. Most popular items are jackets and duffel bags.

Further information

For local travel advice and suggestions on accommodation, the staff are very helpful at the recently opened regional tourist office on Carrera 11, No. 11-35 (tel: 9819 27505).

If you are entering or leaving the country you will need to visit the various immigration authorities for exit and entry stamps (or visas if necessary):

Colombian Immigration (DAS) Office Calle 9, Mon–Sat 07.00–12.00 and 14.00–18.00.
Brazilian Consulate Calle 13, Mon–Fri 08.00–14.00.
Peruvian Consulate Carrera 11, Mon–Fri 08.30–14.30.

To enter the national parks in the region, you need an entry permit (US$1) from the Colombian National Parks Authority (UAESPN) at Carrera 11 (tel: 9819 27619).

Choosing a jungle tour

As most travellers visit Leticia for the jungle, the primary objective is to find a good tour operator with reliable guides and decent prices. This is easier said than done, especially if you have been spoilt for choice in Manaus, Iquitos or Quito. Tours from Leticia are costlier and the options are fewer compared with more popular tourist spots. In Leticia you have few tour operators and a handful of freelance jungle guides to choose from.

In the offices next to the Hotel Anaconda are three tour operators: **Anaconda Tours**, **Amaturs** and **Amazon Explorers**. These companies specialise in day trips to Monkey Island, city tours and bookings.

There are a few freelance guides operating in the area who can guide more adventurous deep forest trips. For up-to-date recommendations on freelance guides, ask around at hotels as well as the aforementioned local tour operators.

If you are in Leticia, ask at the Hotel Anaconda for **Luiz Valera**. He's a white-haired but fit-looking gentleman of short height, stocky build and amiable character. Besides leading city tours for local tour operators, he arranges and leads expeditions into less travelled parts of the interior.

Sr Valera once trained Colombian air-force officers in jungle survival and now offers trips by covered canoe deep into remote tributaries to encounter tribes rarely contacted by the outside world. He takes the minimum of supplies and relies on

BUYING EMERALDS

Colombia is the emerald centre of the world, producing the finest gems and in greater quantity than any other country. Even those who don't profess to be gemmologists should consider an emerald as a unique souvenir. But how do you know if you're buying the real thing?

When making a purchase the rule is that quality is better than quantity. It is better to buy a small fine stone, rather than a large one of dubious quality. The finest emeralds are deep sea-green and flawless. Black spots or 'gardens' are normal in all but the very best stones. Flaws, specks or opacity indicate authenticity.

Be wary of apparent bargains. A perfect-looking dark green stone for less than US$1,000/carat (1 carat = 2 grams) may be glass. More commonly, low-quality emeralds are artificially darkened and then sold for more than they are worth. They have a bluish hue and return to their original colour after a few weeks. The fakes are very difficult to spot and when they fade it's too late to return and get a refund.

One good shop, Agata in the small arcade adjacent to the Anaconda lobby, is run by Sr and Sra Almir and Gloria Da Silva. These people are impeccably reliable and offer certificates of authenticity, but their prices are inflexible and the price of the gems reflects the quality of their reputation... high.

Rodrigo Valderrama is a roving gem dealer, who sets up shop by the Hotel Anaconda swimming pool or in souvenir shops. Recognised by his withered right arm and somewhat shifty countenance, he seems reliable and is happy to entertain reasonable offers.

A flawed but genuine emerald is within most budgets. Souvenir-quality half-carat emeralds cost US$20–50. The novice buyer should definitely stick to the low end of the price scale. Among the most valuable gems, emeralds sometimes cost more than diamonds. A top-notch one-carat emerald can easily dent your wallet by US$2,000–3,000, even in Colombia. Perfect specimens cost as much as US$15,000/carat. Be as sure as possible that you know what you are buying and if you are paying by credit card, check the receipt. It is easy to be ripped off. With few exceptions, it is better to pay a little more for a certified gem from a store, rather than pay less for something dubious from someone you'll never see again.

the jungle and river to provide food for the party. The charge is reasonable: US$60–100 per day, depending on group size. On his trips sightings of large land mammals, manatee, black caiman, anaconda or giant otters are possible. If Luis is not around, then **Amazon Jungle Trips** (Av Internacional, #6-24; tel: 9819 27377), on the Tabatinga road, is recommended for good jungle trips lasting several days.

When booking a jungle tour of this kind follow the advice given in Chapter Two. Make sure you stipulate what you are expecting from the trip, where you want to go and what type of accommodation you are expecting. These trips are only for the truly adventurous, willing to put up with some discomfort and privation. You travel by *colectivo* (motorised covered canoe) and paddled canoe, and you might have to trek miles through jungle and sleep in a hammock or temporary forest camp. Expect heat, sweat, effort, thirst and hunger. The reward is to merge into wilderness, one step closer to the mystery that is the Amazon.

Jungle trips to Amacayacú National Park

In the wedge of rainforest reaching down to the Amazon River in southernmost Colombia, Amacayacú is the only national park in the Amazon Basin to include a portion of the mainstream. This was the first national park in the Colombian Amazon. Established in 1975, it encompasses much of the watershed of the Río Amacayacú, which joins the Amazon River about 65km west of Leticia. Its large area, some 1,700km^2, covers a representative portion of lowland rainforest ecosystem.

Within the park are a wide variety of typical tropical flora and fauna. Plants include teak, mahogany, capirona, a wide variety of acacias and uncounted herbaceous plants and epiphytes. Large mammals include jaguar, anteater, armadillo, sloth, tapir and peccary, with pink dolphin and manatee along remote tributaries. Reptiles include anaconda, caiman, river turtles and the green iguana. Some 500 birds are known from the park, a third of Colombia's total.

A few areas can be visited on foot but access is greatly reduced at high water; as elsewhere in the Amazon, you generally travel around by canoe. To explore the area on foot, the best time to go is at low water from August to January.

Natives of the Ticuna tribe live in the park, particularly around the main settlement, San Martín. This is a three-hour walk from Puerto Nariño, which may be difficult or impossible at high water between February and June.

At the visitors' centre you can hire a guide to take you along the well-marked trails into the forest. Some trails are easy and you might be tempted to set out on your own but, unless you know what you're doing and what you are looking for, a guide is essential to point out all the birds, plants, animals and organic minutiae you may otherwise miss. Certainly the 'jungle experience' here is on a par with those described for remoter parts of Peru and Ecuador.

Due to immigration regulations, tourist riverboats from Peru do not visit the park. To visit from Peru you must first clear Colombian immigration authorities in Leticia.

To get there, take a two-hour river taxi from Leticia to Puerto Nariño (Expreso Amazonas, US$10 one way), the closest village to the park and easily accessible from the mainstream. If you want to organise your own transport for a small group, *colectivos* can be hired for US$100 per day. Trips to the park have to be booked and paid for in Leticia at the UAESPN offices.

Tour agencies in Leticia can make arrangements for tours to the park, or freelance guides will offer less expensive trips. In either case check what's included. Whether you choose this option depends on your confidence level, as it's very straightforward to book yourself, through the UAESPN offices in either Leticia or Bogotá.

Tourist facilities in the park are basic but acceptable. Relatively new accommodation is in communal rooms costing around US$10 per night for a bed, or less if you use one of their hammocks.

Other Amazon towns

As other towns in the Colombian Amazon are smaller than Leticia, they have fewer facilities and are less accessible from the Amazon mainstream and hence not so popular for jungle trips. This section includes towns and villages most likely to be visited when approaching Leticia from the Colombian highlands. These towns are well-served by domestic air carriers, with reasonable fares. Bus links provide overland access, but the local buses, colourfully painted *chivas,* are slow, unreliable and often crowded. If you're not in a hurry, they're the best way to get around on the cheap.

Florencia

This is the biggest town in the Colombian Amazon, with a population of around 100,000. Founded at the beginning of the 20th century, by Italian missionaries from Florence, the town is not as inspiring as its namesake, with little to commend it to the tourist. It is most important as the centre of development for the region but suffers acutely from water shortages and power cuts. The main reason to travel here is en route to Leticia or Mitú on the border with Brazil. The rainforest all around has been seriously degraded and the vast tracts of pristine forest east of Florencia are inaccessible to the average traveller. If you intend going further east, you are better off heading down the Caquetá from the nearby village of Curillo; or instead go south to Puerto Asís, for a trip down the Putumayo to La Paya National Park (near Puerto Leguízamo).

The tourist office (Instituto de Cultura y Turismo, Calle 15, #10-11), open weekdays 07.00–12.00 and 14.00–18.00, will help you organise accommodation, tours and so on. The best hotel in town is the **Hotel Plaza** next to the Banco de República. If it is full try the **Hotel Metropol** at Carrera 11, #16-52; or **Hotel Chairá** on the corner of Calle 16 and Carrera 13. These have private bathrooms and fans...when there's electricity. Low-budget travellers should try the **Hotel Central** at Carrera 11, #15-26, near the central park. The accommodation near the bus station is even cheaper but not very pleasant.

The **Ethnographical Museum** (Museo Etnográfico) is worth a visit for its collection of tools, weapons and crafts used by local Indians, primarily the Witoto and Coreguajes tribes. It is next to the cathedral and opens weekdays 08.00–12.00 and 14.00–17.00.

Florencia is served by several flights daily from Bogotá (US$85 one way) and three or four flights a week to Puerto Asís (US$35). To get to the airport on the La Montañita road take any bus heading out that way or a taxi (US$3 from the centre). For travel overland, the Bogotá buses, costing US$15 one way, depart from Carrera 10. These are comfortable and air-conditioned – a civilised enough way to travel the 12 hours on appalling roads to Bogotá.

Excursions from Florencia

For destinations within the Colombian Amazon, there are several buses daily to **Getucha**, for around US$6, taking five or six hours. For the same price you can get a *chiva* to **Curillo**, from where you can take a boat down the Río Caquetá. Further downstream is **La Tagua**, south of the **La Paya National Park**. Further down the Caquetá is the small town of **Araracuara**, from where you can take a trip into Colombia's remotest lowland rainforest national park. Below Araracuara the Caquetá is unnavigable due to rapids. From here you may be able to get transport into Brazil, and eventually the Amazon mainstream, but this territory is very inaccessible and not for the inexperienced or budget traveller.

An easier trip is to go the short distance by road from **La Tagua** to **Puerto Leguízamo** on the Putumayo and then south to **Arica**, and eventually over the Brazilian border. You can't get to Leticia on these rivers except by the long downstream journey into Brazil and then back up the mainstream of the Amazon.

Puerto Asís

Located a few miles north of the Ecuadorian border, this dusty, ramshackle town is the biggest port on the Putumayo, but offers the traveller little by way of amenities or entertainment. The main reason to be here is en route between Lago Agrio in Ecuador and Mocoa, or to take a trip down the Putumayo River.

LA PAYA NATIONAL PARK

Covering some 4,220km², La Paya is a new park established in 1994 to protect an area of the Putumayo and Caquetá rivers, adjacent to the Ecuador border. Aside from Amacayacu this is the only national park that is accessible to the average traveller. The best way to reach it is travelling by boat from Puerto Asís to Puerto Leguízamo or taking the short road trip to La Tagua. Both work well as a base for day-trips into the park. The park has no permanent tourist facilities so you have either to satisfy yourself with day-trips or take camping equipment.

Founded in 1912, Puerto Asís (population around 20,000) has rapidly outgrown its original infrastructure and the effects show. The area is pervaded by drug and anti-drug activity and can be dangerous for tourists. Leave extra time to get through police checks, which are normally thorough. Puerto Asís is most useful as a point from which to launch off into the jungle by boat, although there are not many options. If wildlife and nature are your interest, then take the trip to La Tagua for La Paya National Park. If you are travelling to Brazil or Leticia, you have a long journey of ten or fifteen days, and some tough negotiating and considerable expense. It is cheaper to fly to Leticia if you are simply trying to get from A to B.

If you need to stay in Puerto Asís there are lots of hotels but mostly of low standard, catering to local sailors in port. Two of the better ones are **Hotel Camba Huasi** at Carrera 22 between Calles 10 and 11, and **Hotel Continental** on Calle 12.

The airport is practically within walking distance of town, if you have little or no luggage, and served by several flights daily to/from Bogotá (US$100–120). There are three flights a week to Florencia (US$35) and connections with most Amazon towns with airports. If you aren't up to the more arduous but undoubtedly more interesting overland journey to Ecuador, Aires has a cheap quick flight three times weekly to Lago Agrio (US$15, one way).

By bus you can get to Puerto Asís from Ecuador (about six hours, US$6.50) via the small town of San Miguel on the Colombia-Ecuador border. This route is rarely used by foreigners so take care. Bus connections to the highlands leave daily for Pasto (US$12) going through Mocoa.

If you are looking for a boat you may have to wait a couple of days. To take a boat from Puerto Asís to Leticia is an adventure but trying to book passage can be an ordeal. There are no scheduled passenger services and making arrangements before you arrive is impossible. So you have to rely on your wits and luck to get a suitable berth. Two places to check for arrivals and departures are at Transportes Fluviales del Amazonas on Carrera 20 and Calle 10 or the Oficina de la Inspección Fluvial at the Alcadia Municipal building on the Central Plaza. There are two port areas. One is on the riverfront in Puerto Asís and the other, the Port of Hong Kong (!), is 2.5km to the west along Calle 12. The latter serves larger ships and the military but both have vessels departing for Leticia.

You will probably end up on a cargo boat as military vessels leave only once or twice a month, so a hammock is essential. Negotiate the fare with the captain, and be sure to check if it includes food, although you might want to consider taking your own if you have the equipment to prepare it. Expect to pay US$100–150 for the ten-day trip downstream and make sure you get a receipt or ticket when you hand over your cash.

Mocoa

This town is capital of Putumayo province which forms half of Colombia's frontier with Ecuador, but such status confers no additional reason to stop here. The town centre is small, as the majority of the 15,000 population live in outlying homesteads. Although friendly to strangers, the inhabitants couldn't care less about tourism, as theirs is a market town and centre of distribution for local farm and forest products. As the surrounding country is heavily altered by agricultural activity, nature seekers will find little to please them in the immediate vicinity of the town. In reality visitors to Mocoa are usually transiting between Puerto Asís and towns further north. A beautiful drive to Pasto through the pass to the west gives access to the good roads through central Colombia and up to Bogotá. The town has few amenities, a handful of hotels and several places to eat. If you are heading for Ecuador through Puerto Asís or San Miguel you need to get your passport stamped at the DAS office in the town centre. Buses to nearby towns are frequent, with three or four a day making the trip to Puerto Asís for under US$5.

Curillo

This small town on the banks of the Caquetá is a nondescript jungle settlement – a speck among the vastness of trees and rivers. It's mostly a through-town, with most visitors on their way to or from Mocoa or Florencia. This is the only other place beside Getucha to look for a boat down the Caquetá to La Tagua, but if you want to go elsewhere you have to make your own arrangements with a local boat owner. If you're thinking of heading to Mitú it will be a challenge. If cost is a factor you're better off flying from Bogotá, as boat passage is expensive at US$75 or more per day. If you want to get to Brazil, travelling the Putumayo from Puerto Asís is a cheaper option.

Mitú

Capital of Vaupés province with a population of 5,500, this small town in lowland rainforest was established to consolidate Colombia's claim over one of the remotest parts of the Amazon. You go there to take a boat to Brazil down the Río Vaupés, or perhaps if you fancy the challenging journey to Puerto Inirida, a distant outpost in the northern Guainia region close to the Venezuelan border. Flights to Bogotá are relatively inexpensive (US$78 one-way), given the distances, and offer the only realistic opportunity to visit this back of beyond. As a rule of thumb, Colombian Amazon settlements such as Mitú are so remote or hard to reach as to be cost-ineffective in terms of dollars spent for wilderness experienced. Unless you are on a special project, working as a doctor, biologist, missionary or prospector, there's not much reason to visit Mitú.

NATIONAL PARKS AND WILDLIFE RESERVES

More conscious of conservation than most other Amazon countries, Colombia was the first and only country to establish a national park along its portion of the Amazon River. Since a major reshuffle in 1994, management of the national park system has been with the Ministry of the Environment through UAESPN (Unidad Administrativa Especial del Sistema de Parques Nacional), or Unidad Administrativa for short. Several new protected areas have recently been declared, including three in the Amazon, bringing Colombia's total number of national parks to 33. Altogether, including protected reserves, about 8% of the country is set aside for conservation. In Colombia, which values its relatively small portion of rainforest highly, sale of wild-captured game and under-sized fish is illegal and laws are strictly enforced. However, there is little money for patrolling parks and the small number of staff are insufficient to manage a combined area bigger than Wales. Information on Amacayacú National Park and La Paya National Park are in the sections on Leticia (page 230) and Florencia (page 231) respectively.

Cahuinari National Park

The second and newer of Amazonas' two national parks, Cahuinari is even more remote and unspoilt than Amacayacu. It covers a larger area, some 5,750km^2 (2,220 miles^2) of tropical lowland rainforest along the middle reaches of the Río Caquetá. The park can be reached two ways, but both are difficult due to the lack of regular transport. First and more practical is via Puerto Guzman (catch a boat) down the Río Caquetá to Araracuara. From Araracuara you can hire a guide to take you to the park. The other way, you start in Manaus, and take a boat up the Japura River to the border to La Pedrera, where the river now becomes the Caquetá. A permit to enter the park must be obtained in Bogotá or Leticia before you set off. Within the park there are no tourist facilities so full camping equipment and food supplies must be taken.

Chiribiquete National Park

This is Colombia's biggest national park, protecting some 12,800km^2 in Caquetá. Between the Yari River and its major tributary the Apaporis, the park habitat is primarily moist tropical rainforest, with the usual array of flora and fauna. The diversity of plant life is as high as anywhere in the Amazon, and due to the park's size extensive sub-habitats of flooded forest are also included within the boundaries. As well as the largest protected area, this is also the most inaccessible. The park has no infrastructure within its boundaries and there is no recognised way of getting there.

Monkey Island

This is the only private reserve in Colombia's lowland Amazonia. Its bizarre history could only happen in Colombia. Along with the Anaconda Hotel and other establishments in and around Leticia, the reserve was set up in the 1970s by Mike Tsalakis, an American businessman. He drops out of the story in 1987 when he was sentenced to a long term in a US jail for cocaine smuggling. Today managed by the Hotel Anaconda, the reserve remains open to the public. Tour operators in Leticia can arrange guided day-trips there, costing around US$20.

About 10km long and 2km wide – the exact size depends on the river level – Monkey Island is located in the Amazon mainstream, about 40km west of Leticia, and is home to a variety of monkey and marmoset species. The various species were brought in when the reserve was set up. Most individuals were yellow-footed titis and now their descendants populate, indeed over-run, the island. Plans are afoot – not a yellow foot – to re-open the island's single lodge, but exactly when this will happen is anyone's guess.

9 Ecuador

Divided between the north and southern hemispheres by the line of the Equator which passes just north of Quito, Ecuador justifies its name perfectly. Excluding the Guyanas, Ecuador has the smallest area of lowland Amazon and is the fourth smallest country in South America. The country covers 284,000km^2, not much bigger than Britain. Despite Ecuador's size, its variety of plant life represents one of the planet's greatest stores of biodiversity. In mountainous cloudforest and undisturbed lowland rainforest, the species diversity of plants, birds, mammals, amphibians and insects is among the world's highest.

FACTS AND FIGURES

Geography

As with Peru and Colombia, Ecuador's territory includes the Pacific *costa* to the west and the Amazonian *Oriente* to the east. These two regions are separated by the Andean *sierra* region bisected by a high central valley where Quito lies.

Among Ecuador's Andean peaks is Cotopaxi at 5,897m, the world's highest active volcano. At Cayembe, northeast of Quito, the Equator reaches its highest elevation around the globe (5,800m). Numerous peaks of 5–6,000m form two parallel chains running from the north of the country to the south. The eastern one, being of lower elevation, forms the Amazon Basin's westernmost rim.

Comprising about half of Ecuador's land area, lowland rainforest has a

BASIC FACTS

Official name República del Ecuador
Area 284,000km^2 (110,000 miles^2)
Population 12 million
Capital Quito (1.3 million)
Largest city (population) Guayaquil (1.5 million)
Main Amazon city Coca/Puerto Francisco de Orellana
Official language Spanish
Date of independence August 10, 1830
Major industries petroleum, agriculture, wood products, tourism, fisheries, textiles and beverages
GDP per capita US$691
Currency sucre (S/4500: US$1, S/7400: UK£1)
Major attractions Galápagos Islands, Otavalo Market, the Amazon
National holidays Jan 1, Jan 6, Carnival (week before Lent in March or April), May 1, May 24, Aug 10, Oct 12, Nov 1, Dec 24, Dec 25

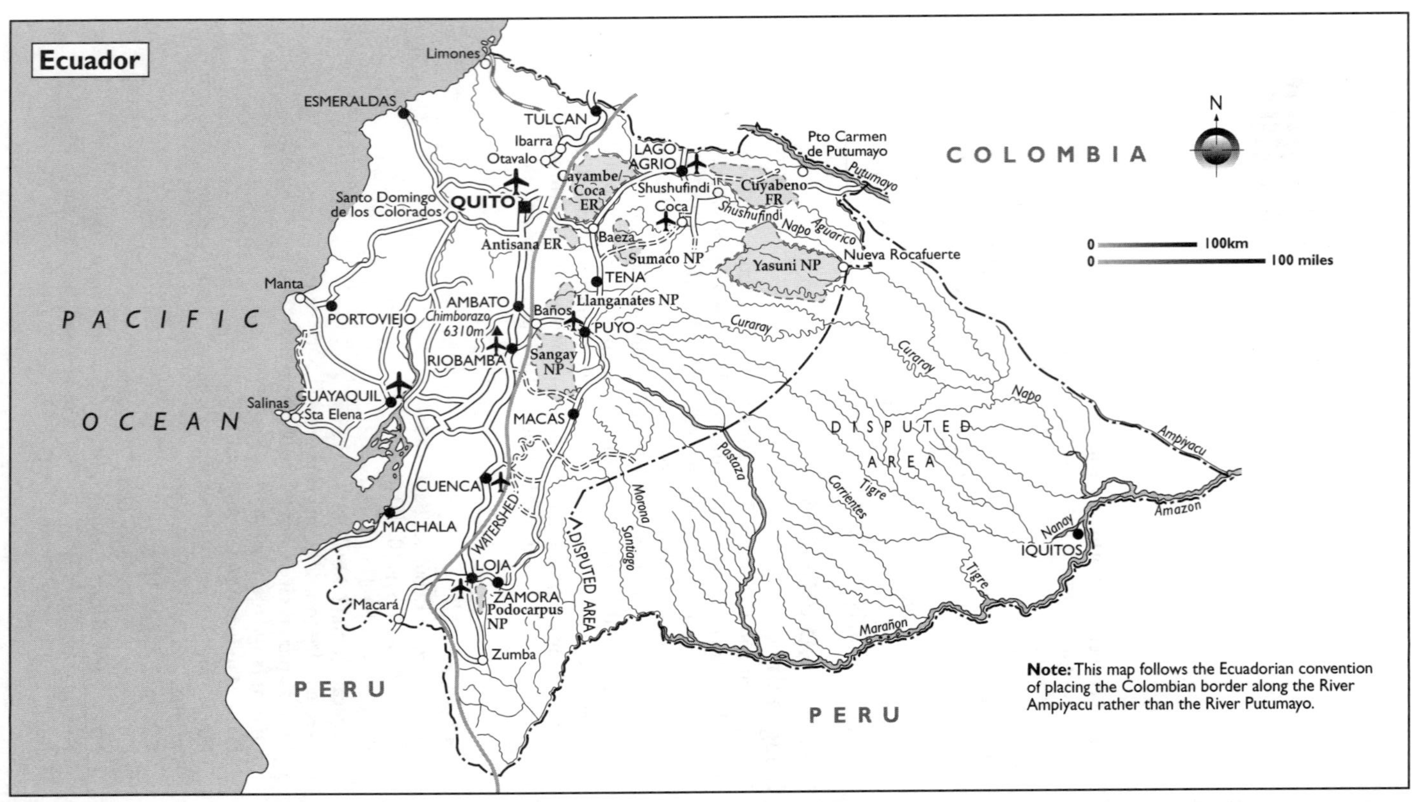
Ecuador
Limones
ESMERALDAS
TULCAN
Ibarra
Otavalo
LAGO AGRIO
Pto Carmen de Putumayo
Putumayo
COLOMBIA
N
Cayambe/ Coca ER
Shushufindi
Cuyabeno FR
Santo Domingo de los Colorados
QUITO
Coca
Shushufindi
Napo
Aguarico
Baeza
Antisana ER
Sumaco NP
Yasuni NP
Nueva Rocafuerte
0 100km
0 100 miles
TENA
Manta
Llanganates NP
AMBATO
Baños
PACIFIC
PORTOVIEJO
Chimborazo 6310m
PUYO
Curaray
Curaray
RIOBAMBA
Sangay NP
Napo
GUAYAQUIL
Salinas
Sta Elena
OCEAN
MACAS
DISPUTED AREA
Ampiyacu
Pastaza
Corrientes
Tigre
CUENCA
WATERSHED
Morona
Amazon
MACHALA
DISPUTED AREA
Santiago
Nanay
IQUITOS
LOJA
Tigre
ZAMORA
Podocarpus NP
Macará
Marañon
Zumba
PERU
PERU
Note: This map follows the Ecuadorian convention of placing the Colombian border along the River Ampiyacu rather than the River Putumayo.

disproportionate share of natural resources, and oil extraction in the Oriente is causing major problems for local indigenous people.

The Galápagos Islands are a group of 13 major islands and many small ones, 1,000km off the coast of Ecuador. The archipelago consists of volcanic rock and is famous for its unique wildlife.

Rivers

Hydrologically, the Ecuadorian Amazon is dominated by the Napo-Aguarico watershed east of the Andes. Except for the Río Guayas that flows through Guayaquil, virtually all Ecuador's major lowland rivers originating in the Andes head in the same direction: east, then southeast before joining the Amazon mainstream. Most important from a commercial standpoint is the Río Napo, which crosses the Ecuador-Peru frontier at Nova Rocafuerte to enter the Amazon mainstream just below Iquitos. To the south is the Río Zamora valley in the disputed border region between Peru and Ecuador.

Strategically important, the Putumayo forms the Colombia-Ecuador border east of the Andes to Peru.

Climate

Ecuador is equatorial and relatively small so latitude and season have little effect on climatic variation, making the dominant factor topography.

Oriente temperatures range between 18–25°C. Maximum rainfall is between April and July, peaking in June, while it is driest in January and February. The lowlands are the wettest region of Ecuador with annual rainfall of 3,000–6,100mm.

Coastal regions are somewhat hotter and humid – around 25–30°C – with the highest temperatures between December and May. Despite the humidity the coastal region is quite dry; Guayaquil gets annual precipitation of just 1,000mm.

The climate gets cooler with altitude producing a temperate zone with rainfall of 750–2,000m. Up in the central valley the weather is likened to perpetual spring. Upland Ecuador is driest between June and September, with rainfall of 1,000–2,000mm.

Surrounded by ocean, the Galápagos Islands have a quite different climate from the mainland. Temperatures average around 30°C. From June to December, the cooler months, the *garúa* mist brings in masses of low stratus cloud. Lowlands are dry, but regions above 600m are usually wet. In the lowlands, rain is most frequent from January to April.

EL NIÑO

Long-term weather patterns dominate the country's climate from time to time. Most notable is the El Niño phenomenon, a climatic anomaly with a five- to eleven-year cycle, seven on average. One of the 20th century's most serious events was in 1982–83, during which heavy rainfall and subsequent floods caused widespread damage. Wildlife was hard hit, especially on the coast and in the Galápagos Islands. Weather in the Amazon Basin is also altered during El Niño events. Temperatures drop to 15°C or even lower as cool northerly winds blow from frigid Patagonian plateaux.

The country was hard hit by the severe El Niño event of 1998, which meteorologists say was even worse than that of 1982–83 event. In just one week, the death toll from El Niño-related causes was 600. In the Amazon, lower rainfall and higher temperatures characterise an El Niño event.

Flora and fauna

Ecuador's mainland wildlife comprises typical Andean and neotropical flora and fauna. The Galápagos Islands are a unique ecosystem of plants and animals specially adapted to life on remote, rocky oceanic islands.

Ecuador's lowland rainforest wildlife consists of all major Amazon fauna: jaguar, tapir, caiman, anaconda, poison-dart frogs, morpho butterflies, howler monkeys, sloths, pink dolphin, river otter and lots, lots more. Ecuador has dozens of endemic bird and amphibian species and thousands of insects.

Land use

In the highland sierra, farming, llama herding and handicrafts are major rural occupations. Here land is intensively cultivated to raise an astonishing range of crops, including some 300 varieties of potatoes. Lowland tropical areas are extensively planted with cash crops, notably bananas and oil palm.

There is little heavy industry in Quito which has allowed its rival and the country's biggest city, Guayaquil, to become the industrial centre. On the coast near Guayaquil, extensive areas are devoted to export-based shrimp farms where mangrove swamps, normally used as nurseries by many fish species, are cleared for shrimp farms.

Ecuador has a vibrant tourism industry and is increasingly concerned with tourism and conservation. Some 40% of Ecuador remains forested, mostly in the Amazon lowlands, and is now increasingly protected.

The people

Population and ethnic groups

South America's seventh most populous country, Ecuador has its share of population problems with the continent's highest population density at 44 people per km^2. Half the population is concentrated in towns and cities, with Quito and Guayaquil home to one fifth of the whole population. Population density in the Oriente is lower than average for the whole country and vast tracts of lowland rainforest remain virtually empty.

As questions of race are not included in Ecuador's censuses, the population's ethnic composition is poorly known. The majority of people are of mixed Indian and Spanish descent. Most Caucasians (10% of the population) are pure-blood descendants of Spaniards who arrived during the 16th to early 19th centuries. Slaves brought from Africa during colonial times are ancestors of the small black population.

Languages

Spanish is the official language and spoken by almost everyone. Survival Spanish should be enough for most situations, but unless you are fluent you need to make an effort to acquire an ear for regional accents. English is quite common in popular tourist areas like Quito and the Galápagos, and at the better Amazon lodges.

Ecuador's linguistic heritage comes from numerous aboriginal native tribes that inhabited the land prior to arrival of the conquistadors. The *lingua franca* among Indians is Quechua, spoken by most tribes. The main linguistic group in the Ecuadorian Amazon is the Achuar (Jivaro) complex of dialects.

Tribes of Amazonia

Most inhabitants of the Ecuadorian Amazon are aboriginal Indians at varying degrees of assimilation into the outside world. Ninety per cent of the Amazon population is either Indian (comprising 50%) – mostly Quechua-speaking – or mestizo (40%), who together number about half a million, 4% of Ecuador's population.

The largest single group is the Achuar or Shuar – also called Jivaro, meaning savages – who live in deep forest in remote southeast Ecuador between the Santiago and Corrientes rivers. They were the last major indigenous group in the Ecuadorian Amazon to remain isolated until the discovery of oil in the 1970s. The Achuar have the disputable honour of being one of the best-known Amazonian tribes who formally practised head-hunting.

Education

Standards in Ecuador's schools and universities are among the highest in South America. Spanish is the language of instruction, though classes are also held in Quechua, and English is widely taught as a second language. For all children between ages 6 to 14, education is free and compulsory. Higher education is valued. Indeed, the country's largest university, the Central University of Ecuador in Quito, is one of South America's oldest, established in 1586.

In the Oriente, isolated schools teach local children the three Rs, but little more. Teachers try hard but school supplies are meagre and travel conditions make regular attendance difficult. During the 1997–98 El Niño, schools had to extend the rainy season holiday by two whole months.

THE 'NOBLE SAVAGE'

Hilary Bradt

A totally honest look at the Indian culture can prove disappointing to some. The 'Noble Savage' is demystified and sometimes emerges as being more pragmatic and less spiritual than many writers would have us believe. During a story-telling session round the fire over which half a peccary carcass was being smoked, Randy Borman (see page 259) gave an example of how myths about Indians come about:

> 'An old man from the village was stopped in Lago Agrio by one of those smart, intelligent army officers on assignment in the jungle and waiting to return to Quito with some good stories. "Tell me about jaguar-hunting," he said. The old man was instantly on his guard, knowing that the army was actively involved in the campaign to stop the trade in jaguar pelts. So he answered to save his own skin: that they never killed jaguar except in self-defence, that if they had to kill one they would apologise to it "because we are brothers", that the spirits of dead Cofans go into jaguars ... and so on.
>
> 'The Indian went back to his village and said: "You should have heard the stories I told that army officer!" Everyone laughed. The army officer went back to Quito and said: "You should have heard the stories I learned from an old Indian shaman!" Everyone listened. He wrote up the stories – with embellishments – and they were published. Generations from now, when the Indians have lost their culture, they will read these stories and assume it is their lost inheritance. After all, it's happened in North America!'

It is worth adding, though, that many tribes still have a powerful respect for the jaguar and sincerely believe that they are 'brothers'.

Religion
The dominant religion, according to national statistics, is Roman Catholicism, to which 93% of the population subscribe. The remainder are Protestant, Evangelical or members of Indian groups with a different belief system.

A brief history
Pre-conquest
Very little is known of Ecuador's earliest inhabitants. By 5,000 years ago, diverse tribes of sedentary agricultural Indians occupied most of the country. Of these, the Caras came to dominate, establishing their capital at Quito. The Caras were conquered in the late 15th century by the Incas and Quito became the main city of the northern half of the empire. The death of Inca Huayna Capac divided the empire between his two sons with Atahualpa taking command of Quito. A divided empire created crucial weaknesses that were easily exploited by the Spaniards when they arrived in 1532.

Conquest
Peru took the brunt of the Spanish conquest, intercepting Atahualpa, one claimant to the Inca Empire, in Cajamarca on his return to the northern kingdom centred on Quito.

The Spanish went south to conquer Cusco before returning to Quito to quash the rumours of rebellions building in the north under the lieutenancies of Sebastián de Belalcázar and Diego de Almagro. They founded the city of Quito in 1534.

Colonialism
As in Peru and other Spanish possessions, extraction of wealth relied on Indian labour working on vast estates. Spain ruled Ecuador as part of the Viceroy of Peru until 1740, when it became part of the Viceroyalty of Granada. In 1809, rebellion shook the country as dissatisfaction spread among working classes, voiced most clearly by an emerging Creole middle class. Independence was declared, but the leaders were executed and the uprising was crushed.

Independence
At the Battle of Pichincha in 1822, Antonio José de Sucre, helped by the great liberator Simón Bolívar, defeated the Spanish and Ecuador became part of liberated Gran Colombia. In 1830 Ecuador seceded from the union and adopted its own constitution. In the same year, Ecuador and Peru signed a treaty establishing international boundaries between their Amazon possessions.

Post-independence years were marked by rivalry and infighting among various powerful families and armed factions. Civil disorder was widespread and governance next to impossible for succeeding regimes. Focus of the struggle for power was rivalry between Quito and Guayaquil.

The 20th century
Increasingly authoritarian administrations dominated by the military continued to govern the country until the 20th century. In 1941 a politically and economically weak Ecuador was invaded by Peru along the Amazon portion of the frontier. The Río de Janeiro Protocol resolved the conflict and in 1942 Ecuador lost territory, an outcome still disputed and which frequently flares up in border skirmishes between the two countries.

After World War II government was relatively democratic but economic difficulties and continued political instability hindered significant progress.

Between 1944 and 1972 President José Ibarra completed only one of his five terms.

The 1970s experienced a small economic boom from petroleum profits and an upsurge in drilling exploration in the Oriente. Standards of living improved but lasting benefits were offset by severe inflation. The 1980s saw little improvement as the economy suffered under massive external debt, exacerbated by low oil prices and continued high inflation.

Economic difficulties were compounded by a series of natural disasters. In 1982–83 a devastating El Niño resulted in extensive flooding of farm land. In 1987 a powerful earthquake caused much loss of life and extensive damage. Then, in March 1993, the country suffered its worst-ever catastrophe when a huge landslide dammed the Paute River, burying hundreds and cutting off communication between Guayaquil and Quito. Thousands were made homeless and the eventual cost of damage was put at over US$100 million.

Ecuador is governed by a representative democracy elected for a four-year term. All citizens over 18 years of age are required by law to vote. Ecuador has many political parties and it is rare for any one to win a controlling majority, with the result that the ruling government is composed of coalitions. The country is divided into 21 provinces, each subdivided into cantons and parishes.

Politically, the country suffered an embarrassing episode in February 1997 when President Bucaram was deposed on grounds of mental incompetence after having been in power only six months.

Money

There are no currency restrictions on import or export of foreign or Ecuadorian money. Ecuador's official monetary unit is the *sucre* (written S/), which has devalued significantly in recent years, making travel to Ecuador relatively inexpensive and favoured among budget travellers. At the time of writing (March 1998), the exchange rate is about S/4500 to a dollar on an upward trend.

It is difficult and expensive to buy sucres outside the country so wait until you arrive. Dollar bills and travellers' cheques are widely accepted by hotels, shops and restaurants in Quito and tourist-oriented towns such as Otavalo, so bring US$100 or so in US$1 and US$5 notes.

Changing money in the Oriente region often attracts a high commission so, before you leave Quito, change enough to last while you are out of town. If your tour is prepaid you'll need only spending money for souvenirs, tips and bar bills. Figure on about US$10–25 per day while in the jungle.

The best place to change money in Quito is at the *cambio* houses of which there are several in the Mariscal Sucre area. Traveller's cheques receive a better exchange rate than dollar bills but again the difference is negligible.

Highlights

Ecuador's diverse natural and cultural resources present ample opportunities for all travellers no matter what their interests. Wildlife is abundant in rainforest, coastal and montane biomes, but what really puts Ecuador on the nature traveller's map is the Galápagos Islands, renowned for unique birds and reptiles.

Tourist facilities are widely available and of good quality. Compared with neighbouring countries, Ecuador's Amazon region is relatively well-developed for commercial travel. Overland and air connections are straightforward and efficient with numerous tour operators providing a wide variety of organised packages to the many excellent lodges.

If you're willing to go off the beaten path, much of Ecuador's lowland rainforest remains undiscovered by the travel industry. Independent travellers will appreciate

AMAZON AND GALÁPAGOS?

One dilemma for both independent and package travellers is whether a Galápagos Islands trip should include the Amazon at the beginning or the end. Trying to 'do' the Galápagos and Amazon in one trip is possibly doing too much and dilutes the experience of both. These two places are among the world's greatest natural treasures. Much better to spend two weeks (or more) in the Amazon region and save visiting the Galápagos for another year (or vice versa).

However, time and money are limited. If you have to combine the two, visit the Galápagos after the Amazon. You'll have earned the rest! Barry Boyce's *A Traveler's Guide to the Galápagos Islands* (available from Galápagos Travel) is highly recommended; also *Galápagos Wildlife* (Bradt Publications).

the ease and efficiency of Ecuador's public transport system. Buses are relatively safe and reliable, frequent and inexpensive, as is domestic air travel.

Otavalo market gets visitors from all over the world, shopping for the high-quality and cheap woven goods and handicrafts.

Jungle tours

Dozens of tour operators sell jungle trips to suit every pocket and schedule.

If you are just after wildlife, go to the remotest areas possible. For botanising, the best place is in remote areas of the lower Andean foothills, such as undisturbed parts of the upper Aguarico and Napo watersheds. In these forests, as lowland and highland habitats merge, Amazon (indeed global) biodiversity reaches its zenith.

Many, but not all, tours include visits to indigenous communities – sure to interest photographers and those wishing to include a cultural component in their rainforest experience. These tours may include interesting observations of shamanism, herbalism and the daily life of a rainforest tribe.

Several lodges have recently opened in the Ecuadorian Amazon, and a few have made outstanding attempts to fulfil the ideals of ecotourism. Tour operators in Ecuador sell many different Amazon trips. Major lodges have their own programmes so you can get a convenient all-inclusive package. Alternatively you can easily travel around the region and arrange your own transport, lodgings and meals.

The best lodges work out at over US$100 a day, priced beyond the financially-strained traveller. Most people who stay at these places are with tour groups from North America or Europe. With airfare to and from Quito included, a three-day stay at Ecuador's best jungle lodges will cost US$500–750.

With a bit of planning and negotiating, you could do something similar for US$150. You would take a bus and camp, in the native-style *cabañas* (raised thatched huts without walls), or sometimes in a tent. Of course, on a basic trip you do without luxuries. You won't get gourmet food or the most educated guide, but you might still get the best experience of your life.

Tour operators

There is no shortage of tour operators offering organised trips to the Amazon Basin in Ecuador. The selection below offer a range of trips covering all-inclusive packages from abroad or options that can be arranged once you're in Ecuador.

In Ecuador (Quito)

Andemoto Adventures Robles 528 y Reina Victoria; tel (cellular): 09 722408; fax: (00 593 2) 224 975. Fully escorted and equipped on- and off-road motorcycle tours throughout Ecuador.
Cuyabeno Tours J L Mera y Washington; tel/fax: 00 593 2 522 768. Have an interesting six-day tour to Dureno, east of Lago Agrio, involving road and river travel along the Aguarico and Cuyabeno rivers.
Ecotours 9 Octubre 599 y Carrion; tel: 00 593 2 224 483; fax: 00 593 2 593 9 735504; email: ecotours@uio.satnet.net; net: www.contacto.com/~ecotours/; postal address c/o Norby Lopez, PO Box 71-21-965, Quito. Have 'Nature and Adventure' trips from their cabañas at Pañacocha.
Emerald Forest Amazonas 1023 y Pinto; tel/fax: 00 593 2 541 543/526 403. Tour agency for freelance guide Luis García, who runs trips in Misahuallí-Coca area.
Explorer Tours Reina Victoria 1235 y Lizardo García; tel: 00 593 2 522 220/508 871. Owners of Sacha Lodge and other property on the Napo River.
Jatun Sacha Foundation Río Coca 1734 y Isla Fernandina; tel: 00 593 2 253 267; fax: 00 593 2 253 266; email: alinahui@sacha.ecx.ec. postal address: PO Box 17-12-867, Quito. A non-profit organisation dedicated to rainforest preservation. Takes bookings for Cabañas Aliñahui on the upper Napo River. In the US contact **Health and Habitat** tel: 415 383 6130; fax: 415 381 9214; email: alinahui@jsacha.ecuanex.net.ec; net: www.igc.apc.org/healthhab; c/o Dr Sandy Ross, 74 Lee St. Mill Valley, CA 94941, USA.
Jumandy Explorers Tours Wilson 718 y J L Mera; tel: 00 593 2 220 518/541 453; tel (Tena): 593 6 887181. Organise stays with indigenous family communities around Tena and bookings for Jumandy Hotel in Tena.
Kleintours Av Shyris 1000; tel: 00 593 2 430 345/432 178; fax: 00 593 2 442 389. The second largest tour operator with a number of programmes at luxury lodges.
Metropolitan Touring Amazonas 329 y 18 de Septiembre; tel: 00 593 2 506 650/464 780; fax: 00 593 2 560 807; postal address: PO Box 17-17-1649, Quito. Ecuador's biggest tour operator, they organise tours to several jungle lodges in and around the Cuyabeno Reserve and take bookings for the Flotel *Orellana*. **Amazon Explorers** in the US take group and individual bookings for the *Orellana* (page 244).
Native Life Joaquin Pinto 446 y Amazonas; tel: 00 593 2 505 158/550 836; fax: 00 593 2 229 077; email: natlife1@natlife.com.ec; net: www.natlife.ec. Postal address; PO Box 17-03-504, Quito. Organise rainforest adventures from their base in the southern Cuyabeno Reserve.
Naturgal Reina Victoria y Foch; tel: 00 593 2 522 681; in Tena tel: 06 886 434/887 181. Takes reservations for staying with indigenous communities.
Neotropic Turis Robles 653 y Amazonas; tel: 00 593 2 527 862/521 212; fax: 00 593 2 554 902. Take reservations for Cuyabeno Lodge.
New Life Travel Foch 713 y J L Mera; tel: 00 593 2 543 956. Sells a wide range of budget tours all over Ecuador, including to Cuyabeno, Yusuni and Misahuallí.
Nuevo Mundo Expeditions Amazonas 2468; tel: 00 593 2 552 617; fax: 00 593 2 565 261; postal address: PO Box 402A, Quito. Excellent tours to Cuyabeno Reserve.
Safari Tours Calama 380 y J L Mera; tel: 00 593 2 552 505; fax: 00 593 2 220 426; email: admin@safariec.ecx.ec. Wide range of adventure travel: mountain biking, trekking, rafting and climbing. 4WD vehicle safaris to remote areas.
La Selva Gustavo Recalde, 6 de Diciembre 2816. PO Box 171235, Quito; tel: 00 593 2 550 995/554 686; fax: 00 593 2 567 297; email: laselva@uio.satnet.net. Take bookings for their first-class lodge on the upper Napo River, near Coca.
Yachana Lodge 188 y Diego de Almagro; tel: 00 593 2 543 851; fax: 00 593 2 220 362; email: dtm@pi.pro.ec. Arranges trips with indigenous communities.
Yuturi Tur Zulema Sanmiguel, Av Amazonas 1324 and Colon; tel/fax: 00 58 2 504037/503225/544166; email: yuturi1@yuturi.com.ec; net: www.yuturi.com. Take bookings for the Yuturi Ecotourist Complex and Reserve east of Coca.

In the US

Amazon Explorers 197 Wall St W, Long Branch, NJ 07764; tel: 908 870 0223/800 631 5650; fax: 908 870 0278. For the Flotel Orellana.
Forum Travel International 91 Gregory Lane, #21 Pleasant Hill, CA 94523; tel: 510 671 2900; fax: 510 671 2993; email: forum@ix.netcom.com; net: www.ten-io.com/forumtravel. For La Selva and Sacha Lodges.
ROW Expeditions PO Box 579 Coeur d'Alene ID 83816; tel: 800 451 6034/208 765 0841; fax: 208 667 6506; email: rowinc@aol.com; net: www.rowinc.com. Offer unique river-rafting expeditions down the Río Upano from Macas (Sep to Mar only).
Wilderness Travel 1102 Ninth St, Berkeley, CA 94710; tel: 510 548 2488/0800 247 6700; fax: 510 558 2489; email: info@wildernesstravel.com; net: www.wildernesstravel.com. Organise trips to Sabolo.

In the UK

Overland Latin America 13 Dormer Place, Leamington Spa, Warks CV32 5AA; tel: 01926 332222; fax: 01926 435567; email: worldlspa@aol.com.
Tribes Travel 7 The Business Centre, Earl Soham, Woodbridge, Suffolk IP13 7SA; tel: 01728 685971; fax: 01728 685973; net: www.tribes.co.uk.
Worldwide Journeys 8 Comeragh Rd, London W14 9HP; tel: 0171 381 8638; fax: 0171 381 0836; email: wwj@wjournex.demon.co.uk. Organise cruises that begin in Brazil and travel the Amazon.

If you want to include the Galápagos on your itinerary try the following.

Galapagos Travel 783 Río del Mar Blvd, Ste 47 Aptos, CA 95003, USA; tel: 800 969 9014/831 689 9195; fax: 831 689 9192; email: galapagostravel@compuserve.com; net: www.galapagostravel.com/galapagos.)
Galápagos Adventure Tours 37-39 Great Guildford St, London SE1 0ES; tel/fax: 0171 261 9890; email: pinzon@compuserve.com.

Both specialise in the Galápagos but can organise jungle extensions as well.

GETTING THERE AND AWAY

Weather need not really be a consideration as there is not much difference year-round in climatic conditions. If you want to keep away from the tourist crowds and finances are tight, avoid the high seasons (June to August, and December).

By air

From the US

International flights arrive in Quito and Guayaquil. Quito is the best arrival point for visitors to the Amazon and has direct flights by American Airlines, SAETA and Ecuatoriana from Miami. American also fly direct from New York, while Continental has daily flights from Houston.

From Europe

British Airways flies from London into Miami for connections with American Airlines direct to Quito. Cities in Europe with direct flights include Amsterdam (KLM), Frankfurt (Lufthansa), Paris (Air France) and Madrid (Iberian).

Mariscal Sucre International Airport is within the city, 10km north of the central commercial district in downtown Quito, somewhat confusingly called Mariscal Sucre as well. Departure tax is US$25 on international flights.

By boat

There are no passenger boat services into coastal Ecuadorian ports, although military vessels and some cargo shipping lines occasionally take passengers.

Reaching the Ecuadorian Amazon by riverboat from Iquitos is not possible as the Amazon border with Peru is closed.

Overland

The Pan-American Highway runs the length of the country from the northern frontier with Colombia and continuing south to Peru. Both frontiers are served by international buses and large numbers of private vehicles make the crossing.

In the northern lowlands it is possible to cross between the Ecuadorian town of Lago Agrio and Colombia, arriving, eventually, in Puerto Asís.

There are several crossings from southern Ecuador in the Zamora district that fall within the disputed border region between Ecuador and Peru and are currently closed.

Customs and immigration

A **passport** is required. Upon entry you get a 60-day **visitor's permit**, and 90-day **visas** are available if you wish to stay longer. If you need to stay over the allotted time get an extension from the Ecuadorian Immigration Authority who have offices in Quito at Amazonas 2639.

Getting around

By bus

Ecuador has a good public transport system and service throughout the country is usually reliable and inexpensive. Prices are very low – from Quito to the Amazon is less than US$10 – and the better buses come equipped with air-conditioning, reclining seats, onboard toilets and TV.

Buses to the Amazon Basin from Quito leave from the Terminal Terrestre in the south of the city. Direct buses are available to most Amazon towns.

By air

From Quito connecting flights for Amazon travellers are to either Tena, Coca, Lago Agrio or Shell-Mera near to Puyo on the military-affiliated Ecuadorian airline TAME. Offices are at Av Amazonas 1354 and Colon, tel: 02 509382.

By boat

Transport to and from popular tourist facilities is usually via motorised *colectivo* or small motorboats. With increasing wealth due to oil and tourism, conventional motorboats are common on the mainstream of the Napo, and the leisure industry now makes extensive use of Ecuador's rivers.

Maps

There are few maps of Ecuador available outside the country. In Ecuador, the best place to get maps is at the Military Geographical Institute (IGM) in Quito (Calle Paz and Miño; tel: 00 593 2 522 066) who have a variety of maps at different scales.

COMMUNICATIONS

Mail

Post from Ecuador takes up to three weeks and on the whole is reliable and relatively inexpensive. A postcard within the Americas costs about US$0.45, or further afield US$0.55. The post office is in the main commercial district on Av Colon at Reina Victoria. International courier companies offer a more reliable service for packages.

Telephone and fax

Phone and fax are widely used by most businesses and public telephones are available in commercial areas of all cities and large towns. Many public phones now only take pre-paid 'smart' cards that are widely available in the city. The cheapest place to make international calls is at one of the branches of the state-owned telephone company EMETEL. There is an office at the airport and the main office is on the corner of Colon and Av 10 de Agosto.

At present, Ecuador's telephone system is expanding fast and in the process of updating. Telephone numbers are liable to alter over the next couple of years so check with the international operator for any change in codes if you are experiencing problems getting through.

The international code for Ecuador is 593.

Internet

Many tour operators in Ecuador now use email. If you have access to the service this is the most efficient way to pre-book jungle trips with agencies based in Ecuador. Many larger tour operators and lodges now have websites so you can check conditions and prices from home.

Cenfei.net at Av 10 de Agosto, on the corner with Riofrio, Building Benalcazar Mil, Office 101 first floor in Quito, has online services. Open Mon–Fri 08.00–20.00, weekends 09.00–20.00.

Television and radio

Ecuadorian television and radio consists of several state-run and private stations. Programming consists predominantly of current affairs although sports are also popular, mainly soccer. Occasional educational programmes are shown, while evening slots are occupied with game shows or music videos. Some of the larger hotels have satellite TV.

Newspapers

All widely circulated newspapers and weeklies are in Spanish. Quito newspapers include *Hoy, El Comercio* and *El Tiempo. Hoy* prints daily weather reports and TAME airline schedules with internal flights from Quito to Amazon towns.

US and European newspapers are not widely available but may be stocked at airports and some of the larger hotels.

South American Explorers Club

All of the above in one place… SAEC members can receive mail, phone calls, faxes and email at the Quito clubhouse at Jorge Washington 311 y Leonidas Plaza; tel/fax: 00 593 2 225 228; email explorer@saec.org.ec; net: www.samexplo.org. If you're not a member you can join when you arrive. See page 44.

QUITO

Close to the Equator and nestled 2,820m (9,300ft) up in a high central Andean valley, Quito's climate is properly described as 'eternal spring' with average daytime temperatures of 15°C. The city is surrounded by lofty snow-capped mountains including the active volcano Mount Pichincha (4,760m).

For travellers to the Amazon, Quito has historic relevance as the departure point for the first-ever full-length Amazon voyage, by conquistador Francisco de Orellana. Geography and growth have seen Quito divide into two cities, New and Old. The Old City, to the south, filled with colonial buildings, was declared a World Heritage Site by UNESCO in 1978 and is governed by strict building regulations.

Today, the Old City looks much as it did when Orellana departed on that cold morning in 1541, less than half a century after Columbus first set foot in the Americas. Red-tiled roofs, atop whitewashed stucco buildings, stretch into the distance, punctuated here and there by cathedral spires and curly wisps of smoke rising into the bright morning sky.

Orientation is along a north-south axis constrained by the narrow mountain valley. Compacted within this groove Quito is easier to navigate than many other sprawling South American capitals. The airport is at the far north in the New City, the long-distance bus station – *terminal terrestre* – is at the far south in the Old City and the hotel and commercial area is roughly in the middle.

At the airport

There are plenty of yellow taxis clustered outside the airport. The 25-minute ride to your hotel in the New City should cost US$4–6. Alternatively you can catch a bus from across the airport into town for about US$1 to the city's main commercial area on Av Amazonas.

WARNING Quito's elevation may cause symptoms of altitude sickness. These range from mild headache to nausea and dizziness. Sleeping may also be difficult. Be sure to minimise exertion, especially for the first day or two, and keep alert for symptoms. (See *Chapter Four*, page 86.)

City transport

The cheapest way to get around is by bus which costs up to US$0.25 for a trip within the city. The buses follow set routes advertised on plaques in the front window. The conductors yell out their destinations, you can yell back and, if they go where you're going, the bus stops and you get the ride.

A new tram system runs along the north-south axis of the city making an easy connection between the Old and New Cities. The standard fare is US$0.25. The nearest stop to the heart of the Old City is Santo Domingo.

Taxis are widespread and should not cost more than US$4 for even the longest journeys. If you take a taxi, make sure the meter is working in the cab, and if there is no meter agree on a price beforehand.

Where to stay

It is easy to find accommodation in Quito, as there are hundreds of hotels, *hostales*, *residencias* and *apartmentes* to choose from. They are loosely concentrated around Mariscal Sucre in the New City, with quite a number in the Old City. Your best bet if new to Quito is to base yourself in the New City – simply because it is safer and easier to get around.

First class

Hotel Alameda Real Esq Amazonas y Roca; tel: 02 562 345; fax: 02 565 759. In the heart of Mariscal Sucre on Amazonas, the five-star Alameda is one of the city's top hotels. Rooms start from US$125.

Colon Hilton Internacional Amazonas y Patria; tel: 02 561 333. Adjacent to Parque El Ejido. As you would expect for a Hilton, it has the works. Used by upmarket tour operators. From US$150 per night.

Hotel Tambo Real 12 du Octubre y Patria; tel: 02 563 820; fax: 02 554 964. Overlooking El Parque Ejido, luxurious for the price and boasts a casino. Upper floor rooms have good views. From US$90.

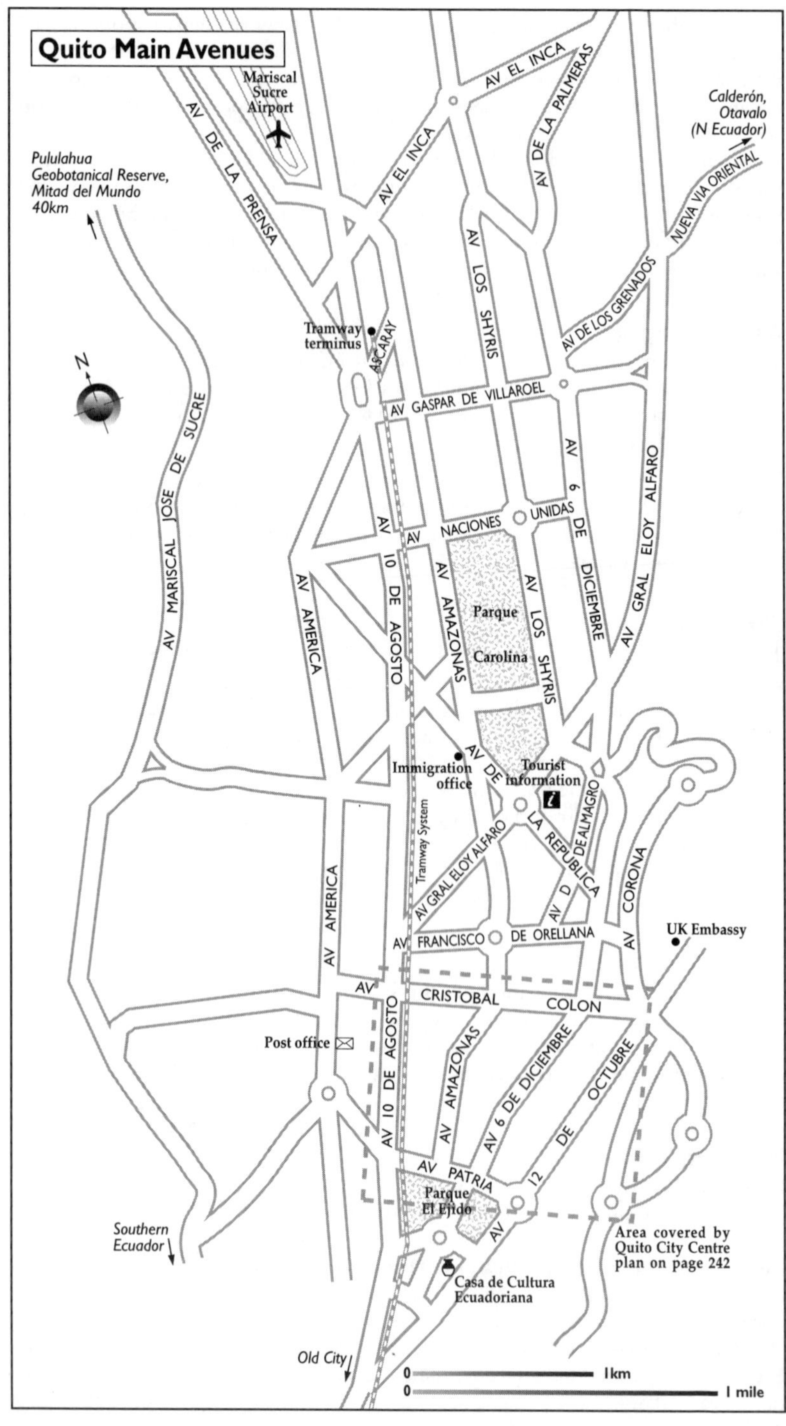
Quito Main Avenues
Mariscal Sucre Airport
AV EL INCA
AV DE LA PALMERAS
Calderón, Otavalo (N Ecuador)
AV DE LA PRENSA
Pululahua Geobotanical Reserve, Mitad del Mundo 40km
NUEVA VIA ORIENTAL
AV LOS SHYRIS
AV DE LOS GRENADOS
Tramway terminus
ASCARAY
AV GASPAR DE VILLAROEL
AV MARISCAL JOSE DE SUCRE
AV 6 DE DICIEMBRE
AV GRAL ELOY ALFARO
AV NACIONES UNIDAS
AV AMERICA
AV 10 DE AGOSTO
AV AMAZONAS
Parque Carolina
AV LOS SHYRIS
Immigration office
AV DE LA REPUBLICA
Tourist information
AV DE ALMAGRO
Tramway System
AV GRAL ELOY ALFARO
AV D
AV CORONA
AV AMERICA
AV FRANCISCO DE ORELLANA
UK Embassy
AV CRISTOBAL COLON
Post office
AV 10 DE AGOSTO
AV AMAZONAS
AV 6 DE DICIEMBRE
AV 12 DE OCTUBRE
AV PATRIA
Parque El Ejido
Southern Ecuador
Area covered by Quito City Centre plan on page 242
Casa de Cultura Ecuadoriana
Old City
0 1km
0 1 mile

Hotel Sebastián Almagro 822 y Cordero; tel: 02 222 400; fax: 02 222 500; email: hsebast1@hsebastian.com.ec. Probably the most ecoconscious of the luxury hotels. Laundry is washed environmentally and organic fruits and vegetables are used in the restaurant – a great hotel for the price, from US$75.

Middle range

Madison Hotel Roca 518 y Reina Victoria; tel: 02 508 617. This mid-priced hotel is ideal if you are looking to get away from busy, anonymous five-star hotels. The Madison has gourmet dining, cable TV, gaming and saloon style bar. Rooms from US$45.

Café Cultura Robles y Reina Victoria; tel: 02 504 078; tel/fax: 02 224 271; email: cafecult@ecuadorexplorer.com; net: www.cafecultura.com. A converted colonial house in Mariscal Sucre. Rooms are spacious and beds sumptuous, finished off with artful neo-traditional decor. There is a café on the ground floor. US$35 for a single or US$45 for a double.

Budget

Villa Nancy Carrion 335 y 6 de Diciembre; tel: 02 563 084; fax: 02 549 657; email: npelaez@pi.pro.ec. Run by a Finnish-Ecuadorian couple, this is an excellent B&B. Rooms are very comfortable and there's a small back garden for relaxing. US$10–15 for a single, US$20 for a double. Nancy is very helpful with travel information.

International Youth Hostel/Centro Hostelling International Pinto 325 y Reina Victoria; tel: 02 543 995; fax: 02 508 221; email: ecuatori@pi.pro.ec. Basically furnished but welcoming. Restaurant, café and laundry. They keep luggage and fax, post and email. From US$9.

Magic Bean Foch 681 y JL Mera; tel: 02 566181; e-mail: bhunt@ecnet.ec; net: www.ecuadorexplorer.com/magicbean/home. Currently the most fashionable hotel/restaurant among young, trendy travellers, with dormitory (US$7 per night) or private (US$10 per night) rooms.

El Cafécito Cordero 1124, just off Reina Victoria; tel: 02 234 862. In a good spot, this comfortable café-hostel is run by friendly Ecuadorians. Useful for travel information and meeting fellow backpackers. Prices start at US$6 per night.

Hostal Eva Luna Pasaje de Roca 405, Calle Roca, between Amazonas y JL Mera; tel: 02 234 799/220 426. Quito's only all-women hostel. Convenient, quiet location, inexpensive, dormitory accommodation. US$9 per night.

Staying in the Old City

The Old City is said to be less secure than the New City, although there are very few incidents in reality. Romantics will enjoy the **Teatro Internacional** (near the theatre at Guayaquil) 1317 y Esmeraldas; tel: 02 216 195. Another mid-range hotel in the same area is the **Real Audencia** Bolívar 220; tel: 02 512 711, while budget travellers should enjoy the **Grand** at Rocafuerte 1001; tel: 02 210 192. The **Hotel Belmont** at Antepara 413 and Vicente Leon, tel: 02 513 247/516 235; fax: 02 516 235, is a block from Plaza San Blas (trolley stop Hermano Miguel). Nice views from the terrace.

Where to eat

For the gourmet or glutton, trencherman or connoisseur, there's no shortage of opportunities to guzzle and quaff in Quito. Virtually any culinary desire can be sated, whether it's for local dishes or for a global range of international cuisine.

One speciality Ecuadorian food is *llapingachos*, a type of cheese and potato rissole accompanied by hot peanut sauce. *Empañadas* are delicious pasties filled with potato and meat, sold hot by street vendors and posh restaurants alike. *Humitas* are made from mashed maize with seasoning, wrapped in maize leaves and steamed. A

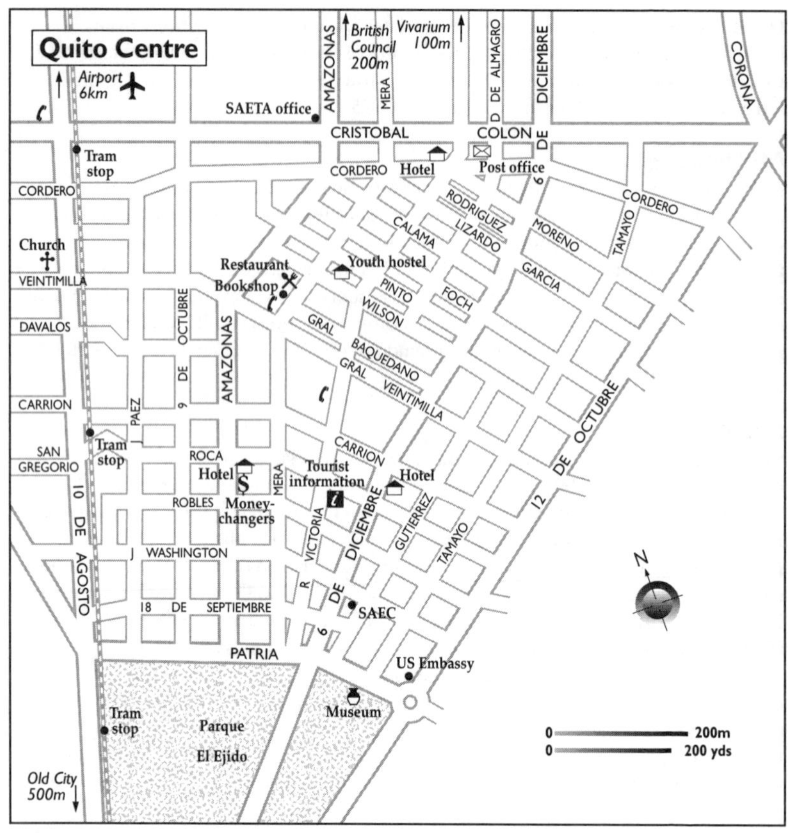

traditional highland dish is *cuy*, roast guinea-pig. *Ceviche* is a popular seafood dish and fresh-caught fish is available daily at the better restaurants.

Note that some restaurants do not accept credit cards even though they have the sticker in their window. Traditional dishes are served at **Rincon La Ronda**. At **La Choza** (1831 Av de 12 de Octubre) decor is interesting and the food is good. The best *ceviche* is at a restaurant of the same name, **Ceviche** (1232 JL Mera). For a variety of seafood dishes, focusing on shrimps, try **Puerto Camaron** (6 de Diciembre 5052 y Granaderos; tel: 250213). **Meson Español** (Carrion 974; tel: 225585) serves Ecuadorian and Spanish meals.

Some very classy restaurants provide foraging for gourmets. Good French food can be found at **La Marmite** (287 Mariano Aguilera) and **La Peche Mignon** (338 Bello Horizonte). Italian food at **El Hornero** (854 Amazonas and Veintemilla) is very good. **La Gritta** (246 Av Santa Maria) is also recommended. For a less expensive Italian meal try **Spaghetteria Romulo y Remo** (JL Mera 1012 y Foch).

The **British Council** (1534 Amazonas) does good vegetarian food. **Superpapa's** (JL Mera 741 y Veintimilla) serves excellent vegetarian food alongside continental or American/English breakfasts. Vegetarians in the Old City can take refuge in **Casa Naturalist** (Lizardo García 630) which has healthy and nicely prepared food.

The **Victoria** (Reina Victoria 530 and Roca) is a British-style pub complete with pub-grub and English beer for less than a dollar a pint. Several other restaurants cater to a more exotic palate including a number of Indian restaurants such as the **Taj Mahal** (San Ignacio 953 y Gonzáles Suárez; tel: 225126) and the **Café Hindú** (Lizardo García 580 y Reina Victoria). Chinese food is very popular; try **Pekin** (197 Bello Horizonte).

Sightseeing

If you have little time you should consider a city tour, to make sure you get the best of what the city has to offer. Most places of historical interest are in the Old City. A half-day itinerary costs US$35–50 per person (excluding lunch), and should include a museum or two, the **Virgen de Quito**, a cathedral and the **Plaza de Independencia**. Visit **Calle de Morales** for examples of early colonial architecture. This is one of Quito's oldest streets, with some of the buildings dating back to the 17th century. This whole area is at the foot of Panecillo Hill so can be combined with a tour of the Virgen.

Plaza de Independencia is a large, open space among the winding cobbled streets of the Old City. Surrounding the plaza are some of the city's most architecturally impressive buildings including the Palacio Municipal (City Hall), Palacio Arzobispal (Archbishop's Palace), Palacio de Gobierno (Presidential Palace) and the Cathedral. From the Plaza de Independencia, you can see Panecillo Hill and Quito's most visible and famous landmark – the **Virgen de Quito**. – said to represent the Virgin of the Americas. Crowned with a circlet of twelve stars, the figure holds a chained dragon under foot. The hill presents a panorama of the Old City and on clear days across to Cotopaxi. You see best from the statue itself, which is hollow and accessible for about US$1 (S/5000).

It's safest to visit by taxi or with organised tours as the route to the top of Panecillo Hill is widely reported to be dangerous.

Museums

Quito boasts literally dozens of fine museums, most of which are in the New City and generally focus on the history and culture of Ecuador. Admission fees are very reasonable. The best and most relevant to visitors to the Amazon are:

Museo Amazónico (Amazon Museum) at 12 de Octubre 1430 y Wilson. Interesting displays from Indian cultural life with the Achuar well-represented and some flora and fauna exhibits. Open Mon–Fri 11.30–12.30 and 13.00–17.00; Sat 11.30–12.30.

Museo de Sciencas y Historia Naturales (Science and Natural History Museum) at Rumipamba 341 and Shyris. Located within La Carolina Park, this small but informative museum has sections on Ecuador's geology, geography and biota. Open Mon–Fri 08.30–13.00, 14.00–16.00; Sat 09.00–13.00; Sun 09.30–14.30. US$1 admission.

Casa de Cultura Ecuatoriana (House of Ecuadorian Culture) at 12 de Octubre and Patria. Near Mariscal Sucre in the New City on the east half of Parque El Ejido, this is Quito's flagship museum. It comprises five museums in one, covering archaeology, ethnology, art, musical instruments, and religious and colonial art. Open Tue–Fri 10.00–18.00; Sat 10.00–14.00.

Vivarium/Gustavo Orcés Fundación Herpetológica (Herpetological Foundation) at Reina 1576 y Santa Maria. Email: fherpeto@pi.pro.ec. An interesting collection of live snakes with several specimens from the Oriente along with caiman, turtles and some poison-dart frogs from South America. Well worth a visit to see some species unlikely to be encountered in the wild. Open Tues–Sat 09.00–13.00 and 14.30–16.00; Sun 11.00–18.00. US$1 admission.

Shopping

Quito is paradise to the keen shopper or souvenir hunter. The city is choc-a-bloc with shops, stalls and kiosks selling clothing, handicrafts, curios, antiques, leather goods, coins, semi-precious stones and any manner of knick-knacks and bric-a-brac. If the timing is right go to Parque El Ejido (at the south end of Amazonas) at the weekend for paintings and woollen goods from Otavalo.

Shopping in the Old City is best around the Avenida 24 de Mayo, worth a visit if only for a look into the local way of life.

Additional information

Several widely available city guides include lists of hotels, restaurants and interesting visitor sites. CETUR (Corporación Ecuatoriana de Turismo; Reina Victoria 514 y Roca; tel: 00 593 2 527 002/074) has an excellent tourist map of Ecuador. The Military Geographical Institute (Calle Paz and Miño; tel: 00 593 2 522 066) also has various maps of Ecuador.

National park permits can be bought from offices in towns near the parks or from INEFAN (Instituto Ecuatoriano Forestal y de Areas Naturales y Vida Silvestre) at the Ministerio de Agricultura y Ganadería, 8th floor Amazonas and Eloy Alfaro; tel: 00 593 2 548 924.

Excursions from Quito

You can leap from the southern to the northern hemisphere at **La Mitad del Mundo** (The Centre of the World) where a conveniently marked line divides the world in two. Located 25km north of Quito, the monument is easily accessible with a day-trip from the city costing US$15–45. Alternatively you can catch a bus to the monument from Av America in the Old City, cost about US$0.25 (S/1000).

Otavalo, some 100km north of Quito, is probably South America's most famous arts and crafts market, despite – or perhaps because of – its popularity with tourists. Local people's characteristic dress sets them apart from non-Otavaleños.

Many goods flow from the Otavalo area to other parts of Ecuador, South America and indeed the world. Woollen goods, many made from alpaca, are good quality and excellent value. If you've had your fill of arts and crafts, you can immerse yourself in local life at the animal market (early to mid-morning), west on Av Calderón in Barrio San Juan, or the produce market (morning to early afternoon) at the west end of J Montalvo, at 31 de Octubre.

Stand-up chefs prepare traditional dishes over charcoal briars, but for more conventional fare several restaurants and hotels are located near the market. VAZCambio on the Plaza de Ponchos changes money if you run out and bargaining is the order of the day.

If you are in Ecuador for more than a day or two, the Otavalo markets should be on your itinerary. Tour operators in Quito have day-trips costing from US$45.

THE ECUADORIAN AMAZON

As yet, no settlement in the Ecuadorian Amazon could properly be considered a city – none has a population over 25,000. Most jungle towns are relatively new, having been established in the 1970s and grown since on account of nearby oil or gold exploration. Many of these rough-and-ready hamlets are not at all geared to tourists and are small, enclosed by jungle and hard to reach.

Many Ecuadorian Amazon towns share common characteristics: dusty streets, poverty-stricken inhabitants and in some cases lack of the most basic amenities. Ecuador's oil riches have come at a high environmental cost. Travellers must endure transit through oil boom towns of stunning ugliness, pervasive pollution and faulty infrastructure, luckily being only stopover points between jungle visits. It seems that none of the oil wealth ever gets back to its place of origin.

Here we describe the most important towns of the Ecuadorian Amazon, starting in the northeast.

Coca (Puerto Francisco de Orellana)

If any town in the Ecuadorian Amazon is a 'must' on the itinerary of the Amazon tourist, it is probably Coca, officially called Puerto Francisco de Orellana. Though other towns are bigger, Coca is nearest to primary rainforest and the region's best lodges. On the upper Napo, some 1,000km upstream from where the river joins the Amazon proper, the town is unimpressive. Built for oilworkers and associated support services, rough-hewn out of the jungle, it consists of cheap concrete buildings bounded by unpaved streets of potholes and puddles, and sidewalks of rubble and rubbish.

Its importance is based on the oil pipeline and drilling activity, the amount of tourism generated by nearby lodges, and its function as a military base. Oil industry activity in the area has conservationists concerned for the condition of the upper Napo, which locals say has already degraded on account of oil spills around its watershed.

Fortunately outside the town are some areas of pristine Amazon rainforest which quickly help you forget the experience of Coca.

Getting there

Getting to Coca is easy enough by air, with at least one flight daily (except Sundays) with TAME direct from Quito. The flight is inexpensive – US$53 one way – but often full so book in advance. The TAME office is opposite Hotel Auca at Napo y V Rocafuerte (tel: 06 881 078).

If you don't want to wait or if you have time for the journey, the easiest and most interesting way to Coca is by bus from Quito (departs from Terminal Terrestre). The 11- to 12-hour journey costs around US$8 (S/35,000) one way and involves a long but spectacular drive over the Andes via Baeza and passing close to Lago Agrio. Buses also connect to Tena to the south.

Where to stay and eat

Most of the accommodation in Coca consists of ultracheap *residencias*, but even the best hotels are within the average budget. Top of the range is **La Misión** (tel: 06 880260), with rooms overlooking the riverfront, away from the central bustle. The hotel has a pool and, for the energetic, a basement nightclub. US$20 (S/90,000) for a room with A/C, US$18 (S/80,000) for one with a fan.

The next best in town is the **Hotel Auca** halfway along the main street on the corner of Napo y García Moreno (tel: 06 880600). With a good restaurant and pretty gardens, including a small aquarium with resident fish and turtles, the Auca is a bargain at US$8 per night. It's also a good place to meet fellow travellers to make up a group for a jungle trip. For about the same price as the Auca, accommodation is better at the **Hostería Amazonas** (Espejo y 12 de Febrero; tel: 06 881 215/880 444, or in Quito; tel: 02 441 533), away from the centre of town on the riverfront.

Eating out in Coca presents a challenge. The cheapest places are dubious from a health standpoint... what you save on meals you might end up spending on medicine. The restaurants in the **Auca** and **La Misión** hotels at US$3–5 for a main meal are quite good. **Papa Dan's,** run by a couple of Americans, serves excellent cocktails from US$2.

Additional information

Opposite the Auca is the office of Ejarsytur (Julio Jarrin, CC Espiral Local 154, J Washington and Amazonas; tel: 06 569852, fax: 06 233245), a local company with trips to the beautiful yet rarely visited Lake Pañacocha, four hours by boat from Coca. Trips take a minimum of three days and cost from US$45/day all inclusive.

Jungle lodges near Coca

La Selva Lodge

La selva means 'the forest' and it is an appropriate name for this beautiful lodge, established in 1986. On the north bank of the Napo River about 100km downriver from Coca, it is reached by company *colectivo* on a three-hour trip. The lodge is close to the northern boundary of Yasuni National Park and is ideal for birdwatchers – over 520 recorded species – and nature-lovers. The surrounding forest is crawling with life and there are thousands of different types of plants – more, according to resident scientists, than anywhere else on earth.

The lodge is well-supported by English-speaking local and US naturalist-guides, essential to lead you along the excellent trails extending for several kilometres into the rainforest beyond the lodge. Itineraries at La Selva combine guided trail walks, and dugout canoe rides as well as specialised birding programmes.

The most popular trail takes you on a short, moderate hike to the forest tower, a wooden structure 40m high reaching up to the massive boughs of a 45m kapok tree. From here you get a parrot's-eye view of unbroken canopy and the chance to spot birds rarely seen at ground level, such as the cobalt-winged parakeet and spangled cotinga.

Hikes on the 'Amazon Light Brigade' leave the main lodge and stay in cabañas at Sloth Camp among beautiful forest, near Mandicocha Lake. The trails are excellent. Go far enough and you get to really unexplored areas. The 'Light Brigade' itinerary features moderate to difficult trekking along forest trails, and sometimes you might be walking for up to eight hours at a stretch so a good level of fitness is needed.

Be sure to take at least one night hike or canoe ride (preferably both). A 'must see' close to La Selva is the parrots' clay lick, on a high exposed bank of the Napo, where thousands of parrots flock across the wall and surrounding vegetation, squabbling for the inscrutable nutrient they crave in the earth. It's best to go in the early morning to appreciate the spectacle.

Current studies at the research station are focusing on the life history of tropical butterflies, and visitors are allowed access to the butterfly-raising facility which houses magnificent pierid and heliconid butterflies.

Guests at the lodge stay in one of 16 double cabins built in native Indian style. The dining room and bar overlook the lake, its tea-dark waters fringed by an unbroken swath of vegetation. The buffet meals are very good, catering admirably to the Western palate. Vegetarians are catered for if advance notice is given. Guests will find La Selva very comfortable, even luxurious by 'rustic Amazon' standards.

Prices start from around US$604 for a four-day programme, including transport to and from Coca. If money is no object, the 'full package' includes two nights at the Hotel Colon in Quito for US$964. The seven-day Light Brigade costs US$1,584 including transfers and hotel in Quito.

You can book a stay at La Selva through Forum Travel (see page 244) in the US. Most Quito tour operators will make reservations for you, or you can just go into La Selva's Quito office (see page 243).

Independent travel to the lodge is possible but the cost of the canoe – US$229 one way – and the day rate of US$169 means it is likely to be cheaper to pre-book the package and a lot less hassle. Arriving in Coca under your own steam will make the trip a little cheaper.

Sacha Lodge

Eighty-five kilometres down the Napo from Coca, Sacha Lodge is rated among the best lodges in the Oriente. The facility is set within 1,500ha of pristine lowland rainforest, which covers a variety of different habitats. Flooded forest, *terra firme*, slopes and level areas are inhabited by tens of thousands of plants. Birdlife, currently recorded at over 500 species, is equally rich.

Excursions feature paddling in hand-hewn canoes with small groups of five or six. Within the lodge grounds a viewing platform made of natural materials overlooks the surrounding forest, and a trail behind the lodge area leads to Sacha's tree tower which gives great views across the rainforest.

You can choose a five-day programme starting Mondays (from Coca), or a three-day option starting Fridays. Book through Explorer Tours in Quito (see page 243) or in the US through Field Guides (see page 40) or Forum Travel (see page 244).

Yuturi Ecotourist Complex and Reserve

Some 180km (106 miles) east of Coca, this is among the largest private preserves in the Oriente, comprising about 2,000ha of fluvial lagoons among primary tropical rainforest with typical lowland fauna.

Four- or five-day programmes feature guided jungle hikes and canoe rides, day and night, as well as early morning birdwatching and visits to the local Samona indigenous communities, followed by a trip to Monkey Island. A great night hike follows a trail around Parahuaco Lake. 'Yuturi' refers to the giant ants (*Paraponera* spp.) found in the area, and you see them come out at night, forming small savage bands. Bird count for the area? About 500.

The complex consists of 15 tastefully decorated cabins and a restaurant on the shores of Cariyuturi, one of a series of lakes connected with the Yuturi River, a tributary of the Napo. Cabins, with comfy mosquito-netted beds and shaded veranda with space for a hammock, face on to a large lawn area. Food is simple but tasty and well-prepared.

All-inclusive prices from Coca are US$288 for three nights, or US$580 for eight nights. Book through Yuturi Tur in Quito (page 243).

Pañacocha Amazon Lodge

On the edge of the beautiful Pañacocha Lake, five hours from Coca by boat, Pañacocha Amazon Lodge consists of several thatched *cabañas* in which guests are housed in small two-person tents. The *cabañas* are located on the shores of a large outlet where Pañacocha Lake enters the Napo.

Four- and five-day trips with biology-trained naturalist-guides cost US$44/day, including transport from Coca. The food is good, mostly brought in from Quito. Book through Ecotours in Quito (page 243).

Nova Rocafuerte

On the border between Peru and Colombia on the banks of the Napo River, this small town marks the frontier between Peru and Ecuador. It can reached by boat from Coca but the boat ride is very long and expensive. The military occasionally fly to the small airstrip but in any case written permission from the military is needed to enter the area due to the border dispute with Peru.

Lago Agrio (Nueva Loja)

Capital of Sucumbios Province, the northernmost Amazon territory and LA of the Oriente, Lago Agrio is among lowland rainforest, with the foothills of the Andes to the west and the Colombian frontier 20km to the north.

The town itself has a languid energy; everyone seems hot and anxious, and on their way to someplace else. With the joint income from oil and tourism, the place prospers, although little of the development seems planned in any way. Lago Agrio is the bona fide oil capital of the Ecuadorian Amazon, with perhaps 15,000 inhabitants and growing fast. On the outskirts of town are huge storage tanks, minor refineries and numerous well-sites with massive burn-offs around the clock. Scattered debris sticks to the oiled road, mixing in after heavy rain to create a greyish porridge-like sludge. No amount of rain washes away the aura of dirt that pervades the town. People-watching is the main entertainment but Lago Agrio is certainly not a place you want to stay in for long.

Despite the grime and tackiness, lots of tourists come here as it is the gateway town for trips to indigenous communities at Dureno and the Cuyabeno Reserve along the Río Aguarico, and the many lodges and cabins near the reserve. Many tour groups head for the Flotel Orellana, a 48-passenger floating hotel.

Getting there

Lago Agrio is easy to reach from Quito. By bus it's a slow but interesting eight- to nine-hour journey (US$5–10) from Quito's Terminal Terrestre. Lago Agrio is three hours from Coca (about 75km, US$4) or nine from Tena (US$8).

TAME fly to Lago Agrio twice a week (Mon and Sat, US$53 one way). The TAME office is at 9 de Octubre y Manabi; tel: 06 830 981/830 982.

Where to stay

Most hotels are along Av Quito, the main road through town where the long-distance buses stop and where you'll find the moneychangers and post office. Phone services are at the EMETEL office (18 de Noviembre and Orellana), about 500m from Av Quito.

Even the best hotels seem beat-up and grungy from the outside, as in the jungle paint peels in no time and even concrete rots. Better hotels include the **Araza** (Av Quito 604; tel: 06 830 223) and **El Cofán** (12 de Febrero y Quito; tel: 06 830 009). The latter is most popular with tour groups and is generally considered the best hotel in town. Rooms with private bath, hot water and fans are US$24 (single) and US$42 (double). The restaurant food is adequate.

Lago Agrio has several economy establishments including the **Hotel Lago Imperial** (Av Quito; tel: 06 830 453; fax: 06 830 460) with nice clean rooms for US$11–18, and the **Machala 2** (Av Colombia 122; tel: 06 830 073) which is safe, welcoming and clean for US$10.

Jungle lodges near Lago Agrio

Grand Cuyabeno Lake Lodge

This lodge has an itinerary leaving Quito for Lago Agrio on a 10.30am flight with TAME. A bus ride from Lago Agrio takes you to the Cuyabeno River followed by a two-hour motorised canoe ride through pristine rainforest to the Grand Cuyabeno Lake Lodge, on an island within the Grand Cuyabeno Lake. You travel on small backwaters, rather than the main rivers that are home to most of the wildlife. Excursions feature trails and canoe trips day and night to admire the forest life and look for nocturnal creatures.

The thatched raised cabins are built of treated wood from outside the reserve and the spacious dining area is simply but adequately furnished. The lodge is at present installing solar power.

Programmes are well-priced at US$350 for two people for four days all inclusive (including transport from Lago Agrio). There is a US$10 park entrance fee for admission to the reserve. Book through Neotropic Turis or Cuyabeno Tours in Quito (page 243).

Trips include excursions to Dureno to meet Cofan Indians and visits to the Siona at Eno and the Secoya at Katecilla. Other itineraries include unique trips along the Quihuaro, Curaray and Cononaco rivers, comprising visits to pristine rainforest and native tribes who have had very little contact with outsiders.

Flotel Orellana

Plying the Río Aguarico within the Lower Cuyabeno Reserve, the Flotel *Orellana* is a purpose-built, three-decked vessel that visits parts of the reserve between Dureno and Sabalo. A motorised canoe takes you to various spots to begin forest hikes with Cofan Indian guides to Cofan communities. Daily briefings and talks on relevant topics are given by naturalist-guides and the generous library has plenty of books, magazines and videos on Amazon natural history.

Travel to the Flotel is from Lago Agrio. The Flotel sleeps 48 in 20 double and two quadruple cabins. Beds are arranged as upper and lower bunks and all cabins are equipped with shower, toilet, hot water and electric fan.

The Flotel has amenities and service as good as any other operation in the Ecuadorian Amazon. A typical four-day trip, all-inclusive from Quito, costs US$700 plus. Bookings can be made through Metropolitan Touring in Quito (page 243) or Amazon Explorers in New Jersey (page 244).

Imuya Camp and Iripari Camp

These are two small lodge-style camps in the Río Aguarico watershed, about four hours downstream from Lago Agrio, which offer unique itineraries for eight days of rainforest trekking in the Río Aguarico area.

The camp is on Imuya Lake, one of several interconnected lakes amongst pristine rainforest that form a huge complex of lakes called Lagartococha. These lakes are home to the majority of large Amazon aquatic fauna including pink dolphin, manatee, paiche, giant catfish and four species of caiman.

Imuya Camp is a small facility, well-designed for environmental friendliness and built of natural materials. Rooms and living areas are comfortable and clean, though not luxurious. The ten double cabins accommodate 20 guests in privacy but showers and bathrooms are shared. Electric light is supplied by solar panels and waste is treated by 'biodigestors'.

Iripari Camp is similar in plan and design to Imuya but in a different habitat. Iripari Lake is surrounded by *terra firme* forest. Here are the Amazon's large terrestrial and arboreal fauna, notably howler monkeys, hundreds of birds, and with luck tapir or even jaguar. The area is rich in birdlife – 550 is the present count.

For an even more adventurous and physically demanding experience, try the Aguarico trekking programmes, within the Cuyabeno Reserve. These take advantage of the 90km of trails and three basic camps. Lodgings are in typical Cofan stilt huts with mattresses, bedding, mosquito nets and towels provided. This is close to real camping, minus the tents.

The itinerary includes one night at both camps, with the first and last night spent at the Aguarico Base Camp, on the banks of the river. This is a very comfortable lodge with 20 double rooms (shared bathrooms). Although used by tourists its primary purpose is to serve as a base for researchers and scientists. Programmes begin in Quito with departures any day of the week except Sunday. Reservations at the camps or for the trekking can be made at Metropolitan Touring in Quito or Amazon Explorers in the US (pages 243, 244).

Native Camp

This basic facility in the southern Cuyabeno Reserve is among outstanding nature, reached by motorised and paddled canoe along the Aguarico River and surrounding tributaries. The company's best trip is a seven-day 'deep jungle' adventure in the Cuyabeno. Based at Nativo Camp, the first night includes an exciting nocturnal hike. You camp for successive nights on Capirona Island and at the Redondococha Lagoon, part of the Lagartococha River system. Four days are spent exploring this remote and utterly unspoiled area by canoe and on foot before you make your way back to civilisation.

Tours are excellent value with all-inclusive prices and transport from US$200pp for five days in the low season to US$860pp for the seven-day deep jungle expedition. Book through Native Life in Quito (page 243).

Dureno and Sabalo

East of Lago Agrio and 21km along a rough road, Dureno is a village with nearby villages of Cofan Indians. In town there are a few basic *residencias*. Guides are available at the Indian village, for about US$20–35 a day. Take a hammock and/or sleeping bag, cooking equipment and food, and be prepared for some very primitive conditions.

About 130km from Dureno, down the Aguarico, is the small village of Sabalo which is inhabited by Cofan. Visitors are eager to meet the tribal chief, American Randy Borman, protagonist in the book *Amazon Stranger* by Mike Tidwell. Read the book to get some idea of the unpaid environmental cost of Amazon's black gold. Borman and his people literally put their lives at risk to halt illegal oil exploration. Due to his efforts, and those of several other concerned groups, the upper Cuyabeno appears safe from further oil drilling for the time being. (See box opposite.)

A number of Quito tour operators run jungle trips to Sabalo and Dureno. If you choose wisely you will no doubt have a total adventure and, if your mind-set is right, a life-changer. In the US, Wilderness Travel (page 244) have several departures a year on eight-day trips to Sabalo, led by Mr Borman. From US$1,995–2,295 (land cost only), these are outstanding trips in the Lower Cuyabeno and proceeds go directly to the Cofan, to conserve the jungle and their way of life.

Tena

One of the more interesting towns of Ecuadorian Amazonia, Tena is at the confluence of the Pano and Tena rivers. On a clear day you can see Volcán Sumaco some 50km to the northeast. Besides the scenery, the town is distinguished by its heritage, stretching back to its founding in 1560. Established by the Spaniards as a remote trading post for trading goods from the rainforest, Tena's isolation made it vulnerable and prone to attack. Sacked several times by forest Indians, its biggest upset came in 1578 when the Quijos tribe, led by Chief Jumandy, rebelled against the colonials and stormed the fledgling town. As always the uprising was swiftly quelled and the town soldiered on.

Today Tena is capital of Napo province with a population of 15,000, who rely primarily on farming and tourism although oil is also important. More tours are operated in this area than in Coca, despite the greater difficulty in getting to pristine natural areas. Although it's not a bad base for jungle trips, the main reason to go to Tena is to get to Misahuallí, a stepping-stone to the jungle, where most tour agencies in this area base their operations.

The town has banks, an EMETEL phone office and post office. For information in Tena you can try the CETUR office on Bolívar.

RANDY BORMAN

Hilary Bradt

Randy Borman was born and raised with the Cofan Indians of Ecuador. His parents were missionaries from the Wychcliffe Bible Translation Society in the United States, and came to Dureno in the 1950s, shortly before Randy was born. There they began the long and laborious process of learning the Cofan language. Unlike some missionaries who maintain a Western lifestyle, the Bormans lived like the Cofans and their children grew up with all the skills of their playmates. By the time he was five, Randy was competent with the blowgun (a skill he was to use effectively in his college days in America, supplementing his frugal diet with squirrel meat) and as a teenager he wrestled with alligators and anacondas. He also learned how to use the products of the forest for medicine, food and shelter. In this respect he is completely Indian. But as a jungle guide, he is all-American, understanding the very different culture and consequent needs of visiting tourists. In his words, 'What I want to emphasise is that this is the real thing. We show visitors what the Indian way of life is all about. Of course we have to make some concessions to comfort and hygiene, but I'd never want to promote the sanitised "Jungle Lodge" type of experience. I'm not putting it down – this type of comfortable accommodation is just right for most tourists – but I do feel that we can offer something unique.'

Randy's tours last from five to seven days. During the short tour, visitors stay in a 'camp' which is reached in six hours by motorised dugout canoe. The emphasis here is on learning about the Indian culture and their use of the rainforest. Colourful birds and monkeys are seen, but for more spectacular wildlife visitors must go another full day downriver where many species of monkey, peccaries, tapir and even ocelot may be found. This is where Randy has established a small Cofan community, away from the increasing spread of Westernisation, where he hopes to maintain the traditional Cofan lifestyle – but using some benefits of civilisation – for as long as possible.

Randy may be contacted at Casilla 6089, Quito, Ecuador; tel/fax: (5932) 437 844.

Getting there

By air, flights from Quito land at the nearest airstrip which is in Shell-Mera, from where you catch a bus to Tena.

By bus the most direct route from Quito uses the northern pass, through Baeza, and turns south at the Lago Agrio turn-off. A dozen buses make the Quito–Tena run each day, departing from Quito's Terminal Terrestre and charging around US$5. Buses also travel from Baños (two hours), Ambato (six hours) and Riobamba (six hours; US$5) to the west. In the Oriente there are regular connections with Coca (six hours; US$6.75) and Lago Agrio (one a day; 10 hours; US$9). Local buses to Misahuallí leave hourly.

Where to stay and eat

Los Yutzos (Augusto Rueda 190; tel: 06 886 458), located on the Río Pano, overlooks the river and is comfortable and immaculate (US$15–20). Many of

Tena's hotels are along 15 de Noviembre in the east of town across the footbridge, or along Olmeda. In the mid-range, **Media Noche** (15 de Noviembre 1125; tel: 06 886 490) is near the long-distance bus terminal and has rooms from US$15. **Hostal Traveler's Lodging** (15 de Noviembre 438; tel: 06 886 372), on the riverfront, is clean and modern, and is run by the reputable tour operator Amarongachi Tours. Its best rooms sport private bathrooms with hot showers. Dormitory accommodation is also available (US$7–15).

If these are too pricey, try the **Villa Belén** (on Jumandy; tel: 06 886 228; US$8), in the El Dorado district; **Jumandy Hotel** (Amazonas y Calderon; US$6), run by the Cerda family, which includes a good breakfast in the price; and **Enmita** (Bolívar 447 y Montalvo; tel: 06 886 253; US$4), which is simple but well-kept and has a café.

There are few places in Tena that meet the standards of a gourmet's palate but several where you can get a decent gut-stuffer for a couple of bucks. Most of the hotels have places to eat and there are some acceptable restaurants. For vegetarian food try **Cositas Ricas** next to the Hostal Traveler's Lodging.

Excursions from Tena

Although some distance from pristine rainforest, Tena is a good place from which to begin exploring the jungle. Tour operators in Quito and Tena will happily offer suggestions, but among the more interesting options is to stay at one of the indigenous communities in the vicinity. One of the most popular is Capirona. Most of the communities have facilities to run jungle tours and, with the available expertise, take you to places and give insights not on the itinerary of larger tour operators.

Excellent jungle trips, including village stays, are sold by **Amarongachi Tours** (15 de Noviembre 432, PO Box 278, Tena; tel: 06 886 372; fax: 06 886 015). This company has tours lasting from one day to a week, including stays at their own jungle cabins.

A short bus ride from Tena are the splendid Jumandy Caves, once off-limits as tribespeople held strong beliefs against exploring them. The caves are fascinating, with vampire bats among their more familiar inhabitants, but look also for bizarre troglodytic insects. The interior is weirdly beautiful, with extensive stalactite formations. A swimming complex complete with restaurant has been built nearby.

Misahuallí

In the south of Napo province, this town (pronounced Mi-sah-oo-ah-yee) is at the confluence of the Napo and Misahuallí rivers. Its former importance as a major access point for the Napo River has declined in recent years and the town's economy is now based almost entirely on tourism.

Although quite small, Misahuallí (population 4,000) is an important centre for jungle trips. Birds and butterflies are plentiful and diverse, but little unspoilt habitat is found near the town and little wildlife. There are few facilities aside from hotels. If you can change money, the exchange rate is very poor, so take plenty of sucres with you.

Getting there

First travel to Tena, by bus or plane, and then on by bus to Misahuallí (see *Tena*, page 259), in total taking seven to eight hours from Quito or five from Baños.

Where to stay and eat

In town, there are plenty of choices for accommodation. Several of the hotels offer a room rate or accommodation packages which include excursions. **Hostal**

LIVING WITH AN INDIGENOUS COMMUNITY

Numerous opportunities exist in Ecuador for the student, researcher or traveller to stay with an Amerindian family in an indigenous community. Programmes vary in cost, facilities and guides. Don't let the price put you off as several of these communities have volunteer programmes that may include room and board for significant discounts.

One indigenous Quechua group based near Coca include night hikes and canoe rides in their village stays. Contact the Amasanga office on the Coca dock.

There are many volunteer opportunities with indigenous communities near Tena, such as the Capirona community. The settlement is reached by bus, canoe and a four-hour trek. You are met in Tena and escorted through the forest by a member of the community.

The Indians' Cooperative appeals to adventurous younger people. The community welcomes volunteers, who would probably benefit more than short-term visitors. Accommodation is simple and food is basic. The programme reflects the community's commitment to preserving the forest and sharing cultural traditions with visitors. Visitors also participate in communal work projects. Tours are operated by the community with benefits shared equally among community members. For information write to: Sr T Tapuy, C Augusto Rueda, PO Box 217, Tena; tel: 06 886288. To stay at Capirona normally costs US$35 a day.

Also near Tena is Amarongachi (tel/fax: 06 886 372; cost US$25) where you can work on a number of community projects, and Ricancie (tel/fax: 06 886 614) based on a group of ten communities who operate programmes lasting from three to six days, for US$25–65 per day depending on group size.

Familia Cerda at 9 de Octubre 356 in Tena is an indigenous family whose tours vary in length. Trips stay at Cabañas Sacharicsina with bedding provided. The guides speak German and some English and focus on the indigenous cultures and plant life of the area.

Cabañas Pimpilala is based in a Quechua community for guests to enjoy two- to four-day programmes (cost US$35 per day). You can meet a shaman to learn about medicinal plants and have an 'esoteric bath' to increase your energy. Deeper forest trips visit Huorani and Auca tribes, travel downriver on native-constructed balsa rafts and include a special excursion for photographers. Three- to eight-day trips are available for US$40–50 per day including bus transport from Quito, river transport, all food and lodging. Based out of Tena, the areas visited include beautiful, unspoiled rivers such as the upper Napo, Cusano, Nushino and Shiripuno. Staff will meet you in Tena if you are expected. More information from Naturgal, in Quito (see page 243).

Dayuma (Calle Principale; tel: 06 584 964) has first-class, by Amazon standards, lodgings in relative comfort for US$20. **Albergue Español** (Juana Arteaga; tel: 06 553 857; fax: 06 584 912) is in a similar class and price bracket.

Cheap favourites include **El Paisano** (near the military guardpost) from US$4 and **Fifty** (near the plaza) for US$2.50. Both have good restaurants, with vegetarian meals for under US$3.

Accommodation in the jungle nearby

There are a number of pleasant jungle lodges in the area. Although none is in truly pristine forest, they are excellent facilities among natural beauty – you rough it in comfort. Among the best is the **Misahuallí Jungle Hotel** (Frente Puerto Misahuallí; tel: 06 520 043; fax: 06 454 146), which consists of lovely cabins on the river-front equipped with electric light and private bath. Cost is around US$60 per night (US$165 for three-day package).

Medium-priced establishments (US$15–25) to choose from include: **Jungle Lodge El Jardin** (on the Minas road; tel: 06 522927) which has cabins in nice surroundings; the **Dayuma Lodge** (tel: 06 584 965) not to be confused with the hotel in town; the **Jungle Lodge Albergue** (tel: 06 553 857) and **Txalaparta** (tel: 06 545 131).

There are a couple of interesting, moderate-level trails close to town along the Río Latas, about 7.5km west of Misahuallí. Walking through dense jungle and some swampy areas for about 5km you reach waterfalls with clear swimming holes nearby. To get to the trail, catch a bus from Misahuallí to the third bridge out of town and then head upriver.

English-speaking freelance guide Luis García specialises in tours from Misahuallí down to Pañacocha (see *Coca*, page 253). He charges US$80 per day including meals and all services and should be advance-booked through the Emerald Forest agency in Quito (page 243).

Jungle lodges near Misahuallí

Cabañas Aliñahui/Butterfly Lodge and Jatun Sacha Biological Station

Jatun Sacha Biological Station is dedicated to rainforest conservation, research and education. The site of 2,000ha was bought in April 1994, a purchase made possible with contributions from individuals and organisations. Proceeds are returned to the community for rainforest purchase and protection, ethnobotanical research, training of naturalist-guides, school programmes and field studies for Ecuadorian biology students.

The research station and cabins are about 10km downriver from Misahuallí, amid virgin tropical rainforest on the upper Napo River. Diversity counts show 100 tree species per acre, 68 amphibian, 358 bird species and 750 butterfly species. Over 100 types of orchids and 14 species of heliconia grow in the vicinity. The station has publications and courses on Amazon ecology and a number of science projects aimed at pure research and applied methods to secure local people's future.

Medicinal plants are cultivated at the experimental nurseries of the Conservation Center for Amazonian Plants. Activities include guided night and day walks, canoe trips, and opportunities for birding, botany, photography, swimming, gold-panning or just plain relaxing. Visits to indigenous communities, hiking in and canoe-ride out, are arranged by prior reservation. Evening education programmes are presented by lodge staff, local shamans, herbalists and visiting scientists. English- and German-speaking guides are available.

The solar-powered station and cabins are on a bluff overlooking the Río Napo. The open-air dining room has well-prepared food with dishes from Ecuador, Europe and the US. Cabañas Aliñahui accommodates up to 45 guests in 26 rooms. These are in a set of eight wooden cabins built with simple modern materials but in traditional form.

Cost is very reasonable with a choice of nine packages. A four-day package costs US$245. Group discounts are available and under-11s pay 60%. Each night at the lodge without excursions costs US$50. For transport, you can either make your own way there or use a US$75 door-to-door service from Quito. This is more expensive than a bus but then you have a knowledgeable driver-guide to make the journey more interesting. To book contact Jatun Sacha's Quito office (page 243).

Yachana Lodge

This well-run lodge in the village of Mondaña is halfway between Misahuallí and Coca on the Río Napo. Access is usually from Misahuallí by two-hour motorised canoe ride downstream. The lodge was planned as part of the Mondaña Project, run by the locally controlled FUNEDESIN Foundation.

The aim of the foundation is to help 30 indigenous communities build schools and a clinic, install running water and sewers and develop sustainable agriculture. They are 'dedicated to finding workable solutions to the dilemmas presented by rainforest preservation and the realities of daily life for the local people'. Projects to date include organic farming education, a schools network and a women's bee-keeping cooperative.

Situated in a swath of 350ha of mixed primary rainforest, secondary forest and agricultural land, the lodge offers comfort in a beautiful setting, with 12km of trails into surrounding greenery. The layout is hotel-style, with plain but clean and comfortable rooms lit by hurricane lamps. The dining area, part of the two-storey central building, contains several tables with simple wooden benches. A hammock hangs outside each cabin, a perfect shady spot to relax for the warm part of day.

Programmes include the usual forest trails and canoe rides with visits to an indigenous community. A nice change is the tour of a nearby coffee plantation, where you watch beans roasting in a clay bowl over an open fire, and a visit to the beehives.

For the cost, Yachana is great value for money and has excellent nature opportunities, although you don't get the trimmings of the more expensive lodges. Price is US$50pp per day with US$10 extra for a private cabin. Children are half price. Make reservations for Yachana through the Quito office (page 243) or at most Quito tour operators.

Baños

Literally on the edge of the Amazon Basin at an elevation of 1,800m, this attractive town is a stopping point for many visitors to central and southern Ecuador on their way between the highlands and the Amazon. Well above the mosquito line and well below the snow line, this is pretty close to Shangri-La. Billed as a 'mountain spa' this town of 20,000 inhabitants has hot springs. Your enjoyment will be greatly enhanced by the luxuriant greenery, spectacular landscape and what seems to be permanently perfect weather.

If you enter the Amazon from Ambato, about 100km south of Quito, heading for Puyo or perhaps Tena, you come through Baños, and it's certainly worth stopping a night or two if you have time.

The accommodation varies from basic to excellent. In the middle price-range are **Hostería Monte Selva** (Halflants; tel: 02 740 566; fax: 02 854685) for US$30–35. One of the best is **Palace Hotel** (Montalvo 20-03; tel: 02 740 470; fax: 02 740 291), from US$25. Less pricey but very nice is **Hostal Isla de Baños** (T Halflants and Montalvo; tel: 02 740 609) for US$12 per night.

If you decide to stay in Baños, there's a lot more to do besides soak in water, such as cycling, horse-riding, or river-rafting. If you're already there and want to take a jungle tour it's a good place to find partners for a group.

One good company based in Baños which offers good value is **Tsantsa Expeditions** (Oriente y Alfaro; tel: 02 740 957, fax: 02 740 717). They run several tours from Baños, starting at US$45 per person per day (including meals) for a group of four with reductions for larger groups. In the same price range, **Rainforestur** (Ambato y Maldonado; tel: 02 740 423; fax: 02 740 743) can arrange tours to lowland Amazonia.

Puyo

Largest town in the Oriente and capital of Pastaza province, Puyo grew around missionary settlements to its present-day population of around 25,000. This uninspiring oil town functions primarily as an oil storage depot, tourist gateway town and trading centre for Indians bringing agricultural and wild-collected forest products to barter for Western goods. The town lies east of the Andes, by a tributary of the Pastaza River which joins the Marañon, some 500km west of Iquitos (in Peru).

There's not much to do in Puyo, unless you're into oil or religion. It has banking facilities, a phone company office and a post office, all within easy walk of the town centre.

Getting there

There are no scheduled commercial flights direct to Puyo, although the military may sometimes have a plane going. Otherwise you can fly to nearby Shell-Mera and take the bus (30 minutes, US$0.25). Buses link Puyo to major cities including Baños (two hours; US$1.75) and Quito (eight hours; US$8), and to several destinations in the Oriente including Tena to the north and Macas to the south. The Terminal Terrestre is in the southwest of town on the road to Baños.

Where to stay and eat

Hostería Turingia (C Marin 294, at Villamil y Orellana; tel: 03 885 180; fax: 03 885 384) is considered the best with small chalets set in an attractive garden; from US$20. **Hostería Safari** (tel: 03 885 465, fax: 03 823 588), about 6.5km along the Tena road, has a restaurant and a pleasant garden. Rooms come with private bath and hot water from US$20. **El Araucano** (C Marin 576; tel: 03 883 834; fax: 03 885227) is well-managed and centrally located charging US$12 per night. **Hotel Chasi** (9 de Octubre; tel: 03 883 059) has rooms at the same price.

For refuelling, your favourite pitstop is going to be the **Europa Internacional** (9 de Octubre and Orellana; tel: 03 885 407), which besides its pretty fine restaurant has nice rooms. The **Rincón Ambateño** (along 29 de Julio) has definite airs and graces and not bad food.

If you have time to spend in Puyo, you can cool off with a swim in the Río Puyo close to the bridge, about 1.7km out of town, and visit the nearby **botanical**

JURI-JURI ECOLOGICAL RESERVE

Located at the headwaters of the Río Curary and Conambo Rivers, Juri-juri is part of a conservation project and offers natural forest pools, waterfalls, trees and animals among pristine tropical rainforest. Accommodations are provided in the native community of Guyacocha. Here you can learn something of the herbalism and language of Amazon Indians.

Access is via Puyo in the southern province of Pastaza. Contact Sergio Gualinga, Juri-juri Ecological Reserve, Casilla 16-01-816, Puyo, Pastaza; tel: 03 795 117; email: j.kneeborn@hcjb.org.ec. In the US P Shriman, Newton Elementary, 16411 Curtis St #111, Detroit, MI 48235-3202; email: ag621@detroit.freenet.org.

gardens (Parque Pedagogico Ethnobotanico; tel: 03 883 001), to look over their collection of herbal plants used by shamans.

Several tour operators sell jungle tours out of Puyo. One of the better ones is **Entsa Tours** (tel: 03 885 500), offering a variety of trips from single-day excursions to week-long jungle tours. A nice day-trip is to the Tropical Forest Reserve (Reserva de Bosque Tropical), about 16km along the Macas road. Lovely trails and a waterfall make for a relaxing but fascinating day. It is possible to stay at simple shelters within the reserve, for just over US$1 per day. Take your own food, cooking equipment and sleeping bag, but you don't need a tent.

Jungle lodges

Kapawi Lodge and Ecological Reserve

Here is Ecuador's closest approach to the perfect 'eco-lodge' and it is a fine attempt by local people to benefit the community while preserving their lands. Begun in 1993, the project is a cooperative venture involving FINAE (Federation of Ecuadorian Achuar Indians). The research facility is a centre for Achuar culture and a biological field station. The aim of the venture is to benefit the Indians and, in 15 years, all the facilities will be owned by the Achuar themselves.

From the lodge on the shores of Kapawi Lake, pink dolphin and giant otters are commonly spotted. Anhinga, horned screamer and hoatzin are usually present as are macaws, parrots and hundreds of other bird species. The mammal life is similarly rich, including sloths, monkeys and several cat species.

A nicely produced booklet has checklists of mammals and some birds and especially interesting information on the Achuar people, with helpful notes on Achuar etiquette; for example, 'The Achuar are very jealous. If you are a man, you should never look directly at a woman's face.' This is useful information as the naturalist guides are Achuar, said to be living encyclopaedias in their knowledge of the forest.

Easy programmes include short hikes (up to three hours) through the forest, or longer treks to visit Achuar communities. Canoe trips are also available with overnight stays in tents. Longer trips last several days, camping in the rainforest with porters carrying food and camping supplies. Some treks include visits to virgin forest and rafting down remote rivers.

Kapawi has 20 double cabins, each with private bathroom, and showers with sun-heated water. Without sacrificing comfort, the native-style buildings are constructed so as to satisfy the purist ecotourist – 'not a single nail was used' claims the company. Seventy-two solar panels, each supplying 75 watts, meet 80% of required power… and the list of ecosensitive considerations goes on.

Two larger central cabins make up the reception area and bar, and a well-stocked library has paperbacks, magazines and books. Guest cabins are located along the shore, so each has a clear view of the lake. Food is tasty, with a combination of international and Ecuadorian dishes, plus the usual array of exotic tropical fruit juices.

Among pristine forest on the Capahuari River, a tributary of the Pastaza, the lodge can only be reached by air, flying first to Shell-Mera and then to Sharamentsa by small plane (5–12 passengers). After landing at Sharamentsa, you take a canoe ride for two hours, until reaching the branch of the Capahuari.

Considering the experience, US$725 for four nights at Kapawi is great value. However, transport is a considerable expense adding about US$200 return from Quito. Reservations for Kapawi can be made through their office in Guayaquil. In the US, specialist birding trips to Kapawi can be booked through Victor Emanuel Nature Tours (page 278) or Field Guides (page 40).

Macas

In the central province of Morona Santiago, Macas is a centre for oil development, with tourism steadily increasing. Founded as a mission station in 1590, the town's religious tradition continued with the completion of its new modern cathedral in 1992. Today its populace, numbering some 10,000, confer upon the town a calm, dignified air. Scenically this is one of the best towns in Ecuadorian Amazon, with the huge Volcán Sangay, still active, smoking in the distance.

At 1,000m altitude in the low hills of the Upano River valley, Macas's climate is very pleasant, typified by balmy days and cool nights.

Getting there and away

Unless you fly from Quito (TAME, three times a week; US$53 one way) getting to Macas is not so pleasant. The bus to Macas from Puyo is a bouncing six-hour ride.

Where to stay and eat

No first-class hotels grace Macas's streets, but there are a few decent *hostales* and *residencias*. All are in a comparable price range, under US$20. **Peñon de Oriente** (Domingo Comín 837 y Amazonas; tel: 07 700 124; fax: 07 700 450; US$5–10) is popular with the few travellers who pass through Macas. Most expensive in town is **Esmeraldas** (Cuenca 6-12 y Soasti; tel: 07 700 160), which is very comfortable and worth US$16 per night.

Eateries in Macas include a Chinese restaurant (near the Peñon). A couple of excellent cafés, both on Amazonas, the **El Jardin** and **Eros**, serve great meals under US$3.

Sucúa

Sucúa is a small town on the banks of the Río Puni, and is the main base for visiting remote tribes of Achuar Indians. The town can be reached from Quito by air or, for the more adventurous (or less hurried), by bus from Quito travelling through Macas. There's not much to it, and virtually nowhere to stay in Sucúa. Your best bet is the new Hostal Karina close by the main street near the plaza.

Not far from Sucúa, about a one-hour (3.5km) walk, is the Río Upano which rewards you with beautiful nature experiences. Morpho butterflies are commonly seen. River-rafting expeditions down the Río Upano are promoted in the US by ROW Expeditions (page 244), and the ride downstream is a spectacular contrast of habitats as you descend from whitewater Class III and IV rapids (V is the roughest) to the level, placid curves typical of lowland rivers.

Zamora

Officially about 10,000, Zamora's population is rather spread out and semi-migratory as many inhabitants belong to recently contacted forest tribes. Principle tribal groups in the area are Achuar and Saraguro Indians.

The southernmost town in the Ecuadorian Amazon, Zamora was founded in 1549 and abandoned shortly after, following repeated attacks by forest tribes. A mission station was set up in 1800 and the town remained a remote backwater, gaining minor importance and not much in size, when in 1953 it was declared provincial capital of the country's southernmost province, Zamora Chinchipe.

Located where the Bombuscara and Zamora rivers meet, the town currently has some tourism but its importance to Ecuador lies with its strategic value in the ongoing border dispute with Peru. Before travelling to this area get up-to-the-minute information.

Anyone with the time and energy to undertake a journey to Zamora is rewarded with nature opportunities in some very remote and pristine rainforest. However, it takes a special outlook on life to appreciate the gold-mining town of Nambija, with its frontier-like atmosphere and brusque inhabitants. South of Zamora is Podocarpus National Park, renowned for its natural beauty and wildlife, and the destination of most visitors to the southern province.

Getting there and away

Several buses travel from Loja in the highlands to Zamora daily, taking four hours for a journey that tests the skills of the most expert Andean bus driver. There is a direct bus from Cuenca taking eight hours. Alternatively you can make your way down the main Amazon road via Tena, Puyo and Macas.

The nearest airstrip to Zamora is in Loja which has daily connections with Quito (US$53 one way).

Where to stay

Facilities are limited to a handful of hotels, none especially noteworthy. The **Internacional Torres** (Francisco de Orellana; tel: 07 605 195) is fairly new for US$20. At the bottom end is **Seyma** (24 de Mayo y Amazonas; tel: 07 605 583). It's simple, clean, welcoming and good value for US$3.50.

NATIONAL PARKS AND WILDLIFE RESERVES

Ecuador has an enviable system of government-run nature reserves and parks, with 25 officially protected areas administered by the government agency INEFAN. Nine are national parks, five of which are in the Amazon watershed.

In all, the protected area covers a fifth of the country. Supplementing government conservation efforts, private organisations run a number of small biological reserves, some of which are in the lowland Oriente.

All national parks charge an admission fee. To get into Amazon national parks, which include all those featured in this section, you have to get permits (US$20) in advance from INEFAN at their offices in towns throughout the Oriente or in Quito. See page 252. The agency's offices also have more detailed information about facilities within the parks.

Cuyabeno Faunistic Reserve

Established to preserve one of the world's biodiversity hotspots, Cuyabeno holds the world record for plant diversity, with 277 tree species recorded from just one hectare. Some 1,275 bird species are recorded from the reserve, 15% of the world's total. The forest canopy is home to toucans, parrots and macaws along with over a hundred hummingbird species and many more equally brilliant relatives.

Protecting 242,162ha of lowland tropical rainforest in the Sucumbios Province of northeastern Ecuador, the reserve is easy to reach, only 318km from Quito. Within the boundaries are significant portions of the watershed of the Aguarico River, a major tributary of the Napo, and hence of the Amazon itself.

The reserve is reached from Lago Agrio where you can get information about transport from the local INEFAN office.

Cayambe-Coca Ecological Reserve

Covering a rectangle approximately 83km by 62km, this is Ecuador's largest reserve and second largest protected area. The reserve straddles the Cordillera Oriental. Protected habitat types include tropical rainforest on the easternmost flank of the park up to sub-tropical forest, cloud forest and *paramo*. Many animals and birds can be spotted along the trails.

Visits to Cayambe-Coca Reserve can be arranged through Quito tour operators, or alternatively you can get off the bus to Lago Agrio close to the Río Reventador and stay in the basic cabins before entering the park to camp. Information is available from INEFAN in Quito and Lago Agrio.

Yasuni National Park

Between the middle Napo and upper Curary rivers, and most readily accessed via Coca, this is the largest preserved area in Ecuador. Its western limit is only 305km from Quito. Recently extended to 970,512ha Yasuni protects an area of typical tropical lowland rainforest flora with riparian vegetation, *várzea* and *terra firme* forest. Important trees are balsa, cercropia, chonta palm, jacaranda – a few among the 700 woody species so far identified. Animal life is correspondingly diverse, comprising some 200 types of mammals and 500 of birds.

Numerous endemic species are found in this biodiversity hotspot, which scientists say is a relic of the Pleistocene age. Within the park, Huaorani (Waorani) Indians inhabit the area, living a traditional lifestyle with little or no impact from the outside, much as they have done for thousands of years. Aside from a few lodges on the edge of the park, tourism is undeveloped, though some camping facilities are available.

Sadly the future of this park is still not secure. In 1991, Conoco were awarded drilling concessions within the boundaries of Yasuni.

Limoncocha Biological Reserve

This reserve protects a small area along the middle Napo River. About 370km from Quito, it is reached via Coca and a 45km boat ride down the Napo. It is relatively small, with 5,300ha, designated primarily to protect Limoncocha Lagoon, an ancient lake within a unique natural area with 347 recorded bird species. Surrounded by *várzea* forest, the lake is lined with semi-aquatic and aquatic plants. Microscopic phytoplankton in the lake's water give it an odd lemon-green colour.

Sumaco National Park

In Napo province to the north of Tena, this is Ecuador's newest national park, established in 1992 to protect a unique ecosystem of lowland rainforest. The protected region encompasses Volcán Sumaco, which rises 3,732m like a giant pimple from an ocean of green, isolated from its Andean siblings to the west. In the upper Napo watershed, the park covers 205,250ha of mixed forest, rivers and an abundance of wildlife including jaguar and spectacled bear.

To get there you need to travel to Baeza, then take the southern fork to Tena and drive 30km south to the Coca turn-off. Head east along here for 21km to Huamaní, a small village where you can hire a guide.

Sangay National Park

Declared a UNESCO World Heritage Site in 1984, this park protects a unique ecosystem in the heart of Ecuador. Rising to 5,230m, Volcán Sangay is Ecuador's second highest active volcano, erupting continuously. More often than not the volcano's peak is cloaked in moist clouds. A look at the stratified vegetation shows that the volcano supports representative habitats of all the major biomes, from tropical rainforest to alpine. Bisecting the park in a west–east direction is the Río Palora, a tributary of the Pastaza.

From the Amazon, the best way to get here is via Macas, to the south and nearest the mountain. You can access the southeast of the park from Macas. Take the road to the village of 9 de Octubre and the park entrance. Ample nature opportunities present themselves along the variety of trails around the volcano's lower reaches.

Podocarpus National Park

Located in the provinces of Loja and Zamora and named after a species of indigenous pine that grows there, Podocarpus National Park is the southernmost of Ecuador's national parks and the hardest to reach. Covering 146,280ha, at elevations over 3,000m, the park protects extensive cloudforest and diverse wildlife. Cloudforest is characterised by an abundance of epiphytes – mainly orchids, ferns and Spanish mosses ('old man's beard'). Aside from endemic trees and epiphytes, many bird species are also found here.

As well as the Andean cock-of-the-rock there's the Amazon umbrella-bird and several endemic hummingbirds. Of mammals, the usual cast of Amazon fauna are present, but if you're very lucky you might see spectacled bear, which are not found in the lowland rainforest.

The nearest INEFAN office is in Loja and issues permits only for day-trips to the park. From Loja you can travel to Villacamba or Zamora. In the US, you can book birding trips to Podocarpus through Field Guides (page 40) or in Quito through several tour operators.

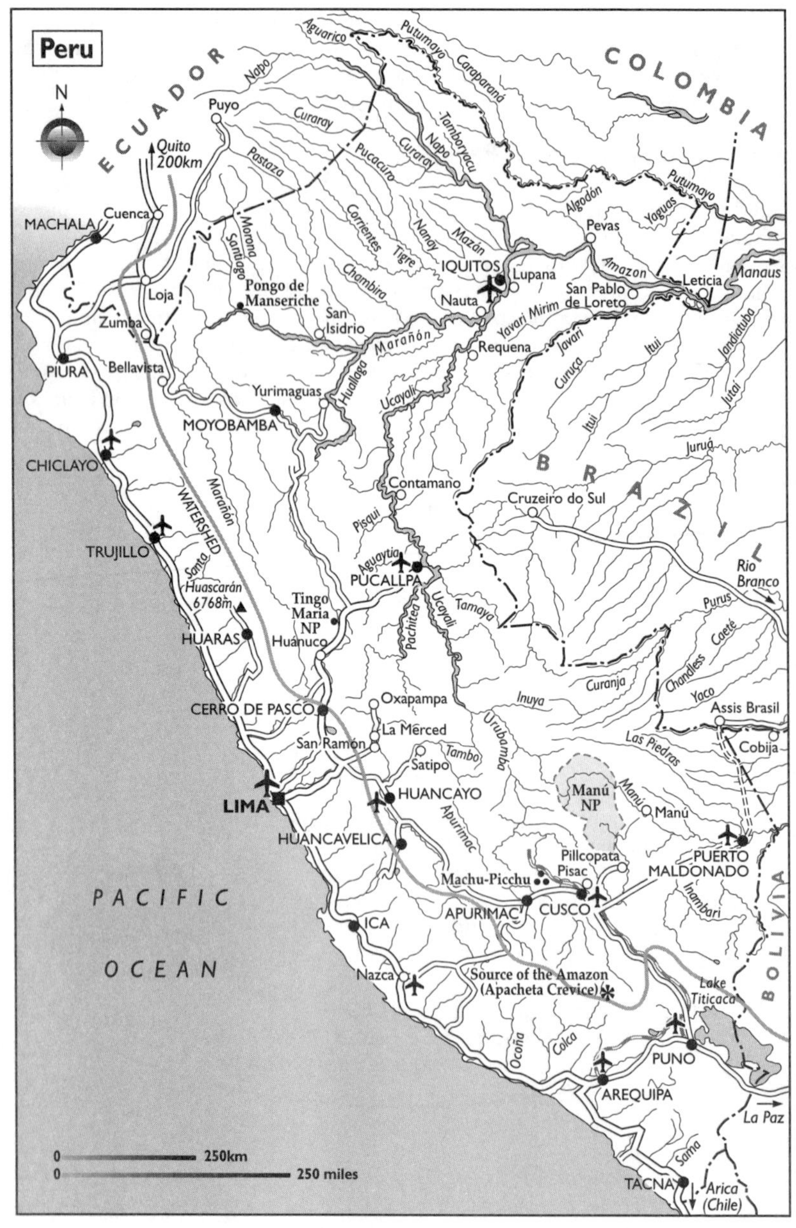

Peru
N
ECUADOR
COLOMBIA
BRAZIL
BOLIVIA
PACIFIC
OCEAN
Quito 200km
Puyo
Cuenca
MACHALA
Loja
Zumba
PIURA
Bellavista
Pongo de Manseriche
San Isidrio
IQUITOS
Lupana
Nauta
Requena
Pevas
San Pablo de Loreto
Leticia
Manaus
Yurimaguas
MOYOBAMBA
CHICLAYO
TRUJILLO
WATERSHED
Contamano
Cruzeiro do Sul
PUCALLPA
Rio Branco
Huascarán 6768m
Tingo Maria NP
HUARAS
Huánuco
CERRO DE PASCO
Oxapampa
La Merced
San Ramón
Satipo
LIMA
HUANCAYO
HUANCAVELICA
Assis Brasil
Cobija
Manú NP
Manú
PUERTO MALDONADO
Pillcopata
Pisac
Machu-Picchu
APURIMAC
CUSCO
ICA
Nazca
Source of the Amazon (Apacheta Crevice)
Lake Titicaca
PUNO
AREQUIPA
La Paz
TACNA
Arica (Chile)
0 250km
0 250 miles
Aguarico
Putumayo
Caraparaná
Napo
Curaray
Pucacuro
Tamboryacu
Pastaza
Morona
Santiago
Corrientes
Tigre
Nanay
Mazán
Chambira
Algodón
Yaguas
Amazon
Marañón
Huallaga
Ucayali
Yavari Mirim
Javari
Curuça
Itui
Jandiatuba
Jutai
Juruá
Pisqui
Aguaytia
Pachitea
Tamaya
Purus
Caeté
Chandless
Curanja
Yaco
Inuya
Urubamba
Las Piedras
Tambo
Apurimac
Inambari
Santa
Ocoña
Colca
Sama

10 Peru

The name 'Peru' conjures images of a remote, far-off land, but Peru is today one of the most popular travel destinations in South America. Yet, despite its popularity, Peru rarely seems overcrowded with tourists, except perhaps at the best-known places like Machu Picchu.

FACTS AND FIGURES

Geography

Peru is a big country, the third largest in South America, covering 1,285,216km^2 (496,225 miles^2) – more than twice the size of Great Britain. It has frontiers with five Amazon countries, a situation which provides Peruvians with a perennial source of worry over ongoing border disputes with Ecuador and tensions with Colombia about possession of the Putumayo and Napo watersheds. To the east is Brazil, while Peru's southeastern border with Bolivia rises from the Amazon Basin to cross Lake Titicaca, the highest navigable lake in the world at an altitude of 4,000m.

The district of Loreto covers most of the lowland rainforest east of the Amazon. Its total area is 348,177km^2, over a quarter Peru's total. Loreto is the biggest department of Peru, with Iquitos as the regional capital. In 1980, Loreto was re-zoned, creating the new department of Ucayali to the south, with Pucallpa as the administrative capital.

BASIC FACTS

Official name República del Perú
Area 1,285,216km^2 (496,225 miles^2)
Population 24 million (1997 est)
Capital Lima
Largest city (population) Lima (c 6.5 million)
Main Amazon city Iquitos
Official language(s) Spanish, Quechua
Date of independence July 28 1821
Major industries petroleum oil, fisheries, lumber, agriculture, mining, tourism
GDP per capita US$1,432
Currency nuevo sol (US$=S/2.5: £1=S/3.90)
Major attractions Machu Picchu, Nazca Lines, Sipán
National holidays Jan 1, Jun 24 & 29, Jul 28 & 29, Aug 30, Oct 8, Nov 1, Dec 8, Dec 25

Rivers

Due to the aridity of the Pacific coast, Peru's main rivers are in the east of the country, flowing into the Amazon Basin. Most important is the Ucayali-Amazon system, rising in the Andes near Arequipa. Formed by the confluence of the Apurímac and Urubamba rivers in east-central Peru, the Ucayali meanders north before heading northeast into the densely forested eastern floodplains. After some 1,500km it joins the Marañón, just below Nauta, some 90km southwest of Iquitos.

Forming part of the Peru–Brazil border, the Río Javari flows northeast for 870km joining the Amazon near Benjamin Constant, Brazil.

The Río Marañón's source lies above Lake Lauricocha, near the town of Huanaco in central Peru, some 250km northeast of Lima. Also, here in the windswept Andes, merely 150km from Peru's Pacific coast, the source of the Amazon (see page 4) flows northwest across high plateaux some 3,500m in altitude and joins the Marañón before it carves a deep canyon through the lower Andean ranges. Some 1,416km in total length, it passes through a series of unnavigable falls and rapids before plunging to the floodplains.

A major tributary is the Huallaga River which joins the Marañón as it winds eastward before it meets the Ucayali. A major river in itself, the Ucayali follows a course that splits into the Huallagu-Urubamba system. The Huallagu River reaches high into the central Andes, to a point once considered a source of the Amazon. Lacking this distinction, but nevertheless a magnificent river, the Urubamba originates near Cusco.

East of the headwaters of the Urubamba, the Madre de Dios flows eastwards across the Bolivian border, eventually joining the Madeira River, a tributary of the Amazon which enters the mainstream 100km east of Manaus.

The Napo River is among the best known of Peru's rivers. It was first explored by Orellana in 1541. Originating high in the Ecuadorian Andes, it drops eastwards toward the Peruvian border, turning south before joining the Amazon some 80km downstream from Iquitos. The 885km Napo is mostly navigable and used for transport.

The Putumayo River flows through densely forested lowlands, forming the frontier between Colombia and Peru.

Climate

Peru's complex variety of climate zones can be broadly defined by three geographical areas: the narrow, dry coastal plain to the west; the cool arid highlands of the Andes; and the moist tropical lowland rainforest occupying the east of the country.

The coast is a cool desert, with temperatures of 19–22°C. Rainfall is very low; however, humid winter fog (*garúa*) from March to October provides some moisture. In the mountains temperatures range between 1–14°C but vary greatly. Rainfall is heaviest in the eastern forests at between 1,900–3,200mm per year.

On an irregular cycle of five to seven years, Peru's climate suffers an about-turn, caused by the poorly understood El Niño phenomenon. Typically, the coastal areas are deluged with rain, while lowland forests experience plunging temperatures and prolonged drought afflicts the southern highlands. Severe El Niños cause extensive ecological and economic damage. Bird and fish populations are particularly affected. The El Niño event of 1997–98 has been the strongest ever recorded, causing heavy flooding in Peru and several other South American countries.

Flora and fauna

At the last count, Peru's diverse habitats support a total of 361 mammal species. In the selva and lower sierra, carnivores are well-represented by the jaguar, puma, ocelot and margay. Primate diversity is among the highest of any country. Peru is home to 1,800 bird species, about one-fifth of the world's total. Hummingbird diversity reaches its highest in the cloudforests of the eastern Andean slopes.

The rainforests in particular have an exceedingly rich invertebrate fauna. Peru has more butterfly species than any other country, around 4,000 species, and at least 20,000 moths. Peru's flora is astounding with at least 1,300 orchids.

Land use

Owing to unfavourable climate, unsuitable terrain or poor soils, only 3% of land is considered arable. Tropical forest is subject to the traditional 'slash-and-burn' technique. Main crops are manioc, bananas, maize and beans. The land is beginning to feel the impact of growing populations and industrial activity but, even today, forest still covers over half the country, most of it pristine rainforest in the Peruvian Amazon.

Most land in the Amazon departments of Loreto and Ucayali remains pristine virgin rainforest. Along rivers and floodplains fertile soils offer better conditions for settled agriculture. In areas above floodplains, traditional slash-and-burn methods are used. On a small scale, this need not damage the forest as a whole but, as ever larger areas are cleared to provide for growing populations, it becomes harder for the forest to regenerate.

In some places, large-scale lumber and mining operations have caused local environmental damage, but not on the scale seen in parts of Brazil. Peruvians increasingly appreciate rainforest as a renewable natural resource that will look after itself if not over-stressed.

The people

Population and ethnic groups

With a population of 24 million Peru's population density is fairly low at 18 people per km^2. In Loreto the population is around 700,000 with a density about one tenth that of the country as a whole. Over one fifth of Peru's inhabitants lives in the capital, Lima – South America's fifth most populous city. Most of Peru's population is urban following large-scale migration to cities during the 1950s.

Native Indians comprise about half of the population. As well as Witoto Indians, visitors are likely to encounter the Bora and Yagua along the mainstream around Iquitos. Matses and Marubo Indians live along the upper Río Javari and remain largely unassimilated. In the uplands, despite considerable Western influence, Shipobo continue their way of life in many ways unchanged.

Catholicism is the main religion, practised by nearly everyone. In remote areas, the Christian rites are overlain with remnants of tribal religions.

Languages

Spanish is the dominant language throughout Peru. Quechua is the second language with Aymara still spoken in isolated pockets. Witotoan is the most widely spoken Amazon Indian language but over 300 other languages and dialects are found in Peru's lowland rainforests.

Education

The country has a strong emphasis on learning and supports more than 30 universities nationwide, including one in Iquitos. Lima boasts South America's oldest university, the National University in Lima (founded in 1551). Schooling is compulsory where practicable and for children aged 6–15 no fees are charged.

As Lima controls the purse strings and educational policy, Amazonian schools end up implementing national schemes totally inappropriate for life in the rainforest. This policy has led to absurd situations where jungle-dwelling children are taught to programme a computer, despite the nearest computer being hundreds of miles away.

Culture

Western art flourishes alongside pre-Columbian creations of pottery, weaving and metalwork. Peru's Chavin, Chimu, Moche and Inca cultures produced brilliant works in gold, and their pottery is stunning in its expressivity. Modern-day folk arts are continued by rainforest Indians, whose basketwork and pottery are of excellent quality.

Soccer is the national sport and is played with rare devotion and enthusiasm. World Cup matches are followed avidly, even in the middle of the jungle, and more so when Peru's team is playing. Virtually every village and town has a soccer pitch, most matches being played on Sundays.

A brief history

Pre-history

To start at the beginning, archaeological finds confirm human habitation of coastal areas of Peru dating back at least 12,000 and possibly even 20,000 years. These populations were primarily hunter-gatherers but soon developed sophisticated civilisations with advanced agriculture and architecture.

By 1,000BC, several advanced civilisations had developed along the central and northern coastal valleys near present-day Chiclayo and Trujillo. Other significant peoples were the Nazca, Tiahuanaco, Chavín and Chimú. Little is known about the settlement of the Amazon Basin at this time as organic remains quickly rot in the humid climate.

In the coastal and mountain areas, the Inca Empire consolidated and unified the region. By the time the Spaniards arrived in the early 1500s, their empire included all of present-day Peru, Bolivia and Ecuador, and large parts of northern Argentina and Chile. The population of the Inca empire has been at around 12 million.

The conquest

Because of the strategic importance of Inca strongholds at Cusco and Lima, Peru saw early and aggressive incursions by the Spaniards. Deception, betrayal, murder and pillage were all in a day's work for the conquistador, firm in the belief that being non-Christians, the Indians could be disposed of at God's will.

Setting up base in San Miguel on Peru's northern coast, Pizarro crossed the Andes to meet the Inca emperor Atahualpa, recently victorious in a civil war against his half-brother Huascar. Pizarro and Atahualpa met in Cajamarca.

Ridiculously outnumbered with a force of just 150 against Atahualpa's 30,000, Pizarro arrested the Inca when he refused fealty to the Spanish crown, demanding payment in gold for his release. With the ransom paid Pizarro promptly executed Atahualpa for the murder of his brother Huascar and installed Huascar's brother, Manco Capac, as puppet Inca. By late 1533 the conquistadors had occupied the Inca capital of Cusco.

Colonialism

Manco Capac proved less pliable than the Spanish expected and in 1536 led an Indian rebellion which inevitably was mercilessly crushed. The Spaniards squabbled over the spoils of war, and this led to the assassination and execution of several of the conquistadors.

The Spanish crown attempted to introduce the *encomienda* system to placate the warring conquistadors, but nearly a decade passed before a sense of calm prevailed, with the 1568–81 administration of Viceroy Francisco de Toledo which established protocols for administering the Indian population. The system allowed local chiefs to rule over their traditional lands in return for paying tribute and providing free labour.

Independence

Nationalism and notions of freedom from imperialist powers were born early in Peru's colonial era. After several uprisings, in which numerous natives were slaughtered in brutal reprisals, José de San Martin, helped by pan-national hero Simón Bolívar, led a final revolt and in July 1821 Peru declared independence from Spain.

The 20th century

In 1922, Peru's claim to the Putumayo region was put to rest as it ceded the curious wedge-shaped portion that gives Colombia access to the Amazon River. Peru made no such concession to Ecuador and in 1942 the Rio de Janeiro Treaty established the present-day border, the southern portion of which was not ratified and remains a disputed area experiencing sporadic clashes.

The 1933 constitution granted power to the president and congress but military juntas ruled the country for three decades. In 1963, Fernando Belaúnde was freely elected but was overthrown by an army coup in 1968. Military rule lasted until 1980 when the army returned Peru to civilians, but economic problems founded in the policies of the military junta worsened soon after Belaúnde's re-election.

The situation reached its lowest point during the office of Alan García Perez, president from 1985 to 1990. The economic and social disaster engendered by García's socialist experiment eventually forced Peru to default on its massive foreign debt. The World Bank froze aid to Peru and imposed international boycotts on goods and arms. Sanctions had a devastating effect on the economy. Inflation spiralled sky-high, peaking at 2,600% per annum in 1989. Unemployment afflicted two-thirds of the working population in some cities and crime shot up. Travel and foreign investment plummeted.

Under such awful conditions a number of revolutionary organisations emerged, mostly bent on violent overthrow of the regime. Best known of these is Sendero Luminoso (Shining Path).

In 1991 the current president, Alberto Fujimori, was democratically elected. One of Fujimori's top priorities was to eliminate the Shining Path. He took emergency powers in April 1992, dissolved Congress, suspended the constitution and restricted civil liberties. In late 1992, the rebel leader, Abimael Guzmán, was caught and sentenced to life imprisonment. Since then guerrilla activity has significantly declined and ceased to be a threat to daily life. A national referendum approved a new constitution in October 1993 which promotes free enterprise and democracy.

Since then Fujimori has turned the economy around. Today, Peru has a lower national debt and is repaying foreign loans. Unlike previous rulers, Fujimori has not neglected the Amazon. His government provided every village with a motorised boat – vastly improving local trade and communications. Cocaine trafficking, once a serious problem, is now heavily suppressed. Conservation laws are more strictly enforced, allowing the return of wildlife, and tourism has reached all-time highs. Around Iquitos and surrounding districts, the economy grows steadily.

Peru hit the international headlines in December 1996 when a faction of the Tupac Amaru Revolutionary Movement took control of the Japanese ambassador's residence and held hostages, demanding the release of political prisoners. The episode ended violently in April 1997 when special forces stormed the building, killing all the guerrillas and saving all but one of the hostages.

Today Peru's constitutional government has an elected president who is also head of state and commander of the military. Presidential decrees and draft bills are reviewed by a cabinet and prime minister appointed by the president.

Money

Peru's monetary unit is the nueve solé which replaced the inti. The new currency has remained relatively stable since introduction in 1992.

US dollars are widely accepted but you will need to change money once you are in the country. Take plenty of small-denomination bills – US$75 to US$150 in ones and fives – for tips and buying handicrafts.

Take another US$200 in US$10 and US$20 bills if you are a keen souvenir-hunter. US dollars are readily accepted in most shops but travellers' cheques and credit cards are not. Bring a credit card for emergencies.

Hotel rooms in the Peruvian Amazon are expensive. Budget US$45–50 if you are travelling independently and staying at the expensive hotels, US$25–30 for the cheaper ones.

As in other South American countries, locals in Peru will not accept notes with even the tiniest tear, so make sure all the dollar bills you take with you are in good condition.

Highlights

For birdwatchers and nature-lovers there are opportunities throughout the Peruvian Amazon. Staying at jungle lodges, taking trips on tourist river-boats and walking guided jungle tours are the best ways to make the most of these opportunities in as much ease and comfort as possible in the middle of the rainforest.

For those who just want to 'do the Amazon' and travel to interesting parts of the Amazon Basin, Peru has three basic options available.

From Iquitos, for an easy tour of the area, you can take the round trip down the mainstream to Leticia, and perhaps visit the ACEER canopy walkway, in ten days or so (about US$150 per day). Another popular route takes you southwest from Iquitos, up the Ucayali to Pucallpa and then to Lima by plane or bus (10–14 days, US$200 per day). Various tour operators offer trips lasting several days up remote tributaries in the area south of Iquitos. From Lima or Machu Picchu/Cusco, the nearest place to visit the Amazon is Manú National Park and Tambopata Reserve, which protect parts of the remote and pristine Madre de Dios region. Abundant diverse flora and fauna cloak rolling hills along snaking river valleys in habitat quite distinct from the lowland rainforest around Iquitos (and most of the Amazon).

Besides the rainforest areas covered in this guide, visitors come to experience the rich pre-Columbian history west of the Andes, in particular Machu Picchu and the Nazca Lines. Other such impressive sites as Chan Chan and Sipán, on the northwest coast, offer further evidence of the sophistication of pre-Columbian civilisations. You could spend several months in Peru and still feel as if you've left important bits out.

Tour operators

The international airport at Iquitos makes the city a very popular destination and many travel opportunities can get booked up well in advance. There are plenty of tour operators who will just reserve jungle lodges or organise independent trips.

In Peru

Amazonas Explorer PO Box 722, Cusco, Peru; fax: 00 58 84 236826; email: amazonasexplorer@compuserve.com; net: www.amazonas-explorer. Has whitewater rafting expeditions in the headwaters of the Amazon near Cusco on the Apurimac and Tambopata rivers. Also have expeditions down the Tuichi in Bolivia.
Explorama Lodges Av La Marina #340, PO Box 446, Iquitos, Loreto, Peru; tel: 094 25 2530; fax: 094 25 2533; email: info@explorama.com; net: www.explorama.com. For direct information and bookings for Explorama Lodges. (Also have an office in the US).
Rainforest Expeditions Galeón 120, San Borja, Lima, Peru; tel: 01 421 8347; fax: 01 421 8183; email: rainfore@amauta.rcp.net.pe; net: www.perunature.co. Organise trips to Manú National Park.

In the US

For riverboats and cruises

Amazon Tours and Cruises 8700 W Flagler, Ste 190, Miami, FL 33174; tel: 800 423 2791; fax 305 227 1880. Own and operate several riverboats out of Iquitos.
Eco Summer Expeditions 936 Peace Portal Dr, PO Box 8014-20, Blaine, WA 98230; tel: 800 465 8884; fax: 604 669 3244.
International Expeditions, Inc One Environs Park, Helena, AL 35080; tel: 205 428 1700/800 633 4734; fax: 205 428 1714; email: intlexp@aol.com; net: www.ietravel.com/intexp. Can arrange group and independent trips throughout the Iquitos.
National Wildlife Federation Expeditions 8925 Leesburg Pike, Vienna, VA 22184; tel: 800 606 9563. Take bookings for riverboat cruises from Iquitos.
Nature Expeditions International 6400 E El Dorado Circle, Ste 210, Tuscon, AZ 85715; tel: 520 721 6712/800 869 0639; fax: 520 721 6719; email: naturexp@aol.com; net: www.naturexp.com.

For jungle lodges

EcoExpeditions, Inc 13031 SW112 St, Miami, FL 33186; tel: 305 387 8713; fax: 305 387 8717; email: ecoexpedit@aol.com. Organise bookings for Peru's most ecofriendly Lodge Yacumama.
Explorations Inc 27655 Kent Rd, Bonita Springs, FL 33923; tel: 941 992 9660/800 446 9660; fax: 941 992 7666. Organise biologist-led trips to Explorama facilities and the canopy walkway near Iquitos.
Explorers 197 Wall St W, Long Branch, NJ 07764; tel: 908 870 0223/800 631 5650; fax: 908 870 0278. Take bookings for Explorama.
Sol International 13780 SW 56 St, Ste 107, Miami, FL 33175; tel: 800 765 5657. Takes bookings for the remote Tambo Amazonico Camp upstream from Iquitos.

For Manú National Park and Tambopata

Forum Travel International 91 Gregory Lane, #21 Pleasant Hill, CA 94523; tel: 510 671 2900; fax: 510 671 2993; email: forum@ix.netcom.com; net: www.ten-io.com/forumtravel. Arrange trips to Manú National Park.
Holbrook Travel 3540 NW 13 Street, Gainesville, FL 32609; tel: 800 858 0999; fax: 352 371 3710. Has travel itineraries for Manú National Park.

Volunteer programmes

Oceanic Society Expeditions Fort Mason Center, Building E, San Francisco, CA 94123; tel: 415 441 1106/800 326 7491; fax: 415 474 3395. Carry out a volunteer programme researching pink dolphins in the Pacaya-Samiria Reserve.
Rainforest Health Project PO Box 624, Deer River, MN 56636; tel: 218 246 9555/800 870 8325; fax: 218 246 9674; email: amazon@northernnet.com. Combine travel and volunteer opportunities while bringing basic health to the Pacayu-Samiria National Reserve.

Birding

Audubon Society Nature Odysseys 700 Broadway, New York NY 10003; tel: 212 979 3066. Offer specialist birding tours to Peru.
Tours International, Inc 12750 Briar Forest Dr, Ste 720, Houston, TX 77077; tel: 281 293 0809/800 247 7965; fax: 281 589 0870; email: toursintl@aol.com; net: www.astanet.com/get/toursintl. If you fancy celebrating the dawn of the millennium on the Amazon give this company a call.
Victor Emanuel Nature Tours PO Box 33008, Austin, TX 78764; tel: 512 328 5221/800 328 8368; fax: 512 328 2919; email: VENTBIRD@aol.com; net: www.VENTBIRD.com. Provide top quality birding trips to Manú National Park.

In the UK

Most of the tour operators mentioned in *Chapter Two* (page 41) have trips to the Peruvian Amazon.

Guerba Expeditions Wessex House, 40 Station Rd, Westbury, Wiltshire, BA13 3JN; 01373 826 661; fax: 01373 858 351. Organise weekly trips to Explorama Lodges.

GETTING THERE AND AWAY

Many towns in the Peruvian Amazon are quite isolated from the outside world. No railroads or highways connect most settlements or villages in the region. Indeed, Iquitos, a city of 600,000, is accessible only by ship or aeroplane. Iquitos and several other towns have airports or at least a landing strip.

By air

From the US

The easiest way to reach Lima is by air, with most Western visitors flying in from Miami, a competitive route served by several US and South American airlines. Prices vary but expect to pay US$600 return for a regular airfare. Several other US cities have direct flights to Lima. Los Angeles to Lima is operated by AeroPerú (stopover in Mexico City).

From the US direct flights to Iquitos, Peru's largest 'concrete island' in the sea of green, go from Miami. There is one flight a week non-stop with AeroPerú (around US$500). It is the only city between Manaus and South American western coastal cities to have direct flights from the US. There are rumours that American Airlines have plans to start flying this route.

From Europe

Several European airlines offer flights to Lima including KLM, Lufthansa, Iberia and Alitalia. If you join one of the European flights you travel through its European capital. Flights from London with American Airlines are routed through Miami. From Miami you can fly to Lima or direct to Iquitos. Prices start from £530 return rising to £680 in the high season. Most flights include at least one stopover so check with your travel agent to see how many South American cities you stop over at before reaching your final destination.

Overland

By road

Connections with neighbouring countries are in the highlands. To the north the frontier with Ecuador is served by regular buses. To the south the options divide, taking you south into the arid deserts of northern Chile – far away from the Amazon – or east to Bolivia crossing the frontier near to Lake Titicaca.

Land crossings to Brazil and Bolivia are possible from Puerto Maldonado in southern Peru or from Pucallpa in central Peru. Both are considered arduous or adventurous depending on your perspective.

By boat

The only other feasible route to the upper Amazon around Iquitos is by boat from Brazil. You can sail westwards from Brazil, upstream from the mouth of the river at Belém or Manaus. Both these cities are served by international flights from Miami. The long river route to Iquitos from Manaus is possible by local riverboat but requires the traveller to have a suitable budget, strong constitution and flexible schedule. A couple of tourist riverboats run portions of this route with schedules that include side-trips for nature viewing. Luxury passenger liners and expedition ships turn around at Iquitos after coming all the way up the Amazon.

The cheapest option is by local riverboat. Rough conditions and worries about safety and health discourage most travellers. You provide your own hammock and manoeuvre around sleeping people, dogs and chickens, doing your best to dodge the swinging bunches of bananas. Meals may be included in the price, but even if they are you will need to take your own food to supplement the basic fare on offer. Using local cargo riverboats may be faster and better for getting from A to B but leaves no time for sightseeing beyond brief stops at a few ports and villages. You can book short passages between villages but this often works out to be quite expensive.

A trip from Manaus to Iquitos on local river transport will take a minimum of ten days. Progress will depend on local schedules, flood conditions and the vessel's reliability and crew. The only certainty is that it takes less time to go downstream, with the current in your favour, than upstream.

Another route, starting in Puerto Asís, in southern Colombia on the border with Ecuador, is down the Putumayo River into Brazil, doubling back along the mainstream into Leticia and then upstream to Iquitos. This route takes you through undisturbed virgin lowland rainforest into remote areas far from civilisation; perfect if you want to get well off the beaten tourist path and are willing to put up with rough accommodation, mediocre food and unreliable conveyances.

A good compromise between local banana boats and luxury liners is to take a tourist standard riverboat fitted out to accommodate the foreign traveller. Oriented toward natural history, these trips run between Iquitos and Leticia. Down the Amazon mainstream, the voyage to Leticia takes three days. Tourist riverboats have a naturalist-guide aboard and make stops along remote pristine tributaries for birding and hiking, and may stop at night for night hikes or canoe rides.

Customs and immigration

You need a **passport** valid for six months from the time of travel. US citizens and nationals of European Union countries do not need a visa to travel to Peru unless staying for more than 60 days. When entering Peru you fill in an immigration form which has a carbon copy that you must keep until you leave. Keep it with your passport as you need it to get out of the country.

If you are travelling by boat into Peru through Leticia, you'll find the Peruvian Consulate next to the Hotel Anaconda.

It is important to keep US$20–50 in hard currency to pay airport departure taxes. The international departure tax was increased to US$25 in 1996. Departure tax for internal flights is US$3. If you are visiting several different places the costs do mount up.

Getting around

By bus

Long-distance buses are cheap and reliable, but bus stations are picking grounds for casual thieves so you should buy your tickets in advance, without the distraction of bags and backpacks. There is no central long-distance terminal in Lima so you have to find the company's terminal and office. Ormeño is the biggest bus company (Carlos Zavala Iquitos 177; tel: 01 275679), with routes to major cities along the coast. TEPSA (Paseo de la República 129; tel: 01 731233) is the best company in Lima but also the most expensive. It has fewer routes than Ormeño and costs more, but you'll appreciate the extra comfort. There is no way to get to the Iquitos area of the Amazon by bus. However, you can start a trip in Pucallpa on the upper Marañón, accessible on Empresa Transmar and Transportes León de Huánaco bus companies, both on 1500 block of Plaza 28 de Julio (US$35 one way).

By air

Domestic air connections in Peru are good, so you can fly direct from Lima to destinations in the Amazon, including Iquitos, for about US$100 return. Faucett make the trip and AeroPerú has daily flights in rather old B737s between Lima and Iquitos (US$65 one way). Get a window seat as the flight treats you to spectacular views of the snow-capped Andes.

To get to Manú or Tambopata in southern Peru you can fly AeroPerú from Lima to Puerto Maldonado (US$95 one way). If these flights are full or cancelled due to bad weather, fly to Cusco (US$60 one way) with AeroPerú and Faucett and complete the remainder of the journey overland.

Iquitos is served by private air carriers and military flights (available to civilians) from Tabatinga on the Colombia-Brazil border and Manaus in Brazil.

AeroPerú have a TUMI Airpass which serves Iquitos, Pucallpa, Puerto Maldonado and Cusco. The routes must be specified in advance but dates can be changed. Single airtickets and the airpass can be bought and booked at most travel agents in Lima and throughout Peru. Airlines and tour operators constantly change schedules and routes. Tariffs suddenly increase without notice. Planning in advance should minimise disappointments.

By boat

One option to reach the mainstream is by river-raft down rapids of the Apurimac River, a tributary of the Ucayali, on waters that originate from the Amazon's source high in the Peruvian Andes. The ride starts on a series of rapids and proceeds through lowland forest, joining the Ucayali and ending up in Iquitos.

The rapidly growing capital of Ucayali department, Pucallpa, is a good point to join the mainstream if you want to complete a full-length navigation of the Amazon. No tourist boats serve Pucallpa so you will have to catch a cargo boat, hang your hammock and relax in style.

COMMUNICATIONS

Mail

Postal services in Peru are slow, inefficient and expensive. It will cost around a dollar (S/2.5) to send a postcard back home, more for a letter. Make sure you have local currency, as post offices do not accept dollars or travellers' cheques. Letters and postcards often go astray. There are many reports of incoming and outgoing packages being lost or opened.

Phone, fax and email

Most hotels in cities have phone services but international calls can be expensive due to hotel surcharges. To get the best rate you should go to the Telecom offices, present in all cities and most towns and villages. Most public telephones are equipped to take phone cards bought from Telecom offices.

Fax machines are available at most hotels and tour operator offices, but charges may be high (up to US$5 per page). Many Amazon tour operators have email facilities: the easiest way to communicate with outside countries.

The international country code for Peru is 51.

Television and radio

Public television and radio emit a stale supply of government-run programming – mostly upbeat news and current affairs with some sports, mostly soccer. Picture quality is correspondingly bad. The best TV – programming and reception – is on cable or satellite, which only the best hotels have. For news and sports addicts, international channels such as CNN and ESPN are available on cable.

Newspapers

The country's main papers are all produced in Lima, the most prestigious of which is *El Tiempo* with right-wing views. Also published in Lima is *El Libro*, said to cater for a more centrist viewpoint. A number of regional newspapers are published for local consumption and focus largely on rural concerns. For the best unbiased news, reviews and commentary, the magazine *Caretas* is really on the ball.

LIMA

Lima is dusty, badly polluted, overpopulated and full of life… just how you'd expect a South American city to be. Lima presents a paradox. From afar, gleaming office blocks declare the city's commercial prowess. Closer-up, in the old plaza, you see a heritage of rich colonial architecture. Yet away from the centre small children and their families pick their way through piles of garbage, scraping together a living from the rubbish of over six million people. Lima has some very plush districts, but outside the centre it seems to be one huge shanty-town.

Lima's proximity to the ocean and the influence of the cool current makes winters (May to October) cool and humid, with sea-fog blanketing the city most mornings. Exacerbated by pollution this leads to the *garúa* white sky that hangs over Lima for most of the day. During summer, most days are sunny and rain is infrequent as Lima is on the leeward side of the Andes, and so protected from prevailing moisture-laden airflows from the Amazon. Temperatures average 18°C (65°F) year-round.

At the airport

The Jorge Chávez International Airport is 12km from the centre of town, 16km from Miraflores. There are buses to town from the street outside, but unless you're confident where you are going it is probably best to get a taxi, which costs US$10–15.

The airport has a couple of banks, a few restaurants, a long-distance telephone office and a left luggage service.

City transport

Within Lima, buses are a good way to get around if you are on a tight budget and have little or no luggage. During rush hour they are crowded and busy – not always a comfortable experience for those unused to South American bus travel. Most local

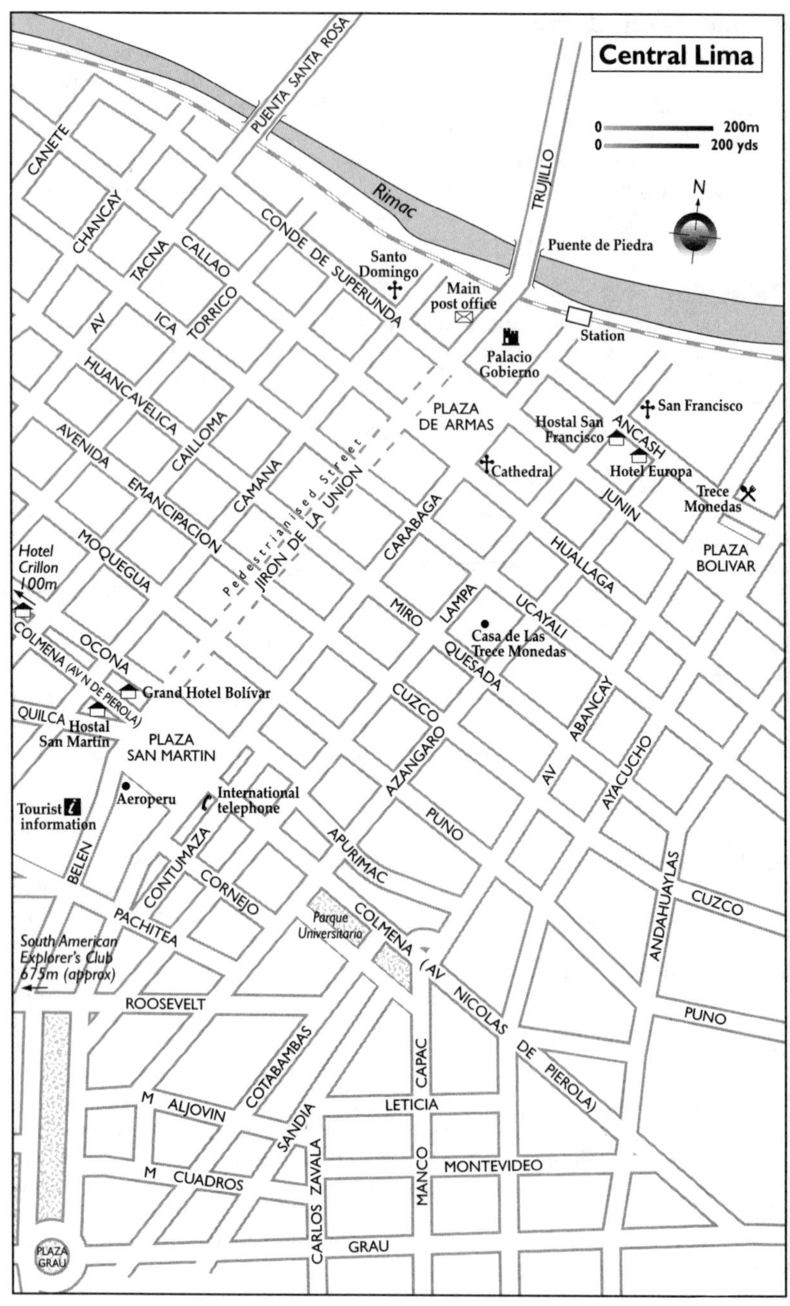

buses have signs indicating their destination and, although there is a system of bus stops, you don't need to use them; just flag the bus down. Within the city, a bus trip costs US$0.25–1.00 depending on how far you go.

Taxis are numerous, cheap and very often the easiest way to get around. As usual, agree the fare before you start the journey.

Where to stay

There are lots of options for accommodation in Lima; choose a place with good security and start by staying in a safe part of the city. Those on a low budget should set aside US$15 per day as survival money, while US$25 a day makes life more comfortable and luxuries affordable. For the best five-star hotels, consider US$100 per day as a starting point.

The hotels mentioned here are all in the historic centre of the city, within walking distance of most city museums and historic sites. There are numerous hotels – and some of the nicest – in the quiet residential district of Miraflores but you will have to travel into the centre if you want to do any sightseeing.

Grand Hotel Bolívar Plaza San Martín; tel: 00 51 1 4272305; fax: 00 51 1 4287674. Near the top of the Lima hotel scale, this is a sumptuous building erected in the 1920s on one of Lima's liveliest plazas. Tour operators rarely use it because of the risk from pickpockets in the area, but with caution there's no reason not to enjoy a stay at this resplendent fossil. Luxury does not come cheap and rooms in the Bolívar start at US$125 per person.

Hotel Crillon Av Nicolas Pierola 849; tel: 00 51 1 4283290. Another luxury hotel, this is arguably better than the Bolívar but does not quite have the atmosphere of faded glory. If cuisine is important the Crillon is a good choice on account of its 'Restaurant With a View', said to be among the city's best for traditional Peruvian food. US$95 per night, single.

Hostal San Martín Av Nicolas Pierola 882 Piso 2. Right on Plaza San Martín near the Bolívar, this hotel is a good deal at US$25pp.

Residencial Francia Samuel Velarde 185. About the same price and standard as the San Martín, the Francia offers comfortable rooms which are affordable for the average budget. It's in a nice quiet area in a spot away from the crowded hotels of central Lima. Bed & breakfast US$22pp.

Hostal San Francsico Ancash 340. Popular with young people and a great place to meet fellow travellers, here is a good budget option in a good location close to the Plaza de Armas. US$5 and up. If it's full the **Hotel Europa** is almost next door.

Youth Hostel Av Casimiro Ulloa 328, Miraflores; tel: 00 51 1 4465488. With pleasant rooms, this is a good place to get travel information or meet companions. It's the cheapest place to stay in the Miraflores district which has plenty of amenities nearby. Members pay US$5 for a dormitory bed. Non-members can stay for a couple of dollars extra.

Where to eat

As Peru's capital, Lima offers a wide variety of places to eat out. Most tourist-standard hotels have acceptable food but, for a change of diet, you can sample some of the local dishes or try a unique variation on a more familiar food. Restaurants are listed in *El Tiempo* and *El Libro,* the latter of which gives ratings, but ask locals and you might find a hidden culinary treasure.

Among the best seafood restaurants is the expensive **La Costa Verde** (Barranquito Beach in Barranco district). The restaurant is set in pleasant tropical gardens and serves the best lobster in Lima. For local dishes, try **Manos Morenos** (Av Conquistadores 887) where the *criollo* food is highly recommended, or the **Hotel Crillon** (Av Nicolas Pierola 849) for *anticuchos*. For international food, many locals recommend the very classy **Carlin** in Miraflores (Av La Paz 646). It is invariably busy and rather expensive.

Criollo and international food is excellent, but somewhat expensive, at **Las Trece Monedas** (Ancash 536), set in a historic colonial mansion and popular for formal dining. For a quieter pace try one of the Chinese restaurants on a weekday, in particular **Chifa Lung Fung** (Av Rep Panama 3165, in San Isidro). The restaurant has tranquil interior gardens and some of the best – and more expensive – Chinese food in Lima. For vegetarian food, **Govinda's** (Av Callao 480) has wholesome dishes at unbeatable prices and **Natur** (Moquega 132) is recommended. Also try **Vrinda Café** (Av Javier Prado 185), which serves fruit with live yogurt – very good if you've had an upset stomach.

For cerviche, try the excellent but expensive **Al Fresco** in San Isidro, Miraflores or the old town. Or the cheaper but very good **Segundo Muelle Pescados y Mariscos** (Av Pezet 1455, San Isidro) where the owner speaks good English.

Additional information in Lima

The government tourist office in Lima was closed some years ago so your best bet is to head for the South American Explorer's Club (SAEC) at República de Portugal 146, in the Breña district; tel/fax: 00 51 1 425 0142. For members they have up-to-date information on travel conditions to the Amazon lowlands and throughout the country and elsewhere in South America. Open Mon–Fri 09.30–17.00. See page 44.

What to see

To orient yourself in Lima, the huge Plaza de Armas is a good place to start. It's well-served by buses, every taxi-driver knows where it is and it's popular with the local citizens. Most notably it's used by a few homeless people who live in or around the square. In the centre of the plaza is a huge intricately cast bronze fountain dating from 1650. The plaza is bordered by several important buildings. The **Palacio de Gobierno**, built in the 1920s, is Peru's seat of government. Rebuilt in the same period, the **Archbishop's Palace** with wooden balconies ranks as an impressive example of period architecture. The **Hotel Simón Bolívar**, a 19th-century relic itself, is an architectural treasure. Also on the plaza is **Lima Cathedral** – the city's oldest colonial building with the earliest parts dating from 1555. Holding the remains of the founder of Lima, Francisco Pizarro, the cathedral is located on the southeastern side of Plaza de Armas, and is open 10.00–13.00 and 14.00–17.00.

Historically the most significant of Lima's churches is the church of **San Francisco**, the most intact to date from early colonial times. The building itself is a beautiful mix of styles, and for the morbidly inclined the catacombs hold some 70,000 bodies. On the corner of Lampa and Ancash, hours are 10.00–12.45 and 15.00–17.30 daily, admission US$3.50. One block west of the Government Palace, on the first block of Camaná, is **Santo Domingo**. The building is constructed on land Pizarro granted to his friar in 1535. Work began five years later but was not completed until 1599. Now resplendent within, redecorated in the 17th and 18th centuries, this church is notable for its two towers that have resisted earthquakes for some 400 years. It opens 08.00-13.00 and 16.00–18.00, admission US$0.50.

Museums

For the capital of a country of such impressive cultural and natural resources, Lima is endowed with a suitable number and variety of museums. Most museums open 09.00–17.00 Tue–Sat. Admission charges range from nothing to a few dollars.

Museo de Antropología y Arqueología (Museum of Anthropology and Archaeology), Plaza Bolívar in Pueblo Libre. Ancient Peruvian cultures including the Moche, Chimú and Inca are represented with over 80,000 artefacts including fabric, jewels and gold. Excellent! Opens 10.00.

Museo del Oro (Gold Museum), Av de Molina 1110. One of South America's most impressive collections of pre-Columbian goldwork and jewellery, yet still privately owned. Most metalwork pre-dates the Inca. If you only have time to see one museum in Lima this is the best option. It's difficult to reach without patience and a good understanding of Lima's bus system, so take a taxi. Opens 12.00.
Museo de Historia Natural (Museum of Natural History), Av Arenales 1250, Aptdo 14-034, at the University of San Marcos (Universidad Nacional Mayor de San Marcos). An especially impressive insect collection although the mammal and bird specimens are somewhat moth-eaten. Closes 15.30 (13.00 on Sat).
Museo Amano, off Av Santa Cruz, Miraflores. Very good for textiles and culture.

Parque las Leyendas

On the road to Callao (catch bus No.75 from Jirón Azangaro), this is Lima's zoo, with fauna from Peru's three major habitat types: tropical forest, arid coast and cold highlands.

Shopping

In the comfortable district of Miraflores, at Benavides 305, there are state-supported local artesanias, small handicraft and cottage industries, selling crafts and clothing from around the country. In San Isidrom there is a similar set-up at Jorge Basadre 610. Woollen and leather goods are excellent value and very good quality, as is hand-made silver and gold jewellery.

Several markets in central Lima offer a wider selection and cheaper prices than Miraflores souvenir shops, but you'll have to search the markets hard to match the store quality. For souvenirs, the best place is the Artisans' Market, on Avenida de la Marina, from block 600 onwards.

THE PERUVIAN AMAZON

For visitors to the Amazon Basin the city of Iquitos in the northwest of the country's Amazon gives you direct access to the great river's mainstream. Opportunities for travel are numerous. Several jungle lodges with trails and a canopy walkway are within easy access of Iquitos which has direct international flights to and from Miami. Tourist riverboats travel the main channel upstream and downstream from Iquitos.

Cargo boats from Pucallpa in the central Amazon travel through Iquitos to the triple frontier with Colombia and Brazil and further downstream to Manaus. In the southern Amazon, Manú National Park and Tambopata Reserve give access to two of the planet's last great wildernesses.

Iquitos: gateway to the jungle

Most people have never heard of Iquitos despite its being a major port, the fourth largest city in Peru and the third largest on the Amazon after Belém and Manaus. Named after a local Indian tribe, Iquitos is a bizarre place – brash and noisy at first but, like a root from some parasitic jungle plant, it grows on you. Iquitos amazes, delights and shocks. The only large town for hundreds of miles, it is an important commercial centre for locals and retains a cosmopolitan feel from its large influx of foreign visitors and status as a busy port. This is the starting point for thousands of visitors every year on rainforest ecotours.

Hotels are pleasant, and shopping for souvenirs, food and travel supplies is good. Iquitos has an international airport and dock facilities. The sprawling city covers most of a large rise at the confluence of the Amazon and Nanay rivers. To the west is a large island (Padre Isla) about 16km long and 8km wide, in the mainstream of the Amazon River.

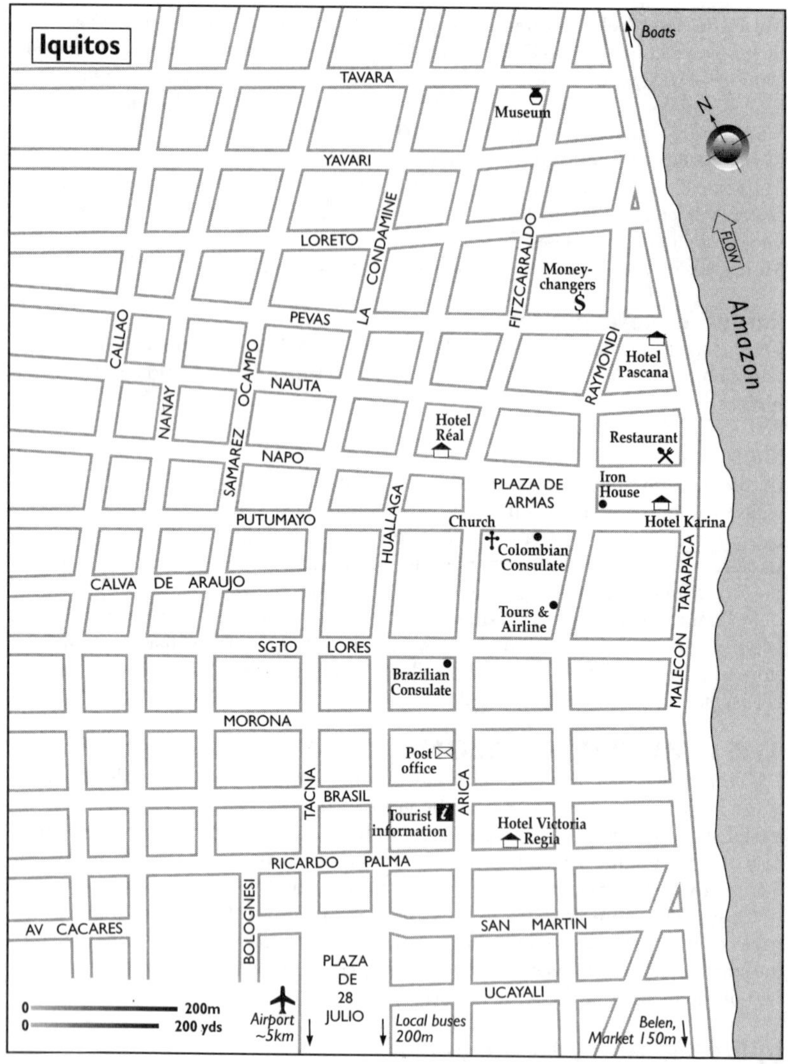

Iquitos is remarkable for being inaccessible by road – the only way in and out is by air or ship – and for being the world's most inland river port and naval base. Ships must sail upstream from the mouth of the Amazon for 3,701km (2,300 miles) to reach the city, yet it is only just over halfway along the river's length with another 2,848km to the Amazon's source. Despite its location Iquitos is only 115m above sea level.

Founded as the Jesuit mission of Santa Maria de Iquitos in the 1750s, the town remained a remote backwater trading post. During the rubber boom it grew rapidly from the 1880s to the early 1890s when huge fortunes were made almost overnight. Many of the city's buildings reflect the prosperity of the past, with fine tile and iron work imported from Europe

The discovery of oil has led the latest boom which, combined with ecotourism, has seen the city's population rise rapidly to 600,000 compared with 250,000 in the 1970s.

Iquitos' other economic activities include small ship-building, fisheries and lumber. Most important of the exported woods are mahogany and Spanish cedar. Jute is exported for use in fibre products. Fish exports include varieties for fish markets in Lima and dozens of species coveted by aquarists the world over. Worth several million dollars annually, natural rubber is still exported from Iquitos.

Getting around

In Iquitos there are taxis and buses some of which look as if they were rescued from a junkyard! There are also three-wheeled motorised rickshaws, or *motocarros*. Basically small Japanese motorcycles with two-wheel cabs on the back, *motocarros* are the best option for speedy cheap travel around the city but not recommended for long distances or carrying a lot of luggage.

Agree on a price before you get in. The usual cost is one solé (about US$0.40) for a ride in the city, or four to five solés for an hour's ride around the city.

Inadequate spending on roads, local drivers' etiquette and the natural elements conspire to make the trip a fairground ride – you weave here and there, bone-jarringly bouncing in your seat, deafened by shouts and blasts on the horn exchanged between irate drivers. It's fun!

Where to stay

Most people stay in Iquitos just a night or two, in transit to one of the many jungle lodges or riverboats in the area. Conditions are simple compared with those of modern Western hotels, but acceptable in most places, and surprisingly good considering that you are in the middle of the Amazon jungle, hundreds of miles from the nearest Hilton or Sheraton.

Hotel Victoria Regia 252 Calle Ricardo Palma. The city's most expensive hotel and air-conditioned throughout. Rooms are small but there is a good restaurant and an indoor swimming pool. Quiet, with courteous, English-speaking staff. A double room sleeping two is US$90 per person, while a single costs US$95. Travel with a partner!

Hotel Dorado Napo and Arica. Slightly lower in standard than the Regia, but rooms all have air-conditioning. The top floor houses the restaurant, while on the ground floor there's a small swimming pool. Price US$75 (single), US$90 (double).

Hotel Réal Malécon Tarapaca. In the best location in town – right on the river front – the building is a bit dilapidated but a relic of the colonial era, with expansive hallways and wide staircases. Staff are helpful but speak little or no English. Street noise can be irritating so get a room on the other side. Rooms are basic but reasonably clean and comfortable. US$80 for a double and US$65 for a single which includes continental breakfast.

Hostal Karina Putumayo 467. Favoured by backpackers and budget travellers, this welcoming hotel offers good value for simple rooms with fan and private bathrooms. US$7.50.

Hostal Excelsior Arica 379. Another clean and friendly budget hotel. From US$7.50 per night.

Hotel La Pascana Pevas 133. Clean and inexpensive, this is one of the better budget hotels. US$7.

Mi Selva Hostal Napo 701. A relatively new budget hotel with extensive tropical gardens. Rooms include double bed, cable TV and fans. Easy walk to the riverfront. US$5.

Where to eat

There's no need to book at the informal **El Meson** (Napo 116), half a block from the river. Caiman and turtle (both wild) are on the menu but have become very rare locally; better options are the delicious fish and manioc dishes. A meal costs US$5–10 and there is no charge for the proclaimed *ambienta distinguido* which makes this a popular meeting place for locals and foreigners alike.

Further down Napo and to the right on the river front is **Le Malecon**, across the street from the Hotel Réal. Built on stilts over the steep river bank, the restaurant juts out over the river with great views at sunset. The food is less remarkable, for the price: US$5–10 for a good evening meal.

Best value in town, with cheap and excellent lunch menus, is a small area down Ricardo Palmo, about four blocks from Prospero, which houses a number of small restaurants including **El Callefan** and **La Paulina**, serving huge portions of fish, yuca and chonta (palm hearts) for less than US$3.

Bread, canned foods, vegetables and fish can be bought at markets and supermarkets on every other street corner throughout Iquitos. Especially recommended are cookies, pastries, cake and drinks at the Iron House on Plaza de Armas. Just ask around for **La Casa Ferro**. You cannot mistake the place.

Ariburger, also called 'Gringolandia', is a hamburger joint on the edge of Plaza de Armas. There are some Chinese restaurants around Plaza de 28 Julio near the miniature locomotive.

What to see

The notable lack of vehicles lends a slower rhythm to Iquitos which rarely displays the frenetic pace typical of most Latin American cities. The **waterfront** and **market** are ideal for taking in the mood of the locals. At the city market, just about everything is sold from fluorescent pink plastic shoes and bootleg tapes to unidentifiable animal parts awaiting the pot.

The market can be exhausting if you want quiet and relaxation. A riot of sights, sounds and smells, it is crowded, noisy, smelly and dirty, but well worth it. For insight into the lives of local people, this is the best one or two hours you can spend. The main market, Belen, is high on a ridge, well above maximum flood levels.

Near to the market is the Floating City or **Ciudad Flotante** of several thousand shacks, hovels and huts that float, rising and falling with the river. From the market you get a good view of this Floating City, at the bottom of a long flight of dilapidated concrete stairs which takes you from Belen down to the shanty town. Watch out for robbers here, especially at night.

Close by the waterfront is the Plaza de Armas. On one corner of the square is the **Iron House**, a two-storey edifice with iron panels painted silver-grey supposedly designed by Gustav Eiffel and imported to the city during rubber-boom days. A wealthy rubber baron bought it after the Paris Exposition of 1886 and had it shipped in pieces and reassembled. Locals say the building was destined for Quito in Ecuador, but there was a mix-up of names... and, as they say, the rest is history. The Iron House is a nice spot to take in the atmosphere of the city, with coffee and cake for about US$2.

The **aquarium** at 151 Sn Martin has literally dozens of fish species from the Amazon, many of which owner Antonio F Wong Mendez exports all over the world. Even if not an avid pisciphile, you might enjoy getting some idea of the amazing variety of fish inhabiting the waters of the region.

The **miniature locomotive**, on display in Plaza de 28 Julio was once used to haul raw rubber from deep jungle to the river where it could be floated to market for sale. In contrast, the same square has a very modern church, with striking geometric architecture and a bold mosaic. An appropriate last spot to visit in Iquitos is the **city cemetery** for the interesting tombstones and mausoleums.

Shopping

There is some good shopping in Iquitos besides the usual jungle souvenirs which you can buy or barter for on the river and at Indian villages. If you leave souvenir buying until towards the end of your trip you'll have a better idea of what you want.

Good buys are tonics prepared from plant roots infused in rum, known as *siete rais* (seven roots) and *viente-un rais* (twenty-one roots), the numbers signifying how many different plants are used to make the brew. Vendors in Belen market claim the tonics have aphrodisiac or healing properties. In any case they make a fine aperitif or nightcap, a great party drink or an exotic flavouring for desserts and cakes. A large bottle of *seite rais* is US$5–7, a small bottle US$3–5.

These local herbalists, both men and women, are a priceless asset, with a lifetime of knowledge on the properties of hundreds or thousands of plants. They have a remedy for practically anything, from a sore throat or upset tummy (recommended: *yerba luisa*, lemon grass) to skin tumours (*uña degato*)!

In town shops and impromptu outdoor exhibitions you will see local artists' paintings, usually rainforest river scenes, in colourful oils and ridiculously inexpensive. Some of the old skills are alive and well, and pottery is one of them. A good place to observe the age-old 'coil-method' in action – nothing to do with contraception – is at Indiana, a village half an hour by boat downriver from Iquitos. Another bargain is beautiful and delicately painted Shipobo Indian pottery – not widely available outside Iquitos, unless one travels the 650km (384 miles) halfway up the Ucayali River to Pucallpa, to the tribe's territory. This is the centre of the Shipobo tribe who make some of the best pottery in the region, renowned for its thin sides and traditional geometric designs of compelling mystical quality.

In Iquitos, many shops sell Shipobo pottery, but if you have time it is worth looking around for a store with a good selection, where prices will tend to be lower. Reasonable-quality hand-made Shipobo pottery such as plates, bowls and vases can be obtained for US$5–20. Larger pieces are available for US$100 or more.

Excursions from Iquitos

Some 15km (9 miles) outside Iquitos is a small zoo, **Quistacocha Park**, with a variety of local wildlife in various conditions of health, mostly bad. An expensive tour of the zoo taking around two hours can be arranged with local tour operators. You can slash the cost if you catch a bus there (US$2), from Abato on the block between Aguirre and Grau.

An excellent, though expensive, activity is to take a **fly-over of Iquitos** in a small plane. You will need half a day. This is a must if you can afford it as the 30-minute flight is spectacular, takes you over the town and allows you to grasp the true size and complexity of the river here. Although the flight takes you over some impressive woodland it's not 'virgin' as there is no primary rainforest in the vicinity. The cost for a party of four is US$85. Flights can be booked with most Iquitos tour operators.

For most visitors, Iquitos is just a start- or end- point for their river cruise or jungle trip. If you are taking the tourist riverboat the next largest city you visit is Leticia, on the Colombia–Brazil border.

River transport

Given the near complete absence of ground transport in the jungle, to move beyond the city one must use rivers, which in the Amazon serve as highways.

Local riverboats

The local 'banana' boats that run between Leticia and Iquitos and to various other cities in the western Amazon are sometimes the only option to get from one city to another. Local riverboats are the cheapest way to travel on the river but often break down, are usually overloaded and very occasionally sink.

If you are undeterred, a local riverboat captain will charge US$30–45 from Leticia to Iquitos, meals included. Food aboard the local vessels is rarely inspiring so take your own if you'd prefer, in which case ask for a discount off the ticket price. If you have to eat aboard, take along extra food in case you are served up something really unpalatable. You can usually buy canned goods and bread, crackers, fruit and sweets at small villages and towns en route.

You'll need a hammock, which you can buy in Iquitos (or Leticia). Take the upper deck to get the best sleep. Even then, you can end up being squeezed between other hammocks, so try to get an outside spot, which is cooler. On some boats cabins are available but they tend to be hot and cramped. It's safe enough but keep an eye on your belongings. Some boats have locked storage for belongings, so you don't have to stand guard all day.

On riverboats, you do not take any nature excursions, the object being simply to get from A to B. However, most vessels make frequent stops and, if you're not in a hurry, these are a great chance to see how local people live. Also, as you will not be with a big group, locals are less intimidated and more inclined to have a chat. A trip on a local riverboat can be the highlight of a visit to the Amazon.

Small local boats and canoes

Locals use small long-boats, or *colectivos*, in the same way we use cars. *Colectivos* serve as private transport or river-taxis. These are long wooden canoes, 6–12m long, fitted with a palm thatch roof and small outboard motor. They are often loaded with vast quantities of bananas or firewood, bicycles and chickens – or even another canoe! – stacked on top. When the canoe is fully loaded, the water-line can be within a hand's-breadth of its gunwales, making you wonder how the vessel goes anywhere without being swamped.

With the exception of tour company *colectivos* (which lack the chickens and intimate waterline), this mode of locomotion is not highly recommended. Only the young, adventurous and budget-minded should seriously consider it. If you are into this, you can just head down to the dock area in Iquitos and ask around.

Express taxi-boats

For rapid transit between cities there is a small but well-run fleet of 16-seater express taxi-boats. These dash from Iquitos to Leticia in under a day. However, speed and not comfort is emphasised. Seating only is provided, with little room for luggage and no toilet facilities aboard. Taking around twelve hours, the trip costs about US$50.

Book with Expresso Turística Loreto in Iquitos (Loreto 151, Raymondi 384; tel: 238652) or Leticia (Avenida Marechal Mattel).

Jungle towns

Independent travellers who arrive in Iquitos must plan on taking a couple of days to organise a jungle trip of their liking. With the exception of river cruises and the ACEER walkway, most tour operators offer itineraries that include jungle treks, canoe trips, night-time excursions to look for caiman and stays at lodges which range from simple to comfortable. Visit as many different companies as possible and beware hyperbole and potential rip-offs.

Towns and villages downstream from Iquitos

Indiana

This is a typical Amazon riverside settlement, inhabited by about 1,000 people. Founded by Franciscan missionaries, it is some 16km downriver from Iquitos on the mainstream. Visits are by *colectivo* boat from Iquitos (around US$5 one way). Indiana is a mission town with schools and a small hospital where laid-back residents drape across concrete verandas, eyeing strangers in town while engaged in basketry or pottery. Several trails lead to the Napo River, the most attractive being the Pipa Trail, close to the Explorama Inn.

Sapo Playa

In this small village daily life is typical of that seen everywhere on the Amazon. About 50 miles downriver of Iquitos on the Amazon mainstream, close by Explorama Lodge, is not on the itinerary of official tours but guests at Explorama often visit. It is not served by the tourist riverboats but river-taxis can stop here.

Francisco de Orellana

This settlement, although hardly a village, should be visited by all those travelling in Orellana's footsteps. The village is notable only for its name and the monument after which it is named, in tribute to the Spanish conquistador who made the first recorded journey down the full length of the river. He is said to have landed at this spot. Located on the banks of the Amazon mainstream, the village is close by Sapo Playa and Explorama Lodge. From these places, it is easily reached on foot, or by canoe during high water. There is nowhere for travellers to stay overnight.

Pevas

Pevas (or Pebas), at the mouth of the Ampiyacú River, about a third of the way from Iquitos to Leticia, is said to be the oldest European settlement in the western Amazon. The earliest date associated with the town is 1542 and it is easy to believe that Pevas has changed little since its founding. Its population remains small, around 2,000, but it's a popular stop with the tourist riverboats because of its proximity to native Indian settlements.

The riverfront path is lined with houses built on stilts that sit in the water when it is high. On a sunny day, townsfolk spread gutted fish on bamboo platforms to dry. The method effectively preserves the fish as ultraviolet from the sun naturally irradiates the food. The taste seems unaffected – much of the fish served at restaurants in the Amazon is preserved this way.

From the riverfront, you need to climb up a long, long flight of steps to reach the town square where a large *calliandra* tree stands in the plaza providing welcome shade and, at the right season, a snack as its large purple flowers are edible. You eat the mass of feathery anthers – quite tangy and refreshing.

Facing on to the plaza, a large Catholic church dominates the rise above the Ampiyacu River. Though it is built only of wood, plaster and corrugated tin, the simplicity of the church makes it worth a visit. Inside there are posters depicting Jesus as an Amazon Indian growing up in the jungle.

Around the corner from the main plaza is a small souvenir shop where you can buy soda or beer and, of course, blowguns and palm-fibre hammocks. Inside the store, in the kitchen and cooking area, are a green parrot and spider monkey and occasionally more exotic animals.

Behind the church is a single-storey schoolhouse, painted yellow. Facilities are basic, though typical: a blackboard, a few wooden desks and stools. This is a good place to donate books or writing materials. The main school holiday is between

YAGUA SETTLEMENT

You can walk here from Pevas, about half a mile along a moderate trail (steep, mud) beyond Grippa's. Most visitors arrive here to coincide with the pre-arranged dance/barter sessions included by a tourist river boat on its standard itinerary.

Communal huts are the traditional mode of dwelling for the forest Indian. Several families would live in each, dividing up living space. Now there are individual houses for each family, an arrangement which arises from the European model. *Yagua* means red and comes from the tribe's practice of face-painting. Dramatically daubed with bright red pigment from seedpods of *achiote* (*Bixa* sp) to ward off evil spirits, the men, women and children join in a traditional dance. During simple, roughly-executed moves, they variously chant, beat drums or blow on bamboo flutes and pan-pipes, with varying degrees of skill and enthusiasm. The Yagua usually wear 'grass' skirts (really made from split palm fibres), over Western dress.

Native dress is worn only for the performance and, although somewhat artificial, the dances provide the Indians with an income and a reason to keep up old traditions, which would quite possibly die out otherwise.

Most Yagua people live by hunting and fishing, and cultivating a few crops. Their economy of exchange is based on barter. Recently, in areas visited by tourists, the sale of handicrafts, such as seed necklaces, blow-guns and ritual masks, has become important to their economy.

A Yagua settlement similar to the one near Pevas is visited by guests of Explorama Lodge who follow a trail to the Yagua Reserve.

April and July, when teachers and schoolchildren stay home because of the difficulty of getting to school during flood season. Many pupils, both Indian and *mestizo*, live in remote jungle villages several kilometres or more away.

Beyond the school, the path leads down to a creek, across a small wooden bridge to the native-built studio house of the famous Peruvian artist, Señor Francisco Grippa, who offers any visitor a gracious welcome. With lovely views of the river, his gallery and its fine paintings are the major attraction for visitors to Pevas. Aged 49 and a native of Peru, Grippa trained in Paris, London and New York and exhibits in the US.

Besides board and conventional canvas, he paints on a cloth, unique among established artists, made of bark from the fig tree *chuchuara*, (*Ficus yoponensis*), working in traditional media of oils and acrylics. His present goal is to interpret Amazonian life in art and his style has elements of early impressionists combined with techniques of Jackson Pollock. But as he says, 'Grippa is Grippa, and no-one else…'

Francisco makes guests welcome without an appointment, whether or not they buy a painting. There is something here for everyone including tapes of specially composed music, postcards, prints and original work in various colourful media (from US$1 to US$100).

The only accommodation is the **Casa de la Loma** lodge close to Pevas, which offers basic comforts among some fine natural areas. It is run by Scott Humfeld, a medical nurse originally from Roseburg, Oregon, who came, like so many, to the Amazon as a tourist but, like very few, stayed to spend his life helping natives battle the wide variety of common afflictions, notably respiratory diseases, parasite infections and snakebite.

He has been in Pevas several years, running the clinic. He started the lodge to help fund the clinic, the only free service in Pevas, severely short of funds and constantly hindered by bureaucracy. Hence donations to Scott's clinic are welcome. Of course, staying at the lodge also helps and it easy to reach Pevas by express taxi-boat or on the tourist riverboats.

Tourist riverboats stop in Pevas for day-visits before visiting nearby Witoto-Bora and Yagua settlements. To stay overnight, if travelling on your own, you can take the tourist riverboat then catch it on the return journey to Iquitos three days later. Alternatively you have regular river transport in the uncomfortable river-taxis or a choice of the unpredictable but frequent local cargo boats.

The surroundings of the town are mostly secondary rainforest, although there are some pristine areas close by. Scott at Casa de la Loma can help arrange a guide (US$45/day) for visits in motorised canoes. For a longer trip you will have to supply all food and camping equipment. If you want to explore the area intensively, you should organise the trip from Iquitos for a better choice of guides and more competitive prices. At times of lowest water (between October and February) the Ampiyacu giant water-lily trail may be inaccessible. This is visited by tour groups and comprises a lake up a tributary of the Río Ampiyacu, close to Pevas. Here you can see giant water-lilies and interesting birds, especially horned screamer and, if you're lucky, hoatzin.

Pijuayal

Just downriver from Pevas is Pijuayal (pee-hyoo-ah-yahl). Pijuayal is an army garrison and checkpoint, where all river traffic must stop to submit papers. Should a boat pass the checkpoint and fail to stop it is, as local guide Daniel Rios put it, 'Blown out of the water'. This somewhat drastic policy is to prevent drug-running down the river.

The tourist boat arrives early in the morning and there is often a beautiful dawn… Wake to the reveille and, if you're lucky, spot pink dolphins cavorting offshore that don't seem too bothered by the sound of the wake-up call! As you stroll the deck, this idyllic scene may be spoilt by the presence of numerous sandflies or 'no-see-ums', which are abundant.

As the garrison is behind the high riverbank you cannot see much of the installation: a couple of brightly camouflaged wooden pillboxes and a walkway, with perhaps one or two armed guards. It is unwise to point a camera in their direction, however cheerful they may seem or unimportant the facilities may appear.

Jessonia

This tiny settlement, with a population of about ten, barely qualifies as a village. Standing at the confluence of the Río Shishita and the mainstream, 64km east of Pevas, the town consists of a couple of ramshackle stilt houses in a clearing – quite typical of many settlements along the river.

Only tourist riverboats stop here regularly as there is little reason for anyone else to stop with any other business. There is no way to get here except by prior arrangement with a local riverboat captain or river express boat owner.

Named after Jesson, an American who ran jungle expeditions for many years during the seventies and early eighties, this hamlet used to have a small lodge for tourists. Today only a local *mestizo* family remain as caretakers of land which is a natural preserve. The main reason to visit is for a launch ride up the Apayacu River, which travels along a beautiful stretch of unspoiled river, to a series of trails. As trails are unmarked, a local guide is necessary to explore them. Ask for José. Regularly used by tour operators, some of the trails are eroded in places but, as a rule, the area is unspoiled by development of any sort and surrounded by pristine forest. Wildlife

WITOTO AND BORA SETTLEMENT

A few miles down the Ampiyacu River, the Witoto and Bora Indian village settlements can be reached by canoe from Pevas (US$5). Several boats a day make the trip.

With their ancestral homelands originally in Colombia along the upper Putumayo, the Witoto and Bora Indians were forced by the government to move to the area in the 1930s following border changes made in 1922. Distinctions between the two tribes are being lost, as they have lived together and been subject to continuous outside influence for most of the last century.

There are some differences, such as the style of face-painting and clothing. Notably, during their dances for tourists, Bora women go bare-breasted whereas Witoto cover themselves. Pre-European native costumes made from wood-bark, chambira palm fibre and various animal parts are used as adornments. Indians play a type of slit drum, also found in Africa and among Pacific Islanders. The Amazon Indians say the drums represent human or animal bodies. The traditional slit-drum of the Witoto has a woman's head at one end and a caiman's tail at the other.

You can trade Western goods for souvenirs such as blow guns, paddles, bark paintings, carved gourds and seed necklaces. The ecopurist may decry the practice of trading, and it is true that selfish exchanges can damage relationships between visitors and Indians and have a negative impact on some people in the village. On the other hand, the local Indians do have the right to choose whether or not to barter for our goods. Should we take the moral high ground and withhold the possibility because we are somehow afraid of tainting them?

From legal and ethical standpoints, it is advisable not to buy items with significant amounts of feathers, teeth or skin or any animal products in general.

includes monkeys, sloths, iguana and a variety of forest birds, while flora consists of mixed secondary and primary rainforest, including some very impressive specimens of kapok (*ceiba*) and fig trees over 50m high and at least 150 years old.

San Pablo

This town of about 2,500 inhabitants is around two-thirds of the distance from Iquitos to Leticia, on the southern bank of the Amazon River. Tourist riverboats stop here for a short excursion, giving two or three hours for the visit. Otherwise you can reach here from towns up or downstream on cargo riverboats or by river taxi.

There are no hotels in San Pablo suitable for the Western traveller although basic accommodation can probably be found – ask the nuns. There are several small bars where you can get a meal.

San Pablo's prominence is as a so-called 'leper colony', which was moved to San Pablo by the government. Sufferers who have no family or money are still sent to this Amazon outpost. There is a basic hospital with a few dozen patients in the latter stages of Hansen's Disease – as leprosy is properly called. In fact by far the majority of people in the town have never suffered from the disease.

The most noticeable legacy of the patients is a thriving industry of wood-carvers. Vividly coloured, varnished or unpainted, the simple carvings are of rainforest animals such as anteaters, parrots and fish. Some of the carvings are often so newly finished, the varnish is still sticky. They sell for outrageously low prices of US$3–6.

San Pablo is worth a visit for a couple of hours. Look around and you can always discover something of interest: an exquisite tropical flower, a postcard view across

At the Witoto village is a shaman, Gabriel, who always has a wad of coca powder in his gum. He is a rich source of knowledge on herbal remedies from rainforest plants, with a cure for practically anything.

Of course, the efficacy of Gabriel's treatments is not guaranteed but it is certain that some of his medicines work. He contributed significantly to the researches of Richard Evans Schultes, founder of the science of ethnobotany. If you are suffering from an ailment or fever, Gabriel will be happy to prescribe and create a remedy for US$10.

At some time during your visit to the villages you will probably be offered coca leaf to chew, locally called *ipadú*. The raw ingredient for cocaine, only the leaf is used by natives. In the highlands it is chewed raw or served as a tea but in the Amazon coca is prepared differently. It is ground to a dust and then added to cercropia leaf, which is similarly powdered and contains alkaloids to enhance the active ingredient.

The greenish-brown powder is taken with a suitable leaf or piece of card, about a thimbleful at a time, and poured into the space between the cheek and the teeth. Despite a gritty texture and earthy taste it's not unpleasant and makes your teeth a little numb. The wad is kept in the mouth and encourages saliva which is spat out, along with some of the powder. Only men use it and swear that it enhances performance in hunting expeditions or during their work in the fields. Apparently, they use it for twenty years or more without ill-effect or addiction.

Numerous other drugs available from the rainforest are used for intoxication, in particular hallucinogens, such as *ayahuasca*, taken as an infusion, and snuffs made from the virola vine. Hallucinogens play a significant role in the religious life of rainforest tribes, even today.

the Amazon, bright yellow corn drying on the pavement, kids squabbling over the pen a tourist gave them, silent pain in the eyes of a leprosy patient, a caiman skin drying in the sun.

Caballococha

Caballococha is the last town downriver from Iquitos visited by boats before Leticia. Your best bet is to come here on a pre-arranged tour or make all travel arrangements in Iquitos. Tour boats stop here for just an hour or two and moor while their passengers go off in motorised canoes to explore the nearby lake. If you're stuck here, there's a very basic hotel, a handful of shops and bars, but not much else to do.

This small town (population 2,500) has little to distinguish it except the fact that it is a welfare or even warfare town of strategic importance. Caballococha is the main town in Peru on the stretch of river which borders Colombia and only 80km from Leticia, and the town is bolstered with official funds to deter Colombian military adventurism. Most households receive cash handouts from the Peruvian government.

Besides having more streetlights than any town between Iquitos and Leticia, Caballococha has a gigantic satellite dish, with global communication ability. With good timing, you can watch the Olympics and other global events in the middle of the Amazon. Close by is an ENTEL office with public phones.

The town has little of major interest. The centre of activity is the main plaza, one side of which is the riverfront. Men sit around in the shade of a mango tree, chatting and drinking beer; a couple of urchins run around; dogs squabble over a scrap on a trash heap, joined by a flapping platoon of black vultures.

Caballococha, or at least the area around it, is not entirely uncharming – the Caballococha Lake just south of town is home to pink dolphins and a wide variety of fish. This impressive body of water is fed by the Río Marichi before it flows into the mainstream of the Amazon. The lake area is important ecologically, with water birds and caiman in the vicinity. The setting is a splendid back-drop for spectacular sunsets. Of interest botanically are brazil nut trees, just by the outlet to the lake. Close by is a stand of bamboo, of unusual variety, with long, claw-like thorns on thin stems.

Tributaries leading away from the lake are choked with floating vegetation ideal for piranha fishing and caiman spotting at night, when you can listen to the sounds of amphibians, night monkeys and the chorus of innumerable insects.

Chimbote

This is another checkpoint at which tourist riverboats and other mainstream river traffic must stop before proceeding on to Leticia. Chimbote checkpoint, with shades of Checkpoint Charlie, is located on the southern bank of the mainstream, close by the Colombian border. Passengers are not permitted ashore. Watch where you point your camera.

Santa Rosa

Across from Leticia is Santa Rosa, the final point for riverboats from Peru. Peruvian entry and exit border control is based here. Santa Rosa is a small settlement on an island in the middle of the Amazon River, opposite Leticia. It is the easternmost point of Peru. With views overlooking the river toward Leticia is a small bar. Its avant garde owner, Sñr Hugo Hoyos, a Brazilian, installed solar panels for electricity, which makes it the most ecologically correct establishment in the vicinity. A restaurant and lodge are planned, which should make it an ideal location for a stopover when heading for a connection in Leticia. Hugo is also master of the riverboat *M/V Joandra* which is often tied up by the riverbank here. Behind Hugo's bar lies the village itself, small and with no amenities for visitors.

Upstream from Iquitos

Pucallpa

Capital of the Ucayali department, Pucallpa lies on the Ucayali River. Although large, with a population of some 170,000, it still retains the atmosphere of a frontier town. Indeed, though founded early in the colonial era, the town remained isolated until 1945, when the 846km railway from Lima was completed. However, Pucallpa is easiest to reach by air (it has an airport) or road. It is also accessible by river from Iquitos, and travellers trying to journey along as much as possible of the Amazon's navigable length may start or end their voyages here. See pages 285–9.

Like many Amazon towns, Pucallpa has electricity, but most streets are unpaved and sewers are inadequate. Industries include rosewood oil processing, lumber and oil refining. An oil refinery is connected by a 76km long pipeline to the Ganso Azul oilfields. Missionary activity is ongoing in Pucallpa and other groups have their headquarters there, such as organisations involved in settling the area.

Jungle lodges

Several companies operate lodges in the Peruvian Amazon and have more or less the same protocols for tours. Usually included in your trip price are: being met at Iquitos airport by local staff; transfer for you and your baggage by bus to a town hotel or to the dock and then on to the lodge; a bilingual, English-speaking, local guide who accompanies you throughout your trip and on each excursion.

The places mentioned are those most likely to be used by visitors on trips to the Peruvian Amazon between Iquitos and Leticia. In most cases they cannot be booked directly so trips must be arranged through tour operators in Iquitos (or from your home country). Stays at jungle lodges in Peru are expensive, varying from US$75 to US$150 per night, out of the range of budget travellers.

For budget travellers options are few as most trails and rainforest worth visiting are controlled by tour operators, and it can be difficult to strike off on your own due to the lack of transport and public tourist amenities.

The majority of lodges – though not all – are run by Explorama (see page 277), based in Iquitos. Several reliable US tour operators have been working with the group for years and can make reservations for any of the Explorama establishments. The Audubon Society (page 278) offers trips led by expert birders, while Explorations Inc (page 277) have trips accompanied by more broadly-based scientists. The longest established tour operator, International Expeditions (page 277), also have regular trips without tour-leaders to Explorama lodges.

Rainforest lodges and camps are constructed the same way as native houses. Roofs are made of palm-thatch – remarkably watertight and insect resistant. Frames, walls and walkways are built from incredibly hard palm wood and other lumber. The structure sits on stilts raised above the highest flood level. Beds are simple cots or even mattresses on the wooden floor, and usually with mosquito nets.

Explorama Lodges

One of the first such companies to set up in Iquitos, Explorama has been running lodges in the area for some 25 years. Reflecting the growing popularity of the region, Explorama now has four facilities: Explorama Lodge, Explornapo Camp, Explorama Inn and ExplorTambo. Each one provides a different level of service. The company was also instrumental in seeing the ACEER canopy walkway developed.

Explorama Lodge Explorama Lodge is the company's main facility, and oldest, established in 1965 and, though given a facelift in 1989, beginning to show its age. The lodge facility is up the small Yanamono tributary, close to the Amazon mainstream about 80km downriver from Iquitos. The Bushmaster Reserve belonging to Explorama protects around 195ha of forest around the lodge. Nearby is the 1,600ha Yagua Reserve, where visitors are taken to visit a small settlement of Yagua Indians.

The area close to the lodge has been cleared and you are free to stroll and admire resident birds and animals, plus orchids and bromeliads collected from the forest and put on display. There is direct access to a number of nature trails radiating into the nearby forest. However, the company won't take responsibility for guests who wander beyond the lodge grounds unaccompanied. Well-trained English-speaking Explorama staff lead excursions on the trails and add immeasurably to your experience, as they point out birds and plants which you could easily miss.

Morning nature walks are excellent for birds and invertebrates, such as insects, spiders and snails. Expect few mammals but with some luck squirrel monkeys or tamarins may be seen. Nevertheless, the huge variety of vegetation will certainly give you the feeling you are deep in the Amazon rainforest.

Technically, the forest can be divided into seasonally flooded *várzea* and upland *terra firme* forest. Around Explorama most forest is fully-grown secondary forest with some primary rainforest that has never been logged. Without a bit of practice you'll struggle to tell the difference. This is certainly an authentic jungle experience, although it is lagging behind state-of-the-art ecolodges such as Yacumama Lodge.

The downstream journey from Iquitos takes just over two hours by company-owned *colectivo*. These long, covered motorised canoes are built in the traditional form with palm-thatch roof. The return journey against the current is somewhat longer, four to five hours.

At high water, access to the lodge is directly by launch which leaves the mainstream going up the Yanamono and pulls up to a floating platform a short way from the lodge. At low water access is restricted so it is necessary to disembark from the *colectivo* on the Amazon River, which makes for a steep muddy climb up the riverbank which can be very slippery. From here you walk for 15 to 30 minutes to the Lodge. Some of this is along a well-built wooden walkway – essential to avoid tramping through a swamp – while the second portion of the walk is along forest trails.

Close by the low-water disembarkation point is the small village of Sapo Playa, home to lodge staff and their families. On the main river bank is a still for the distillation of the sugarcane used to make the local rum (*ron*). A primitive mangle is used to squeeze out the juice which is poured straight into a long wooden canoe and left to ferment. The liquor is extracted and distilled through a 2m-high bulbous copper still. Adjacent to the still shed, you can sample the fiery product at the tastefully decorated ramshackle bar.

On the walk to Explorama Lodge you pass cultivated areas planted with maize, manioc (locally called *yuca*), bananas and sugarcane. A large pond complete with wallowing water buffalo is reminiscent of a scene in southeast Asia, from where these bovids were imported after World War II.

Surrounded by forest, the lodge sleeps 150 guests in relative comfort in half a dozen thatched buildings. Each cabin has two single beds with mosquito nets. Adjacent to the lower cabins is a hammock area where you can sleep at night or relax after jungle walks.

Water is provided, along with a washbowl, as there is no in-house plumbing. Washing water in your cabins and the showers is filtered but not safe to drink. Showers and toilets are a short walk from the cabins and the water is unheated, not totally unwelcome given the temperatures! If unheated shower-water bothers you, it is warmest in late afternoon.

Located in separate buildings from the cabins, the communal latrines are simple with non-flush (and sometimes smelly) toilets. There is no electricity here. Lighting is by paraffin lamp so keep a flashlight handy for night excursions to the toilet.

Food is prepared on open fires, and can leave vegetarians hungry, over-stressing meat dishes. Some fresh fruit is served, the quantity and variety depending on seasonal availability, while excellent salads are dished up year-round. On the whole, Explorama food is very good, though not gourmet. Filtered water is available, along with hot water for tea or coffee throughout the day. In the main dining area, hanging from a rafter is a bunch of bananas to feed the resident scarlet macaws.

Between meals or after nature activities you can visit the bar. Presumably because of the absence of electricity, there is no ice. Local handicrafts for sale in the bar include masks, flutes, blow-guns and paddles.

Accommodation is less than perfect and the nature is not totally pristine but Explorama Lodge will not disappoint. The accommodation is comfortable, the food acceptable and the nature opportunities endless. The price is not cheap, at US$365 for a three-night package. Book through Explorama offices in Miami or Iquitos. A number of US tour operators can also make bookings for you. Try Explorations Inc, International Expeditions, Nature Expeditions International or Explorers. Details are on page 277.

Explornapo Camp Tucked away among trees and shrubs on the River Sucusari, a tributary of the Napo, Explornapo Camp is the base for trips to the ACEER laboratory and the canopy walkway. Constructed in 1982 it provides facilities among rainforest more preserved than in the immediate area around Iquitos.

From Explornapo you can take half-day motorboat trips up the Sucusari River to go piranha fishing, birdwatching and dolphin-spotting. But look closely around you and, as always in the rainforest, you can find something unusual to occupy you – like the flocks of sulphur-yellow butterflies dancing around a patch of mud, sucking up minerals and salts, or a ball of bristling ants collecting at the top of a young cercropia stem as the waters rise and flood their home. Because of Explornapo's remote location, the forest here is less disturbed than around Explorama Lodge and extensive primary forest remains.

At high water, your boat ties up right next to the main facility. At low water, however, the gently sloping bank presents a hundred metres or so of mud. It's an easy, but slippery and muddy, walk unless the staff have cut logs for a walkway.

Compared with Explorama Lodge, Explornapo Camp is smaller and accommodation facilities more primitive which appeals to some travellers. As the company's brochure says, 'The Camp is... often the favourite of our lodges'. Beds are mattresses laid dormitory-style on the wooden floor of a large native-style building. Only the mosquito nets offer privacy and not much at that! Toilet and shower facilities are shared and in a separate block.

Food is cooked over an open wood fire. Beer and soft drinks are kept in a cooler, and you can help yourself, an honour system trusting you to mark what you take and settle the tab before departure.

Explornapo offers a real 'away-from-it-all' experience and has its charms. In the lounge area hang dozens of plaques left by previous groups or individual travellers – far more interesting record than a visitor's book! Here also are a couple of hammocks where you can doze or peacefully relax, watching for birds and animals who curiously investigate the grounds.

Of course, the main reason to stay at Explornapo Camp is en route to the canopy walkway (see below). The price is the same as for Explorama Lodge and booking is through the Explorama office in Iquitos or via US tour operators.

Explorama Inn Closest of Explorama's lodges to Iquitos and the most luxurious, with electricity and individual private cabins, Explorama Inn is close to the village of Indiana. Accommodating about 50 people in all, this facility is for those with only a day or two or who want a more 'civilised' jungle experience. There are half a dozen or so easy trails with lots of plants, insects and birds, but most large mammals are gone. Unfortunately no maps are available but in any case guests are not permitted to walk trails without a guide. It is about 90 minutes by boat from Iquitos, or two hours on the return trip upstream.

The facilities here are more developed than at other Iquitos lodges. Built on concrete foundations, the lounge, bar and dining rooms have electric light and overhead fans. Rooms have twin beds with electric light, fans and conventional plumbing for the toilet and shower. Concrete walkways connect the cabins and dining room. Other amenities and food are similar to those of Explorama Lodge and Camp.

This is the most economical of Explorama's establishments, available on a per-night basis from US$95 per person (includes meals, accommodation), plus US$28 for transfer (one way) from Iquitos, arranged by Explorama. They take bookings in Peru, while from abroad you can book through the US tour operators mentioned for other Explorama facilities.

ExplorTambo *Tambo* is a Quechua term meaning resthouse, and in the Amazon applies to a simply built small 'cottage'. Here, Explorama have extended the concept to their new facilities, opened mid-1997 for the slightly more adventurous, and lower budgeted (US$175 for three days). A 3km hike from Explornapo Camp takes you through verdant primary rainforest to the *tambos*. Bedding is provided, with mosquito nets, while catering and latrine facilities are similar to those at other Explorama camps.

Remo Caspi

For a friendly, personal service integrated with local villages and certainly less expensive, try the lodge of Felice Cosentino called Remo Caspi at Mishana, Río Nanay. A few pleasant hours from Iquitos, it's a very different set-up.

ACEER (Amazon Center for Environmental Education and Research)

If you have a week to spend you can stay in the Amazon to experience the only tropical rainforest canopy walkway in the Americas at the ACEER facility some 140km from Iquitos. This is the location of the famous tree canopy walkway – depicted in numerous TV nature specials. It is undoubtedly the best way to get a feel for what life in the canopy is like. Forty-six metres above the forest floor you come face-to-face with life's diversity at its most extreme.

The site is within the privately owned and managed Amazon Reserve, set up by a joint effort of scientists, officials and tour operators. ACEER is reached by a 3km hike from Explornapo Camp. The walk creates no problems for the moderately fit person.

Accommodation at ACEER is pleasant and comfortable, with room for 20 visitors. There are two wings of rooms around a central dining area. The two beds per room have mosquito nets. Washing and drinking water is available in jugs – there is no plumbing in the rooms. Lighting is by paraffin lamp. The bathroom facilities are communal latrines and showers, a short walk from the room. Food at ACEER is typical jungle lodge fare – acceptable but not gourmet.

Overall ACEER is comparable with other good jungle lodges, although the five-star treatment is dispensed with. Everyone is interested in nature and discovering things rather than being pampered. If you're weighing up whether to visit here, any shortcomings are more than compensated for by the outstanding birding, insect life and stunning diversity of plants.

Explorama handle all booking arrangements in Peru. International Expeditions, Explorations Inc and several other tour operators offer all-inclusive trips from Miami. Expect to pay at least US$2,000 and upwards for these seven- to ten-day trips, which usually include two or three days at ACEER, with the rest of the time spent at other Explorama facilities.

Because of the relatively high cost of transport and accommodation, it won't be much more expensive than arranging the trip yourself and you might not have so much fun. The natural luxury of ACEER does not come cheap, at US$275 for a three-day package (including transport from Iquitos). The canopy walkway is the highlight of any visit.

Canopy walkway

You can literally walk among the treetops right in the middle of the rainforest canopy, the site of the highest biodiversity in the world, strolling among the leafy branches and enjoying the 'high life'.

The walkway is among *terra firme* forest, atop a ridge. The steps take you around and up trunks and branches – through the lush vegetation, to the tops of immense trees. Built on a slope, from the walkway's higher points you can see over the trees: a rolling ocean of multi-hued green, unbroken forest stretching as far as the eye can see. It is an awe-inspiring sight.

At dawn you can watch the sun rise over the treetops, as wisps and tendrils of mist waft up like ethereal smoke above the breathing trees. In the domain of epiphytes, such as orchids and bromeliads, and animals that never touch the ground. High above the ground, you are cooled by refreshing breezes as you leisurely inspect plants and animals you could otherwise never see. Take time to watch for wildlife, look at the rare plants or just ponder the wonder of it all.

NOTE You are permitted to use the canopy walkway only with an ACEER guide. You can make arrangements at the lodge for walkway tours at any time of day.

The walkway is an engineering marvel around 430m long and 32m up in the trees. Every effort was made to minimise harm to the surrounding forest. For the US$10-million project scientists and engineers teamed up to give visitors the ultimate rainforest experience. You need no specialised climbing equipment – the facility is designed and built with safe, easy access as a priority.

Amazon Camp

Another good jungle lodge in the Iquitos area is Amazon Camp, managed by Amazon Tours and Cruises who operate the two main tourist riverboats and handle bookings for the Camp. Most visitors here are on their way to or from one of the vessels or a city hotel. The camp lies about half an hour's boat ride from Punta Buenavista, the southernmost point of Iquitos.

A group of palm-thatched dwellings on stilts, the lodge is on the banks of the Momón River, a tributary of the Nanay that feeds into the mainstream. At the mouth of the Nanay River there is a 'meeting of waters' where the Nanay's black water flows into the Amazon's brown, not mixing for some miles. Where the two waters blend, the surface has the appearance of black-brown marble.

This spot is a pleasant and peaceful retreat. The lodge buildings and facilities are laid out neatly along the riverbank. There is an easy landing platform and steps up to the lodge. The accommodation is comfortable with twin beds in mosquito-proofed cabins and en-suite wash basins and flush toilets. Water is unheated, the showers are communal and there is no electricity. Lighting is by paraffin lamp. For relaxing and cooling down you can swim in the river; the landing platform is a good place from which to dive in.

Amazon Camp has better prepared food and a healthier menu (eg: fresh heart of palm, fresh fruit, excellent fruit juices) than other lodges, though to be fair there is not a lot of difference. On the early morning walk a guide takes you through the forest behind the camp along a pleasant trail. The area around the camp is less impressive in terms of pristine forest but is surrounded by miles of mature secondary rainforest recovering from selective logging many years ago.

A night at Amazon Camp booked direct through Amazon Tours and Cruises (page 277) costs US$95 (single) or US$125 (twin), although it might work out cheaper (eg: US$65) to book through US tour operators who run tourist riverboats.

Yacumama Lodge

Located on the banks of the quiet Yarapa River, some 145km from Iquitos as the toucan flies, Yacumama Lodge competes for the title of Most Ecosensitive Lodge in the Amazon. Here are features common to the best Amazon lodges and camps – pristine forest, by a river, birds and tree-dwelling animals. Sited far from human habitation, Yacumama is surrounded by rainforest offering abundant wildlife and a wide diversity of large trees. All this comes at a lower environmental cost, as the company's brochure says: 'To minimise our impact on this pristine area we employ recycling, composting, organic gardening, sewage treatment, biodegradable detergents and solar power.'

The usual procedures are followed to get there: the company representatives meet and greet you at Iquitos airport. You are transferred to a city hotel and the next day by *colectivo* to Yacumama Lodge. The lodge sleeps up to 30 in twin or single cabins, which have en-suite flush toilets and shower.

Raw sewage is processed and cleaned before release into the river. This fine example will hopefully be followed by other lodges who currently pipe raw sewage directly into rivers. Yacumama is solar powered so there is no disruptive generator noise to disturb your dawn reveries. Given the abundance of sunshine and the expense of petrol, solar power makes economic as well as ecological sense.

To arrange a stay at Yacumama book in advance through EcoExpeditions in Miami (page 277). From Iquitos, a three-day all-inclusive package costing US$595 is good value for the combination of outstanding service, ecofriendliness and nature opportunities which are among the best of those of any tourist lodge in Amazonia.

Sinchicuy Lodge

Downriver from Iquitos, the 29km trip to this pleasant lodge takes around two hours, depending on flood conditions. Plantings of orchids and other tropical plants in a small garden allow close-up inspection of species otherwise out of sight or reach. Nearby nature-spots include a beautiful lake and nature trail. Your stay includes a nocturnal canoe ride to listen to the sounds of the night.

Camp staff meet and greet you at Iquitos airport and escort you by canoe to a camp, usually via Swiwa Lake with a short trail walk to the local Bora Indian village. On the banks of the Sinchicuy River the dwellings are built in the native fashion. Rooms have private bathrooms (sharing showers), while spacious dining and bar areas let cool breezes waft through the buildings. Rooms and public areas are lit with kerosene lamps.

Due to its proximity to Iquitos this lodge is popular with tour operators but still offers excellent cultural and nature experiences. A stay at Sinchicuy can be booked from most tour operators in Iquitos, from US$75 per night and upwards depending on the quality of the guide and whether transfers are included. You can book in the US through Sol International (page 277) who offer fully inclusive eight-day trips from US$1,750 per person including return airfare from Miami to Iquitos.

Tambo Amazonico Camp

Located beside the Yarapa River, close by the confluence of the Ucayali and Marañón, some 210km upstream from Iquitos, Tambo Amazonico Camp is surrounded by pristine rainforest. A stay here can include a 'camp-out' where participants set up camp using branches and tree leaves to build a simple shelter, spending the night on mattresses, protected by mosquito nets. The camp surroundings offer tranquillity among the sights and sounds of the forest, while outings include a day-trip by canoe to the Cumaceba Lagoon, inhabited by pink dolphin. Huge kapok and fig trees covered with epiphytes, and numerous other species, crowd the edges of the lagoon. The usual array of visits to local tribes, piranha fishing, birdwatching excursions, jungle hikes and nocturnal canoe rides are also available.

Bungalows built of natural materials in native style house dormitories of six simple beds, each provided with mosquito nets. Showers and latrines are communal and water is river temperature. The dining area is bug-proofed so you can enjoy the food without waving your hand over your food every five seconds or plucking out unidentifiable wrigglers that drop in for a taste. Lighting is by paraffin lamp.

The lodge can be booked through tour operators in Iquitos for US$55 (single) or US$90 (double). In the US Tambo Amazonico can be booked through Sol International.

Other jungle lodges

There are a number of other jungle lodges and campsites which may offer better or worse facilities than those described here, but they are all roughly comparable. With the increase in tourism to the area there are bound to be more lodges opening.

Air expeditions

This totally different type of trip for the adventurous takes you to remote areas more rapidly than you can reach them by river. At Iquitos you board a small plane for a flight far into the forest, landing by a remote tributary. By prearrangement, your canoe is waiting with all the basics provided. You sleep in hammocks, small camp beds or temporary sleeping quarters, either tents or huts with a thatched roof. The seven-night Tacha Curaray air expedition (cost US$1,695 for 2–3 people; US$975 for 4–6; US$820 for 7 or more) from Amazon Tours and Cruises (page 277) takes guests to remote parts of the Curary River, some 200km northwest of Iquitos.

Freelance guide

Operating out of Iquitos and usually hanging around the airport, Andres Peña offers outstanding trips, suitable for the highly adventurous. Andres speaks fluent English and grew up in the jungle, so he's familiar with virtually every animal and plant. His six-day (five-night) canoe trips begin with a trip down the Amazon to a base camp (mosquito nets provided) and proceed with camping overnight in the jungle, while days are occupied with forest hikes, fishing for piranha and meeting native tribes. Bring boots and rainwear. These trips are well-run and excellent value for US$200, or US$40 per day with all meals, accommodation and transport included.

Trails and nature walks

Here we describe the popular trails and nature walks found on or near the mainstream and easily accessible from Iquitos. The focus is on trails used by operators of tourist riverboats as these are the ones most likely to be visited by readers. Note that, in virtually all cases, there are no signs marking the trails described, making it imperative to have a guide.

Jessonia Trail

Behind the huts in the village of Jessonia is a 2.5km trail. It starts with a path through the banana groves managed by the family. José, the headman, will lead you around the trail using his machete to hack away at the undergrowth. Not much of a talker, he can be recognised by a cataract in one eye, large rubber boots and ragged clothes.

The trail paths are reasonably well-kept and cleared for easy access. After heavy rain they can be very muddy or even partially flooded.

On the trail there is fascinating vegetation typical of *várzea* – lowland flooded forest. Look for strangler fig, monkey-ladder vine and the two enormous kapok trees. Many palms inhabit the forest, including the moriche palm (*Mauritia* sp) with its huge leaves and delicious fruit. Numerous smaller shrubs and herbs are of great interest to the botanist because of their use by native tribal shamans.

Toward the end of the walk is a stand of crab-claws (*Heliconia* spp) notable for their large red and orange flowers, shaped like crab-claws, pointed out and often with a bold fluorescent anther.

Río Shishita Trail

From the riverbank opposite the settlement of Jessonia leads a trail rather drier than the Jessonia trail. It leads further downstream along the Shishita heading into the *terra firme* forest, which is never flooded, and watered only by rain. This is relatively undisturbed although villagers harvest wild products. Along the path is diverse vegetation, including several species of tree, numerous lianas and palms – vegetation of a different composition to that found in the *várzea* forest. The path takes you 3.5km or so from the tributary eventually to a tree which is a favourite scratching post for a jaguar and has obvious claw marks. Most walks stop at this point and return the same way.

As elsewhere, most big animals have been hunted out so to see a jaguar or other large game such as tapir or anteater, you would need to hike for another two days into the jungle. You may be able to hire a guide at Jessonia. Certain monkeys, sloths and numerous bats and rodents are common, and of course hundreds of different birds, reptiles and amphibians, and countless invertebrates.

The Río Shishita itself is a small tributary but exceedingly beautiful. Fish thrive in the river, although they are not always abundant because they migrate away during seasonal high waters. Bizarre and convoluted root formations of large trees among the mud and riverbank fascinate and confuse the eye. Numerous epiphytes adorn every tree, as though some mad gardener had randomly thrown orchids, bromeliads and lilies at every place that would hold a plant.

An early morning boat trip is very rewarding and will most likely produce sightings of the metallic-blue morpho butterfly, a troop of saddleback tamarin cavorting in a huge *ficus* and several other rainforest dwellers.

Ampiyacu Water Lily Trail

This is located among undisturbed lowland *várzea* forest, close by a tributary of the Ampiyacu River, about 30 minutes upstream from Pevas and not far from the Witoto-Bora village. The trail varies in length depending on the flood level but doesn't exceed 500m. Approaching by small boat, the ride to the site is through narrow channels, bordered by overhanging vegetation and thick epiphytic growth. At low water this stream is sometimes blocked off by vegetation and water weeds.

The site itself is a gem among the natural treasures of the Amazon. The trail opens to a beautiful small lake, surrounded by trees and shrubs. The dominant plants on the water margin are spiny palm, equipped with vicious spines arranged in parallel circlets up the trunk.

Fed by whitewater rivers, nutrient levels are high. The lily pads grow to enormous sizes, two metres or more across. With luck the plant will be in flower, and you will get to see the spectacular blooms, the size of a football. Depending on the season, there is also a good chance of seeing the horned screamer, hoatzin and more common waterbirds such as the striated heron.

Amazon Camp Trail

Access to this trail is from Amazon Camp by the Momón River. The start is just behind the lodge dining area, through a small grassy clearing in which grows tufts of lemon-grass. The walk is about 3.5km in length, easy to moderate, but some parts may be muddy.

This is secondary rainforest but in an advanced state of regeneration, and there is lots to see, with a wide variety of vegetation and fungi. Wildlife consists mostly of birds and invertebrates, including the splendid morpho butterflies. You can take night walks from Amazon Camp.

You have to negotiate a couple of muddy slopes and a rickety wooden walkway on the final part of the trail before a clearing in which stands a communal native hut. Here the walk ends with a dance by Bora Indians. Dances are based on traditional forms, to honour such animals as jaguar and caiman, and spirits of the forest.

From the village, a boat takes visitors back to Amazon Camp. At low water, a 1–2km walk may be necessary to reach the river.

Medicine Walk Trail

This trail through *terra firme* forest is close to the ACEER facility and easy to find.

On the walk visitors can find some of the vast number of plants used by natives for medicinal and other purposes. The easy walk, a mile or so on a well-marked path, takes about an hour, or more if you linger. This is where the diversity of the plant life really hits home. Besides everyday uses, there seems to be some plant cure for every ailment you can think of.

Plants are marked so you can identify them easily, and ACEER provides a printed guide to the numbered plants, so you can discover more about a species' particular uses.

Yagua Reserve Trail

This is the trail taken by most visitors to Explorama Lodge. From the lodge you walk through beautiful rainforest for about 1.5km. It's an easy walk, without steep rises, though muddy and slippery in places. It leads to a clearing with a traditional Yagua dwelling, built in a round shape of bamboo and palm thatch. The place is used only for holding dances to entertain tourist riverboat groups.

Tourist riverboats

A popular way to see the Amazon, and the only tourist-class transport between Iquitos and Leticia, is to take one of the riverboats operated with Western tastes in mind. These vessels offer privacy and relative peace with reasonable food and at reasonable prices (around US$175 per day).

Bookings are made through Amazon Tours and Cruises (page 277), the only company to run scheduled tourist riverboat departures between Iquitos and Leticia. Run by the North American Paul Wright, this company operates the most popular riverboat trips in the region. Costing US$595–1,695 (depending on cabin and vessel) for the three-day trip it's not the cheapest way to make the journey, but you certainly get to see some good wildlife and meet some relatively unacculturated tribes.

If you're booking from the US or Europe, you have the choice of a dozen or more tour operators, who offer the same trip for varying prices. Among the better-known companies in the US are Nature Expeditions International (page 277) and Explorations Inc (page 277, who both send a qualified scientist as tour leader. Tours International (page 278) have a Millennium Package during which you get to spend the Big Moment on *El Arca*. Prices are unavailable at the time of going to press but expect to pay US$2,500 and upwards.

Two vessels regularly make the six-day Iquitos-Leticia round trip. With the charm of old paddle-steamers without the paddles, the *M/V El Arca* and the *M/V Río Amazonas* are similarly equipped with ship-to-shore radio, 220V electric system and air-conditioning. All cabins are fitted with en-suite toilet and shower, and provided with soap, towels and bedding. The ships tow a small motorboat for excursions to reach small tributaries and remoter parts of the forest while travelling along the mainstream.

On any riverboat, noisy engines may take some getting used to and can be a problem for some people, especially at night, so take along earplugs. The best cabins from this point of view are as far from the engine-room as possible, on upper decks, toward the prow. But after a couple of nights you will probably barely notice the gentle soothing chug of the engine.

Both boats follow the same itinerary and schedule, leaving from Iquitos at 15.00 on Sunday afternoons and arriving in Santa Rosa (with shuttle to Leticia-Tabatinga) at 08.00 on Wednesday mornings. They return to Iquitos the following Saturday, arriving around 07.00. They usually carry groups of tourists, occasionally local passengers, and are available for private charter.

El Arca

Built locally in the 1970s, the *M/V El Arca* is the smaller but faster of the two meaning that there is more time for excursions, so the wildlife and nature opportunities tend to be better with this ship. However, at 30m and 208tonnes, it is less spacious. With its full complement of 32 passengers, the dining and bar areas seem cramped, especially at meal-times. Food is good but not fantastic.

Although it provides a fine platform for admiring passing scenery, the top deck is not covered, a drawback in view of the sometimes harsh sun and heavy rain.

Each cabin holds two passengers in bunk beds, with air-conditioning provided by one unit to two cabins. The cabins are quite small, about 3.0 by 2.4m and the windows are too small to enjoy the view from inside. However, accommodations are comfortable, built of local tropical hardwoods.

The ship has an onboard local guide who leads excursions. Señor Daniel Rios is one of the Peruvian naturalist-guides on *El Arca* and with 30 years experience is one of the most knowledgeable guides in the western Amazon.

The price of a trip on *El Arca* has risen recently, reflecting the increased interest in travel to the Peruvian Amazon. The base price for the Iquitos-Iquitos round trip is US$850 (per person, sharing) or US$1,350 (single), or US$495 to US$795 one way between Iquitos and Leticia.

Amazon Tours offers other trips on *El Arca*, for seven and thirteen nights, up the Javari River on the border with Brazil. This area is almost undisturbed and a lot more remote and correspondingly more expensive, from US$1,095 per person for seven nights.

NOTE Do not plan just to arrive and take a trip on this vessel – chances are you will be disappointed as it is often booked months in advance. Many dates are closed as *El Arca* is taken by charter groups. If you cannot get a place on the dates you prefer you could try one of the many US tour operators who use this boat regularly.

Río Amazonas

The *Río Amazonas* is a spacious vessel, comfortable by Amazon standards. Its sedate pace has a charm of its own. Larger than *El Arca* at 44.5m, the *Río Amazonas* is slower, limiting time ashore and some visits and excursions. But this ship will delight those not in a hurry or who prefer more room. You can choose from several nice places on the boat to relax and watch the forest's splendour as it passes by. Engine noise is less of a problem on the *Río Amazonas* because of its larger size.

The vessel holds 42 passengers in twin-bed cabins each with piped air-conditioning and private bath/shower. The cabins have large windows from which you can view the scenery as it slides by. On the middle deck is a bar and dining room. Food is good, about the same as on the *El Arca* and served as a buffet. It is healthy and safely prepared.

The *Río Amazonas* is easier to book than *El Arca*. It is bigger and rarely chartered. Usually you can get a cabin if you book just a month or two ahead.

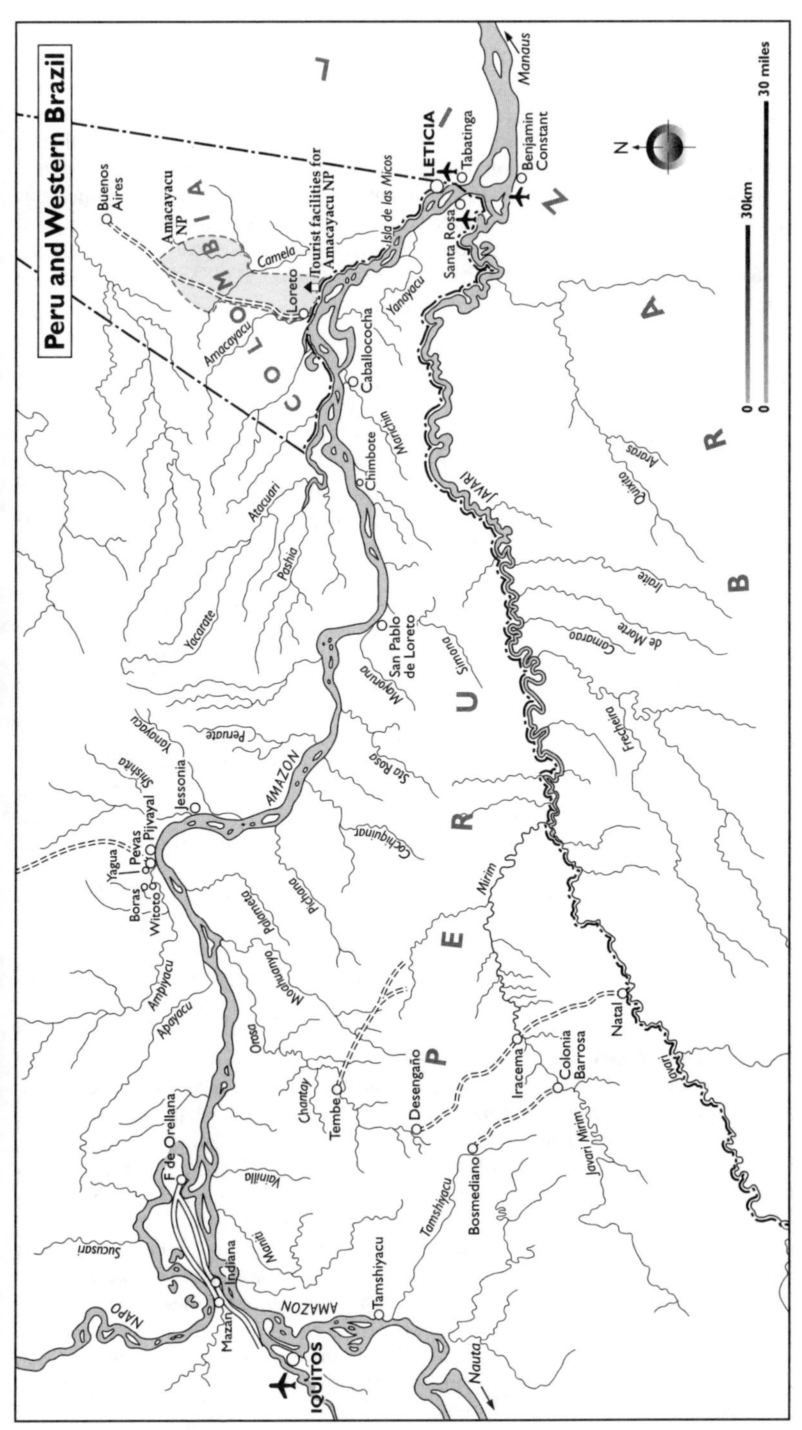
Peru and Western Brazil
COLOMBIA
PERU
BRAZIL
Buenos Aires
Amacayacu NP
Camela
Tourist facilities for Amacayacu NP
Loreto
Amacayacu
Isla de las Micos
LETICIA
Tabatinga
Santa Rosa
Benjamin Constant
Manaus
Yanayacu
Caballococha
Marchin
Chimbote
JAVARI
Araras
Quixito
Atacuari
Pashia
Yacarate
Itaite
San Pablo de Loreto
Simona
Camarao
de Morte
Mayoruna
Frecheira
Yanayacu
Peruate
Shishita
Jessonia
AMAZON
Sta Rosa
Pijyayal
Pevas
Yagua
Boras
Witoto
Cochiquinar
Mirim
Palameta
Pichana
Ampiyacu
Apayacu
Maniharyo
Orosa
Natal
Iracema
Colonia Barrosa
Desengaño
Tembe
Chantay
Javari
Javari Mirim
Bosmediano
F de Orellana
Vainilla
Sucusari
Manití
Tamshiyacu
Indiana
Mazan
NAPO
AMAZON
Tamshiyacu
IQUITOS
Nauta
0 30km
0 30 miles
N

However, it is more expensive. The base price for an upper-deck cabin on the Iquitos-Leticia round trip is US$950 per person sharing (US$525 one way) or US$1,695 for a single person (US$895 one way). The sun-deck cabins are slightly more expensive.

Budget travellers have an option on this vessel: a bunkhouse with shared accommodation. These are on the lower deck, at water level, with separate bathroom facilities. The windows are tiny and your allotted space is cramped but usually you will be the only person down there and you have the place to yourself. The bunkhouse has air-conditioning which makes life considerably more comfortable. If you are willing to rough it this option costs US$595 per person for the Iquitos-Leticia round trip.

El Arca and Río Amazonas cruises

The two ships have the same itinerary. Cruises include daily excursions to natural areas, native villages and jungle towns. With your fellow passengers split into manageably sized groups and led by a native guide, you roam trails through rainforest and take motorboat trips for bird-watching and piranha fishing. There are also night rides when the engine is switched off and you drift downriver, listening to the sounds of the Amazon night. You go ashore into Indian villages to meet tribal people and take day-trips into various towns en route such as Pevas, Caballacocha and San Pablo.

Not all trips include the best villages, forest walks or tributary rides. Natural areas along the route of the tourist boats, while very beautiful and well worth the visit, are partly disturbed secondary rainforest. Some areas were and still are selectively logged, while most land alongside the river has been inhabited at one time or another.

As you voyage sedately on the river, the forest appears pristine, with unbroken canopy topped by large trees, while below a riot of vines and lianas fight for the easiest route up the trees. Where forest meets river, birds and butterflies dance through the air in splashes of colour. Innumerable insects and amphibians sound out nature's symphony, especially around nightfall: a cacophony of different squeaks, chirps, whistles and grunts.

In isolated spots along the river bank are palm-thatched huts on stilts, home for the local *mestizo* people but tiny in the immensity of the landscape. *Mestizos* living along the sparsely inhabited river have adopted the way of life of their Indian predecessors, with a simple existence of fishing, farming and hunting, adapted to the rhythms and cycles of nature.

Other Amazon river journeys

Several other vessels, smaller than the *Arca* and *Río* operate in the area and offer a more intimate look at the rainforest, as they are able to access shallower tributaries and hence probe deeper into virgin forest.

Operated by Amazon Tours & Cruises, the *Delfin* sails west out of Iquitos to remote areas upstream. Trips on the *Delfin* promise lots of game and go to remote areas to find it. Cabin accommodation with bunks, shared shower and air-conditioning cost about the same as on *El Arca*. The boat is 19.8m long and carries 20 passengers. It has scheduled departures and is also available for charter. You can book direct with Amazon Tours and Cruises (page 277) or through a US tour operator. The non-profit Rainforest Health Project and Oceanic Society Expeditions (page 277) both offer eight-day volunteer positions for research on the pink dolphin in the Pacaya-Samiria Reserve, from around US$1,900.

Amazon Explorer and Amazon Discoverer

Smaller still are the *Amazon Explorer* and *Discoverer*, two similar vessels operated by Amazon Tours, both taking 16 passengers and available for charter. These vessels have itineraries to the Tahuayo River up to the confluence of the Ucayali-Marañón rivers. The trip proceeds up the remoter tributaries such as the Yarapa River to the Pacaya-Samiria Reserve. As this is to a more remote area you may get to see more animals, although your score depends as much on luck and season – high water is better – as on location. Trips on these vessels are booked through Amazon Tours and Cruises in Iquitos or direct in the US.

Joandra

For an intimate, close-up look at rainforest life try the six-passenger *M/B Joandra* which operates out of Santa Rosa. Master of the vessel is Sñr Hugo Hoyos, a Brazilian guide with twenty years of experience leading jungle expeditions. The vessel is ideal for families or small group charter costing about US$75 to US$135 per person per day depending on group size and trip length. The itinerary takes guests on a cruise of the Javari River to the remote area of Quishito. Bookings through Amazon Tours and Cruises.

Esmeraldas

The 16-passenger *Esmeraldas* is available exclusively through the US tour operator International Expeditions (page 277). This vessel goes to remoter areas: upstream of Iquitos to undisturbed areas, westwards to the Ucayali-Marañón confluence and to the Tapiche and Tahuayo Rivers. Each cabin, with two beds and private bathroom, is equipped with creature comforts such as hot water, shower and air-conditioning. The dining area is air-conditioned too, and has floor-to-ceiling windows so you can admire the scenery as you eat. For after-meal relaxation aboard, you can rest in the deck chairs on the partially covered observation deck. For further research, use the ship library's maps and books.

It's a step up from the Amazon Tours vessels and more expensive. Approximate cost is around US$1,500 for seven days on the river from Iquitos.

Turmalina

This 28-passenger vessel is the sister ship to the *Esmeraldas*. She's about the prettiest riverboat in the area, decorated in 19th-century style, with carved arches over the doors and very comfortable cabins. The top deck has a viewing point offering all-round views and, at night, the guide operates a powerful spotlight to catch the eye-shines of nocturnal animals. The itinerary varies according to season and local river conditions. Generally, the boat travels west from Iquitos, up the Ucayali River along the southern border of the Pacaya-Samiria National Reserve. It visits villages such as Requena and explores remote tributaries including the Río Tapiche.

Prices and on-board facilities are on a par with the *Esmeraldas*. Bookings and enquiries through International Expeditions or National Wildlife Federation Expeditions (page 277).

NATIONAL PARKS AND WILDLIFE RESERVES

Northern Peru

Pacayu-Samiria National Reserve

Astoundingly, there is only this one officially protected area in the district of Loreto which is entirely within the lowland Peruvian Amazon – and Pacayu-Samiria National Reserve does not even have the status of a national park. However, it is the largest protected natural area in Peru, with an area of 2.80 million hectares –

10,800 square miles! In Peru only Manú National Park comes close in size at just over half of that with 1.53 million hectares.

The boundaries of Pacayu-Samiria National Reserve form a triangle with the Ucayali River to the south and the Marañón River to the north. The western boundary follows the border between the districts of Loreto and San Martin. The reserve is named after the Río Samiria, a tributary of the Marañón.

The park is a long way from Iquitos and expensive to get to. Most tour agencies in Iquitos charge US$50 or more per day to travel here, where there are no lodges or fixed accommodation. Access is by motorised canoe upriver from Iquitos. As this is not a common trip you will have to organise it on your own or through one of the tour operators in Iquitos. Unpredictable low water levels can hinder access to the park so visit between April and August during high water level to minimise disruption. Take care when researching whether to take this trip – which is not practicable for solo travellers – as Iquitos tour operators can be very keen to offer things you're just not going to get.

The US-based Rainforest Health Project (page 277) has a medical team working to bring basic health care in areas around the park. They offer travel opportunities (eg: US$2,500 for seven nights, including airfare from Miami) combined with volunteer work.

The best way to visit the park there is to book a trip through a US tour operator, which is expensive, but also relatively hassle-free, leaving you time to enjoy a very special part of the Amazon. See above for details on week-long cruising trips in the riverboat *Turmalina* up the Ucayali and Tapiche Rivers in and around the National Park. This trip costs US$2,600, all-inclusive from Miami.

Amazon Reserve

This is a private reserve of 100,000ha, whose owners hope to raise money with donations and income from ecotourism to buy more land and expand to 400,000ha. At present the reserve encompasses the watersheds of the upper Apayacu and Sucusari Rivers, around which is some of the area's most pristine rainforest. The reserve was set up by a joint effort of scientists, officials and tour operators. The initial US$60,000 needed for its inception was raised by International Expeditions' First International Rainforest Workshop, held 1991. The major attraction of the reserve is the ACEER canopy walkway, a direct outcome of the workshop.

Southern Peru

Tambopata Candamo Wildlife Reserve and Manú National Park are the only government-protected rainforest areas in southern Peru. Located southwest of the upper Amazon region, both areas are relatively undisturbed and offer unrivalled opportunities for wildlife viewing and wilderness. However, they are not directly connected by air or river to major airports, making them less accessible and more expensive. The best time to visit the region is between May and December when it is slightly drier.

The gateway for the region is through Cusco which is well-known for its proximity to Machu Picchu, the Lost City of the Incas.

Manú National Park

This is one of the last great wilderness areas on the planet. Protecting the headwaters of the River Manú, the park of 1.53 million hectares is home to staggeringly diverse flora and fauna. It is also home to indigenous groups that until recently had been completely uncontacted. Difficult to get to and with restrictions

Previous page Cofan Indian in traditional dress, Ecuador (PO)

Above Riverboat hammocks (PH)

Right Large riverboat on the Rio Madeira, Brazil (PH)

Above Quichua Indian making canoe, Ecuador (PO)

Left Quichua Indians in motorised canoe, River Napo, Ecuador (PO)

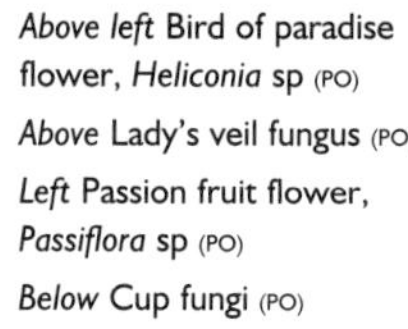

Above left Bird of paradise flower, *Heliconia* sp (PO)

Above Lady's veil fungus (PO)

Left Passion fruit flower, *Passiflora* sp (PO)

Below Cup fungi (PO)

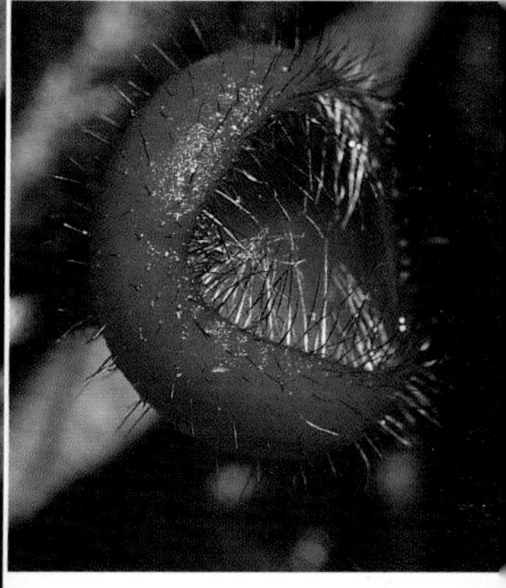

Left Strangler fig buttress roots (PO)

Right Giant water lily, *Victoria amazonica* (RH)

Below Rainbow over Madre de Dios River, Peru (PO)

on the numbers allowed to visit the area, the park offers the chance to see several different rainforest mammals which, with luck, include the giant otter, black caiman, jaguar and ocelot. It is also home to at least 13 different types of primate. Manú has for a long time been highly prized as a destination by ornithologists and the current bird count has just topped the thousand mark. There are several small macaw and parrot clay licks in the reserve.

Manú Biosphere Reserve is accessible from Cusco and visitors stay at Manú Lodge, the only tourist facility actually in the reserve.

This is not a destination for those on tight budgets. Travel in this area is expensive and time-consuming. Due to Manú's international reputation its limited, though excellent accommodation is often full. The best way to avoid disappointment is to book well in advance through a tour operator (eg: Eco Summer Expeditions, Forum Travel, Holbrook Travel, see page 277). Victor Emanuel Nature Tours offer outstanding trips for serious birders (two weeks, US$2,750). Otherwise book with a reliable tour operator in Lima; the best is Rainforest Expeditions. For the minimum three-night trip from Puerto Maldonado, expect to pay a minimum of US$525. Adventure trips with jungle huts and tents to sleep in cost US$25–75 a day depending on what's included, the number of people, and the quality of accommodation, food and guides.

Tambopata-Candamo Reserve

The major attraction here is the colpa clay lick, where hundreds of colourful macaws and other parrots gather to nibble on the clay cliffs, a scene said to be one of nature's greatest spectacles. Birds perform this intriguing behaviour mainly from July to September, a cycle that is related to the seasonal decline of preferred foods. Ingesting the clay helps the birds digest less palatable food and survive during a period when they might otherwise go hungry.

Parrots included, this reserve holds the highest 24-hour bird species count in the world: 331 species. The total list is 570 bird species along with 91 mammal species. It also has record species of invertebrates, including butterflies. Marked trails and trail maps help the visitor explore the rainforest which is permitted without a guide.

For most people the gateway to Tambopata is Puerto Maldonado, on the north edge of Tambopata reserve. This small but growing town is served with flights from Lima or Cusco. Road access from Cusco is possible but likely to leave you in need of another holiday.

TREES: CONSERVING TAMBOPATA

TReeS was founded in 1986 to promote the conservation of the area on a sustainable basis in the long term. The society supports Peruvian biologists to enable them to undertake field research and applied investigations; works with the local native people to empower them to retain their traditional activities, especially with respect to health care; supports the responses of local representative organisations to explorations within the region by multi-national oil companies; and provides advice to those visiting the area from abroad. Resident Naturalist Programmes offer a few places annually to biology graduates, enabling them to undertake research while guiding tourists to the lodges. Further details from TReeS, c/o 64 Belsize Park, London NW3 4EH, UK, or c/o 5455 Agostina Court, Concord, CA 94521, USA.

This upland wilderness is largely undisturbed virgin rainforest. The Madre de Dios region to the west of Cusco along the Brazil/Bolivia border is recognised as a World Centre of Plant Diversity by the Worldwide Fund for Nature. Part of the region is protected within the Tambopata Biosphere Reserve. According to David Childress the region could also be the site of the Lost City of Akakor, said to date from 12,000 years ago.

Visitors to Tambopata have two choices for accommodation, both quite similar to the Explorama Lodge near Iquitos in standard: Explorer's Inn (Peruvian Safaris) or the Cusco Amazónico Lodge. These lodges vary in price from US$250 to US$500 for three-day stays, although five or more days are really needed to make the most of the forest. In Lima, ExplorAndes (Bellavista 518, Miraflores; tel/fax: 445 0532) can arrange Tambopata tours, while several US tour operators offer all-inclusive trips from Miami (seven full days in Peru, starting at US$1,750). Other tour operators likewise include Tambopata as part of a longer trip incorporating Cusco and Machu Picchu. In the US try Holbrook Travel or Forum Travel (page 277).

11 Bolivia

Bolivia is a relative newcomer to the travelling scene having for a long time lived in the shadow of its more ambitious and vocal South American neighbours, Peru and Brazil. But the quiet one in the middle is being explored more and more by visitors who are prepared to risk a few of the comforts of life in the hope that they may experience something special, and the overwhelming majority acquire an endearing affection for this less well-known country.

FACTS AND FIGURES

Geography

Simón Bolívar's wave of liberation came to a halt in Bolivia, the country that bears his name in tribute. Its most northern part lies just 9° south of the Equator, with the southern tip of the country just north of the Tropic of Capricorn. At just over one million square kilometres, Bolivia is landlocked by five nations: Brazil to the north and east, Paraguay and Argentina to the south, and Peru and Chile to the west.

Bolivia encompasses a broad range of biomes, as you might expect from a country ranging in altitude from 6,500m above sea level down to just 175m. The Andes split in two before entering the country from Peru, creating a vast central plateau which stretches south from Lake Titicaca for over 800km. At an average altitude of 3,750m, the *altiplano* is a harsh environment.

BASIC FACTS

Official name República de Bolivia
Area 1,098,581 km^2 (424,165 miles^2)
Population 7,237,000
Capital Sucre
Largest city (population) La Paz (784,976; over 1,119,000 if the neighbouring city of El Alto is included.)
Main Amazon cities Santa Cruz de la Sierra and Rurrenabaque
Official languages Spanish (60%), Quechua (25%), Aymara (15%)
Date of independence August 6 1825
Major industries mining, natural gas, petroleum, agriculture
GDP per capita US$839
Currency boliviano (US$1=Bs5.20; £1=Bs8.50)
Major attractions Salar de Uyuni, Lake Titicaca and Madidi, Manuripi Heath and Noel Kempff Mercado National Parks
National holidays Jan 1, Carnival (week before Lent), Easter, Aug 6, Oct 12, Dec 25

To the north and east of the Andes, the mountains quickly fall away. Rivers cut a network of steep-sided valleys, in the north called the *yungas,* and the dry barren vegetation of the *altiplano* is soon replaced by cloudforest, montane forest and, eventually, tropical rainforest.

As the last few hills of the Andes ripple out across the eastern and northern lowlands, tropical rainforest and savannah take over. The Amazon lowlands of Bolivia constitute 54% of the country's territory.

Rivers

Waters from three quarters of Bolivian territory eventually flow into the Amazon Basin, including the world's longest tributary, the Madeira-Mamoré-Grande system. Starting as a small stream to the south of Santa Cruz, the river quickly grows to form the Grande, travelling 3,200km before joining the River Amazon mainstream downstream from Manaus. The three other major rivers in Bolivia all join this river before leaving the national territory.

The Río Iténez, starting in the lowlands close to Noel Kempff Mercado National Park, marks Bolivia's northeastern boundary with Brazil. The River Beni's headwaters flow from the northern slopes of the Eastern Cordillera, descending rapidly into lowland gold-mining towns before meandering at a more leisurely pace through the jungle towns of Rurrenabaque and Riberalta to join the Mamoré. The Madre de Dios River begins life in Peru's Manu National Park,

UP IN FLAMES

One strong human influence on the climate is the *chaqueo*. Every year in September, land is burnt to clear and prepare it for the next year's crops and to bring on the seasonal rains. This annual burning is carried out throughout Bolivia. It is difficult to know whether the *chaqueo* plays any role in speeding up the arrival of the rainy season, but it isn't difficult to see that the skies of Bolivia are filled with smog when the burning starts. The government has tried to outlaw the practice but traditions are rarely changed as a result of government dictates. Meanwhile, much cloudforest has been destroyed by out-of-control fires.

crossing the border into Bolivia at Puerto Heath and then travelling east to join the River Beni north of Riberalta.

Climate

The rainy season, lasting from November to April, coincides with the southern summer. As altitude decreases clouds are more likely to produce rain. The *altiplano* experiences a wide diurnal range, with comfortable day-time temperatures regularly falling to below freezing at night.

The comfortable year-round temperatures of the *yungas* consistently hit the mid-20s celsius with regular rainfall between December and March.

In the northern lowlands, comfortably warm winter temperatures in the high-20s contrast with hot and oppressively humid summer months. Between December and March, tropical storms can change the streets of Santa Cruz and other lowland towns into rivers and streams.

Flora and fauna

Bolivia is among the world's top ten countries in number of vertebrates species. It is seventh in the world for bird species richness, with more than 1,300 species.

The country is host to more than 220 species of reptiles and more than 100 species of amphibians. Over 40% of known neotropical mammals, 316 species, are found in Bolivia, with ten of them being endemic to the country. These include the rare short-eared dog, which has been sighted in both Madidi and Noel Kempff Mercado National Parks. In the less-populated parks of Bolivia, jaguars and smaller members of the cat family are still to be found, while to date 20 species of primate have been identified throughout the country.

There are more than 22,000 species of plant recorded in Bolivia, including over 2,000 species of orchid and 90 different types of palm.

Land use

Geography and weather conditions play the greatest role in deciding land use. Around one quarter of the country is so high that only the hardiest crops survive, while the steep-sided slopes going down to the lowlands make intensive farming difficult. Lowland areas have seen the introduction of farming and ranching where roads provide sufficient access.

People

Population and ethnic groups

Nearly 60% of Bolivia's population of 7,237,000 lives in cities and towns which are growing at over 4% a year, while the country's population overall increases by just 2.4% annually.

Bolivia, like many South American countries, includes a culturally diverse mixture of peoples. The main groups are of *mestizo* (30%), Quechua (25%), Aymara (17%) and European (12%) descent. Urban Indians or *cholos* make up a significant proportion of the population of La Paz and many other cities.

In rural areas, particularly in the lowlands, it is estimated that there are between 180,000 and 220,000 indigenous people, made up of over 40 different ethnic groups including the Chiquitano, Mojeño, Chimane, Baure and Itonama. Comprising at least 11 linguistic families, these lowland communities lack the coherence and the numbers of highlands Indians. It is within these groups that the worst provision of education and health care is to be found and only recently have they begun to protest at their unfair treatment within the Bolivian political system.

Languages

Spanish is the official language of Bolivia, spoken by over 60% of the population. Quechua, the language of the Inca empire, is the *lingua franca* for some 25% of the population particularly in highland areas. A slightly smaller percentage speak Aymara, the language used throughout the Bolivian highlands before the arrival of the Spanish or the Incas.

Language in lowland areas reflects the diversity of ethnic groups. Many indigenous languages have been lost, reflecting the dominance of the country's three major languages and the extent of migration within the country.

Education

Bolivia's education system has recently undergone several changes, pushing for better and more appropriate teaching. Elementary education is free and, in theory, compulsory… although getting to a school from some of Bolivia's many remote areas is impossible, so lessons are broadcast on the radio to outlying areas, with outreach workers travelling the country to support the programme schedule.

There are eight state-funded universities, the largest being Universidad Mayor de San Andrés (UMSA) in La Paz, and a further ten private universities.

Culture

While archaeologists argue over the birth of South American pottery, Bolivians are happily telling the world that the true home of ceramics can be found in the Bolivian Andes with the Tiahuanaco culture, which dates back to 500BC. A contentious claim is also put forward that the geometric designs of the Tiahuanaco III era – lasting from 300BC to the first century AD – were the inspiration for one of the 20th century's great painting movements. Allegedly a friend, on returning from a trip to Bolivia, told Picasso of the geometric animals seen on ceramics near Tiahuanaco.

Weavings are also an inspiration and delight. Detailed *aguayos*, essentially square pieces of cloth woven with ornate designs used for carrying anything from babies to fruit, vegetables and firewood, are in common use throughout the country. Older *aguayos* are available on Calle Sagárnaga, some of which are genuine antiques and may be priced accordingly. Modern weaving techniques have seen the introduction of mass-produced *aguayos* fashioned from an array of day-glo colours.

Music includes the haunting melodies of the panpipe and woodwind instruments, more correctly called the *quena*. The frantic strumming of the *charango* is another typical sound of the Andes. This small guitar-like instrument was, until recently, commonly made using the plates of a (dead) armadillo as the sound box.

Lowland cultures tend to take second stage to those of the highlands. To the north of Santa Cruz, attention focuses on the mission towns encompassing

Chiquitania which at Easter attract large numbers of pilgrims. The main cultural expression is through fiestas.

If there is a reason to have a party Bolivians will find it. The majority of fiestas merge the complexities of Andean mythology and history with a large dollop of Roman Catholic religion; experiencing one of the Bolivian festivals is unforgettable.

In the lowlands, the Fiesta del Santo Patrono de Moxos overruns the small town of San Ignacio de Moxos, between Rurrenabaque and Trinidad. Ornate costumes and feather head-dresses, accompanied by dancing and the near-compulsory drinking, attract thousands of visitors to the normally quiet town at the end of July.

The main national carnival of the year is La Diablada in Oruro on the *altiplano*. A procession paying tribute to the Socavón de la Virgen ('Cave of the Virgin') winds its way up the hill to the church overlooking the town where the Virgin resides. Thousands of dancers dressed in elaborate costumes dance, drink and meander their way along the 8km route on the last weekend before Ash Wednesday.

In La Paz the procession of El Señor del Gran Poder, a similar style of carnival, fills the city's streets at the beginning of May.

Independence Day on August 6, or the weekend closest to it, is carnival time throughout the country. Very similar to other festivals, the Independence Day parade in La Paz tends to be a slightly more formal occasion with government officials and dignitaries in official attendance.

Religion

Bolivia is nominally 95% Roman Catholic. But a quick trip to the witches' market in La Paz will give you a pretty good idea that other forces are at work. In rural and urban areas, particularly among Indian communities, there are still strong beliefs in the power of *pachamama*. This Mother Earth figure, if duly respected, protects those who live on or in her. Several rituals paying tribute to *pachamama* throughout the year are sufficient to keep her on your side.

A brief history

Pre-conquest

Remaining monuments suggest the Tiahuanacans of the *altiplano* had reached a high degree of sophistication and organisation, having developed irrigation, complex ceremonial textiles and ceramics. The remains of the city itself, with tightly fitting stonework and lintel doorways, suggest the Tiahuanacans were the antecedents of the Inca empire. Archaeological evidence suggests that environmental changes led to the sudden decline in the empire around AD1100 and its breaking down into a number of smaller autonomous Aymara kingdoms.

In smaller groups the Aymaras were unable to stop the advance of the well-organised and expansionist Incas around AD1350. The Inca empire stretched throughout the Bolivian *altiplano* and as far east as Samaipata near Santa Cruz. Although the Incas introduced Quechua as the *lingua franca*, the smaller Aymara kingdoms retained much of their character as well as their Aymara language.

Post-conquest

The conquest of the Inca empire began in 1532. The Spanish conquistadors reaped such golden rewards from Peru in such a short period of time that the hunger to continue exploration quickly brought the Spanish into the territory of Alto Peru – modern-day Bolivia.

Although the Spanish failed to find the legendary gilded city of El Dorado, they could content themselves with the riches of Cerro Rico in Potosí. The quantities of silver taken from the *Rich Hill* financed the rapid development of an administrative infrastructure within Bolivia, including the cities of La Plata, now called Sucre (1538), and La Paz (1548).

Independence

As with much of South America, the French and North American revolutions of the 18th century encouraged the *Creole* population – the descendants of Spanish immigrants – in Bolivia to push for independence. But it wasn't until the liberation wave of the Venezuelan Simón Bolívar reached Alto Peru in 1825 that the country was free to determine its own future. On independence the country was renamed República de Bolívar and Bolívar's General Antonio José de Sucre became the country's first president.

With so many newly formed countries in South America, it is hardly surprising that most tried to extend their boundaries. Between 1835 and 1935 Bolivia's neighbours acquired national territory that reduced the size of the country by half.

The rubber boom of the late 19th century that swept through Amazonia saw Bolivia, as home to some of the most productive rubber stands producing the best quality rubber, enjoy a brief flurry of prosperity, and brought the country to the world's notice. At considerable cost, a railroad was to be built from the north of the country to transport rubber down to Porto Velho in Brazil, removing the need to carry cargo over several sets of rapids along the Mamoré and Madeira rivers. In return for the railroad Bolivia ceded the rubber-rich state of Acre to Brazil. Work began in 1890 and resulted in the death of over 6,200 workers. By 1910 the rubber industry showed signs of imminent collapse. Demand diluted, the source of income for Bolivia's lowlands was thwarted, and the railroad was never completed.

The 20th century

The Chaco War (1932–35) proved costly to Bolivia. An area of 243,000km^2 was lost to Paraguay and 65,000 soldiers, mainly *campesinos* or peasants, were killed in the fighting. Indeed the war set the stage for the political developments of the 20th century.

Increasingly disgruntled by their treatment at the hands of wealthy landholders in the name of national pride, *campesinos* rallied behind the newly formed Movimiento Nacionalista Revolucionario (MNR). The 1952 revolution saw the MNR leader Víctor Paz Estenssoro take power, and nationalisation of the mining industry and agrarian and educational reform followed. The revolution changed the consciousness of the country's population. It is still easy to get grass-roots support for a city-stopping march or a road-blocking protest.

The 1970s and 1980s saw an exhaustive number of military coups. The lowlights include seven years of presidency for General Hugo Banzer Suárez, ending in 1978, whose term saw thousands of political dissidents imprisoned while he handed out favours to the agricultural nouveau riche of his home department Santa Cruz. His legacy to the nation was US$1.8 billion of foreign debt.

Crippled economically, Bolivia limped through three presidential elections and five military coups between 1978 and 1982. The government of General Luís García Meza, with the assistance of former Nazis including Klaus Barbie, ruled over a period of torture, human rights abuses and disappearances. Bolivia's image as a plaything for the ruling classes was reaffirmed as Meza and his cronies amassed huge personal fortunes through coca production and cocaine trafficking.

The 1980s saw Bolivia shift its support behind the democratic process and aim for economic stability. Annual inflation of 25,000%, over-staffed state industries and high unemployment demanded drastic austerity measures. Plans to return state industries to the private sector led to huge numbers of redundancies, industrial disputes and increased hardship, with few foreign investors interested in taking up the opportunities.

The presidency of MNR chief Gonzalo Sánchez de Lozada, beginning in 1993, saw the introduction of capitalisation to the Bolivian economy, moving responsibility for nationalised industries into the private sector. Although not booming, the Bolivian economy experienced several years of growth with inflation at just 10%.

In August of 1997, Hugo Banzer and Paz Zamoro's coalition ticket returned Banzer to the presidency. The reformed president, elected as a committed democrat, has already introduced a price hike of 30% on basic food staples and fuel, resulting in inflationary pressures. Banzer's commitment to eradicate coca production by the end of his term in 2002 is likely to lead to increased social friction.

The price increases will not make travel in Bolivia prohibitive for visitors, but for people living and, more importantly, earning in Bolivia, they will affect the standard of living.

Money

The boliviano depreciates slowly against the dollar. Take cash dollars or American Express dollar travellers' cheques. Sterling is difficult to change.

If you want to change travellers' cheques or cash you can go to one of the exchange houses on La Paz's Avenida Camacho. If you have any problems with travellers' cheques the American Express offices are in Turismo Magri on Avenida 16 de Julio 1490, Edificio Avenida, 5th floor.

Changing cash dollars outside the main cities is usually possible if you look hard enough, but the best option is to change as much into bolivianos as you think you will need before reaching the next city. Changing travellers' cheques outside of cities is difficult.

Budget travellers can easily get by in Bolivia on US$20 per day, but may have to choose between excursions. A more realistic figure placing no limits on activities would require around US$40–50 per day.

Highlights

Bolivia's Amazon region has several national parks which are home to virtually untouched rainforest. Madidi National Park and Manuripi Heath Nature Reserve are north of La Paz. Both parks can be visited with organised tours or independently, but a knowledgeable guide will give a far greater insight into special sites. Trips can be land-based, travelling short distances each day to go on trekking excursions. Alternatively rafting trips lasting up to three weeks and travelling through the parks give a fantastic close-up of life on the river.

To the east, Noel Kempff Mercado National Park is home to untouched rainforest and the drier Precambrian sandstone plateau that rises abruptly to an altitude of 550m. Also in the east is the Ríos Blanco y Negro Wildlife Reserve, completely away from the beaten track.

Boats travel many of Bolivia's rivers but opportunities for independent travel are somewhat limited as there are very few regular boat services. If you have time to wait and try your luck, travelling down any of the larger rivers should be possible although you may have to take several different boats.

The only flotel – floating hotel – in Bolivia travels from Puerto Villaroel, south of Trinidad, along the Río Mamoré through a system of rivers and lagoons amongst rainforest and savannah ecosystems.

Ecotourism has only recently begun to take off in Bolivia which may mean agencies and travellers alike will experience occasional teething troubles, but with tourism in Bolivia still in its infancy most of the national parks are still totally unspoilt. If you can handle a little less comfort, the extra effort required to travel to the Bolivian Amazon is truly worthwhile.

Away from the Amazon Basin, Bolivia has a fantastic array of landscapes to choose from: trekking and hiking in the spectacular Andean mountain range, or excursions to the historically important mining town of Potosí and, further south, to the pure white expanses of the salt flats of Uyuni.

Tour operators

In Bolivia

Academia Nacional de Ciencias de Bolivia Av 16 de Julio 1732, La Paz; tel/fax: 00 591 2 350612; email: cmiranda@ebb.rds.org.bo; postal address: Casilla 5829, La Paz, Bolivia. Coordinates trips to Beni Biosphere Reserve.

EcoBolivia Foundation Calle Colombia, Plaza San Pedro; tel/fax: 00 591 2 315974; email: ecob@megalink.com; postal address: Casilla 8505, La Paz. Arranges trips to Chalalan Ecolodge in Madidi National Park.

EcoLogical Expeditions Sagárnaga Esq Mutillo 189, Galería Dorian Local No 13; tel: 02 365047; fax: 02 314172; email: ecological@bone. Trips to Madidi Park, particularly birdwatching.

Fremen Tours Calle Libertad 320; tel/fax: 00 591 3 360265; email: vtfremen@caoba.entelnet.bo; net: www.andes-amazonia.com. This family-run company, with offices in all major Bolivian cities, arranges trips to Chalalan Ecolodge and Noel Kempff, and runs flotel trips down the Río Mamoré.

Fundación Amigos de la Naturaleza (FAN) Km 7 on the road to Samaipata; tel: 00 591 3 523921; fax: 00 591 3 533389; email: fan@fan.rds.org.bo; net: www.scbbs-bo.com/fan/; postal address: Casilla 2241, Santa Cruz, Bolivia. Organises trips to Noel Kempff Mercado National Park.

In Peru

Amazonas Explorer PO Box 722, Cusco, Peru; fax: 00 58 84 236826; email: amazonasexplorer@compuserve.com; net: www.amazonas-explorer. Has rafting trips through Madidi National Park but these must be booked in advance.

In the UK

Overland Latin America 13 Dormer Place, Leamington Spa, Warks CV32 5AA; tel: 01926 332222; fax: 01926 435567; email: worldlspa@aol.com.

GETTING THERE AND AWAY

By air

From the US

American Airlines (tel: 1 800 433 7300) and Lloyd Aero Boliviano (LAB) (tel: 1 800 327 7407) are the only airlines offering direct services between Miami and La Paz or Santa Cruz. The cost is currently around US$600 return. The service provided by American Airlines is daily, with LAB flying the route several times a week.

From Europe

There are no direct flights from Europe to Bolivia. The most direct flight is with American Airlines, changing at Miami and stopping at Santa Cruz en route. Argentinas Aerolíneas, Varig and AeroPerú all travel from Europe to their home countries and link to Bolivia with connecting flights. Some of the connecting times leave you waiting for up to 24 hours so check the connection times with your travel agent.

Return prices from London start at £740 in low season (April to June), rising to £989 in the high season (July to September). Prices and tickets can be picked up from Journey Latin America in London, tel: 0181 747 8315; fax: 0181 742 1312; email: tours@journeylatinamerica.co.uk.

Overland

Overland crossings into the lowlands are from Peru or Brazil. From Brazil, you can travel from Corumba in the Brazilian Pantanal to Santa Cruz on what has affectionately been labelled the death train. If possible try to book your ticket a couple of days before travel from the new station on Avenida Brasil. If you need a visa to enter Brazil the Brazilian consulate in Santa Cruz is at Av Busch 330.

Slightly to the north, a crossing links the town of San Matías to the Brazilian town of Cáceres.

On Bolivia's northern border the main crossing to Brazil is through Guayaramerín. A short speedboat journey takes you across the Río Mamoré to the Brazilian town of Guajara-Mirim. Border details in Bolivia can be sorted out in the Immigration Office by the ferry terminal. In Brazil border formalities are completed at the offices of the Federal Police a few blocks behind the ferry terminal on Av Pres Dutra 70.

Those finding themselves well and truly off the beaten path, or indeed any path at all, can cross at Cobija into Brasiléia. Crossing into Peru close to the Madre de Dios is also possible but, since there are no border officials of either nationality, locals may view you with some suspicion.

Customs and immigration

Visas of 30 days are offered as standard but if you require longer you can ask for 90 days at your point of entry. If you need an extension, visit the Immigration Ministry on Av Camacho in La Paz.

Getting around

Major cities and towns are often connected by good roads but any deviation from the main routes leads to dirt roads. Much of overland travel in Bolivia can firmly be put in the adventure sector.

By bus

Buses are the most commonly used mode of transport. Intercity buses are straightforward, usually air-conditioned and comfortable. There is normally a central terminal for departing and arriving buses. Timetables exist and work.

Buses travelling to smaller, out-of-the-way places are a different story. Journeys last for 15 hours or more in a vehicle that seems designed for children and bounces its way over potholes jarring every bone in your body. This is what travelling in Bolivia is all about. It'll bore you to tears, amaze you with new sights, smells and sounds, and stun you into disbelief. That first Bolivian bus experience is unforgettable. Once you've done a few, you'll feel like an old-timer, and probably want to fly.

On all but intercity buses the schedules are theoretical. Departure times are fantasy, arrival times are absent and seat numbers are changeable even as you sit in them. In the northern lowlands travel is even worse!

Buses stop at meal times. If you are happy eating from roadside restaurants there's the normal selection of *almuerzos* and *cenas* to choose from. Alternatively you can buy fruit or biscuits to nibble. Bottled water is available at most stops.

Hitching

One step down the comfort ladder is hitching in the back of a truck or *camioneta.* There is a small charge for being transported. Sharing in this mode of travel can take you through the highs and lows of Bolivian culture as it is a common way for Bolivians to travel.

By air

Those seeking a little more comfort can use the relatively inexpensive but extensive network of internal flights provided by LAB, AeroSur and TAM – the military air service. Most towns, even the smaller ones, can be reached by one or more of these airlines. La Paz to Rurrenabaque, for example, costs US$50. This option does have the added benefit of fantastic views.

The simplest way to buy tickets is on arrival in La Paz through one of the airline offices: LAB (Av Camacho 1456-60; tel: 0800 3001), or AeroSur (Av 16 de Julio, Edif. Petrolero Mezannine; tel: 354435).

TAM provides occasional passenger services on routes to the smaller towns (tel: 379285).

There is a Bolivia Airpass available from LAB, valid for one month and costing US$160; but destinations are limited to the major cities of Santa Cruz, Cochabamba, La Paz, Sucre, Tarija and Trinidad.

By train

Two rail lines connect Bolivia to Brazil to the west and Chile to the south, leaving from Santa Cruz and La Paz respectively. There are no train services in Bolivia's Amazon Basin.

COMMUNICATIONS

Mail

By comparison with other countries in South America, the Bolivian postal service is quite good. It takes about a week for incoming and outgoing mail to Europe and slightly less for the US. Postcards cost about 75 cents. Package rates can be costly so it's far better to try to squeeze that little bit of extra luggage in the bag and carry it home.

If you are writing to a Bolivian postal address do not forget to include the *casilla* or box number. Individuals and organisations collect mail from the post office boxes. Conversely, to visit an office you need the full address – the postal address will take you only to a little metal box!

Telephones, fax and internet

The Bolivian telephone system has undergone a near revolution in recent years. Modern telephones using phonecards (*tarjetas telefónicas*) are found in many hotels, bars and on the street. *Tarjetas* range in value from Bs5 to Bs50 and can usually be bought from someone in the vicinity of the telephone.

International calls can be made from these phones but be sure to buy the higher value cards. (Bs50 buys approximately three minutes to Europe.)

Faxes can be sent from the better hotels or from the central telephone office on Calle Ayacucho 267 near the post office.

Bolivia has been quick to catch on to the benefits of email and cybercafés are beginning to open up. WaraNet is in La Paz on Calle Yanacocha #372, on the ground floor of Edificio Cristal.

Television and radio

Television and radio are good ways of keeping up with the news if your Spanish is up to it. Some of the better hotels in La Paz and Santa Cruz have cable, providing international news from CNN and BBC World.

Newspapers

A range of broadsheet and tabloid papers are available. It's worth picking one up if you want to improve your Spanish. If you have a bilingual dictionary they aren't that difficult to understand.

The English-language newspaper *The Bolivian Times* is available in many tourist areas, and provides a mixture of news and cultural pieces which may give a little more insight into what is happening in the country.

LA PAZ

La Paz is a dramatic city. Nestled in the canyon created by the Río Choqueyapu, the city is overshadowed by the beautiful snow-topped mountain of Illimani (6,439m). La Paz possesses a cosmopolitan air. The flashing neon signs are a stark reminder of Westernisation, but away from the main street of El Prado you will see the strong tradition of the urban Quechua Indians, still in traditional dress, who make up 40% of the city's population.

At an altitude of 3,600m, it is quite likely that visitors arriving by plane will experience altitude sickness. The symptoms of *soroche* include tiredness, loss of appetite, headaches, nausea and vomiting. Symptoms can take a few hours to appear and the best remedy is to rest and have a cup of coca tea. Fortunately, the steep hills of La Paz discourage too much activity.

Orientation is relatively easy with the city being divided into three levels. At the top is the urban sprawl of El Alto which offers fantastic views over the city below. Dropping a level, and descending some 400m in altitude takes you to the heart of the city with the main street, the Prado, running straight through the middle. Most things of interest to the visitor are close to the Prado. Dropping another step is Zona Sur, the wealthiest part of the city, with a slightly milder climate and certainly the worst views. Bolivia is often difficult to fully comprehend.

At the airport

It is a 30-minute drive to La Paz. A taxi to the centre costs about US$8 and gives you the option of stopping to take pictures of the city. Buses leave the airport for the centre of town every ten minutes or so and cost US$0.50. They wait just outside the arrivals building until full and drop you in the centre of town along the Prado.

Airport departure tax is US$20.

City transport

Radio taxis are efficient and can be hailed in the street or booked by telephone. Numbers are posted in hotels and on the side of vehicles. Short trips cost Bs5 (about US$1), longer trips Bs10. In La Paz shared taxis called *trufis* flying green pennants run along set routes – a slightly quicker option than the buses but more expensive. City buses, charging Bs1 for travel throughout the city, have their destination signposted in the windscreen.

Where to stay

There are plenty of hotels in La Paz. Those below are close to the centre of town.

First class

Hotel Plaza Av 16 de Julio; tel: 02 378311; fax: 02 343391. A 5-star hotel providing all the comforts you'd expect and seemingly a world away from the city outside. Fantastic views from the top floor restaurant. (Single US$130, double US$150.)

El Rey Palacio Av 20 de Octubre; tel: 02 393016; fax: 02 367759; email: hotelrey@wara.bolnet.bo. Off the main street, this is a very good hotel popular with tour groups. (Single US$70, double US$80.)

Middle range

Hostal República Calle Comercio 1455; tel: 02 355617. A restored colonial building with comfortable rooms and a pleasant forecourt for whiling away quiet moments.

Hotel Galería Calle Santa Cruz 583; tel: 02 371565; fax 02 316857. A new hotel a couple of blocks up from Calle Sagárnaga with good rooms, an airy restaurant and bar area. (US$15 per person.)

Budget

Hostal Austria Yanachocha 531; tel: 02 351140. Popular with travellers and often full, it has a kitchen and lounge. (US$6 per person.)

Hotel Torino Calle Socabaya 457. Redecorated, the Torino has good and reasonably priced rooms. At weekends the forecourt restaurant, popular with families in La Paz, has kitschy floor shows complete with bontempi keyboards – a must-see. (US$4 per person.)

Where to eat

At midday, hundreds of small restaurants serve a set meal or *almuerzo*. Usually three courses, the meal ranges from the unforgettable to the undesirable. An evening set meal is harder to find so you may have to visit a larger restaurant.

Hotel Gloria near to San Francisco Plaza has a vegetarian restaurant on the ground floor, a good restaurant upstairs and an excellent coffee shop on the way out. The **Hotel Plaza** restaurant on the hotel's top floor provides a good mix of European and Bolivian dishes, is reasonably priced at US$15pp and has stunning views. Arguably the best restaurant in La Paz, **Restaurant Vienna** on Federico Zuazo 1905 serves European cuisine and is popular with expatriates.

Andromeda, on Av Arce and Aspiazu, serves good food with vegetarian options.

An essential part of the Bolivian way of life includes the mid-morning snacking of *salteñas*. Readily available on the street, the best in La Paz are from **Snack Valerie's** at Av 6 de Agosto No 2187, a few blocks down from Plaza Estudiante.

La Paz has a range of entertainment options. The traditional outing, for many, would include a trip to a *peña* which provides traditional Bolivian food, dancing and music. **Peña Naira** on Calle Sagárnaga is popular.

Refreshments can be found throughout the city in a host of drinking bars. If you don't want to leave it to chance, two recommended pubs include the **Pig & Whistle**, near the centre of town on Calle Goitia, and the **Britannia** between Calle 15 and 16 in Calacoto, Zona Sur.

Lively and popular with *paceñan* trendies is the **Café Montmartre** on Fernando Guachalla in Sopocachi. **Mongo's** on Hermanos Manchego 2444 is good for US-style food.

A new piano bar is **Cambrinus** at Av 20 de Octubre #2453 on Plaza Avaroa. Owned by Dr Fernando Arispe, this bar, fantastic in all its detail and perversities, positively oozes atmosphere and, at times, good home-brew beer.

What to see

Most things of interest to the passing tourist are in the centre of the city within a couple of blocks of El Prado, the main street. Architecturally the area around **Plaza Murillo** is of greatest interest, and is home to the **Cathedral** and **National Congress**. The restored colonial street of **Calle Jaén** is worth a visit and is home to four different museums looking at Bolivian history and art.

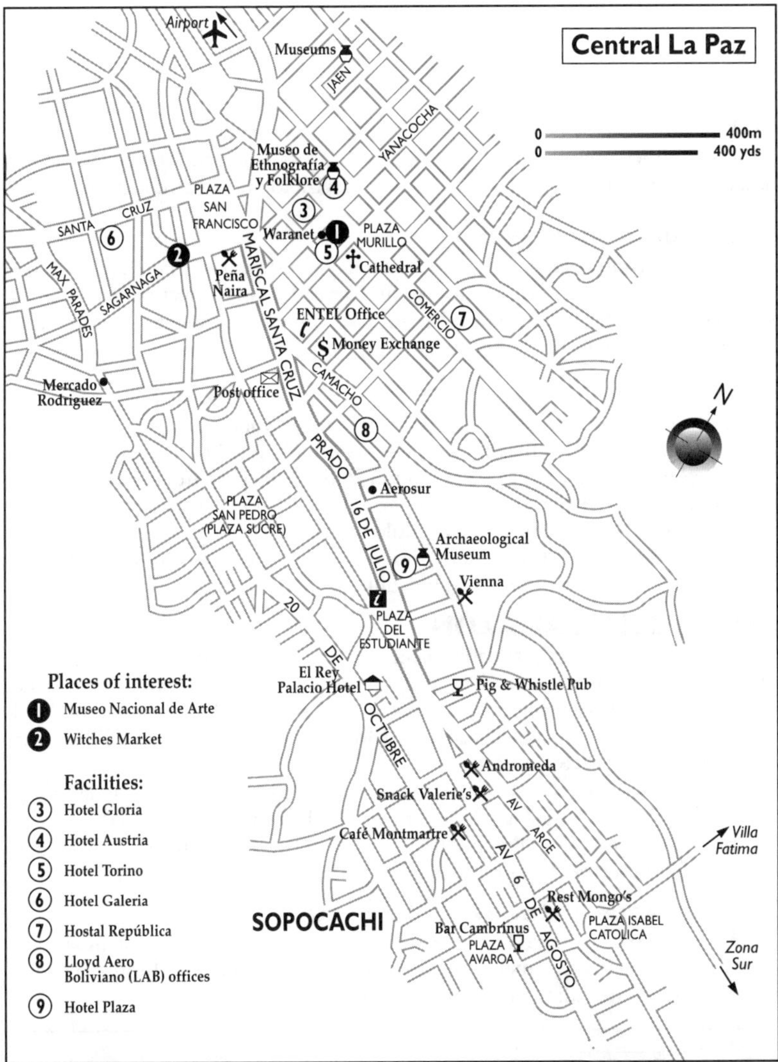

The **post office** is a rather impressive building in the style of Frank Lloyd Wright on the Prado. A few blocks behind this is the colourful **Mercado Rodriguez**, selling dry goods, fruit, vegetables, fish and meat. It's a wonderfully chaotic mixture of sounds, smells and colours, and is best on a Saturday as there are more stalls.

Up the hill from the post office is **Plaza San Francisco** with the 16th-century church of the same name. The plaza in front fills with hawkers and pedlars selling all sorts of remedies to the world's illnesses. City buses will also take you to visit the strangely eroded **Valley of the Moon** to the south of the city.

Shopping

A visit to Calle Sagárnaga beside San Francisco church, to buy clothes, textiles, jewellery and ceramics, is a must. Bartering is common. Traditional *aguayos* are sold alongside more modern goods. Most items of clothing can be bought including waistcoats, jumpers, trousers and hats; along with jewellery, rugs and blankets. The list is endless and the prices are ridiculously low.

Off Sagárnaga is the *Mercado de los Brujas* selling all manner of items, some of which would certainly be picked up by customs on your way home.

On the same street there are several travel agents who can arrange city tours, local excursions and trips to the Amazon if you wish to organise these from La Paz.

Excursions from La Paz

Easily arranged and needing no more than a day is a short trip to the pre-Inca site of **Tiahuanaco**. An impressive display of Tiahuanacan architecture and designs occupies the site itself and a new museum goes some of the way to showing how the site would have looked at the height of the empire.

Leaving town

The daily buses to Rurrenabaque (US$10) and beyond leave La Paz around midday from the Villa Fatima district. They are often full so buy your ticket the day before if you can. The journey takes around 20 hours if there are no roadworks en route. Buses for Riberalta and Guayaramerín leave from La Paz and can take up to two days although 36 hours is the scheduled time.

Buses to Trinidad and Santa Cruz leave from the main bus terminal at Plaza Antofagasta – check your driver is not drunk.

THE BOLIVIAN AMAZON

While no single town can justifiably claim to be the centre of the Bolivian Amazon for visitors, **Rurrenabaque** is the most popular and the easiest spot to visit in the rainforest. Several agencies have offices in the town making it a simple and economical base for planning a trip. Most trips organised in La Paz use Rurrenabaque as a starting point.

An alternative entry point to the Amazon, with direct international access, is **Santa Cruz**, which is used as a base for organised excursions.

Large towns throughout the lowlands buzz with the hum of the tropics but few have organised tourism opportunities.

Rurrenabaque: gateway to the north

On the banks of the River Beni the small town of Rurrenabaque, with around 7,000 inhabitants, is very much a jungle town. The river squeezes through a ravine upstream before spreading out to drift past Rurre, as locals call it.

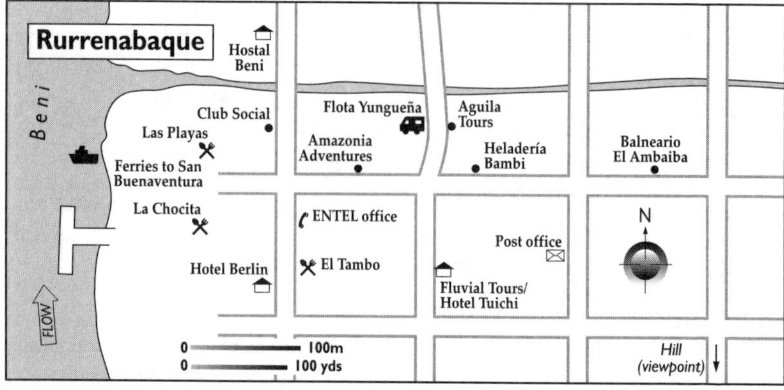

Originally a trading and transit point for river traffic, the town has developed to become a supply post for surrounding communities, the logging industry and, in recent years, oil company exploration including the French company Total. Until recently logging has remained small-scale, but as with other parts of the Amazon the future may not be so optimistic.

Despite the logging activity the sense that the jungle is just around the corner never leaves. Travelling salesmen occasionally set up stalls near the waterfront market selling all-powerful medicinal concoctions.

Rurre has grown in recent years and the rainforest's salvation could be the arrival of tourism. You need at least a week to enjoy the area without feeling too rushed. The centre of town is so small you'll struggle to get lost. Although lots of travellers use Rurre as a base for rainforest trips, most people are out of town for several days so the place keeps a sleepy feel.

Getting there

A daily bus to and from Rurre stops right in the centre of town. The journey to La Paz takes you through stunning scenery which sadly you cannot see once night falls. Taking twenty hours along a terrible road, the trip costs US$10. Not surprisingly, the internal air flights are becoming more popular, with the added bonus of having spectacular scenery as you fly down to the lowlands through gaps between the mountains. TAM flies between Rurrenabaque and La Paz three or four times a week; US$45 one way. The flight is often booked up two or three days in advance so book early if you want to fly. The airport is a dirt landing strip just outside town. Trucks and taxis meet the 40-seater plane when it comes in to land.

Where to stay

The **Hotel Tuichi** (US$3) is very popular, often full and the best cheap hotel. The **Hostal Beni** (US$5–8) on the riverfront is slightly more expensive and very clean with a patio for relaxing. There is also, of course, the **Hotel Berlin** (US$4–6) for those wanting to be part of Rurre's history.

Those seeking to just relax away from the town may want to try out the **Selva Tambo River and Lodge** upriver from Rurre. Isolated rustic lodge accommodation is available either on the banks of the River Beni or in a jungle clearing. The lodge can be used as a base for short guided tours into the jungle or for river trips. The dormitory accommodation provides beds and mosquito nets and you can opt to cook for yourself. Transport is only by boat; ask for details at the Restaurant El Tambo.

Where to eat

Eating is often more function than flavour in this jungle town. Having said that, spectacular fish dishes like *dorado* or *surubí* may surprise you on any of the riverfront restaurants. The **Club Social** – which always looks closed – on Calle Comercio is popular with regular visitors to the town providing big portions of traditional Bolivian dishes from US$3.50.

Restaurant El Tambo is targeting the traveller market with 'good gringo food'. It's a bit pricey but you can't get pancakes and maple syrup in every jungle town.

Heladería Bambi provides excellent ice-cream, perfect at any time of day.

Excursions from Rurrenabaque

If you climb the small hill behind the town, after leaving the main plaza heading away from the river, you'll have a fantastic view of the Amazon lowlands, the river and the town below. Boats cross over the river to San Buenaventura. Nothing of specific interest awaits the visitor there, but for soaking up atmosphere, attitude and chance encounters it's ideal just to see what might happen.

After a few days of sweating it out in the jungle your best option is to spend the day at the swimming pool, Balneario El Ambaiba. It costs US$2 for the day and you can come and go as you please.

If you have a little longer you could venture upstream to the busy gold-mining town of Guanay. The eight-hour boat trip to Guanay costs around US$20 per person.

Jungle adventures

Several agencies provide guided trips into the jungle up the River Tuichi, a tributary of the River Beni. The most popular trip is four days and three nights, leaving early in the morning and returning in the afternoon of the fourth day. Jungle trips need a minimum of four people. Heading upstream for four hours or so, you set up camp in the lowland tropical forest just off the beaches of the River Tuichi. A night under canvas, in reality little more than a tarpaulin, tests out the mosquito nets. The following three days and nights will take you on hikes along primary rainforest trails exploring remoter areas. Agencies follow different paths on every trip, but you should see several animals including waterbirds, toucans, macaws, and with luck monkeys, caiman, snakes and capybara.

Included in the trips are camping, fishing and bushcraft skills, learning about edible and medicinal plants from the rainforest, canoeing to remote channels for bird and animal watching, and night treks.

Agencies will tailor trips to your needs and interests so, if you have a particular interest such as birdwatching, discuss it with the agent.

Increased pressure from tourism has seen the River Tuichi and its tributaries explored further upstream. Jungle trips are beginning to include circular routes which enter one tributary, trek across to another and rejoin the canoe before heading towards Laguna Santa Rosa. The lagoon is an excellent spot to see snakes and caiman and to fish for piranha.

Pampas tours

For a change from sticky, humid jungle consider a trip to the pampas grasslands close to the town of Santa Rosa. A network of river channels is home to hundreds of water birds, river turtles, pink dolphins, capybara and many other animals. Many people find the open freshness of the pampas grasslands a more relaxing trip than the jungle. Without the dense vegetation of the rainforest it's a lot easier to see or hear the wildlife. As with the jungle trips, it is possible to arrange tours of any duration but three days is long enough for most people.

Choosing an agency and guide

Until recently tourism development has been unrestricted along the course of the River Tuichi and its growth has been based on demand. The creation of Madidi National Park, to the west of Rurrenabaque, is in response to the greater awareness of the region's impressive biodiversity and aims to conserve the area.

Competition between agencies has led to price cuts, and concern for the ecological systems that attract visitors seems, at times, to have floated down the river. Agencies tend to offer the same kind of deal so competition is based on price. Trips currently cost as little as US$25/day, although agencies are trying to secure an industry minimum of US$35/day for the area.

RURRENABAQUE NOW AND THEN

Cynthia Thompson

In 1975, no roads led to Rurrenabaque and the only way to reach the village was by river. Mario Sarabia and I travelled from La Paz through the Yungas down to Puerto Linares where we finally found a boat willing to take us to Rurre. It took six days to reach the village. We arrived sunburnt and exhausted having travelled the last day downriver through a series of difficult rapids. Just before the village of Rurrenabaque, the mountains rose tall and narrow like stage sets, then fell steeply. From the village onward nothing could be seen but the muddy Beni river disappearing into a flat green plane of steaming jungle.

The Hotel Berlin stood on the bank just up from the river – the first and, at the time, only hotel in town. Doña Aury greeted us warmly. Foreign travellers passing through were rare then and we caused a stir of interest and curiosity. Everyone knew each other in the village and the strong sense of community among the people was apparent. The houses were constructed of bamboo with thatched roofs, and only a few were made of wooden planks. The doors were never locked.

To reach San Buenaventura on the opposite shore, you had to search for someone with a canoe and ask for a ride. There were no telephones and electricity was available for only a few hours after dusk. Since no road entered the area, neither did motorised vehicles and most people travelled by horse or ox-drawn cart. Rurrenabaque's streets were worn footpaths through the grass. The Río Beni was its highway and means of communication with the rest of the world.

At night, the darkness was filled with a deafening chorus of frogs and insects, and fish could be heard leaping in the river. In the early morning, the pandemonium of birdcalls, dominated by the raucous cry of macaws flying across the sky in resplendent pairs, woke the village and set the day in motion.

Twenty years later, the trip from La Paz to Rurrenabaque takes just one day by bus or one hour by plane. I took the bus down and hardly recognised the village when we pulled in that morning. Motorbikes, trucks, buses and jeeps raised clouds of dust as they drove through the town.

A large group of tourists sat at an outdoor café with a menu board written in English and Hebrew. More than a dozen new hotels had sprung up and still others were being constructed. I looked for the Hotel Berlin. That old haven of hospitality to river travellers was still standing, looking worn and crowded in between new buildings. Doña Aury, the original owner, was making plans to renovate it in order to keep pace with the times and the competition.

Ferry boats crossed the river to San Buenaventura every fifteen minutes. Discos and karaoke bars offered night-time diversion, competing with the night-time chorus of frogs and insects. The village has a telephone office now, a beautiful, clean, public swimming pool, numerous restaurants, and several ecotourism offices catering to tourists who want to see the jungle wildlife and travel the rivers of the region.

Cynthia Thompson travelled down the River Beni on a raft in 1975. Twenty years later she returned to repeat the trip.

When choosing an agency try not to focus on price alone. Think about what it is you would like to see and whether the impact of your visit will significantly reduce the prospect of following visitors seeing the same things. Make sure all rubbish is carried out. Ideal group sizes are between four and eight people.

Some of the guides can speak a little English but it is far better to have someone in your group with at least some knowledge of Spanish.

Tour operators and agencies

At present Rurre agencies do not have their own telephones although they are expected any day. If you want to book in advance call the town's telephone exchange (tel: 083 2999) and someone at the exchange will go and fetch someone from the agency. But in reality you can just turn up in Rurre and organise a trip to leave immediately.

Fluvial Tours is one block from Flota Yungueña – the bus company. It is popular with travellers, and recommendations are consistently good. The husband-and-wife team run a hotel, which makes it easy to sort out accommodation for your return from the jungle.
Aguila Tours opposite the bus company is reported to have friendly and informative guides.
Amazonia Adventures on Calle Santa Cruz. A new operation that is aiming to provide ecologically sensitive tours. Amazonia can also organise extended adventure trips to Madidi National Park (see below). Minimum number of people is five, maximum ten.

WARNING Unfortunately there have been a couple of incidents in Rurrenabaque that travellers should be aware of. A guide by the name of 'Negro' Israel Janco, formerly with Eco-Tours, has sexually abused at least two female travellers. That agency has now closed down and 'Negro' is on the run from the police. His tactic relies on drugging victims senseless. Do not take drugs, sweets or drinks from anyone.

NATIONAL PARKS OF THE NORTH

Madidi National Park

Created in 1995 and with its boundaries still to be legally recognised, Madidi National Park is being hailed as one of the world's most diverse national parks. It is now just opening up to ecotourism.

The diversity within the park is staggering. Geographically the park borders Bolivia's western frontier with Peru stretching southward from Puerto Heath in the Amazon Basin to join the Ulla Ulla National Reserve on the Bolivian *altiplano* – a highland reserve created in 1972 to protect the shrinking vicuña population. Stretching eastwards, the 1.9 million hectare park encompasses the River Tuichi basin which flows out through Rurrenabaque. The park ranges in altitude from 6,000m above sea level down to just 250m.

Conservation International carried out a Rapid Assessment Programme (RAP) of the park in 1990. The park is home to more than 50% of all neotropical bird species. Nearly 1,000 bird species can be found in Madidi National Park, 11% of all bird species on earth, as well as 44% of all neotropical mammals and 38% of all neotropical amphibians. Madidi's floristic richness is also very high and the region is a major centre for plant endemism. The park encompasses diverse habitats including montane cloudforest, rare tropical dry forest, savannah and lowland tropical forest.

The low population density of this part of Bolivia has directly contributed to lower pressure on land than elsewhere, thus providing points of refuge for animals in the region.

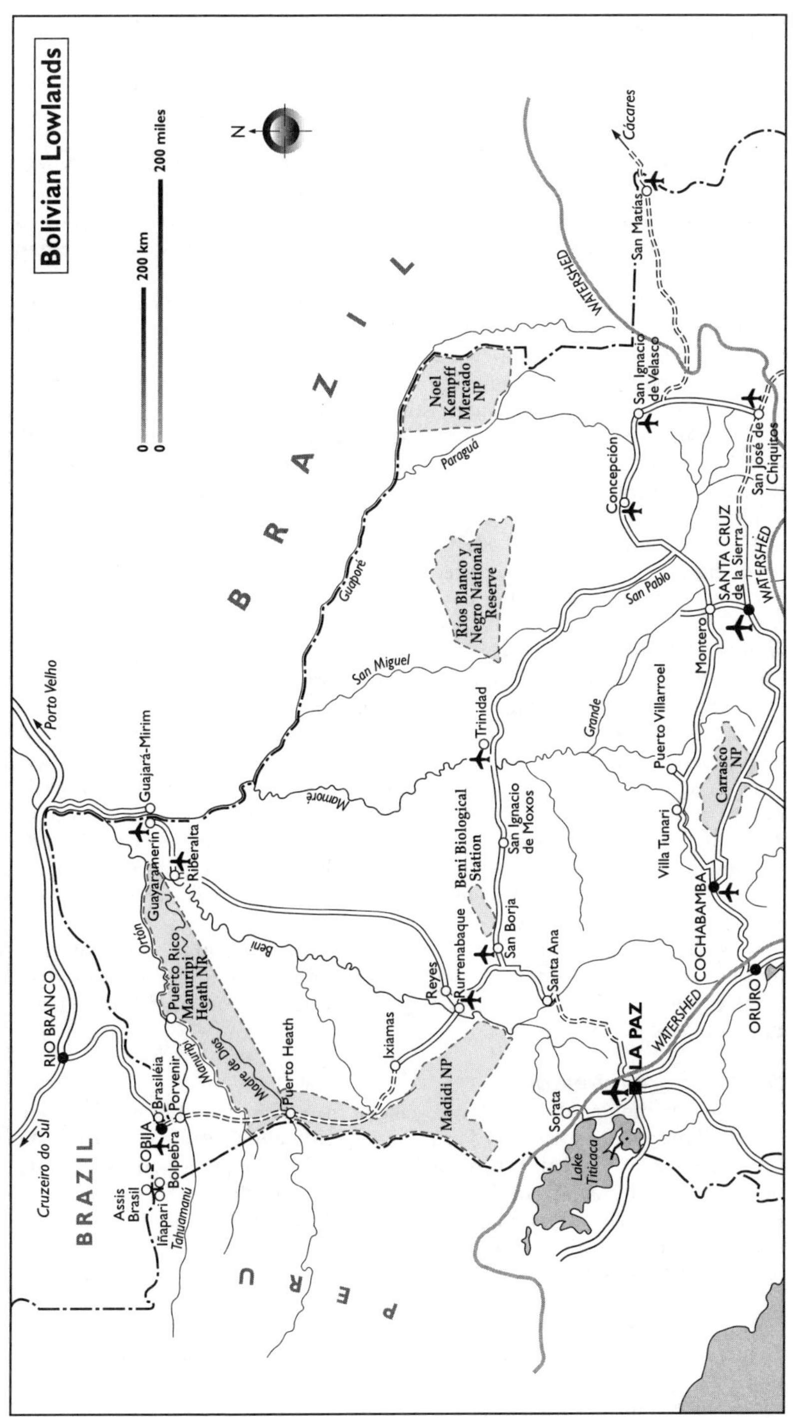
Bolivian Lowlands
0 200 km
0 200 miles
N
BRAZIL
BRAZIL
PERU
Porto Velho
Guajará-Mirim
Guayaramerín
Riberalta
Orthon
Puerto Rico
Manuripi Heath NR
Manuripi
Madre de Dios
Puerto Heath
RIO BRANCO
Cruzeiro do Sul
Brasiléia
Porvenir
COBIJA
Bolpebra
Assis Brasil
Iñapari
Tahuamanu
Beni
Ixiamas
Reyes
Rurrenabaque
Madidi NP
San Borja
Beni Biological Station
Santa Ana
San Ignacio de Moxos
Trinidad
Mamoré
San Miguel
Guaporé
Ríos Blanco y Negro National Reserve
Noel Kempff Mercado NP
Paraguá
Concepción
San Ignacio de Velasco
San Matías
Cáceres
WATERSHED
San José de Chiquitos
SANTA CRUZ de la Sierra
Montero
San Pablo
Grande
Puerto Villarroel
Villa Tunari
Carrasco NP
COCHABAMBA
ORURO
LA PAZ
Sorata
Lake Titicaca

Getting there and where to stay

If out-of-the-way is what you are looking for, stay at Chalalan Ecolodge. After travelling to Rurrenabaque, where you will probably need and want to spend at least one night, it's a five-hour journey upriver. Once dropped off, a 30-minute walk takes you to the lodge.

Two agencies can arrange trips to Chalalan although neither has offices in Rurre. (See page 320.) It is probably best to book in advance from La Paz. One agency, **EcoBolivia Foundation**, played a vital role in raising awareness of the region and lobbied the government hard for its status as a National Park. The second, **Fremen Tours**, is a family-run company that focuses on ecotourism.

Trips are tailored for each group and prices reflect the length of stay and the number in the group. Four people visiting the lodge for a four-day trip with Fremen costs approximately US$160pp, including transport to and from the lodge and all meals. Transport to Rurrenabaque from other parts of Bolivia is not included in the price and neither is accommodation while in Rurrenabaque.

Chalalan Ecolodge has three palm-roofed, wooden lodges with accommodation for up to 24 persons. The sleeping quarters are mosquito-proof and decorated with local crafts. Showers and bathrooms are provided. It is clean but basic.

Meals are provided using a selection of foods harvested from the forest such as brazil nuts, organic vegetables, coffee and chocolate. The dining room has a view of the lake along with a relaxing area complete with hammocks.

Travel opportunities

All the tour operators taking tourists to the park are keen to avoid ecosystem destruction. The 500 Quechua-Tacana Indians living in the village of San José de Uchupiamonas have lived in the Tuichi valley for over 200 years with little impact on the local habitat.

From the lodge visits to nearby Lake Chalalan, the Tuichi River and the Eslabón River can be planned. In the immediate area there are ten jungle trails, totalling 20km in length, incorporating several different ecosystems. The trails are signposted and information is posted en route about flora, fauna and the distance travelled. The longest trail takes you to the Eslabón River, close to a site frequented by several species of monkey.

In addition to providing a visit to pristine rainforest, the project aims to improve the socio-economic conditions of the community of San José. Conservation-based initiatives encourage the village to grow food for the lodge and train local people as guides.

For the more adventurous

If you are fit enough, the best way to take in the park's natural beauty has to be by raft. Amazonas Explorer in Peru arrange whitewater rafting trips from the headwaters of the Tuichi. Setting out from La Paz, groups jeep and trek to the small community of Virgin del Rosario from where the river flows down to Rurrenabaque. The trip passes through cloudforest before paddling through tropical dry forest and, of course, primary rainforest. Nights are spent camping on the river's beaches. Days are spent paddling while you try to convince yourself that the world around you, in all its beauty, is real.

Trips need to be organised in advance. They cost around US$1,800 (£1,100), excluding international flights. For details contact: **Amazonas Explorer**, PO Box 722, Cusco, Peru; fax: 00 58 84 236826; email: amazonasexplorer@compuserve.com.

Manuripi Heath National Reserve

Close to the northern border with Brazil is Manuripi Heath Nature Reserve. Formed in 1973, the park is lowland tropical rainforest. The boundary of the 1.8 million hectare park is contained by the Peruvian border to the west. The River Manuripi marks the northern border, with the southern border roughly following the River Madre de Dios to its confluence with the River Beni near Riberalta.

At just 200 metres above sea level, climatic variations are minimal with the annual temperature range a mere two degrees: fluctuating between 25° and 27°C. Annual rainfall is around 1,650mm, with the dry season between June and August receiving sporadic rainfall.

Although research carried out in the park is not comprehensive, approximate species counts yield 800 types of birds, including the harpy eagle. Mammals include tapirs, capybara, giant anteaters, at least six species of primate and various types of lowland cat including the elusive jaguar.

Human impact on the park is minimal, principal activities being brazil-nut and rubber extraction. Pressure from logging is increasing with the improvement of roads from Cobija to the north.

Getting there

The nearest town of significance is Cobija. Bordering Brazil along the River Acre and with a population of 15,000, this capital of the Department of Pando has nothing to differentiate it from any other Bolivian frontier town.

Oppressively hot in the summer months and with regular afternoon showers, the climate may tempt you to take a refreshing swim across the River Acre to Brazil. There are no border controls along the stretch of river in the town to stop you, but stripping for the swim attracts swarms of vicious sandflies.

Overland routes to Cobija are feasible but only for the masochist. It's a 12-hour, bone-shaking bus journey from Riberalta in the dry season. Air travel is the only real option. AeroSur and LAB fly to Cobija from La Paz several times a week. The cost is US$150 return.

Where to stay and eat

Accommodation options are limited with the two best options being close to the main plaza. **Hostal Sucre** provides clean rooms and efficient service for Bs50 (US$10), and the **Residencial Cocodrillo** (Bs20) has basic rooms.

Travel opportunities

A foray into the virgin jungle of Manuripi Heath offers many opportunities for the independent traveller. Either of the two main rivers would be interesting routes to consider for a boat trip, with the added bonus of ending up near the town of Riberalta, an easy exit point with regular planes and buses to and from La Paz.

Logistically, however, a trip to Manuripi Heath is difficult to organise. Letting someone else take the strain is a good idea. Eli Rush of **Rainforest Expeditions** (tel: 00 1 916 265 0958; email: rainfst@netshel.net) guides kayaking trips in the area. A 21-day trip with Eli is around US$3,000 land costs – international flights to Bolivia are extra. Rainforest Expeditions provide several trip options travelling on the River Tahuamanu and to Lago Bay on the border of the park, with plans to launch exploratory trips to Manuripi Heath National Park.

Millicent Foreman of the US who visited the area with Rainforest Expeditions is in no doubt that the region is well worth the effort.

'For eight days we paddled over 200 miles spending our nights in tents on small sandy beaches. We saw monkeys more than once each day and more caiman than I could count...hundreds. We saw scarlet macaws and flocks of parrots. One evening, when we were looking for a place to camp, we came across a huge, standing dead tree covered with hundreds of storks flapping their wings and mumbling to themselves.

'One beach we camped on was littered with jaguar tracks with a long snake track leading down to the river. We saw capybara and once saw one hauling ass to get away from us…it prompted me to think how useful a book of animals' backsides would be for identification.'

Building on the success of the Madidi Park, **EcoLogical Expeditions** in La Paz is constructing five jungle lodges in the park. (See page 320.) The agency specialises in birdwatching tours, but can tailor trips for individuals or groups wanting to visit the park. Prices start from US$40/day.

Santa Cruz: gateway to the east

Santa Cruz is the natural access point to the eastern lowlands of Bolivia, with direct flights from Miami. Having grown rapidly in just a couple of decades, this city of over 700,000 is expected to become Bolivia's largest city early in the next millennium.

Its rapid growth is officially explained by the development of oil reserves in the region. As oil isn't *that* prominent in Santa Cruz it is fair to assume that some of the profits from the coca-producing Chapare region have been invested in property! Agribusiness in the area has increased rapidly, with soya and other products grown for export to Brazil and Argentina.

Travel opportunities

Santa Cruz is the ideal starting point for visitors interested in travelling to either Noel Kempff Mercado National Park or the Ríos Blanco y Negro Wildlife Reserve.

Organised trips to either one of these large biological reserves can be organised by Fremen Tours (see page 320) or most established tour operators in Santa Cruz.

Unfortunately, it is difficult for independent travellers looking for an Amazon experience to organise trips on their own. A trip to Noel Kempff Mercado National Park can easily be planned by visiting the offices of Fundación Amigos de la Naturaleza (FAN) – the conservation organisation in charge of the administration and management of Noel Kempff – at Km. 7, Carretera Antigua a Cochabamba; tel: 03 524921; fax: 03 533389; net: www.scbbs-bo.com/fan/. FAN has an information packet for independent travellers interested in visiting the park, but you shouldn't even consider it unless you have more than a week to dedicate to the trip.

Boat trips which travel down the Río Ichilo from Puerto Villaroel are one option for the independent traveller, as is exploring the savannah region between Trinidad and Rurrenabaque.

Other places to visit in the region include the beautifully restored Jesuit Missions and the pre-Inca site of Samaipata close to the town of the same name.

At the airport

Viru Viru airport, serving national and international destinations, is 15km north of the city. Buses and taxis provide transport for the 30-minute journey to the city centre throughout the day.

City transport

Taxis are priced in a similar way to those in La Paz; short trips cost Bs5 (about US$1) and longer trips Bs10. Maps of the city are available from most bookshops.

Where to stay

As with any large city there is no shortage of hotels.

First class

Los Tajibos Hotel Av Santa Marta 455; tel: 03 421000; fax: 03 426994. A luxury 5-star hotel with swimming pool and virtually every indulgence you can think of. (Single US$146, double US$164.)

Las Américas 21 de Mayo esq Seoane; tel: 03 368778; fax: 03 336083. Comfortable, central and half the price of Los Tajibos. (US$60 per person.)

Middle range

Hotel Viru Viru Junín 338; tel: 03 335298. Comfortable and with a swimming pool. (Single US$30, double US$35.)

Hotel Bibosi Junín 218; tel: 03 348548. In the centre of town. (Single US$25, double US$34.)

Budget

There is lots of budget accommodation of varying standards around the bus terminal. For example, try **Residencial RM Pantanal** Av Omar Chávez Ortíz 1043; tel 03 330084. Just south of the bus terminal. (Single US$6, double US$10.) Closer to the centre of town is **Residencial Bolívar** Calle Sucre 131; tel: 03 342500. (Single US$8, double US$12.)

Where to eat

You can trust the locals or *cruceños* to know where the best places are. Recommendations include **Castalñuelas** on Calle Velasco 308 esq Pari (tel: 334679) which is a popular Spanish restaurant.

Victori is on Calle Junín esq 21 de Mayo (tel 322935). Centrally located in the Casco Viejo on the first floor, this Italian coffee-place serves good cappuccino and cakes and is an ideal place to hang out during the day. Very central.

La Casa del Camba is slightly out of town on the second *anillo* (ring-road) on the corner with Avenida Alemana at Cristobal de Mendoza 539 (tel: 427864). They serve good meat in the traditional way. Almost next-door is another meat place: **La Buena Mesa** (tel: 421284).

Leonardo Avenida Warnes 666; tel: 338282, serves good Italian food but is a little pricey.

Tapekua, on the corner of Calle Ballivian and La Paz, is a Swiss-owned restaurant with live music. There is a small cover charge when bands are playing but the food and atmosphere are good. Open Wed–Sun.

Going out

Cultural centres include the **Instituto de Cooperacion Iberoamericana**, known as the ICI, on Calle Arenales 583 and has exhibitions and free movies. The **Casa de la Cultura** on the main square has classical concerts, theatre and other events. **Cine Arte Videas** has recently opened on Calle Andres Manso 1095 and may be screening a Bolivian film.

The **Irish Pub** almost on the corner with Avenida Banzer and the third *anillo* is very popular with gringos, is spacious and has good music.

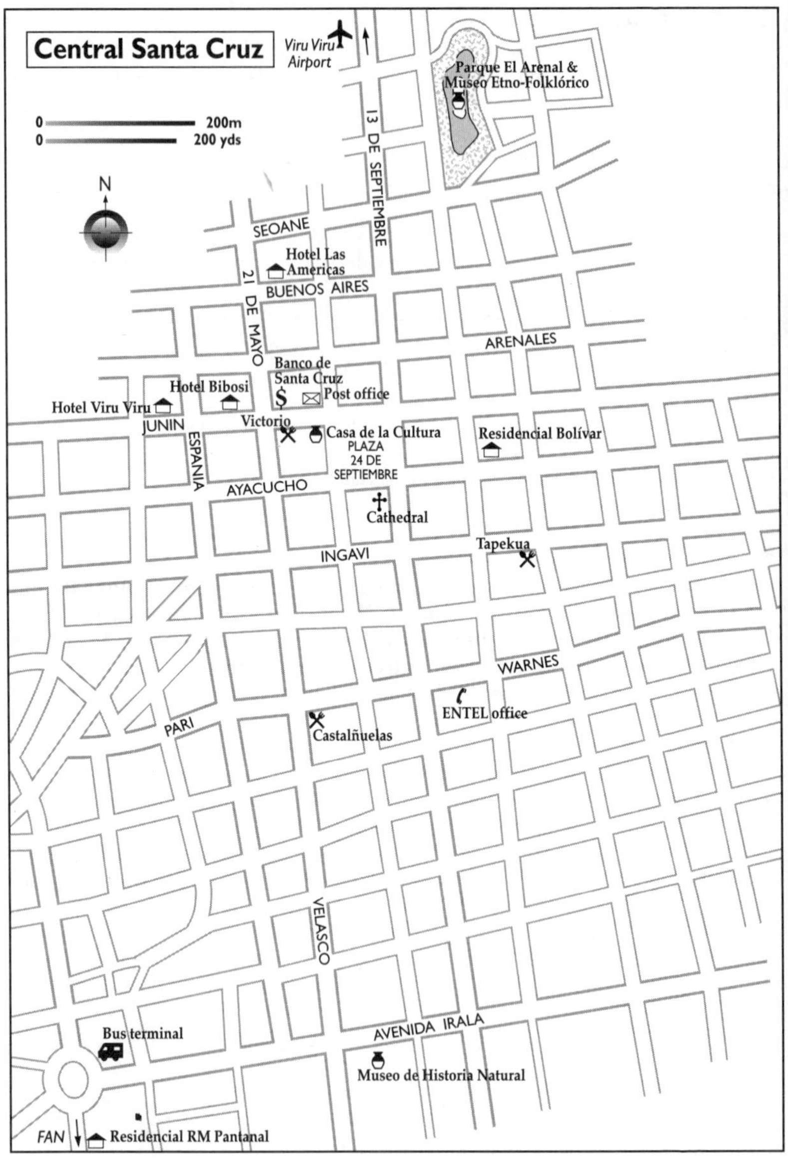

What to see

The trees in the main plaza are home to a few sleeping sloths. Parque el Arenal five blocks north of the main plaza centres on a man-made lake with several stalls around the lake selling souvenirs and a small Indian museum on the island in the middle.

The **Natural History Museum** is found on Av Irala 565, Edif UAGRIM, close to the bus terminal, housing a fantastic display of all the creepy crawlies that you would love to avoid. Open 09.00–18.00, closed for lunch.

Leaving town

All buses leave from the main bus terminal on Av Cañoto esq Av Irala.

Excursions west of Santa Cruz

El Puente Jungle Hotel

Villa Tunari is 300km west of Santa Cruz and is the nearest town to the Hotel El Puente, a comfortable jungle hotel that makes a pleasant start or end to a trip in the Bolivian Amazon.

Much of the surrounding area has been affected by logging, but the hotel is within 40ha of preserved jungle. The area is rich in birds and butterflies and has several viewing towers, jungle trails and a number of swimming holes. In addition to being an ideal place to relax, day-trips to the nearby waterfalls and Inca ruins can be arranged. Trips to Carrasco National Park take you to the southernmost point of the Amazon Basin.

The hotel has a restaurant, bar and lounge and a hammock room for relaxing. All rooms have private bathrooms. Prices start from US$22 for a single and US$28 for a double. Bookings can be organised through Fremen Tours in Santa Cruz or La Paz (see page 320).

Organised boat travel

Fremen also provide Bolivia's only floating hotel, the ***Flotel Reina de Enin***. Comfortable but simple, the *Reina de Enin* travels a circular route along the Mamoré and Ibare rivers taking in evergreen riverside forest, the Moxos savannah and the palm-tree savannah, intermingled with swamps and rainforest-covered islands. Caiman, river dolphins, river turtles, monkeys and capybara are common in the area, and studies have documented over 2,000 varieties of plants, many mammals and more than 400 species of birds.

In addition to just being able to relax, activities include jungle walks, horseback riding, canoeing, swimming and fishing for piranha. Fremen have embraced the essence of ecotourism by supporting and encouraging the involvement of local indigenous groups in the company's activities. Groups visiting riverside communities have local guides who explain the way of life for such communities in the Bolivian savannah.

Alice Walter travelled aboard the Flotel and strongly recommends the trip.

> 'The Flotel had seemed an enticing prospect if only for its clever name, but we had not expected so many enchanted moments watching Technicolor sunsets from deckchairs, spending lazy afternoons at the helm looking for sloths among the massive trees, or inspecting the beautiful *baku* bought off local fishermen for our gargantuan dinners.
>
> Life on the *Reina de Enin* takes on another dimension: swimming with pink dolphins and the odd piranha; taking off, in our pyjamas, for a spur-of-the-moment birdwatching trip downstream in one of the dugouts, swinging in hammocks with a well-deserved cool beer in hand after riding fiery horses through marshland, or most amazingly coming face to face with an adult puma valiantly swimming across a mile-wide lagoon.
>
> 'Not even the clouds of merciless mosquitoes or the rather cramped cabins – I recommend the ones on the lower deck - could spoil the magic of this intoxicating, unmissable experience.'

Tours last up to six days at a cost of US$450. The price includes all food, accommodation and transport from Trinidad. Fremen can also arrange your transport to and within Bolivia.

Independent boat travel

One option for independent travel that receives contradictory reports ranging from 'best time of my life' through to a cursing 'I waited four days for a boat', is to take a cargo boat from Puerto Villarroel downstream towards Trinidad, and maybe as far north as Guayaramerín on the border with Brazil. Boats travel down the Río Ichilo before joining the Río Mamoré, taking at least four days to reach Trinidad.

Buses do not make the journey from Santa Cruz to Puerto Villarroel. To get there you'll need to find a bus from Santa Cruz which passes the junction and will drop you at the turn-off. The journey to the junction takes about four hours so make sure you leave early in order to complete the trip before night. From the junction you can hitch a ride with a truck.

This trip gives you the best opportunity of any in Bolivia for travelling on the river while you relax in a hammock. Buy a hammock up in Santa Cruz or you may be able to get one in Puerto Villarroel. Information about sailings can be obtained from the Captain's office on the riverfront or from Transportes Fluviales just off the river. Boats are normally fairly regular but you may have to wait for a few days if you're unlucky. The trip to Trinidad, including food, costs about US$30. Take along a few extra things to eat because, as with all commercial riverboat travel in the Amazon Basin, the menu's variety leaves much to be desired.

Travelling by river has a calming and therapeutic element. With so little to do on board, life develops into a series of gentle routines. Gazing at the water and the jungle as you drift by, you see macaws and waterbirds. Pink dolphins, caiman, capybara may all make brief appearances. But even if none of these animals shows up, the gentle

PUERTO VILLARROEL TO TRINIDAD – 1973

Hilary Bradt

Bradt Publications was born on the Río Mamoré between Puerto Villarroel and Trinidad. No wonder I have fond memories of that journey. George and I had nothing to do except sit in our hammocks writing alternate chapters of *Backpacking along Ancient Ways in Peru and Bolivia* and birdwatch. The birdlife was the best I've seen on any major river trip, maybe because at the end of the dry season the boat went so slowly and hit so many sandbars that we had more time to watch. The most exciting species was jabiru, but there were numerous kingfishers and other colourful birds.

The journey took five days, and each day was centred round the quest for food. Apart from bananas and rice, the cook had brought nothing with him. Once the crew and all the passengers went ashore to collect turtle eggs. These days I would have had a conscience about eating them, but in 1973 I was anxious to try a new taste. Strange things… the white never properly hardens whilst the yolk is like stale sponge cake. We also ate turtle meat and the enormous (and tasty) eggs of the rhea.

We arrived in Trinidad which, in those days, had no road connection with the outside world. There were smaller planes out, but these were fully booked for many days ahead. We had to stay ten days. The town boasted a typing school, and each evening after the students had gone home, the proprietor allowed George to type up our book while I stayed in the hotel working on the maps and illustrations. When it was finished we mailed the typescript to George's mother and took a motorbike taxi to the airport.

movement of the boat, the companionship of similarly ensconced passengers and a supply of books to read while resting in a hammock are relaxing enough.

If you want to stop in Trinidad, then jump ship at Puerto Barador and catch a truck or bus to Trinidad. Long-distance buses regularly make the journey from Trinidad eastwards to Santa Cruz, or westwards to La Paz. Less frequently, three or so a week, are buses heading to Rurrenabaque.

Boat enthusiasts may want to continue the journey downstream through to Guayaramerín on the Bolivian/Brazilian border. The trip takes up to a week and costs around US$30. Make a short bus trip to Abunã or Porto Velho in Brazil, and you can complete your journey all the way to Manaus and the mouth of the River Amazon in Belém.

Trinidad

This town of 60,000 is a dusty, jungle sprawl. A selection of hotels and restaurants can be found around the centre if you're planning to stay. The town is a good base to explore the *Llanos de Moxos* to the south of Trinidad.

Archaeologists have found large numbers of anthropomorphic figures and ceramics in artificial mounds or *lomas*. Built close to the rivers, the mounds were constructed to allow cultivation on the elevated land at times of flooding.

There are around 20,000 *lomas* in the region, dotted amongst 100km of canals dating back to the Enin Empire that flourished in the region over 4,000 years ago. Despite the wealth of knowledge hidden within the *lomas* there is very little information available about them and limited opportunities for travellers. One exception is a trip to Santuario Chuchini, 14km out of town. This 8ha artificially raised mound has a small museum displaying artefacts and sculptures excavated from the site. There are small bungalows costing US$70pp if you want to stay on the site. Details from Loreno Hinojoso, Calle 25 de Noviembre 199 in Trinidad (tel: 21968).

Well away from any towns, Chuchini is an ideal base for walks through the rainforest to nearby lagoons. There is no regular transport to Chuchini so you will have to hitch (Sundays are best) or take a taxi.

Heading west from Trinidad

San Ignacio de Moxos

Buses travel the road heading west to the small town of San Ignacio de Moxos, a small town where just enough roads – four – converge to create the all-important plaza. On the square the Jesuit mission – built in 1689 – is currently being restored, in a project that has so far taken two and a half years at a cost of US$75,000. It should be finished in four years.

The region is the traditional territory of Mojeño Indians and the town has a significant indigenous population. Very few Indians live traditionally, having adopted small-scale farming and fishing, as well as labour on nearby ranches, as an alternative way of life.

Just out of town (a 20-minute walk) is Laguna Isirere, which is ideal for swimming. Legend has it that a small child was abducted by a spirit in the lake, and at certain times can still be heard crying within the waters of the lake.

The town comes alive every year on the last day of July for the Fiesta del Santo Patrono de Moxos, probably the most colourful celebration in the Bolivian lowlands. The fiesta is a reason for flamboyance and feathers. Costumed dancers parade the streets in extravagant masks and the town fills with people gathering to see the passing parade, or just keen to partake in the dancing and copious amounts of alcohol that are an essential ingredient of Bolivian carnivals.

NOEL KEMPFF MERCADO NATIONAL PARK

Tim Miller, Fundacíon Amigos de la Naturaleza, Santa Cruz

Noel Kempff Mercado National Park, named after a scientist murdered in the area by drug barons, is a biological reserve located in the extreme northeastern corner of Bolivia in the Department of Santa Cruz; it shares an international border on the north and east with Brazil. The park is situated in an ecological transition zone that bridges the rich, wet Amazon Basin from the north and the drier ecological communities of the Gran Chaco and *cerrado* to the south and west respectively, with the Andean highlands found further to the west. As a result of its remote and unique geographic location, the relatively unstudied 1.5 million hectares of Noel Kempff are believed to contain some of the highest levels of biological diversity found in the world.

The most outstanding physical feature of the park is the Huanchaca Plateau, a Precambrian (750 million-years-old) sandstone escarpment which represents the southernmost limit of the Amazon rainforest. The plateau rises abruptly from the dense, wet rainforests approximately 550m to an elevated plain of grasslands and dry *cerrado* forests, which are similar in appearance and structure to the savannahs found in Africa. The Huanchaca Plateau is drained by numerous perennial rivers which flow over the plateau, giving rise to more than 20 spectacular waterfalls. In combination with its waterfalls, this unique formation framed by the rugged backdrop of mesas, rivers, and dense forests has blessed Noel Kempff with some of the most awe-inspiring scenery found in Latin America. The impressive size and landscape of Noel Kempff is matched only by the flora and fauna found within its borders.

The wide range of habitats and geologic formations found in Noel Kempff has resulted in an extremely high diversity of bird species residing within the park. To date a total of 613 have been identified. However, experts estimate that once a comprehensive bird study of the entire park is completed, more than 700 species of resident and migratory birds will be recorded. The

Beni Biological Station Reserve

Still further west towards Rurrenabaque by bus or truck along a steadily deteriorating pot-holed dirt road is the Beni Biological Station Reserve in the Department of Beni. Its 135,000ha of protected land contain tropical rainforest, pantanal and open savannah offering a broad range of ecosystems for the visitor. There are over 100 species of mammal in the reserve including jaguars, more than 470 different species of bird, 45 species of amphibian and over 2,000 recorded plant species.

In addition to serving as a scientific research station, the Reserve acts as a buffer zone to the Chimane Indigenous Area to the north, aiming to reduce the impact of outside influences on the Chimane Indians.

The Station has begun taking in groups who wish to visit the area and the surrounding forests. The Reserve Station building is in the south of the Reserve just off the road from San Ignacio de Moxos. Spending at least four days in the Reserve will get you to the pristine forests in the north of the park; seven days would provide enough time to explore much of what the reserve has to offer. Travel is by foot and accommodation is camping. It's basic and simple. But a great way to get close to nature.

avifauna is one of the park's main attractions. With little effort, one can spot and hear many species: from small hummingbirds to harpy eagles, toucans, macaws, over 20 species of parrots, multicolored tanagers, and at least seven species of cracids, a group with many threatened species throughout the neotropics.

There is also an incredibly rich fauna found within the park's borders which is indicated by the frequent sighting of large mammals during hikes into the park's savannahs and forests or while travelling along the extensive river and lagoon systems. An extensive species list of over 150 mammals includes such notable species as the South American tapir, capybara, jaguar, black spider monkey, black howler monkey, silvery marmoset, bush dog, giant armadillo, the rare maned wolf, and a number of cat species including the margay, jaguarundi and ocelot.

The rivers are equally rich, with common sightings of freshwater dolphins (pink and grey), giant otters, and both spectacled and the endangered black caiman.

All proceeds from tour operators that work in Noel Kempff Mercado National Park go directly to the ecotourism department of Noel Kempff (FAN), a private, non-profit Bolivian organisation founded in 1988 to help conserve the biodiversity of Bolivia. Under agreements with the government of Bolivia, FAN is responsible for the management and protection of more than 2.6 million hectares in two national parks and a large biological reserve, including Noel Kempff Mercado National Park which is currently the focus of FAN's ecotourism department.

The mission of the ecotourism department is to provide ecotravelers with the best possible opportunity to visit and learn about the unique natural history of Noel Kempff Mercado National Park. The primary goals of the ecotourism programme are to create a high conservation awareness among visitors, keep physical impacts on the park's natural resources to a minimum, and provide direct economic and educational benefits to members of the local communities that surround the park.

Trips can be organised through the Academia Nacional de Ciencias de Bolivia based in La Paz: Av 16 de Julio 1732; tel/fax: 02 350612; email: cmiranda@ebb.rds.org.bo; postal address: Casilla 5829, La Paz, Bolivia. Prices depend on the number in a group and the length of a trip.

NATIONAL PARKS OF THE EASTERN LOWLANDS

Noel Kempff Mercado National Park

Guaranteed to compete with Madidi National Park in Bolivia's ecotourism market is Noel Kempff Mercado National Park with over 1.6 million hectares under protection. Tucked away in the far northeastern corner of Bolivia, Noel Kempff is one of the country's largest protected areas and is home to a stunning combination of dramatic scenery and exotic wildlife – a large percentage of which is rare or endangered. Given Noel Kempff's remote location, its incredible natural and aesthetic beauty, and the existence of a well-developed infrastructure providing relatively easy access, Noel Kempff offers an excellent opportunity for a unique travel experience. It also offers the chance to participate in an ecotourism project truly dedicated to the conservation and sustainable development of one of the largest protected areas in Latin America.

COCA AND BOLIVIA

One of the more lucrative crops grown in Bolivia is coca – the raw material used in the manufacture of cocaine. There are two different species of coca creating a confusing status for the plant in Bolivia. One plant is a vital part of the nation's heritage with a wide range of cultural and medicinal uses. In the *yungas* the plant is grown legally, producing coca leaves for chewing or to make a tea; either of which alleviates altitude sickness and fatigue.

In the Chapare region between Cochabamba and Santa Cruz a different species of coca grows too well, in fact like a weed. Its cultivation requires no training yet it produces crops valued at US$7,000 per hectare – the nearest legal crop yields US$1,400 per hectare. The Chapare provides significant inputs of illegal raw materials into the international cocaine trade and these allegedly account for the sudden and rapid growth of Santa Cruz.

Getting there

There are two main lodges in Noel Kempff: Flor de Oro and Los Fierros. Since its beginning, Flor de Oro was designed to become the centre for ecotourism, scientific research, and park protection in Noel Kempff and has been developed accordingly. Located in the extreme northern section of the park, the comfortable lodge provides access to a range of habitats: large expanses of *cerrado* vegetation, periodically inundated savannahs, *terra firme* and *igapo* rainforests, ox-bow lakes, semi-deciduous woodlands and the Arco Iris and Ahlfeld waterfalls found on the Paucerna River. The only reasonable access to Flor de Oro is by plane.

Los Fierros, on the other hand, is located in the heart of the park and is accessible by land (450km and 11 hours from Santa Cruz) or air. Los Fierros is a converted and upgraded ranger station and provides easy access to similar habitats to those in the north and the savannahs found on top of the Huanchaca Plateau. It is possible to hike up the side of the Huanchaca Plateau and visit the El Encanto waterfall via Los Fierros.

The park's ecotourism programme includes a number of trips ranging in duration from three to ten days, and priced from $210 to over $2,000 (not including transportation to and from the park). The trips include food, lodging, all transportation within the itinerary, and bilingual naturalist-guides.

Those interested in visiting the park should get in touch with the ecotourism department of FAN (see page 320) for more information. They will coordinate your trip within Noel Kempff and provide you with a list of local tour operators who can help with logistics outside the park.

Perseverancia – Ríos Blanco y Negro Wildlife Reserve

The Perseverancia Centre for Tourism and Scientific Research lies in the centre of the Ríos Blanco y Negro Wildlife Reserve. Some 350km from Santa Cruz, Perseverancia is only accessible by light aircraft from Santa Cruz.

The wildlife reserve covers some 1.4 million hectares including flooded *várzea* and *terra firme* forest, permanent marshes and a number of ox-bow lakes. Over 300 bird species have been sighted in the reserve including the harpy eagle, red-and-green macaw, southern screamer and hoatzin.

Mammals are also well represented in the area. Giant river otter, tapir, capybara and jaguar have all been sighted.

Activities in the park are varied. Over 50km of trails are prepared with especially designed birdwatching trails, and travel along the rivers is in dugout canoes or with low-impact electric-powered motors. Horse riding is also available.

Private or shared accommodation is available. Water heating systems are solar-powered. The food is good quality and snacks and refreshments are available throughout the day.

Amazonas Adventure Tours (3er Anillo Equipetrol frente a la Normal Enrique Finot #756; tel: 03 422760; fax: 03 422748; postal address: Casilla 2527, Santa Cruz, Bolivia) are the sole operators of the Blanco y Negro Reserve.

Trips are tailored for each group so prices vary. Make sure that you state your requirements in advance as getting supplies to the park at short notice can be difficult. As with other jungle trips, larger groups on longer trips benefit from the economies of scale.

Brazil
CARACAS
VENEZUELA
ATLANTIC OCEAN
Orinoco
GUYANA
BOGOTA
COLOMBIA
PUERTO AYACUCHO
Guiana Highlands
SURI-NAME
Fr Guiana
BOA VISTA
WATERSHED
Neblina 3014m
Branco
Putumayo
Amazon
Negro
LETICIA
MANAUS
SANTAREM
BELEM
SÃO LUIS
FORTALEZA
TABATINGA
TERESINA
NATAL
AMAZON BASIN
Purus
Madeira
Tapajós
Xingu
Tocantins
RECIFE
RIO BRANCO
PORTO VELHO
MACEIO
São Francisco
Guaporé
Mato Grosso
SALVADOR (BAHIA)
BOLIVIA
Lake Titicaca
CUIABA
BRASILIA
PERU
LA PAZ
Pantanal
Brazilian Highlands
Sucre
Corumbá
Altiplano
CAMPO GRANDE
Chaco
Iguaçu
PARAGUAY
SÃO PAULO
RIO DE JANEIRO
PACIFIC OCEAN
ANDES
Gran
Asunción
Uruguai
ARGENTINA
Paraná
PORTO ALEGRE
N
Santiago
CHILE
URUGUAY
Montevideo
Buenos Aires
Rio de la Plata
ATLANTIC OCEAN
0 1,000km
0 1,000 miles

12 Brazil

Brazil is the biggest country in South America and the fifth largest in the world. Often chaotic, sordid and depressing, it nevertheless affords the visitor endless opportunities for exploring the Amazon.

FACTS AND FIGURES

Geography

Brazil's huge size is as much a burden as a blessing. Difficulties in governing such a vast territory, much of it inaccessible with modern vehicles, have hampered development. The Brazilian Amazon has international borders with all Amazon countries apart from Ecuador. Brazil's largest state of Amazonas (1.6 million km²) touches Venezuela, Colombia and Peru. The northwestern Amazon state of Roraima borders Venezuela. To the east is the state of Pará stretching north to the border with French Guiana and Guyana, with Mato Grosso to the southeast and Rondônia to the south bordering Bolivia. Acre to the southwest has a frontier with Peru and Bolivia.

The capital of Amazonas is Manaus, where the Rio Negro meets the Amazon's mainstream. It is the biggest lowland Amazon city, with over a million inhabitants. Other major conurbations in the region include Boa Vista, the capital of Roraima, and Barcelos on the Negro River. South of Manaus is the city of Porto Velho and at the mouth of the Amazon is the port town of Belém.

Compared with much smaller South American countries, Brazil has pretty boring topography. The Amazon watershed within Brazil is generally less than

BASIC FACTS

Official name República Federativa do Brasil
Area 8,511,965km² (3,286,488 miles²)
Population 153 million
Capital Brasilia
Largest city (population) São Paulo (20 million)
Main Amazon city Manaus
Official language Portuguese
Date of independence 1822 (Portugal)
Major industries mining, coffee, forestry, manufacturing
GDP per capita US$2,451
Currency real (US$1=R$0.95; £1=R$1.49)
Major attractions Iguassu Falls, Rio carnival, the Amazon
National holidays Jan 1, Apr 21, May 1, Sep 7, Oct 12, Nov 2, Nov 15, Dec 25. Carnival is the week before Ash Wednesday.

250m in altitude while none of western Brazil exceeds 90m above sea level, except for the extreme northern borders, where Neblina Peak rises to Brazil's highest elevation just over 3,000m.

Only to the south and north of the country are significant rises encountered. From the Amazon River's northern bank, mostly intact forest stretches for 1,000km until hills and valleys rise to form the vast Guyanan Shield, one of the oldest rock formations in the world. South of the mainstream the Brazilian Shield creates an eastern limit to the Amazon watershed. These two rock formations are rich in gold deposits. Sediments washed down during millennia into Amazon watersheds underlie much of today's present lowland rainforest. Transported sediment has seen some of the most dramatic gold-rushes in recent history with almost every settlement in the Amazon experiencing a gold boom in the last thirty years.

Rivers

Of course the Amazon mainstream is the region's dominant waterway. Major Amazon tributaries in western Brazil are the south-flowing Iça/Putumayo and Japurá/Caquetá, both running through Colombia, and the Negro, originating in the Guyanan highlands.

Flowing north are the Javari, Juruá, Purus, Madeira and Tapajós rivers. The south-flowing 2,100km Negro, in terms of volume, is the biggest mainstream tributary and also carries most river traffic, while the Japura and Iça are important arteries for traffic to Peru and Colombia. South of Tabatinga, the Javari forms the top half of Brazil's border with Peru.

The Madeira is the Amazon's longest tributary and provides an important link with the southern Amazon town of Porto Velho.

Climate

Weather in northwest Brazil is dominated by a tropical moist climate, with little variation throughout the region or from season to season. In the Amazon, days are warm and humid from December to June, accompanied by high rainfall. Day temperatures virtually never fall below 22°C, and night-time lows are 18°C or so. During certain years, the cold *friagem* blows north from the Patagonian steppes. On such occasions, usually associated with El Niño events, day temperatures dip as low as 15°C, placing severe stress on the rainforest flora and fauna. July to November are the hottest months when shade temperatures can rise to over 38°C, but 26°C is average. Highlands toward the north and the southern basin are cool and pleasant, at 10–25°C.

Rainforest rainfall rarely exceeds, 3,500mm annually, but some wetter places along Brazil's Atlantic coasts record as much as 5,000mm (over 16ft!) in a year. The Amazon interior is considerably drier, not the constant deluge we typically have in mind. Along the upper mainstream around Manaus, around 1,500–2,500mm falls over twelve months. The rainy season lasts from December to May, with daily rain likely. June to November are drier months, with dry spells often lingering for several days. In recent decades deforestation in Brazil has shortened the rainy season and decreased its intensity.

Flora and fauna

Ever since reports emerged from early expeditions, Brazil's flora and fauna have awed and mystified laymen and professional naturalists alike. Yet even today, these biological riches are among the most unexplored in the world, relative to their diversity. The Amazon's size and inaccessibility, and the lack of expertise, seriously hinder efforts to assay the country's biological wealth. Primary ecosystems are *igapo*, *várzea* and *terra firme* forest. To the extreme north and west of Amazonas, as the land rises, dominant vegetation changes to dry tropical forest and to savannah, dotted with patches of montane rainforest. These areas are remote and good for seeing large animals but the tourist infrastructure is sparse.

All South America's tropical vertebrate groups are represented and invertebrates are exceptionally diverse. Brazil is home to 68 primate species, more than any other country in the world. Discovered in 1993 was the Río Maués marmoset (*Callithrix mauesi*), dressed in a faded striped coat and with tufted ears. Barely big enough to sit in your hand, it weighs less than 250g. Since then, three more species have been discovered, bringing the total to seven since 1990.

Land use

Most of Amazonas remains pristine tropical rainforest, sparsely inhabited by a few indigenous Indians, settlers and missionaries. Rural activities occupy little land. Most crops consist of soybeans, maize, sugarcane, manioc and bananas. Primarily, crop production is along rivers in cleared areas of flooded forest where the land is regularly fertilised with silt deposited by annual floods.

Outside of Amazonas large portions of lowland rainforest have been set aside for development projects. Most notorious of these were government assistance programmes for cattle-ranchers, whose tenure was marked by laying waste to large areas of forest in exchange for two or three years of good pasture. These devastated large parts of Mato Grosso, Acre and Roraima. The land-grant practice ceased in 1995, but other plans allocated large chunks to road-building and urban expansion, or hydro-electric schemes, while mining and lumber operations continue with few controls.

The people

Population and ethnic groups

In Brazil as a whole, whites of direct European descent comprise around 55% of the population, whereas 35% are *caboclos,* descendants of mixed Indian and European or African blood. Ten per cent are black, descended directly from Brazil's West African slaves. The remainder are indigenous Indians or immigrants from Europe – especially Germany – and Asia.

Despite Brazil being South America's most populous country, rural areas are largely empty, so the average population density of 17 per km^2 is much less in jungle areas. Indeed, much of Amazonas is uninhabited, being the country's most thinly populated state.

Population composition is somewhat different in the Amazon where proportions of *caboclos* and Indians are higher than average. Of indigenous peoples, a number of fairly intact cultures are in Brazil's far northwest, while in the east and along the mainstream, virtually every tribe is being rapidly assimilated into the dominant way of life.

For visitors interested in visiting less culturally contaminated tribes, the most important group are the Yanomami along the upper Negro to Brazil's northern border with Venezuela. The nearly extinct Omagua live south, along the Juruá River. Other tribes include Tikuna, from the Colombian border area, and Waiwai, Arawete, Kayapo, Carajá and Xavante.

Languages

Portuguese is the official language, a legacy of Brazil's unique colonial history. Attempts to speak Portuguese, no matter how amusing, are much appreciated.

BRAZIL'S INDIGENOUS INDIANS

Depending on whose figures you believe, the Indian population is currently between one tenth and one fiftieth of the original population when Columbus arrived. Today some 150–200,000 Brazilian Amerindians survive. While many have adopted the *caboclo* or *rivereño* culture of subsistence farming and fishing, others remain unacculturated, still very isolated from the Brazilian way of life.

Incredibly, the wholesale extermination of indigenous peoples during the 19th century continued in Brazil until very recently and still does in more subtle ways. Even those responsible for carrying out such programmes appear not only uninterested in preserving their country's cultural and natural heritage, but positively bent on its destruction.

There is very little that is funny about FUNAI (Fundação Nacional dos Indios), the government organisation charged with looking after the welfare of Brazil's indigenous Indians. The history of FUNAI officials includes reports of ineptitude, corruption and even violence against the Indians, the very people they are sworn to protect. The worst outrages, documented by official public enquiry, include 'donations' of disease-ridden blankets, exploiting the vulnerability of Indians to Western diseases. Settlers were thus rid of a big obstacle to their land claims. Recent shake-ups in the organisation have put an end to such atrocities, but the same myopic mentality prevails and resources are few.

There remain a few peoples with relatively intact cultures in Brazil, as in Peru, Ecuador and remote parts of other Amazon countries. Reservations are off-limits without hard-to-obtain permission from FUNAI (Joaquim Nabucu 473, Manaus; tel: 234 7632).

Some 200 indigenous dialects are currently spoken; mostly among tribes virtually assimilated into dominant Brazilian society. Linguistic fragments brought over by African slaves have found their way into common usage and in some regions are the basis for local dialects. Nevertheless, the present linguistic diversity of Brazil is but a shadow of what once was.

Education

Theoretically education is free and compulsory from ages six to 16, but Brazil's ideal of education for all has not yet even been approached. Some 15–25% of 13 million school-age children have no schooling at all. Availability of schooling in urban areas is limited by lack of teachers, while in outlying areas insufficient funds are available to build even a few badly needed schools. The University of Amazonas is one Brazilian educational success story, as the region's most prestigious higher education establishment. Likewise, the internationally respected INPA researches important questions in tropical biology.

Culture

Brazil is a country of music. From salsa to rumba, Brazilian dance music is heard around the world. The country has also produced its share of talented classical musicians, while in rural areas, simple rhythms of working people provide raw material for constant innovations to the Brazilian music scene.

Also defining Brazilian culture is the obsession with football. South America as a whole is fanatical about the sport, but the passion of the Brazilians makes the interest of others seem like a mere hobby. As with music, football crosses all cultural boundaries, creating one of the few unifying forces in Brazilian culture. When Brazil win the World Cup, the nation is happy; when they lose – as they did in the World Cup in France to the host team – it is a time of national mourning.

Religion

Roman Catholicism is the dominant religion but numbers of Protestants are rising and currently make up 15% of the population. Afro-Brazilian religions such as *candomblé* and *umbanda,* which are also popular, have their origins in western Africa.

Fiestas

There can be few people who have not heard of the Rio carnival: one of the biggest song-and-dance festivals in the world when thousands of dancers in varying states of undress move to the hypnotic beat of hundreds of drummers. Rio Carnival is samba time and, if you can handle large crowds, it's a spectacle not to be missed.

A brief history

Unwritten history

Dominant tribes encountered by Portuguese explorers on the coast were Tupi-Guarani and Gê. Further inland Arawak, Carib and others were encountered by other early explorers. Two to five million indigenous people comprised the pre-European population.

Following a semi-nomadic, hunter-gatherer lifestyle, these tribes are known to have had sophisticated cultures, with their own language, religion, diets and mode of dress. We have little hard evidence but can infer the foods they ate by study of extant tribes. In charming water-colours by early artists we have glimpses of clothing; from nothing at all to elaborate adornments of rainforest bird feathers and animal teeth. From such glimpses, and written accounts of early traders, we presume there were trading links between some of these tribes and hostility between others.

The Europeans

In the year 1500, the Portuguese captain Pedro Cabal landed on Brazil's northern Atlantic coast and claimed the territory for Portugal. Others, notably Amerigo Vespucci, navigated further down the coast and were the first Europeans at the mouth of the Amazon. Neither knowing nor believing it was a river, they called it Rio Mar – 'River Sea.'

The conquest of Brazil and the Amazon was not achieved through direct warfare as throughout much of South America. The colonisers trickled in, at first unsure of how to live in the new surroundings and relying on coastal Indians for labour and assistance.

Of the region's inhabitants, Francisco de Orellana knew nothing when he left Quito for his first navigation of the river in 1541–42. His exploits and those of other post-conquest explorers did little to belie the legends and superstition that so impressed Western minds: tales of female 'Amazon' warriors, lost cities and other bizarre entities.

Aside from a few missionaries, and the Portuguese explorer Teixeira who travelled upriver, for the world at large the Amazon's interior remained a mystery until the age of explorer-scientists, who described the place in realistic and plain language, revealing a potential bonanza of natural resources.

For its hardwoods the region became renowned and the country took its name from the reddish *pau do brasil* hardwood. By the mid-1800s, around Manaus and further upstream the development of rainforest commerce was based first on *chicle,* then on rubber.

Independence

Brazil's struggle for self-rule was virtually over in a day and night and was totally bloodless, unlike the massacre-laden independence movements in Spanish colonies. When Napoleon captured Lisbon in 1807, King of Portugal Don João VI fled to his biggest and least-tamed colony and declared himself emperor. Returning to Portugal in 1821, he left behind his son Pedro as prince regent. Dom Pedro I became emperor of an independent Brazil in 1822 before abdicating in favour of his five-year-old son Pedro in 1831.

Taking command in 1840, Dom Pedro II took his new title seriously but went too far when in 1888 he declared slavery was to be abolished, or he would abdicate. His ploy worked, but the political price was high and Dom Pedro II was forced to flee to Paris. Brazil was declared a republic in 1889.

Scientific developments in the Amazon began with La Condamine, who noted how Indians used sap from the *Hevea brasiliensis* tree to make waterproof shoes, bouncing balls and syringe-type instruments. Following hot on the heels of geographic knowledge, Victorian scientists scrambled into the jungle's depths in search of new and usable plant and animal species. The French botanist d'Orbigny and English scientists Alfred Wallace and Henry Bates visited Manaus in the mid-18th century. By this time, the collapse of the sugar trade had weakened Brazil's ruling classes and rubber had come to dominate the country's external trade. For the first time real power was centred in the Amazon and Manaus flourished in the spotlight, while labourers and Indians slaved away tapping the vast Amazon forest for rubber.

The 20th century

Brazil's 20th century will be remembered as one of change and growth, chaos and environmental degradation. From a half-forgotten ex-colony, during the late 19th century Brazil grew, assisted by the boom in the rubber trade, to become an industrial power to be reckoned with a century later.

Coffee grown in the southern state of São Paulo supplanted rubber as Brazil's main income earner early in the 20th century. The wealth from coffee financed early industrialisation in southern Brazil, creating powerful coffee barons. Despite attempts by the military to take control the coffee-producing oligarchies of the south obstructed any change. Unrest amongst the working classes and dissatisfaction with the dominance of the coffee producers brought the military dictator Getúlio Vargas to power in the 1930s on a wave of populist support. Vargas introduced a minimum wage, improved working conditions and set Brazil on the path to full modernisation while systematically removing opposition and torturing political prisoners.

World War II cut Europe off from its Asian rubber plantations, and European overtures saw Brazil recruit 30,000 tappers to harvest latex from the Amazon, thus temporarily reviving the flailing industry. World War II also saw the US begin the development of the Brazilian steel industry. The rapidly industrialising country continued down the road of modernisation but when Vargas, now the elected president, created the large state oil company Petrobras in the early 1950s the military and international community saw this as a step too far towards communism. Media pressure grew and Vargas, feeling increasingly isolated, was forced to stand down in 1954 and committed suicide shortly after.

Juscelino Kubitschek took power in 1955 and began an intense period of expansion that saw Brasilia built in three years and the first road link to central Amazonia

THE BALBINA PROJECT

The gates of the Balbina hydroelectric dam 200km north of Manaus were sealed in October 1987 damming the Uatumá River. The project flooded 236,000ha of tropical forest and displaced one third of the remaining indigenous Waimiri Atroari Indians. The cost of the project was put at US$750 million, while the value of timber flooded was around US$400 million. Nearly 300,000 animals had to be rescued from the unnatural inundation, and even the fish have survival problems as the decay of forest biomass has turned the water fetid, acid and low in oxygen.

The benefits of the project? Eighty megawatts of power, just 32% of the installed capacity, produced at a financial price that is four times the amount considered to be reasonably competitive.

running from Belém to Brasilia. Kubitschek also left the legacy of spiralling inflation which only increased demands from the burgeoning working classes to adopt leftist policies. Pressure for land reform in the northwest and populist policies for the south worried conservatives and the military alike, with the almost inevitable outcome of a military coup. The US considered Brazil under military rule to be an important ally in the Cold War of the 1960s. An 'economic miracle' transformed Brazil to such an extent that, when power was handed back to a civilian government in 1985, the economy had grown to be the tenth largest in the world. The military regime gave rise to the first Amazon colonisation plans, as agricultural labourers displaced by mechanisation in the south and drought in the north demanded action. The social costs of the regime were heavy, with over 20,000 Brazilians imprisoned, tortured and 'disappeared', while thousands more sought exile abroad.

Despite Brazil's return to democracy, the 1980s offered little hope as hyperinflation gripped the economy and foreign debt rose to a staggering US$120 billion. The election of Fernando Collor de Melo on an anti-corruption ticket was seen by many as a way out of the intractable economic problems. His currency stabilisation programme would hurt, but the Brazil that emerged would fully live up to the notion of 'order and progress' proudly displayed on the national flag. When Collor was finally impeached for a scam costing the treasury billions of dollars in a country where corruption is a part of daily life, few were surprised.

The finance minister, Fernando Henrique Cardoso, was the mastermind behind the stabilisation programme and used its success as a platform for his election to the presidency in 1995. While Cardoso's 'Real Plan', pegging the Brazilian *real* to the US dollar, has hurt the poorest sections of society, his presidency has seen the economy continue to grow, as state industries have been privatised and regional trade organisation has continued to remove trade barriers between the southern nations of South America.

Elections in October 1998 were likely to return Cardoso to power. But the growing support from the poorer sections of society for the former trade unionist 'Lula' Inácio da Silva of the Worker's Party suggest that the fear of social unrest will continue to play a part in the continuing development of a democratic Brazil.

Brazil's system of government is a representative democracy headed by the president with a four-year term, requiring at least 51% of electoral support to secure office. If first-round voting does not establish a clear majority, a second round of voting with fewer candidates takes place. Congress is composed of a 513-member Chamber of Deputies and an 81-member Senate. Voting is compulsory for eligible adults aged 18–70, voluntary for the over-70s.

Although when travelling in the Amazon it is sometimes difficult to believe, the Brazilian economy is an industrial powerhouse that produces over 1.5 million cars, exports nearly 400,000 of them, builds aircraft and tanks, and in the mid-1980s stopped just short of becoming a nuclear power.

For the future, minerals are destined to become Brazil's economic mainstay as it makes the most of its significant deposits of bauxite and around a third of the world's iron ore reserves. Carajás, south of Belém on the River Tocantins, is one of the world's largest mine complexes producing significant exports of iron ore and several other minerals for Brazil.

In the Amazon, mining projects are less ambitious, although a major gold-producing area south of Roraima flanks the Rio Branco, its exploitation facilitated by the Caracas-Manaus highway, soon to be completely paved. In the far west of Amazonas, along the frontier with Venezuela, lie further gold bearing formations and the world's richest deposits of niobium (a strategic metal used by the aerospace industry).

The region's exports are funnelled through Manaus from where most products end up in Brazil's industrial centres for processing and export. Considerable quantities of raw materials are exported direct to North America, Japan and Europe.

Money

Brazil's currency problems are a case-study in classic economics. With sky-punching inflation rates reaching 1,000% annually during the 1970s and mid-80s, money became truly worthless. The *real*, Brazil's present currency, is doing better than its predecessors. Cardoso's 'Real Plan' has introduced a degree of stability to the currency and foreign exchange reserves are at an all-time high.

Brazil is currently one of the most expensive Amazon countries to travel in. Acceptable budget accommodation starts at around US$15 and the cost of travel, although good value, tends to be high due to the great distances involved. Budget travellers can probably get by comfortably on a minimum of US$40–50 a day. If you're looking to do the occasional excursion and stay in more comfortable hotels, then spending over US$100 a day is easy.

Dollars are accepted in places aimed at tourists but as soon as you leave the set itinerary you will have to use reals. The best places to change money are at branches of Banco do Brasil and foreign exchange houses. In Manaus, Banco do Brasil has branches at Rua Marechal Deodoro in the centre and at the airport where you can cash travellers' cheques and change currency.

Travellers' cheques and major credit cards are widely accepted at all banks and in most large hotels and restaurants. By far the easiest way to get money is with a credit card at the ATMs (Automatic Teller Machines) that are sprouting out of banks' walls in some of the most surprising places throughout the country.

If heading off into the jungle for several days, change as much money as you think you'll need. In smaller towns you may have problems changing travellers' cheques or using your credit card over the counter. In the very smallest towns and villages you will have to work hard to convince people that the piece of paper called a dollar that you are holding is worth anything.

Highlights

The Amazon in Brazil overall is underdeveloped for nature tourism. Most rainforest visitors to Brazil go to Manaus, where the Rio Negro joins the Amazon. Here and along the mainstream, especially eastwards, deforestation has ruined vast tracts of once pristine rainforest.

Major rivers in eastern Brazil up to Manaus are where much mining and industrial development in the Amazon has taken place. To get to unspoiled areas, you need to go upstream toward Tabatinga on the Colombia-Peru border, or far up the Negro towards the Venezuela border. Heading south along the Madeira there are few opportunities unless you make them yourself.

Except for a few adaptable birds, wildlife is largely absent in the immediate vicinity of towns and villages, having been seriously over-hunted. Yet not too far from Manaus it is still possible to see a wide variety of birdlife, a caiman (*jacaré*) or sloth and perhaps a monkey or two.

For **group travellers**, Brazil may feel passé, as though there's always something better over the horizon; but by carefully selecting a tour operator's itinerary you should be able to get to spectacular places, although they won't be cheap.

For **independent travellers** opportunities are endless but can be expensive. You just need to decide what you want to do, look at a map and have a rough idea how you want to get there. There is usually a way if you have enough time and money.

Most visitors to Brazil's Amazon go to Manaus one way or another; whether you love or hate it, a stop at the city is an essential part of any visit to the heart of the Amazon. First-time travellers should study carefully to see if a trip there will suit their interests, staying-power and wallet. For those lacking confidence about travel in the Amazon, Manaus is a great place to put a toe in the water. To travel to remote areas it is necessary to go beyond Manaus, four or five days by boat, but the city is fine to look for guides and equipment or to rest up after a jungle trip.

Tour operators

Several overseas tour operators organise trips along the Amazon and take bookings for the lodges found throughout the area. In other areas you have to go direct to operators in Brazil.

In the US

The following companies take bookings for partial and full-length trips along the Amazon mainstream.

Brazil Nuts 201 8th St, Naples, FL 34102; tel: 800 553 9959. Boat trips along the River Negro upriver from Manaus.

Bryan World Travel PO Box 4156, Topeka, KS 66604; tel: 913 272 7511/800 255 3507; fax: 913 272 6244. Take bookings for a small 12-passenger boat travelling the Negro to places unreachable in larger vessels.

Ecotour Expeditions PO Box 1066, Cambridge, MA 02238; tel: 617 876 5817/800 688 1822; fax: 617 876 3638; email: nature@tiac.com. Arrange trips on a small boat cruising the Negro.

Explorers 197 Wall St, W Long Branch, NJ 07764; tel: 908 870 0223/800 631 5650; fax: 908 870 0278. Arrange trips originating in Boa Vista travelling by river down to Manaus.

Field Guides Inc PO Box 160723, Austin, TX 78716; tel: 512 327 4953/800 728 4953; fax: 512 327 9231; email: fgileader@aol.com; net: www.fieldguides.com. Amongst other trips throughout the Amazon, have trips to the King's Island Lodge near São Gabriel in northwest Brazil.

Forum Travel International 91 Gregory Lane, #21 Pleasant Hill, CA 94523; tel: 510 671 2900; fax: 510 671 2993; email: forum@ix.netcom.com; net: www.ten-io.com/forumtravel. Bookings for a number of trips throughout the Brazilian Amazon.

Lifelong Learning 101 Columbia, Ste 150, Aliso Viejo, CA 92656; tel: 714 362 2900/800 854 4080; fax: 714 362 2075; email: lllexpo@aol.com.

Maxim Tours Ltd 50 Cutler St, Morristown, NJ; tel: 970 984 9068/800 655 0222; fax: 973 984 5383; email: maximtours@earthlink.net. Have a number of different options available for the Brazilian Amazon including cruises and lodge accommodation.

Nature Expeditions International 6400 E El Dorado Circle, Ste 210 Tucson, AZ 85715; tel: 520 721 6712/800 869 0639; fax: 520 721 6719; email: naturexp@aol.com; net: www.naturexp.com. Have trips navigating the length of the Amazon combining cruise boats, canoes and flights.
OdessAmerica 1700 Old Country Rd, Mineola, NY 11501; tel: 516 747 8880/800 221 3254; fax: 516 747 8367; email: oac@odessamerica.com; net: www.odessamerica.com.
Rod & Reel Adventures 3507 Tully Rd, Modesto, CA 95356; tel: 209 524 1220/800 356 6982. Fishing expeditions departing from Manaus.
Tours International 12750 Briar Forest Dr, Ste 720, Houston, TX 77077; tel: 281 293 0809/800 247 7965; fax: 281 589 0870; email: toursintl@aol.com; net: www.astanet.com/get/toursintl. Take bookings for jungle lodges along the Amazon mainstream.

In the UK

Fred Olsen Cruise Lines White House Rd, Ipswich, Suffolk IP1 5LL; tel 01473 292 222; fax: 01473 292 345. Occasional luxury cruises travelling the Amazon leaving from England.
Journey Latin America 12–13 Heathfield Terrace, Chiswick, London W4 4JE; tel: 0181 747 3108; fax: 0181 742 1312; email: sales@journeylatinamerica.co.uk. Have organised tours that travel to Manaus.
Kumuka Expeditions 40 Earls Court Rd, London W8 6EJ; tel: 0171 937 8855; fax: 0171 937 6664; email: sales@kumuka.co.uk. Expeditions that include boat trips down the Amazon.
Passage to South America 12 Noyna Rd, London SW17 7PH; tel: 0181 767 8989; fax: 0181 767 2026; email: psa@scottdunn.com. Can arrange bespoke trips to the Brazilian Amazon and throughout South America.
Worldwide Journeys & Expeditions 8 Comeragh Rd, London W14 9HP; tel: 0171 381 8638; fax: 0171 381 0836; email: wwj@wjournex.demon.co.uk. Take bookings for full-length and sections of Amazon cruises.

When to go

Any time of year is good, but those averse to heat should avoid the hottest months, during October to January; the heat sometimes lingers into February. The dry season is the time of lowest water, when fishing is better, but high water (April–July) gives you the chance to take a boat through the flooded forest.

During Brazilian holidays from December to March, coastal resorts are busy and Manaus gets crowded. Foreign tourists are most numerous during times of holidays in the northern hemisphere, ie: in the middle of summer (June–July). Therefore the best times to visit are May and August, as September is Brazilian holiday season. A bad time is from September onwards for a couple of months when farmers and loggers put large areas of rainforest to the torch. Fishing is best during low water (September–March), but the Victoria water-lilies die down during this season.

Health

Technically Brazil requires the yellow fever vaccination if you have travelled through other endemic countries such as Peru or Colombia. The immigration authorities don't usually check but for peace of mind, get vaccinated, and keep the yellow World Health Organisation card with your passport.

Security

Crime is an increasingly serious problem facing Brazil. It is less severe in the Amazon area than in notorious conurbations like Rio de Janeiro and São Paulo, but visitors are well advised to keep up their guard. Certainly in Manaus a 'big city' mentality will go a long way to keeping the baddies at bay.

GETTING THERE AND AWAY

By air

From the US

The easiest and most popular way to reach the Brazilian Amazon is to fly from Miami to Manaus. Varig, Brazil's national airline, flies the route three or four times a week. It's an evening flight taking four hours to Belém with another two for Manaus. People on organised upstream full-length Amazon cruises or those wanting to take the normal passenger boats get off at Belém. It's worth checking your luggage is labelled correctly.

LAB (Bolivian Airlines) flies non-stop from Miami to Manaus once a week. As this flight goes on to La Paz it is often crowded. Other international flights to Manaus come from Los Angeles (VASP).

From Europe

Several airlines fly to Brazil from Europe once or twice a week but most fly to Rio. The cost from London is between £560 and £670. Flying to Rio with Varig you can get a connecting flight to Manaus or Belém for another £50 or so. Aeroflot have the cheapest fares, but their safety record is not confidence-inspiring.

LAB offers two flights weekly from Bogotá, La Paz, Caracas and Iquitos. You can fly from Georgetown, Guyana, once a week, via Boa Vista.

By ship

Reaching Brazil by cargo ship is possible but in reality you pay a heavy price for the experience. Although almost 2,000km inland by river, Manaus is accessible by ocean-going vessels as many visitors on luxury cruise ships or foreign-registered expedition vessels find out. However, without significant amounts of time and money it is not practicable to take a ship simply to get to and from Manaus.

The triple frontier where Brazil, Colombia and Peru meet is one access point by ship although you have to change if you are travelling on national vessels.

Overland

The only way to get to Amazonas by road is from Venezuela. The border crossing is at Santa Elena, some 200km north of Boa Vista. There is a road from Guyana into Boa Vista but I have heard it is terrible. This route and others are only sporadically available. To the south there are several road connections with Bolivia, the most commonly used being Porto Velho to Guajará-Mirim on the border (four hours by bus, US$10).

Frontier crossings by river in all other places apart from the triple frontier are not commonly used and any passport formalities, such as exit and entrance stamps, will have to be dealt with before you arrive at the frontier or the next large town after crossing the border.

Customs and immigration

Brazilian bureacracy makes life more difficult for travellers than other Amazon countries. Its strict reciprocal visa policy requires **visas** of citizens from countries who require Brazilians to have a visa. US citizens need a visa to travel in Brazil (unless on a day-trip), but UK and German nationals do not. (See *Preparations and planning,* page 29).

All visitors who stay over 90 days require a visa. They are no longer sent by mail, therefore you have to apply in person at your nearest consulate or use a visa service agency. Getting the visa in your home country is the easiest option but you can get one from Brazilian embassies and consulates in neighbouring countries.

When entering Brazil complete the **disembarkation card** issued on your flight or vessel and keep the copy that has to be handed in when you leave. In Manaus the immigration offices are at the airport or, if you are disembarking from a ship, at the floating dock next to the tourist information office.

If you are crossing a land border, **customs formalities** are available in the immigration office, at the border crossing or, in most cases, at the local police station. If entering or leaving Leticia, Colombia, you need to get your passport stamped in Tabatinga.

If you need to stay longer than allowed by your entry visa, you must extend it at the offices of the Policia Federal 15 days before it expires. Overstays on a visa will cost $1 per day for up to 75 days.

Getting around

By bus

Bus services are the only sensible way to travel by road in Amazonia. The *rodoviária* (bus station) for long-distance buses in Manaus is at the junction of Rua Recife and Avenida Constantino Nery, some 6km from the town centre (US$5 by taxi). Bus services into Manaus come from Boa Vista in Roraima, but the unpaved road is notoriously unreliable, especially during the rainy season. The 20-hour journey (US$40 one way) has to be among the most gruelling in the annals of travel. No less tough is the theoretical road to Manaus from Porto Velho to the south, which is invariably impassable due to flooding. Some of it is newly paved, and when complete should provide more rapid, but less tale-worthy, transit between the two cities. Santarém and Manacapuru are other towns with irregular and unreliable bus services to Manaus.

The trans-Amazonian highway was supposed to open up the Amazon to motorised land transport. But the dream has been denied by weather, terrain, remoteness and absence of money for regular maintenance. Travelling the highway is possible but the road is served only by very occasional transport and you need to use river transport for the section immediately west of Itaituba. Venturing into the inner Amazon with anything resembling a motorised vehicle is only for the serious expeditioner.

By air

Internal flights in Brazil are efficient and inexpensive; with the air-taxi system you pay fares of US$100 or less between many cities on regular flights. If you are planning on visiting a number of different places, the Brazilian airlines Varig and VASP have airpasses that link up several of the larger cities in the Amazon.

By boat

ENASA (Empresa de Navegação de Amazonia), the state shipping line, offers regular passenger services between Belém and Manaus and throughout the Amazon. However, their vessels are not particularly recommended as they are large, crowded and impersonal. They are a useful source of information for finding a local riverboat for passage up the main rivers, with schedules of locally registered vessels.

From Guyana or Venezuela, one can travel overland to Boa Vista then transfer to Caracaraí on the Rio Branco to take a riverboat down to Manaus. It's relatively easy to make this river trip solo. For the two- to three-day voyage, several boats daily depart the Boa Vista docks for Manaus (US$50–75 one way, sleeping in a hammock).

From Iquitos, via Leticia, luxury ships come downriver and cross into Brazil at Tabatinga, and their passengers simply have to admire the scenery and attend the evening cocktail, with no worry about immigration formalities. Those on local boats will need to change at Tabatinga or Benjamin Constant as most local riverboats only travel as far as the borders. Dozens of boats depart on this route daily so you should find it easy to get a berth. From Tabatinga, Manaus is around a five-day cruise on the local riverboat and costs US$75.

From Porto Velho the journey downstream to Manaus costs around US$70 and takes four days when the conditions are right, far longer when things go wrong.

Travelling the Amazon on a luxury cruise is one option, and the trip has to be organised from outside Brazil. Your first tough decision is whether to do the 'full monty' and travel the full length of the Amazon from Belém to Iquitos or whether to head downstream. Up is better, because you travel from developed land near the mouth of the river towards pristine forest upriver. As the currents are slower closer to the riverbank, that's where you tend to travel. Cost is from around US$4,000pp and up depending on the quality of your cabin. If your funds don't stretch that far you can do a half-length cruise from Manaus to Iquitos, which is the best for wildlife and sightseeing, or Manaus to Belém which is not especially recommended. Your cruise agency will let you know details of dress code and ship cuisine.

COMMUNICATIONS

Mail

All towns and many smaller villages have post offices (*correios*) but the post is generally slow and prone to disappearing in either direction. Be prepared to pay two or three times more for postage than you would back home. Even airmail letters or postcards cost upwards of US$1, taking five days for US destinations and about ten for Europe.

General delivery is reported to be unreliable so to receive mail use your hotel address. American Express members can use the local Amex office. The main post office in Manaus is on Rua Marechal Deodoro. The post office is open weekdays 08.00–17.00 and on Saturdays in the morning.

Telephone and fax

Phoning is most convenient and most expensive from the hotels (eg: US$10–15 for a three-minute call to the US). If you don't mind the long queues at the TeleAmazon office at Rua Guilherme Moreira or Getulio Vargas it's much cheaper (eg: US$5 for a three-minute call; UK £1.50/minute). International operators at Embratel speak English if you are having problems.

Fax is the most popular and convenient way to communicate with Amazon businesses, although a few are adopting computer-based communications systems. But to send an international fax *from* Manaus can be horrendously expensive: US$10–15 per page with a commercial fax service. Most TeleAmazon offices have a fax service that is cheaper, charging around US$1 per page.

The international phone code for Brazil is 55.

Internet

The electronic age has not yet reached the Brazilian Amazon in a significant way. A few enlightened tour operators are beginning to create websites and use email but this still remains the exception rather than the rule, a situation that will no doubt quickly change. Any email addresses that are provided for out of the way places are likely to be relayed to their ultimate destination by fax so don't rely on a speedy response.

TV and radio

Brazilian broadcast media are largely unintelligible to the non-Portuguese speaker. There are over 250 TV stations throughout the country and almost 3,000 radio stations. TV is no more exciting than anywhere else but Brazilians are blessed with the gloriously melodramatic soap *A Indomada* – essential viewing throughout Brazil.

For media addicts posher city hotels have English-speaking programmes including BBC World, CNN and ESPN, available via satellite.

Newspapers

Highest-circulation Río papers are *Globo* and *Jornal do Brasil*, copies of which you will see in Manaus and other large Amazon cities. At international airports and big city hotels, English-language newspapers and magazines from the US, or more rarely the UK, are available a day or three out of date.

PASSING THROUGH RIO

The three main international points in Brazil – Rio de Janeiro, Brasilia and São Paulo – are a long way from the Amazon River. If the main focus of your trip is the river itself, there are a number of airlines that fly directly from the US to Belém and Manaus. From Europe, meeting a flight in Miami opens up the same possibility. Most direct flights to Brazil from Europe go to Rio de Janeiro which is over 3,200km from Belém and 4,300km from Manaus. All Brazilian international airlines connect with most regional cities and the extra cost on your ticket and the extra time saved travelling make the option worth exploring.

Galeão International Airport is on Governor's Island around 15km north of the centre of the city. If you need to change money Banco do Brasil on the third floor is open 24 hours. It's also worth picking up maps of the city and other tourist information from the registered Riotur or Embratur information desks. Other desks, although providing useful information, are working for a particular chain of hotels.

As at all international airports the open arms and heart-warming welcome of crowds of taxi drivers are sweet and quite touching, but there are a couple of alternatives to running the gauntlet with a private taxi.

Executive buses operated by Real Auto Onibus make the journey to the centre of town every 30 minutes until midnight, leaving from outside the terminal and charging US$5. The bus weaves its way through most city districts of interest to the visitor including the centre, where most sites of historical interest are found, the hotel districts of Glória, Flamengo and Botafogo south of the centre, and the more expensive areas of Copacabana and Ipanema.

If you are in a group, buy a taxi ticket from Transcoopass or Coopertramo who have several desks in the airport. They sell pre-paid journeys to different parts of the city. A taxi carrying up to four people to the centre costs around US$20, slightly more to Copacabana.

For getting back to the airport your hotel will help you book a taxi through Transcoopass or Coopertramo. Hotel staff will also be able to direct you to the nearest pick-up point for the airport bus.

Where to stay

As you would expect with an international city of Rio's status, accommodation is available at all levels and prices. City guides and various other books provide hotel listings. With places of historical interest in the centre and the must-visit beaches of Copacabana and Ipanema to the south, Glória, Flamengo and Botafogo are perfectly positioned districts along the efficient and quick metro line. These districts are full of economically priced hotels, restaurants and bars. Down in Copacabana and Ipanema the hotels are more expensive.

Right next to Glória metro station is the clean and reasonably priced **Cândido Mendes** at Rua Cândido Mendes 117 (US$30). **Turístico** at Ladeira da Glória 30; tel: 225 9388 is also close to the metro. It's one of Rio's most popular budget hotels and often full (US$25). If you are looking for a little self-indulgence at the beginning or end of your trip, **Hotel Glória** Rua do Russel 632; tel: 205 7272, is possibly the best hotel in Rio (US$100). If you are travelling from the airport by bus ask the driver to drop you at the nearest point, or get off at Cinelândia metro stop and travel south one stop to the Glória.

Down in Copacabana there are plenty of hotels, most of them quite expensive. **Hotel Martinique** at Rua Sá Ferreira 30; tel: 521 4552 comes recommended at US$40 for a good room.

What to see

If you do have time to stop in Rio you'll find it worthwhile. Most hotels can arrange trips up Corcovado Hill from where Christ the Redeemer has stood, arms outstretched, preaching his silent sermon on the mount, for nearly seventy years since first taking up residence on this dramatic spot. Excursions to Sugar Loaf Mountain can also be arranged. You can walk or climb up either of these hills; or there are transport systems that will take the strain if you'd prefer.

Then it's off to the beach to quietly hum the tunes of Manilow and Sinatra. As the sun sets over Copacabana the only thing left to do is think about what tomorrow may bring.

If you need tourist information, **Riotur** are in the centre at Rua da Assembléia 10, ninth floor, and have a multilingual telephone service (tel: 00 55 21 542 8080).

MANAUS: GATEWAY TO THE AMAZON

Most people going to the Brazilian Amazon travel into Manaus and strike out from there. So we start in the city and head west.

Bona fide capital of Amazonia, Manaus is so far west (1,200km) of Brazil's coast that it is in a different time zone (one hour behind). Manaus is the only city in the central Amazon area with over a million inhabitants. Located at the confluence of the Negro and mainstream, the two largest rivers in Amazonia, it is a focus for regional trade, tourism and administration. Although 1,320km from the river's mouth, Manaus lies only 32m above sea level. Today it has a rough-and-tumble but benign atmosphere, somewhat unsettling for first-time visitors or those just returning from a two-week jungle trip.

The city began life as Barra, a fort built by the Portuguese in 1669. Its fortune waxed and waned with those of *pau do brasil*, quinine and other easy-come, easy-go products. When the French botanist d'Orbigny visited in 1830 he saw a bedraggled settlement of 3,000 inhabitants. This changed practically overnight in the 1850s, with the discovery of new ways of using rubber latex and its subsequent application in the inventions of rapidly industrialising northern countries.

By 1870, 3,000 tons of rubber were being exported annually, and the population had mushroomed to 50,000. By the century's end, annual rubber exports totalled 20,000 tons and Manaus' growth reflected the astounding wealth.

Manaus' excesses of luxury became a byword for extravagance. Never did the phrase 'from rags to riches' ring so true. Tatters were exchanged for clothes tailored in Paris and London. According to Anthony Smith, the worst spendthrifts even sent their wardrobes back to the Continent just to be laundered!

Gold was the accepted medium of exchange, with business transacted in spacious, luxuriously furnished offices, toasted with champagne and cognac served by bartenders brought over from Europe. Indeed, servants were not the only immigrants: bankers, musicians, artists and eligible ladies along with women of lesser repute were among the passengers of cargo ships returning from Liverpool or New York for another load of rubber.

There was no apparent attempt to seek economical solutions. Portuguese stone was imported to pave marshy areas, along with work-crews to lay the slabs. In 1896, an opera house to rival anything in Europe or America was erected, equipped with orchestra, full company, and guest performances by world-renowned singers. Whatever the truth behind the claim of Caruso's appearance at Teatro Amazonas, it is certain that electric trolley-cars were rattling through the streets in 1897. In the same year the latest-technology telephone exchange was installed, to serve the city's 300-plus telephones. Together with a huge floating dock, in 1902 the British built a customs house on the waterfront in a solid classical style, entirely of stone imported from England. It is still in use today. Intact also is the Municipal Market, constructed mostly of glass and wrought iron, copied from Les Halles in Paris.

In 1908–10, over 80,000 tons of rubber were exported, the income from which covered two fifths of Brazil's balance of payments. Yet the human price was steep, as thousands of indigenous Indians were virtually enslaved, and Chinese work gangs were imported to power the rubber industry. Demand for Amazon rubber slumped through competition on the international market; rubber from Manaus found no buyers; and in 1912 one business after another fell into bankruptcy. By 1923, the collapse was complete, and Manaus seemed destined to become a ghost town.

It was not until the middle of the 20th century that prospects perked up. Amazon rubber's high quality sustained a small market and prevented the industry's total disappearance. During World War II, attrition by Japanese forces of Malaysian plantations led to a rapid rise in demand as the Amazon became the Allies' only reliable source of rubber, essential to the war effort. The town emerged from its generation-long depression.

Manaus' tax-free status, established in 1967, and more recently its growth in tourism, have boosted local fortunes, while the dock facilities promise a role for Manaus in the area's commerce and travel industry for a long time to come.

At the airport

Manaus airport is Eduardo Gomez International, an unremarkable enough place except to exit from as quickly as possible. Of the two terminals, international flights are normally served by Terminal One – but check.

You pay about US$15–20 for the 20-minute taxi ride into town. Fend off as best you can the offers of cheap accommodation, tours and so on, and don't take a hotel bus unless on a pre-booked tour. To avoid taxi rip-offs you can buy a set-price ticket for your destination from a booth in the airport close by the exit. On the way back you can buy a ticket from your hotel – most are familiar with the system. Never leave luggage in a taxi alone with the driver.

There is an hourly airport bus service to and from the centre of town between 07.00 and 23.00. Buses heading for the airport are marked Aeropuerto Internacional and leave from R Tamandaré near the cathedral.

On the whole Brazilian airlines are safe, well-run and reliable. National routes are served from Rio, São Paulo, São Gabriel and Tabatinga, by VASP, Varig and several smaller domestic carriers.

Emamtur (the Government tourist office) has an office at the airport.

City transport

Transport in Manaus can be a nightmare if you want to do a lot of sightseeing. The best way of getting around is taxi. Make sure the taxi goes where you want, not where they want. Buses are frequent, inexpensive and easy enough; just use enough sign-language and say in Portuguese where you want to go. On the downside, most are crowded, old and smelly with erratic schedules.

Where to stay

Lodgings in this city, increasingly oriented to the tourist, come in a wide range of price and quality. With hundreds of hotels, choice is not a problem except at busy times of year. You get roughly what you pay for, although it will seem expensive for the standard. But then Manaus is in the middle of the jungle!

Luxury

Hotel Tropical Estrada de Ponta Negra; tel: 092 238 5757. This five-star wallet-emptier ranks as Manaus' most prestigious hotel. Accessed through a maze of corridors, palatial rooms are decked with antique furniture and bathroom fittings with modern conveniences. Dark wood floors, whitewashed walls, and floor-to-ceiling cabinets and wrought-iron lanterns are from another age.

Innumerable amenities include a swimming pool, sauna, disco, modest library, video game arcade, running tracks and tennis courts. The hotel's Taruma restaurant is one of the city's best. During the dry season the receding river reveals a nice beach. Within the hotel grounds is a small and somewhat primitive zoo, with a collection of representative mammals, birds and reptiles.

The Tropical will set you back at least US$150pp. Pre-book your rooms and the hotel staff will meet you at the airport or in the city. Day guests are welcome if you fancy dropping in for an afternoon to use the pool. The hotel is located 5km from the airport and about 40 minutes' drive from the city centre (US$10–15, US$5 with hotel shuttle).

First class

Hotel Amazonas Praça Adelberto Valle; tel: 092 232 2957. This four-star upmarket hotel is not quite in the Tropical's league but it tries hard. It's just a couple of minutes' walk from the dock in the centre of town. The hotel has 182 large rooms, with canned air, private bathroom, hot water and TV. Facilities include a swimming pool and inexpensive but unimaginative buffet. Better value than the Tropical at US$85 per night.

Middle range

There are dozens of medium price range (US$20–50) hotels in Manaus. If you are already in the city, a morning stroll around Manaus' main commercial area between 7 de Setembro and Dos Andrades, east of the dock, will cover most of the options. The following are given as examples of what's available rather than as a specific recommendation.

Rei Solimoe Rua da Moreira 119; tel: 092 234 7374. Has cool, clean, apartment-size rooms with private bathroom and phone. US$25.
Hotel Krystal Rua Barroso 54; tel: 092 233 7305. A new hotel, similar to the Rei Solimoe.
Hospedaria de Turismo Rua 10 de Julho; tel: 092 232 6280. Has comfortable rooms at US$28.

Budget

Youth Hostel Rua Silva Ramos 685; tel: 092 234 6796. Members US$11. Non-members are welcome but pay around US$2 extra per night.

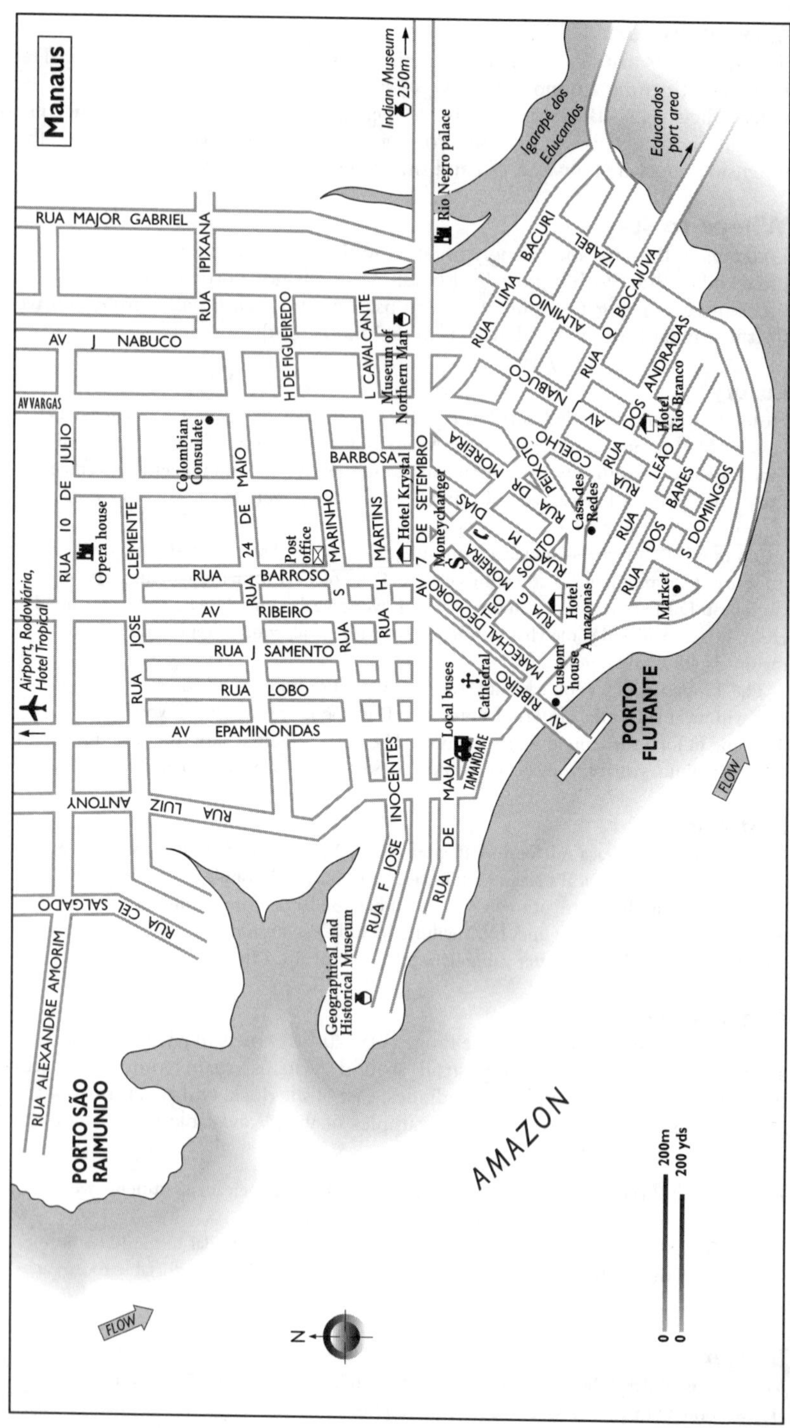

Manaus
Indian Museum
250m
Rio Negro palace
Igarapé dos Educandos
Educandos port area
RUA MAJOR GABRIEL
RUA IPIXANA
AV J NABUCO
AV VARGAS
H DE FIGUEIREDO
L CAVALCANTE
Museum of Northern Man
RUA LIMA BACURI
IZABEL
ALMINIO
RUA Q BOCAIUVA
NABUCO
AV
RUA DOS ANDRADAS
Hotel Rio Branco
Colombian Consulate
RUA 10 DE JULIO
Opera house
CLEMENTE
24 DE MAIO
BARBOSA
Post office
MARINHO
MARTINS
Hotel Krystal
AV 7 DE SETEMBRO
Moneychanger
MOREIRA
DIAS
PEIXOTO
COELHO
RUA DR
M
RUA SOUTO
RUA LEÃO
Casa des Redes
BARES
RUA DOS
S DOMINGOS
Market
RUA BARROSO
AV RIBEIRO
RUA J SAMENTO
RUA LOBO
AV EPAMINONDAS
RUA JOSE
RUA S
RUA H
MOREIRA
TEO
MARECHAL DEODORO
RUA G
Hotel Amazonas
Custom house
AV RIBEIRO
Cathedral
Local buses
TAMANDARE
RUA DE MAUA
INOCENTES
PORTO FLUTANTE
FLOW
Airport, Rodoviária, Hotel Tropical
ANTONY
RUA LUIZ
RUA F JOSE
Geographical and Historical Museum
RUA CEL SALGADO
RUA ALEXANDRE AMORIM
PORTO SÃO RAIMUNDO
AMAZON
FLOW
N
0
200m
0
200 yds

Hotel Río Branco Dos Andrades 484; tel: 092 233 4019. Centrally located and a favourite among gringo backpackers. It's safe and clean. Even if you don't stay here it's a great place to meet fellow travellers and pick up titbits of information (US$7.50 per night, including breakfast).

For those on a minimalist budget, other cheap hotels are concentrated around the dock area.

Camping

With little to no camping in or around Manaus, you need to travel to remote areas with beaches to pitch a tent. If you're camping to save money, you are better off staying in jungle shelters with a hammock. Ask tour operators and make sure you have a good guide.

The best place reasonably close to Manaus is **Praia da Ponte Negro**, some US$15 by taxi from town near the Tropical Hotel. Here there is a nice beach with toilet and washing facilities, a restaurant and boats for hire. Swimming is relatively safe and enjoyable except at weekends and during high season when the site is heavily used by locals. Hang on to belongings at all times. There is no charge for slinging a hammock or pitching a tent.

Where and what to eat

Given that the jungle is barely a spear's throw away, you might be forgiven for expecting dull cuisine and you'd be partly right. Restaurants, clean and inexpensive, offer a wide range of international dishes and of course, fresh fish is the regional speciality, but prepared with little imagination in most cases.

Less frequently nowadays *tambaqui* is on the menu – hardly surprising since the species has been seriously overfished around Manaus, alarming some conservationists. Proposals to farm *tambaqui* are currently in the pipeline and could be the salvation of this most tasty of fishes.

A staple dish is rice with beef, chicken or beans. You should try some Brazilian specialities. *Feijoada* consists of cuts of salted or smoked meats with seasoned vegetables, eaten with dried manioc (*farinha*) and grated kale and orange slices as a relish. It is most often served as the main meal for Saturday lunch. The Amazon version is called *maniçoba*. Another traditional meat dish is *churrasco*, a grilled steak and other meats with roasted manioc. Downriver, *empanhidas de camarão* are popular: shrimpburgers with heart of palm and olives. Another shrimp dish is *tacacá* – shrimp with manioc and hot sauce. *Mixira* is meat from the endangered manatee and *pirarucu* is a heavily overfished species which could do with a break from the menu listings.

Un-aged sugar-cane rum, *aguardiente,* is the traditional alcoholic refreshment, called *cachaça* or in polite company *pinga*. A surprising choice of wines is available to accompany a meal. Brazilian wines are not wonderful, but not bad either, and should be sampled, if only out of curiosity. Still, choose carefully as a good bottle costs US$25–30.

A popular non-alcoholic rainforest fruit beverage is *cupuaçu* juice, while *guarána* has enough caffeine (7%) to top up even the most dedicated coffee drinker. Other fruit juices are cashew, guava, passion fruit and the lesser-known chirimoya and sapote.

The Hotel Tropical's **Tarumã Restaurant**, serves world-class international and local dishes. The desserts are excellent. A speciality is crêpes stuffed with tropical fruits and flambéed bananas. To keep you going in between bouts of foraging at the restaurant, the hotel's pool bar serves drinks and a range of snacks. If it is really hot, you can always opt to have your drink served in the pool. Outdoor barbecues are held pool-side as an alternative to the restaurant.

If you get tired of hotel restaurants head for **La Barca** (Rua Recife 684), with fine upmarket international dining and excellent fish. Other good fish restaurants are **São Francisco** (Blvd Rio Negro 195), **Panorama** (Blvd Rio Negro 199; tel: 624 4626) by the river, or the most expensive: **Caçarola** (Av Rio Maués 188; tel: 233 3021). **Bufalo** (Av Joaquim Nabuco 628) specialises in meat dishes. **Miako** (San Luis 230) serves good Japanese dishes, and for Chinese try the **Mandarin** (Av Eduardo Ribeiro 650). For non-carnivores, the **Vegetariano** (Av 7 de Setembro 752) is recommended, while good vegetarian food is served at the Indian restaurant **Chapaty** (Rua Costa Azevedo 105). Many eateries close late Sunday and all day Monday, or all weekend.

For cheap food to eat on the move, the fish market has fish and meat cooked on skewers, or various savoury or sweet snacks cooked alfresco over wood burners. They are tasty and safe enough when eaten straight from the fire and thoroughly cooked. Fresh fruit provides endless amusement as you figure out how to deal with the various alien species; it should be peeled before you eat it.

What to see

The majority of interesting sights are within 15–25 minutes walk of the central area. This busy, bustling part of town is fascinating, with lots of shops, a couple of museums, the fish market and the floating dock. The area is quite safe to walk around during daytime, if you keep a close eye on the unstoppable traffic. After dark, sensible caution is required: walk around only with companions, dress casually, and conceal any valuables, purses and so on. Going any distance is best done by taxi.

Formerly a dingy backwater trading post, Manaus owes much of its success and status to the huge **floating docks**, completed in 1902 by the British to accommodate ocean-going ships during the rubber boom. The Punta Flutante – or more formally the Punta Escadoria dos Remedios – was essential to increasing trade through the port of Manaus.

Today, despite nearing its centennial and having suffered ship collisions and fire, the ageing edifice continues to perform sterling service on behalf of the city's shipping. Construction began in Glasgow before pieces were shipped to Manaus and assembled *in situ*. The docks are 150m long and designed to rise and fall with the annual flooding of the river, accommodating a change in water level up to 12m. It remains an engineering marvel and, even if you are not interested in tonnage capacity or shipping schedules, is worth a visit just to observe the press of human life. Riverboats and cargoships, cruise ships and canoes, *caboclos* and foreign crews, tourists and tribespeople, hawkers and hookers, all flock to the riverfront. The docks are central to Manaus, physically and spiritually: the city's true heart. If your ship or riverboat doesn't actually berth there and you come into town by bus or plane, any local can tell you where the dock is located.

Parisian-inspired, the airy, high-vaulted design of **Manaus fish market** deserves a mention in guidebooks, but it's a great biology tutor too. The grandly titled Mercado Municipal is an education, where you can major in ichthyology, minor in Brazilian economics and take in some post-renaissance French architecture at the same time. On any given day you will spot dozens of different types of fish. Look for popular species: *tambaqui*, *dourado*, peacock bass and armoured catfish. Depending on the season, other water animals are on display; caiman and river turtle in variously advanced states of dismemberment. Hopefully you won't see parts of the endangered manatee. Besides fish and meat, numerous different types of vegetables and fruits are sold, some more familiar than others; squashes, maize, beans, manioc, avocado and dozens of herbs and nuts, primarily cashews and Brazil. You'll recognise bananas although there are several different varieties; also plantain, citrus fruits, pineapple and, when in season, mango. Less familiar are *chirimoya*, *sapote*, *guarána* and *cupuaçu*, all used in delicious juices. It's easy to spend lots of time speculating about a fruit… just buy it and try it. Vendors in the market sell fruit juices, but take care as they do not use purified water to make them.

A resplendent monument to past glory, the **Amazonas Opera House** (Praça São Sebastiao) is surely among the most splendid edifices in the Amazon. Today, just over 100 years after it opened, the building dominates its surroundings situated atop a small bluff. Its luxurious features were paid for with wealth earned by the slaves who enriched rubber barons. Its pink-and-white-wedding-cake style is surely testament to its sponsors' confidence and arrogance, if not taste.

Over the four years it took to erect, the Opera House so beloved of its builders was adorned with no expense spared: marble from Italy, a massive four-storey dome covered with glass tiles imported from Alsace in France, and gold plating elsewhere. The inside is decorated with English china and baroque French furniture. Enthusiastic guides will tell you the Opera House, which opened in 1896, hosted the world's greatest artistes at the time, such as Pavlova and the legendary Caruso.

Built as it was with the profits made from rubber, the Opera House was an early victim as the rubber barons' empires crumbled. The price of rubber collapsed in 1910 and in 1912 the doors of the Opera House closed, 16 years after they had so proudly opened. The theatre itself remained, but without a company or performances, mute testimony to a bygone age and in imminent danger of sinking into the Amazon. Restoration began in 1974 and in March 1990 the Opera House re-opened, but holds only a couple of performances each year. Tours of the theatre are 09.00–15.00; Tue–Sun; admission US$3. You can walk there from the floating dock, a short but hair-raising, high-traffic-density stroll. From the dock's main gates head straight up the hill past the post office and across Av 7 de Setembro, then along Av Eduardo Ribeiro a couple of blocks and the theatre, on Praça São Sebastiao, is right in front of you: unmissable in both senses of the word.

The headquarters of the **Instituto Nacional de Pequisas da Amazonas** (INPA – National Institute for Amazon Research – Alameda Cosme Ferreira/Estrada do Aleixo 1756) is the centre for much of Brazil's rainforest research. There are pleasant botanical gardens and a visitor facility with labelled trees. Wildlife to enjoy are manatees, otters, caiman and lots of birds. It has fewer but better-kept animals than the zoo. Stroll along the well-constructed, modern walkway through the tree-tops. At the Science House (Casa de Ciencas), there are exhibitions of INPA's world-class research into Amazonian ecology, and of ongoing projects to study practical applications of ecological research, especially into effects of development and notably dams and mining.

Of particular interest to entomologists is their world-famous insect collection (Colecáo Sistemática de Entomologia). A visit here will give you some idea of how much you are missing if you don't think much of insects. It is near Est de Aleixo (take any bus to Aleixo), near the Natural Sciences museum.

The **Jardim Botânico** (Botanical Garden), Av André Araujo, is a small garden dedicated to Chico Mendez, the murdered rubber tapper and trade union leader. It's a pleasant retreat from Manaus' bustle, with a fine selection of Amazon plants containing many species which home gardeners will recognise. Open 08.00–12.00 and 14.00–17.00 daily.

Parque Zoologico do Centro de Instruçao de Guerra en Selva (CIGS Zoological Park) is at Est Punta Negra 750. This modest establishment is run by the Brazilian Army to show soldiers rainforest animals, because the reality is that most

Brazilians have not seen even a wild monkey, let alone a jaguar or anaconda. So the zoo's a good place to see the animals you won't encounter on an average jungle tour.

However, many of the cages are small and the animals receive poor diets. The occupants vary but monkeys, parrots, snakes, armadillos, tapir and jaguar are usually present. Conditions are poor compared with those of our modern zoos and some visitors find the place depressing. From town take a taxi for around US$4 or a bus ('Punta Negra' or 'São Jorge') to Est Punta Negra 750, some way beyond the Hotel Tropical. Open Tue–Sun 09.30–16.30.

Museums

Before venturing into the jungle, first-time visitors should take a day to tour the main museums dotted around the city centre, as these will broaden your perspective of the region's wildlife and culture. They close weekends (or Sun–Mon) and most charge a small fee.

Museu do Instituto Geográfico e Histórico (Geographical and Historical Institute Museum). From the floating dock, turn left along Rua M de Santa then left again all the way to the west end of Av 7 de Setembro on the waterfront. The contents of this historic building feature displays of mounted animals, ancient artefacts and fossils. It has a library, most of which is in Portuguese. Open Mon–Fri 08.00–12.00.

Museu de Ciêncas Naturais da Amazônia (Amazonian Natural Sciences Museum). To get there from the town centre direct, take a taxi (US$3–4) along Estrada Belém. A visit to this museum will give you some idea of rainforest biodiversity, with displays of butterflies and a huge variety of beetles and ants. A large *pirarucu* is on show at the aquarium. Post-tour, you can head for the museum shop to buy handicrafts. It's best combined with a trip to INPA (above) by bus, after which you can continue to the museum by taxi. It's worth the effort. Open Tue–Sun 09.00–17.00.

Museu de Minerais e Rochas (Museum of Minerals and Rocks) Est do Aleixo 2150. This geological museum is worth a visit for a better understanding of what is under your feet. Open Mon–Fri 08.00–12.00 and 14.00–18.00.

Museu do Indio (Indian Museum) Rua Duque de Caxias near Av 7 Setembro. Run by the Salesian Mission, this ethnic museum is one of Manaus' most popular repositories of memorabilia including pottery, woven goods, traditional dress and art objects. Best represented are the Tikuna and Waiwai tribes, with some material from the Yanomami along the upper Negro. A small gift shop sells postcards and crafts. Open Mon–Fri 08.00–12.00 and 14.00–17.00; Sat 08.00–12.00.

Museu do Homem do Norte (Museum of Northern Man) Av 7 de Setembro 1385. A general museum, especially focused on depicting the *caboclo* way of life, culture and history, with perspectives on local economy and social structure. Among the exhibits are photographs, models, pottery, clothing, utensils and weapons. Mon–Fri 09.00–12.00 and 13.00–17.00; Sat 13.00–17.00.

Other sites of interest

One of the city's most impressive buildings, dating from the late 19th century, the **Rio Negro Palace** was one-time home of Waldemar Scholtz, a wealthy rubber baron, and is the place to go if you have trouble believing the stories of Brazil's rubber wealth. Those days are now long gone, but the building lives on as the home for the administrators of Amazonas' state government. The Palace is located on the east side of town at the end of Avenida 7 de Setembro where it meets Rua Major Gabriel. It is not open to the public but is worth a look from the outside.

The **British Customs House** is a fine example of 19th century British architecture, showing the solid confident style typical of contemporary government buildings. Built square-shaped of English sandstone, the Customs House serves in much the same function for which it was originally intended; as an office for Manaus' inspector of port taxes. It's not open to casual visitors, although it is used today for port business, as it has been since its construction which coincided with that of the floating dock, whose traffic it was built to administer. The customs house is unmistakable and easy to find: just inside the entrance to the floating dock, left as you go through the gate.

In the **Port of Manaus Museum** (Rio Vivaldo Lima 61) you can have all your questions on the minutiae of the construction and running of the port facilities answered. The displays include photographs, maps, instruments and log-books. The museum will fascinate anyone interested in the story of the Manaus dock construction. Open Mon–Sat 07.00–11.00 and 13.00–17.00; Sun 12.00–17.00.

Excursions from Manaus

Along the confluence of the Amazon and Negro is the so-called **Meeting of the Waters** (Encontro das Aguas), some 12km from Manaus. The Rio Negro is, as its name suggests, black, or at least very dark brown, the colour of *café noir* and classified as a blackwater river. The Amazon mainstream is classified as whitewater, somewhat misleadingly, being the colour of *café au lait*. Anyway, where the rivers join up, and for several kilometres downstream, the two differently coloured waters remain distinctly separate, intermingling in all sorts of interesting circular, spiral and wavy whorls and eddies.

Most tour agencies will arrange trips to see the Meeting of the Waters. The most economical option is to go by a taxi or bus (No. 617 'Vila Buriti') to the Careiro ferry dock and take the car ferry across the river.

About 8km outside Manaus (20 minutes by taxi, US$15), the **Salvadore Reserve** protects a lake of the same name which is a haven for numerous aquatic and forest birds, plus reptiles, amphibians and the odd lucky monkey or two (they are heavily hunted outside reserve areas). You have a good chance of seeing all of these, as the wildlife can be readily viewed from a floating deck, to which the birds especially seem quite accustomed. The reserve is best experienced early morning or around dusk but there is no accommodation so you need to coordinate transport to get you there and back. Any of the Manaus tour agencies (page 370–6) will be able to provide more information or can book tours to the reserve.

The **Amazon Ecopark** is a private nature reserve with a visitors' centre and a variety of animals. Their Brazilian ranger leads a course on jungle survival offering you the best way to learn how people 'live off the land' in the jungle. Figure on US$30–35 for a day-trip (no accommodation here), including the 30-minute launch trip from Manaus. To make a booking enquire at the Ecopark office in Praça Auxiliadora 04, third floor, in the city centre. Separate from, but adjacent to, the Ecopark is the **Monkey Jungle**. This small wildlife centre run by the Living Forest Foundation is dedicated to the care of confiscated and abandoned animals. Most people come here as part of their visit to the Ecopark. Book at the Ecopark office.

Turislandia is a sort of arboretum, sure to enthral students of tropical agriculture who want to see plantation crops such as those you will encounter on a typical three- or four-day jungle trip. There's a few large jungle trees, unusual herb or epiphyte species or foreign flora. But on a one- or two-hour tour, you have a good chance of seeing some plants and birds hard to find in the jungle. Guided visits can be arranged at most Manaus tour agencies (US$15–20) but you can do it a lot cheaper yourself (US$0.75 by bus, US$1 admission). You'll need a half day to visit the arboretum, located approximately 25 minutes' drive from the city centre, in the Aleixo neighbourhood.

Shopping

Brazil manufactures world-class aircraft and mass-produces VW Beetles by the million...but tourists are usually after more practical souvenirs. For those whose bank balance can meet the challenge, Brazil is renowned for its range and quality of precious gems. Top of the range are precious stones and exotic minerals.

Street hawkers and curio shops sell wood and soapstone carvings, basketry and pottery and little paste sculptures used to make figurines and all sorts of imaginative small objects. Leather goods are a more practical buy. Of less desirable acquisitions, preserved piranha heads, shoddy carvings and craftwork, snakeskin and cat furs are widely available. Trade in pelts and skins is illegal as are products with feathers or teeth so don't waste your money.

For one-stop souvenir shopping try the **Casa da Arte Indigena** on dos Andrades between Marcilio Dias and Dr Moreira. This sells most types of folk art and handicrafts you are likely to see in the region. The shop, close to Hotel Amazonas, is run by FUNAI and profits are said to help Indians maintain their traditional way of life. Try **Casa de Beija Flor** (Rua Quintino Bocaiuva 224) for native handicrafts such as blow-guns, masks and pottery and tropical fish.

If you are going to the Indian Museum their craft shop sells a few handicrafts, wood-carvings and Indian hammocks. More practical cloth hammocks can be bought from a shop in front of Hotel Amazonas. Among several other places to buy handicrafts, try **Central Artesano** on Rua Recife. **Casa des Redes** conveniently located on Rua dos Andradas (corner of Rocha dos Santos) is a good place to pick up general items for a jungle trip: hammocks, eating utensils, rubber boots and so on.

The Tropical shopping arcade has a branch of **H. Stern** with the best – but not cheapest – selection of gemstones and semi-precious stones. This Stern chain is Brazil's biggest and best known jeweller and a visit to their shop at the Hotel Tropical is an education in itself, with most items way beyond the pocket of mere mortals.

Leaving Manaus

Getting out of Manaus into the jungle on your own by boat or road using local transport is a very different ball-game from booking a day-trip or lodge at a tour agency. Bus, boat or aeroplane are the main options. There's not much to Manaus' bus connections so we'll deal with those first.

By bus

The bus station for long distance travel is at the *rodoviária* 6km outside the city. To get there, you can catch a 507 bus (US$0.50) from the town centre or take a taxi (US$5). Buses leave Manaus for Boa Vista along the BR174; the best bus company is União Cascavel. Otherwise there are few options for exploring the area this way. Recently, the Porto Velho–Manaus bus route has been cut from schedules.

By boat

For long journeys on the river you can choose anything from a luxury passenger liner to a rusty old banana boat. The latter are charmingly called *gaiolas* by locals. Here we refer to them as local riverboats to distinguish them from luxury liners or live-aboard tour boats.

On local riverboats your concerns will be survival-based. Most of these vessels are extremely basic. They certainly make you appreciate the simple things of life such as a solid bed, decent food and clean water. There are cabins on some boats – 20–50% more expensive than travel in a hammock – available for passengers. But most people sling a hammock. Taking your own food and water is a good idea if you don't want to risk eating and drinking the boat's food which is almost certainly going to result in stomach upsets. Security on these vessels can be a concern but most problems occur when you are in port or stopping over for a few hours. While the boat is actually travelling a thief can't go far with a complete bag. A small lock should prevent any opportunistic dipping.

Four docks operate in Manaus. Which one you use depends on your vessel, destination and flood level. The floating dock (Porto Flutante) is used throughout the year for destinations along the Amazon mainstream: Tefé and Benjamin Constant to the west or Santarém and Belém to the east. For boats up the Rio Negro during high water the main port is Ponte São Raimundo on the west side of town along Igarapé de São Raimundo (from town centre US$0.50 by bus, US$5 by taxi). During low water boats for the Rio Negro depart from the similarly named Bairro São Raimundo (about 2.5km). For trips down the Madeira to Porto Velho, use Bairro Educandos, at the end of Rua Quintino Bocaiuva in the southwest of Manaus, about 1km from the floating dock. If you are uncertain as to which dock you need, head to the floating dock and ask; someone will point you in the right direction.

Up the mainstream, several local riverboats depart from Manaus' floating dock for Tabatinga leaving a couple of times a week, usually Wednesdays and Saturdays, taking six to ten days for the trip. Departure times and schedules change often. These boats are more expensive than you might expect – Tabatinga costs around US$70–100 for one-way hammock travel. If roughing it is not your thing and you can't afford a luxury cruise ship (eg: Iquitos to Manaus US$3,250), slightly less expensive expedition cruise ships and cargo vessels operate during high water. Maybe you could hitch a lift.

For boats up the Rio Negro, go to the port at São Raimundo. Most vessels depart Wednesdays and Thursdays. By local riverboat to São Gabriel this worthwhile trip costs US$60–75 with hammock. Santa Isabel, Barcelos, Carvoeiro, Moura and Novo Airão are stops along the way.

ENASA is the government shipping line, based out of the floating dock. It operates vessels carrying up to 600 passengers between major Amazon cities. Boats depart when ready and have no fixed schedule. If you're considering a trip on one of these vessels, think again. They look horrible and are unpleasant inside, with crowded, unsanitary conditions and inedible food. It is the cheapest way to travel on the river in Brazil but for a few dollars extra you will have a much better time mentally and physically aboard a *gaiola*.

Once you're ready to travel, check the ENASA bulletin board at the floating dock (for destinations along the mainstream) or at São Raimundo (to the town of São Gabriel and up the Rio Branco) for sailing and arrival times. Try to get to the ship after it has unloaded or arrive early the next day. If you can't find details relating to your destination just ask someone.

Get to the boat as early as possible to give yourself the best chance of getting a good hammock spot. But as you will quickly find, multi-level hammock hanging is the norm and the boat may not leave until the deck is packed with hammocks filling every space. If your boat doesn't leave until the next day you are normally allowed to stay on board overnight but don't leave luggage unattended.

Most passenger boats take cargo, so expect to be accompanied by bananas, dried fish, exotic fruits and fuel. Fellow travellers, invariably locals, bring along their entire household including dogs, chickens, pet monkeys and anything else that might make their journey a little more amusing or painless.

Cabins are more expensive, hot and insulating, and can be claustrophobic, offering marginally better security which in reality is just psychological. Most have fans but no air-conditioning.

By air

Amazon towns and cities are well-connected by domestic air services, in particular the air-taxi system connecting Manaus with Brazil's main cities and São Gabriel, Belém, Boa Vista and Tabatinga. Various air taxi companies (eg: Taba) operate out of Manaus. Air travel gets you to remoter parts quicker, and for equable cost, but misses the fun and romance of boat travel for a week and the education of going from a city to arable areas through recently cleared forest and into untouched primary forest.

On domestic flights airport departure tax is US$2–3; for international flights it is US$20 payable in hard currency.

TRAVELLING THE BRAZILIAN MAINSTREAM

From the dynamic city of Belém at the river's mouth, along the mainstream through tropical rainforest in variously ravaged states, passing the towns of Santarém and Alter do Chao and then the teeming metropolis of Manaus, you perceive how people live, the extent of habitat destruction and the conflict between Brazilian and Western values. Peasants cut down forest in order to sell wood, and land is cleared for ranching or plantations. Expanding populations have created serious problems of litter and sanitation which threaten to pollute the mainstream, as does the danger of contamination from mine waste and industry. Cattle run unchecked through wetland habitat, disturbing nesting birds and contaminating water. The river's riches are forced from it by nets stretched across the mouths of tributary streams, dynamite fishing and the killing of dolphins for their believed aphrodisiac properties. It's not a pretty picture, but it is real and is as much part of the Amazon as the rainforest. Workable solutions have to be found to these problems.

As you voyage further westwards and beyond Manaus the population thins, towns become less frequent, villages are smaller, the pollution decreases and the rainforest reasserts itself. People are less reliant on manufactured goods and still use the forest and river in more traditional ways, with sustainable hunting and gathering and cultivation of small plots using multi-species methods. The trend continues up to and beyond the Colombia–Peru border, where the mainstream – now named Solimões in Brazil – narrows and, beyond Iquitos, splits up into feeder tributaries. For practical details, see page 65.

JUNGLE TOURS AND LODGES

Choosing a jungle tour

First, do as much research as possible before you go. When you get to Manaus get some tourist information from **Emamtur** who have offices at the airport, floating harbour and in town. Their staff speak some English and they offer advice on getting around Manaus, as well as the harder job of navigating through Manaus' jungle of tour operators.

If you are hoping to arrive, stay a day and be straight on your way to the jungle, prepare for a let-down. It is possible but, if you book with the first representative you see, there is a good chance of getting a bad tour. If you want a run for your money it could take three or four days of sifting through, checking and comparing tour agencies. Ask and shop around for the best deal.

The tour operators mentioned below provide good service and are generally ecologically friendly but are still expensive for budget travellers. Expect to spend a minimum of US$100 per day for a nice boat trip, or from US$60 for hotels and US$100–150 for lodges. The cheapest accommodation is BYOH (bring your own hammock), travelling by riverboat or staying at primitive lodges, for US$15–50 a day. Motorised canoes take you to riverside accommodation, sometimes no more than a hut. Enquire beforehand what supplies you need to bring. Solo travel is most expensive, group travel on a pre-booked tour is cheapest. Pair up with a fellow tourist just to share rooms or take a jungle trip together and the savings quickly add up.

Manaus offers a wide choice of day-trips or overnighters, many seeming overpriced for what you get. Tours range from luxurious to cheap, but price is no guarantee of enjoyment. Generally the more expensive tours have better boats, more educated and environmentally aware guides, better food and, if overnight, better accommodation.

The feeling among tour operators and knowledgeable travellers is that Manaus and the immediate surrounds are rapidly spoiling as nature travel destinations. Aside from a few responsible companies, the evocative logos and eco-names of local tour operators are largely just lip-service.

The only sensible way to experience the Amazon in this part of Brazil is to take an inexpensive, well-organised three- or four-day trip (minimum) heading to the northwest. Aim to spend at least five or six days in the Amazon with two or three nights in a remote jungle lodge. Anything else is not worth the airfare. In Manaus, look hard and you can find good tours to remote lodges. It will be worth the extra effort.

Planning a tour

Know what you want, know your physical and financial limits, know what to expect, and even then still expected the unexpected. Decide before you go what sort of jungle trip you want and what you can afford, ie: will you want to focus on birdlife, or flora, or perhaps fishing? If you are culturally oriented make sure you will visit a couple of Indian villages (where indigenous tribespeople live, perhaps with a semblance of their original lifestyle). Visits to *caboclo* settlements provide a different insight as to how people eke a living out of the rainforest by subsistence farming, ranching on marginal land and clearing forest. The cultural experience is often disappointing for visitors as visits to Indian villages are normally oriented towards the tourist market and can seem false. If you want contact with 'authentic' unacculturated Indians you need to go far beyond Manaus to remote hinterlands, such as along the upper Negro around São Gabriel. Whatever your intentions, research carefully trips that claim you will meet 'native Indians'.

Other details you need to check are the type of accommodation and whether you need to take a hammock, as well as the quality of food and water, whether the guide speaks English. Meeting the guide before departure and having him explain the itinerary is an ideal way of judging his quality and linguistic ability. What sort of trails are involved for walking in the jungle, and are these included as standard? Whether you take a day-trip or a week-long river journey, spend as much time as you can in the rainforest because, no matter what sort of adventures you have, once you leave you will want to go back.

On a day tour beyond Manaus you should visit the tree-lined *igarapé* creeks. You won't see big animals but the bird life and plant life are rich. Ask about scenic spots. Lago Janauário and the *igarapé* lagoons have better birdlife and more diverse plant

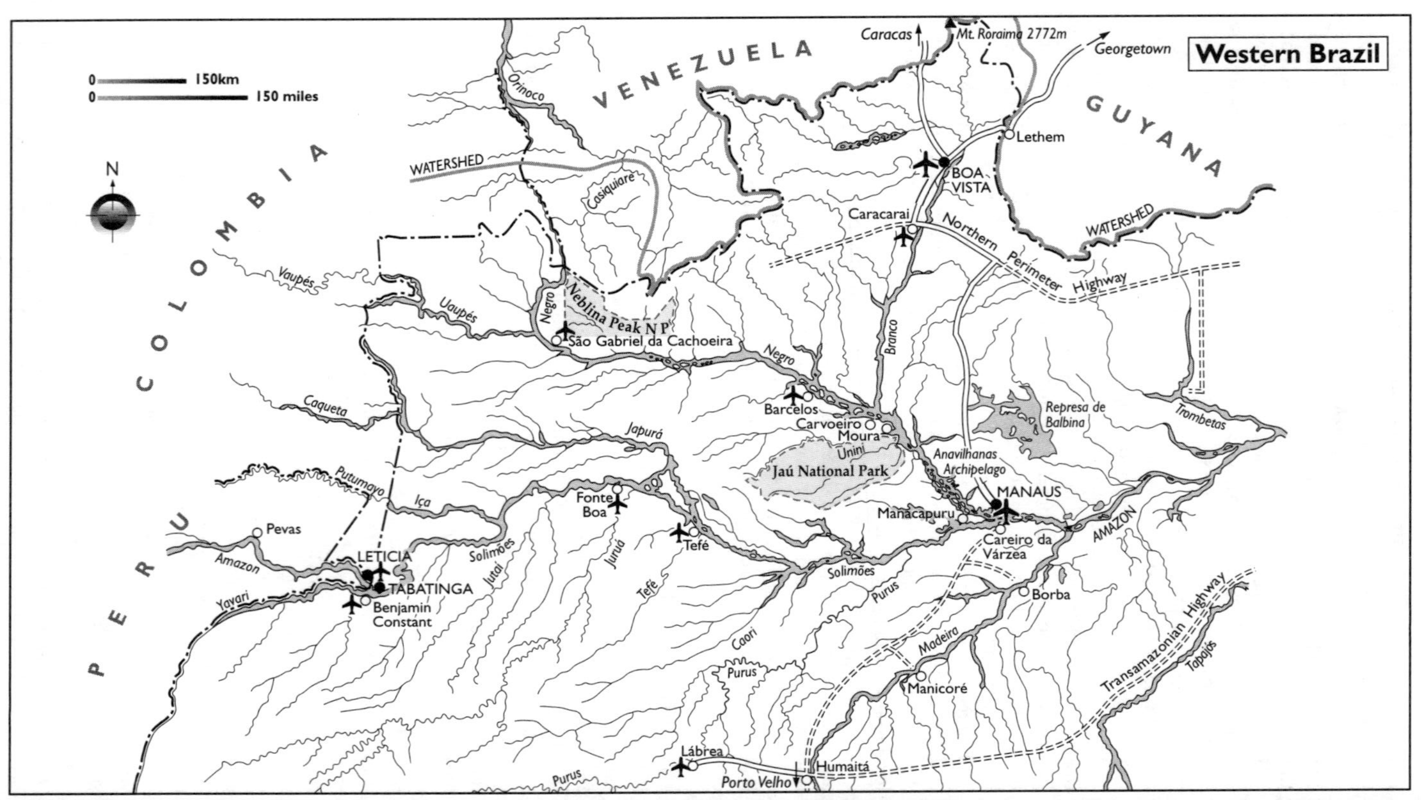

Western Brazil
0 150km
0 150 miles
N
VENEZUELA
GUYANA
COLOMBIA
PERU
Caracas
Mt. Roraima 2772m
Georgetown
Lethem
BOA VISTA
Caracaraí
Northern Perimeter Highway
WATERSHED
Orinoco
Casiquiare
Vaupés
Uaupés
Negro
Neblina Peak N P
São Gabriel da Cachoeira
Branco
Barcelos
Carvoeiro
Moura
Unini
Jaú National Park
Represa de Balbina
Trombetas
Anavilhanas Archipelago
MANAUS
Manacapuru
Careiro da Várzea
AMAZON
Borba
Caqueta
Japurá
Putumayo
Içá
Fonte Boa
Tefé
Juruá
Jutaí
Solimões
Pevas
Amazon
LETICIA
TABATINGA
Benjamin Constant
Yavari
Purus
Coari
Madeira
Manicoré
Transamazonian Highway
Tapajós
Lábrea
Humaitá
Porto Velho

life than along big rivers. During the rainy season, several waterfalls beyond the city (Cachoeira do Tarumã, 30 minutes and US$0.75 by bus, US$15 by taxi) offer a relaxing opportunity to spot more unusual plant life, although the falls themselves are worth visiting only during the rainy season.

Trips to the São Gabriel region can be made independently or through a Manaus tour operator, or booked in advance through an overseas tour operator. Birders can book through Field Guides, Inc (page 353) who offer fully inclusive trips to King's Island Lodge (US$2,895pp from Miami including airfare). Another option for exploring the area is four or five days up the Napo or, better still, the Caqueta or Putumayo – these routes are available only through local tour operators.

Selvaturs (Hotel Amazonas, Praça Adelberto Valle; tel: 092 232 2957) have four- to five-day tours along the Rio Negro, in a floating hotel (US$230/day). Besides operating Amazon Lodge and Amazon Village (pages 374 and 375), **Transamazonas Turismo** (Rua Leonard Malcher 734; tel: 092 232 1454) offer well-organised trips aimed at medium-budget travellers. Their trips along the Rio Negro last from three to four days and cost from US$125 a day. **Safari Ecologico** (R Monsenhor Coutinho 119; tel: 092 233 6910) Week-long tours for the upmarket traveller, emphasising ecotourism. They can be booked in the US with Brazil Nuts (page 353).

Amazon Nut Safaris (Av Beira Mar 43, São Raimundo; tel: 092 671 3525; fax: 092 233 0154) run outstanding tours to the Anavilhanas Archipelago, several hours journey by boat from Manaus, for US$70 a day. This haven for birdlife is a complex of hundreds of islands formed by a series of convoluted streams connected with the Rio Negro.

Amazon Wild Tours (Rua Quintino Bocaiuva 425; tel: 092 233 9308; fax: 092 633 1626) offer three- to seven-day tours up the mainstream or up the Rio Negro to São Gabriel. Their boats feature hammock accommodation so are somewhat cheaper (from US$45 per day).

Tours in the Novo Airão area along the Rio Negro are offered aboard the *Amazon Clipper* and *Selly Clipper* tourist-standard riverboats. The vessels cruise up the Pagodo River, a tributary of the Negro, and via Acu Creek to Anavilhanas and Novo Airão – where the *Clippers* were built. Trips on these vessels leave from the Tropical Hotel on Wednesdays and Mondays. As these boats are often booked months in advance it is best to make reservations from your home country. In the US contact **Maxim Tours** (page 353) who offer four-day, three-night cruises (US$629pp, sharing).

For a comfortable, ecosensitive trip try **Iaraturs** (R Mundurucús 90; tel: 092 232 2949), who run and take bookings for Malocas Camp, several hours' boat ride from Manaus. Unostentatious, amid lush tropical forest, the camp offers fine food and all amenities expected of a modern jungle lodge, although at a price (US$85 per night).

Smaller operators

As soon as you start walking the streets of Manaus you will be approached by someone who wants to sell you a trip on this or that boat. Heed the cautions already given and use commonsense if you choose to buy from a smaller operator. The plus side is that they offer lower prices and, if you choose well, more personal service. Recommended is **Moaçir Fortes** (R Miguel Ribas 1339, tel: 092 232 7492) who operates the 12-passenger *MV Cichla Ocellaris* – named after his favourite fish – from the floating dock. Moaçir cruises along the Rio Negro to places rarely visited by other tour operators. His speciality is small fishing trips. The *Cichla* is well-kept with pleasant amenities, fresh food and cold drinks, and Moaçir is among the most sought-after guides in Manaus, fluent in English and

German. Trips on the *Cichla Ocellaris* can be booked direct in Manaus or through several tour operators in the US; try **Bryan World Travel** (page 353). Another vessel popular with overseas tour operators is the *Tucano* which plies the Rio Negro to the Anavilhanas islands and also travels the Rio Branco, spending two or three nights on this remote and beautiful river. Six- to ten-day trips are available at US$175–250 per day. In the US, book through Ecotour Expeditions, Forum Travel or Maxim Tours page 353).

Personal service is given by **Marco Valério Teixeira** for day-long canoe trips to Lago Janauário, or for overnight trips there is a simple jungle camp (book at Hotel Internacional, Rua G. Moreira 168; tel: 092 234 1316). **Amazon Explorers** (Rua Quintino Bocaiuva 189; tel: 092 232 3052) is a small, locally owned and run company offering good-value day tours around Manaus. They have a boat available for charter. For fishing trips along the Rio Negro, **Rod & Reel Adventures** in the US (page 354) offer a week-long trip aboard a comfortable boat for US$1,695 from Manaus.

Jungle lodges

New jungle lodges and small hotels far beyond Manaus are springing up along some very remote rivers; in other words, where you want to go. For the lodges west and north of Manaus, prices are generally higher than downriver, partly determined by proximity to the city and the cost of moving food, equipment and staff. In decreasing order of price and standard we describe recommended lodges. Prices are minimum per person sharing on a three-day package, with meals and bottled water – bar drinks extra. To get the 'Amazon experience', you should take at least a jungle walk or two (with at least one at night), a piranha-fishing expedition and a couple of birdwatching canoe rides. Transport from Manaus is extra in most packages. Unless otherwise noted, accommodation mentioned below can be booked only through Manaus tour operators. In many cases bookings will be part of a package.

King's Island Lodge

This is among the best jungle lodges in northwestern Amazonas, near São Gabriel. The sedate journey takes five days up the blackwater Rio Negro, along wide, sparsely inhabited stretches of forested riverbank. The cruise is a good way to spend the time but it is possible to fly inexpensively to São Gabriel and take transport from there to the lodge. Birdwatching excursions are highly rewarding as most of the visible wildlife consists of aquatic birds. Bats and nightjars come out at dusk, and the sharp-eyed observer can pick out half-hidden forest birds. Trails and canoe rides provide good chances to spot monkeys, sloth or *jacaré*. Book through Nature Safaris (Rua Leonardo Malcher 734; tel: 092 622 4144/235 2840; fax: 092 622 1420) in Manaus or in the US through Field Guides (page 353). If you book locally a stay at this lodge costs about US$150 per day. Tour operators invariably fly guests from Manaus as part of a package but the river journey makes a fascinating trip.

Amazon Lodge

This relatively small luxury lodge is situated on the Parana do Mamori River system, among mature secondary forest 80km downstream from Manaus – five or six hours in a launch. On the Lago Juma, the dwellings (comprising 14 rooms in small cabins) float on platforms, offering unique chances to observe Amazon aquatic life up close. Rooms are screened for mosquitoes and there are communal cold water showers and toilets. It's quiet here as there are no generators; power is from batteries and light from hurricane lamps. Air-conditioned rooms are available when there is power. Beyond the lake several trails go into the surrounding forest, while canoe rides, piranha fishing and caiman hunting are included in the standard package. Set aside US$130 per day for a three-day excursion if booked locally through Nature Safaris (Rua Leonardo Malcher 734; tel: 092 622 4144/235 2840; fax: 092 622 1420) in Manaus. Maxim Tours (page 353) offers three-day packages, with transfers from Manaus, for US$405 per person (double) to US$570 (single).

Acajatuba Jungle Lodge

On the shore of the large blackwater Lago Acajatuba, several hours by boat east of Manaus, not far from Irandula, the Acajatuba Lodge is amidst beautiful mature secondary forest. This pleasant lodge has cabin-style accommodation with fan, private bathroom and mosquito nets and is good value at US$80 per day. In Manaus, book at Ecotéis (Rua Doutor Alminio 30).

Ariaú Jungle Tower

A nature-lover's delight, the main feature is a raised walkway through trees and across a swampy area connecting a succession of platforms and ending with a 50m-high observation tower. The walkway is great for birdwatching especially in the morning. The complex is sited by Lago de Ariaú in the Arquipélago das Anavilhanas. From Manaus, the journey of 35km takes about three hours. A whole day (two nights) is the minimum needed to take in the area around the tower. Accommodation is US$120 per day, booked through Río Amazonas Turismo (Hotel Monaco, Rua Silva Ramos 41). In the US, you can book 2–4-day packages (starting at US$185) from Forum Travel (page 353).

Tropical Lodge

This well-run lodge is the Hotel Tropical's country cousin. The facilities are located by Lago do Salvador, in the Igarapés dos Guedes. It's about 30km from Manaus, and the trip there takes around an hour by launch. Here is where to stay if comfort and ease are your main priorities. It has a good restaurant and nice rooms, but not much wildlife so nature enthusiasts may question the price: about US$120 per day. Most guests come here through the Hotel Tropical where you book with Selvaturs in the hotel lobby.

Amazon Village

Situated on the banks of the Lago Puraquequara, Amazon Village is a luxury jungle lodge some 30km up the Rio Puraquequara. From Manaus the journey takes three to four hours by boat.

A central lodge area is surrounded by 16 twin-bedded cabins with private bath and patio, with a ready-hung hammock for dozing during siesta time. There is no generator (as there is at most lodges in Brazil) and energy is supplied by solar panels. Meals are at the lodge restaurant, with refreshments for quaffing at the well-stocked bar. Standard activities include a variety of jungle treks, canoe trips, piranha fishing, caiman-spotting and visits to *caboclo* villages.

It gets crowded during the high season, being popular with foreign tourists, within easy reach of Manaus and somewhat less expensive than average. Reservations are recommended. Nature Safaris in Manaus charge US$90 per night. From the US you can book through Maxim Tours; US$326 per person double, US$381 single. Tours International in the US offer three nights at Amazon Village as part of a twelve-day round-Brazil tour. (See page 354.)

Anavilhanas Creek Lodge

This luxury lodge is 80km northwest of Manaus on the banks of the Igarapé do Marajó, a tributary of the Negro. Each of the modern bungalow-style cabins has private bath, air conditioning, minibar, phone and intercom system. A roofed patio for each cabin allows guests to admire scenic views of the river after lunch (international and local food) at the restaurant. A swimming pool gives you the chance to cool off after the various jungle trails and canoe rides are offered as part of packages, usually a two-night minimum. Bookings can be organised through Manaus tour operators but the lodge is often fully booked so reservations are recommended. In the US, try Maxim Tours whose trip (two nights, US$390pp sharing, US$475 single) includes activities during which you can 'taste the milk of a rubber tree, swing from a vine or search for hairy tarantulas or lethal fire ants'. Good luck looking for 'lethal fire ants', but if you don't see them you're sure to see a lot of other ants, zillions of birds and with luck, perhaps a pink dolphin, caiman or monkey. The tour runs from Manaus, including transfers from the airport to the lodge.

NATIONAL PARKS AND WILDLIFE RESERVES

Historically, Brazil has not cared much for the notion of national parks and even today government officials seem barely ecoconscious – there is little in the way of information for protected areas. Given the size of the territory, much of it still pristine and undeveloped, Brazil has allocated a minute amount of land for conservation. However, the protected areas are remarkable wildernesses, as yet untouched by man. The effort to travel there will be great, but then so will the reward.

Parque Nacional Jaú

This is the only fully protected area of tropical lowland rainforest in the state of Amazonas. Covering a total 27,000km^2 it is basically an unofficial reserve for Yanomami still living a relatively traditional way of life. Indeed it is the closest place to Manaus where you can see Indians in a natural setting – otherwise you have to go north up to the remote area near the Venezuela border. Covering a large area west of Manaus, between the rivers Solimões and Negro, the easiest way to get there is to proceed to Novo Airão (via boat from Manaus), from where you can hire a boat to take you to the park area. A guide is essential for any visits to the park.

Rio Negro Forest Reserve

This official reserve covers a huge and very remote triangular area from the headwaters of the Negro down to the Rio Uaupés on the Colombia border. The reserve is about half a day's travel, by motorised canoe (US$35) upriver from the small town of São Gabriel. In town you can hire a guide for about US$20 per day. Camping is the only option for accommodation, with you bringing bedding and all necessary utensils. As the area develops, permanent accommodation may become available so check in Manaus for the latest opportunities.

Parque Nacional do Pico de Neblina

This relatively small park protects the mountainous area in the far northwest of Amazonas on the Venezuelan border. The area includes Neblina Peak, Brazil's highest point 3,014m above sea level, which only experienced climbers should attempt. The Neblina Peak is highly inaccessible, with no roads or navigable rivers close by, and reaching the foothills takes several days' hike through dense jungle. From Manaus, the National Park is remote and hard to reach, but all efforts will be amply worthwhile. São Gabriel is the closest town to the park. Once there, a couple of tour operator offices can arrange a guide (US$20 per day and up) for camping trips into the park. You must supply bedding, food and utensils for yourself and usually for the guide as well.

Amazon National Park

With over one million hectares close to the town of Itaituba (page 396), south of Santarém, Amazon National Park is relatively easy to reach and completely off any beaten track.

The park is primarily *terra firme* forest but also includes *várzea* forest encompassing a number of different watersheds. It has high biodiversity. Park authorities have recorded over 40 species of tree per hectare and large numbers of orchids and bromeliads. The park is home to spider, howler and cebid monkeys, four different species of marmoset, collared and white-lipped peccaries, giant river otters, anteaters, tapirs, caiman and jaguar. Seeing any of these is down to luck and depends on how long you can spend in the park.

There are cabins at the park entrance in Uruá with basic cooking facilities and beds, or you can camp. Whichever option you choose you have to provide your own food so bring it canned or dried from Itaituba. You can explore the park on your own but getting lost is a very real possibility. Alternatively talking to the park staff will reveal the best places to go and you can strike a deal with one of them to guide you.

What you get out of a trip to the park depends on what you put in. A couple of days gives you a feel of the place but spending up to a week gets you to some of the least disturbed areas.

Permission needs to be obtained from Ibama's offices on the outskirts of Itaituba – get a taxi to take you there from town. Charges to visit the park are US$20 per day, plus US$20 administration fee, which is payable at Banco do Brasil in town. Transport to Uruá can be arranged through Transportes Itaituba. Their jeeps pass the entrance, 50km out of Itaituba, on the way to Buboré.

TOWNS AND VILLAGES WEST OF MANAUS

Along the Solimões

Immediately upstream from Manaus, the landscape differs little from that downriver; patches of secondary rainforest among sprawling, dirty villages, their attendant planted areas, grazing fields and newly hacked-down forest. Not a pretty sight, but it is less severe than east of Manaus and does not continue for long. As you get further west beyond the conurbation, the vegetation reasserts itself and begins to crowd in on the river. Only every now and then are the tall, dense woods broken by shacks and huts, usually atop stilts. Some of these merge into *bona fide* towns, most of them visited by river boats at least once or twice a week. Some of the hamlets listed below are on the itinerary of international cruise or expedition ships.

Manacapuru

This typical Amazon river port is usually missed by the cruise ships, being less than a few hours' sail from Manaus. The smaller riverboats usually stop here to trade goods or make repairs – a frequent event – after all the town is 85km upriver from Manaus! Manacapuru is remarkable only for its obvious poverty. Although you may not come here for nature or beauty, you should visit it for insight into the living conditions of the vast majority of Brazilians who dwell in the Amazon Basin away from major settlements. There is not a lot for the visitor to see or do, except take in the atmosphere; a bit smelly near the river, where a lot of sewage is dumped straight down the bank.

The town itself has two or three hotels suitable for the less fussy traveller who can put up with sharing a room with the unseen critters scurrying around at night. One establishment with a below-average density of cockroaches is **Hotel Coqueiro**, where local dishes are served. Not gourmet, but good value.

Manacapuru is about US$12–15 by launch or riverboat, or can be reached by ferry from São Raimundo docks and then a bus, but boat is better. Going upstream from the town, some riverboats stop at Anon and Codajas. Further upstream is Coari, a village at the confluence of the Rio Coari and lying on the shore of the surprisingly named Lago Coari.

Tefé

After Manacapuru, Tefé is the next sizeable town up the Solimões, 600km from Manaus; it is actually the biggest town between Manaus and Tabatinga and marks the halfway point of the mainstream between Manaus and the Colombia-Peru border.

This town is a good starting point for jungle tours, available for from three to seven days. A minimalist camping or jungle shelter trip using hammocks costs US$40–50 per day. During the high-water season, every week or so, foreign-registered cruise ships stop here; during which time 70 or 80 tourists descend, to mingle with somewhat bemused locals. There is no permanent dock so the cruise ships moor some distance offshore and send in their passengers by inflatable Zodiac dinghies.

As tourists are only here twice a month, you'll enjoy the beach on the riverfront and the Monday morning market. At a Franciscan convent, nuns sell small crafts and embroidered cloths. Of the two or three decent hotels, **Anicelis** (Santa Teresa 294) has air-conditioned rooms, and is clean and inexpensive. If it is full try the **Panorama Hotel**.

It's a fairly boring journey, as most of it is along the broad river, and after a while the forest begins to look much the same mile after mile and you ache to get off and explore. Still, some nice boats run between Tefé and Manaus. One-way the voyage costs around US$50 for first class on a better riverboat, with nice clean cabins and safe if not gourmet food. Varig has flights between Tefé and Manaus which can be booked at their Tefé office on the airport road, Est do Aeropuerto 269.

Fonta Boa

Nothing sets this typical jungle town apart; it's just a stop for local riverboats to trade goods and stock up before the final leg to Benjamin Constant. It takes some time by boat, after you leave Tefé, to make the 180km to Fonta Boa. The route upriver takes you past major tributaries, notably the Jutai and the Iça. From Fonta Boa, boats arrive and depart up the Rio Juruá, eventually to Cruzeiro do Sol, in the Andes foothills, on Brazil's southern border with Peru.

Benjamin Constant

This town is the end-point for all upriver travel through Brazil and the starting point for trips downriver. There's not much to distinguish the place; some shops, travel agencies, a bank and a few hotels. Visit the rubber plantation nearby to see rubber tappers at work. Benjamin Constant is the departure point for trips down the Javari River, which offers excellent nature experiences among pristine lowland rainforest. This journey is highly recommended for birdwatching and wildlife (tourist boats heading down the Jivaro also originate in Iquitos). For most people, the main reason to be here is just to be passing through upriver to Leticia or down to Manaus. You can pick up a boat down to Manaus, but if you are coming from Leticia, you might as well sail from Tabatinga.

Tabatinga

Just inside the Brazil–Colombia border is Tabatinga, Siamese twin to Colombia's Leticia, but more sprawling and unkempt. The two towns are one; indeed the whole area, including Santa Rosa across the Solimões in Peru, is a free-trade zone. Tabatinga is Brazil's westernmost town along the Amazon River, and a far-flung outpost it is indeed.

Raw, shabby and virtually ignored by tourists, Tabatinga's citizens collectively suffer an inferiority complex, derived from having busier and wealthier Leticians as their immediate neighbours. Tabatinga's couple of hotels and handful of restaurants are OK, but you can find much better food, accommodation and generally friendlier people just next door with a quick taxi ride into Leticia, Colombia, with no border formalities. If you must stay in Tabatinga, the **Hotel Martíns** (1220 Av da Amizade; tel: 412 2128) is acceptable for the foreign traveller: basic but clean and comfortable.

To change money in Tabatinga, go to Avenida Internacional, just past the border, where you have a choice of two *casas de cambio*, but the rates are invariably better in Leticia (see page 227). If entering or leaving Brazil, get your passport stamped at the Policia Federal at Avenida da Amizade (the airport road). It's open daily, 08.00–12.00 and 14.00–18.00.

From within Brazil, Tabatinga is easily reached, with three flights a week from Manaus with Varig (US$150, one way). To continue to Iquitos, you can fly from Tabatinga for US$125 (one way) with two flights per week. Irregular military flights depart for Iquitos from Santa Rosa in Peru. To continue on local boats you have to book further passage in Leticia. A choice of vessels from tourist riverboats, river taxis and local riverboats ply the Iquitos–Leticia route. From Manaus, a river boat costs US$150–190 with a hammock, or US$200 plus per person for a double cabin on a six- to ten-day journey.

Most westbound Brazilian-registered vessels turn around at Benjamin Constant. To continue west in this case you must disembark and pick up a river-taxi ride (US$10, one hour) from Benjamin Constant to Tabatinga. Alternatively make sure your boat is going through to Tabatinga. If you're heading into Colombia and staying there over 24 hours, be sure to stop at the immigration post in Tabatinga before proceeding into Leticia.

To return to Manaus from Tabatinga you can take a local riverboat and do the reverse trip. Most of these leave Tabatinga Wednesday or Saturday mornings, passing through Benjamin Constant in the same afternoon.

If you're looking for something to do in or around Tabatinga don't get your hopes up. There just isn't much. No tours are operated from the town as all this business is in Leticia. Likewise for accommodation, virtually every visitor heads over the border for the better choice and quality. There is one exception.

Most day-trips with an excursion to Leticia involve a bus ride to Tabatinga's only tourist attraction… **the market**. On the riverfront, multiple plastic-covered shacks sit around a tiny square. Unable to contain itself, the the market's constructions continue alongside stilt-supported walkways edging the precipitous riverbank.

If you can get over the flea-bitten, scrawny and down-trodden mongrels, the market proves to be a lively, colourful, bustling place, and a good spot to observe local life. The shopping is nothing remarkable but the activity levels are at their highest early in the morning.

A gathering of shacks and stalls sells the ubiquitous plastic goods, fishing equipment and straw hats. If you're peckish, local goods include Brazil nuts, passion fruit, mango and wild-harvested berries.

For non-vegetarians, hot snacks are cooked on open fires; catfish sliced open and plonked on a grill or small, skewer-roasted squares of meat. If curiosity can overcome repulsion, you may want to look at what it is you might be eating, displayed without consideration for the squeamish. On the slab is turtle meat or capybara; hanging 2m down from rafters are salted *piraruca* fillets, in enamel bowls lie a dozen or so armour-plated catfish or cuts of wild peccary meat.

Along the Rio Negro

Northwestern Brazil is among the wildest, least inhabited parts of the Amazon. The main route into the area is up the Rio Negro, biggest Amazon tributary and a great river in its own right. The Negro is a blackwater river, with *igapo* flooded-forest vegetation along its banks. Due to the water chemistry, the flora is distinct from vegetation along the whitewater mainstream.

Numerous Manaus tour operators offer boat trips up the Negro. Especially popular are fishing trips for peacock bass (*Cichla ocellaris*). This species is prized for its fighting abilities and good taste. Along the Negro, record sizes are caught. The Negro fulfils the aesthetic as well as the sporting instinct, for in its dark, tea-coloured waters swim highly sought-after aquarium fish. Short day-trips are possible but these do not get far enough beyond Manaus to see the interesting wildlife in the region.

A hundred kilometres or six hours by motorised canoe upriver from Manaus you reach Anavilhanas, the world's largest freshwater archipelago, comprising some 400 islands. The area offers some of the best birding sites in the Amazon and is relatively easy to reach. Tours can be booked from Manaus, with the best time for trips at low-water being between August and December.

Another option, two days upriver from Manaus, is Jaú National Park, accessed through Novo Airão. As you travel up the Negro, far beyond the outreaches of Manaus, the population thins out and the riverside becomes largely uninhabited. Only a few villages with a few huts here and there hug the shore. Across a vast flat plain, barely above sea-level, the flora is relatively intact, pristine in many places or at most lightly logged in the more accessible areas. Birds and animals are abundant, with good chances to see sloth, caiman, river dolphin and monkeys.

You can take an adventure trip in a local riverboat up the Negro as far as São Gabriel. This town gives access to Pico Neblina National Park on the Colombian border and the tantalising prospect of navigating the Braza Casiquiere that links the Orinoco River system in Venezuela; a connection first discovered in 1800 by Alexander von Humboldt, one of the Amazon's greatest explorers.

On local riverboats you must provide your own hammock and may want to consider taking your own food. If you are unable to speak Portuguese, you'll need a good phrasebook to help you wander around this remote river. If you are not on a pre-arranged tour you can usually hire a local guide (around US$20–30 per day) to take you on jungle trails. A definite plus for the area is the acidity of the Rio Negro which deters mosquitoes from breeding, thus allowing you to camp on beaches without getting attacked. There are still a few, though, and malaria is present so keep up with your malaria pills and anti-insect protection.

Novo Airão

Situated on the Negro's western bank, this small town of some 2,500 inhabitants is two days by launch from Manaus and has little to recommend it except as stopover for destinations further upriver. Consisting of typical nondescript shanty dwellings, it is worth wandering around for a bit, especially if you will not have another chance to visit any other small Amazon towns. Riverboats on their way to Boa Vista or Barcelos often visit here as a first stop after Manaus.

Novo Airão's main industry is boat construction. Along the main street are small shops where you can buy bread and biscuits and there is a market selling fish and vegetables. The town has unreliable international telephone facilities. For Amazon adventurers, the main reason to visit here is as a launch point for a visit to Jaú National Park, accessed via the mouth of the Rio Jaú, a tributary of the Negro.

Moura

You won't ordinarily visit this nondescript settlement of a couple of hundred military personnel three days upstream from Manaus. However, should any problems arise for travellers, the camp has telephone links, medical facilities and an airfield for emergency evacuation... but don't have an accident at high water, as the airfield is only operational at low water.

Carvoeiro

The first major town after Novo Airão is Carvoeiro opposite the mouth of the Rio Branco, three or four days upriver from Manaus. There are not many reasons to stop here: except as a break from travelling by riverboat en route to São Gabriel, or to catch a boat up the Rio Branco to Boa Vista if your boat is heading for São Gabriel. The town has a hotel (US$7.50) where you can stay before catching a boat up to Caracaraí for Boa Vista. If you're going there during August you might want to time your arrival to coincide with the town's annual festival.

Barcelos

Biggest town on the Negro between Manaus and São Gabriel, Barcelos takes three to four days by riverboat from Manaus. The trip costs US$20 and up. Boats departing upriver from Barcelos to São Gabriel (US$15–25) leave Saturdays: a four-day journey in the rainy season, double that during the dry season. If you are travelling to São Gabriel, you just pass through Barcelos, after which your boat continues up the Negro, passing Tapurucuara, Içana and a handful of other settlements.

Barcelos is the first sizeable town beyond Manaus around which you can take tours into the surrounding forest, which remains intact in most places. You are more likely to see animals such as caiman and pink dolphin here than downriver. The Nara family operates jungle tours from Barcelos (including meals and cabin-style accommodation), but you must book in Manaus before making the trip. (Dr Anita Nara, c/o Unidad Mista, Barcelos, Amazonas 69700; tel: 092 721 1165.)

São Gabriel da Cachoeira (Uaupés)

Banks edged in overflowing green with butter-yellow beaches in places are the typical scenery along the Rio Negro around São Gabriel. A closer inspection reveals the river banks marked only with the trident feet of wading birds or perhaps the tracks of a *jacaré* (caiman) or river turtle.

To São Gabriel, the 900km journey is five to eight days by boat from Manaus. By plane, the flight takes only three hours. São Gabriel is Brazil's biggest town near the Venezuela-Colombia border, located close to Pico de Neblina National Park. About 25km upstream the Negro meets the Rio Uaupés, which heads west, past Taraqua and the Colombian border. This route offers the prospect, with another day's journey, to head along the border to the Colombian town of Mitú. There are no tours on this route, so logistically this trip is tough going – you must organise all the transport, paperwork and supplies.

São Gabriel is the place to come to escape. The town's one hotel is modest and unremarkable but pleasant enough, well-run and good value (US$12). A dozen or so small shops sell a few staples and daily essentials. There are no currency exchange services at the town's two banks, so before leaving Manaus make sure you get enough reals.

From the US, trips up the Negro to São Gabriel da Cachoeira are offered by Field Guides (page 353) whose ten-day trip includes accommodation at King's Island Lodge. The tour features small groups and an itinerary tailored for birdwatchers, with ornithologist guides who point out species normal mortals would never spot. The land cost from Manaus is US$2,895.

For independent travellers, excursions from the town are organised by a couple of tour operators with independent guides who offer the chance to visit the Yanomami people. Many of these people remain in remote, far-off villages but a few come from their lands around the headwaters of the Orinoco down to the Brazil-Venezuela border and into São Gabriel, the biggest settlement for hundreds of miles. Politically the area is tense, due to conflict between gold mining *garimpeiros*, who are illegally settling the protected land of the Yanomami as they search for gold.

Along the Branco

This Rio Negro tributary is a whitewater river creating a meeting of waters at the confluence. This area has more insects than around the Negro, so stock up on repellent before you set off. But by way of compensation, the bird life is richer, wildlife is more abundant and fishing is better compared with those of blackwater rivers. The river's watershed is mostly uninhabited and a journey up to Boa Vista is highly rewarding for naturalists. For this reason don't use the bus service to Boa Vista unless you are short of time; take the boat instead. For those not strapped for cash, the best way to visit this area is aboard the tourist riverboat *Tucano* (see page 374). Aside from the wildlife and unspoilt scenery, this trip is off the tourist-beaten path and gives you the chance to feel that you really are exploring!

Santa Maria

Two days by river boat up the Rio Branco gets you to Santa Maria, a small settlement of four or five hundred, mostly army personnel manning an airfield. Although not often used, the facility maintains regular radio contact with Manaus. Other residents scratch out a meagre existence from increasingly infertile plots of recently cleared rainforest. A few general stores, rarely open, and a couple of small churches are among the village's other attractions.

TOWNS AND VILLAGES NORTH OF MANAUS

Boa Vista

Largest town on the Rio Branco, Boa Vista is the capital of Roraima state. The BR174 from Manaus is partly paved but still difficult and unreliable in the rainy season. As state capital, Boa Vista is home to many civil servants. The city's founding fathers approved an amazing town plan, laying the city out in impressively wide avenues following neat geometric arrangements. It must have been fun to draw up the blueprints of such aesthetically pleasing patterns, but it is less than fun for the pedestrian. Unless you can afford wheeled transport, you are doomed to wander the airy, expansive streets for many hours. Boa Vista struggles with its isolation from the rest of Brazil. The well-ordered layout of the city is surrounded by poverty and there's not much of interest except to students of architecture and town planning.

Getting there and away

Boa Vista's main importance for Amazon travellers is as the northern gateway to Venezuela. It is the largest city between the Amazon mainstream and the frontiers with Venezuela and Guyana, whose overland routes into Brazil merge here. The road from the Venezuelan border to Boa Vista is fully surfaced and offers easy access to the Caribbean; but to take a bus to Bonfim (Guyana) is difficult as this road is often reported impassable. It is easier to fly into Georgetown from Boa Vista. Heading south, it's a short drive to Caracaraí from where you can take a boat down the Rio Branco for the river trip to Manaus.

Boa Vista's international airport is 4km from the city centre, US$10 by taxi or you can take a bus ('Aeropuerto') for US$1. Varig (Avenida Getúlio Varga 242; tel: 095 224 2226) has daily flights to Manaus (US$125 one way) or take an air taxi (MMTA at airport), with three departures a week. The cheapest way to/from Manaus is by bus on a whole day's journey. It's gruelling but, for US$45–50, it is half the price of a riverboat trip or airfare. If you have the time the most relaxing and enjoyable way to go is by bus to Caracaraí and then by boat for the 7–10-day trip down the Rio Branco and Rio Negro to Manaus.

Where to stay and eat

Visitors can get help from the **Tourist Information Office** at Rua Coronel Pinto 241. Ask there about hotels and restaurants (of which there is a pretty good choice), foreign exchange, banking and postal facilities. They can direct you to the city cultural centre, park and beaches, and provide limited information on the better local tour operators. Hotels in the top range begin with **Hotel Aipana Plaza** (Praça Centro Civico 53; tel: 095 224 4800) with sumptuous rooms from US$70 per night. For US$25 per night the **Hotel Eusebio** (Rua Cecilia Brasil 1107; tel: 095 224 0300) is popular with all sorts of travellers. For lodgings under US$10 per night try **Hotel Ideal** (Rua Aranjo Filho 467; tel: 095 224 6342) which has great rooms and OK breakfast. If it's full go to the **Hotel Monte Libano** (Av Benjamin Constant 319; tel: 095 2224 7521).

Excursions from Boa Vista

Beyond the city are plenty of nature opportunities. On the fringe of the Amazon Basin, three habitats come together: tropical rainforest, savannah grasslands and *tepuis* – flat-topped mountains rising from the surrounding terrain. There is lots of unspoiled jungle to the north and west; the south is a major gold-prospecting area. **Jungle trips** from Boa Vista are worthwhile on account of much unspoiled habitat. Typically a standard tour is a two-hour trip to a scenic site and a forest-covered island, followed by a walk through rainforest. Another place to visit is the archaeological site at **Pedra Pintada**, located between Santa Elena and Boa Vista, where you can see huge carved rocks (petroglyphs). Also worthwhile is a day-trip (about $US95) to **Lago Caracaraña** which is fringed by lovely white beaches, good for swimming and shaded by stands of cashew trees. Several hours from town by bad

INDIAN RAIN RITUAL STOPS FOREST FIRES

Exceptionally dry weather, believed to be caused by El Niño, meant that seasonal fires from slash-and-burn agriculture went wildly out of control in early 1998, burning an area of over 33,000km^2 in the state of Roraima. The fires, burning for over two months, destroyed the small farms of thousands of families and threatened to burn through the forest reservation of the Yanomami Indians.

Despite attempts by the federal government to put out the fires, it was rain that finally quenched them. Two Indian Kaiapo shamans from the Xingu reservation in Mato Grosso and known throughout the Amazon for their rain-making skills, performed an ancient rain ritual on a dried-up river. Rainfall came just two hours later.

roads there is an ecological research station at **Ilha de Mara** which you can visit; and nearby is the Fazenda São Marcos Brazilian-style ranch which has accommodation at US$75 per night. Two hours by boat from town is **Forte São Joaquim** (day-trip costs US$35), the ruins of a Portuguese colonial fort, constructed in the 1700s.

River trips along the Rio Branco are highly recommended, as are trips into the **Serra Grande uplands** for patches of rainforest, good game-viewing and lots of birds.

Tour operators

Recommended tour operators in Boa Vista include **Amaturs** (Av Sebastiao Diniz 65/1, Centro Commercial; tel: 095 224 0004; fax: 095 224 0012), **Anaconda Tours** (Av Silvio Botelho 12; tel: 095 224 4132) and **Monte Roraima Tours** (Rua Floriano Peixoto 374; tel: 095 224 9523).

From the US you can book a 15-day trip to Boa Vista, travel the 540km by canoe and riverboat down the Jatapu and Uatamu rivers to Manaus. This trip costs just under US$2,000 (excluding Miami–Manaus airfare) and can be booked through Explorers (page 253).

TOWNS AND VILLAGES DOWNSTREAM OF MANAUS

Santarém

With a population of 300,000, Santarém is a town that has experienced extraordinary growth in the last fifteen years due to gold prospecting and timber. Positioned at the confluence with the Tapajós river, halfway between Manaus and Belém, it's the fourth largest town in Brazilian Amazonia, and is a good spot to rest for a couple of days or to equip an expedition. But despite its size, money changing is difficult, and impossible for travellers' cheques. The staff at the Varig office might change cash.

A good tour guide in Santarém is the North American Steve Alexander at **Amazon Turismo** (Trav Turiano Meira 1084; tel: 091 552 2620; fax: 091 552 1098). He's knowledgeable, helpful, friendly and popular so it's best to pre-book. A good hotel is the **Brasil Grande Hotel** (Trav 15 de Agosto 213), which is clean and has a restaurant. Otherwise try **Santarém Palace** (Rui Barbosa 726) or **City Hotel** (Trav Francisco Correia 200).

The road south to Cuiabá (1,777km) is not paved and makes for an arduous bus journey, especially in the rainy season. Yellow fever inoculations are insisted upon if you travel this road. A good excursion is to Alter do Chao, very peaceful during the week, which is a weekend retreat for the inhabitants of Santarém, with good swimming in the Tapajós. Extensive beaches appear from August to January. The failed rubber plantation of Henry Ford at Fordlândia is also worth a visit.

Belém

Named after the biblical village of Bethlehem, with which it has little in common, this noisy, bustling port serves as the gateway for all Amazon river traffic – as it has for some 400 years since its founding in 1616. Beneath accumulated centuries of grime glimmer a few remnants of this colonial legacy, crammed between shimmering skyscrapers and blotchy grey tenements, adorned with hanging clothes and forests of television aerials.

On the mouth of the Amazon, Belém is the second largest city on the river and the only other in lowland Amazonia with a population over one million. Now state capital of Pará, Belém grew fast with the rubber boom during the late 19th and early 20th centuries, its expansion attributed to its location and good international travel connections.

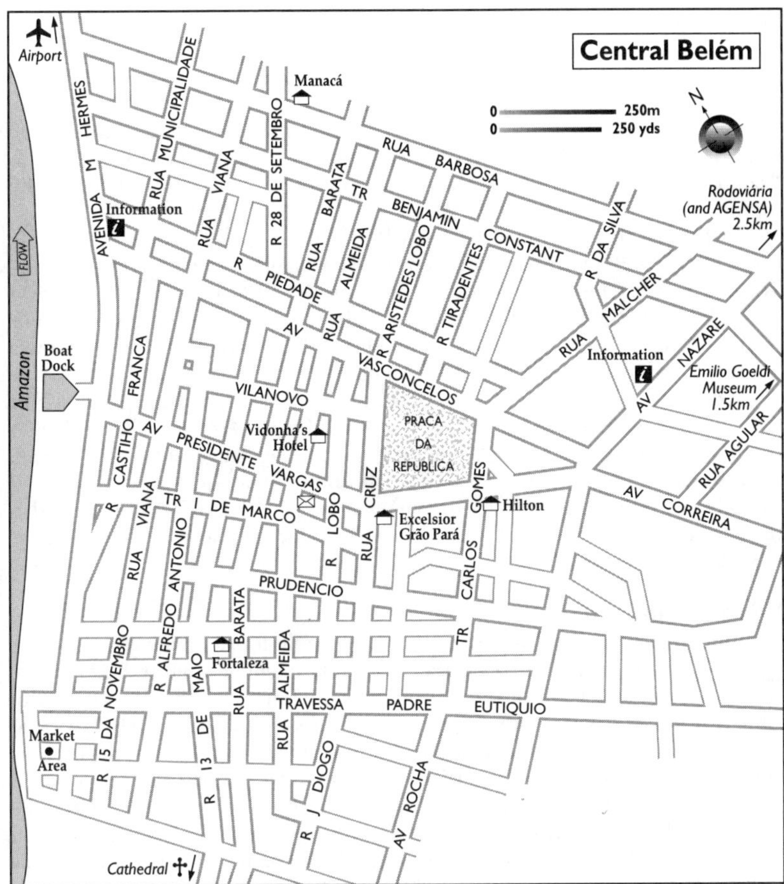

Because of the better nature opportunities upstream, most people arrive in Belém en route to Manaus for the start or end of an Amazon cruise.

Getting there and away

Belém is well served by international flights. From Miami, Varig (Avenida Presidente Vargas 768; tel: 091 225 4222) flies daily with a service that continues to Manaus (US$575 return).

Most people who leave or arrive at Belém by sea do so via *gaiola* riverboat or, at the other end of the comfort and cost scale, by luxury cruise ship, including expedition vessels like the *Explorer*. Travel to Santarém or Manaus by riverboat with hammock accommodation is straightforward though hardly comfortable. Buy tickets at the Agenasa (Agencia de Navegaçao a Serviçio da Amazonia; tel: 091 246 1085) office at the *rodoviária*, on the east side of town, 1km from the town centre along Avenida José Malcher. The three-day trips to Santarém cost around US$75 for hammock space (US$100 per person in a four-berth cabin) or about US$105 to Manaus (US$150 for a cabin). Meals are not included. Agenasa also provide transport from the bus station to the dock. Boats depart Monday, Tuesday, Wednesday and Friday.

Where to stay

Being a port Belém has plenty of accommodation, mostly inexpensive. For convenience, stick to the central area which is quite safe for the most part. However, especially after dark you should not go out alone and always be on your guard against pickpockets, bag snatchers and so forth. The area around the waterfront market – Mercado Ver O Peso at the southern end of Vilha Castilho França – is dodgy, but the sights, sounds and smells make a visit worth the minor risk.

The plushest hotel is the **Hilton** (Av President Vargas 882; tel: 091 223 6500; fax 091 225 2942), with all the luxuries (US$190 single per night) and little soul, as you'd expect. Close by is the rival **Excelsior Grão Pará** (Av President Vargas 718; tel: 091 222 3255), with nice views and very nice rooms at US$75pp. For medium-priced lodgings try **Manacá Hotel** (Travessa Quintinio Bocaiuva 1645; tel: 091 223 3335) for US$25 per night in rooms with fans. It's a little way from the city centre but still within walking distance. The best value in this price bracket is **Vidonho's Hotel** (Rua O de Almeida 476; tel: 091 225 1444), in the city centre with clean spacious rooms including fridge and TV for US$25 for a single room, US$35 for a double. If you're penny-pinching, the **Hotel Fortaleza** (Travessa Frutuoso Guimarães 276; tel: 091 241 5005) is bang-slap in the middle of the city centre and one of the better cheap 'n' cheerfuls for US$10 per night.

What to see

If you're in Belém for a couple of days, there's time for sightseeing. A city tour typically includes the **Teatro de Paz** (Praça de Republica; tel: 091 224 7355), which is Belém's version of the Manaus Opera House and almost as splendid. The **Emílio Goeldi Museum** (Avenida Magalhães Barata 376; tel: 091 249 0163) is a combination of park, zoo, aquarium and collection of Amazon Indian artefacts and mineral specimens. The **zoo** is one of South America's best and a visit is well worth every penny of the admission fee (US$4). Open Tue–Thur 09.00–12.00 and 14.00–17.00; weekends 09.00–17.00. City tours are available from travel agents from about US$25 per person. Try **Mururé Turismo** (Avenida Presidente Vargas 134; tel: 091 241 0891; fax: 091 241 2082) or shop around for the best deal.

Of course, what's of interest to some travellers is what is not included in the tour. These are places – such as the **market** – where you see the daily life of the people of Belém. In the heart of the city, opposite the Hilton hotel, is **Praça de Republica**, a small park – focus for local musicians, tradespeople, craftsmen and bohemians. It's a fun place to wander and watch the local life go by.

Excursions from Belém

There aren't a whole lot of reasons to stay in Belém on its own account, at least not if you're interested in visiting pristine rainforest. The best excursion is a trip to **Marajó Island** in the river's mouth. About the size of Belgium, this is the world's largest river delta island. Although overrun by Asian water buffalo, the island offers excellent birding opportunities. Expedition and cruise ships going from the main stream to Belém take a short cut along the east of the island through the Breves Channel. You can catch a boat from the Belém docks (near Porto do Sal) costing US$3 for the five-hour trip. On the island is a small settlement with simple lodgings at the basic **Hotel Ponta de Pedras** (US$7.50 per night). In the village you can hire a bicycle to explore the island on numerous tracks and trails. Allow at least a full day (two nights) to make the journey worthwhile.

SOUTH FROM MANAUS

South of the mainstream is the realm of the independent traveller. Passenger and cargo boats travel up the Rio Madeira to Porto Velho. Jumping ship in Humaitá you can travel east along the Transamazônica Highway by road. Completing the journey in Porto Velho you can head east through the recently settled state of Rondônia or south and west to Bolivia and Peru.

An almost complete lack of tourist facilities makes it hard to reach those blank spaces on the map. A few towns of notable size are just reference points between large expanses where it's just you and your intuition taking you along.

Boats up the Madeira

Riverboats leave from the main port in Manaus taking around five days upstream at a cost of US$80 including food. Water is provided for the journey but probably comes from the river so sterilise it or take along your own.

You'll need your hammock and a few books to while away the hours. A straw poll of people who have completed this route (totalling a statistically significant three) reveals the boats take longer than scheduled. This is meant to be a five-day trip upstream, four days downstream; the downstream journey took one traveller 11 days.

The food on the boats is very basic. Breakfast is usually no more than crackers and coffee, with lunch and supper being fish or chicken with rice, beans and, on good days, noodles. Sprinkled with the ubiquitous *farinha* this tasty and nutritious diet gets a little trying after a few days – a week of crackers and coffee for breakfast is a distinct possibility – so you might want to take some food with you. There are usually people plying the dockyard in Manaus with some strange looking fruits.

Up the Madeira

The journey first takes you from Manaus down the Amazon before heading south up the Madeira. The boat stops at several towns along the river depending on the destination of cargo, passengers and the mood of the captain. A couple of days from Manaus the town of Manicoré is a regular stop for picking up and dropping off cargo. If the blandness of the food is getting to you there is a small market just off the main square. Other towns along the journey are little more than mission outposts; or a bar with a pharmacy round the back or a palm-frond-thatched hut in the middle of nowhere to which pilgrims trek from the surrounding area to sit and gaze at the flickering light emerging from within: a television.

The next main town of significance is Humaitá, another stopping point for boarding and disembarking passengers. The square beside the river is reminiscent of a ghost town since the road from Porto Velho to the south made the new centre of town the bus station. If you want to experience the ongoing battle between colonisers of the Amazon and the rainforest, travel from Humaitá along the Transamazônica Highway for roughly 1,000km towards Itaituba and on to Santarém.

Travel on this size of boat is unlikely to put you in touch with nature. The river is too wide and the river traffic too great. Tugs push huge barges loaded with over 25 lorries between Manaus and Porto Velho. Any animal seeking a peaceful life would move up one of the smaller, less-used tributaries. But occasionally you can see river dolphins break the surface of the water and caiman basking on the sandbanks.

Life on a riverboat is a fascinating display of Amazon culture. On all but the very smallest boats there is usually a top deck where people gather and while away the hours talking, playing cards, drinking and dancing to music; none of the sobriety of simply getting from one place to another. As the boats move so slowly up the river there seems little reason not to stretch the longest yarns to near breaking point. It's a great exhibition of story telling. Tempers rise and fall, friendships wax and wane. Having spent such an intimate time with so many people, it can seem a little strange, once back on land, to be amongst a throng of nameless faces.

Porto Velho

Capital of the state of Rondônia, Porto Velho has grown at a staggering pace from a small Amazon outpost to a city with over 350,000 inhabitants in just twenty years. As you arrive by boat the small sleepy district close to the port obscures the bustling energy of the city.

At the turn of the century the city was set to become an important centre for the movement of rubber from Bolivia further downstream to Manaus. The long-awaited completion in 1912 of the Madeira-Mamoré rail line from Bolivia to Porto Velho was timed to perfection, just when the boom days of rubber were beginning to fade. In the 1970s the discovery of gold in the area combined with encouragement from the Brazilian government to colonise the Amazon saw a huge influx of immigrants.

Even without the railroad, the city's role as a distribution centre has flourished. Trucks commute the main BR364 artery to the south of Brazil, while to the south and west smaller but equally significant roads stretch out to Bolivia and towards Peru.

The centre of the city – if there is such a thing – is Avenida 7 de Setembro. It's a busy street with hundreds of over-staffed shops selling all sorts of things that nobody even knew they wanted. There are several bars and *lanchonetas* or snack bars along the street, also a cinema. Towards the port is the post office which is the best place from which to send a letter and also has an ATM cash machine for Visa cards. (Failing that the Banco do Brasil on Avenida José de Alencar changes travellers' cheques and cash, and cash advances.)

On the main street towards the port are two places of interest. The **Museu Estadual de Rondônia**, on the corner with Av Farqhuar, has fascinating displays of ceramics, pickled creatures and animal skins from the state. There is also a good display of musical instruments, feather head-dresses, arrows and fighting sticks and language tables explaining the relationship of indigenous groups in the area. There are several Indian groups still living in the state of Rondônia, an area that was once home to 40 different tribes. When the BR364 road from the southeast was built to open up the Amazon frontier there was barely any consideration for traditional lands – with predictable consequences. Despite the introduction of consultation procedures to limit further incursions, new projects continue to threaten remaining traditional lands.

Closer to the river is the **Estrado de Ferro Madeira-Mamoré** which pays tribute to the impressive task of building a railway through the Amazon lowlands. The railway was built to avoid the tedious task of carrying rubber around 18 sets of rapids between northern Bolivia and Porto Velho. But trains in South America are usually late and this railway is no different.

The railway museum itself is as uninspiring as museums get. Even today the display inside looks completely out of place. If you care not one jot for the clackety-clack on the track, if the romance of steam-powered engines billowing out plumes of smoke passes you by, maybe knowing that around 6,000 people died during construction gives the railroad some significance. Building and working with trains has always been hard work. Constructing a track in the steamy Amazon Basin was a hare-brained idea almost certainly doomed to failure from the outset.

The museum is filled with renovated engines and railway equipment. Victorian leather-upholstered chairs sit at worn tables, bureaux bear ink stains over a century old and cabinets hold trinkets and glasses that could not look more out of place.

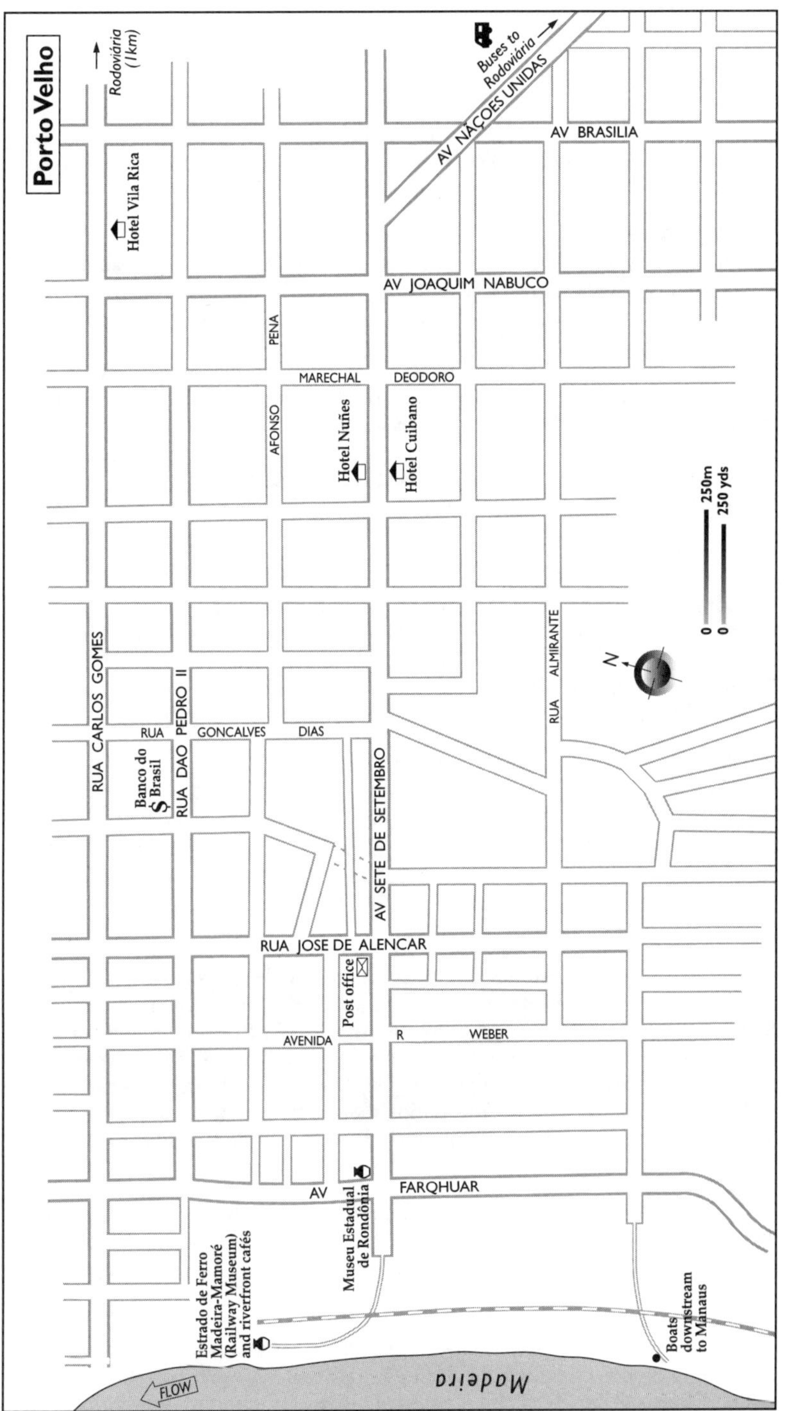
Porto Velho
Rodoviária (1km)
Buses to Rodoviária
AV NAÇOES UNIDAS
AV BRASILIA
Hotel Vila Rica
AV JOAQUIM NABUCO
PENA
MARECHAL
DEODORO
AFONSO
Hotel Nuñes
Hotel Cuibano
0 250m
0 250 yds
RUA ALMIRANTE
RUA CARLOS GOMES
RUA DAO PEDRO II
RUA
GONCALVES
DIAS
Banco do Brasil
AV SETE DE SETEMBRO
RUA JOSE DE ALENCAR
Post office
AVENIDA
R
WEBER
AV
FARQHUAR
Museu Estadual de Rondônia
Estrado de Ferro Madeira-Mamoré (Railway Museum) and riverfront cafés
Boats downstream to Manaus
FLOW
Madeira

There are several photographs of the managers and workers who gave all or part of their lives to the railroad.

The railroad is still the passion of some and part of the line and a couple of engines have been restored. On Sundays several trains depart to make the 7km journey to and from the rapids at San Antonio upstream.

Outside the museum is a terraced area where several stalls serve juices, coconuts and pizzas.

Getting there and away

Travel out of Porto Velho is either by boat down to Manaus, or by road. Humaitá is four hours to the north by bus and the trip costs US$10. Cuiabá along the BR364 is a rather frightening 1,965km to the southeast and is a journey probably worth avoiding in one go unless you're really in a hurry. Buses heading west to Rio Branco (US$26, eight hours) leave along a good road. Going in the same direction, buses turn south off the road to Guarajá-Mirim (US$20) on the border with Bolivia.

Internal flights to most Brazilian cities leave from Ter Guaporé airport 7km out of town.

Local buses to town run from outside the *rodoviária* (bus station). Buses to the terminal leave from 7 de Setembro.

Where to stay

Accommodation in Porto Velho is either grubby or over-priced. Finding something affordable and reasonable is quite difficult. The best in the centre of town is **Hotel Vila Rica** at Rua Carlos Gomes 1616 and Av Joaquim Nabuco (tel: 069 224 3433), easy to find as it is the tallest building in the city (US$100+). **Hotel Nunes** and **Hotel Cuiabano** (US$15) are both considerably cheaper places on 7 de Setembro. If you're arriving at the *rodoviária* late at night or leaving early there are several options around the terminal. **Novo Hotel** on Av Carlos Gomes 2776, two blocks west of the station (tel: 069 224 6555), is clean and tidy (US$36). **Guajará Palace Hotel** on Rua Miguel Chaquian 1468 (tel 069 225 3227) claims to have the best service in Porto Velho (US$32). Budget accommodation along Av Carlos Gomes includes **Hotel Ouro Fino** at #2844 (US$10) and **Hotel Amazonas** which is slightly better at #2838 (US$10). South of the station are a few cheapies, the best of which is **Hotel São Cristoval** (US$7).

Where to eat

One of the smaller mysteries of life is where people in Porto Velho eat. The floating restaurant outside the rail museum serves good fish...when it is open. One recommendation is the **Remanso do Tucunaré** at Av Brasília in the Senhora das Graças district. There are several restaurants close to the Hotel Vila Rica including the **Chinese Oriente** at Av Amazonas 1280. Several stalls offer street food close to Av 7 de Setembro. Near the bus station there are a few *parrilladas* selling meat by the carcass. For beer and drinks take a stroll down Av 7 de Setembro.

Excursions from Porto Velho

There's not much for tourists to do around Porto Velho. At weekends boats cruise up the Madeira and most of the passengers are locals giving you an ideal chance to practise your Latin legwork with a bit of dancing, music and generally having a good time.

An alternative excursion, although in its embryonic stage as yet, is to visit Parque Nacional de Pacaás Novos. Covering over 750,000ha and home to several indigenous groups including the Uru-eu-wau-wau, this national park is 200km south of Porto Velho. The park is primarily tropical forest with transitional zones and savannah. Access is along the BR364, turning off at Ariquemes. There is no public transport to the park, although it is possible to hitch. By the end of 1998 there will be cabins in the park at Campo Novo offering a basic tourist infrastructure, with guides available for arranging trips deeper into the park.

For details contact Carlos Rangel; IBAMA-Rondônia; tel: 069 224 6568; fax: 069 224 6511; Av Jorge Teixiera 3477 (buses from the bus station heading north), CEP-78904-320, Porto Velho, Rondônia, Brasil.

TO GUAJARÁ-MIRIM AND BOLIVIA

Buses from Porto Velho to Guajará-Mirim on the Bolivian border leave almost hourly. The road still has a frontier feel with small towns dotted along it and pockets of rainforest between the cleared farmland. On the northern bank of the Mamoré the town is quiet and ordered. The *rodoviária* is several kilometres out of town; from there you can walk to the centre or catch a bus or taxi. There's a selection of hotels including the **Mini Estrela** and **Fenix Palace** along Av 15 de Novembro, but if you're on a tight budget the hotels on the Bolivian side are cheaper.

If you're crossing to Bolivia for more than a day you'll need an exit stamp from the Brazilian Federal Police on Av Presidente Dutra. A passenger boat service buzzes back and forth across the river charging next to nothing. On the Bolivian side, immigration is next to the ferry terminal. Most accommodation is close to the main plaza a few blocks straight up behind the ferry terminal.

The Rio Guaporé, which feeds into the Mamoré upstream from the town, marks the border between Brazil and Bolivia and, potentially, makes an interesting river trip. Three days upstream by boat is the border post Forte Príncipe da Beira built by the Portuguese in the 1770s to mark the boundary between Portuguese and Spanish territory. With the growth in road transport throughout the Amazon river transport has dwindled. If you really want to make the trip you may have to wait, but with luck you'll find a boat heading upstream. An alternative upriver destination is Trinidad (see page 339).

West of Porto Velho to Rio Branco

Travelling west towards Rio Branco through cleared forest along a good road, opportunities for stopping are limited and there seems little reason to do so. The town of Abunã is close to the Rio Madeira. Barges take all transport across the river and beyond.

Rio Branco, capital of Acre state, is some 550km from Porto Velho. The town itself is bustling with energy. The meandering traveller is barely noticed, let alone acknowledged. The days start early because of the heat so if you arrive midday you may find yourself wondering where the city's 200,000 inhabitants have gone.

Rio Branco is sliced in two by the Rio Acre. The centre of town, with most of the hotels and places of interest, is on the north bank. The bus station and airport are several kilometres south of the river.

Two museums in the town are worth a visit. The **Museu da Borracha**, on Av Ceará, has a range of ethnological, archaeological and historical exhibits on display, and the **Casa do Seringueiro** gives some insight into the realities of the rubber tapper's life, with particular reference to Chico Mendes who was assassinated in the state in 1988.

Getting there and away

The *rodoviária* is about 2km out of town and is served by regular local buses. If you are just passing through there are plenty of hotels around the station that are fine for a night or two.

The airport is another kilometre or so out from the centre of town. Buses run from the end of the airport road. There are regular flights to Manaus and Porto Velho but locations further west can be reached only by air taxi.

Money

Banco do Brasil on the plaza changes travellers' cheques and dollars. If you're heading further west this is probably the last chance for a while so stock up with all the money you need.

Where to stay and eat

In the centre of town at the top end of the range is the **Hotel Pinheiro Palace** on Rui Barbosa 91; from US$80 with swimming pool and A/C. Considerably cheaper, the **Hotel Rio Branco** along the same road (number 193) is also a comfortable option, and slightly cheaper is the **Hotel Loureiro** (Marechal Deodoro 196). The area around the bus station has several hotels including the **Hotel Rodoviária** and **Hotel Nacional** both charging US$8 for a single and US$12 for a double. A little more upmarket is the **Hotel Flor da Mata** at US$18 and US$23.

Casarão at Av Brazil 110, near the bottom of the plaza, is the most popular restaurant in town, serving good fish dishes. **Pizzeria Bolota** is opposite the Hotel Pinheiro Palace. Near the old bridge there is a small food market and a few bars.

Excursions from Rio Branco

Short trips to visit rubber tappers and nearby forest can be arranged with Acretur next to Hotel Rio Branco at Rui Barbosa 193, as can trips to the nearby religious sects including Colonia Cinco Mil.

Boca da Acre to the north of Rio Branco is a good spot for swimming and fishing. The trip downriver to Lábrea takes two days and travels through quiet stretches of *várzea* forest. There is a reasonable amount of river transport but if you're trying to go a long distance you may have to use several different boats. From Lábrea it is possible to jump ship and travel east by road to Humaitá or you can continue further downriver which eventually will lead you to Manaus.

South from Rio Branco

From Rio Branco the dirt road splits. The southern fork takes you to Brasiléia, which links to the Bolivian town of Cobija and on to Assis Brasil on the frontier with Peru. Both crossings leave you in frontier town territory where by and large you have to make your own travel arrangements. Heading west takes you along the last section of the BR364 to Cruzeiro do Sol from where you can just about cross the frontier to Peru near Pucallpa.

Both roads are dirt tracks and can be impassable in the rainy season between November and March.

To Brasiléia and Assis Brasil

The advance of settlers in this part of Brazil is steady. Just a few years ago moving around the area proved difficult, but there are now four buses making the journey from Rio Branco to Brasiléia daily (US$17).

The road itself is dotted with a mixture of ghost towns and thriving settlements some of which are quite pleasant if you have the time to stop. But the backdrop of scenery is a real eye-opener. The area, once rich with rainforest, is now a vast expanse of cattle-pastures interspersed with rainforest. When the road nears the frontier the rainforest comes in to view; this part of Bolivia, for the moment at least, has not been stripped bare by chainsaws.

It is difficult to find someone or something to blame for the devastation. While the ranchers and peasants who work on the land seem to be trapped in or very close to poverty, it is hard to imagine that their circumstances would be any better if the rainforest had been left standing.

Halfway between Rio Branco and Cobija is the turn-off to Xapuri where the rubber tapper Chico Mendes was assassinated. There are a couple of hotels and a small exhibition in tribute to the murdered eco-martyr.

If you're going to Bolivia you'll need to have your passport stamped at the Federal Police offices in Brasiléia near the entrance to town. You can get a Bolivian entrance stamp from the Bolivian Consulate on Rua Major Salinas 205. The bridge that crosses the river into Bolivia is quite a long way through the town, and down the hill.

Accommodation in Brasiléia is forgettable but if you need to stay the **Hotel Kador** is on the way in to town and the **Pousada las Palmeras** is in the centre.

To Assis Brasil and beyond

Like Brasiléia, this frontier town has very little of intrinsic value to the visitor apart from being the place to stop before crossing to Peru. That said, if you were going the other way and fancied an adventure, then getting a canoe and starting your journey downstream passing through Brasiléia would be an ideal way to ease yourself into the idea gently.

Transport from Brasiléia is by bus in the dry season and the road is bad. Once in Assis you can spend the night in the Hotel Aquino or get an exit stamp from the Federal Police and walk the 2km to the Peruvian town of Iñapari, from which trucks leave for the Peruvian jungle town of Puerto Maldonado.

To Cruzeiro do Sol and beyond

From Rio Branco the BR364 continues, in name at least, to Cruzeiro do Sol (population 60,000) some 600km to the west. The road has little chance against the elements and there is no bus service at present, making for a hard journey. The *Quatro Rodas* road map of Brazil says that four-wheel drive is required but it's a fair bet that regular bus traffic will be travelling the road soon.

There are a few cheap hotels, with the **Sandrais** probably being the best, then the **Flor de Maio**, with **Hotel Novo Acre** bringing up the rear.

A visit to Cruzeiro can be rewarding if only because you are one of the few visitors to the area. You'll have to negotiate trips to see rubber tappers but you may get insights that are hard to come by in more accessible places.

From Cruzeiro the quickest way to Peru is to fly to Pucallpa. The flight, costing US$70, is with SASA (Boulevard Taumaturgo 25). The airport is 7km out of town.

Cruzeiro do Sol is about 100km from the border with Peru at Brazil's westernmost point. The town of Pucallpa is a similar distance from the border on the Peruvian side. A land crossing is manageable but most people travelling the route will be up to something illegal so be careful when choosing travelling companions from the region. Having gained an exit stamp from the Federal Police in Cruzeiro you can continue along the road to the border. From there you will need to make your way through the jungle to a river heading down to Pucallpa. Don't attempt the journey without a guide unless you like the idea of getting lost.

THE TRANSAMAZÔNICA HIGHWAY

If boat travel with its laid-back eccentricities and relaxed chaos gets you close to the spirit of the Amazon, travelling along the Transamazônica puts you directly in touch with the indomitable frontier spirit of the Amazonian coloniser. It may not be part of the romantic nostalgia that mythologises the Amazon, but it is a part of the story that gives rise to the myth. No-one has been forced to live along this road but settlers have chosen to move here in the belief that the opportunities are better than elsewhere.

Although the road was first cleared by the government, the presence of migrants led to greater deforestation of the area as they reclaimed land for agriculture and grazing. Along the Transamazônica the trailblazing culture of the frontier sits side-by-side with environmental destruction. The spirit of these colonisers is admirable in a world which rewards those who seek to help themselves, even as their actions destroy the rainforest. Such contradictions are central to the conservation dilemma. If you seek motivation to get involved with environmental organisations that are serious about recognising and tackling them, this is the road to travel.

The road's original blueprint connected Brazil's Atlantic coast at Belém to the westernmost point near Cruzeiro do Sol. At present the road stops in Lábrea, over 1,000km short of its destination. Travel along the road is by bus and truck and is hard and, at times, frustrating. Sections of the road have become impassable as river transport is an easier option. Travel in the rainy season between November and March is likely to be difficult but there is always a way if you have the time! There are very few points of natural beauty along the way; the rewards of travelling this route come with stopping in a settlement to soak up atmosphere.

Apart from a couple of towns, Itaituba and Marabá, there are few opportunities to change or obtain cash so stock up before you travel. Accommodation is basic and food is available in all the towns.

Many settlements between Humaitá and Itaituba are experiencing increases in the number of cases of malaria so take prophylactics. The chances of getting medical treatment are close to zero and it is extremely difficult to leave the area quickly.

Humaitá

A small jungle town of several thousand, Humaitá makes its living supplying nearby ranches and logging. The bus station has become the new centre of town making the plaza alongside the river quiet most of the time.

Regular buses leave Porto Velho for Humaitá (US$10, four hours). Boats also stop off in Humaitá. The road passes through completely cleared rainforest. In the burning season, September and October, the landscape looks like Armageddon and the final battle between good and bad.

On the edge of town is the **Hotel Masadonia** charging US$25 for a double. The **Hotel Brasil** charges US$25 for a single and US$45 for a double. It has a restaurant, bar, and rather strangely a tropical fish tank. These two hotels are surprisingly smart, no doubt waiting for a sudden increase in demand for good-quality hotels in the middle of the Amazon.

The best of the rest is **Hotel Maia** charging US$8 for a single. It is family run and serves food in ridiculously large portions. **Soveteria Tropical** serves life-enhancing ice-cream.

Apart from watching the gentle flow of life there is little to do in Humaitá. The church is a rather ostentatious creation. Towards the ferry crossing there is a saw-mill which you can look round once you've obtained permission from the site manager in the office at the gate. Trees of the rainforest are cut and shaped for distribution to Brazilian and international markets, while the workers operate heavy machinery in flip-flops. Blades that easily slice through trees three metres thick don't have problems with human limbs, a risk the workers are prepared to take for US$300 a month. (The management don't like you taking photographs.)

Beyond Humaitá

There is a regular twice-weekly service to Apuí which takes 12 hours. A more interesting way to travel is to hitch from the riverfront where a ferry transports vehicles across every other hour. An early start increases your chance of making any real dent on the 1,000km to Itaituba.

The road quickly deteriorates. Solitary huts sit patiently alongside it optimistically waiting for the boom. The road travels through the northern extremity of the Tenharim-Transamazônica Indigenous Area before arriving at the creatively named town of Kilometre 180, which has two restaurants and a hut with mattresses that is provisionally called accommodation.

Another 300km down the road is the town of Apuí; its appearance pre-empted by advertising boards promoting the amazing sounds of Radio Apuí.

Paved road surfaces and a number of shops separate the town from the rest of the Transamazônica. The population of around 5,000 lives on ranches and agricultural plots close to the town. Hardworking and industrious, Apuí is a supply town for the region, providing everything from food and clothes through to fishing nets, guns and machetes. At weekends everything and everyone stops, and indulges in the Brazilian passion for football, with teams travelling from hundreds of kilometres away to play. The pitch is a couple of blocks behind the main street, next to the corral which has occasional rodeo festivals.

Accommodation is plentiful, desperate and on (or close to) the main road. Charging US$30 are **Hotel Route 66** and **Hotel Silverado**, both with air conditioning. At the bottom end – and they really are deep down – are **Hotel Goiana** and **Hotel Al Vorada.** There are several restaurants and bars, none of which stands out.

A weekly bus travels from Apuí to Jacareacanga. Alternatively you can try to hitch from the eastern end of town. There is also a twice-weekly cooperative bus that makes the journey to **Sucunduri**, roughly halfway along the road.

Having spent any time in one of these towns, you eventually ask yourself how they came to be created. Sucunduri has, more or less, a valid reason. With Apuí getting too big, a group of settlers decided to push eastwards. On the banks of the Rio Sucunduri this group of 800, attracted by free plots of land, went no further. It's as good a place as any to appreciate the lot of the Amazon settler. Swimming in the river is very refreshing.

A chat with the people of the town might get you on a fishing trip or a short trip upriver in the afternoon. If you're feeling truly adventurous an eight-day paddle upstream takes you to the waterfall of Monte Cristo. You can't really get lost, but you might want to take a guide for the logistics of meals and lodging. Travelling downstream on the Rio Sucunduri, eventually joining the Rio Madeira just south of the Amazon mainstream, is another option, but involves travelling through the Coata Laranjal Indigenous Area which is off limits unless you have a permit from FUNAI.

A hut in Sucunduri at the river end of the town constitutes the full range of hotels. It has been inspected for its suitability as accommodation and miraculously passed. The same place serves meat, rice, pasta and beans.

Travelling onwards requires patience or luck. A weekly bus goes to **Jacareacanga**, 150km (six hours) down the road, or you may get a ride in a truck. The jungle is fighting hard to reclaim this section of the road and may, without more traffic, eventually succeed.

Jacareacanga is a sleepy frontier town stuck in the haze of a Saturday morning lie-in. Living out the last few years of a gold-prospecting boom, in just a few years the town could be empty. There are a couple of hotels and a few restaurants. Air taxis can also connect you to Itaituba (US$90) and Santarém (US$150).

The road between Jacareacanga and Itaituba is often closed. Cargo boats connect the towns regularly, making the two-day trip down the River Tapajós from the port outside the town. The journey costs around US$30 including food. Hammocks can be bought in Jacareacanga. The cargo boats are smaller than those found on the larger Amazon tributaries and are generally cleaner and healthier.

The boats drop off cargo and pick up passengers mid-stream, and stop off at gold-mining settlements. There are several sets of rapids which in the dry season can cause problems. If the water is too low the boat stops in Buboré from where a truck takes you the last couple of hours to Itaituba.

The road to Itaituba passes the entrance to Parque Nacional da Amazônica (Amazon National Park). Entrance permits to use the park are obtainable from IBAMA in Itaituba.

Itaituba

The gold rush that gave this town a rough reputation has been tailing off for several years as the easily obtained gold has mostly been extracted. What remains is a melancholic atmosphere patiently waiting for the better times ahead.

On the gold front they almost certainly will. The state of Pará has large amounts of 'greenstone belt' which has proved to be the richest gold-bearing rock stratum globally and is currently home to 70% of the world's gold production. Multinationals are concentrating on concessions within the Tapajós watershed and several companies expect to announce major operations within the next couple of years.

People in the town have time to talk and are friendly. The waterfront has a colourful market and food stalls. Around the town there are several clean and professionally organised shops buying and selling gold.

Hotels include **Juliana Park Hotel** (Travessa Joãa Pesoa 31A), which is smart, tidy, clean and close to the waterfront. Doubles are US$25. A couple of blocks back is the **Central Plaza Hotel** (Trav 13 de Maio 194) with doubles at US$44, and across the road is the slightly cheaper **Santa Rita Palace Hotel**.

The best of the cheapies is the **Hotel Riozinto (**doubles US$15), right on the waterfront just in front of the market. It appears rough at first but is actually family-run, and the mafia element seems to be there to scare off unwanted customers. The evening barbecue is a feast but you could be put off if you saw how the meat is stored!

The waterfront has several restaurants of different quality. The telephone office is along the waterfront upstream. Banco do Brasil, opposite Santa Rosa Palace Hotel, has an ATM cash machine for Visa cards. The general response to travellers' cheques and cash in all the banks is 'Eh… en Santarém.'

The Amazon National Park at over one million hectares is one good reason for visiting Itaituba. Although some 50km outside Itaituba and relatively easy to get to, the park is completely off any beaten track. (See page 377.)

From Itaituba, boats and buses continue the journey downstream to Santarém; or you can continue along the Transamazônica to Altamira. The boat for Santarém departs from the dockside and the trip takes a couple of days. With the completion of the road to Santarém most Brazilians now travel there by bus, from Miritituba on the east bank of the Tapajós. Miritituba, reached by an hourly ferry service free to foot passengers, is also the place to catch buses travelling further along the Transamazônica to Altamira (US$35) and Marabá (US$60). Hardy fools may want to travel the road south to Cuiabá heading first to the town of Novo Progresso (US$25), from where you can catch another bus on to Cuiabá.

Alta Floresta

Totally off any natural route or circuit, about halfway between Cuiabá and Santarém, is the town of Alta Floresta (population 70,000). As with many other towns in the Amazon, Alta Floresta experienced a gold boom that has now faded.

Alta Floresta has two ecotourism opportunities that set it apart from other small towns: **Cristalino Jungle Lodge** and **Thaimaçu Lodge**. Neither option is cheap, independent travel is not an option and ideally you should book before arriving in Alta Floresta.

Getting there

There are daily flights with Nordeste Airlines to Alta Floresta from Cuiabá; and Cuiabá has connections to Rio de Janeiro (US$780), São Paulo (US$688) and Manaus (US$950). Flights are expensive when bought individually but Alta Floresta is included on Varig's Brazil Airpass.

From Cuiabá in the south buses run to Alta Floresta several times a day, costing US$55 and taking 12 hours. If you're coming from the north, buses make the ten-hour journey on very rough roads from Novo Progresso. The buses go to Sinop – 160km past the Alta Floresta turn-off – but ask the driver to drop you off at the junction for Alta Floresta and then hitch a lift.

Getting into town

Taxis serve the centre of town from the airport, 2km west of town, and the *rodoviária* (bus station), 2km to the south. Two parallel roads make up the main boulevard with most restaurants, bars and hotels found close by.

Where to stay

The best is **Floresta Amazônica Hotel** (Av Perimetral Oeste 2001; Alta Floresta; tel: 065 521 3601; fax: 065 521 2221; net: www.brazilnature.com/cristalinojunglelodge). There is a pool, sauna, excellent air-conditioned rooms and beautifully prepared food. It's close to the airport and rooms start at US$50 for a single. A small nature reserve of 15ha at the bottom of the garden is home to monkeys, toucans and parrots, so you can walk out of the four-star hotel straight into the rainforest at any time of day or night. The Floresta also operates the Cristalino Jungle Lodge and is the base for trips. Other local visits can be arranged here – ask Vitoria.

On the airport road closer to town is **Pirâmide Palace Hotel** (Av Aeroporto 445; tel/fax: 065 521 2400). Rooms are tidy, with A/C and TV as options. Doubles from US$40. On the main road is **Estoril Hotel** (Av Lucovico da Riva 2950; tel: 065 521 3298); its rooms are basic but the staff are friendly and the hotel restaurant is very good and handy. (Doubles US$25.)

Close to the *rodoviária*, which is too far away from the centre of town for convenience, are a few cheapies. The best is probably **Londres Hotel** (Av Ludovico da Riva Neto), in front of the bus terminal, at US$20 for a double.

Where to eat

On the plaza is the **Nova Lanchete da Praça** serving hamburgers, beers and refreshments. On the other side of the main street is **Choparia e Pizzaria Feitico** which is popular and has a pleasant atmosphere. The restaurant next to the Hotel Estoril is a good *churrascaria*, as is the one opposite Pirâmide Palace Hotel on Av Aeroporto.

Excursions from Alta Floresta

In terms of ecotourism, there are a few things under way that may interest the interested traveller.

Projeto Vivero de Mudas de Plantas is a small project researching and promoting traditional use of medicinal plants from the area. Close to this project is the town's zoo which has a small jungle path with named plant specimens. The zoo is very basic, which can be disturbing, but it is one way of promoting awareness of animals in the region.

Jungle lodges

Cristalino Jungle Lodge

This is located in pristine rainforest. The jungle lodge sits in a small clearing on the banks of the Rio Cristalino, a small blackwater tributary of the Rio Teles Peres which flows down to the Rio Tapajós.

Slight variations in terrain, topography and soil type have created a series of ecosystems that support a wide range of plant, bird and animal species.

Eight trails have been laid out through the forest in the immediate vicinity of the lodge and others are a short boat trip away. The trails are easy but quickly immerse you in the rainforest. The Brazil Nut Trail takes you to see these magnificent forest giants draped in lianas, vines and epiphytes. The Sierra Trail takes you up through towering forest, to scrubby, semi-deciduous vegetation, before arriving at the granite summit which provides a panorama of the rainforest canopy. While enjoying the view of the rainforest from above, you can see several bird species moving around the canopy. With luck you may spot a harpy or crested eagle searching the canopy for prey. Other trails take you through bamboo forest, home to antbirds, and sightings of hoatzins are common. Animals in the area include giant otters, tapir, capybara, several species of primate, jaguar and, just beyond the floating deck of the lodge, caiman.

Catch-and-release fishing is also possible at the lodge, but you do need to take your own equipment.

The shortest trip to the lodge is four days, which is enough time to enjoy a few trails at a relaxing pace. If you have longer, a ten-day expedition upriver leads you to Cristalino Waterfall: a dramatic cascade of water in an exuberant setting.

Transit to Cristalino Lodge is arranged by Floresta Tours at the Floresta Amazônica Hotel. A one-hour jeep ride, followed by a 40-minute boat trip, takes you to the lodge. There are eight bungalows with private toilets and sun-heated showers, each sleeping two or three, and a couple of dormitory-style buildings divided into smaller rooms. There are several hammocks hanging around. The restaurant serves an excellent variety of typical dishes and there's a bar for talking the night away.

Such a unique experience isn't cheap, but what price paradise? A week at Cristalino for two costs US$900pp. The price includes airport transfers, accommodation in Alta Floresta and Cristalino and all meals. English-speaking guides are also included in the price.

Thaimaçu Pousada-Lodge

This is a catch-and-release sports fishing paradise on the Rio São Benedito, a 40-minute flight from Alta Floresta. The cabins are just a few metres back from where the 150m river crashes over a small but dramatic waterfall. Above the cataract the mirror-still water reflects the riverine forest.

Close to the lodge is primary rainforest which can be explored with the help of a guide. In the river above the waterfall there are crystal-clear lagoons filled with minute ornately-painted tropical fish. If you don't see the Amazon kingfisher splashing into the water you could see a pair of razor-billed curassow grubbing their way through the shrubby forest floor. Out on the open river, rainforest canopy gives way to open gallery forest revealing flocks of hoatzin scrambling awkwardly through the trees. There are also monkeys, tapirs and caiman in the area.

Around the cabins are several species of macaw nesting in the stumps of fallen trees. The tapir wandering around the river at night was adopted as a youngster after its mother had been killed by one of the jaguar that roam the area.

As you would expect from a fishing lodge, fishing in the area is excellent; some would say world class. Catch-and-release is practised to prevent over-fishing. Some of the fishing is ridiculously easy and it can be a struggle to keep piranha off the hooks. Fish include large numbers of peacock bass and payara, while the more focused angler can concentrate on the deeper spots for giant catfish or a 40kg *jaú* and *pirara*, or even the 100kg *piraíba.*

The air-conditioned cabins at Thaimaçu are comfortable and can accommodate 20 people. The food, grown in the surrounding area, is excellent and beautifully presented. There is also a bar in which to tell those fisherman's tales of the one that got away. The lodge is family-run and is the passion of Carlos Muñhoz, an extremely affable and knowledgeable man who speaks a wonderful blend of Portuñol (Portuguese and Español) and is happiest when chatting with guests about the river, the fish and Brazil.

From Alta Floresta it's a short 40-minute flight to the private landing strip at Thaimaçu Lodge. Flights can be organised when booking through Carlos. Visits to Thaimaçu can be as long as you like. Six nights at the lodge, including the flight from Alta Floresta and all meals, cost US$1,280. The lodge is closed between mid-December and the end of January. For details and booking contact: Carlos Muñhoz, Thaimaçu Pousada-Lodge, Rua C2 #234, Caixa Postal 04, Alta Floresta, Mato Grosso, CEP 78.580-000; tel/fax: 065 521 3587.

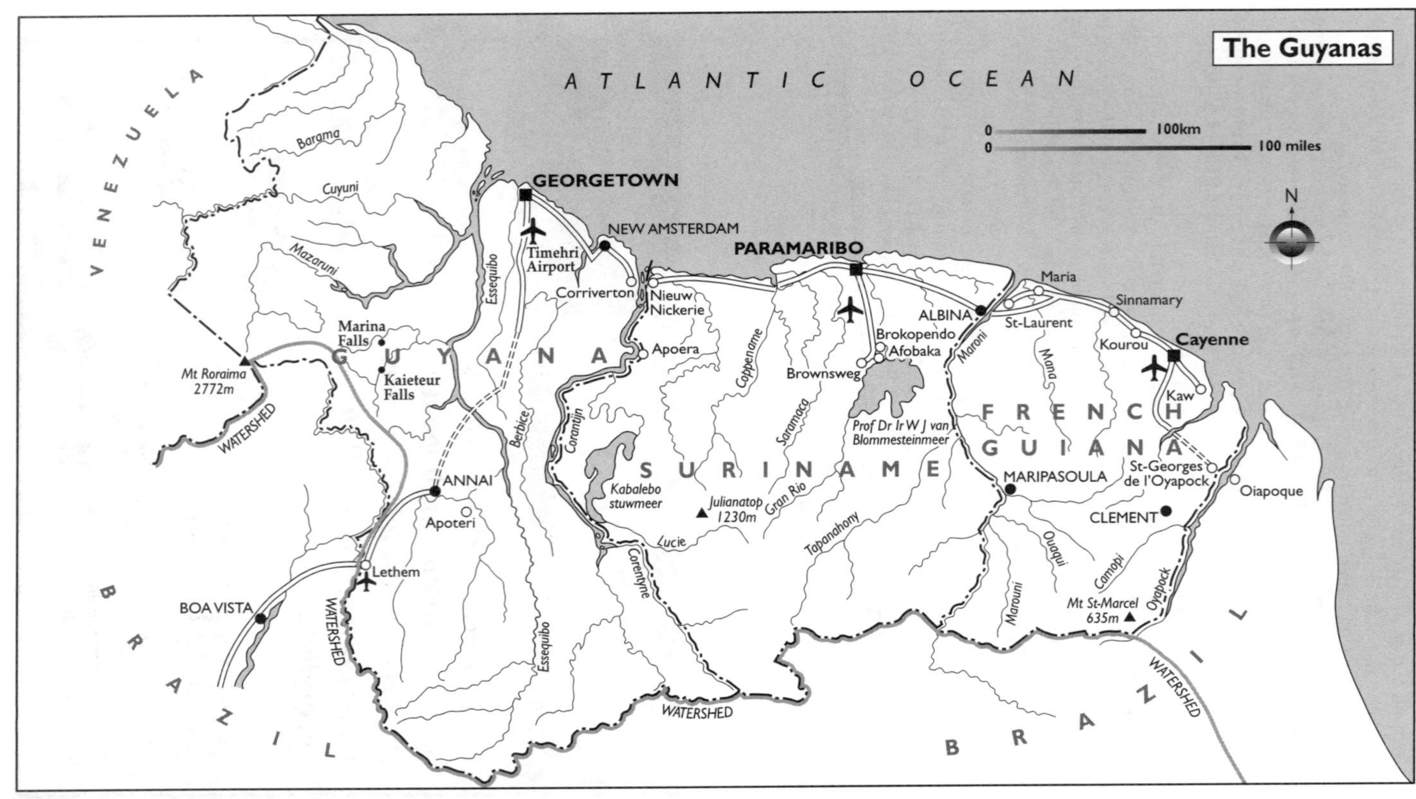
The Guyanas
ATLANTIC OCEAN
0 100km
0 100 miles
N
VENEZUELA
Barama
Cuyuni
Mazaruni
GEORGETOWN
Timehri Airport
NEW AMSTERDAM
Corriverton
Nieuw Nickerie
Apoera
Marina Falls
Kaieteur Falls
GUYANA
Mt Roraima 2772m
WATERSHED
Essequibo
Berbice
Corantijn
ANNAI
Apoteri
Lethem
BOA VISTA
PARAMARIBO
Coppename
Saramaca
Brownsweg
Brokopendo
Afobaka
Prof Dr Ir W J van Blommesteinmeer
SURINAME
Kabalebo stuwmeer
Julianatop 1230m
Gran Rio
Lucie
Corentyne
Tapanahony
ALBINA
Maroni
St-Laurent
Maria
Mana
Sinnamary
Kourou
Cayenne
Kaw
FRENCH GUIANA
MARIPASOULA
St-Georges de l'Oyapock
Oiapoque
CLEMENT
Ouaqui
Camopi
Marouni
Oyapock
Mt St-Marcel 635m
BRAZIL

13

Guyana, French Guiana and Suriname

In this chapter we cover three of South America's smallest countries. Despite their size, the travel and nature opportunities they offer are on a par with those of their giant neighbour, Brazil. Strictly speaking, all three lie outside the Amazon River watershed. However, similarities in natural history and proximity to the Amazon ecosystem justify their inclusion in this book.

GUYANA

BASIC FACTS

Official name The Co-operative Republic of Guyana (formerly British Guiana)
Area 214,969km² (83,000 miles²)
Population 825,000
Capital Georgetown
Largest city (population) Georgetown (175,000)
Official language English
Date of independence May 26 1966
Major industries minerals, agriculture, fisheries
GDP per capita US$356
Currency Guyanan dollar G$ (US$=G$150; £1=G$232)
National holidays Jan 2, Feb 23, Easter, May 1, Dec 25–26

Facts and figures

Geography, rivers and climate

Meaning 'land of many waters', the name Guyana originally referred to the triangle of territory between the three great rivers of northern South America – the Amazon, Orinoco and Negro. The national territory is bordered to the south by Brazil. Venezuela lies to the west and Suriname to the east, and persistent frontier disputes with both countries continue.

With the Atlantic to the north, the country encompasses a wide range of ecological habitats, from coastal mangrove to montane tropical forest in the wild hinterland. The northeastern half comprises a relatively flat coastal strip, 15–60km wide, covered with dense tropical rainforest or mangrove along the narrow tidal belt.

In the central western region the Pakaraima Mountains, forming part of the Guianan Shield, rise to over 2,750m. To the south are the Kanuku, Wassari and Acarai ranges; effective barriers between Guyana and north-central Brazil.

The five major rivers are the Cuyuni, Demerara, Essequibo, Berbice and Amacuro.

Most densely populated of Guyana's administrative districts is East Demerara. Situated in its northwest corner is the country's capital Georgetown, at the Demerara River's mouth. The largest district is Rupununi, a rolling savannah covering the rugged southern hinterland to the Pakaraima foothills.

Kaieteur Falls is one of the country's major tourist attractions. Along the Potaro River, a tributary of the Essequibo, it has a sheer drop of 222m, nearly five times that of Niagara Falls. Yet it is only one of several splendid waterfalls, including Orinduik Falls, on the Ireng River.

Georgetown's average annual temperature is 27°C. The coast experiences two wet seasons, from April to August and November to January. The south of Guyana has only one wet season, from April to August. Rainfall is heavy on the coast. The high interior grasslands receive less, typically 1,780mm per year.

People and languages

Guyana's small population gives it the second lowest population density in South America after French Guiana. The population is concentrated along the coast and in Georgetown.

About half the inhabitants are of East Indian origin while Africans comprise about a third. Mulattoes, Creoles, Amerindians, Chinese, Portuguese and Lebanese make up the remainder. Amerindian tribes still inhabit remote hinterlands. Main ethnic groups include Carib, Arawak, Arrau, Makuxi, Waiwai and Kawaio.

English is the official language. Ethnically, over 80% are African or East Indian but most people speak 'talkie-talkie' or Creole English, while Hindi and Urdu are spoken among the Indian community.

Education is of relatively good quality, with about 95% literacy. All children must attend school (free of charge) from 6 to 14 years of age.

History

Of pre-European history, it is known that peaceful Warrau Indians colonised the Guianan Highlands in the first millennium BC, but were later supplanted by the more warlike Arawaks and Caribs.

Spain largely ignored the area known as the Wild Coast between the Orinoco and Amazon deltas. Europeans first settled there in the early 17th century, when the Dutch established trading posts inland, dating from 1621, and imported slaves from West Africa to farm sugar-cane.

In 1796 the British took over the Dutch town of Stabroek, changing the name to Georgetown, and purchased territories along the Essequibo, Berbice and Demerara rivers in 1814.

Large numbers of slaves were imported by the Dutch West India Company to plant sugar-cane. When slavery was abolished in 1834 many of the 100,000 freed slaves left the coastal zones for the hinterland, leading to a wave of immigration from Portugal, China and India.

In 1962 Venezuela renewed its claim to portions of Guyana, a dispute that went to the United Nations in 1982 and remains unresolved.

Independence was not attained without difficulty. After a decade of civil unrest, proportional representation was introduced in 1964, and the country opted for full independence in 1966 under the leadership of Forbes Burnham. During the 1970s, Burnham consolidated his position and in 1980 declared that his government would follow socialist doctrine.

In 1978 Guyana was the site of a mass suicide committed by 913 members of a religious cult led by the Reverend Jim Jones.

Following the collapse of the Soviet Union in the late 1980s, the Guyanan government adopted free-market policies. An about-turn in the country's fortunes in 1991 led to the highest growth rates seen in decades.

The public sector is dominant, following socialist policies of public ownership through nationalisation; but private economic activity is increasingly important. Despite rich mineral and natural resources, Guyana's GNP has actually declined from the mid-1980s and its per capita income is currently South America's lowest.

Money

Guyana dollars are not available outside the country but US dollars are widely used. It is easy to change travellers' cheques or get credit card advances. Overseas visitors must use hard currency to pay hotel bills and locally purchased air-tickets. Georgetown has several foreign exchange houses with better rates than the banks.

Highlights

The government resisted tourism until the 1990s. Following the general policy reversal, a Ministry of Tourism was created, and efforts began to improve tourist infrastructure.

Visiting the only South American country in which English is the mother tongue will surely appeal to Anglophiles. This makes Guyana potentially easy for independent travellers from the UK and US.

With the low cost of living and favourable exchange rates, travel in Guyana is cheap; but not simple. Tourist facilities are underdeveloped, and the country is not geared to meet the diverse needs of today's international traveller.

You should plan to be on your own unless you organise your own group. Guyana is hardly the world's best known holiday hotspot so few tour operators offer organised tours. Inland trips are real adventure as travel away from the coastal strip is not easy. But the effort is highly rewarding, with rugged, unspoiled scenery, quiet accommodation and the occasional 'discovery' of some unpublicised waterfall or natural area.

When to go

If you can take the heat, the best time to go to Guyana is during the dry season from September through November, although this coincides with the hottest period. Most days, though, temperatures are not high enough to be oppressive. Rainfall in the Rupununi region to the south is low enough that the short rainy season does not provide problems for travellers.

Tour operators

In Guyana

Ecotours Woodbine Hotel, 41–42 New Market St; tel: 02 59430
Tropical Adventures Forte Crest Hotel, Seawall Rd; tel: 02 52853
Torong Guyana 56 Coralita Avenue, Belair Park; tel: 02 65298
Wonderland Tours Tower Hotel, 74 Main St; tel: 02 72011
Wilderness Explorers 61 Hadfield & Cross Sts; tel: 02 77698; fax: 02 62085; email: wilderness-explorers@solutions2000.net

In the US

Field Guides Inc PO Box 160723, Austin, TX, 78716; tel: 512 327 4953/800 728 4953; fax: 512 327 9231; email: fgileader@aol.com; net: www.fieldguides.com.

In the UK

Discovery Initiatives No 3, 68 Princes Square, London, W2 4NY; tel: 0171 229 9881; fax: 0171 229 9883; email; enquiry@discoveryinitiatives.com; net: www.discoveryinitiatives.com.
Trips Worldwide 9 Byron Place, Clifton, Bristol BS8 1JT; tel: 0117 987 2626; fax: 0117 987 2627. Also PO Box 17-12-602, Quito, Ecuador.

Getting there and away

Getting there

By air

International flights arrive and depart at Timehri International Airport 40km outside Georgetown. Several airlines serve the airport including Guyana Airways Corporation, BWIA, Carib Express, LIAT and Suriname Airways. BWIA flies daily direct from Miami and New York. Other direct flights originating in North America are from Atlanta, Miami and Toronto.

With no flights direct from Europe, you must fly to North America first or take another route with a connecting flight. The best and least expensive route is London–Miami–Georgetown. Another easy alternative is London–Barbados–Georgetown, although you will have to overnight in Barbados.

By ship

Georgetown is a major seaport and a passenger terminal for cruise ships and river ferries. Luxury liners sometimes stop here on the way to or from cruises along the Amazon or around South America.

By road

The only way to approach by bus or private vehicle from Brazil is via Boa Vista to Bonfim and then across the border at Lethem, on a difficult road.

There are no road links with Venezuela and just a pedestrian ferry connection with Suriname.

Customs and immigration

In 1994 Guyana relaxed its previously stringent visa requirements to encourage tourism. Citizens of the US, UK and most European countries no longer require visas.

There is a US$8 departure tax from Guyana.

Getting around

Guyana's roads are generally poor, unsurfaced or with tar sprayed on a graded track. Repairs on flood-damaged main highways invariably take several days. Few roads penetrate the interior so the only sensible way to get around is by river transport or aeroplane.

For domestic flights, Guyana Airways Corporation (GAC) is the national airline, though the bulk of internal traffic is now carried by small charter operators. These remain the primary means of connecting towns from the interior with Georgetown. Most internal flights leave from Georgetown's domestic Ogle Airport where you can book cheap charter flights directly.

Canals throughout the coastal region connect estates and villages and are served by passenger services.

Communications

The general post office in Georgetown is on North Road. The service is expensive and unreliable so any important mail is best sent registered or by private courier.

The government exerts practically complete control over its own media; one radio station and a daily newspaper *The Chronicle*. *The Mirror* represents opposition views, while the highly regarded *Catholic Standard* is considered neutral.

Guyana's first television station opened 1988, also under government control, but now two independent channels show US satellite television.

Telecommunications are generally good, with global direct dialling and relatively low rates. The large hotels have international dialling facilities. Calls are cheaper from the Guyana Telephone & Telegraph (GTT) office in the Bank of Guyana building (North Street). For those in a hurry service is quicker but more expensive at the Tower Hotel.

The country code for Guyana is 592.

Georgetown

Awash in moth-eaten colonialism, Georgetown's schizoid personality arises from a bygone era hauling itself into the 21st century. Victorian buildings of imposing, confident architecture still line many city streets.

The town has the air of a rough-and-tumble port peopled by a combination of hurried business people and laid-back stall traders, tourists and street people. Even during the day there's a latent energy capable of tensing all who feel it. Maybe it's an absence of security, given that Georgetown is among the most dangerous cities in South America for theft, muggings and violence.

But somehow, when this background fades, an evening ocean breeze rustles the palm leaves and a spicy aroma wafts across the air, Georgetown can be heaven.

Transport

From Timehri International Airport to Georgetown – a trip that should only be done during the day – expect to pay US$20 for a taxi into town. A fleet of minibuses also make the journey, charging US$1.50.

In Georgetown the visitor finds it relatively easy to get around in taxis and buses. Fares are very low, about US$0.25 for minibus rides anywhere in town. Go to Stabroek Market to catch long-distance minibuses to Linden (US$12) and Parika (US$8). For destinations outside Georgetown buses leave from the station, located between Stabroek Market and Avenue of the Republic.

Where to stay

Accommodation in Georgetown is generally quite expensive compared with that in other Amazon countries. Most hotels are situated in the western part of the city around the main commercial districts. Most foreign tourists go to **Forte Crest Hotel** (Seawall Road; tel: 02 52856), along the seafront: the best hotel in town, and most expensive (US$95). Tropical Adventures have offices in the lobby. A bit cheaper is the **Tower Hotel** (74 Main Street; tel: 02 72011). The **Woodbine** (41–42 New Market Street; tel: 02 59430) is a friendly place but near a rough part of town (US$50). In the mid-price range (US$25 per night), the **Park Hotel** (Middle and Main St; tel: 02 54911) offers the taste of a now long gone colonial life. For budget accommodation try the **Waterchris** (Waterloo Street; tel: 02 71980) or **Rima Guest House** (92 Middle Street; tel: 02 57401).

Where to eat

Most restaurants and cafés are located along Main Street. There is a reasonable choice of places to eat out in Georgetown including European, Caribbean, East

Indian and South American influences. For an up-market meal (US$10–20) the better establishments are **Del Casa** (232 Middle Street) and **Caribbean** (175 Middle Street). Also recommended as one of the best in Georgetown is the **Cabazon** (74 Main Street; tel: 02 72011) in the Tower Hotel.

What to see

The railway station, an interesting example of mid-Victorian architecture, is at the north end of Carmichael Street. St George's Anglican Cathedral has a towering spire 43.3m high – among the tallest in South America. National cultural institutions centre on Georgetown, notably the Parliament Building (a block west of Stabroek Market) and the Presidential Residence at the southwest corner of the botanical gardens. City tours can be arranged for around US$30.

Encompassing a large park area in the southeast of Georgetown the **Botanic Gardens** (admission US$0.10) provide the setting for the city zoo. The zoo is quite impressive considering the limited finances. Birders will appreciate the bird collection, including a hyacinth macaw. Many specimens of tropical South American animals are represented so you can see a number of species from Amazon areas which you may have missed during jungle tours.

In the commercial centre of Georgetown is the very good **Guyanan Museum**. Much of the museum, inside and out, is ageing, and the contents have hardly changed since British colonial times. However, the place is not moth-eaten, rather growing old gracefully. Overall the displays and collections tell a full story of the country's past and natural history.

Shopping

Avid souvenir hunters have much to occupy their attention in Georgetown. Handicrafts are of a quality and price not seen along the more tourist-beaten path. The Amerindian Handicrafts Centre (1 Water St) has a wide selection of weapons, native costumes and adornments. Stabroek Market (on the Demerara riverfront) has some handicrafts, including baskets and hammocks, plus more prosaic machetes and rubber boots, along with a wide variety of local agricultural produce.

More information

Once you're in the country, the best source of information is the industry-funded Tourism Association of Guyana (Church and Carmichael Streets, Georgetown; tel: 02 702647). They publish a travel guidebook which has a map and information on upmarket hotels and lodges throughout the country.

WARNING Parts of Georgetown are very dangerous and must be avoided even during daylight. Especially notorious is the Tiger Bay district.

Beyond Georgetown

Close to Georgetown, one option is a trip to the mining town of Linden (population 75,000), the second biggest town in Guyana. It has a few decent hotels (US$10–25) which cater to the traveller of reasonably modest expectations.

Several Georgetown tour operators offer a variety of options to explore the wild Guyanan hinterlands already described. Another option is to explore the coastal region which has the advantage of relatively easy access. However, this area is hot and humid so many people prefer to go further inland.

River rafters will love four days of river rafting on the Cuyuni River. Rapids along the Nekuima Canyon, requiring seven days, are among the most spectacular scenery in the area, and provide thrills, in between relaxing at accommodation in riverside jungle camps and lodges.

Guyana's 'Amazon'

Most of Guyana is rainforest and the interior is practically uninhabited. Where extractive operations are absent, the forest is pristine and the wildlife abundant.

Guyana's backcountry has few towns or villages that could be considered 'gateways', as most are isolated from road traffic, and accessed usually by small plane or, nearer the coast, by launch or dug-out canoe. The few establishments that do exist are top-notch and, if you can afford the price, well worth the effort to travel beyond the coastal plain. In turn this region offers excellent opportunities for birding and exploring tropical rainforest.

Jungle towns and villages

Lethem

This is the main town for trips to the central Rupununi savannah region, notable for expansive rolling grasslands, ideal for birdwatching and horse-riding. The town is set within a valley formed by the Pakaraima Range to the north and a huge arc of high peaks of the Serra Acari Range to the west and south.

Lethem is a modest market town with buildings varying from quaint to horrible and streets with a smattering of shops supplying the basics needed for life in what is still very much frontier country: maize meal, machetes, sugar, tea and hammocks. In Lethem itself the climate is cool at night and warm during the day. Shorts and T-shirt are usually fine from mid-morning to early evening but you'll need jeans and sweatshirt to keep the evening chill at bay. Because of the cooler temperatures, biting insects are not bothersome. With the valley and mountain landscapes and variety of savannah and tropical forest habitat, the nature is outstanding.

The twice-weekly, hour-long flight to Lethem from Georgetown with Guyana Airways costs US$65 one way.

Tours are arranged through Georgetown tour operators who offer swimming, angling and horse-back excursions. Birdwatching in the extensive grasslands surrounding the town is excellent and the open grasslands make a nice contrast with the lowland tropical jungle to the north where vegetation obscures much of the birdlife.

Close to Lethem is Guyana's earliest established Amerindian village of Annai. The Waiwai and Macushi tribes are largely acculturated but still retain some traditional handicrafts such as the use of colourful feathers in ceremonial costumes. Ask in the village for a guide (US$10) to take you on a 20-minute walk from the village to Mocomoco falls, a beautiful cascade surrounded by thick vegetation.

Another pleasant trip several hours' drive from Lethem is Lake Pan, located in the lower Rupununi Valley. The place is popular with locals for its temperate clean waters, lacking in significant currents and offering most enjoyable swimming and snorkelling. The lake's fish life is diverse, including the Amazon's biggest freshwater fish, *arapaima,* and a local species, *lukunani*, said to make good eating. With greater technical skill than required of hook and rod, natives shoot the huge *arapaima* fish with simple bow and arrow.

A trip to Mocomoco Falls or Lake Pan costs around US$150 per day, with a minimum three or four days needed to make the most of the nature and culture opportunities. In remoter areas, accommodation is a combination of camping and simple forest cabins with transport from Lethem costing US$35–100.

Imbaimadai

In the west of Guyana, this town is the gateway to the Pakaraima Range. Visitors can enjoy clear rivers running down valleys with sheltered patches of montane elfin forest among expansive grasslands. Although Imbaimadai is not far from the Venezuelan border, there is no way to cross officially from the town. It is, however, a popular starting point for trips to the Pakaraima Range and Kaieteur Falls National Park.

There is little to see or do in this frontier mining town along the Mazaruni River, apart from watching a gold-rush in action as gold and diamonds are dug from the alluvial sediments of the riverbanks.

Ask your tour operator to arrange Indian (Kawaio) guides to the nearby Maipuri Falls. Sometimes tour operators include this in the itinerary with Kaieteur Falls. Further on are 700-year-old Indian cliff drawings, a 30-minute hike from the falls. It is very difficult, if not impossible, to make it here on your own from town.

Bartica

This is an old gold-mining camp, gaining importance as a stopover before and after jungle trips. Though not far from Georgetown, it lies on the coastal plain's innermost portion on a promontory at the confluence of the Essequibo, Mazaruni and Cuyuni rivers. Between the Essequibo and Mazaruni rivers, the Hinterland Road heads south with various routes taking you to several small jungle towns. There is little to do in Bartica but if you have to overnight here there are a handful of very basic hotels from US$10 per night.

Jungle lodges

No stilt-borne, palm-thatched, solar-panelled 'luxury ecolodges' grace Guyana's wilderness, but the prepared traveller will enjoy the simple camps, and small but very pleasant hotels, ranging from modest to sumptuous. Popular places to stay have all the amenities expected of tourist-standard lodges and accommodations.

Comfortable, ranch-style accommodation near the middle Essequibo is provided at **Shanklands**. This fine lodge on the northern edge of the Rupununi savannah, is surrounded by an area incredibly rich in birdlife. Built in an elaborate Victorian style, Shanklands is a converted villa set among attractive gardens. The veranda and balconies of the comfortable rooms overlook vast grassy plains with beautiful views. Activities include birding, horse-riding and trekking along remote open trails. For US$115pp (sharing), you can book a room at Shanklands through Georgetown tour operators. The newly opened **Rockview** is also on the Essequibo and said to have similar standards and prices to Shanklands. From the US, Field Guides run a specialist birding tour with Shanklands and Rockview as part of a two-week Guyana itinerary leaving from Georgetown and costing US$3,950.

Among the most highly regarded establishments in the hinterlands is **Timberhead**, a trio of thatched lodges on the Kamuni River. For the luxury-minded traveller, this place offers the most comfortable jungle accommodation in Guyana and at US$150 per night with meals and transport included (three-night package US$450–600) is relatively good value.

Recently completed is the **Sapodilla Organic Farm** on the Berbice River, 145km from the capital, which has simple cabins for US$45 per night. The food is outstanding due to the organically grown vegetables and well-run restaurant. The least expensive stay in lowland rainforest within easy reach of Georgetown is the **Rainbow River Safari** – a hammock camp on the banks of the Mazaruni River.

On the same river is **Jacaranda Camp**, 50km upstream from Bartica. Facilities here are basic, costing from US$30 per night with self-catering and excluding transport.

As with lodges in the interior it is best to arrange transport and reserve accommodation through tour operators in Georgetown (page 403). New businesses are opening and closing with high frequency, so you should ask at the Tourism Association of Guyana (PO Box 101147, Georgetown; tel: 02 70267) for recommended companies, hotels and lodges.

National parks and wildlife reserves

The most important government-protected area is **Kaieteur National Park**, established to protect the watershed of the Potaro River, down which tumbles Kaieteur Falls. The park is home to a vast area of pristine tropical vegetation supporting a wide variety of tropical fauna. Accessible by road from Bartica, the nearest town to the falls is Mahdia from where you will have to try to catch a lift. There is no accommodation in the park so take your own camping equipment.

On the Ireng River, a tributary of the Negro and part of the Amazon proper, Orinduik Falls is a spectacular waterfall, ranking with Niagara Falls for majesty and beating it hands down in terms of unspoiled natural beauty. On package tours a visit to Orinduik Falls and the nearby Patamona Indians is usually included with a trip to Kaieteur Falls (US$175–200 from Georgetown for three days).

On the northern edge of the northern Rupununi savannah is the recently established **Iwokrama Forest Reserve** measuring 360,000 hectares. Here the birdlife is among the richest in the country, with expanses of primary rainforest which are home to a number of typical Amazon species including scarlet macaws, curassows, parrots and numerous antbird species. New accommodation is now available for short stays in the reserve.

FRENCH GUIANA

BASIC FACTS

Official name Département de La Guyane
Area 91,000km² (35,135 miles²)
Population 130,000
Capital Cayenne
Largest city (population) Cayenne (42,000)
Official language French
Status Overseas Department of France
Major industries fisheries, forest products, gold
Currency French franc (US$1=Ffr6; £1=Ffr10)
Major attractions Îles du Salut, Kourou Space Centre
National holidays Jan 1, Easter, May 1, July 14, Aug 15, Nov 1, 2, & 11, Dec 25

A small enclave on the northeast coast of South America, French Guiana is the smallest country in South America, dwarfed by giant Brazil on the south and east and big brother Suriname to the west. Nevertheless it remains an anachronistic testament to colonialism.

Facts and figures

Geography, rivers and climate

Over the aeons rivers have eroded the underlying crystalline rock of the Guiana Highlands leaving a coastal terrain that is flat for the most part. To the northwest, ancient riverbeds underlie a savannah-type habitat. East of Cayenne, more recent alluvial deposits form swampy plains, ending in mangrove flats on the coast. Occupying the country's south towards Brazil, the Tumuc-Humac Mountains (Massif des Tumuc-Humac) form rolling hills, up to elevations of 850m, covered with tropical evergreen woodlands.

Running northwards from the highlands are five major rivers of which Fleuve Oyapock's 500km length defines the eastern boundary with Brazil. The 725km-long Fleuve Maroni forms the border with Suriname to the west. Recent proposals to dam the central Mana, Oyapock and Sinnamary rivers for hydropower were met with strong protests by environmentalists.

With no high mountains and a humid, warm climate, dominated by heavy rain, much of French Guiana is covered with dense tropical rainforest, habitat for a rich variety of typical Amazon birdlife and large animals including cats, tapir, manatees, turtles, caiman, but not pink dolphin. Due to low population and lack of access about 90% of this forest remains pristine.

This is among the wettest places in South America averaging 3,800mm annually. Rainfall is heaviest around Cayenne, peaking from December to July. Warm all year round, average temperatures at Cayenne are 25–27°C.

People and languages

Like its independent English-speaking twin, French Guiana has a low population density. The majority of Guianans outside cities and towns are subsistence or part-time farmers.

The population is 90% Roman Catholic, whereas East Indians and Southeast Asians practise Buddhism and Islam.

Diverse ethnic communities form the basis for French Guiana's varied cultural life. Black people and native Indians, primarily in rural areas, take their heritage from African and indigenous influences. In urban areas, the main culture is mixed-Creole. Amerindians mostly constitute the rural population especially away from the coast. Among the important groups are Arawak, Wayana, Oyampi, Galibi, Emerillons and Palikors.

French is the national tongue. A crash course or at least a bilingual dictionary is indispensable for non-French-speaking independent travellers.

History

French Guiana is among the earliest settled parts of South America, with Spaniards recorded as exploring the region as early as 1500. French presence in the area was established by merchants who set up a trading post in 1624 at Sinnamary.

Getting the country off to a good start, the community for freed slaves at Mana set an example of humanitarianism rarely equalled at the time. However, in 1846 the community was closed and Guiana became the main French penal colony. In 1852, Napoleon III decreed that convicts with sentences over seven years were to serve time in French Guiana, a policy that remained until the prison stopped admissions in 1945. It finally closed in 1953. The year 1877 saw representation of free Guianans in the French Parliament and in 1946 the colony became a *département* of France. Major postwar developments were the rocket launch facility at Kourou (1968) and the Green Plan (Plan Vert), a 1970s project to increase agricultural production and timber harvests.

French Guiana attains distinction as the only territory on the continent that is not an independent nation, and indeed the continent's smallest 'country'. It is ruled by the French government, subject to the French constitution and with the president of France as head of state.

As a business concern, France's colony fights a losing battle. Its trade deficit continues to grow, imports outweighing exports by ten to one. Inflation is often rampant and unemployment rates are usually in double figures. Yet, bolstered by regular injections of cash and industrial aid from France, French Guiana has one of the highest per-capita GNPs in South America.

Money

French Guiana's medium of exchange is the French franc, divided into 100 centimes. Because the French franc counts as hard currency you can easily obtain it before arriving in the country. You normally get a better exchange rate in your home country than in French Guiana. If you have a credit card you can get francs from ATMs throughout Cayenne and in larger towns.

Expenses in French Guiana are higher than in France and most South American countries so budget accordingly. The frugal traveller will spend US$50/day. Lodgings start at around US$20. Budget around US$3 or US$4 for each meal. Tours and travel services are correspondingly expensive.

Highlights

French Guiana is still relatively under-used by major tour operators, delightful for travellers looking for the unbeaten path. Organised tours are few and far between and the tourist infrastructure is undeveloped, making French Guiana well-suited to the independent, flexible traveller. Getting up remote rivers – there are no significant roads into the interior – takes some perseverance, but is worth the effort.

Nature opportunities abound. Over 80% of the country's forest cover remains intact. Wildlife includes all the major Amazonian mammals, reptiles and hundreds of bird species. Watered by seasonal rains, rivers rise and fall in the lowlands of French Guiana, as they do in the Amazon proper, resulting in flooded and *terra firme* forest.

Most people start in the coastal region, where travel is relatively cheap and accommodation is easily available. Wildlife and nature thrive on the nutrient-rich mud that is deposited by tides and rivers dropping their loads as they flow into the ocean, supporting a diverse mix of sea, shore and forest birds. Leatherback turtles nest on several beaches, notably at Aouara from April to July.

To get to really remote rainforest, your best bet is to book a canoe trip through a tour operator in Cayenne. If you're travelling independently, your only option is to fly to one of the isolated towns of the interior. Saül is almost bang-slap in the middle of the country, on the Inini River and within a day's journey of Montagne Machoulou and Pic Coudreau, French Guiana's two highest mountains. Maripasoula is even closer (about 10km) to Montagne Machoulou and provides easier access than Saül. Maripasoula is a small jungle town on the Maroni River, which forms the border with Suriname, and offers among the best nature and adventure travel opportunities in the interior.

Especially recommended for the adventurous is the jungle trip to Mount Rorata in the Montagne de Mahury Range, occupying the southern half of the country. After a long, leisurely motorised canoe trip 100km up the Sinnamary River, you take long rewarding walks (moderate to difficult) through mountainous landscape dotted with groves of elfin forest, abounding in orchids, butterflies and tree-ferns.

The hike eventually takes you to three lakes of Mount Rorata. Also in the area are a number of river trips, with nights spent in hammocks at jungle shelters.

When to go

If rain is not a bother, any time of year is good, given the uniformity of temperatures from month to month. The rainy season from December to July really ought to be avoided, unless you have a specific desire to get wet.

Tour operators

In Cayenne

Chez Modestine St Georges St Laurent; tel: 00 594 370013; fax: 00 594 370214.
JAL Voyages Boulevard Jubelin and Av Pasteur; tel: 00 594 316820; fax: 00 594 301101; email: JALVOYAG@mail.change-espace.fr; net: www.change-espace.fr/JALVOYAG/.
Takari Tours Hotel Novotel; tel: 00 594 311960; fax: 00 594 315470.
Youkaliba Expeditions tel/fax: 00 594 341645.

A useful contact in French Guiana is Kris Wood, who runs a conservation organisation called Pou d'Agouti (email: POU-AGOUTI@Mdi-guyane.fr). Trips with English-speaking guides on the Creek Portal and Creek Irakoumpapi cost US$50 a day per person, excluding hammock and mosquito nets (email: KRIS.WOOD@Mdi.guyane.fr).

In the US

Lifelong Learning 101 Columbia, Ste 150, Aliso Viejo, CA 92656; tel: 714 362 2900/800 854 4080; fax: 714 362 2075; email: lllexpo@aol.com.

In the UK

Journey Latin America 12–13 Heathfield Terrace, Chiswick, London W4 4JE; tel: 0181 747 3108; fax: 0181 742 1312; email: sales@journeylatinamerica.co.uk.

Getting there and away

By air

French Guiana's La Rochambeau International Airport is about 19km outside Cayenne. Flights arrive from the US, and from several South American and Caribbean countries. Air France is the main airline with four flights weekly from Miami. Air France departs three times a week for Cayenne from Paris, and weekly from Lima. The Brazilian airline Cruzeiro del Sol has two flights a week from Belém.

By ship

Some ships call in to French Guiana before or after Amazon cruises, sailing northwest to Îles du Salut, where cruise passengers disembark and go to Cayenne for the return flight home. In the US, contact Lifelong Learning (see above) for details on their end-of-Amazon-cruise itinerary in French Guiana.

By road

By the coastal road, access to French Guiana is from either Brazil to the southeast or Suriname to the west, although there is no car ferry from Suriname. No viable roads penetrate French Guiana's backcountry from Brazil.

Customs and immigration

Citizens of the EU, the US, Canada and Japan do not need visas to enter the country.

Departure tax is US$5.

Getting around

Paved roads are very good in most places but deteriorating in areas which are less travelled. Most roads outside the coastal zone are unpaved and a four-wheel-drive vehicle is essential to get around on your own.

The public transport system is inadequate, with too few vehicles and routes. Fares tend to be expensive, so if you intend to travel along the coast, consider hiring a car in Cayenne. Alternatively have a tour operator make your local travel arrangements between jungle sites and towns. If either is beyond your budget, or inclination, you can make do with communal taxis (*collectifs*) for road transport between towns and motorised launches or hand-paddled canoes (*pirogues*) for travel to the Guianan interior.

Internal flights are available but few routes are served, flights are often fully booked days in advance and fares are high.

Communications

Postal services are efficient, with letters taking about a week to reach international destinations. French stamps and rates are used. The main post office (Poste Centrale) in Cayenne is at Route de Baduel about 20 minutes' walk from the town centre.

As you might expect in a country which has South America's only space-port, French Guiana's telephone system works well and is available in most towns. Coin-operated telephones take 1Ffr and 5Ffr coins but are rapidly being replaced by ones taking phone cards. Faxes can be sent from most hotels.

The international country code for French Guiana is 594.

La Presse de Guyane is the principle newspaper. English publications are not widely available.

Cayenne

Almost exactly on the fifth parallel above the Equator, Cayenne is by far the French colony's most important urban development.

On the site of present-day Cayenne, in 1643, the settlement of La Ravardière was founded by merchants from Rouen and Paris. In 1777 the Dutch renamed the town Cayenne after a local Indian tribe that also gave its name to a hot red pepper from the region. Since then, Cayenne has remained the country's administrative and economic centre. Home to around 50,000 people, Cayenne's events and culture dominate the country.

Tourism facilities in Cayenne are expanding fast in response to increasing numbers of travellers who are attracted by the surrounding unspoiled nature, and the outstanding hotels and restaurants.

Getting around

Taxis and rental cars are available in the city and at the airport. Taxis from the airport cost US$7–10 (no bus).

Small *collectif* taxis, minibuses, run between major coastal towns. Though inexpensive, they are often full and run an erratic schedule.

Transport problems mean plane or motor-launch and *pirogue* are the only way to travel sensibly around the interior.

Where to stay

The handful of tourist standard hotels in Cayenne are well run and of high standard, but expensive. Most popular with business travellers and upmarket tour groups is the **Novotel** (Rue de Montabo; tel: 303888) 3km out of town. The most expensive in town at US$125 it has a swimming pool, restaurant and bar.

More centrally located and less expensive is **Hotel Amazonia** (28 Av du Général de Gaulle; tel: 310000), from US$60 (single) to US$66 (double). Relatively new is the 35-room **Central Hotel** (corner of Rues Becker and Mole; tel: 313000). Cheaper accommodation includes **Neptima** (21 Rue F Eboué; tel: 301115) with air-conditioned rooms and private bath, is about the best value in town for US$25 per night (single).

Close to the airport is **Green Tourism Camp**, tel: 280089; fax: 300682. Run by Joep Moonen, this upmarket lodge is used mostly by Dutch and American clients.

What and where to eat

Given the great culinary tradition of France, it is perhaps not surprising that French Guiana has plenty to offer the gourmet. From upmarket restaurants to cheap and cheerful streetside cafés, the range of countries and food types represented is truly global.

Novotel's restaurant, the **Angelique**, is among the best and most expensive. Fine French dining is to be had at **La Belle Epoque** (88 Rue Lalouette) but you'll pay less at **Le Saloon** (21 Rue Christophe Colomb). For Creole food, **Le Paradis des Amis** (5 Rue Mole) or **Restaurant le Tatou** are both good. For Asian food at good value, **Le Chateau de Asie** (21 Rue Lieutenant Brasse) or **La Rivière des Parfums** (10 Rue Justin Catayée) are suggested.

What to see

Cayenne's city sights offer interesting perspectives on its past and present ties with France. The city's compact enough to walk around but, to see most or all the sights mentioned below, you should take a city tour (US$25). The **Hall of Prefecture** was the **Governor's Palace** during early colonial times. Dating from 1750, built by Jesuits, it faces on to **Place Grenoble**, near the port area in the west end of the city. In the same square is **Montravel Fountain**. The oldest remaining evidence of early colonial settlement is found at **Ceperou Fort**, built 1643 by Charles Poncet de Brétigny. Members of the French Foreign Legion are based there to this day. If you're in town, a good place to people-watch or do some shopping is **Place des Palmistes** in the city's far northwest corner.

Also included on city tours is Cayenne open market, first held in 1910 on the Place du Coq. It's a bustling mass of people, mostly locals doing their weekly shopping for fish, fruit and vegetables.

The **Pasteur Institute** is an important research centre that employs about 100 scientists specialising in tropical diseases. Their highly regarded work includes investigating cures for malaria and screening rainforest biota for medically useful properties.

In the town centre, the **Franconie Museum** (Av de Gaulle) named after deputy Alexandre Franconie, is housed in a building dating from 1901. Collections of historic papers and pamphlets documenting Amerindian lifestyle and arts are interesting. Near Place des Palmistes is the **Musée Departemental** (Rue de Remire) with models of Cayenne and the Îles du Salut to give a sense of perspective.

More information

For the latest travel, lodgings and restaurant information and details on new tour operators, as well as free city maps and brochures, contact the **Tourist Office** at 12 Rue Lalouette (tel: 300900), open Mon–Fri 08.00–12.00 and 15.00–18.00, with English-speaking staff. You can also try the Comité du Tourisme de Guyane, tel: 266500; fax: 309315.

Beyond Cayenne

Most towns of any note in French Guiana are situated along or near the coast, and are therefore easy to reach by vehicle. However, a number of towns a short way inland offer ready access by motorised canoe into deep forest. To the untrained eye this habitat is virtually identical to the steamy, dark jungle typical of much of lowland Amazonia, and much of it is pristine. All this wilderness does not come easy and if you take a tour into the backlands don't expect luxury treatment. These trips use temporary jungle shelters for accommodation, with simple food.

Kourou

There can be few sights as incongruous as a space rocket blasting off from the middle of the jungle. Yet at Kourou the lucky (or carefully planning) visitor can sometimes arrange to observe this awesome spectacle.

Kourou was chosen as the launch site for the European Space Agency's Ariane due to its equatorial location. You can tour the Space Centre (Centre Spatial Guyanais), but the guide only speaks French. Ask at the tourist office (Av des Roches in Kourou) to reserve a place on the tour. Book several days in advance, from Cayenne if necessary. Entrance to the Space Centre is free; open Mon–Thur 08.00–12.00 and 14.00–17.00, closed Wednesday afternoon.

Travellers have the choice of six or seven hotels and *auberges* from US$25, centred around the main Rue de Gaulle, including **l'Hotel des Roches** with two restaurants, the posh **Edouard Le Thym** or the more casual and less expensive **La Cage Milk Bar**.

To the west of Cayenne, Kourou is easily accessible on a good surfaced road after a 20km drive.

A good road takes you from Kourou 210km west along the coast to the town of St Laurent de Maroni – point of departure for trips up the Maroni River to Maripasoula. Takari Tours (tel: 311969) have offices in town.

Roura

Some 20km southeast of Cayenne via the town of Matoury, Roura is located about 18km inland up the Mahury River estuary. This small town provides access to the Montagne de Kaw region, a beautiful formation rising a couple of hundred metres above extensive coastal forests, swamps and marshes lying between the Mahury and Approuague estuaries. This area is rich in waterbirds, amphibians and reptiles. A paddled canoe ride, included in a standard US$100-a day-tour, is a memorable experience. You are serenely propelled through broad marshes, fringed here and there with thick tropical jungle. Ask tour operators in Cayenne about these trips.

South from Cayenne the road to Roura first goes through Matoury and then about 10km out of town is the turn-off to Stoupan. This settlement marks the point on the Mahury River from which a ferry crosses to Roura (US$1 passengers, US$5 vehicles). Further on from Stoupan is the **Hotel Relais de Patawa** (36km from Cayenne; tel: 319395), a pleasant boarding-house on the Roura–Kaw road. The owners have an impressive insect collection which they are happy to show guests. Comfortable rooms at the hotel are available for US$15 per night or a place to hang your hammock for US$5 per night. The food is outstanding, but meals are rather pricey. Further southeast from Roura, about 40km along a variously tarred and dirt road, pretty bad in places, is the country village of Kaw. Day-trips from Cayenne cost US$75 or more but time spent here is highly rewarding as the village, on the banks of the Rivière de Kaw, is sure to reward photographers, birdwatchers and all nature-lovers. Primates, sloths and dozens of forest birds inhabit the high canopy, while the waters are infested with caiman. Tours in this area are available from

Cayenne tour operators but they are expensive. JAL Voyages offer overnight birdwatching tours for US$220. Independent travellers should enquire at tourist information offices for budget camp and cabin accommodation.

St Georges d'Oyapock

This small town, 152km southwest of Cayenne in the low lying valley of the River Oyapock, serves as the main transit point for overland traffic between the Guianan and Brazilian frontiers. Travellers heading for Brazil should get visa-related paperwork completed in Cayenne. A couple of basic hotels and restaurants provide basic facilities for accommodation and meals, along with some duty-free shops.

Mana

This small town, graced by quaint colonial buildings, is situated on the coast at the mouth of the Mana River, 200km by road northwest of Cayenne. Mana's relaxed atmosphere makes it a pleasant diversion just to relax and enjoy the ambience. Jungle tours visit Acarouany, inhabited by villagers from the Vietnamese Hmong tribe.

Mana attracts travellers who want a break on the way between Suriname and Cayenne. The Suriname border crossing is at St Laurent de Maroni, 40km to the south along the river. Surrounded by mixed mangrove and tropical rainforest, the area around Mana offers plenty of birding, wildlife and natural history opportunities. Night rides in canoes looking for caiman are always successful, while night birds, frogs and insects have so many different calls that it is difficult to tell whether a chirp or whistle comes from a tiny hyalid frog or a small tropical owl.

Aouara

This small Indian village is situated some 22km northwest of Mana along the coastal road. If you're not here on a package tour, your best bet is to hitch a ride from Mana. Aouara offers the nature-lover get-away-from-it-all jungle living, with the bonus of beautiful beaches and friendly tribal people. Once in Aouara ask for directions to the beach hut where you can stay for a paltry US$5. Facilities at the beach include covered beach shelters of palm and bamboo sleeping ten people. You must bring full camping equipment and mosquito nets with fresh water. Bathrooms and toilets and some simple foodstuffs are available at the site.

Aside from a rich birdlife and abundance of shore animals, the beach is a nesting site for turtles that lay their eggs in the nesting season between April and June.

St Laurent de Maroni

With a population over 5,000, this town on the Suriname border remains a tranquil colonial backwater. Somewhat run down, its fascinating past connects it with the colony's history as a penal colony. Today the town serves as a border crossing for overland travel into Suriname and also as the main departure point for package trips and commercial traffic up the Maroni.

The few hotels and restaurants are good, but no less expensive than those of other towns in French Guiana. For mid-range accommodation try the **Star Hotel** (109 Rue Thiers; tel: 341084), costing from US$25 per person. For a bit more there is the **Relais de Barcarel** (Avenue Félix Eboué; tel: 341023) at US$30 per night. A couple of cafés provide cheap eats while the Indonesian outdoor stalls cook all sorts of spicy delights, with a satisfying meal of noodles and fish stew costing US$5.

If you have some time in town, be sure to visit the original prison site and centre for convicts, the Camp de la Transportation, with buildings dating from 1857.

Collective taxis and buses provide public transport to and from Cayenne, 250km southeast, costing from US$15 one way, and leaving from the ferry pier at the southern end of Avenue General de Gaulle.

The ferry pier is also, logically enough, the departure and arrival point for overland travellers to and from Suriname. Customs and immigration procedures for the crossing into Suriname are very security-conscious.

Leaving from the pier, river trips along the Maroni take you south deep into primordial jungle through some 400km of sparsely settled, dense rainforest, to the jungle town of Maripasoula. On package tours, bilingual naturalist-guides point out the natural history of the river as you proceed past the small village of Apatou, 60km downstream from St Laurent. Guides accompany you along two or three trails a day. Numerous forest birds and waterbirds inhabit the river's edge: anis, kiskadees, kingfishers, herons and the jabiru stork. Transport is in comfortable motor launches. Booked through Takari Tours in Cayenne (see page 412) a six-day voyage up the river in a safe comfortable launch will cost upwards of US$600 per person, excluding airfare back to Cayenne (US$125 one way). In St Laurent, Guyane Adventure (2 Avenue Carnot; tel: 342128) and Youkaliba Expeditions (3 Rue Simon; tel: 341645) offer similar trips.

Maripasoula

Located in the hinterlands on the Suriname border, Maripasoula is accessible via a daily flight from Cayenne. Most people fly from the town back to Cayenne, having arrived on a riverboat cruise. If you're not on a package tour, you may be able to scrounge a ride on one of several small cargo boats leaving for St Laurent daily from the pier. Passage is difficult to arrange as vessels are usually fully loaded, but with perseverance and a couple of days to spare you may get lucky. US$75–100 for passage.

Travel further upriver requires written permission from the police in Cayenne.

Jungle lodges

Places to stay in the jungle are clustered around Cayenne and St Laurent de Maroni, and serve as points from which to enjoy jungle trails, birdwatching, canoe-rides, caiman spotting and botanical instruction. To travel beyond areas with roads, many tourists experience French Guiana's natural wonders on the move, via river. From Cayenne and Kourou it is only three hours' drive to St Laurent Maroni so it is usual to overnight at a hotel there and then board a boat the next day.

Association Yawo Ya Délé tel: 341414/343253. In Awala.
Chez Maryse tel: 342855. In Saut Sabbat.
CISAME tel: 280109; fax: 280062. In Approuague.
Maripas tel/fax: 320541. Near Kourou.
Quimbé Kio tel: 270122; fax: 270148. In Cacao.
Saut Sonelle tel: 314945. In Maripasoula.
Tolenga Jungle Lodge tel: 00 87 1761 373520; fax: 00 87 1761 373522, Cayenne tel: 0594 294894. This jungle lodge is on the Inini (a tributary of the Maroni just south of Maripasoula.

Places of interest

One is surely forgiven for wondering why the Islands of Salvation are so-called when their purpose was the incarceration and inhuman treatment of people. Indeed the name given to one of them, the Devil's Islands, seems more appropriate.

Located about 12km off the Guianan coast, the Îles de Salut group comprises three islands. Île Royale is the most interesting island as it was used for the main incarceration facility. The autobiography of Henri Charrière, *Papillon,* who spent ten years (four of them in solitary confinement) on the islands, is now familiar to millions throughout the world.

Pale statistics fail to convey the impression of this place. Of 50–70,000 convicts, the only ones to leave alive were the 5,000 there when the prison closed.

The Îles de Salut are not the most accessible or joyous holiday destination. To spend a night there could be trying on one's psyche, at least. However, the visit is an education. The islands' palpable atmosphere and notorious past are sure to leave a lasting impression.

The **Hotel Auberge Îles de Salut** (tel: 321100) has airy comfortable rooms, with private bathroom and wooden storm shutters on the window, for US$30 (single) and US$20 (double) per person. Trips can be booked with tour operators in Cayenne or you can make your own way there.

SURINAME

Located on the central eastern coast of northern South America, Suriname's western border is with Guyana, while to the east is French Guiana and south is Brazil. Suriname is the smallest independent state in South America.

BASIC FACTS

Official name Republiek Suriname (Republic of Suriname)
Area 163,820km² (63,251 miles²)
Population 410,000
Capital Paramaribo
Largest city (population) Paramaribo (201,000)
Main 'Amazon' city Paramaribo
Official language Dutch
Date of independence Nov 25 1975 (The Netherlands)
Major industries bauxite, food processing, wood products
GDP per capita US$870
Currency Suriname Guilder, Sf (US$1=Sf411; £1=Sf635)
Major attractions Dutch colonial architecture, national parks and nature reserves
National holidays Jan 1, Holi Phagwa (Mar), Easter, May 1, July 1, Nov 25, Christmas

Facts and figures

Geography and climate

Topographically, the country's north comprises a narrow coastal plain, about 365km long from east to west. This is formed of mudflats and sandbanks deposited by equatorial currents from the Amazon's mouth. Developed areas in the low-lying coastal zone lie below river flood levels and require extensive drainage. Inland to the south lies extensive dense forest, covering hills and low mountains, for for about 80% of Suriname's territory. To the southwest lies a region of upland savannah. Little land has been cleared and around 90% of the original forest cover remains intact. Most deforestation is in the coastal region and river valleys.

Flowing northwards, all the country's major rivers discharge into the Atlantic, their upland stretches characterised by numerous falls and rapids. Major rivers are the Corantijn, marking the border with Guyana, the Coppename, the Suriname and the Maroni, which marks the border with French Guiana.

Suriname's climate is equatorial maritime: humid year-round but with refreshing northeast breezes. Rainfall is relatively high but occurs mostly in the mountains. These receive an average 3,000mm per year. The coast is somewhat drier, getting 1,900mm over a year. In the northern populated regions, four seasons of alternating wet and dry periods are recognised. Heaviest rains are from April to August, with a minor rainy season from November to February, the months between being relatively dry. In the south there is no distinctive wet or dry season.

Annual mean temperatures hover around 27°C, varying little throughout the year.

Flora and fauna

Suriname's flora is highly diverse, with over 4,000 fern and higher plant species from the coastal zone. Four-fifths of the land remains covered with its original tropical rainforest from which at least a thousand tree species are known.

Suriname's vertebrate fauna is typically neotropical with 150 recorded mammal species in all. The rare black-tailed hairy porcupine (*C. melanurus*) is found in Suriname. Five species of marine turtles, protected by law, breed on coastal beaches along the coast and estuaries. Around 650 bird species are recorded from Suriname and 350 or so kinds of fish are known from coastal and fresh waters.

People and languages

Second least populous country in South America, Suriname's population actually declined during the 1970s and 1980s by a third because of migration, mostly to Holland. Four fifths of the population live in Paramaribo and the surrounding areas.

Minority ethnic groups include Amerindians, blacks, Dutch and Chinese. Major groups are East Indians, Creoles and Javanese. The Bush Negroes (Boesch Negers) have returned to a West African way of life, adopting its customs, religion and slash-and-burn agriculture, together with hunting and fishing.

Dutch is the official language, learned as a second language by most Surinamese though English is widely spoken, along with Sranan or Taki-Taki – a Creole dialect – and a variety of Asian, African and Amerindian languages. Sarnami is spoken by East Indians. Trio and Wayana are two important linguistic groups.

All the world's major religions are practised. Around two thirds of the people are Christian; East Indians are generally Hindu, although a few are Muslim, as are most Javanese. The Chinese practise Confucianism. Judaism has been practised in Suriname since the 16th century. Native Indian and African religions thrive among indigenous peoples and Bush Negroes.

History

Suriname's earliest inhabitants were the indigenous Surinen, after whom the country is named. In 1593 the Spanish claimed Suriname but the Dutch were the first (in 1602) to set up a trading post and fort. In 1682 the Dutch West India Company introduced coffee and sugar-cane, along with African slaves to cultivate the crops. Brutally treated, many slaves escaped to the interior where they remained free, were eventually recognised as such and were awarded lands.

Apart from two brief spells under British colonial rule at the beginning of the 19th century, Suriname remained a Dutch colony. In 1863, a slave revolt lasting two years led to the abolition of slavery. To overcome labour shortages, indentured workers were hired from China, Java and India.

Constitutional reforms in 1948–51 led to the creation of two-party self-government in 1954. When Suriname declared its intention to separate from Holland in 1973, the skilled and professional Dutch classes emigrated en masse.

A military coup in 1980 led by Colonel Dési Bouterse established martial law in Suriname. Following the execution of 15 political opposition leaders in 1982, raids by the National Army on forest villages saw the death and detention of many Bush Negroes with almost 15,000 seeking refuge in French Guiana. Rebel activity around Albina closed the economically important border with French Guiana in 1986.

A new constitution, approved by the electorate in 1987, forced Bouterse to take a back seat. Following the military-led bloodless coup in 1990, Johan Kraag was made president. The French Guiana border re-opened in 1991 and violence subsided. In May 1991, peaceful elections were held, with the New Front coalition, led by Ronald Venetiaan, winning 30 seats. Peace accords between rebel guerrillas and the government were successfully negotiated in August 1992.

Relatively high standards of living compared with the South American norm are enjoyed by Surinamese. People are generally well-off and poverty is scarce.

The economy is based on private and public sector development, with bauxite, alumina and aluminium production dominating the industrial sector. One in five workers are occupied in agriculture.

Money

Suriname guilders are the main currency, divided up in to 100 cents, although a guilder is worth about a quarter of a US cent. The black market rate from exchange houses is 5–10% better than the official rate given by banks and hotels.

Costs in Suriname are reasonable; it's far less expensive than French Guiana and not much pricier than Guyana. Some payments must be made in US dollars. Budget travellers can figure on US$5 per night for decent accommodation and about the same for food when eating out.

Highlights

Up until recently, Suriname was absent from the itineraries of most travel agents and tour operators. In 1993, the Suriname government welcomed tourists for the first time in ten years.

Paramaribo offers insight into the legacy of Dutch colonialism, the only such opportunity in the Americas. Most obvious Dutch influence is in the architecture and language. Streets are lined with four- or five-storey houses, fronted with the curved, feminine gables typical of colonial Dutch buildings. As a beach resort, the city offers more to wildlife enthusiasts than to leisure seekers; nearby rivers and tidal conditions conspire to keep the beaches muddy and the ocean water murky, and mosquitoes often reach unbearable numbers.

Beyond the city, the tropical flora and fauna remain largely intact, partly because the interior is so inaccessible, with just a few hotels and restaurants beyond Paramaribo. Conditions are difficult for independent travellers. Full board is rarely available, accommodation is basic, and even the better-off will have to take a hammock, mosquito net, and quite often their own food.

The rainy season (April to August) is unpleasant for rainforest excursions. Prices are higher and lodgings harder to find during the high seasons: mid-March to mid-May, July to September and then the year-end holiday.

Getting there and away

By air

Paramaribo's Zanderij or Johan Pengel International Airport, in operation since 1934, is served by several international airlines. Flight prices vary dramatically. The minimum return airfare from Miami is US$500 while the regular fare is US$750 and up.

Suriname Airways (SLM) has two flights a week from Miami and one a week from New York, Amsterdam and Curaçao. Dutch airline KLM has one flight a week from Amsterdam. Air France flies from Cayenne once weekly providing the cheapest way of reaching Suriname from Europe.

Departure tax is US$25 payable in dollars.

By ship

Paramaribo is Suriname's main port-of-call for cruise ships navigating up or down the coast, on their way from the Caribbean wintering grounds to the Amazon or the South Atlantic.

By road

From French Guiana, it is possible to drive by road *to* Suriname, but not *into* it, as the ferry from French Guiana across the Maroni has no facilities for vehicles. Around one third of the country's 2,750km of road are paved along the coast. No major roads enter the interior. A new ferry is planned for the crossing along the Corantijn, with a terminal just outside Niuew Nickerie.

Customs and immigration

Because of internal conflict and serious border disputes, Suriname is wary of visitors and is only now getting used to the idea. A **passport** valid for six months is required and **visas** are needed for citizens of most countries.

Getting around

Internal air transport is efficient and usually the best way to reach remote back-country areas. Road transport is under-developed and limited to the coastal region. An east–west highway runs along the coast connecting the borders of French Guiana and Suriname.

Wide rivers along the coast admit ocean-going vessels, chiefly to Paramaribo. River navigation along interior waterways is hampered by rapids and falls in upland regions.

Communications

The main post office in Paramaribo is on the corner of Wagenwegstraat. Mail is reliable and inexpensive (US$0.50 for a postcard within the Americas), though slow. Telephone, telegram and fax services are available but costly.

The international country code for Suriname is 597.

Two daily Dutch-language newspapers and one Chinese publication are available in Paramaribo and larger towns. Of the two television stations, the official channel is STS. There are six radio stations, two of them government controlled.

Paramaribo

Imagine a 1950s Amsterdam (minus canals), transport it to tropical jungle and allow it to decay for thirty or forty years. Paramaribo is a city whose dominant feeling is one of decadent, worn-out post-colonialism. Yet grandeur remains. Rows of houses, fronted with typically colonial Dutch gables, lend an exotic air to the city.

Paramaribo itself has its attractions: fine architecture, rich history and a highly diverse, cosmopolitan culture. The major sights are within a small area in the centre, located in a triangle bounded by Waterkant to the south, Rust en Vredstraat to the northwest and Gravenstraat-Soldatenstraat to the northeast.

Transport

Most international flights use Zanderij International Airport, 45km south of Paramaribo (US$10–15 by taxi). Some domestic flights and others to nearby countries depart or arrive at Zorg en Hoop Airfield just outside the city (US$1 by taxi). Domestic destinations are served by SLM and Gum Air.

Generally, transport in Paramaribo and Suriname is very inexpensive but not widely available. Around Paramaribo taxi prices are very low: US$1–2 for a ride across the city. The city's major streets have bus routes. Fares are very cheap (US$0.10–0.50). Long-distance buses heading east from Paramaribo leave from the ferry terminal near Waterkant, and westbound buses depart from the corner of Hostraat and Dr Sophie Redmondstraat.

Where to stay

Choice of Paramaribo hotels for the foreign traveller is somewhat limited. The **Toarica** (L J Rietbergplein 1; tel: 471500) is the most expensive (US$50 per night) but has a great coffee shop and restaurant. In the Leonsburg district, 7km outside Paramaribo, is the **River Club** (around US$1 by taxi from the town centre). This hotel has good-value rooms (US$35 per night) and a nice restaurant, with good meals at reasonable prices. **Graaf van Zinsendorff** (Gravenstraat 100) is centrally located for US$15 per night, while **Balden** (Kwathweg 183) is a little further out of town but cheap at US$7. A good budget choice is the centrally located **Lisa's Guest House** (Burenstraat 6; tel: 476927) with rooms for US$7.50.

Where and what to eat

Food here is tasty, varied and wallet-friendly. One of the best up-market restaurants is **Sarinah** (Verlengde Gemenelansweg 187), about 20 minutes' ride from the city centre (US$1 by taxi). They serve really hot Indonesian food, the way it should be – you have been warned. Another good Indonesian restaurant is **La Bastille** (Kleine Waterstraat 3), easy to walk to from downtown, near Waterkant, behind Palmentuin. They serve outstanding food: under US$5 for a full meal. Other restaurants include **New China** (Verlengde Gemenelansweg 136). **Sunshine** (Wilhelminastraat 23) has very inexpensive and tasty Creole food. For the best breakfast in town try the **Toarica's Plantation Room**.

What to see

To get a rush of sights, sounds, colours and smells in one location, **Waterkant Market** on the riverfront has the works – a great place for shopping and people-watching. The **People's Palace** on Gravenstraat, built in typical Dutch colonial style, dates from the mid-1700s. It's in the main city centre park, the Palmentuin (next to Waterkant). In front of the Palace is **Unity Square**, the heart of the city centre and a good place to begin orienting yourself around Paramaribo.

Paramaribo's religious buildings hold some interest. The Roman Catholic cathedral, on Gravensraat (close by Wulfingstraat), is said to be the largest wooden building in the western hemisphere and is currently being restored.

For a perspective on Suriname's heritage, visit the **Surinaams Museum** (Commewijnstraat 18, Zorg en Hoop) on the outskirts of town. Displays feature Amerindian relics and artefacts and the latest exhibition. Open 07.30–14.00 weekdays, except Friday and weekends 17.00–20.00; admission US$0.10.

An interesting place to visit near the capital is **Niuew Amsterdam**, site of a ruined fort built to guard the confluence of the Commewijne and Suriname rivers. It's easy to reach from Paramaribo. Catch a No.4 bus from the city centre to

Leonsberg. There is a free open-air museum describing the area's history and efforts to conserve the ruins.

Shopping

Local handicrafts are of good quality and not too touristy. In simple stalls erected along the airport road, Bush Africans sell carvings and basketwork. Of course, in the towns are the usual array of curio shops selling handicrafts and local art. The main native handicrafts are drums, baskets and wooden carvings.

More information

Recovering from the damaging civil war and now encouraging tourists, Suriname is changing fast and new accommodation, restaurants and tour operators are setting up all the time. Up-to-date tourist information is available from the Tourist Department office at Cornelius Jonbawstraat 2; tel: 471163. Another excellent source for information on travel beyond Paramaribo is **Stinasu** (office at Cornelis Jongbawstraat 14; tel: 475845), a local conservation organisation which can take bookings for all the places mentioned below.

Beyond Paramaribo

Albina

This small town, 140km east of Paramaribo, exists primarily to serve border traffic crossing between Suriname and French Guiana. Almost deserted in the late 1980s on account of rebel activity around the town, Albina has recovered somewhat since 1991 when the border with French Guiana was re-opened. The town is easily reached from Paramaribo on fairly good roads with regular buses (four to five hours, from US$5 one way). Basic accommodation is available at the nearby town of Moenga (US$2 by taxi).

For motorised canoe trips up the Marowijne, you can hire an independent guide (US$10–15 per day) for day-trips or overnights at temporary jungle shelters. Camping equipment is essential for these excursions. On the river, heading deep into the interior, beyond habitations and cultivated areas, you travel to pristine lowland rainforest harbouring a variety of plants and animals on a par with anywhere in the Amazon.

Stoelmanseiland

This small settlement on the Lawa River, a tributary of the Maroni, is set in a beautiful landscape of rivers and forested rolling hills, some 150km downriver from Albina in the west of Suriname. Lodgings are provided at the pleasant Stoelmanseiland Guest House, with bedding and meals provided (US$15 per night). Make reservations for the lodge and transport (US$28 one way from Paramaribo) with tour operators, who offer four- to seven-day packages from US$25 per day. By motorised canoe it takes about two days to get here from Albina.

Apoera

About 120km inland on the Corantijn River, Apoera is a small port town accessible to ocean-going ships. No buses ease the effort of getting there but you can try to hitch along the Paramaribo–Apoera road (about 325km).

En route is Marie Blanche Falls, formed by the River Nickerie. Nearby you can stay at the **Dubois** guest house (US$25). Opportunities for nature activities are very good, with chances for outstanding birdwatching, easy-to-moderate trekking and swimming in clear forest rivers. The Dubois can be booked in Paramaribo through any of the listed tour operators.

To reach Guyana you need to catch a river taxi to Nieuw Nickerie from the Apoera wharf.

Nieuw Nickerie

This town of 8,250 on the border with Guyana is 5km inland on the Nickerie River, and is of most interest to travellers as a point to cross the border into Guyana. The town has half a dozen hotels ranging in price from moderate to cheap. One of the best in town is **Ameerali** (GG Maynardstraat 32), with great rooms from US$10. Cheaper is the **Luxor** (Gouverneurstraat 22). The best place to eat is at the Ameerali restaurant, although a couple of cafés in the town centre are good for a quick snack.

Jungle lodges

The choice of jungle lodges in Suriname is lacking, but then so are tourists. Certainly Suriname will suit those in search of a real jungle wilderness experience, where the wildlife and scenery are more important than your accommodation. To get off the beaten track, enjoying motorised and paddled canoe safaris through dense tropical jungle, with a decent guide to point out animals, birds and plants, you are best off consulting the local tour operators. Packages are affordable for budget travellers.

Brokopondo

About 120km inland south from Paramaribo, Brokopondo is a small settlement on the edge of the Brownsberg National Reserve. The drive takes about two hours along a surfaced road but no buses come this far. The village is most often visited on package tours to the nearby reserve from Paramaribo (book through the Paramaribo tour operator Stinasu).

Inexpensive (US$10 per night) accommodation is at a government resthouse, spartan but clean, with bedding and simple utensils provided. The facility is self-catering so take food. The main reason to be here is to take excursions into the park, including walks along easy-to-moderate trails. For a guide you must book a package tour in Paramaribo. The huge Afobaka dam can be reached a few kilometres down the Brokopondo Dam road and is the main point to begin exploring the WJ van Blommestein Meer – one of the world's most extensive man-made bodies of freshwater (area about 1,500km^2), created by the dam.

Brownsberg Chalets

Situated in the high rolling hills of the Brownsberg National Park 100km south of Paramaribo, a handful of small, simple chalets offers visitors comfortable lodgings, surrounded by wilderness. Each dwelling sleeps 8–10, with cooking facilities, shower and beds, for US$10 per person per night. Reservations are made through Stinasu in Paramaribo, who can arrange all-inclusive two to three-day guided package tours to the park from US$30 per day. You can get there by bus (US$5) from Paramaribo. Set among a grove of trees with well-kept gardens, the chalets are a good base to explore surrounding montane rainforest for birds and wildlife, notably by the WJ Blommestein Meer that marks the park's eastern boundary.

Matapica Beach

Situated on the boundary of the Wiawia Nature Reserve, some 50km east along the coast from Paramaribo, Matapica Beach offers basic lodgings for visitors to the reserve. These are simple beach huts and definitely not for the comfort-lover, although nature-lovers will be in heaven. You must provide your own bedding and food, but it's inexpensive; around US$5 per night. Book stays and arrange transport through Stinasu, whose package includes an English-speaking guide to take you along the reserve's trails through a variety of swampy lowland habitats from tropical rainforest to coastal mangrove and tidal estuaries.

National parks and wildlife reserves

Suriname has an impressive system of natural habitat protection, with several very large reserves and parks protecting a variety of different ecosystems, from mangrove swamp to upland rainforest. Most protected areas have written guides (in Dutch), available from tourist information offices and simple accommodation either inside the boundaries or close by. The national parks included below are readily accessible and have accommodation nearby. Three inaccessible reserves not mentioned – Tafelburg Nature Park, Eiferts de Haan Nature Park and Sipaliwini – are located far in the southern interior of the country.

The 6,000ha **Brownsberg Nature Park** is the most accessible of Suriname's inland reserves, being only two hours' drive on tarred road south of Paramaribo. The park is accessed via the village of Brownsweg. The reserve protects a variety of montane forest habitats, rich in epiphytic plants such as orchids, ferns and bromeliads. This is a perfect home for a typical array of neotropical rainforest fauna, including several monkey species, sloths, ant-eaters and spotted cats. The cane toad (*Bufo marinus*) is abundant. Indeed, the species originated in the region, and has now spread to tropical regions throughout the world. A guide to the park and the reserve's birds is available from Stinasu (US$2.50) and a guide to trails can be bought from the park headquarters in the park (US$1).

Wiawia Nature Reserve, 36,000ha in extent, encompasses significant areas of coastal beach along a narrow coastal strip, some 53km from Paramaribo. This undisturbed area is ideal for nesting sea-turtles who come ashore to lay eggs. Five species of turtles are found. The commonest are green turtle, leatherback and Ridley's. Birdwatchers have lots to look out for including large flocks of flamingo, scarlet ibis and storks. Simple accommodation is available at Matapica Beach.

Galibi Nature Reserve is a small area of seashore set aside for the benefit of marine turtles. Located along a part of the lower Marowijne Estuary, the reserve can be reached from Albina, 133km from Paramaribo. Take a river taxi from Albina to the reserve for a day of birdwatching and walking easy trails. There is no accommodation in the park.

About 150km (89 miles) southwest of Paramaribo, **Raleighvallen Voltsberg Reserve** protects 57,000ha of pristine mixed tropical montane and wet rainforest and river habitat along the middle Coppename some 111km inland from the coast. Within its boundaries are Mount Voltsberg (which offers hard but exhilarating hikes) and Foengoe Island, on the Coppename River. The closest town is Witagron, located where the road crosses the Coppename.

Half-an-hour's drive (35km) west of Paramaribo along a good road, Coppename **Estuary National Park** protects the lower Coppename River. Along the river are a couple of jungle camps and a thatched restaurant. Ask Paramaribo tour operators to book accommodation or for details on package trips up the Coppename, among the most rewarding natural history experiences in the country. Canoe rides along the river and its associated wetlands are highly rewarding for flora and fauna. Shore and water birds are particularly abundant and diverse.

Appendix 1

EMBASSIES

In Venezuela

Australia Quinta Yolanda, Av Luis Roche, entre Transversal 6a y 7a, Altamira, Caracas; tel: 00 58 2 263 4033
Canada 6a Av Entre 3a y 5a Transv de Altamira, Edificio Omni, Caracas; tel: 00 58 2 264 0833
Netherlands Edif San Juan, piso 9, San Juan Bosco y Av Transversal 2, Altamira; PO Box 62286; tel: 00 58 2 266 6522
UK Apartado 1246, Torre Las Mercedes, 3rd Floor, Caracas 1010-A; tel: 00 58 2 993 4111
USA Calle S y Calle Suapure, Colinas de Valle Arriba, Caracas; PO Box 2291; tel: 00 58 2 977 2011

In Colombia

Canada Calle 76, No 11-52, Bogotá; tel: 00 57 1 313 1355
Netherlands Cra 9, No 74-08, piso 6, Bogotá; tel: 00 57 1 211 9600
UK Torre Propaganda Sanco, Calle 98, No 9-03, piso 4, Bogotá; tel: 00 57 1 218 5111
USA Calle 22D No 47-51, Bogotá; tel: 00 57 1 315 0811

In Ecuador

Canada Edif Josueth González, 6 de Diciembre 2816 y James Orton, piso 4, Quito; tel: 00 593 2 543 214
Netherlands 9 de Octubre y Orellana, Quito; tel: 00 593 2 567 606
UK Av González Suárez 111 Quito; casilla 314; tel: 00 593 2 560 309
USA Av 12 de Octobre y Av Patria, Quito; tel: 00 593 2 562 890

In Peru

Australia c/o Inversiones en Tourismo SA, Av República de Panama 3055, Oficina 21-A, San Isidro, Lima; tel: 00 51 1 211 8073
Canada Calle Frederico Gerdes 130, antes Libertad, Miraflores; tel: 00 51 1 444 4015
Netherlands Av Principal 190, San Borja; tel: 00 51 1 476 1069
UK Edif El Pacífico Washington, 12th floor, Arequipa 600; tel: 00 51 5 433 5032
USA Av La Encaldada cdra 17 s/n, Surco, Lima 33; tel: 00 51 1 434 3000

In Bolivia

Canada Av 20 de Octubre 2475, Plaza Avaroa, La Paz; tel: 00 591 2 375224
Netherlands Calle Rosendo Gutiérrez 481; Casilla 10509; tel: 00 591 2 392064
South Africa Calle Rosendo Gutiérrez 482, La Paz; tel: 00 591 2 367754
UK Av Arce 2732, La Paz; casilla 694; tel: 00 591 2 357424
USA Av Arce 2780, La Paz; casilla 425; tel: 00 591 2 350120

In Brazil

Canada Edificio Top Center, Av Paulista 854, 5th floor, 01310-913, Sao Paulo; tel; 00 55 11 287 2122
Netherlands R M Leão 41, Manaus; tel: 00 55 92 234 8719
UK Eduardo Ribeiro 520, Sala 1202, Manaus; tel: 00 55 92 622 3879
USA Geral Recife 101, Manaus; tel: 00 55 92 234 4546

In Guyana

UK 44 Main Street, Georgetown; tel: 00 592 2 65881
Canada High and Young Streets, Georgetown, 00 592 2 72081

In Suriname

UK c/o VSH United Buildings, Van't Hogerhuystraat, PO Box 1300, Paramaribo.

LANGUAGE

English-Spanish glossary

A brief list of commonly used words and phrases with Spanish equivalents, including weekdays, months and numbers. Phonetic pronunciation is given for each word. The list gives a visitor with no knowledge of Spanish enough to get around, find luggage, ask the time, look for food and communicate other basic needs.

English	***Español***	***Pronunciation*** (accent on underlined syllable)
hello	*ola*	oh-la
goodbye	*adiós*	ah-dee-oss
how are you?	*¿como está usted?*	coh-moh eh-stah ew-stayd
see you later	*hasta luego*	astah lew-aygoh
good day	*buenos dias*	boo-eynohss dee-ahs
good afternoon	*buenos tardes*	boo-eynohss tarr-dayz
good evening	*buenos noches*	boo-eynohss noh-chayz
morning	*mañana*	man-nya-na
afternoon	*tardes*	tarr-dayz
evening	*noches*	noh-chayz
very good	*muy bien*	mwee bee-en
thank you	*gracias*	grah-see-ahs
please	*por favor*	pohr fah-vor
excuse me	*perdóneme*	pehr-dohn-ay-may
many thanks	*muchas gracias*	moo-chas grah-cee-yahs
yes	*sí*	see
no	*no*	noh
what is your name?	*¿como se llama?*	koh-moh say jah-mah
my name is…	*mi nombre es…*	mee nohm-bray ays
I don't understand	*no comprendo*	noh cohm-prayn-doh
do you speak…	*Habla…*	a-blah…
…English	*…Inglés*	…en-glays
I'm hungry	*tengo hambre*	ten-goh am-bray
how much?	*¿quantos?*	kwahn-tohss
that's expensive!	*¡está caro!*	eh-stah kar-oh
that's too much!	*¡está todo mucho!*	eh-stah toh-doh moo-cho
I want	*quiero*	kee-eh-ro
I don't want	*no quiero*	noh kee-eh-ro
I would like	*quisiera*	kee-see-eh-ra
I am lost	*estoy puerde*	eh-stoy pwehr-day
to the right	*a la derecha*	ah lah day-ray-chah
to the left	*a la izquierda*	ah lah eez-kwee-ehr-dah
where is…	*¿donde está…?*	dohn-day eh-stah…
restaurant	*el restaurante*	el reh-staw-rahn-tay
bathroom	*el baño*	el bahn-yo
hotel	*el hotel*	el oh-tehl
bedroom	*la habitación*	la ab-ih-tas-yon
towel	*la ropa*	la roh-pah
soap	*el jabón*	el zhah-bohn
telephone	*el teléfono*	el tay-lay-foh-noh

currency exchange	*la casa de cambio*	la kasah deh cahm-bee-oh
bank	*el banco*	el bahn-coh
river	*el río*	el ree-oh
forest	*la selva*	la sehl-bah
airport	*el aeropuerto*	el ahy-roh-pwahr-toh
Indian village	*el pueblo de los Indios*	el poo-weh-bloh day loss een-dee-oss
boat	*la barca*	la bar-kah
bus station	*stación del autobús*	stah-see-ohn dehl ow-too-boos
street	*la avenida*	la ah-vehn-eedah
house	*la casa*	la cah-sah
guide	*el guía*	el gee-yah
luggage	*equipaje*	eh-kee-pah-hey
what time is it?	*¿que hora es?*	kay orah ays
what time is…	*¿que hora…*	kay orah…
the meal	*la comida*	la koh-midh-ah
breakfast	*desayuno*	day-say-ooh-noh
lunch	*almuerzo*	ahl-moo-ehrt-soh
dinner	*cena*	say-nah
what is your…	*que es su…*	kay ays soo…
phone number?	*número de teléfono?*	nume-eh-row day tay-lay-foh-noh
address	*dirección*	dee-rek-shee-yon
Weekdays	**Días laborables**	
Sunday	*domingo*	doh-min-goh
Monday	*lunes*	loo-ness
Tuesday	*martes*	mahr-tess
Wednesday	*miércoles*	mee-ehr-coh-less
Thursday	*jueves*	hoo-ay-bess
Friday	*viernes*	bee-err-ness
Saturday	*sábado*	sah-bah-doh
Months	**Meses**	
January	*Enero*	ay-nay-rho
February	*Febrero*	fay-bray-roh
March	*Marzo*	mahrso
April	*Abril*	ab-reel
May	*Mayo*	my-oh
June	*Junio*	hoo-nee-oh
July	*Julio*	hoo-lee-oh
August	*Agosto*	ow-go-stoh
September	*Septiembre*	sayp-tee-aym-bray
October	*Octubre*	ock-too-bray
November	*Noviembre*	noh-bee-aym-bray
December	*Diciembre*	day-see-aym-bray
Numbers	**Números**	
zero	*cero*	zay-roh
one	*uno*	oo-noh
two	*dos*	dohs
three	*tres*	trayss
four	*cuatro*	kwat-roh
five	*cinco*	seen-koh
six	*seis*	says
seven	*siete*	see-aytay
eight	*ocho*	oh-cho
nine	*nueve*	noo-ay-bay
ten	*diez*	dee-ayz
eleven	*once*	ohn-say
twelve	*doce*	doh-say
thirteen	*trece*	tray-say
fourteen	*catorce*	kaht-ohr-zay
fifteen	*quince*	keen-zay

sixteen	*diez-y-seis*	dee-ayz ee says
seventeen	*diez-y-siete*	dee-ayz ee see-aytay
eighteen	*diez-y-ocho*	dee-ayz ee oh-cho
nineteen	*diez-y-nueve*	dee-ayz ee noo-ay-bay
twenty	*veinte*	bay-ihn-tay
twenty-one	*veinte-y-uno*	bay-ihn-tay ee oon-o
thirty	*treinta*	trayn-ta
forty	*cuarenta*	kwahr-ehn-ta
fifty	*cincuente*	seen-kwen-tay
sixty	*sesenta*	says-ehn-ta
seventy	*setenta*	say-tehn-ta
eighty	*ochenta*	oh-chen-ta
ninety	*noventa*	noh-ben-ta
one hundred	*cien*	see-ehn
two hundred	*doscientos*	dhos see-ehn-toss
one thousand	*mil*	meehl
one million	*millón*	meeh-jee-ohn

English-Portuguese glossary

A brief list of commonly used words and phrases with Brazilian Portuguese equivalents, including weekdays, months and numbers. Phonetic pronunciation is given for each word. The list gives a visitor with no knowledge of Portuguese enough to get around, find luggage, ask the time, look for food and communicate other basic needs.

Stress

If a word ends in a vowel with a tilde (~), stress the last syllable, unless another vowel in the word is accented.

If a vowel has an acute (´) or circumflex (^) accent, stress that vowel no matter where in the word it comes.

If a word ends in r, stress the last syllable, unless there's an accented vowel somewhere else.

Otherwise, in words of two or more syllables, stress the penultimate vowel.

English	***Português***	***Pronunciation***
hello	*olá!*	ol-lah
goodbye	*adeus!*	er-deoosh
cheerio	*tchau!*	chow
how are you?	*como vai?*	comb-oh v-eye
see you later	*até breve!*	er-teh-brev
good day	*bom dia!*	bom dee-er
good afternoon	*boa tarde!*	bow-ah tardee
good evening	*boa noite!*	bow-ah noy-chee
morning	*manhã*	mer-nyah
afternoon	*tarde*	targee
evening	*noite*	noy-chee
very good	*muito bem*	mween-too bem
thank you	*obrigado/a*	oh-bree-gah-do/dah
please	*por favor*	poor fah-vor
excuse me	*desculpe*	dish-koolp
many thanks	*muito obrigado/a*	mween-too obri-ga-doo/er
yes	*sim*	seem
no	*não*	nawm
what is your name?	*¿como se chama?*	koo-moo set sha-mmer
my name is…	*chamo-me…*	sha-moo mer
I don't understand	*não entendo*	nawm ayn-tay-doa
do you speak…	*fala…*	fa-ler
…English	*…Inglês*	een-glaysh
I'm hungry	*estou com fome*	e-stoo com fom
how much?	*¿quanto custa?*	kwan-too cush-ter
that's expensive!	*e caro*	eh ka-roo
that's too much!	*muito caro*	mween-too karoo
I want…	*queria…*	ker-ree-er
I don't want…	*no queria…*	No ker-ree-er

I am lost	*estou perdido/a*	ish-toh per-dee-doo/er
to the right	*á direita*	a dee-ray-ter
to the left	*á esquerda*	a ishkairder
where is the...	*onde é...*	ond eh.....
restaurant	*o restaurante*	o rish-tow-rawnt
bathroom	*a banho*	a ba-nyoo
toilet	*a banheiro*	a bah-nyay-ro
the hotel	*o hotel*	o ot-tehl
bedroom	*o quarto da dormir*	o kwar-too der door-meer
towel	*a toalha*	a too-al-yer
soap	*o sabonete*	o ser-boo-nayt
the telephone	*o telefone*	o ter-ler-fon
currency exchange	*o câmbio*	o kawm-byoo
bank	*o banco*	o bawn-koo
river	*o rio*	o ree-oo
forest	*a mata/a floresta*	a floo-resh-ter
village	*a aldeia*	a al-dag-ea
airport	*o aeroporto*	o eh-ro-poartoo
boat	*o barco*	o bar-koo
bus station	*a rodoviária*	a hodo-vyar-rhea
street	*a rua*	a rhu-a
house	*a casa*	a ka-saa
guide	*a guia*	a gee-er
luggage	*a bagagem*	a ber-gaz-haym
can you tell me the time?	*dizia-me as horas*	dee-zee-er mer er zor-ush
a meal	*comida*	co-mee-dah
breakfast	*café da manhã*	ka-feh dah man-yah
lunch	*almoço*	al-moa-soo
dinner	*jantar*	yan-tar
can I have your…	*pode dar-me o seu…*	pod dar-mer oo se-oo
phone number?	*número de telefone?*	noo-me-roo der ter-ler-fon
address?	*endereço?*	arn-der ray-soo
Weekdays	**Dias**	
Sunday	*domingo*	doo-meen-goo
Monday	*segunda-feira*	ser-goon-der fay-rer
Tuesday	*terça-feira*	tart-ser fay-rer
Wednesday	*quarta-feira*	kwar-ter fay-rer
Thursday	*quinta-feira*	keen-ter fay-rer
Friday	*sexta-feira*	says-ter fay-rer
Saturday	*sábada*	sa-ber doo
Months	**Meses**	
January	*janeiro*	zher nayroo
February	*fevereiro*	fer ver ray-roo
March	*março*	mar-soo
April	*abril*	er-brill
May	*maio*	mig-hoo
June	*junho*	zhoo-nyoo
July	*julho*	zhoo-lyoo
August	*agosto*	er-goash-too
September	*setembro*	staym-dro
October	*outubro*	oh-too-broo
November	*novembro*	noo-vaymbroo
December	*dezembro*	der-zaym-broo
Numbers	**Números**	
zero	*zero*	ze-hroo
one	*um/uma*	oom/er
two	*dois/duas*	doysh
three	*três*	traysh
four	*quatro*	ka-troo

five	*cinco*	seen-koh
six	*seis*	saysh
seven	*sete*	set
eight	*oito*	oy-too
nine	*nove*	nov
ten	*dez*	desh
eleven	*onze*	onz
twelve	*doze*	doaz
thirteen	*treze*	trays
fourteen	*catorze*	ker-toarz
fifteen	*quinze*	keenz
sixteen	*dezesseis*	dzer-saysh
seventeen	*dezessete*	dzer-set
eighteen	*dezoito*	dzoy-too
nineteen	*dezenove*	dzer-nov
twenty	*vinte*	veent
twenty-one	*vinte e um/uma*	veen-tee oom/er
thirty	*trinta*	treen-ter
forty	*quarenta*	kwer-rayn-ter
fifty	*cinqüenta*	seenkwayn-ter
sixty	*sessenta*	ser sayn-ter
seventy	*setenta*	ser tayn-ter
eighty	*oitenta*	oy tayn-ter
ninety	*noventa*	noo vayn-ter
one hundred	*cem*	saym
two hundred	*duzentos/as*	doo-zayn toosh/ush
one thousand	*mil*	meel
one million	*um milhão*	oom mee-lyawn

Appendix 3

FURTHER READING

Travelogues

Cousteau, J Y and Richards, M, *Jaques Cousteau's Amazon Journey*, Harry N Abrams, New York (1984). A coffee table book replete with colour photos telling the story of Cousteau's 1981 Amazon expedition.

Fawcett, Col P H, *Exploration Fawcett*. Hutchinson, London (First ed. 1953). Reprint Century, London (1988). Follows the legendary explorers travels in the lowlands of Bolivia and his ultimate disappearance in Mato Grosso.

Ghinsberg, Y, *Back from Tuichi*, Random House, New York (1993). The true story of an Israeli who went missing for three weeks in the jungles of Bolivia.

Gordon, N, *Tarantulas, Marmosets and Other Stories: An Amazon Diary,* Metro, London (1997). A highly readable account of travelling in the rainforests of Venezuela and Brazil based on the wildlife filming of the author in the Amazon.

Harrison, J, *Up the Creek*, Bradt Publications, London (1986). Out of print, but essential reading for anyone planning an independent canoe trip who needs a little preparation.

Jordan, Tanis and Martin, *Out of Chingford*, Frederick Muller, London (1988). In turn scary, awe-inspiring and hilarious, the authors describe journeys by inflatable boat in the rivers of Peru, Suriname and Venezuela..

Kane, Joe, *Running the Amazon*, Knopf, New York; Pan, London (1997). A now-classic account of the full-length voyage by kayak and essential reading for anyone doing whitewater trips in the upper Amazon.

Kelly, B and London M, *Amazon*, Harcourt, Brace Jovanovich, New York (1983). The authors describe travelling the main stream by plane and boat during the pre-tourist boom era in the 1970s, with a chapter each devoted to descriptions of Iquitos and Leticia at the time.

Morrison, T, *Lizzie: A Victorian Lady's Amazon Adventure*, BBC, London (1985). Follows the journey of Lizzie Mathys who travelled with her husband up the Amazon through Peru, taking the Madre de Dios to reach Bolivia and work for the rubber baron Nicholás Suárez.

O'Hanlon, R, *In trouble again: A journey between the Orinoco and the Amazon*, Penguin, London (1997). The author's detailed account of travels in the Venezuelan rainforest.

Shoumatoff, A, *The Rivers Amazon*. Sierra Club Books, San Francisco, (1986). The author's tale covers his voyage up the full length of the Amazon from its mouth to Pucallpa, Peru.

Van Dyk, J, *The Amazon*, National Geographic 187: 2-39 (1995). The author describes a riverboat journey along the full length of the Amazon.

History

Gheerbrant, A, *The Amazon: Past, Present and Future*, Harry N Abrams, New York (1992). A well-written and beautifully illustrated book that tells the story of the Amazon from its early discovery to the present day. Has a full chronology of events in Amazonia, mostly in Brazil.

Hemming, J, *Red Gold: The Conquest of the Brazilian Indians*. Macmillan, London (1978). A detailed and highly readable historical analysis of the exploitation of the Indians of Brazil and the Amazon.

Hemming, J, *Amazon Frontier: The Defeat of the Brazilian Indians*, Macmillan, London (1987). Continuing the story set in *Red Gold* explaining the continued decimation of the Indians of the Amazon from 1755 up to 1910.

Smith, A , *Explorers of the Amazon*, Viking/Penguin, New York (1990). The most comprehensive history of the Amazon from early discoverers to the rubber boom.

The Latin American Bureau have an *In Focus* series providing a guide to the people, politics and culture of each country bordering the Amazon Basin. International mail order available. Contact Latin America Bureau (LAB), 1 Amwell Street, London EC1R 1UL; tel 0171 278 2829.

Ethnology

Allen, R, *Amazon Dream*, City Lights, San Francisco (1993). A first-hand account of the author's travels to Pucallpa, Peru, to study the pottery of the Shipobo tribe living along the upper Marañon.

Chagnon, N, *Yanomami: The Last Days of Eden*, Harcourt Brace Jovanovich, New York (1992). A French anthropologist gives an excellent sympathetic account of this Indian tribe living in the remote forests of southern Venezuela and Brazil.

Descola, P, *The Spears of Twilight: Life and Death in the Amazon Jungle*, Flamingo, London (1997). A detailed insight into the life of the Achuar Indians of Ecuador based on the anthropologist author's two years spent living close to the banks of the Pastazo.

Popescu, P, *Amazon Beaming*, Penguin, New York (1992). Describes the author's adventures among the 'Cat People' Amazon tribe of southern Venezuela.

Tidwell, M, *Amazon Stranger*, Lyons Press, New York (1997). A reporter's touching account told with wit and sensitivity of the Cofan, a small Ecuadorian Indian tribe, and their American chief's battle to save the Cuyabeno Reserve from the big oil companies.

Up de Graff, F W, *Headhunters of the Amazon: Seven Years of Exploration and Adventure*, Garden City Books, New York (1923). A fascinating account of the upper Amazon at the beginning of the 20th century, including descriptions of Iquitos at the time, as well as graphic descriptions of the now-outlawed practice of headhunting.

Wheeler, J, *The Adventurer's Guide*, David MacKay Inc, New York (1976). Describes, among other things, the author's year-long experience living with Shuar Indians of the Ecuadorian Amazon. Lots of detailed information on how he prepared for his adventure.

Conservation

Caufield, C, *In the Rainforest: Report from a Strange, Beautiful, Imperiled World*, University of Chicago Press, Chicago (1984). This book highlights the causes and consequences of rainforest destruction, with emphasis on the fate of the Amazon.

Cousteau, J Y, *The Cousteau Almanac: An Inventory of Life on Our Water Planet*. Doubleday, New York (1981). An encyclopaedic source of information on all aspects of the aquatic realm, with comparative data on the world's rivers and a useful section on Amazon conservation.

Collinson, H (ed), *Green Guerillas*, Latin American Bureau, London (1996). A study of environmental conflicts and initiatives in Latin America and the Caribbean with several chapters looking specifically at the Amazon.

Fisher, R (ed), *The Emerald Realm: Earth's Precious Rainforests*, National Geographic Society, Washington DC (1990). A general treatment of rainforests, with lots of beautiful photos to illustrate brief but informative articles by separate authors on ecology, tribes, uses and conservation of rainforest worldwide.

Hecht, S and Cockburn, A, *The Fate of the Forest: Developers, Destroyers and Defenders of the Amazon*, HarperCollins, New York (1990). Rainforest conservation is the major theme of this outstanding book in which the authors do a fine job of untangling the knotty issues and personalities.

Lewis, S, *The Rainforest Book*, Living Planet Press, Berkeley Books, New York (1990). Accessible to school-age children, this is a useful source book on rainforest conservation issues.

Stone, R, *Dreams of Amazonia* (2nd edn), Penguin Books, New York (1993). The author uses the theme of failed megaprojects in Amazonia to illustrate the futility of unbridled development of rainforest habitat.

White, P T, *Nature's Dwindling Treasures: Rain Forests*, National Geographic 163: 2-48 (1983). An article sounding a relatively early warning alarm of rapidly increasing destruction of tropical rainforests.

Natural history

Ayres, J M, *Scarlet Faces of the Amazon*, Natural History 3/90:33-40 (1990). An article describing research on the red uakari, an unusual and very rare monkey living only in flooded forests of western Brazil.

Bates, H W, *The Naturalist on the River Amazons,* University of California Press, Riverside (1962). A classic Victorian travelogue and natural history of the author's years spent in Brazil during the middle of the nineteenth century.

Conniff, R, *Tarantulas*, National Geographic 190: 98-115 (1996). Fascinating article on physiology and ecology of giant Amazon spiders.

Duke, J A and Vasquez, R, *Amazonian Ethnobotanical Dictionary*, CRC Press, Boca Raton, FL (1994). Essential research material for those interested in native use of wild plants, containing a list of some 1,400 plant species, each with a description of ailments treated.

Emmons, L H, *Neotropical Rainforest Mammals: a Field Guide*. Chicago University Press, Chicago (1990). A must for scientists and naturalist-guides interested in Amazon mammals. Every known mammal species is fully described and illustrated in colour or black-and-white, with scientific name.

Forsyth, A and Miyata, K, *Tropical Nature: Life and Death in the Rainforests of Central and South America*, Scribner & Sons, New York (1984). Just about the most readable text on tropical rainforest ecology and evolution. The authors draw on extensive experience in Ecuadorian and Costa Rican rainforests to paint a dramatic and sometimes amusing picture of the inner workings of tropical plants and animals.

Goulding, M, *Amazon: The Flooded Forest*, Sterling Publishing Co., New York (1990). Based on a BBC documentary series, this book is written for the layman (eg: no scientific names) interested in the flooded forest habitats of the Amazon.

Hallé, F, *A Raft Atop the Rainforest*, National Geographic 178: 128-138 (1990). A Frenchman describes his new technique for exploring the rainforest canopy in French Guiana.

Hilty, S L and Brown W L, *A Guide to the Birds of Colombia,* Princeton University Press, Princeton, NJ (1986). Although it technically covers only Colombia, this is the most comprehensive field guide (some 1,500 species described with hundreds of colour drawings) of the upper Amazon avifauna and will be useful for birdwatchers visiting Ecuador and Peru.

Kricher, J C, *A Neotropical Companion*, (2nd edn), Princeton University Press, Princeton, NJ (1997). Written for the informed layman, it offers useful insights into rainforest ecology and evolution.

Line, L, *Silence of the Songbirds.* National Geographic 183: 68-91 (1993). A sobering article on how migratory songbirds are declining in population due to deforestation in Latin American rainforests.

Marshall, E, *A deadly parasite spurs up-to-the-minute biology*, Science 267:811 (1995a). A summary report on the status of Brazilian research into Chagas' disease, transmitted by a biting insect.

Marshall, E, *Homely fish draws attention to Amazon deforestation*, Science 267:814 (1995b). This short article describes the present status of fisheries in the middle Amazon, with special reference to the highly sought fish called tambaqui.

Moffett, M W, *The High Frontier: Exploring the Tropical Rainforest Canopy*, Harvard University Press, Cambridge, MA (1993). A scientifically rigorous and excellently written text describing the latest research on the biodiversity, ecology and evolution of the rainforest canopy, with examples from the Amazon and Latin America.

Moffett, M W, *Poison-dart Frogs: Lurid and Lethal*. National Geographic 187: 98-111 (1955a).

Moffett, M W, *Gardeners of the Ant World*. National Geographic Vol. 188: 98-111 (1995b).

Munn, C A, *Winged Rainbows: Macaws*. National Geographic 185: 118-140 (1994). A summary of recent research into the ecology and conservation of scarlet macaws at Tambopata Reserve in Peru.

Murawski, D A, *Passion Vine Butterflies: a Taste for Poison*. National Geographic 184: 122-137 (1993). The author describes her studies into the ecology of Heliconiid butterflies and their evolutionary interaction with their host plant.

Prance, G T and Lovejoy, T E, *Amazonia*, Pergamon Press, New York & London (1985). An excellent photo-essay of the Amazon's floral and fauna wealth, written by two of the world's foremost tropical biologists.

Rettig, N, *Remote World of the Harpy Eagle*. National Geographic 187:40-49 (1995). Describes the ecology and conservation status of the Amazon's largest bird of prey.

Wheatley, N, *Where to watch birds in South America*, Princeton University Press (1995). A comprehensive guide to birds and the best birding sites throughout the Amazon and South America.

Wilson, E O, *Rain Forest Canopy: the High Frontier*, National Geographic 180: 78-107 (1991). Excellent introductory material to the structure and function of the canopy layer of rainforest.

Wilson, E O, *The Diversity of Life*, W W Norton, New York (1992). The founder of sociobiology and world's foremost ant expert takes a broad perspective to show the importance of biodiversity, with several useful examples from Amazonia.

Travel guides

If you intend staying in one country a long time and travelling beyond the Amazon, you will find a country-specific guide useful as these cover areas outside the Amazon Basin. Bradt's travel guides cover general travel information to specific countries (eg: A Bradbury, *Guide to Brazil,* and H Dunsterville Branch, *Guide to Venezuela*) or specific activities within a country (eg: R Rachowiecki, *Climbing and Hiking in Ecuador*). All the main Amazon countries have been covered by Lonely Planet. These guides emphasise information on accommodation, eating out and transport and really help you stretch your travel dollar. Footprint (Bath, England) publish the *South American Handbook,* lovingly referred to as The Bible by many travellers, and have several new country guides giving information on virtually everything you could hope to do in a country. Insight Guides on Peru, Ecuador, Brazil and Venezuela have lovely photographs, but the information is very selective and practical travel information is somewhat limited.

Index

Page numbers in italics refer to maps